THE AUTHOR

THE ELEVENTH HOUR

A call for British rebirth

by

JOHN TYNDALL

ALBION PRESS
LONDON

In gratitude...

...To my colleagues and friends John Morse and Ronald Rickcord, who have rendered invaluable help to me in the preparation of this book.

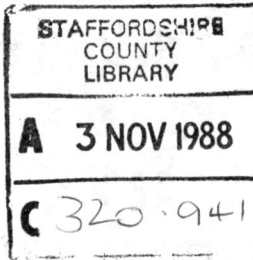

CONTENTS

	Foreword	1
1	Origins and early life	6
2	Army service	26
3	The call of politics	41
4	British Nationalism	67
5	Is there a conspiracy?	92
6	The cancer of liberalism	117
7	The left	141
8	Conservatism in surrender	155
9	Years of political apprenticeship	178
10	The National Front	208
11	Roots of the British sickness: the political system	258
12	Freedom: the illusion and the reality	292
13	The role of the media	323
14	Beyond capitalism and socialism	348
15	A new land and a new people	397
16	The racial controversy	412
17	What is at stake in Ulster	439
18	The imperial imperative	457
19	Britain and the world	500
20	Scenario of war	543
21	The British National Party	557
22	The way ahead	585
	Index	611

INTRODUCTION
by Ronald Rickcord

THE IMPRISONMENT in 1986 of John Tyndall, leader of the British National Party and editor of *Spearhead*, and of John Morse, editor of *British Nationalist*, was an outrageous attempt to silence two patriotic Britons who had dared express views which may no longer be openly discussed in this country. It is indeed ironic that the two men were both imprisoned for publicising the truth in a country that prides itself on having taught the world that 'freedom of speech' is a sacrosanct right belonging to all citizens of a civilised land.

Doubtless the ruling and influential individuals, many of alien extraction, who comprise the conspiratorial clique which today determines the fate of the British people, hoped that the imprisonment of Messrs. Tyndall and Morse would deter them and other like-minded patriots from uttering views which are potentially so popular that they must be suppressed at all costs. However, if they imagined that such men could be silenced, they were mistaken; for both emerged from prison unbowed and quite unrepentant.

Just how far the inquisitors had miscalculated the resolve of British Nationalists to go on spreading the truth was shown by the continued publication of *British Nationalist* during their imprisonment, and the publication of *Spearhead*, which was resumed immediately after Mr. Tyndall's release. But, above all, the magnitude of the nationalists' victory over the totally unrepresentative establishment, which seeks to control our thoughts and opinions as well as our actions, is more than amply testified by the appearance of this absorbing and penetrating book.

In one sense it can be said that by imprisoning John Tyndall the enemies of British Nationalism did us all a favour by providing him with the rare opportunity for writing *The Eleventh Hour*, a book which many nationalists had hoped would be forthcoming for a long time. Mr. Tyndall's enforced leisure afforded him the peace and quiet that are necessary for writing an important book of this kind — luxuries which his duties as leader of the British National Party and editor of *Spearhead* seldom, if ever, permit. So, to use a colloquialism, it can be said that Mr.

Tyndall's enemies "scored an own-goal," and we nationalists and, indeed, all people concerned with the future of our country are the beneficiaries.

Although most Britons who take an intelligent interest in domestic political matters will doubtless have heard of John Tyndall, few of them, apart from those who are his own colleagues and supporters, actually know the man or fully understand his political beliefs and aspirations. The reason for this widespread public ignorance is that there has been a co-ordinated conspiracy waged by the political establishment to suppress such beliefs — an establishment which is fearful of the potential popularity of Mr. Tyndall's views. This suppression is further reinforced by the activities of the hostile news media, which have successfully persuaded the less discerning majority to believe that Mr. Tyndall is some sort of ogre who, given half a chance, would subject his compatriots to a totalitarian dictatorship.

Besides providing Mr. Tyndall with a means of answering his critics, the publication of *The Eleventh Hour* will also enable those who are genuinely interested to discover for themselves what he really stands for. By reading this book, they will not only discover the truth that lies behind many of the events in which Mr. Tyndall has been involved but they will also learn about his background and early struggles, his political beliefs and the evolution of the British National Party which he now leads. I believe that all who read *The Eleventh Hour*, even those who hold views diametrically opposed to Mr. Tyndall's, will agree that the book makes fascinating reading and goes a long way towards dispelling some of the myths that have surrounded those of us who subscribe to the cause of British Nationalism.

There can be little doubt that had John Tyndall chosen any other walk of life than he did he would have made his mark. I am quite convinced that, with his outstanding powers of oratory, and his abilities as a writer, administrator and leader, he would have risen to the top of any of the major political parties if he had had a mind to join one. But unlike so many of those politicians who today infest the British political scene and unfortunately dominate the political destinies of our people and our country, Mr. Tyndall is no careerist or self-seeker. Unlike them, he is not concerned with self-aggrandisement or power for power's sake; if those had been the forces that motivated him he would surely have joined one of the established political parties long ago. And, unlike so many of the politicians of today, he is, above all, a man of principles.

In all the years that I have known John Tyndall I cannot recall a single occasion when he compromised any of his principles in order to gain any momentary advantage, to curry public favour or as a matter of political expediency. As a young man, he made a conscious decision to take up the cause of British Nationalism and give his whole life to it, and he has for more than a quarter of a century remained faithful to that cause despite the sometimes almost insuperable obstacles that have been placed in his way. To my certain knowledge, he has never deviated one iota from the lonely, and at times dangerous, task which he has set himself.

I am convinced that all fair-minded readers, whether they agree with Mr. Tyndall's opinions or not, will have to admit that his sincerity, integrity and probity are evident in every page of this book. But those are not his only virtues; he also possesses in large measure courage, persistence and an unrelenting dedication to the future well-being of the British people. Despite the conspiratorial efforts of his enemies and the numerous ploys they have used to thwart his legitimate aspiration to see the control of his native land restored to his fellow countrymen, John Tyndall has, by sheer tenacity, forged a political movement in this country which, in spite of many obstacles and setbacks, is, in my opinion, the most potent weapon we have to bring about the resurgence of our nation and the salvation of our people.

Mr. Tyndall is a realist, and he has always warned his supporters that the struggle in which they are engaged will be long and arduous. He knows that the nationalist victory for which he has so ardently and valiantly fought all his political life may not materialise quite so soon as many would hope. However, sooner or later British Nationalism **will** triumph; and when it does John Tyndall's name will endure as that of its principal architect. Indeed, I predict that John Tyndall will be remembered long after the political pygmies who are now so busily engaged in plotting our national decline and racial suicide are forgotten.

The Eleventh Hour not only provides us with a blueprint for the salvation of our country; it also tells the inspiring story of what can be achieved by one remarkable man of vision who has set his face implacably against the national death-wish with which so many of our so-called leaders seem to be afflicted. It is a book that should be read by all Britons who have a genuine love of their country, and indeed by patriots all over the world who feel about their own countries in the same way. The book may not become a best-seller in the immediate future; but I believe that in the years beyond it will take its place as the most outstanding testament written by a British Nationalist.

RONALD RICKCORD (APRIL 1988)

ISBN 0 9513686 1 3

THE MAIN PART of the contents of this book were written while the author was serving a term in Wormwood Scrubs Prison, in West London. In the preparation of the final copy for the printer, however, some further insertions were made, as a result of which the reader will occasionally find references to events that took place after Mr. Tyndall's release from prison in November 1986.

THE PUBLICATION of this book was not backed up by large financial resources. One symptom of this is that the typesetting was carried out with the use of elderly equipment. The equipment was for the most part adequate to the task but it did not contain a mechanism for reproducing accentuation marks to go with foreign words on the few occasions on which these were used. The reader is therefore asked to excuse this omission where it is encountered.

Printed and published by Albion Press, PO Box 446,
London SE23 2LS
Second Edition, 1988

FOREWORD

ON THE 16th JULY 1986 I took up residence in Wormwood Scrubs Prison, in West London, having been consigned there from Crown Court in consequence of my having been judged to have broken the law under Section 5a of the Public Order Act, in that I had published words deemed to be liable to stir up 'hatred' against certain racial groups in Britain. For the first time in a long while, I found myself with the time to complete a project that had been in the pipeline for some years and which I had in fact started a short time before my imprisonment. I refer of course to this book.

For some time my friends and collaborators had been urging me to write the book, and I had agreed with them over its desirability. My problem had been that of fitting the work into my very intensive programme of duties. Now, with a number of months of enforced absence from those duties before me, the chance existed which may not occur again for a long time — to pursue the work to its conclusion in conditions of solitude and absence of distraction. The chance was too good to miss, and I took it — in a spirit of gratitude to those to whom I owed the opportunity.

Right from the beginning, I have been preoccupied with the question of what form the book should take. Should it be a straight presentation of the political aims for which I have worked during most of my adult life? Or should it be an autobiography? The author of any book of the latter kind always runs the risk of appearing presumptuous that he is a figure of greater public interest than is the case! On the other hand, it is often helpful, in expounding a particular belief, to be able to relate the process by which one came to hold that belief, and this involves, unavoidably, some narration of personal history and development.

After much thought on the matter, I have decided to make this work a combination of the two themes. The book is mostly a political manifesto, as is proper, but it contains throughout an autobiographical element. Apart from the one reason for this already stated, there is another: this is that in the real world of politics — whatever principle may be advanced to the contrary —

'causes' are in the minds of their followers inextricably identified with certain personages who become their leading advocates and crusaders, and those personages become, inevitably, the focus of some interest and curiosity. It might finally be added, in my case, that someone who has been the object of much vilification by his opponents (and even at times by people who are supposed to be 'allies'!) does perhaps have the right to square accounts by a presentation of the case for his own defence.

With all these considerations in mind, I have decided that this book should not exclude some references to my own life and background, with these being especially prominent in the earlier parts. To those who do not find these references of interest, I can only advise that they skip over them and go directly to the parts of the book that are devoted to the political message — these parts comprising the main meat of the work.

The presentation of the ideas of a reforming movement in print assumes a particular importance today, in view of what is largely a ban on the use of other means of communication. Throughout almost the whole length and breadth of Britain today, my colleagues and I have been prevented from putting our case to the people by means of public meeting. This has been accomplished by the simple practice of our political opponents of threatening mob violence at any meeting held, and thus frightening the owners of meeting halls into denying us the facilities of hire. In the case of those halls owned by public authorities, it might be expected that these authorities would refuse to yield to the threats and would allow us the use of their meeting halls out of the need to defend the traditions of free assembly and free speech that are supposed to be a central part of the British way of life. But no such luck! In fact it has become clear to us that most public authorities have positively welcomed the existence of a threat of disorder at our meetings as a pretext for denying us meeting rights, and in some cases there has been evidence of actual collusion between those authorities and the mobs causing the trouble, for example the presence in violent counter-demonstrations against us of persons recognisable as local town councillors.

More important still, we have, except on very rare occasions, been denied the facilities of television, today by far the most influential means of communication. We have always accepted that the larger political parties, with representation in parliament, will qualify for greater TV coverage than smaller groups with minority support (interpreting that phrase 'minority support' in accordance with vote figures at elections rather than concurrence of views over the major political issues). Nevertheless, it is a principle constantly proclaimed by the controllers of broadcasting in Britain that the views of minority organisations should be given a hearing, if the democratic spirit of broadcasting is to be preserved. In fact numerous minority groups with much smaller public following than our own have been allowed a regular voice in TV current affairs programmes, but we have in recent years been constantly denied the same right.

There is not the slightest doubt in our minds that an invisible censorship exists in modern Britain, a censorship which not only applies to certain types of political organisation but also applies to certain categories of political opinion. It is a censorship which extends also to the press and publishing, which latter tendency made it quite clear to me from the beginning that I would not stand the slightest chance of getting this book produced, advertised, reviewed and sold through the normal publishing and distributive network.

This phenomenon of censorship, amounting virtually to attempted suppression, in a society supposed to pride itself on its traditions of 'democracy' and 'freedom', has monumental implic- ations for our whole view of politics. It forces us to put under serious scrutiny everything we have been taught, right from early adolescence, concerning the nature of democracy as a political doctrine and system, and to be prepared to reconsider many of the most basic ideas that have been instilled into us concerning British society and other Western societies founded, supposedly, on the same principles. What the phenomenon does is expose as a total fraud a set of institutions and beliefs that most us have been taught to regard as sacred — even to the point of being prepared to fight major wars in defence of them! At the same time it opens up the question of the credibility that can be attached to the guardians and advocates of that system concerning **any** matter of importance to our lives, to the world and to history. When a set of beliefs can be seen, by the evidence of one's own eyes and experience, to be founded on sheer lies and humbug, every aspect of those beliefs loses the automatic moral authority we have been accustomed to accord to it, and we are obliged to rethink our whole philosophy and attitude towards a vast range of political questions. This process began with me years ago, and in the course of this book I shall have occasion to relate the various stages through which it passed. In the end, as one perceives the whole gigantic superstructure of lies, deceit and humbug around which our present political state is built, one feels like a man who for years has been holding a picture in his hands which he has imagined to be a photographic print but which now he realises all along to have been a negative — everything thought to be black was white, and everything thought to be white was black!

Perhaps the least difficult of my tasks in this book will be that of persuading the reader that our country, Britain, is in a condition of long and continual decline; this fact is something now recognised by millions. What the book seeks mainly to do is analyse **why** there is this decline and what measures are going to be needed to reverse the process and bring about regeneration. Here is the essence of the controversy. The opinion I shall advance in the forthcoming pages is that these measures will need to be radical and far-reaching in the changes they involve, not only for our political institutions but in respect of the whole way of thinking, the entire national outlook, that has been the dominant orthodoxy throughout the 20th century. Some proposals will go further than many people at the present time are prepared to accept. But I make no apologies for this; I write, not as one of today's conventional political jobbers, pleading for a seat on the merry-go-round of the old party game, but one who sees it as his task to point forward to entirely new horizons of political thought and action, through which a decaying social order may be given the means to new life. If the ideals for which my companions and I now fight are not universally endorsed, then we are prepared to fight on for as long as it takes before they are, though that may be only after years of bitter struggle against all the mobilised venom of the old world.

In certain parts of this book I have had occasion to refer to racial matters. It is necessary for me to ask the reader to bear in mind here that British citizens are today prevented from speaking entirely freely on questions of race by laws prohibiting certain forms of expression on the subject. The way that I have dealt with these matters in this book is conditioned by the need for me to avoid transgression of these laws, if only to protect those others whose help will be needed in the distribution of the book after publication.

In the first part of the book, dealing largely with my own background I make mention of some members of my family. I should stress in this regard that none of these relations had or has any connection with my political views or activities, and that where I refer to sympathies on certain questions which I hold in common with some family ancestors, such as the cause of Irish Unionism, this should not be taken to mean that any of the persons to whom I refer in these respects would necessarily endorse all views on other matters such as I hold today.

It should not really be necessary for me to make these disclaimers, as it should be assumed that none of these people are connected with my politics unless I state specifically that they are. However, I state the position as I have done here in order to leave no room for misunderstanding on this subject and to protect any such family relations as may feel embarrassment as a result of their family connections with me.

This book is written first and foremost for British readers and is addressed to specifically British problems. It is hoped, however, that people overseas will find something in it that they can relate to the problems of their own countries as well. In large part, the illnesses with which we have to deal in Britain are universal, and in particular afflict, in greater or lesser degree, those nations that we are accustomed to grouping together under the heading of 'The West'. In the case of those peoples who share with us the English tongue, I am certain that much will be found here that is familiar elsewhere, and that some of the solutions put forward run largely along parallel lines to the solutions needed for similar problems on their own doorstep.

In going through this book, the reader, inevitably, will encounter some degree of repetition. The book is not a scientifically-composed treatise, put together in absolutely methodical form. Nor are the issues dealt with in it to be seen as isolated from one another; all of them in fact go to make an integrated whole, and it simply is not possible to deal with one without reference back to things said when dealing with another.

I should finally mention that this book, though it resorts regularly in its text to the first person singular, is by no means a lone effort on my part. It has been made possible by the help of many others, not only in the way of sharing my working burdens — as mentioned earlier, but also in that of assisting in providing the means, first for publication and then for distribution. Last but not least, a debt of gratitude is owed to my dear wife, who has patiently tolerated the non-performance of many domestic tasks in order to leave me free to complete the preparation of the book for the printer.

Chapter 1

Origins and early life

I am sometimes asked if politics are in my blood. It is not an easy question to answer; there is some record of political involvement by members of my own and related families, but it is not exceptional. What certainly does run through the strain is a disposition to work for 'causes' of some kind or another, whether political or not.

Tyndall is a Northern English name, originating, as might be supposed, in the Valley of the River Tyne. From there it travelled around the British Isles and later far and wide across the world with the dispersal of the British race, being subjected, as is common with family names, to a number of variations of spelling. The fact that those bearing the name are not great in number increases the probability of ancestral connections between them. What is known about my section of the clan is that they were found in Gloucestershire in the 15th century, bearing the name in its older form of Tyndale. They were mainly farmers and small landowners. One story handed down and mentioned in the Dictionary of National Biography is that these Tyndales were refugees from the Wars of the Roses, occurring in the North earlier in that century, and that to escape identification on occasions they used the name Hutchyns as an *alias*. This latter name was passed down as a middle name to me.

The most prominent of the Gloucestershire Tyndales was William Tyndale (1490-1536), scholar, religious reformer and first publisher of the English Bible, who spent much of his life embroiled in the flames of controversy and eventually was burnt at the stake in Vilvorde, in the Netherlands.

My exact relationship with William Tyndale is not easy to establish at this great distance of time and with the records available, but the fact that he met his death as a heretic against the prevailing orthodoxy of his day carries more than a suggestion of kinship!

Later, in the 17th century, a branch of the family settled in Ireland, and from this branch came Professor John Tyndall (1820-93), physicist, natural philosopher and spare-time mountaineer. In his entry in the Dictionary of National Biography it is stated that his family claimed descent from William Tyndale. He was born in Leighlin Bridge, Co. Carlow and is thought to have shared with my own family a common ancestor in the person of his paternal grandfather or great grandfather. Aside from his main occupation, Professor Tyndall had a strong interest in politics and at one time nearly stood for parliament as a Unionist candidate, in addition to speaking and writing in opposition to Gladstone's home rule policy.

My own paternal grandfather was John Francis Tyndall, whose mother was born a member of the Griffiths family, suggesting a Welsh connection some way back. One of her ancestors was Patrick James Smyth, who was for several years Unionist MP at different times for the constituencies of Westmeath and Tipperary. This is the closest link I can claim with anyone in the fullest sense political.

Grandfather Tyndall was the son of a member of the Royal Irish Constabulary and became in turn himself an RIC man, attaining the rank of District Inspector. The family home was in Co. Waterford. In *The Life and Work of John Tyndall* (the physicist) it is stated that his father also served in the RIC, so that the family would appear to contain a much greater number of policemen than politicians, my father also spending a short time in the former occupation before going on to other things.

From his RIC connections it will be gleaned that Grandfather Tyndall was a strong Unionist, as were, to my knowledge, the rest of the family. He was much occupied with the fight against terrorism in both the South and North of Ireland during the last part of the 19th century and the first two decades of the present one, and there are family memories, passed down, of his having more than once to leave church by the back entrance having received the tip off that gunmen were waiting for him at the front. After dedicating much of his life to fighting what he called 'the rebels', he was to spend his last years in disgust and disillusionment as he saw the British Government, on whose behalf he had served, wine and dine the rebel leaders in Westminster while giving them their 'Free State'. According to my grandfather, this never need have happened, since the RIC had largely won the war against them — something that will find echoes in our own time!

Grandfather Tyndall married Mary Elizabeth Francis, whose maternal relations, the Careys, were newspaper-owners. There were two sons and a daughter, the younger son being George Francis Tyndall, my father. The elder son, my Uncle Charles, attended school with Father at King's Hospital, Dublin. Uncle Charles later attended Trinity College. He first considered an army career and became an officer cadet at Sandhurst. Later he changed his mind and entered the ministry of the Church of Ireland, eventually being consecrated as Bishop of Kilmore and later of Londonderry.

My father, George Tyndall, took longer than his brother to find his intended vocation in life. At 16 he developed a great interest in marine engineering and for a short time believed that therein lay his career. Far from discouraging him in this, his parents allowed him to leave school ahead of schedule and go to work as an apprentice in the yards of Harland and Wolff in Belfast. His disposition to this career was to be short-lived but his spell in the shipyards was to be a valuable part of his development. The ex-public schoolboy was thrown at the deep end into a tough, working class environment and soon got to learn how the 'other half' lived and thought. He grew up into a thoroughly 'classless' person, or so he always seemed to me.

In the 1920s my father, his sister and their parents left Ireland and settled in Hertfordshire, leaving elder brother Charles behind. Still not sure of where his future lay my father enlisted in the Metropolitan Police and was posted as a constable to Peckham Division in South East London. A keen and able rugby player, he became a member, and eventually captain, of the Met XV. At around this time he met, and in 1930 married, Nellie Parker, one of a family of two boys and six girls then living in Penge. 47 years later, by a strange coincidence, I emulated my father in choosing a lady of the same family name of Parker for my own wife.

My maternal grandfather, William Henry Parker, came from Somerset, being born in Bridgwater, the son of a Scot who had moved there from Castle Douglas, Kirkcudbright. The family was in the drapery business, and it was to further his prospects in that business that William Parker moved to London, where he married Nellie Pittock, from a Kentish family one of whose members had been mayor of Sandwich.

George Tyndall decided after four years to leave the police and took a job in a mineral water company, where he rose quickly to a managerial position. He was sent to Devon to take charge of the

Exeter branch of the firm, and it was there, at 4 a.m. on a very hot summer's morning on the 14th July 1934 that I was born.

My parents did not stay long in Exeter, my father being transferred to Hove, where we lived also for a short time and to where, by another strange twist of fate, I was to return many years later.

My earliest childhood memories begin in Finchley, North London, where my father again took a managerial position with his company. Very soon war was upon us, so that the earliest days that I can recall were mostly wartime days. I have a vivid memory of the 'Blitz', when one bomb fell so close by that it rocked Grandma Tyndall, staying with us at the time, backwards off the piano stool.

Too young to appreciate the danger of the air raids, I found them an occasion for considerable excitement and a good excuse not to go to bed on time. I soon learned to identify enemy planes as well as our own by their shapes and engine noises, and used to try to follow the battles up above when I had the chance. I recall our nightly retreat to the Anderson shelter in the back garden of our home in Parkside. Another memory is of the V 1s appearing in the skies and one occasion when, with my mother out shopping, I heard the familar sound of one of these machines. I rushed out into the street to get a better view and watched, enthralled, as it passed overhead seemingly very little distance away from me. Somewhat less enthralled was my mother, who just at that moment turned the corner on her way back from the shops and who must have broken the world's sprint record to catch me and scoldingly usher me inside!

I was very much an outdoor boy and spent much time in the local parks, of which there seemed to be an abundance, and very early on I took lovingly to games and outdoor adventures. The friends with whom I teamed up would go on explorations of the local open spaces, including Hampstead Heath. We often played war games, which I much enjoyed. I soon became fascinated with the bigger, and real, war that was taking place at the time, becoming quite a little expert in uniforms, badges of rank and the guns, tanks and aircraft of the belligerent nations. Precocious in these things, if not in others, I would devour the daily papers to follow the progress of the war in its many sectors. At such an age I could not of course have any comprehension of the political issues at stake in the conflict. I recall only that I was eager always to see the British forces fare well — I gained no satisfaction at all from the victories of our 'allies'!

In these early emotions I can of course now see the first stirrings of the incipient nationalist. At about the same time I also showed, for a small lad, an above average interest in maps. I was always poring over world atlases, and before I was 10 I had a pretty good grasp of basic geography, being aware of the positions, sizes, populations (and national flags) of all the world's major nations. I did not fail to take note of the vast area of the world's surface covered by the British Empire; contrasting this with the modest territorial size of Britain itself, I became, before I reached double figures, an ardent imperialist!

As the war intensified, many children in the South East of England and in the major cities elsewhere, being in the front line of the bombing raids, were evacuated to the country areas. In 1940 my parents enrolled me at Michael Hall School, a Rudolf Steiner institution, and packed me off to Minehead, in Somerset, where I was to stay for two years. I hated being parted from my mother and father and I remember the regular waterworks on the platform at Paddington when they saw me off. The experience was not bad for me, however, as it taught me to stand on my own feet at an early age, and placed me in a healthy semi-rural environment which could only have been to my benefit.

An only child for the first nine years of my life, I was pleased at last to have a little companion when my brother was born a short while after. I will not mention his name here, as I do not want to cause problems for him in his own life. We get on very well personally, but he is in no way connected with my politics.

Soon after my brother arrived, my mother, he and I went to stay for some months with my father's family in Ireland, at first with Uncle Charles, who then was a rector in Dublin, and later with my Grandma and Aunt, who had moved back to Ireland to take over the *Leinster Express*, a newspaper left to them by a deceased relative in Portlaoighise. This period would not be worthy of mention but for a small incident that could be seen as a portent of later development. I was taken by a friend of the family to a variety concert staged at, I think, the Curragh barracks. One of the turns was a character who specialised in monologues. From the beginning to the end of his act he dwelt on Irish nationalist themes, with stories about the brave boys who had fought and died ''for Ireland'' against the ''wicked British.'' Throughout the whole performance the fellow spewed forth non-stop anti-British hate. Little 10-year-old Tyndall sat livid for the duration of the act, anger mounting with every fresh denigration of his country. Returning home afterwards, he did not stop storming about the matter for at least a week!

This was of course very uncharacteristic of the modern-day British, a great many of whom will willingly listen to insults against their nation with an attitude of tolerant stupor. Perhaps, ironically, it was the Irish in the blood coming out here — from the ranks of Irishmen can come those who are the most passionately British as well as those who are the most vehemently anti-British.

We returned home just as the war was coming to an end, and settled in that area where South East London borders on West Kent, living for a while in Bromley, then Bickley and finally West Wickham. It was in this area, as never in Finchley, that I felt I had some roots, and I have retained close connections with it ever since.

During the war my father had at last found his true vocation in life by taking a full-time post with the YMCA. What had drawn him to that work was a basic old-fashioned Christian belief combined with a lifelong interest in young men's welfare and the desire to see youth rescued from an aimless existence and brought into a fraternity where they may combine together for the purpose of mutual self-development of body, mind and character — an ideal that I came to share entirely, although I differed with my father as to the best way to its achievement. My father had a kind of vaguely idealistic faith in the ability of the nations and races of the world to solve problems by coming together in such international organisations as the 'YM' — not itself an objectionable belief except in so far as it is one liable to be exploited, for much less idealistic purposes, by those dedicated to the undermining of nationhood. A world of perpetual peace and brotherhood among the nations is a pretty idea that over the ages has commended itself to some of the very best intentioned of folk. As we come to terms with the realities of human nature and of history, we appreciate the limitations to the realisation of such an idea in practice, and indeed the very grave dangers that it poses to those nations who pursue it to extremes, by assuming that international idealism can be a substitute for national capability.

To be a nationalist is not to take the view that all international concepts are necessarily invalid, only to recognise, firstly, that all things useful that might be achieved at international level rely in the last analysis on the qualities and resources applied to them by the contributing **nations**; secondly, and in consequence, that any international project that is pursued to the detriment of national interest becomes in the end counter-productive to its purpose, by weakening those national assets on which it most relies for its effective promotion.

International idealism, therefore, when not harnessed to cool nationalist realism, becomes a highly risky intellectual indulgence.

My father was never a political animal, and therefore never seriously thought through the YMCA doctrine of universal brotherhood to whose service he gave much of his life. Like many others who worked for these international causes, he would most probably be horrified were he to be able to return to the earth today and see some of the consequences of all this crusading. For instance, when the first black and brown faces began to appear in Britain in the 1950s it never occurred to my father that those concerned were anything other than visitors to our country who had come here to learn the arts of our civilisation and would in due course return home to bestow the benefits of that learning upon their compatriots. In this spirit he made those he met through the YMCA feel welcome and went out of his way to help them. There was much in him of the evangelistic 19th century missionary, who felt it a noble vocation to communicate the refinements of the British way of life to the world's 'less fortunate breeds', believing quite honestly and sincerely that only universal good would come of such a process. That the reverse might be happening, that in fact the 'less fortunate breeds' may indeed be in the process of transplanting **their** way of life into large areas of urban Britain, with the results we were to see in the 1980s, did not occur to my father until perhaps shortly before his death in 1964, when I felt I detected in him the first stirrings of a realisation that maybe the ideal of the brotherhood of man had somehow gone wrong.

Though my father and I did not agree on all things, I remember him as a very fine man, a wonderful parent to me and a devoted husband to my mother. He grew up in an entirely different age and environment to mine, and this has to be taken into account when our differences of outlook are examined.

Shortly after the end of the war I had entered my teens. This period of my life was characterised by two things: a love of outdoor sports and, partly in consequence, a less than zealous approach to school studies. I took quickly and naturally to soccer and cricket, and a little later to rugby, when I enrolled at Beckenham and Penge Grammar School and found the latter game to be the established football code. In the winter I got the best of both worlds by having my rugger game at school in the midweek and then playing soccer for a youth club on Saturdays. A clash between these two loves threatened when someone told me that I would be in line for selection for the school Junior XV if I was interested. That would have meant rugby on Saturdays and the forfeiture of my soccer game, and so I replied negatively. This was a disappointment to my father, as he had hoped I would follow in his rugby-playing footsteps and had been much encouraged when he found I had some talent for the game. Looking back years later, I considered that I might have made a mistake.

In summer, cricket was the dominant preoccupation. Here there was no conflict; I played for the school Colts and later for the First XI. My speciality was fast-bowling and I was reputed to be, by schoolboy standards, pretty quick, although not in the top grade for length and direction — I recall breaking the stump of a batsman in one school match and getting more pleasure from this than if I had taken five or six wickets in the ordinary manner!

At the start of the 1950s Kent County CC were organising a talent-spotting scheme, and I was entered as a candidate by our school cricket master along with another member of the school team. I attended trials, first at Blackheath and later at Canterbury. In the course of these trials I was taken in hand by an old county player, R.T. Bryan, who told me I had the right action and physical requirements to succeed as a fast bowler if I gave my mind to it. He introduced me to the local club, Beckenham, for whom I played a few games between school cricket and after leaving school.

In the meantime I enjoyed my football in the winter and on one occasion managed to get selected for Kent Minor XI, a team made up from youth clubs in the county, and I played a not too distinguished game against Essex Minors at Tilbury in the winter of 1951-52.

Looking back on this period, I could see in later years how sport played an extremely important part in my life then, sometimes perhaps an excessive part. School homework often received inadequate attention as almost every evening and weekend I was either playing matches, practising or training. I became ardent in the pursuit of physical fitness, and this habit has kept with me into middle life. I have a few regrets over the fact that between the ages of about 11 to 17 I got my priorities a little out of balance, with the result that my studies suffered, but it is not all regret: in those days

I laid the foundation of a life style of healthy living and attention to physical well being that has stood me in good stead ever since.

One of the unfortunate tendencies of this world is that men, just when they have 'grown up' a little and are becoming fit for responsibility, are in physical decline. This process cannot be altered but it can be greatly slowed down by the observance of a health- and fitness-orientated living regime, involving regular vigorous exercise, a balanced diet and the avoidance of over-indulgence in things like tobacco and alcohol, the first of which I have never touched and the second always taken in moderation.

Sir Oswald Mosley, to whom I shall refer again in this book, made a similar observation of the men of affairs in his day, and urged that such men should "live like athletes in light training." It is good advice, not heeded enough by public men of his generation or ours. Far too many of them, when they get to an age at which they may be expected to have achieved some maturity of mind and character, are well on the way to being physical wrecks, having by inattention to care of the body aged in that respect far beyond that made inevitable by nature. Our present civilisation and culture, unlike that of the ancient Greeks, sets a very low priority on body health and cultivation — a tendency which to my mind has always been indicative of decadence. Perhaps in the hideous creations of our modern *avant garde* sculptors we see the idealisation of universal, raceless 'liberal' man, which it seems the determination of this age to breed.

As any athlete will know, physical training has a strong and important mental element. When the body is in good trim, such training can incorporate the setting of definite targets of performance, such as, say, the running of five miles within an allotted time. There will be the days when the body will rebel against this, and then there comes a test of the will. That will, if it is in fine tune, will drive the body on, through the fatigue barrier and perhaps to the attainment of the body's 'second wind'. At the end there is not only the physical benefit of having completed the course but the great psychological satisfaction of the will having triumphed over the temptation to give up. No-one will ever persuade me that this is not good nourishment for the mind and spirit, and that it will not produce benefits in the way of a more positive approach to life's challenges and obstacles. It is our misfortune today not to be governed by men in whom are harmonised these qualities of body, mind and will, but by those whose every being betrays a depressing flabbiness.

Life is full of 'might-have-dones'. Had I devoted myself more to school studies during the crucial years, I might have gone to university. In a time and place other than post-war Britain this could have been very good for me, but as things were I have my doubts. In this modern era our centres of higher learning, far from fitting people to play useful roles in the affairs of a successful nation, perform the very opposite function, increasing their isolation from the real world rather than further opening that world up to them. Correlli Barnett, in his book *The Audit of War*, devotes a chapter to what he calls 'Education for Industrial Decline', the contents of which are evident from that title. In a previous book, *The Collapse of British Power,* the same author traces British educational methods back to the days of Dr. Arnold at Rugby in the 19th century, putting under the microscope the tendency, even then, to produce a type of man of affairs hopelessly ill-equipped to achieve international success for Britain, either in the economic or other fields. For a time long before 1945, therefore, British universities and leading schools have had this tendency to isolate their products from the realities of world politics and national survival. I only mention the post-1945 period in the sense that this tendency has in that period gone much further. This is of course a very arbitrary time-division. British universities in the 1950s had not become quite the madhouses that many of them are today, where the mere suggestion that there is more than one point of view on certain 'sensitive' subjects can invite a reaction of mob violence (allowed free reign by dons who have gone scurrying to their funkholes in abject terror of their pupils). Even in the 1950s, however, these seats of learning had long harboured the tendency to have a softening, feminising effect on the young men who entered them. Certainly since the end of World War I, leftish, liberalistic and internationalist influences have predominated in all departments of university teaching concerned with politics, religion, philosophy, history and the arts, and these influences produced the appalling 'intelligentsia' of the 1930s, 1940s and 1950s that turned the British into a nation of self-haters ready for wholesale abdication from empire — and eventually even from control of their own homeland.

There were other reasons for my none too industrious application to the school academic curriculum. As I progressed through my teens, I found myself developing an increasing concern about public affairs. This did not immediately materialise in the form of any political awareness, less still of any thought of ever becoming actively involved in politics myself. Rather was it a feeling, at first merely instinctive, of living in a society that was slowly dying, and in which we had got our values all wrong. I found myself pondering much on questions of morality and religion. The need for a firm moral code was to me self-evident, but was our Church in this age providing any useful guidance in this direction? I found myself repelled by many of the contemporary clergy and the attitudes they struck on many vital questions of right and wrong. In fact what I was witnessing was an early stage of what has today become a headlong retreat of our clergy from moral leadership and into a kind of spiritual marxism, in which the first commandment is that thou shalt always side with thine enemies against thine own kind!

Everywhere around me I sensed an atmosphere of increasing decay in our national life. As I became more interested in the arts, particularly music, I was more and more revolted by the ugliness and formlessness of modern trends. I detested the 'architecture' of the new town and city centres, just as I despised the herd-like disposition of our 'intellectuals' to drool over the diseased creations of a Picasso or a Henry Moore. I brooded over the inclination of our modern composers to produce works that were mere jangling noise, while I could not help but contrast the shallowness of most of the age's popular songs with the quality of those of my grandparents' day. I noted the current trend of the 'anti-hero' of literature and film, while everywhere I was becoming aware of what seemed to be the orchestrated onslaught against the sentiment of national pride.

Attending the cinema quite often in those days, I grew revolted by the products of Hollywood, representing what seemed to me a kind of 'Americanised' cultural imperialism. Later, as I came to know the true identity of most film moguls of the English-speaking world, I realised that the label 'American' was not an entirely accurate one!

Slowly and gradually, the idea began to form in my mind that I was not fated to follow any conventional profession or career but would find my vocation in some kind of reforming work, countering the influences that I could see were eroding the health of society, and promoting alternative ideas and values — ideas and values that would contain the seeds of a rebirth of those qualities that had provided the foundation stones of earlier national greatness. In this regard I would only in fact be following the same trail as a number of other Tyndalls before me, although pursuing perhaps different goals in response to different circumstances and different times. Somehow, I had the premonition that in doing this I would be sailing through stormy seas — perhaps a harkback to the circumstances in which my ancestor parted this world centuries earlier!

That such work would lie in the field of political action was, as I have said, not at first apparent. What was apparent, however, was that the education and training I would require for it would not be obtained by means of the normal academic routes. In this lay much of the cause of my lack of motivation in school studies, though it would be dishonest not to admit that my sporting enthusiasms were a factor also.

Bit by bit, it started to come home to me that the questions causing me increasing concern could only be satisfactorily settled by means of action in the political field. I had not so far been very impressed by what I had seen of politics or politicians. I recall the election of 1950, when the respective party candidates and their helpers came around fishing for everyone's votes. They would call at doors like travelling salesmen, give oily smiles and mouth some meaningless platitude to the effect that they were, or represented, the so-and-so candidate and hoped that they could count on the householder's vote on polling day — just like that! Just why the candidate should be given the vote requested was never explained unless the householder made so bold as to ask that question, in which case some brief banality was trotted out which, examined in the context of the really important national issues, could be seen, even by an unenfranchised 16-year-old like myself, as an insult to the voter's intelligence. Of course the canvasser could not engage in a serious discussion, for that would have taken time. There were hundreds of other doors to be knocked on and hundreds more smiles to be given, so he had to be on his bike! This simply underlined the absurdity of the whole exercise. It was one of my early lessons in the charade that operates under the name of 'democracy', a word which throughout this book I shall frequently enclose in quotation marks because of the great difficulty in interpreting it literally and seriously as it is enacted in modern Britain.

'Democracy' is after all supposed to be a system resting on the assumption that the common people are able to understand the political issues so as to make an intelligent judgement of them on which they then base their decision to vote for this or that candidate in accordance with which one is most closely committed to the policies that they want to see carried out — thus bringing about government that rests on 'the people's will'. Anything further from the reality than this is difficult to imagine. Discussion of the issues on the doorstep at election time is almost zero, and on the few occasions when it does arise it is at a level little higher than the kindergarten. The parties compete with one another in 'selling' their candidates to the electorate in much the same manner as soap-manufacturers compete in selling their washing products. The rest of the paraphernalia of electioneering conform to the same pattern. The posters that scream down from the hoardings telling people to vote for this or that party put across, not arguments, but mere slogans, and as such tell us no more about the product being advertised than those billboards which say: "Guinness is good for you!" or "Go to work on an egg!"

It seems not to occur to the politicians that, by the childish level to which they pander in seeking votes, they contradict, almost every day of their working lives, the very principle which they claim to hold sacred: that in the voice and will of the people will be found political wisdom — the very basis of the democratic ethic.

In defence of these practices it may be argued that candidates and parties fighting elections, even if they do include people with admirable political intentions, have no alternative but to campaign in this way, and that the fact that they do does not necessarily mean that their aims are as silly as suggested by their propaganda. I would accept this point, and indeed the movement with which I am involved today is in just such a position as that described: it is forced to speak largely in slogans and to engage in the same canvassing exercises as its opponents in order to operate effectively within the system that exists.

But that is simply a commentary on the very inadequacy of the system. It means that the party or candidate that succeeds is not the one that has won the support of the majority in an intelligent and reasoned debate on the political issues but the one that has outdone rivals in soft-soaping the public with propaganda and ballyhoo.

Let me straightaway make it clear that I am not one of those who subscribe to the view that a decision arrived at by majority verdict, even after a reasoned debate, is necessarily always the right decision, though the debate may be at a comparatively intelligent level of discussion; the fact remains that some intelligences present may be greater than others and a viewpoint commanding a minority of votes could well be the viewpoint that it is in the nation's best interests to follow.

But if we are to judge things, as we are always urged to do, according to the criteria of 'democracy', and therefore to believe that the majority will, right or wrong, must always prevail, I must reply that scarcely ever is that the way that matters under 'democracy' are decided! The advocates of a particular political system at least deserve some respect if their system operates in a manner consistent with its professed principles. But when it does not do anything of the kind, and these principles become revealed as mere sugar-coating underneath which wholly different principles determine the outcome of events, then this one entitlement to respect is forfeited and the system is seen as one without a single redeeming feature.

The fraudulence of the system is further underlined when it is seen that the elected 'representatives of the people', once they have pocketed the votes they seek and taken their seats in parliament, rarely in any event carry out the policies for which their beloved voters have elected them, as I shall examine in more detail later in this book.

These observations of politics, which I was able to make as a youngster in my mid-teens, did nothing to incline me towards political involvement but, on the contrary, repelled me from ever entertaining the ambition to become a 'politician'.

Nevertheless, the issues that disturbed me would not go away; on the contrary, I found myself becoming increasingly preoccupied with them. More and more I turned to reading in an effort to formulate some coherent picture of the national and world situation. I devoured a vast number of books, pamphlets, newspapers and magazines in order to become better informed and to find answers to the questions that were vexing me. My 'education', which for a while had been neglected, began to catch up — but not in a way that helped me very much to excel at school. Instead of the standard academic textbooks, my reading ranged over philosophy, theology, economics, social questions, military science and — above all — politics, politics and more politics. Even in history, in which I was taking an increasing interest, my studies did not lead to any particularly high exam results. I was always much more interested in the broad sweep of the historical picture, and the lessons it provided for the present day, than in precise details of dates, kings and queens and acts of parliament, which tend to dominate the standard school syllabus.

In all this, two thoughts came into increasing conflict: on the

one side, there was a revulsion against the political process as I
saw it, on the other a realisation that only through some kind of
political process could the many wrongs I cared about be put right.

Through what form of politics could this be done? I closely
examined the political doctrines available for examination in
order to arrive at some determination of my own political position.

A line from a Gilbert and Sullivan opera tells us that every little
infant born alive is either a little Liberal or a little 'Conservataive'.
Swop the word Labourite for Liberal and that description would
fit the early 1950s, when I started to explore the subject of
politics. I was, without realising it at the time, taking my first look
at the two-party hoax, the racket under which the real controllers
of our nation maintain their grip by keeping two political factions
on a lead like two performing dogs, with a third one in reserve in
case needed. When the masses get tired of Dog No. 1 and want a
change, Dog No. 2 is brought out of the kennel and placed on
centre stage. When the dogs meet they yap and snarl at each other
so as to give the impression that they are mutually hostile. The
public witnessing the performance is never allowed to know of
course that both dogs, and the third one in reserve, are the property
of the same owner and perform to his instructions.

But this was not yet clear to me in the early 1950s as I sought to
find out what the two main parties stood for and with which one I
felt aligned. I have referred to election time in the area where I
lived, but this was in fact a mere formality: the Conservative was
always bound to win. What sort of a dolt he was and what political
ideas, if any, he had in his head were of small importance; it has
been said, without too much exaggeration, that if they fetched a
chimpanzee out of the zoo, dressed him up in a city suit and stuck
a blue rosette in his lapel, the electorate of this kind of suburban
constituency would vote for him without a second look. It will
therefore be gathered that the sympathies of the people with whom
I came into contact were overwhelmingly Tory. I started to speak
to some of these people to find out what ideas and thoughts lay
behind their sympathies, to find out why people voted
Conservative.

What I encountered was an almost complete mental void.
Though only at the beginning of my political education at the
time, I had at least applied my common sense to a consideration of
the vital questions determining the success or failure, the strength
or weakness, of nations. I found that on these questions the people
to whom I spoke had scarcely any thoughts at all; the only thing

that came out of my discussions with them was that they had some sort of vague belief in the free enterprise system, in the idea of private ownership of property and wealth, and in the dangerous radicality of socialist doctrines (though none of them admitted to ever having read a book, or even a pamphlet, in support of socialism).

What struck me about all these people was their virtually total preoccupation with material things. The degenerating tendencies in society that had started to cause me much concern hardly bothered them, where they were even aware of them. They were folk completely absorbed in the selfish quest for an improvement of their own positions in life and living standards, to the exclusion of any higher concern for the national good, and their political loyalties clearly were to the party which they saw as most likely to maintain the conditions desirable for their own continued pursuit of material benefits, augmented by various social status symbols, such as a new car every year and a detached house in the most fashionable part of town.

Occasionally one would comment that the Tories were the party of 'patriotism' and that it was 'unpatriotic' to be a socialist. But when I got to the bottom of what 'patriotism' meant to these people I found that it consisted of a smug belief that everything British was perfect and that it was 'unpatriotic' to question that belief. They could not seem to see that a man who passionately wanted his country to excel but was honest enough to admit the fields in which it was second rate, and strove mightly in those fields to improve it so as to bring it up to the level of his highest ideals and dreams, was far more of a patriot than the one who kept a portrait of The Queen on his wall, stood to attention for the national anthem and displayed a national flag on his car bumper, but who, when it came to **doing** something to right the manifest wrongs in his country, would not even admit that they existed!

Patriotism always seemed to me something totally different to what it was in the Tory mind. A true patriot sets the highest possible standards for his country and, when it fails to reach those standards, acknowledges it and gets down to doing something about it — not being too proud to admit that another country may in certain respects be better. A true patriot must be capable at times of cursing his country, even hating it, when it falls from high standards and proves unworthy of his pride. Most of all must he be capable of recognising those times when his country reaches the lowest level of its fortunes and then giving everything he has to the task of raising it up again. He has to be able to hate everything that is mean, rotten, trashy and contemptible in his native land and nation, and to fight against those things with all the ardour with which he would fight against an outside enemy.

But of this the Tories understood nothing. What they did understand — and it was practically **all** that they could understand — was the wholly self-centred and materialistic attitudes of their followers. To these preoccupations the Conservative Party propagandists addressed themselves with all the slickness of professional ad-men, toadying to every greedy instinct by shouting the praises of the material improvements they claimed to have brought to the people and the yet greater material improvements still to come — if the people had the good sense to see where their selfish interests lay and keep voting Conservative!

It was all very depressing.

So what did the other side stand for? What was Labour policy? Though supporters of that party were thin on the ground in my locality, I had the good fortune to get to know an old gentleman living just across the road from us who was a committed socialist. Sensing in me a possible convert, he invited me into his home and explained his ideas. Between times he gave me books to read which expounded the socialist point of view.

On first impression, socialism appeared to me to have a case. To begin with, it opened up a whole world of which hitherto I had been unaware. I had up to that time travelled very little, having seen barely anything of the regions of Britain outside the South East — and indeed not a lot even of the poorer areas of London, though I lived just on the edge of it. I learned something of the appalling conditions under which a large part of the country's 'working classes' had been condemned for many generations to live. This increased my discontent with the political state of things.

The literature I studied spoke persuasively of the evils and failures of 'capitalism'. So far as this went, I had to agree — although of course I was relying on the evidence of what I saw in print, not what I had actually witnessed with my own eyes. What I was of course reading about was international, liberal *laissez-faire* capitalism, which has been the form of capitalism prevailing in Britain for most of the time since the Industrial Revolution; that there could be another, alternative economic concept under which **some** of the aspects of capitalism could be retained and made to work for the general good was not something that occurred to me at the time, as of course it was not suggested in any of the left-wing literature I was studying. Nor had it occurred to me to investigate for myself the practical results of socialist economic doctrines where they had actually been applied; I was content to accept the theoretical picture of the socialist utopia as presented by socialist writers. Remember, I was only in my teens!

For a time it appeared to me as if I might, through socialism, find the solutions I was seeking. I retained an open mind about it all. I was already convinced that the Tories had no ideals worth supporting whatsoever. I detected some idealism, and at least some just dissatisfaction with things as they were, in the polemics of socialist writers, as well as some of the speakers to whom I had started to listen on radio and TV. There seemed to be some degree of crusading zeal in the socialist cause, whereas on the political 'right' there was only self-centredness and smugness.

But something still held me back from accepting the full socialist package of goods and aligning myself with that point of view. What that something was I could not at that time explain, even to myself. Some kind of instinct, rather than clear reasoning, told me that there was something wrong with it all, and deterred me from joining any left-wing organisation and committing myself to that side of politics.

Have you ever focused your eyes on an object, be it a person, a picture or some urban or rural scene, and had the feeling that something about it is not quite right? Exactly what, you cannot say. Undoubtedly, some features of what you are looking at are attractive, but a little voice inside you says: "Don't accept this — there is a flaw in it somewhere!"

That was how it was with me as I looked into the subject of socialism, always bearing in mind that every brand of socialism under my examination at the time was one standing to the left of the political spectrum.

Not satisfied that I could embrace any of these socialist schools of thought wholeheartedly, but not seeing on the horizon any alternative political doctrine that attracted me, I dropped for a time the idea of taking up any definite position in British politics and turned my attention to other matters, devouring more books on political history (in particular modern history), economics and much else.

I had by this time left school with a modest three O-levels (to be supplemented later by two more obtained through private study and tuition). No career beckoned me which I could follow with any enthusiasm. All the world seemed increasingly wrong and I wanted to do something towards changing it. Until such a change had been achieved, I could not see the point of pursuing any ordinary career or profession. Looking back now, I can see that there may have been an element of bohemianism in all this — it has so often been the excuse of young men to escape the disciplines of study and training for a useful occupation that they were exempted from such labours by some special 'call' to reform society, and many a parasitical philosopher who has plagued mankind with quack doctrines of social betterment has in fact, when the wrapping is stripped off, stood revealed as nothing better than a spoilt brat who shirked honest and useful work. In my own case the latter did not occur, however; I found employment in the clerical field very shortly after leaving school. Within a year I was due to enlist in HM Armed Forces as a national serviceman, and it was difficult to form any long-term plans concerning my chosen occupation until that hurdle was over. By then, I reasoned, I may have a clearer picture of what I wanted to do.

In the meantime I spent much of my off-duty hours playing cricket and football, with occasional diversions into other games such as table tennis, which I always enjoyed and was able to play a little. In the course of club cricket I found myself now and again playing alongside coloured cricketers. I did not feel in any way hostile to them — at that time I assumed, like my father, that their presence in Britain was purely a transitory one. I had not yet begun to think very deeply on the subject of race, for the reason that no great presence of people of other races in Britain had yet come to my notice. The Coloureds I encountered, perhaps because they had not yet come to feel strength of numbers, were not obtrusive, and I got along alright with the few I knew. At the same time I did not feel that compulsion that some of my countrymen feel to be friendly to them beyond the normal requirements of common civility; the liberal guilt feelings over imagined imperialist 'exploitation', which seem to induce some folk positively to fawn on anyone with a darker skin, had never touched me. And whilst it did not occur to me to think of these visitors as my enemies, neither did I ever for one moment think of them as my equals — not at least in any collective sense. My race had for centuries been their rulers and they its subjects, a relationship that it was obvious to me had not come about as a result of some toss of a coin. I did not take this as a reason to maintain an excessively overbearing attitude towards coloured people but it did, to my mind, require the maintenance of some degree of 'distance'. At this time my feelings on such matters were instinctive rather than methodically thought out, but everything I have learned since has confirmed that they were right. This same attitude leads me to deplore any crudely offensive behaviour by Whites towards Coloureds in Britain, and any manifestation of that behaviour by members of our movement today is quickly stamped upon on the very rare occasions that it occurs. Apart from any other considerations, that kind of behaviour degrades the White Man by undermining his dignity.

Before coming to the end of this chapter on these early years, it is perhaps appropriate to say a word about a very strong influence on my boyhood life: my mother. Like my father, Mother was not a politician, nor even a member of any political party. She did, however, possess a kind of basic British patriotism combined with a healthy scepticism towards what she read in the newspapers and towards politicians generally. In Finchley we lived next door to a couple who had visited Germany during the Hitler years and seen much to admire. In conversations over the garden fence, they opened Mother's eyes to the forces in this country that were using the weapon of the Big Lie to goad us towards war, and they recommended her to listen to Mosley, who was the leading voice in the country in favour of a no-war policy. My mother did once hear the British Union leader speak at a dinner, and years later told me how impressed she had been. Perhaps most important, she instilled into me at an early age the principle that I should not believe everything I read in print, nor follow 'orthodox' opinion just because it was the opinion everyone about seemed to hold.

Looking back on those years, I have nothing but affection and gratitude towards both my parents. My opponents, in trying to seek some reason for my present heresies, have sometimes tried to attribute them to an unhappy childhood. I am afraid that there they are onto a loser. My father and mother made my young years as contented as any parents possibly could, though they knew how to be strict when the situation demanded it. My mother is still alive today as I write these words. Although she is not connected with my politics, we remain close — as we have always been.

Chapter 2

Army service

I have said that I found it difficult to make long-term plans concerning my future with my scheduled two-year spell in the armed forces ahead of me. In the summer of 1952 I reported for a medical examination and, not surprisingly to me, was passed A1. When asked which branch of the forces I preferred, I opted for the Army and when asked which branch of that said, without quite knowing why, the Artillery. I got my wish.

On the 2nd October 1952 I reported for national service at Park Hall barracks, Oswestry, enlisting as a gunner in the Royal Artillery. I had in the preceding years read enthusiastically on military matters and cultivated a strong admiration of military institutions and conventions, and I welcomed the opportunity to serve a period in the British Armed Forces. Indeed in different times I might seriously have contemplated making the army my career. To do this, however, I would have needed to have confidence that national affairs were in good hands, that the political direction of the nation was basically sound and that therefore the deployment of the armed forces was carried out in pursuit of sound national objectives. By 1952 I had come to the view that this was not the case. I did not therefore for one moment contemplate becoming a professional soldier. I was convinced that my vocation lay elsewhere, though exactly where elsewhere I was not sure.

For all these reasons it did not occur to me to seek a commission. I did not anyway believe that men who were just in the army for a short stay and only had little experience should be given command. Perhaps it may have been to my advantage at the time to have taken a different attitude; the experience of leadership of men might have been valuable to me — although, as I shall shortly relate, I did gain plenty of experience of how **not** to lead by observing officers from the position of a man in the ranks. In addition, the record of having served as a commissioned officer might have been useful to me as a reference in later life. At 18, however, we do not always see things this way. I was placed in a training squad consisting of fellows who, on the basis of background, were considered to be of possible 'officer material', and the nature of our training was such as to familiarise us with the kinds of tasks that would be faced by RA subalterns in the field. We were dubbed 'Technical Assistants Royal Artillery (TARAs)'. The work of a TARA was to assist the commander of a troop (four guns) in the task of achieving accuracy in range and direction for the guns. This was achieved with the aid of ordnance survey maps, compasses, theodolites and various geometrical instruments. I took to it and found it interesting — perhaps here indicating a disposition similar to my distant relative, Professor Tyndall, who spent a part of his early life on survey and map work.

The really keen ones in my training squad went on to become officers, while the rest of us were to spend our time in the ranks. While I have mentioned the possible advantages that might have fallen to me from joining the former, there were some advantages in not doing so, one of which was to have lived and worked for two years with fellows of very different backgrounds to my own, helping me to become, like my father, something of a classless person. To a limited extent, I had had a similar experience before in my youth club soccer team, and this army period was to continue the process a step further, with the additional factor of the wide regional variations among the fellows I knew. I got to know Scots, Geordies, Yorkshiremen, Midlanders, Welshmen, Cornishmen and many others — at first finding some of their accents incomprehensible but in time finding my acquaintance with them a valuable education. These chaps included many factory workers, some farm labourers, shipyard apprentices, bricklayers, fishermen and much else, and a few of them came from mining families. Talking to them about their backgrounds, and some of the social problems they had experienced, I found a whole new world opening up to me. I had read something in socialist literature of deprivation among the poorer classes in Britain, but in the back of my mind was the thought that some of the writers had axes to grind. Hearing of these things from fellows who had, and whose fathers and grandfathers had, experienced them directly, I was inclined to give them more credence than when gleaning them merely from a book.

This was a priceless education and for me perhaps far preferable, in view of my later endeavours, to the officers' mess. By mixing with all classes as well as men from all regional backgrounds, I was able to develop a truly national outlook. I had always of course thought and felt nationalistically, but here my national feelings took on an extra dimension. I suspect that one of the troubles with the Tory Party is the fact that most of its leading lights have grown up in an environment in which they have had little contact with the kind of people with whom I mixed in the army and therefore have not the slightest idea of what they really think. Getting to know these fellows and the problems faced by their families in areas and times of considerable poverty and lack of work prospects, I came to understand what makes people become socialists. Though in due course I was to come to see the utter futility of Labourite and other forms of British socialism as solutions to these problems, the problems remain, and it is well to be aware of them.

Another thing that I quickly came to appreciate was army discipline — I say 'appreciate' but of course in the first place it was the appreciation simply of recognition rather than of liking. For the first two weeks of our lives as soldiers we seemed to spend all our time drilling and polishing. We were under the command of a bombardier, an aggressive Ulsterman. He must have been pretty small, for I remember him looking quite a long way up at me, and I am no more than average height. He seemed to delight in subjecting all of us to the vilest personal abuse, and it was quite a test of one's self-control to have to stand passively to attention and take this from someone of his size in silence.

The process continued when, at the end of this two weeks, I was transferred to another squad, this time under a sergeant. He was a cockney, and a chip off the old block, with a vocabulary of quite amazing range. I recall one occasion when we were engaged in a piece of marching drill during which some members of the squad had not been performing at their soldierly best and our sergeant had been voicing his opinion of their efforts in very loud and outspoken terms, with a torrent of four-letter expletives, some ancient and well known, some quite novel. Suddenly it dawned on him that the regimental padre was standing nearby watching and listening spellbound to this remarkable elocution lesson. Within our earshot but not within the padre's, our sergeant checked himself and said: "Sorry priest!" From then on we started to regard him almost with affection and learned to accept his daily verbal portraits of us as being merely in the line of duty and in no way personal — just simply part of the necessary job of licking us into shape as soldiers.

During the evening we would spend most of our time preparing our uniforms and kit, and particularly our boots, for inspection the

next morning. This seemed to me a thoroughly pointlessly irk-
some chore — as long as things were tolerably clean, I reasoned,
that should be enough; it should not be necessary to polish toecaps
until you could practically use them as mirrors to shave with. I
was of course wrong. These tasks were being imposed upon us for
a good purpose: the idea was to get us used to a regime of tidiness
and cleanliness by comparison with which the later one, when we
were posted to our service regiments, would seem easy. It was
also an aim to instil into us an automatic obedience to authority,
quite irrespective of the wisdom or logic, as we saw it, of the
orders we were obliged to obey. As we sat on our beds and spat
and polished well into the evening, NCOs would strut into the
barrack room, pick up the products of our hours of toil and bark at
us to the effect that the results were not nearly good enough and
that many more hours at the same labour would be required if we
were to escape some dire fate the next morning. All this was interlarded with the usual expletives and uncomplimentary references
to our persons (and occasionally our fathers and mothers). Here
again our self-control was being put on trial. We soon came to
know that if we reacted as we would often have liked to react a
most unpleasant future would befall us, and we learned to suffer in
silence, punctuated just by "yes, bombardier", "no, bombardier" and so on.

This was vastly different to what I had known at school a short
time earlier. There I had not been among the most disciplined of
pupils — in fact the very opposite of a goody-goody. I attribute
this mainly to the weakness of my schoolteachers. Whatever their
competence in the particular academic subjects they were paid to
teach, they were mostly wholly lacking in the force of character
necessary to win the respect of their class members and command
the latter's interest and attentiveness. Many of them were timid
little hothouse plants who had been trained almost solely in the
academic field and very little in boy management. If they came up
against an unruly pupil who was physically fairly strong and, in
addition, of forceful character, they would tend to let him get off
almost with murder. Of course, in recent times things have got
very much worse, and discipline in most of our schools is virtually
non-existent. However, back in my schooldays in the late 1940s
and early 1950s it was far from being what it should have been, at
least at my school. The Army was a world apart. Within little
more than a year of being a none too well behaved schoolboy I
became a very well behaved soldier. I had no choice.

This experience demonstrated to me the value of pure coercive discipline. That of course is not enough on its own; as one gets older some additional element making for discipline has to become present; but it is a necessary start. In most spheres of life in Britain today we have lost sight of this elementary rule, and one reason for this could be the abolition of the institution of national service that was obligatory for nearly every young man of my generation.

I sometimes hear some 'wise guy' from among my contemporaries come on television or radio and relate the 'silliness' and 'pointlessness' of the drilling and spit-and-polish regime to which he was subjected in service days. Very often he is one of these trendy 'radicals' who has made a good living writing books in which ancient codswallop masquerades as modern 'thought'. He imagines his achievement in discerning the 'illogic' of army discipline to be indicative of some superior intellectual and reasoning powers, whereas all he is revealing is a mind that has not developed since his days at nursery school, when he resented not being able to do exactly as he liked.

My training at Oswestry ended, I was posted to the 4th Regiment, Royal Horse Artillery, stationed at Hohne, Germany. I need hardly say that the regiment contained no horses, its name being retained merely out of respect for past tradition. We arrived at Hohne on New Year's Eve 1953, in the midst of much snow. The barracks, like most of those used by British forces in Germany, were formerly the property of the Wehrmacht. Compared with the hastily-built huts in which we had resided at Oswestry, they were most impressive. Hitler, I deduced, must have regarded the provision of good living quarters for his troops as a very high priority. Not only were the billets extremely comfortable but the washing amenities were of the highest standard. As a sportsman, I was also impressed by the sight of two football fields surrounded by running tracks visible just over the road from our barrack room window.

This was to be my home for the remaining 21 months of my service. The time seemed to pass slowly by comparison with preceding and following years. This was probably because we were not kept particularly busy. Looking back, I am bound to say that this was due to a very low quality of officering. A nation that is called upon to pay a high price — and in my view an entirely necessary one — for the maintenance of its armed forces has a right to expect that every day in the life of every member thereof will be spent to the best possible effect. First of all, the men should be kept up to a high peak of physical fitness. At Oswestry PT periods had been regular and tough, and very good for us. Here they were non-existent. Fellows who had been licked into good condition in basic training soon got out of condition again unless, like me, they took part in sports and submitted themselves to voluntary fitness training.

Perhaps it was supposed that we, as gunners, did not need to attain the same fitness standards as infantrymen, but I would disagree. I could easily imagine contingencies of war in which men serving in artillery units would be called upon to perform an infantry role. Supposing that guns were destroyed but manpower was left largely intact, and then the men were required to fight their way across country to a place where they could be regrouped. Alternatively, supposing that a gun position was attacked by enemy infantry — what use would the big guns be then? The unit would have to fight as foot soldiers against foot soldiers. Out of condition and lacking any kind of infantry training, they wouldn't stand a chance!

For these same reasons, it should have been regarded as vital to make our men proficient in the use of small arms. In fact small arms were not issued to the men but kept in an armoury and only taken out on manoeuvres. I recall no more than two or three occasions during my entire two years when my unit went to the rifle ranges for practice — useless as a preparation for war.

Our barracks were situated no more than 30-odd miles from the East/West border. Popular myth had it that the main reason for us being there was to defend Western Europe in the event of a Soviet attack. I often found myself pondering what would happen if the not-so-distant Russians made a sudden lightning raid, perhaps by parachute. Just how capable would we be of resisting them? Even if advance warning was sufficient to enable small arms to be issued to every man in the regiment in time, the majority probably would not be capable of hitting one of the enemy at 50 yards, let alone putting his weapon in order if it broke down!

The men were given some exercise in the functions to which they had been allotted, but this nowhere near filled the hours of time available. Those hours could have been occupied in increasing the versatility of the regiment by teaching each man at least the rudiments of other men's jobs. What would happen in battle, for instance, if the radio operator got killed and no-one else knew how to make his radio work? What would happen if vehicle drivers fell and those surviving could not drive? At one time they did hold driving courses on a voluntary basis for anyone who was interested. I grabbed at this chance to do at the state's expense something which in civvy street I could only do at my own expense, and I thereby learned to drive, obtaining an army licence which, on demob, I was able to swop for a civilian licence without any additional test. Every man, however, should have been taught to drive as a matter of course. The time was available. Why was it not done?

The army, like the devil, was much exercised in finding work for idle hands. The fellows would parade in the morning and the sergeants or bombardiers were left to find them something to do. Those who did not have any definite job to tackle would be assigned to the washing of vehicles and guns. Once this was done, what next? Why, the same vehicles and guns were given another wash, even though the previous wash may have been only four or five days ago.

Naturally, with so much time taken up by this useless activity, which was at the same time boring and therefore demoralising, 'skiving' (dodging work) became something of an art by no means confined to the born loafers, and I engaged in quite a bit of it myself. I was prepared to do my bit as a soldier in terms of essential work, but I was not prepared to waste away my time performing ridiculous and unnecessary functions in order to spare some officer the exercise of finding me a function that was useful to the regiment and at the same time to my training as a member of that regiment.

I soon cultivated the knack of persuading whoever took morning parade that I had a job to do, and I was duly told to go and do it. I would then proceed to the storeroom where the equipment necessary to my trade was kept and, along with my colleague in that trade, would while away the many surplus hours. When we heard footsteps in the corridor heading in our direction we would grab brooms or dusters and be prepared to 'look busy' if one of our superiors entered. Most of this time I occupied reading books from the regimental library and was able thus to continue my study of subjects related to politics, which were absorbing me more and more. Between times I would become involved in political arguments — at least on such occasions as I could find people interested enough in the subject. When I look back over those years and the ones immediately following, I recall that I seem to have spent a great deal of time in political argument, which no doubt stood me in good stead in later years when what had at first been a hobby became a profession, indeed a vocation. One of the things that I learned quite early on was that, with some people, such argument is a pure waste of time: they have an entirely different value system and what they want in politics is a world away from what people like me want. In discussion with them, one can build a case which in pure logic is utterly unassailable; so long as there is something in their emotional make-up which is deaf to such a case, one might as well be talking to the birds. The best thing always is not to bother trying to convince these people but to concentrate one's attention on those in whom one can detect some glimmer of common ground with oneself in the way of basic feelings and values. At the same time it could be said that arguing with one whom one can never 'convert' is at least useful training. Also, if one can argue before an audience it is always possible that there is someone in that audience in whom one can strike a receptive chord. After a while, I developed the technique, when arguing with someone whose attitudes were poles apart from my own, of pitching my appeal, not to my adversary, but to others who may be listening to the discussion while not taking part in it.

All this while I maintained my interest in sports and played for both the regimental cricket and football teams. A side benefit of this was that it gave me a chance to travel around and see some of Germany, including two trips to Berlin on cricketing duties. We took the midnight train across Communist East Germany to get there, an experience I found fascinating.

While I had no ambitions as a soldier, I did come to take some interest, as I have said, in my army trade, and got around to feeling that I may as well better myself in the time I had remaining, so I went on a course in order to obtain a certificate of competence and, as a result of this, was promoted to lance-bombardier. With this I was assigned to a few tasks of slightly greater responsibility than previously and found myself coming into closer and more frequent contact with officers. This enabled me to study the officer corps of the British Army as it was in the 1950s, and my study gave me much cause for serious reflection. Supposing, I pondered, a war started and we ceased just to 'play' at soldiers and became engaged in battles of life and death. These men would be my commanders and my life might depend on their decisions, judgement and competence. Are they the kinds of men I would follow with confidence and who would inspire me to fight to the last drop of blood?

The thoughts induced by these questions were not reassuring ones. Our officers were, with one or two exceptions, an unimpressive lot. They seemed to be wholly recruited from the gentry and upper middle classes and the products of public schools. In the course of field exercises I came to realise that some of them were complete idiots, totally unfit for responsibility of any kind. In only one of them (curiously enough a South African, who was briefly seconded to our unit) did I detect any qualities of leadership. This man, apart from possessing a natural authority and knowing his job, took a personal interest in every man in the unit, praised him when he did a task well and infused him with a desire to please — not of the crawling type, motivated by an eye to personal advantage, but one inspired simply by liking and respect for one's superior and the feeling that he deserved loyalty. But among the officers I knew this quality was rare.

Most of them were hardly ever seen, and we came to regard many of the sub-divisions of our regiment (batteries, troops, etc.) as being run mainly by the warrant officers and sergeants, with the commissioned officers as mere remote figureheads. Frequently, I witnessed a subaltern at a complete loss to deal with a situation and having to rely on the sergeant major to take over and sort it out.

Our officers seemed to me to be having quite a joyride. A great deal of their time was spent on recreational pursuits and this perhaps explained why they had so little time to supervise the daily schedules of the men so that their hours were spent to the very best effect.

Leaders of men in war need to be strong personalities. A great many of these fellows we had to salute daily were nothing better than wimps. They came largely from the idle refuse of the genteel classes. They lacked force of character. A great many of them were stupid. And scarcely one of them could motivate the men under him to do anything other than snigger behind his back. That such people would be leading us in war if that contingency came was a terrifying prospect and gave me much food for thought.

The British Tommy over the ages, when he has had capable leadership, has been a match for any fighting man in the world. All too often, however, this has not been the case — giving rise to Napoleon's quip that the British were ''lions led by donkeys.'' There seemed to me to be something dreadfully wrong with a system that allowed such nincompoops as those described by the First Bonaparte, and their heirs and descendants in our regiment in the 1950s, to rise to positions of command.

I am very definitely not a class warrior; on the contrary, I regard some kind of class structure and divisions as inevitable and necessary in any ordered society, providing always that such divisions are a reflection of true superiority on the part of those in the upper echelons. But it seemed to me that the British forces were making the error of recruiting their leaders much too exclusively from the ruling classes just at a time when those classes had grown effete and needed urgent replacement in the way of new blood. A lot of twaddle is talked about 'meritocracy' these days, particularly on the political left, so often ignoring the value to a nation of men born to high position and bred from childhood for public duty. There is no doubt in my mind, however, that a military hierarchy should be very largely, if not totally, meritocratic, with men from the humblest backgrounds able to become generals if they have the necessary leadership qualities. In the case of Britain in the 20th century, this truth applies with extra special force. Why should a ruling class that has led us in the wrong direction in every other field of national life be expected to lead us in the right direction on the battlefield?

My army service was the first opportunity I had had to travel outside my own country (Ireland not being a place which, in my own mind, I was ever able to put in that category). At the time I joined up, British forces were stationed in many parts of the world, and it therefore seemed likely that I would get some overseas posting. Of all the postings that I contemplated, Germany was the one that most appealed to me, and it was therefore my good fortune that this was the one I got. My childhood years had been dominated by talk of what was going on in Germany, and from this talk one might have formed the view that the Germans were Satan's emissaries on earth. Even in schoolboy comics this was the trend, with the soldiers of that nation depicted as hard-faced robots peering hatefully at you from under coal-scuttle helmets. Indeed most wartime British and allied propaganda was more or less at this schoolboy comic level; when one watches the films and reads the newspapers of that period, one winces at the degree of corn employed. Did our opinion-moulders really have to insult the British public's intelligence to this extent, or had we indeed become the nation of morons implied by the language thus used to keep our war resolve up to scratch?

I well remember an occasion near the war's end when I was travelling with my father in his car and we found ourselves behind an army truck filled with young fellows with rather tattered greenish uniforms. "They," Dad pointed out, "are German prisoners."

I stared, fascinated. They actually looked human! In fact they resembled nothing so closely as the older boys in my neighbourhood. I had been encouraged to view them as one would creatures from another planet, yet here they appeared as if just the same race as us! From then on I tended to react to the familiar media stereotypes of Germans with increasing derision.

By the time I was called up, I had begun to develop a great love of classical music, and it had not escaped my notice that a very large portion of the music I enjoyed most was written by German or Austro-German composers. This did not square with the picture of the 'nation of barbarians' that was in popular vogue in the wartime and early post-war years; indeed the label 'barbaric' would be far more appropriately applied to the collection of jungle noises now being promoted, with great profit, by the burgeoning electronics industry that has taken over the management of our cultural life in the 'democracies'.

I therefore placed my first foot on German soil comparatively uncontaminated by the prejudices against that country held by many of my compatriots. I had not yet formed any particular views about the Nazi period, as I did not feel that I was sufficiently knowledgeable thereon to make a judgement. It had occurred to me that, if a highly civilised and intelligent nation, as the Germans very obviously were — Lord Beaverbrook's opinions notwithstanding, wholeheartedly embraced a leader and a doctrine as the Germans for a time did Hitler and National Socialism, then the period in which that leader and doctrine held sway deserved some serious and objective study.

I could at least make a start by looking at the country in the not too distant aftermath of the Nazi collapse and observing its people close-up. I therefore welcomed the opportunity to spend nearly two years in Germany.

In 1953 the Germans were still picking up the pieces from the wartime devastation. The rebuilding they had achieved by that time was impressive. I recall the times when we went on field exercises and might sometimes be proceeding in convoy through a village or small town in the early hours of the morning. Even at 6 o'clock there was plenty of activity, with many people on their way to work. Nowadays the Germans, having achieved their 'economic miracle', do not labour quite such long hours — indeed

I understand that their working **year** (when holidays are taken into account) is less than ours in Britain. At that time, however, they certainly seemed to deserve the reputation for super-industriousness given to them.

Since these times I have travelled in a number of countries and observed many races. I have not changed the view that I formed then — that the Germans are as admirable people as can be found anywhere. It is indeed a tragedy that we have spent so much of our recent history fighting them. Had the British and German races in the 20th century been able to come to an understanding, how much better world we might now be living in!

It was not easy to talk to the Germans about their recent past. For one thing, I knew at that time almost nothing of the language and could only therefore communicate with those of them who spoke English. For another, they were extremely wary of expressing their opinions about the Hitler period with any openness or frankness — and for very good reasons, as I came to learn when I became acquainted with the laws of the then infant Federal German Republic against any manifestation of pro-Nazi sentiments. We had of course 'liberated' these people from totalitarianism and bestowed upon them our glorious 'freedom'. Yet here they were, forbidden and afraid to say anything even only mildly favourable to their country's previous management. It gave me much upon which to ponder.

What I could see about the Germans is that they conducted themselves in a manner that could not possibly be bettered, in view of the fact that their country had comparatively recently been conquered and was, at that time, officially, under forces of occupation. They had suffered overwhelming defeat and appalling destruction, but they had not lost their dignity or their pride. Very few behaved towards us with any sort of ingratiation, let alone servility; on the other hand, they were mainly courteous and not lacking in friendliness, as long as one did not attempt to push them around or patronise them. If our country were ever to suffer the catastrophe of defeat and conquest in war, I would hope that our people would bear themselves with the same honour towards those who became their occupiers.

I have mentioned earlier how I put to use the abundant time on my hands to continue my book-reading. Indeed my whole 21 months in Germany provided the ideal conditions for study, observation and meditation. We were in a remote, sparsely populated part of the country. A small village called Bergen was situated about three miles down the road. The nearest town of any size was Celle, to which we might go on a Saturday out every two or three months or so. Generally speaking, there was not a lot with which to fill off-duty hours. One had to become fairly self-reliant in the way of keeping occupied. Apart from my participation in sports, most of my time was spent reading and thinking, the latter pursuit often engaged'in on long and solitary walks.

This period enabled me to augment, better arrange and clarify the jumble of ideas that had started to form previously as a result of my pre-army observations and studies. I was still at the stage of believing that, possibly, some sort of socialism may provide the remedy to the ills of society that troubled me, but I continued at the same time to be put off by something in the stance of the political left. I tried to analyse more carefully what it was about the left which inspired this doubt. Gradually, little shafts of light began to penetrate through the fog.

Being placed in a foreign country, I was not only able to broaden my outlook by observing that country and its people; I was also able to see my own country in new perspective. One of our great poets (was it Browning?) once said: "He little knows England who only England knows." Apart from my dislike of the tendency to speak of 'England' when referring, usually, to Britain, I find much wisdom in those words. For my own part, being abroad — and particularly in an advanced and civilised country which I came greatly to respect, served to heighten and bring into bolder definition my own national consciousness. That consciousness had always been there, as indicated earlier. But during this period of my life it began to come more and more to the forefront of my thinking. I had somehow taken it for granted before that Britain was a great and proud nation, with a heritage and a position in the world second to none. I had from a very early age taken a great pride in the achievement of the British Empire, and formed the firm belief that this empire should in the main part be retained and welded even more closely than in the past to the Mother Country.

This is not to say that I was unduly enamoured of the thought of Britain binding herself for ever to rule, defend and take responsibility for a vast network of colonies, the majority of whose people had no special ties of kinship with ourselves. I did not consider we had lost anything of concrete value by getting out of India, although I disliked the whole manner and style of our withdrawal, just as I was disgusted by the tendency of so many of our 'intelligentsia' to drool over shamans like Gandhi, as they did any and every former imperial subject who had twisted the tail of the British Lion and thus fed their endless appetite for national masochism.

I viewed all these territories where the British Race had ruled other races as possessions to be evaluated on a pure profit/loss, asset/liability basis. If they were not useful to us from some sound economic or strategic point of view, we should get out — without delay and without ceremony, with the view taken that their protection was not worth the life of one single British serviceman. If they were useful from either or both of these points of view, we should hold onto them and defend them with all means necessary — and for as long as the criteria by which we deemed them useful to us continued to apply. At least along these lines there lay a firm and unambiguous policy. But from what I could see no post-war British Government had any policy at all on the matter, other than one of long-term surrender in all sectors, confused, in the short-term, by panic reaction to each and every emergency as it occurred, sending troops to quell a disturbance here, then there, and always seeming to be swept along by pressures from 'world opinion' as well as various sections of opinion at home, rather than any prudent and far-sighted consideration for the British interest.

The vital elements of the Empire always were the Dominions. In these lands there were substantial populations belonging to the British Race, albeit here and there mingled with other white racial groups, mostly assimilable. The countries in question possessed, with Britain, nearly every natural economic resource, together with space for an almost limitless expansion of population. It should have been regarded as the prime task of British statesmanship to weld this White Empire and Commonwealth together into an unshakable combination of national power. Yet it was clear that there had been a total failure to do this — not on account of any insurmountable difficulties in the task itself but because of total lack of will in Britain to undertake it.

In the ranks of Conservatism there had in earlier years been a kind of lip service to the imperial idea but no sign of any practical policy for imperial organisation and development. Tories in the first half of the present century had been full of wind about the 'Empah' but very lacking in any signs of action to exploit its immense possibilities for the British Race that had built it. By the 1950s it was becoming clear that these Tories were starting to abandon even the pretence of being an imperial party. On the Labour side, on the other hand, such a pretence had never been adopted in the first place. The left had always been implacably hostile to any imperial concept, as indeed to any other concept of national greatness. On the contrary, all patriotic causes were anathema to those dedicated to socialist causes.

This latter fact began to come home to me with increasing emphasis as I turned back and re-read some of the socialist literature I had perused earlier, together with newer and more up-to-date writings. That which had deterred me from aligning myself with the left of politics, at first only vaguely perceptible, now loomed large and clear. Every school of socialist thought with which I had become acquainted repudiated any concession to nationalism or patriotism — or at least to **British** nationalism or patriotism; socialists were quite prepared to champion national or patriotic causes of other nations, and most enthusiastically of all when those causes ran contrary to the interests of Britain!

,. In October 1954 my army service came to an end. I was glad to get back to civilian life but glad at the same time to have had this army experience. I have ever since retained the view that a period of service in the armed forces is good for a young man, just as the institution of national service is good for the country. Today when I watch the yobbish behaviour of some of our youthful generation I am constantly struck by the thought that had they had a background of experience in the forces the instances of such behaviour would be greatly reduced.

Chapter 3
The call of politics

I returned from Germany to be demobilised formally at Woolwich Barracks. By this time my father had taken over the administration of a YMCA holiday centre in Skegness, Lincolnshire. I spent a week or two with my family before returning to civilian employment. They had kept my old job in London waiting for me and I resumed duties there, not with too much enthusiasm, as it was clear to me that it was no more than a temporary phase in my life before I went on to other things. It did at least enable me to keep solvent, however, while I was sorting out what eventually I wanted to do.

I took a room at the Central YMCA in London's Tottenham Court Road. The rent was cheap. The position was handy for my work, involving me in no more than a 10-15 minute walk mornings and late afternoons. In addition, the YMCA had a well equipped gymnasium, where I was able to engage my passion for keeping fit, and here I started for the first time another healthy pursuit, weight-training, of which I still do a bit today.

This period of living alone in Central London provided much in the way of a further education for me. I continued to do a vast amount of book reading, and in between started to acquaint myself with the big city itself. Previous to this I had been essentially a suburbanite, living on the outer periphery of the metropolis and commuting in and out daily in the course of my work. Now I found myself with many spare hours on my hands right in the centre of the nation's capital, and I took the opportunity to observe it close-up. I took many long walks around London's maze of streets, taking in the scene with studious intent. The more I saw, the less I liked.

One of the first things to earn my distaste was the higgledy-piggledy design of the city. London has many magnificent buildings, but they have been thrown up in a completely unco-ordinated process of development, so that the city has no plan and no symmetry. Most of the streets are far too narrow. Fine pieces of architecture are situated next door to drab and ugly constructions which spoil much of their effect. There is a depressing shortage of noble vistas, and of course, in later years, there has been a far worse disfiguration with the coming of gigantic and hideous office blocks.

I had my own idea even then of what the capital city of a great nation should look like, and I could not in all honesty deceive myself that London came anywhere near it. Yet indeed most of the centuries of the city's development were centuries in which Britain was as wealthy as, if not wealthier than, any other nation in Europe. Why then did so many continental cities, one or two of which I had seen in Germany and several more I had read about and studied in pictures, far excel London in generosity of planning and construction? It could only be because those administering them had greater national and civic pride, and perhaps because the necessary political means were in their hands.

My travels about the city gradually began to reveal to me the depths of degeneration to which our society was sinking. Everywhere one could see the cinemas and theatres catering to human depravity. Everywhere prostitution was prominent. Then a new phenomenon began to appear — new at least to me, who was then much of an innocent in such matters. I began to be troubled by the profusion of effeminate-looking men everywhere, unmanly in their facial expressions, in their speech, in their dress and in their bearing. What is the breed of Drake and Cook coming to? I thought. What I did not immediately know, but took time to awaken to, was that these specimens were the advance guard of the 'gay' plague that later was to sweep through society like a poisonous virus. Before long I came to realise that these creatures had whole industries running to cater for them, such as the industry printing the many picture books with young men in 'body beautiful' poses, presented as 'physical culture' but in reality produced to pander to the tastes of the growing queer fraternity.

The smell everywhere was one of decadence. I began to realise that my idea that the British were a great nation was becoming alarmingly out of date. The decadence I had of course begun to recognise some years before, as I have related on earlier pages, but the full extent of it only started to dawn on me when I lived right in the centre of the 'Great Wen'. At about the same time I obtained a book summarising in precis form Gibbon's *Decline and Fall of the Roman Empire*, and I could not help being struck by the similarities between this great writer's descriptions of that long past tragedy and the evidence I saw with my own eyes all around me.

And yet we were still in the comparatively early aftermath of a war which we had reputedly fought in defence of some 'superior' way of life and values, having defeated the 'dark' and 'evil' forces that had threatened our 'civilisation'. If this was really what millions of men had given their lives for, one wondered the purpose of the sacrifice!

And what, in the face of this sin and filth, were the leaders of our society doing? What, for a start, was the Church doing? Where were those men of the cloth prepared to come forward and crusade against all the moral rottenness around us? It became clear to me that, apart from a few pious words from the pulpit on Sundays, they were doing virtually nothing. What were the politicians doing? Apparently, nothing either!

It was during this period that I first started to become acutely conscious of the huge alien presence in our capital. Everywhere around were faces which by no stretch of imagination could be regarded as British. Equally obviously, they were not just people on a temporary stay in our country; here they regarded as their home! I began to notice that a large proportion of the nasty little bookshops and places of entertainment disfiguring the landscape were run by these people, though plenty of my own fellow countrymen had their sticky fingers in the rackets too.

I began to make the acquaintance of a few fellows who, like me, were staying at the YMCA. They were largely young students from homes in the provinces and with middle class backgrounds. I started to engage them in political discussions to see whether they shared with me my alarm at the degenerating state of our country, manifest in the loss of its international power and the creeping collapse of society at home. I soon found that I was up against a brick wall of ignorance, apathy and topsy-turvy values.

This was my first close-up experience, on the level of personal contact — as opposed just to the book level, of 'liberalism', the faith once described by James Burnham as 'the creed of Western suicide'.

In the earlier stages of my discussions with these fellows I hung onto the naive belief that by the sheer rationality of my arguments I could eventually win them around to my position! I had by this time, and in the course of experience, developed a better technique of exposition, learning to build up a case methodically, in the manner of a barrister in a court of law. This apart, I was of course much better informed than they were on most of the subjects in question. But it was of no avail. I found that there was no possibility whatever of getting through to these fellows because we were arguing from entirely different standpoints, underpinned by wholly different basic values.

With two people who hold the same things dear, who share the same ideas as to what should be the ultimate goals of society, and whose fundamental concepts of right and wrong are held in common, there is the possibility of eventually reaching common ground, even if there is disagreement at the start. Both want the same things; all that is in dispute is the best path to the attainment of them. Here is the basis for a useful debate.

But if that essential of a shared set of sentiments is lacking, if the two sides have entirely opposite goals, discussion becomes hopeless. It is like two men, one of whom wants to get to London and the other to get to Manchester, arguing about what is the best route!

This is how I found it with these 'liberals'. I started by thinking that I could easily appeal to their patriotism and national pride by showing how the policies of a succession of British governments had resulted in one national surrender after another, one national humiliation after another. Surely they would see! But they didn't. In time it came home to me that in appealing to their patriotism and national pride I was appealing to things that simply didn't exist — they had none of either; on the contrary, they thought that such things were strangely archaic, even evil, ideas! If I tried addressing myself to their instincts of race, I experienced the same result: they had no such instincts. In fact some of them would quickly turn on me and accuse me of being a 'hater' of other races, though I had said nothing whatever to justify such an assertion, having only spoken in terms of a love and loyalty to my own race, their race. It was baffling: trying to get reason out of these fellows was like trying to get blood out of a stone.

I did not give up easily. After one argument in which certain points had come up, I would go away and think things out, perhaps rearranging the presentation of my case, taking into account some of the claims they had made, ensuring I knew my facts about them, then coming back with answers to those claims. In particular, I remember an argument about national independence and self-determination. They were always singing the praises of these things when alluding to the various nations, real or imagined, which at some time or another the British had ruled. Why then, assuming they were reasonable men, this surely would mean that they would be in favour of **British** national independence and self-determination, now coming under real threat with the increasing tendency of our governments to concede sovereignty over British affairs to international bodies. But no! These people did not believe that **Britain** had a right to national independence and self-determination, only other nations!

I then tried answering their 'anti-colonialist' argument by saying that, if it was right for the British to get out of India, Malaya, Cyprus and our various African colonies as these lands were the property of the native inhabitants, they could not then possibly object to the proposition that the many foreign migrants we had in Britain should get out of **our** country and leave it to the native inhabitants. But no again! When this point was raised, they would turn a principle on its head and throw back at me the accusation that anyone who could make the latter proposition was guilty of inciting 'racial hatred' — though of course it was not 'racial hatred' for Indians to demand that the British get out of India or Africans that they get out of Africa!

We talked about 'democracy', which of course they all thought was a self-evident good. I challenged them to tell me how they defined democracy. Well, they would say, under democracy the majority rules! They would sometimes go on to amplify this point by stressing how necessary it was for us British to hand over control of places like Kenya and the Rhodesias to the Blacks — because, after all, they were the majority!

Using a lawyer's technique in court cross-examination of a witness, I would draw them further and further into this line of argument by getting them to stress, again and again, and by a mounting weight of examples and emphasis, how absolutely right it was that at all times and in all situations the will of the majority was sacrosanct and should always prevail over that of the minorities.

Having lured them into this trap of self-committal, I would then put it to them: "What do you therefore think about 'minority rights', another supposed cornerstone of any democratic system?" By any rational yardstick, they had tripped themselves up completely, for by defending 'minority rights' after their previous commitment to the rule of the 'majority' they would in fact be arguing in complete contradiction of themselves. To illustrate the point, I asked them, presuming that what they wanted came about and the Blacks took over the countries in Africa mentioned, what would be the rights of the white settlers who lived there? They would not acknowledge that these people had any rights, for of course they had been party to a wicked colonialist system under which the natives had suffered — they deserved all that was coming to them!

I tried the same technique in a slightly different sector of argument. These fellows were firmly convinced as to how right it was that Britain recognise the 'independence' of our colonial territories, as earlier mentioned. Parallel with this, we must recognise, they would claim, that our colonial subjects belonging to different races to ourselves were really 'equal' to us in basic capability, having the same intelligence, the same inventiveness, the same industriousness and the same stability of character. All that had previously held them back was the fact that we had ruled them and not allowed them their freedom.

Leaving the subject there, and without any counter-argument, I would then switch the discussion onto overseas aid, citing certain countries that had already been given their independence or others that always had been independent, and asking my aquaintances whether we should give them aid, if necessary for the remainder of time. Oh yes we should! For the remainder of time? If necessary, for the remainder of time!

I would then remind them of their earlier assertions that these countries should be 'independent' of the White Man and that, given that status, they would prove the truth that they were in every way equal in capability to us. How then was it that the countries of Africa, Asia and Latin America that had obtained 'independence' from former white rulers or never known white rule were still sunk in chaos and poverty and needed our economic help to stay afloat? Clearly they had demonstrated that they were neither 'independent' nor 'equal' in relation to us. My adversaries had clearly lost the argument by a mile.

But would they acknowledge it and confess: "OK, you're right." Not a bit of it! They would engage in the most incredible mental gymnastics to escape from their predicament. Alongside this, they would sometimes get angry and shout abuse — these preachers of 'tolerance', who were always singing the praises of their liberal faith in that regard. When you had wiped the floor with them in argument, the mask of tolerance would drop off and they would spit and snarl at you like demented vixens manoeuvred into a corner.

Yet these fellows were, by comparison with most others at that time, 'well educated'. They had in some cases been to the best schools. Currently they were attending universities or colleges of higher learning, where, supposedly, an atmosphere of logic, reason and objective enquiry prevailed — or so one was supposed to believe. In fact I could get much more sense out of a common navvy in an East End pub who had had virtually no education at all. With the latter, an appeal to reason and common sense was possible, while basically healthy sentiments like patriotism and national pride were still there. Not so with these middle class 'clones' at the YM and other places where I met them. It started to come home to me that these fellows had been not so much 'educated' as 'processed' — like some creatures injected with drugs in a laboratory which made them perform in exact accordance with the directions of some master manipulator, who had taken away their brains and their wills and substituted his own. It was nothing less than sinister. I had heard of Orwell's *Nineteen Eighty Four*, but had tended to dismiss it as something which might happen in far off parts of the world but not here in Britain. I began to wonder otherwise.

In relating this process of awakening now, I may give the impression that the stages of it were precise and clearly defined, a step-by-step development in which all had been darkness before each stage and all light thereafter. It was not really so simple as that as it happened. The encountering of a barrier of unbelief and hostility would often lead me to go back and reconsider my own ideas, being prepared to entertain the thought that perhaps it may be I who was the one in the wrong. There is a certain loneliness in this kind of isolation, particularly for a very young man, as I then was, and there comes with this a great temptation to 'conform' to certain ideas in fashion, no matter how much one's instincts and reasoning may rebel against them. But in my case, whenever I retired to rethink some of the positions I had adopted, perhaps fuelling myself for this exercise with further study, I would only return convinced even more strongly that I had been right. Before this period of my life had begun I was deeply worried about the general state of things in Britain. At the end of it I had come to realise that things were worse, much worse, than even I had imagined. The British people — or at least that part of them from which the leaders of society came — had seemingly been infused with a kind of national and racial death-wish. The downward slide of our nation in world affairs was no ordinary misfortune. We had willed it that way!

Two aspects of my personal life were in my thoughts at this time. I was still unsettled in the matter of a career. After some further thought, I decided that I would try to get into a training college for teaching. It was not that a conventional life as a schoolmaster appealed to me very much, but I felt that I ought to qualify at something, and this might be a stepping stone to some vocation in which I would have the opportunity to communicate my ideas to others, particularly young folk. I had the thought of concentrating on the two subjects of history and physical education, the first allowing me to teach the version of past events that I believed correct — by contrast to the false version, as I perceived it, that was being taught at the time, while the second would enable me to capitalise on my competence at certain sports and my great enthusiasm for fitness and exercise.

To enable me to be considered for one of these colleges, I would have to obtain two further GCE O-levels. I went to evening classes and studied for these, eventually obtaining them. Becoming dissatisfied with life in London, I moved to live with my parents and brother, then living in Lincolnshire. I soon found it difficult to get employment there, but my father came to my rescue, giving me odd jobs around the YMCA holiday centre that he managed. I did a bit of painting and decorating, cement-mixing and store-keeping — the spot of partially manual labour involved here doing me no harm. My father was prepared to be helpful now, seeing that I appeared to be more ready than in the past to attempt to qualify for some kind of profession.

The other quest in my life by this time was to find and support some political organisation sharing my ideals. I could not bring myself to join any established party. The Tories and Liberals had never attracted me. For a time I had wondered if I might find a home in the Socialist camp, as I have said, but by now I was thoroughly set against the left and harboured no further illusions that my path might lie in that direction. Wherever I belonged, it looked as if it was to be, for the moment at least, on the unorthodox 'fringe' of politics. This I was quite prepared to accept — it was clear that nowhere could I align myself with any of the established orthodoxies.

I knew almost nothing of such 'fringe' organisations as then existed. The one exception was Union Movement, led by Sir Oswald Mosley, the latter better known of course as the leader of the pre-war British Union of Fascists. Somewhere I read in a newspaper that Mosley had started up in politics again and that his new policy was 'Europe a Nation', the merging of all the European states into a single super-state. By this time I had begun to take an interest in Mosley and wanted to find out more about him and his ideas, but on hearing of this 'Europe a Nation' concept I was immediately put off. I had certainly come to believe that the policies of the pre-war gang of British leaders leading to the division of Europe and then to war had been disastrously wrong — a subject to which I shall return later — and that a more enlightened foreign policy would have been directed towards achieving a state of European harmony which would have spared us the 1939-45 conflict, at least in the West. Harmony among the nations of Europe remained, and still remains, a good thing — though it ill becomes the Common Marketeers to talk of the need to unite Europe now, when these people are the direct political descendants of the generation that divided Europe in the 1930s.

But a single European Nation was, and is, out of the question, being wholly undesirable and not remotely possible. Any thought, therefore, of support for Mosley in respect of his post-war politics was killed at birth.

Then one day I heard a television news report of a demonstration by a group calling itself the 'League of Empire Loyalists', and this report was followed shortly after by an interview with one of the LEL officials, who explained the group's policy of opposition to the (Tory) Government's disengagement from empire.

As I will have made clear, imperial doctrines had become a very central part of my own political thinking, and I would not consider supporting any political group from which such doctrines were excluded. This group immediately caught my interest, although I thought its choice of name a little archaic — I had come to the point of believing that the Empire, though it should be preserved in substance, needed to be up-dated in form, with some of the old terminology discarded. I decided anyway that I would try and locate this group and find out more.

At that time I was still living with my family in Lincolnshire, where I presumed the LEL had no local branch, but I was planning to return to London, and I promised myself that I would then investigate the League.

This I duly did, tracing the group to a basement office in Bridge Street, Westminster, just opposite Parliament. As I entered the room, I took a step that was to have profound consequences for my future life.

A tall man with a beard greeted me and we had a talk. His name was Austen Brooks. From our discussions I learned about LEL policies. It was made clear to me that the group was not a political party and did not intend to become one; its strategy was to act as a pressure group to influence political opinion — which in effective terms meant Conservative opinion, since there was not the slightest prospect of LEL ideas ever being embraced within the Labour or Liberal parties.

The League was not entirely the sort of organisation with which I had had it in mind to become involved. Its imperial and patriotic orientation attracted me, but on some issues its policies did not seem sufficiently radical, while on others it did not attempt to formulate any policies at all. First and foremost, I did not share its faith that anything could be achieved by attempting to influence opinion within the existing political structures, for I had by then come to believe that all of these, the Tory Party included, were rotten to the core. I believed in the necessity for an entirely new political party, though I was under no illusion that the road forward for it would be other than long and hard.

On the other hand, if not the League — then what? I realised that I was much too young and inexperienced to form a political group of my own, besides entirely lacking the means to do so. In the League, on the other hand, there existed the nucleus of something which might develop more in the direction I wished in the fullness of time. Also, by participating in it I would be able to get the apprenticeship in active politics that I needed, as well as make the personal contacts necessary to the achievement of something of greater scope in the future.

I took some literature home for study and devoured it eagerly. From it I came to realise that the leading light in the League was A.K. Chesterton, a man of whom I had never heard. I later met AKC and liked him. He was the Editor of a small journal called *Candour*, of which I soon became an avid reader and from which I gained some entirely new insights into politics that I had been denied previously.

Candour brought me face-to-face for the first time with what is sometimes called the 'Conspiracy Theory', the idea that the great events of recent history and of the present were not chance occurrences or indeed the products of the causes popularly attributed to them but were, and are, the outcome of conspiratorial forces, directing world affairs in a manner entirely different to that explained to, and believed in by, the masses.

This theory of politics came to me by no means as a bolt out of the blue. For some years I had been forming the opinion that some kind of conspiratorial forces were at work behind political events, by the simple reasoning that those events had no other rational explanation. To begin with, I could not see how a nation such as the British, which had displayed qualities second to none over the centuries, could in our century become inflicted with a kind of mass madness, by which policies manifestly disastrous to our nation in every respect were applauded as the ultimate in wisdom. I had been struck by the 'processed' minds of the liberal-leftish students to whom I referred earlier, which simply could not have been filled with such self-contradictory balderdash unless some other minds, much cleverer than their own, had concocted the nonsense they were spouting. The whole of the panorama of British and world politics in the 20th century seemed to contain about it the aura of dark and sinister powers at work, contriving British and Western destruction, while keeping public protest at bay with a quagmire of deceptions and lies.

Here, arranged in clear and logical order by a mind much more experienced than mine, was confirmation of all that I had hitherto suspected but not been able conclusively to prove. I felt grateful to Chesterton for doing this, and he was to become a man who in the coming years had a very considerable influence on my understanding of politics.

I decided I would join the League of Empire Loyalists and help the spread of A.K. Chesterton's ideas — and perhaps, when I was older and a bit more mature, contribute to them myself.

A short time after this I embarked on a venture that might seem strange in the case of someone now committed to this political course. In a sporting magazine I saw an advertisement for a specially organised group trip to Moscow, for which the participant only had to pay £43. While no communist, I had always been interested in Russia and would have welcomed the opportunity to see a bit of it on the cheap. I contacted the organisation promoting the trip and expressed the desire to be included. I was still then in some respects naive and did not immediately recognise that this was one of the various red front organisations operating in Britain in the Kremlin's service. But, be that as it may, as long as there were no strings attached to my using the opportunity for this very cheap and interesting holiday, I saw no reason not to do so.

The Russian trip was certainly interesting, but of much more significance to my political education was the experience of the journey there and the company I encountered on that journey. We went by train the whole way from Ostend to the Russian capital, this taking three days. That time afforded plenty of opportunity to talk with the people accompanying me, who were almost entirely far left-wingers. The same exercise was of course repeated on the three-day journey back, as well as the brief boat-trips across the Channel and the train journey over Kent — a lot of time spent in the company mentioned.

I have explained earlier my youthful interest in socialist ideas and my thought that possibly some salvation might lie in them. I have later explained my growing doubts on this score, enforced by realisation of the consistently anti-patriotic stance taken by socialists on the issues I considered to be of major importance, and the further revulsion experienced in my discussions with students in London in my immediate post-army period. Well, if there still remained in me, after all this, just a grain of hope that something good might be found on the left of politics, that was eliminated for all time by my impressions of, and discussions with, the people who shared with me that long train journey to Russia and back again.

This experience just happened to come at a time when new political horizons had opened up to me through the reading of literature to which previously I had had no access. Reflecting on the personal impressions I had gained of these far leftists and on the conversations I had had with them, and then putting this together with the knowledge gleaned from my new reading, I recognised at last the full extent of the evil inherent in left-wing ideology. I now saw this, not just as a jumble of rather naive and impractical fantasies, not capable of realisation in the real world, but a foul poison the stench of which made one positively sick with revulsion. Here, in all its vile ingredients, was the recipe for the destruction of civilisation.

Some short time before this experience, and through contacts I had made in the LEL, I had obtained and begun to read some books and pamphlets on what, for the sake of simplification, I might best refer to as the 'Jewish Question'. 'Anti-semitism' had of course been a live issue from way back, and I had heard talk of it as a boy without really having any idea as to the meaning of the term. Had anyone suggested to me that a particular race or religious group should be singled out for special ostracism, let alone persecution, merely because of their identity and without any rational basis in the way of anything that they had done, I would, like nearly everyone, have rejected such a proposition. I had had very little to do with Jews in my personal dealings up to that time and was not aware of any special role played by them in politics.

In the literature that I had recently acquired there was much talk of the Jews' political role, of their involvement in 'conspiracies' and of their being the originators of communism. Some of this literature betrayed in its general style and its resort to ludicrous exaggeration that it was clearly written by cranks — for instance, some prominent public figures were described as 'secret Jews' who quite manifestly were not Jews. I was therefore extremely cautious, not to say sceptical, in accepting these authors' conclusions.

In the writings of A.K. Chesterton, however, whom I knew to have a thoroughly balanced and objective mind, some of the same themes appeared, in this case in language that indicated that the author's views had not been reached without a great deal of scientific enquiry. I decided that I should investigate this subject, taking care to steer clear of the lunatic fringe among its practitioners, who tended to blame the Jews for everything, even including the weather.

As I gathered written information, so I also observed, and I did not neglect to turn to Jewish sources to obtain contradiction of the claims of the 'anti-semites'.

Bit by bit, it started to come home to me, in the form of incontrovertible evidence, that there was present in Britain and around the world a definite Jewish network wielding immense influence and power — through money, through politics and through its strong foothold, in some sectors amounting to virtual monopoly, in the mass media.

But were such influence and power necessarily wrong? Could it not be that they were simply the natural and just rewards for hard work, for intelligence, for enterprise and ambition? I tended to despise those natural 'losers' among my fellow men who were always resenting the success of others with greater drive and talent than themselves, and then rationalising that resentment by ascribing to such successful people all manner of diabolica tendencies. Was 'anti-semitism' just the jealousy of the little mar towards those who had climbed to the top of the pile by merit? Or did it have some more reasoned foundation?

The answer would surely depend on two considerations. In the first place, had the wealth and power of the Jews been achieved by genuine service to the community in the way of constructive works, enriching the nation industrially, technologically, culturally and in other positive ways? Secondly, was such power, once it had been attained, wielded in the national interest, that is to say exercised in the service of truly patriotic causes'?

My further studies revealed to me that most of the most success-ful members of this community had risen to the top through commerce, rather than through the productive sectors of industry — as property developers, middle-men, import-export traders, high street chain-store owners, gold, silver and diamond merchants, financiers and bankers. In addition, they were to be found among the leading barons of the mass communications industry, including publishing and popular entertainment, above all the cinema.

Even at this early stage of my political awakening, it was obvious to me how enormously influential the mass media were in setting the tone of national taste and opinion. That a racial minority should wield such power over these means of commun-ication was alarming, to say the least.

Of course to suggest that these areas of activity were not in any way necessary to the nation's life would be ludicrous, but it must be said that within them there are far more opportunities to make money and become successful, without actually enhancing the nation's wealth or welfare, than is the case in the productive sectors of the economy, i.e. manufacturing, farming and the provision of minerals and energy products. This is particularly the case in the financial field, where a clever speculator operating on an international level, can make a vast fortune without actually contributing one small jot to the prosperity of his own country-men. Likewise, in the property field there were huge opportunities for enrichment without providing any useful service to people, indeed by doing the precise opposite, as exemplified by the enterprises of Mr. Peter Rachman and his type. Importers did not necessarily promote national prosperity, particularly if the products they brought into this country resulted in loss of business for home producers. As for the mass media and popular entertain-ments industry, whether these rendered a useful service depended entirely on the nature of the material purveyed.

As far as the popular entertainments industry was concerned, I had by this time come to the opinion that a large portion of the products of that industry were pure garbage, and that those who made money out of them, whether Jew or Gentile, rendered no service to society whatever. If things have changed since that time, it is only that they have become far, far worse. Now the garbage predominates over the good products in a ratio of about four to one. Apart from the puerile mental level to which these products appeal, they have increasingly become the germ-carriers of the vilest propaganda, practically all of it leftist-orientated.

Looking at the productive sectors of the economy that I have mentioned, I was not able to perceive any particularly remarkable degree of Jewish contribution. Very few were to be found among the outstanding inventors, pioneers of real science, engineers and builders. On the cultural level, they had not been particularly prominent among the truly great novelists, poets, painters, composers, sculptors or architects — though on the entrepreneur side of the arts, and as agents, financial backers and critics, they were to be found everywhere.

Looking over the whole picture, I was of a mind not to deny any Jews credit where they had made money and obtained influence by rendering genuine public service in the activities in which they had succeeded, but I was bound at the same time to observe that many had enriched themselves in ways that had contributed little, if anything, to national prosperity, material or otherwise. It goes without saying of course that some Gentiles can also be put into this same category.

Then what of the uses of Jewish wealth and power? I set to work studying the political orientation of Jewish writers in the press, Jewish book-publishers, Jewish political leaders, political philosophers and academics. I investigated the various causes to which Jewish money was being donated.

The truth was inescapable. In not one single case could I find any prominent, powerful and influential Jewish personage who identified himself or herself with any cause complementary to the interests of the British Nation, to patriotism, to race or to Empire. Quite the contrary, every cause inimical to these things seemed to have Jewish participation and backing. Looking back to the political arguments I had had earlier, it now occurred to me, as it had not done at the time, that the most vociferous and aggressive opponents of all I believed in had been Jews.

I became aware of a strange paradox. While Jews were to be found among the most ardent and committed opponents of British Nationalism and British race-loyalty, they were at the same time the most passionate champions of nationalism and 'racism' on the part of their own people. What they denigrated in Britain, they applauded in Israel and among Zionist communities the world over.

I have to stress here that I am not speaking of **all** Jews. I am certain that there are many of that race who earn their living usefully and do not seek to wield influence and power to the detriment of Britain or whatever host country they may live in.

I am only saying that in respect of certain prominent and important Jews, and of the existence of a definite Jewish network exercising great financial and political power, that doctrine derisively referred to as 'anti-semitism' is something possessing a definite foundation of reason and fact. I believe that there are great numbers of men in public affairs who well know this but, precisely because of their awareness of the massive power of this community, are terrified to acknowledge it publicly.

My Russian trip gave me some chance to put to the test of observation the theory that Jews have provided a large portion of the leading activators of the political left. The group with which I travelled from Britain was about 2,000 in number, and for the purpose of easier management was sub-divided into smaller sections of about 30 or so, each section designated as a 'team' and given a 'team leader'. It became clear to me that an exceptionally high proportion of these team leaders were Jews.

In the many discussions and arguments in which I became engaged during the trip I noticed again that the most aggressive and committed proponents of the far left, pro-marxist viewpoint were Jews. On one occasion I had the temerity to ask one of them how he managed to square his antagonistic attitude towards everything patriotic in the British context with the ultra-nationalistic outlook of his own people on every question affecting themselves. The answer came not in the form of a reasoned argument but of a bout of screaming abuse ending in a threat to 'do me over'. It was perhaps fortunate for me at the time that I was, and looked, in pretty good physical condition. Probably the fellow would not have even made the threat if he had not had three or four of his cronies nearby. I looked him squarely in the eye and invited him to carry it out. He looked at them, then back at me, muttered some excuse and then walked off.

Wherein lies the appeal of socialism?

My earlier interest in socialist ideas was prompted by a revulsion against the self-centred outlook underlying the doctrines of the Conservative Party as it had evolved in mid-20th-century Britain and remained since. 'Social Order' and 'Social Justice' were two themes regularly expounded by writers of the left, and to these I could not object. Could not any concept that acknowledged the mutual interdependence between all members of society and recognised the existence of social reponsibility for the welfare of all be described as 'socialist'?

To this, the Conservative will reply that the idea of social responsibility for the welfare of all will discourage individual initiative and self-help. That is all very well and good in situations where people are hard up through their own fault, where there is ample work available at decent rates of pay for anyone who cares to go and find it. In that case the man who is too idle to go and find a job deserves to suffer, and society should have no responsibility for him.

But in the vast majority of cases of poverty in 20th century Britain this factor of personal idleness and lack of initiative has not been the cause. Whole areas of the country have been economically blighted by the closure or retraction of old industries and the absence of new ones, depriving industrious and energetic men of any possibilities of employment during the prime years of their lives. To say that society has no responsibility for the welfare of these men and their families is to talk evil rubbish.

Conservatives have gradually come around, in the main, to accepting this truth and upholding the broad framework and principle of the welfare state. Yet there remains in the Conservative mind, deeply ingrained, an idea that individual initiative is the factor needed to restore such areas to prosperity, thus alleviating the strain on welfare services needed to keep the unemployed.

Of course individual initiative can create work and generate wealth in a few isolated cases. One of my own political colleagues of later years, made redundant by the furniture store in which he was a manager, did not want to stay idle and so set up in business cleaning windows. Such a case will of course be offered by Tories as a model as to what the ordinary man should do when one avenue of employment closes: he should create another.

But in areas where tens, even hundreds, of thousands have depended for employment on some traditional large industry, and then are thrown out of work in vast numbers as that industry declines, to say that they can all go out and find work for themselves as window-cleaners or in some other similar small business occupation is absurd. The economic facts of life simply do not permit this.

It is at this point that the Conservative will switch from the method of laying individual blame to that of laying collective blame. These traditional large industries, he will claim, are declining and closing down because they are not internationally competitive, and that must be the fault of the workers in those

industries. If they want to create work opportunities for thems-
selves again. they must work to make their local industries internationally competitive. That is the way to prosperity!

In fact this is sheer economic abracadabra. For one thing it
ignores the fact that there are numerous factors that can result in an
industry being outpriced and outsold by its international competitors which have nothing to do with the work performance of those
employed in them. for instance the ability of those competitors to
employ very cheap labour or a policy of subsidies given to them
by their governments.

And even where their own work performances may be. in
whole or in part, to blame for their industries' loss of business and
their loss of jobs. of what help is it to the situation to say: "Ah
well, let them rot on the dole!''?

By the same token, the government of a country at war might
say that if the enemy happens to produce its guns, its tanks and its
aircraft more efficiently than can industries at home, the white
flag should go up and the enemy be handed victory!

These thoughts led me at an early age to a complete rejection of
capitalist economics, as exemplified in the Tory policy of leaving
everything to 'free market' forces, and to a belief in the necessity
for government to organise industry so as to ensure work for all
who wanted work.

This is not to say that no effort should be made to improve
efficiency where it needs improving, but rather that the preservation of industry and jobs should come first.

As a very young man I learned to understand this doctrine as a
socialist doctrine, and I therefore believed that, in that respect at
least, the way forward might lie in socialism.

Other questions, too, encouraged me to turn with a receptive
ear to socialist teachings. It was clear to me that a great number of
the people in Britain who possessed social privilege and inherited
wealth were utterly unfit for those things. The idea was therefore
attractive to me that such privileges and the institutions of inherited wealth should be done away with, and wealth and social
position based entirely on merit.

To this sentiment socialism appealed. I was of course, as I have
said, very young. Later in life I came to realise that a total 'meritocracy' in which everyone's income and social rank was related
with absolute accuracy to their contribution to society was an
impossible dream, although in certain sectors — of which I have
mentioned the armed forces — it is practicable and desirable.

A more mature consideration of the question of social rank and privilege, together with the related question of inherited wealth, led me to recognise that there were some advantages in those things. The world owes much to true aristocracies, meaning of course family dynasties in which the inherent qualities of parents are passed down to their children and thereafter to each succeeding generation and these qualities can be put to use in genuine public service. As part of this, inherited wealth can have a good use in as much as it can provide a background of financial security enabling the public servant to concentrate single-mindedly on his or her duties without the distraction of having to make a living at jobs that other people can do. It also creates a class of people much less vulnerable to financial corruption.

But the vital precondition for this system to work is that such classes that enjoy this rank and privilege **are** of the quality of genuine aristocracies. In 20th century Britain this can no longer be said except in a very few rare cases. If it were otherwise, our aristocratic classes would have asserted their natural superiority and leadership and acted to combat the forces that have brought about Britain's decline. They have not done so, and for the most part they have therefore proved their unfitness for their position.

It is therefore hardly surprising that the young idealist with a social conscience, when he sees great numbers of people at one end of the social scale rotting in poverty while observing those at the other end swanning around at Ascot or on the grouse moor, not in the meantime lifting a finger to provide the nation with real leadership, should feel that the whole system is wrong and thereby find an echo of his own sentiments in socialist doctrine, which calls for the elimination of aristocracy altogether. Such a policy of course is not the answer; the answer is a new structure of aristocracy comprised mostly of new families, earning their rank in the beginning by outstanding public service on the part of the first generation and then preserving the quality of the blood by wise marriages, with some department of state existing to carry out a constant pruning process whereby families whose heads do not fulfil their proper responsibilities and maintain their proper standards are cast out and replaced.

Conservatism, which in Britain, has been the party most aligned with the aristocratic tradition, has failed to bring about such changes, and in this failure — as in so many others — has provided a breeding ground for socialism.

From an early age I was a thorough supporter of the National

Health Service, as well as of most other social services, and I remain so today despite the abuse to which so many of those services have been put. Somehow in my young mind I equated these social advancements with the left of politics, though in fact almost all of them were present as far back as the time of the Germany of Bismarck. In fact there is no earthly reason why the left should be allowed to claim credit for any of the positive achievements of the welfare state, let alone a monopoly of the social ideals that led to it. Socialist propaganda in the early 1950s, however, persuaded me otherwise, and, looking back, I can see that this was in large measure due, again, to the essentially self-centred philosophy of Conservatism as I perceived it at the time.

But not only did I regard it as the responsibility of society to care for the sick, I saw it as being at least an equal responsibility to nurture the healthy. As a youngster keen on exercise and fitness, I was appalled at the very low physical standards of many of my fellow countrymen and -women. A very large number of the men reared in the 1920s, 1930s and 1940s were undernourished and under-sized. The latter deficiency has now largely been made good but not the former; men are now on average bigger but not fitter. I felt in those earlier days the necessity for the state to take a lead in promotion of national health and fitness, with the provision in every locality of well equipped sports centres providing facilities for every kind of sporting and training pursuit. Many other countries had been far ahead of Britain in this development, as could be evidenced by our failure to pull our proper weight in many fields of international sporting competition. I saw some awareness of this need among socialist writers but none at all among Conservatives, who, as with everything else, seemed to adopt the view that such things were a matter for the individual.

A number of trends of thought, therefore, pointed me in a socialist direction from about my middle teens to my early twenties, but, as I have indicated before, I held back from full commitment. Why I did so later became clear, as I have also explained.

Any social utopia not built on foundations of **national** wealth, strength and power is like a house built on sand. To begin with, arguments about the distribution of wealth must always follow, rather than precede, the **creation** of wealth. This much Tories understand, but they do not seem to understand that the creation of wealth of which they are continually speaking rests first and foremost on possession of the necessary national assets, these being:-

(1) An industrious, skilled, intelligent, innovative, enterprising and — not least — healthy population, moved by a strong patriotic spirit.

(2) A homogeneous population, making for national unity.

(3) A strong and diverse manufacturing base, enforced by a high competence in technology (which must incorporate education for technology).

(4) National security against external attack.

(5) A foreign policy which gives foremost priority to the national interest.

(6) A system of government that provides the best possibility of strong, wise and far-sighted national leadership, invulnerable to the pressures of sectional interests and able to embark on long-term national development and planning.

(6) Efficient organisation of the nation at all levels of government and industry.

In addition to these things, there are three further assets which not all nations can have but which are of substantial advantage to those nations that do have them. These are: (a) independent domestic sources of minerals and energy products; (b) a large domestic consumer market, allowing industry to achieve the maximum economies of production scale; and (c) access to abundant open spaces, allowing for a healthy population increase without overcrowding.

British socialism, in pursuit of its utopia, is about as hopelessly equipped in its understanding of these things as it is possible to be.

All these desirable conditions of a nation's prosperity and welfare require first an underlying attitude of **nationalism**, i.e. the determination to defend and promote the national interest to the utmost and to realise the full potential of national power. The philosophy of the British left runs totally contrary to this principle. It puts its trust in international idealism rather than in national capability. It makes a virtue out of national weakness. It is against racial homogeneity and race quality. It puts a low rating on national defence — when it condescends to permit national defence at all. It surrenders to the foreigner, by its concession of national political and economic sovereignty, the power to determine the conditions under which the people of the nation will survive and earn their bread. In international relations it substitutes the criterion of 'morality' (its own morality of course) for that of national interest, alienating the nation's friends and assisting the nation's enemies by subjecting every international issue to the test of its own warped and bigoted ideology. Finally, it is wedded to a political system that makes effective national government impossible.

And today everything said here about the left might also be applied, in greater or lesser degree, to Conservatism, Social Democracy and Liberalism.

The three additional advantages to nations that I have mentioned as a postcript to the numbered ones preceding are of course advantages that would have accrued to Britain by the exercise, when such a possibility existed, of a vigorous imperial policy. Such a policy was never exercised by any of the established parties forming British Governments. Particular hostility to such a policy was always to be found in the ranks of British socialism.

British socialism, except in the isolated writings of a few of its earlier pioneers — long since rejected by the movement's mainstream, totally failed to grasp any of these principles. In the pursuit of its utopia, it talked ever more romantically about the ends but left itself unarmed and naked in terms of the means.

For these reasons, despite some initial attraction, I could never become a socialist.

A question that I did not ask myself at first but certainly did later was this: was the rejection by the left of realistic national and imperial thinking merely the product of ignorance and woolly-mindedness or was it deliberate?

If, as I now firmly believe, it was the latter, this imposes on us the task of looking afresh and in new perspective at the whole history, traditions and origins of the political left in Britain.

We are guided in this study by what the left has become subsequent to those earlier days of the immediate post-war period. Since then it has become, increasingly, the champion of every conceivable form of national, social and human degeneracy. Every cult, every habit, every disposition conducive to the weakening of society, people, nation and race the left has taken up as a *cause celebre*: homosexuality, ultra-feminism, race equality, abortion, relaxation of drug laws, weakening of the police, soft sentences for criminals, indiscipline in schools, ugliness and decadence in the arts, downgrading of the work ethic, impotence in national defence. Now the left, still not satisfied, is taking up yet crazier causes, such as ruling that Labour Party election candidates may not be pictured with wives and families on the grounds that this is 'heterosexism'!

To many people these increasing incursions into the world of the insane are just recent aberrations, the result of the infiltration of the socialist ranks by 'extremists' in no way part of the normal socialist tradition.

I disagree. I hold that the wild antics of the left today are but a logical and inevitable result of a process of development that has been present in the political left in Britain from the very beginning, indicating merely the advanced stages of a sickness that resided in the body, like a malignant growth, from many years back.

In the process of my own political development I progressed from a position of seeing socialism as a jumble of well meaning ideas, some perhaps practicable, some not practicable, to one of identifying socialism — or perhaps more accurately marxism — as a deadly national and racial poison, formulated for the one purpose of subverting and eventually destroying the British Nation and with it the whole fabric of the civilised world.

Yet it must never be forgotten that all along the line this process has been able to advance forward in Britain because of the abysmal lack of any organised and determined resistance from what is supposed to be the 'right' of politics. All along the line, Conservatism has retreated before this leftward advance, conceding to it ideologically at every point, showing in the face of its nasty and brutal side the most abject cowardice, and creating by the very barrenness and failure of Tory policies the ideal conditions for it to thrive. Conservatism has in effect been the left's most useful ally.

Sometime around 1957-58, and when I was 23 years old, I finally grasped and faced up to the full enormity of the evil forces menacing Britain from all quarters. No longer did I believe, as I had wanted to believe in earlier years, that things would somehow 'right themselves' by a popular realisation that we had been treading the wrong path and a resulting change of national mood; things could only be righted by **political action**, at first by a small number (for then it obviously was a small number) of determined people prepared to dedicate their lives to the task, putting all personal desires, plans, ambitions and pleasures into second place.

I had up till that time still had the idea of pursuing some profession, and had made some moves towards entering a teacher's college, first obtaining the necessary qualifications, as I have related earlier, and then making a few enquiries about the establishments available.

Now the importance of this receded into almost nothing. The political struggle had to take precedence over all. I decided that I would abandon all thoughts of a normal career and concentrate entirely on political activity and continued political studies, working in normal employment only because of the necessity to pay my way in the world and only to the extent of that necessity. Being then a single man and with no marriage prospects or thoughts in sight, I was of course in a better position to make this commitment than some others.

At this time I had no particular thoughts of becoming a 'leader' in the political field. My own position of seniority or otherwise in whatever organisation I attached myself to mattered much less to me than the opportunity to work actively for the things in which I believed and to develop and give voice to political ideas. I had started writing articles, due to A.K. Chesterton's encouragement, and was very pleased to see my first effort appear in *Candour* — probably less due to its intrinsic merit than to his policy of giving me a chance to get started.

A little later I made a start in public speaking. The occasion was a Sunday morning in Bethnal Green, East London, and the facilities consisted of a crudely constructed collapsible wooden platform that had beforehand been carried to the spot from another part of London by means of the Underground. I had gone to the spot with an LEL colleague, John Bean, with the idea of his being the speaker on the occasion and my merely playing a helping role, as had been the case for a number of weeks previously. On this occasion my associate half persuaded and half pushed me into doing a stint on the platform. In a very few minutes I discovered that public speaking was not nearly as frightening a task as I had imagined and that I had some natural capability at it. I persevered and in due course was able to develop as a political speaker in a tough school — street corners, where the first art lay in capturing the interest of people going about their normal private business and inducing them to stop and listen. A forceful style was very necessary to accomplish this first objective, and that set the pattern for my later development in the practice of public speaking.

Such an environment was very different from the cosy lecture room atmosphere in which most would-be speakers start to learn their trade. Right from the beginning, people would turn up who were diametrically opposed to everything my friends and I stood for. Sometimes there were fights and we had to act vigorously to defend the platform and our own persons. Much more often, indeed almost every meeting, there was loud heckling — necessitating the development of a quick-witted repartee in dealing with the hecklers.

I am grateful for having served my apprenticeship as a speaker under these conditions — I would be able to speak to little effect now if I had not.

This time of my life was a time of decision, and in two senses. In the first place, there was the decision, as I have mentioned, to throw myself totally into political work. In the second place, it was a time of decision as to where I stood in political terms. All the preceding years had been a process of probing, groping, exploring and considering, weighing up the merits of one political idea against another, and slowly but gradually clearing a path through the fog towards a full state of awareness. Now was the moment for commitment to a definite political path.

There was now no longer any doubt as to where I stood. I was first and foremost a **British Nationalist**, not in the narrow sense of nationalism as applied to a particular state or territory, but in the much wider **ethnic** sense of a nation held together by bonds of race. This in no way incorporated any feelings of hatred towards other races, as is constantly alleged by the opponents of our thinking, but merely a dedication to my own race **first**, and the preparedness to oppose other races, or sections thereof, who menaced my own race — something entirely different to hatred.

None of this is to say that my nationally-minded viewpoint was a new one; indeed it had been present from as early on as I had been old enough to think. But in earlier years it had been just one of a number of strands in my thinking; now it was the key and central strand, from which all other strands flowed in consequence.

Inevitably, in this process I became part of a tradition of political thought and action that had long preceded me and my contemporaries. It would have been conceited of us in the extreme, to say nothing of being dishonest, to claim that we were innovators of our movement and creed. Quite the contrary, we made no bones about having drawn our ideas from a number of past sources, largely British but not entirely so. In the same way as Conservatism, Socialism, Liberalism and Social Democracy in Britain have drawn from their fonts of universal wisdom, inspiration and experience, so had we; and the fact that we, much more than they, were a national movement did not forbid us learning from the examples of other national movements overseas. Indeed the dedication that we had, and have, to our own nation and people places us a position uniquely suited to understand the similar feelings of men and women of other nations. I have long believed that two nations sharing in common an intense patriotism are better equipped than any others to come to an understanding, even in the event of there being practical conflicts of interest between them. By contrast, wars become much more likely when one nation believes in a national ideal and the other in an international one. History, particularly in our own century, is replete with examples of this.

Chapter 4
British Nationalism

Searching back for a tradition of British Nationalism, we were under something of a disadvantage, and for two reasons. Firstly, such a nation as 'Britain' had only existed for about 2½ centuries, previous to which there were separate nationhoods in our islands but not one single nationhood. Secondly, for the period in which an established British nation state had been in being nationalism had largely been a kind of unconscious, or at the most subconscious, tendency. It had not been, as in the case of a number of countries on the European mainland, an organised movement with a recognisable name, least of all a political party to give it expression. In times of national eminence, security and success, the conscious need for nationalism is scarcely there. It is taken for granted as a factor in the shaping of state policy and generally resides as a strong force in the thinking of most citizens, but the need does not seem to arise for it to go further than that. The time when it develops into an organised movement is a time when there is a deep national yearning for something that does not exist, be it national unity, national independence, national retribution for a past wrong inflicted by an outsider.

As for any ethnic nationalism, the first precondition of this is some clearly discerned foreign ethnic threat, and this was never perceived by British people until early in the present century, nearly all previous migrations into our country being by people ethnically and culturally the close relations of ourselves and therefore quite easily assimilable within a generation or two.

We are therefore much dependent on comparatively modern sources to find examples and a tradition of British Nationalism in organised political form.

The ethnic threat of which I have spoken was avoided for centuries by our advantages of geography. For all this long time, Britain's island position minimised it. Jews had come into this country in the wake of William the Conqueror. By the later part of the 13th century, they had generated wide and deep opposition to themselves and eventually were expelled by an edict of Edward I. They returned by arrangement with Cromwell, who had become indebted to some Amsterdam Jews for financial support. By the second half of the 19th century, their presence in Britain had become an issue of some considerable political controversy. These migrations apart, no racially foreign presence became manifest in our country on any significant scale until the middle of the present century, when West Indian, and later Asian, settlers began to arrive in large numbers.

For all these reasons, British Nationalism does not have a well established political tradition. By this I mean of course nationalism as an explicit concept, as an organised political force and incorporating a doctrine which consciously places the nation-state idea at the centre of everything; implicitly and objectively, nationalism has of course been a strong element in British policy for many centuries, indeed probably the main element up to the time of World War I.

The difference between nationalism in its explicit and implicit, subjective and objective, forms is usually rooted in the different circumstances surrounding the historical development of one nation by comparison with another, as I have said earlier. Broadly speaking, the nationalist idea receives its strongest impetus in conditions of some kind of national adversity, of which the most common is the lack of national independence. But nationalism may receive powerful generation from a particularly disastrous defeat in war, or from a frustrated urge to national unity. It is of course possible for all three of these factors to be present: lack of unity leading to weakness, weakness to defeat in war, and defeat in war to loss of independence. In such an instance there is truly fertile ground for the growth of a strong nationalist spirit, as the history of Europe shows.

In the case of Britain, on the other hand, these conditions have been less in evidence than almost anywhere in Europe. Nearly 300 years have passed since the union of the English and Scottish parliaments that made of these islands a single nation-state, while in the case of its largest component, England, we are able to look back on more than 1,000 years of national unity. Add to this the geographical advantage making for near invulnerability to invasion and the unparallelled commercial and imperial success of the 18th and 19th centuries, and we have the very opposite of the ideal circumstances making for a conscious movement of nationalism.

This is of course very far from saying that nationalism has been absent as a force in British thinking and action; as I have stated, it certainly has not. Rather has it been something residing a little way below the surface of affairs. Until recently, the need to act in accordance with the national interest was something more or less taken for granted in all politics. Britain, however, was seen by most as dealing with the world from a position of such immense strength, prosperity and security that that her national interest was scarcely seen to be in any kind of danger. Nationhood and national freedom were complacently assûmed never to be at risk, as was also the fact of our seemingly permanent imperial position and great power status. Nationalism as such was for those nations not similarly blessed and who therefore felt it necessary to be especially assertive in their pursuit of national rights.

Such a view, it can now be seen with hindsight, was an unduly smug one, assuming as part of the everlasting order of things a heritage of national identity, independence and strength which in fact is a precariously held possession in this world and can only be retained by those peoples prepared to defend it in peace as energetically as in war. Such a defence must lead ultimately to a form of **tribal organisation** in which the interest of the individual becomes subordinate to the welfare of the whole, and indeed in which the former is anyway seen as inconceivable éxcept through the latter.

This is where the Briton's concept of nationhood has, over a large span of history, stood in sharp contrast to that of the continental European, the latter being nurtured under conditions of much greater external danger and therefore demanding much greater internal cohesion. Indeed, Britons have even been deluded into regarding their national identity and their tradition of individual sovereignty as two mutually interdependent features of the national character, the one largely moulded by the other. To be quintessentially British, so the thinking has been, we must be resistant to any political tendency conducive to making us function as a co-ordinated group — except under the extreme duress of war. Thus it was not until half way through World War I that Britain came to see the necessity for universal military conscription — something which, had it been adopted much earlier, might have prevented that war and the sacrifice of over a million of the most valuable British lives.

If we are to go back to a period of our history in which a genuine spirit of nationalism permeated life in this country, we must look to the England of the Tudors. Then, not only was patriotic sentiment strong and national policy governed by patriotic considerations, but the nation was organised in a community regulated by certain civic disciplines, which induced the strict co-ordination of economic activity in the service of the national good. It is perhaps not accidental that this period was one of the most creative and fruitful in our whole island story.

The coming of liberalism destroyed this harmonious fabric. We adopted as a national religion the concept of the 'rights' of the individual — although of course this never amounted to more than mere sloganising, for the effect — as distinct from the theory — of such a doctrine is always that those 'rights' become the possession of self-interested groups, based usually on the power of money, and politics become a struggle between these groups in which national aims are largely lost sight of.

From the onset of liberalism, a strange doctrine took hold of Britain. According to this doctrine, the national interest would best be served by the very minimum attempt by government to organise, regulate and co-ordinate national life. Private interests should be allowed to fight it out in a free-for-all, and by a process of natural selection — a kind of social and economic Darwinism — the best would come to the top, a development that would be of national benefit as well as beneficial to the successful competitors concerned.

This tendency, which dominated British politics during the 19th century, was in sharp contrast to that developing in continental Europe, particularly in Germany but also, in modified form, in France. The trend on the continent was increasingly towards the close co-ordination of all the resources of the nation-state — political, economic, cultural, educational and, not least, military — in a firm strategy for the development of national strength and power. In both Germany and France the need for universal military service, in peace as well as in war, was generally accepted, as well as was the direction of industry and commerce for national purposes. National educational programmes were adopted with a view to providing nations with the skills necessary for success in the modern world, whereas in Britain education remained primarily devoted, as pointed out by Correlli Barnett in *The Collapse of British Power*, to the breeding of "Christian gentlemen." Said Barnett, in drawing a general contrast in national attitudes:-

"...Other great powers did not see the world as one great human society, but — just as the British had done up to the 19th century — as an arena where, subject to the mutual convenience of diplomatic custom, nation-states — the highest effective form of human society — competed for advantage. They did not believe in a natural harmony among mankind but in national interests that might sometimes coincide with the interests of others, sometimes conflict. It followed that they considered that relations between states were governed not by law, nor even by moral principle, but by power and ambition restrained only by prudent calculation and a sense of moderation. War therefore, in their view, was not a lamentable breakdown of a natural harmony called peace, but an episode of violence in a perpetual struggle. European powers looked on armed forces not as wicked, but among the instruments of diplomacy. Indeed, whereas in Britain romantic emotion expressed itself in visions of a world society, in Europe it had given rise to a fervent nationalism. In the late 19th century the world was becoming not less dangerous and anarchical but more so."

Of course, during the 19th century those in Britain who saw the world through the rose-tinted spectacles of liberalism had their own rationale in the almost unbroken good fortune of British policy of most of that period. To quote Barnett again:-

"For half a century after Waterloo the English could afford to ignore the 'animal lust for struggle', at least as between great powers. A moral conscience was the ultimate luxury afforded the middle classes by commercial success and national security. Thanks to the war-making and aggrandisement of the past, they were able now to disdain and condemn unscrupulous self-seeking in other powers, just as the rich are able to rise above envy. The beneficiaries of the broadsides of Trafalgar and the volleys of Waterloo could safely indulge in their humanitarian and peaceable sentiments."

In this atmosphere the British developed a totally illusory picture of the foundations of their success as a nation. These were attributed to liberal-democratic institutions and certain ethical codes of 'moderation' and 'fair play', whereas the true reality was that Britain had become the world's leading power despite, rather than because of, such traditions and habits.

The essential factor working to Britain's advantage up to the first phase of industrialisation was that, due to the nature of the various invasions and migrations from Europe that had occurred over the past two millenia, she enjoyed the legacy of a racial stock which, in its combination of intelligence, physique, courage, energy and breadth of creative talent, was certainly equal, and possibly superior, to any other in the world. Her racial composition, though overwhelmingly Nordic in kind, was diverse in as much as it comprised several branches of the North European tree; in its various Teutonic, Scandinavian and Celtic sub-divisions, this was not a 'racial mixture', as often alleged, but merely a tribal mixture within the framework of a basically common race — an important difference.

To this initial asset were added three further ones, all essential contributions to national power. Firstly, an empire was acquired which differed fundamentally from those of the other European powers, not only in its vastly greater size, but also in the fact that it included huge territories that were to become settled in substantial numbers by people of the same race as those of the metropolitan country. Secondly, partially due to native talent and partially also to the possession of convenient natural resources, first and foremost coal, Britain became the first major manufacturing nation, and in that respect had a lead on others until at least the middle of the 19th century. Finally, Britain enjoyed in that same century a massive increase in population that, by the century's end, brought her manpower resources up to the level of those of France and, with her Dominions taken into account, close to those of the recently unified Germany.

These then were Britain's basic assets in the heyday of the Victorian era — not a sound political system nor a high quality of national leadership, not sound economic or social institutions, and certainly not a sound national outlook or doctrine; for all these things were lamentably lacking. Nourished, as Barnett has said, by the triumphant gains made by previous generations and protected by a 22-mile moat from their continental neighbours, the Victorians felt able to indulge themselves in a head-in-sand complacency regarding their world position that was not justified in reality. By the time of the Diamond Jubilee of the Queen in 1897 there lay, not far beneath the pomp and pageantry of that occasion, a national fabric that was rotting at the seams. As Barnett states in *The Collapse of British Power*:-

> "...there were those in Britain who perceived this. They argued that the continuance of British prosperity and security required more than blind faith in a free market and moral law. They called into question the whole liberal interpretation of British history, according to which British greatness was said to derive

from peaceful economic and constitutional progress. Whereas liberal thought had looked upon the expansionist wars of the 18th century as immoral, costly and useless interruptions of progress, it was now argued that strategy and successful war had been keys to the growth of British power and influence. It was argued that the British Empire ought to be revived as a collective organism for strategic purposes.''

Lest this may sound like a concession of the moral high ground to those of the liberal world view, let it be emphasised that the exponents of this realist conception of politics did not look with scorn on morality *per se*; rather did they regard it as an essential bedrock of stability on the domestic front. They simply understood, as liberals did not, the strict practical limitations of **international morality** when it was not backed up with the implements of sovereign **power** as represented by industrial capability and, where necessary, armed force — something that still had not been learned decades later by those who placed boundless faith in the instruments of the League of Nations.

The people and lobbies to whom Barnett referred as looking on the world as strategists, and who argued for priority to be given to the building up of national strength and power, did not come to prevail in British politics in the Victorian age, but they were in fact forerunners of modern British Nationalism, even if the latter term was one which it never occurred to them to use. What they advocated was in fact a continuation of the national tradition of thought and action that had been dominant in British affairs up to the time of the final victory over the First Napoleon but since then had had to vie in considerations of state with several other criteria in no way influenced by the national interest and sometimes positively detrimental to it: a tradition which recognised the world as being divided, probably permanently, into nation-states engaged in a struggle for power, for most of the time peaceful but at intervals escalating into war, and which therefore accepted survival and success in that struggle as a primary aim of national policy, and without which no other aims, however high-minded, could be achieved with any permanence.

Foremost among British political leaders of the Victorian and Edwardian period who recognised the new needs of Britain and her Empire was Joseph Chamberlain, father of Prime Minister Neville. Chamberlain led a faction within the Liberal Party known as the 'Liberal Unionists', who differed from the established party policy of Home Rule for Ireland. Consistent with his opposition to anything that might weaken Britain's position of strength, Chamberlain also became the main spokesman for the 'Tariff Reform' movement, whose policy it was to oppose the free trade doctrines that were the prevailing Liberal orthodoxy and to institute in their place a programme of protection and imperial preference. Foodstuffs and raw materials that could not be produced from domestic sources would be imported, as far as possible, from the dominions, which were to be persuaded to yield to Britain in return preferential entry for its manufactured products. British manufactures would at the same time be protected from foreign competition by tariff walls.

Closely interwoven with the theme of trade tariffs against goods from outside the Empire was that of stronger political ties with its members. Said Chamberlain in a Birmingham speech in 1902 which anticipated future dangers:-

> "If by adherence to economic pedantry, to old shibboleths, we are to lose opportunities of closer union which are offered to us by our colonies, if we are to put aside occasions now within our grasp, if we do not take every chance in our power to keep British trade in British hands, I am certain that we shall deserve the disasters which will infallibly come upon us."

And again at Birmingham in 1906 in the last great public speech he ever made:-

> "Relatively, in proportion to our competitors, we are getting behindhand, and when the tide of prosperity recedes...and a time of depression follows it, the working classes especially will be the sufferers, and we shall find then that it will be impossible, without a change, to find employment for the constantly increasing population of these islands. The remedy is at hand...we can extend our trade in the best markets, with our best friends. We can benefit them in trading with them while they give us reciprocal advantage in the preference which they give for our manufactures."

Chamberlain closed the same speech with the words:-

> "By a commercial union we can pave the way for that federation which I see constantly before me as a practical object of aspiration — that federation of free nations which will enable us to prolong in ages yet to come all the glorious traditions of the British race...The union of the empire must be preceded and accompanied by a better understanding, by a closer sympathy. To secure that is the highest object of statesmanship now at the beginning of the 20th century. If these were the last words that I

were permitted to utter to you, I would rejoice to utter them in your presence and with your approval.''

Closely parallel to Chamberlain's ideas were those of Professor J.R. Seeley, whose book *The Expansion of England*, published in 1906, incorporated a series of lectures on the worldwide dispersion of the British race. Seeley's book, though interlarded with much of the liberal cant fashionable in his time, pointed the way to an enlightened national and imperial policy in these words:-

> "...It seems possible that our Colonial Empire so-called may more and more deserve to be called Greater Britain, and that the tie may become stronger and stronger. Then the seas which divide us might be forgotten, and that ancient preconception, which leads us always to think of ourselves as belonging to a single island, might be rooted out of our minds. If in this way we moved sensibly nearer in our thoughts and feelings to the colonies, and accustomed ourselves to think of emigrants as not in any way lost to England by settling in the colonies, the result might be, first that emigration on a vast scale might become our remedy for pauperism, and secondly that some organisation might gradually be arrived at which might make the whole force of the Empire available in time of war.''

Part of Seeley's thesis was that modern developments of communication were rendering out of date the long-established idea that movements of population over great distances were bound to result in the end in the severance of the migrating peoples from their original homeland. Strands of nationalist thinking are obvious in his writings. He was much preoccupied with Britain's then rapid increase in population. That this should be checked with methods of 'birth control' was unthinkable; greater numbers for our race were to be welcomed as an augmentation of national strength. But this was not satisfactory if those numbers were to be confined to the small spaces of the home country. They should migrate to where they would find ample living room, but this migration should not mean their loss to our nation — not if those great spaces they were to settle overseas were to be bound to the United Kingdom in a form of effective political and economic organisation which would render the whole a single and indivisible unit. Seeley, while conceding that bigness did not necessarily equal greatness in nations, recognised implicitly the role of size and power in governing international relations. Speaking of the current trend of opinion in favour of jettisoning Britain's overseas possessions, he said:-

"Such a separation would leave England on the same level as the states nearest to us on the continent, populous, but less so than Germany and scarcely equal to France. But two states, Russia and the United States, would be on an altogether higher scale of magnitude, Russia having at once, and the United States perhaps before very long, twice our population. Our trade too would be exposed to wholly new risks."

These two visionaries, though their views gained a considerable audience in their time, did not win sufficient acceptance for those views to prevail. Smugness and ignorance, combined with the power of vested interest — in particular the vested interest of the great banking and mercantile combines which profited by the internationalisation of Britain's economy — prevented the adoption of their ideas as national policy.

Both Chamberlain and Seeley contained in their doctrines, though perhaps more implicitly than explicitly, the theme of devotion to the 'British Race'. By the time of the 19th and early 20th centuries it was possible to speak of such an entity, for by then the various tribal groupings of the British Isles had intermingled to form what was certainly a British ethnic nation. In later times Mr. Enoch Powell has told us that we must regard as a nation a group of people who think and feel themselves to be such. I am inclined to accept this definition as the nearest practical one there is as to what constitutes nationhood. Actually, in Chamberlain's and Seeley's time such an idea was far from unfashionable — not for a long time to come were we to reach the lunatic situation where the championing of one's own race became 'criminal'. Of all the proponents of the British racial idea, one of the most ardent was Alfred Lord Milner, who formed the 'Round Table' society in an effort to promulgate his theme of a special destiny for the peoples of British stock throughout the world — a destiny which Milner, like the others, saw as being fulfilled by means of imperial federation. Said Milner: "My patriotism knows no geographical but only racial limits."

Although faith in the 'British Race' was at this time much in vogue, there was a certain amount of naivety in the matter of what constituted a member of it. Correctly, it should have meant a person descended from one of the indigenous stocks of the British Isles or indeed more than one of these stocks. This could indeed be extended to someone of kindred Northern European stock who had become a member of the British national community and who, to adopt the Powell criterion, 'thought' himself British. In the eyes of some Victorians and Edwardians, however, the concept was rather a cultural than a biological one, taking in people who in the latter respect were outside the British and North European family but who had been subjected to a British education, assimilated — on the surface at least — certain British habits of behaviour and professed loyalty to the British state. In the eyes of many who promoted Milner's society, though probably not of Milner himself, such a definition sufficed, with the result that after the passing of Milner and Cecil Rhodes, another 'Round Table' man who thought very similarly to him, the society ceased to be an organisation with a truly racial objective and became one for the spread of essentially political doctrines that, quite erroneously, were claimed as 'British' and 'Anglo-Saxon'.

There were, however, others with clearer perspectives. In the later half of the 19th century the first major threat to the ethnic homogeneity of the British people began to materialise with the entry of large numbers of Jews from Central and Eastern Europe, these tending to congregate in the major cities, in particular London. In response to this threat there was formed the British Brothers' League, which campaigned vigorously against the immigration in the years preceding World War I. At one time the BBL boasted members of parliament among its supporters. It ran out of steam when the legislation it had fought for, and which was aimed to stop the immigrant flood, failed to get through parliament; but a not insignificant factor in stopping it was the hidden pressure put upon some of its supporters by the pro-Jewish lobby which even then had obtained no small influence in British politics. Men started to find that their political careers, and sometimes their private businesses, were not enhanced by their opposition to this new power in British affairs — a sinister foretaste of what was to come in later years.

All these individuals and groups had one thing in common: in the end they failed to sway the governments of their day. Whatever forces they had working for them, stronger forces were working against them, and the latter in each case came to prevail within the political system. Indeed the very consistency with which that system, again and again in the past century and a half, served to render these wise counsels impotent, while sustaining in power those whose policies have turned out to be disastrous for Britain, highlights the problem that lies at the root of everything — the system itself: the basic set of institutions and governmental procedures by which British politics have been conducted and which have produced the succession of governments with which we have been afflicted over this period. What is clear is that every challenge to prevailing policy that was not accompanied by, and part of, a challenge to the system that produced that policy was bound to fail. As the 20th century got into its stride, what was clearly called for was more than just a series of lobbies and pressure groups to campaign for changes of policy on specific fronts; what was called for was an entirely new and revolutionary political doctrine and movement which would achieve a synthesis of all these various strands, and with it a set of proposals for a change in the entire system whereby Britain was governed and led.

To this call the Great War of 1914-18 gave added impetus, and if we are seeking the roots of modern British Nationalism the forces that came to the surface in that war cannot be excluded.

In the First World War the brutal demands of survival awakened every combatant nation to the necessity for the fullest mobilisation of all national resources, on the home front as much as in the battle zone, in the drive for victory. This necessity was grasped much earlier by the continental powers than by Britain but it came home to Britain in the end. By 1916 the spirit of smugness and lethargy that had prevailed throughout so much of the Victorian and Edwardian periods had disappeared, and the whole British Empire became organised in one massive united effort. Indeed it was the first time that the Empire had functioned as an effective single unit, sending more than 8½ million men to swell the British forces to an unprecedented strength. In the United Kingdom conscription was adopted for the first time, and this involved nearly one-seventh of the whole population serving in uniform, this not including of course the many auxiliary organisations.

For a short time, Britons from all regions of the country and its Empire, and from every social background, came together in a single cause, casting aside all previous political party and class divisions and joining hands in a common comradeship of the trenches.

And for the first time in centuries politicians in this country put aside party warfare and joined forces in working for a single goal. A coalition government was formed in 1916 and proceeded to co-ordinate the whole national life in one mighty endeavour. *Laissez-faire* economics were dropped as Britain found that these methods, practised so long in the years of peace, had rendered her industry hopelessly incapable of producing her needs of survival in this titanic conflict. New industries, such as chemicals, machine tools and optics, had to be built practically from scratch, while others, such as electricity, aircraft and aero-engines, had to be greatly expanded, in order to provide the sinews of war; and this was done mainly on the initiative of the state. By the end of the war, tremendous strides had been made in making good these previous shortcomings of industry. What the theoretical stimulus of the 'free market' had failed to do for decades beforehand was done in just three years of corporate effort, achieved by firm national leadership directing economic resources, and by the whole nation, and Empire, working as a team.

Of all the massive adjustments from peacetime to wartime life, that which left the most profound stamp on all those affected by it was the institution of universal and compulsory military service — not just in Britain but in most of the countries on both sides. Millions of men who previously had spent little or none of their lives in uniform became seasoned veterans of war, living for years under conditions of great material hardship and governed by a military code of rules and ethics. The experience made into men great numbers who previously had been mere children in their awareness of the more brutal realities of life in this world. Millions were able to see close-up what could be achieved by discipline, teamwork, boldness and firm, decisive leadership. Outstanding men of action, rather than verbalisers and wafflers, became the ones looked up to and accorded rank. Perhaps above all, the war heightened national feeling in a generation that had not lacked such feeling in the years beforehand but never experienced it in a way so sharply defined as in that mighty struggle of the nations. Interestingly enough though, this was a more mature patriotism, as it did not incorporate any hatred of the man in a different uniform fighting on the other side. Many veterans of that conflict have testified that the mutual respect, sometimes amounting even to affection, felt by the front line adversaries towards each other contrasted with the contempt many of them felt for their own politicians back at home.

These millions of men returned to civilian life at the war's end destined never to be quite the same men again. They had been through a new and hard school and had acquired wholly new perspectives and values. With a portion of them this change was to have striking consequences in the moulding of their outlook on life.

The heroes recently returned from the front watched the politicians of their respective countries address themselves to the building of the post-war world, and were not impressed with what they saw. In place of valour, there was cowardice. In place of unity, there was division. In place of discipline, there was the collapse of authority. In place of order, there was chaos. In place of patriotic zeal, there was a woolly internationalism.

In certain countries where the dislocation of life at the war's end had become the most acute, the absolute scum of society had come to the surface and, taking advantage of conditions, had brought about red insurrection and civil war in place of the previous national war. Bolshevism had taken control in Russia. Elsewhere, in Germany, Italy and Hungary, it was in imminent danger of doing so — indeed did do so for a short time in Hungary and in the German province of Bavaria. In the face of this red threat, the leaders of the 'democratic' parties demonstrated a conspicuous yellow streak.

Throughout Europe there grew a disillusionment with the old politics and a yearning for a new political ideal that would harness the qualities displayed in the recent war to the tasks of peacetime reconstruction. Could not the super-human efforts displayed on the battlefield in the face of dangerous adversity now be displayed again in the creation, from out of the rubble, of newly born nations?

All over the European Continent new political movements arose which sought to grapple with these problems, movements which owed little to the political traditions of the past, which distrusted an over-preoccupation with theory but gave priority to organisation for action, which distrusted 'politicians' and looked instead to **leaders**. Indeed, in most cases these movements were led by men who had recently served in uniform and seen battle rather than those who had stayed at home and basked in the sunlight of their exploits.

In different countries these movements took different names. In time, however, by their opponents' choice rather than by their own, they came to be lumped together under the generalised term of 'fascist', and this was the term usually applied to the movement in this country that became part of that tradition.

Fascism in Britain never became the same force in the inter-war period as did its namesake in Italy or national socialism in Germany; and of course, unlike the latter movements, it never attained political power. There were a variety of reasons for this, many of them much misunderstood. The breakdown and crises that brought Mussolini and Hitler to power abroad never became quite so acute here as in their countries. In addition to this, those who pioneered the British movement had to face a much more entrenched attitude of reaction among the educated classes than elsewhere, this attitude being the product of a century of liberal illusions nurtured, as has been shown earlier, in the hothouse of imperial wealth, security and isolation. Finally, the interests threatened by, and therefore resistant to, fascism were much more powerful here than on the continent, and placed every conceivable barrier in the way of the new movement, including many that were not encountered on a comparable scale abroad.

Nevertheless, we must account as the main reason why British Fascism did not attain power the simple factor of time. A different national situation to those prevailing in Italy and Germany made it always probable that fascism in Britain would need a longer period of maturation and development before it could be politically victorious. Such a period was never allowed to it, for the onset of World War II brought to an end all normal politics in Britain for six years, after which new circumstances arose in the wake of the defeat of the Axis which ensured that, for some considerable time to come, fascism would have no chance anywhere.

So what was British Fascism and what were its objectives? Has history proved its diagnosis right or wrong? Were its aims good and only its methods evil? Or were its methods in fact forced upon it by circumstances, and in the reality less ignoble than depicted in the popular pess of the day?

A fully detailed answer to these questions would require a whole book devoted to this subject alone. Many such books have been written by the opponents of fascism, and most of those that I have read have been long on condemnation and short on facts. One of the more objective of these books, and which takes its title from the name of fascism's principal spokesman during those years, is *Oswald Mosley*, by Robert Skidelsky, a self-confessed socialist and anti-fascist who nevertheless avoids much of the silly, dishonest and downright hysterical language usually employed on the subject by writers of the left. Skidelsky sets the tone for his examination of Mosley's career by explaining what stimulated his own initial interest:-

"...It was Hugh Gaitskell's courage, in the face of the bitterest denunciations from his own party, in fighting for what he

believed to be right, that really attracted me to Labour politics...
To be drawn into politics by the personality of a leader may
seem immature. Yet there is a sound reason for it. On the
quality of the leadership depends the possibility of action. This
truth has never, it seems to me, been adequately grasped by
social democratic parties. They spend their lives talking about
the world to come; yet saddle themselves for the most part with
leaders who are all too obviously content with the world as it is:
hence the literature of 'betrayal' which pours out in unceasing
flood from social democratic pens...The Mosley of the 1920s
seemed to have all the attributes that I wanted from a Labour
leader — bold policies, unflinching courage, eloquent
language, compassion, popular appeal. As the Labour Government of 1964 staggered from disaster to disaster under an
obviously inadequate prime minister, Mosley took shape in my
mind as Labour's 'lost leader'.''

Sir Oswald Mosley, to give him his full name and title, had
indeed been a rising Labour politician, and before that a rising
Conservative one. He had crossed to the Labour benches after
despairing of the Tories' ability or will to overcome the evils of
poverty and unemployment in post-1918 Britain. Seeing, as many
initially do, some sign of greater crusading zeal on the left, he
aligned himself with the 'Clydesiders', a group containing a
number of men passionately committed to tackling these
problems. In time, however, Mosley came to recognise that in the
ranks of Labour, however ideal the ends, there was a total incomprehension of , combined with an unwillingness to accept, the necessary means. Labour's preoccupation with internationalism, and
its adherence to a mechanism of government geared to inaction
and paralysis, ensured that it too would fail to lead Britain out of
crisis. Mosley's break with Labour came in 1930. In the final part
of his resignation speech in which he slammed the then Labour
Government for its failure to solve the unemployment problem
and for its general lethargy in the face of crisis, he said:-

"This nation has to be mobilised and rallied for a tremendous
effort, and who can do that except the government of the day? If
that effort is not made we may soon come to crisis, to a real
crisis. I do not fear that so much, for this reason, that in a crisis
this nation is always at its best. This people knows how to
handle a crisis; it cools their heads and steels their nerves. What
I fear much more than a sudden crisis is a long, slow crumbling
through the years until we sink to the level of a Spain, a gradual
paralysis beneath which all the vigour and energy of this country

will succumb. That is a far more dangerous thing, and far more likely to happen unless some effort is made. If the effort is made how relatively easily can disaster be averted. You have in this country resources, skilled craftsmen among the workers, design and technique among the technicians, unknown and unequalled in any other country in the world. What a fantastic assumption it is that a nation which within the lifetime of everyone has put forth efforts of energy and vigour unequalled in the history of the world, should succumb before an economic situation such as the present. If the situation is to be overcome, if the great powers of this country are to be rallied and mobilised for a great national effort, then the Government and Parliament must give a lead. I beg the Government tonight to give the vital forces of this country the chance that they await. I beg Parliament to give that lead.''

The lead was never given, and Mosley quit the 'orthodox' parties to go out into the streets of Britain to find the men and women who would help him to give it himself. He first founded the New Party, in whose policies were incorporated many of the new economic proposals he had tried unsuccessfully to get adopted by Labour, but which also included many politicians of the old type, who imagined that their new venture was going to be a joyride. After the party was heavily defeated in the election of 1931, with some of its meetings attacked by violent red mobs, these fair weather supporters melted away, and Mosley was left with a small hard core of people who shared his revolutionary outlook and understood the need, not only for new policies, but an entirely new and different kind of political movement and system. From this hard core was born the British Union of Fascists, which was launched in 1932.

The BUF, as it was known for short, will mainly be remembered for two things: the violence at its meetings and the strong-arm methods adopted to counter it; and the adoption of proposals for a new political system in Britain which invited the allegations that Mosley was aiming to do away with our traditional freedoms and set up a dictatorship. Here Mosley should be allowed to answer for himself:-

"When organised force is used against you, only two courses are open, if authority has already proved unable or unwilling to keep order: to surrender, or to meet force with force and to win. After the New Party experience it was perfectly clear to me that I could blow the red roughs a kiss, pack up and go home, or, after due appeal and warning, eject them from my meeting. It should be remembered that I had no resource except the spoken word: no press, no radio, and little money. Public meetings were our only way of putting over our case, and if our audiences were to hear it we must be prepared to fight for free speech.''

Such an attitude naturally infuriated the ruffians of the left, who by that time had come to regard themselves as the divinely-appointed censors of what political views may or may not be heard in the meeting halls of the country — just as their spiritual heirs do today. What was less natural, but indeed a revelation as to the state of mind that had gained currency in the Britain of that time, was that Mosley's decision to defend his meetings when they were attacked caused almost equal outrage among those who represented 'respectable' opinion. From left, right and centre, he was castigated for not doing the decent thing, which was to abandon all his attempts to make himself heard around the country and go into peaceful retirement rather than stand up to the thugs and risk a fight.

As for 'dictatorship', here Mosley was of course running up against the most abused, and misused, word in the modern political dictionary. What he wanted was nothing more than a political system which gave to government the power to get things done, as he explained in his booklet *Tomorrow We Live*:-

"The will of the people shall prevail. The policy for which the people have voted shall be carried out. This is the essence of good government in an enlightened age. This is the principle which is denied by the system misnamed democracy, which in degeneration is more appropriately called financial democracy. When the government, elected by the people, is incapable of rapid and effective action, private and vested interests assume the real power of government, not by vote or permission of the people, but by power of money dubiously acquired. In recent years the trifling measures which have struggled through parliamentary obstruction have been insignificant in their effect on the lives of people, by comparison with the immense exercise of money power. Decisions and movements of international finance on Wall Street, and its sub-branch in the City of London, may send prices soaring to create a speculator's paradise at the expense of the real wages of the people, or may send prices crashing to throw millions into unemployment, as the aftermath of some gigantic gamble. In terms of the things that really matter to the people, such as real wages, employment, the hours of labour, food prices and the simple ability to pay the rent, finance, under the present system, can affect the lives of the mass of people more closely and more terribly in the decision of one afternoon than can Parliament, with puny labour and the mock heroics of sham battles, in the course of a decade. For the instrument of the money power was designed to fit present conditions and to exploit the decadence of an obsolete system. Parliament, on the other hand, was created long before modern conditions existed to meet an altogether different set of facts.''

Years later Mosley returned to the same subject of dictatorship in *300 Questions Answered*, where he was asked to differentiate between dictatorship and leadership. He said:-

"There is all the difference in the world. The leadership principle is the voluntary acceptance of guidance you desire. Dictatorship implies compulsion to do something you do not want to do. For instance, I accept the leadership principle from somebody else every time I ask a policeman the way and he tells me. He knows something I do not know, and I am very glad to accept his guidance...Getting someone to run the government for you, if you think him good at the job, is really just the same thing. And of course it means in practice getting a team of men to run the government. You are then accepting the leadership principle. This is really all there is to it once we can see through current nonsense to the clear reality behind."

Mosley's concept of how best to put into effect the will of the people of which he spoke in *Tomorrow We Live* was fundamentally different to those of the upholders of the old party racket: he wanted, as has been said, a government with the power to act and for the nation not to be torn apart by party warfare, but he did not envisage the action of that government being contrary to the wishes of the people. As he said in *300 Questions Answered*:-

"There is a very simple remedy against dictatorship in any advanced country. Just stay away from work. If enough people do it, the country comes to a standstill and the government must fall. In other words, no government can carry on if the people really do not want it.
"...In a backward country it is another matter. Any brigand with a gun can rule a desert, particularly if no-one else wants it; or if you begin where people are used to an inefficient tyranny, as the communists began in Russia, the people continue in the habit of accepting a more up-to-date tyranny. But dictatorship cannot work in modern countries that have known freedom. No form of government can last without support of the people.''

We will return later in this book to these questions of methods of government which occupied Mosley in his time and occupy us today — here is not the place to examine them in great detail. Mosley's policies, apart from those concerned with the reform of our system of government, can simply be condensed as follows: Britain should opt out of the anarchical international 'free trade' system and build up her manufacturing industries behind protective barriers. She should negotiate with her dominions to obtain imperial preference under which they would take British finished goods in return for their minerals and food products — though this did not preclude the dominions' development of their own manufacturing industries where they saw this as in their interest. With industry at home protected against cut-price foreign competition, it would be possible gradually and progressively to raise wages so as to create huge new purchasing power at home, which would in turn increase the market for our own manufactures, thus leaving them much less dependent on foreign markets. This, in essence, was the same as the programme advocated by Chamberlain's Tariff Reform movement of thirty years earlier, with some updating to meet new facts of technology and with the additional proposal that entirely new methods of government be introduced to give effect to such a programme. Whereas Chamberlain's policies were proposed in the hope that they would be adopted within established political institutions, those of Mosley were seen to depend entirely on new institutions of government and politics to replace the old. Beyond this, Mosley offered proposals for the reform and regeneration of a whole society. In one case there was simply a set of propositions for the reform of economic policy, while in the other there was a comprehensive political doctrine that embraced every sphere of the nation's life. In the outlook of fascism, economics, politics, social questions, culture, philosophy and morality formed an integrated whole, and that whole was a total challenge to the liberal outlook that preceded it. Fascism was much more than a new political movement; it was a new creed, almost a religion. One may revile it or herald it as the harbinger of salvation; at least it cannot be denied a consistency of logic in the ideas it incorporates.

A history of the inter-war British fascist movement written, for a change, by one who supported that movement would be a valuable contribution towards a redressing of the balance in the propaganda that has surrounded the subject, and I hope that this one day appears. It is not my purpose to attempt the task, for I am writing primarily to signpost the future. I am not anyway the best qualified to be a witness to what happened in that period, for I was only five years old when it came to its end. My knowledge of it has been obtained through study and through many conversations with those who took part. This is not, I will gladly admit, a substitute for first-hand personal experience.

Nevertheless, no study of contemporary British Nationalism would be adequate without some attempt to trace the currents of thought contributing to it, and such a presentation of these currents would be incomplete, as well as dishonest, without some acknowledgement of the part played in the process by the fascist movement of the pre-1939 era. This, along with the other antecedents that I have mentioned, should be given its place of recognition.

If there is a valid criticism to be made against Mosley and his movement of the thirties, it is that they did not go far enough to distance themselves from continental movements in respect of the external imagery adopted. The name 'fascist' was chosen with the same considerations in mind as those accompanying the earlier import of the words 'liberal' and 'socialist', that it was no dishonour to share with other nations a common political language when this was justified by the similarity of doctrines held. That is a perfectly rational argument, but it did not take sufficiently into account that in the practice of politics we are dealing all the time with irrational forces. Somehow the name 'fascist' gave fuel to the irrational view, encouraged by opponents for all they were worth, that the Mosley movement was a 'foreign' import. In retrospect, it may be seen as not the wisest choice.

The same may be said of all the other trappings of the movement, in particular the black shirt and the Nazi salute.

But I make these observations in no spirit of assumed superiority of wisdom; for years later, and with much less excuse, I myself made the same error of associating with a group which employed identical tactics. The observations are made only to point out that the Mosley movement of the thirties should not be regarded as a model to be followed today in all respects. It is merely one part of the family tree of British Nationalism to be considered along with others. It is nevertheless an important part and as such should be acknowledged if we are to keep faith with the spirit of honesty in which I have tried to write this book.

In this analysis of the historical roots of British Nationalism, it must be emphasised that not all of the policies advocated for previous times are necessarily valid or feasible today. The different age in which we are now living calls for the adoption of different positions on a number of issues to those put forward in earlier times. For instance, many factors present in the 1930s situation are no longer present today. At that time events in Germany, and to a lesser extent Italy, dominated the international political scene, for the obvious reason that war with those countries was seen by many to be a coming prospect. Inevitably, therefore, Germany and Italy loomed large in political debate in this country. They did so because our rulers and our press willed it that way. A nation which should at the time have been devoting most of its thoughts to tackling its own immense domestic problems became unduly and obsessively preoccupied with events on the continent. That scenario of debate having been created, no-one could engage in the politics of the time without adopting some position on these continental affairs — even if it was only the position that Britain should keep out of them.

Today that situation no longer exists because those continental movements and regimes are no more. Today the focal points of world affairs have moved elsewhere, calling for different approaches and policies, so that the question of whether we should endorse the whole of the Mosley programme of that earlier period simply does not arise. Some aspects of the debate of that period are relevant to the present day, and this is particularly the case with the debate on the national economy, but other aspects are no longer relevant. We should not remain stuck in the past but should move on. Mosley fascism is an interesting study to those of us today who are searching for solutions to our contemporary problems, but it is not the gospel. We should take from it the lessons that are useful, and leave it at that.

There may be some who will say in reply to all this: Why mention Mosley or Fascism at all? And why, particularly, mention Hitler? Is it not best to ignore them entirely rather than raise up old ghosts from the past to haunt the present? I would reply that it is not I who is concerned to raise up these ghosts: it is our opponents who are determined at every turn to do so. Just as soon as there is any attempt to discuss rationally the problems with which we are beset today, in particular those connected with racial matters, these opponents will immediately seek to prejudice the discussion by evoking the spectres of 'fascism', 'nazism' and Hitler. We could not exclude these questions from the discussion if we wanted to, so we may as well face them and deal with them frankly. At the same time we should, as I have said, not get them out of proper perspective. Least of all should those who are able to unite over the questions of what should be done today oblige their common enemies by falling out over what was done half a century ago.

In the matter of specific approaches to specific questions, British Nationalism must move with the times just as must any political creed or movement; on the other hand, in the matter of fundamental principles of faith, it is unchanging. What then are these principles of faith?

In the first place, we recognise that the world is not — and never can be — one single human family. The theory that it should and can has been a pretty one, attractive to dreamers and fantasy-weavers across the ages, but history in the raw has never fulfilled, and will never fulfil, their hope and prognosis. Such an idea is anyway completely contrary to all evolution of the human species. In the real world of mankind, as in the world of other species, there not only will always be, but must always be, competition — for living space, for resources and, among the higher species, for prestige and honour. As far as resources are concerned, these are finite, while the breeding possibilities of mankind are not. That there should be struggle between the various sections of mankind for possession of these resources may be an idea hard for some to accept, but it is an inescapable reality. The only question of the future to be determined is who will be successful in this struggle and who not.

Man in a civilised state will do everything possible to eliminate the most brutal features of this struggle and to reduce to the minimum its unkind effects on those who are the losers in it. But it is at his peril that he will attempt to defy the laws of the struggle itself and imagine that he can rise above it to some alternative form of worldwide organisation under which it no longer exists.

Nationalism simply arises from the acceptance by a human group of this law of the universe and its will that it should be one of those groups to survive and not one to go under.

From this acceptance will come a form of national organisation best geared to national survival and success. This imperative will precede all others. Private or public ownership of wealth and resources, extension or restriction of individual freedoms and rights, decisions by popular or minority consensus, will all be evaluated according to how they serve that paramount need.

Nationalism is in any community the great unifier, in large part because it is the great synthesiser. The impetus towards national unity in a people is always the greater when it is recognised that the nation's survival in international competition is of over-whelmingly greater importance than the sectarian differences of politics, religion or class that may mark one section of the nation as distinct from another. But, in addition to this, once these priorities of national strength and capability are accepted, it is much easier to reconcile what at first may appear to be sharp divisions of political, economic or social theory. Seemingly contradictory and conflicting concepts, such as 'free enterprise' and 'statism', are seen not as ends but merely as means to an end, and as such can be employed in alternation — one in one place, the other in another place — according to what is expedient.

In the simplest terms, nationalism is no more than team spirit. Just as the school, the firm, the regiment and the rugby XV need, each in its own way, to be infused with a pride of identity and a desire to win, so must nations, if they are to be effective forces for the furtherance of their own interests and for their survival in the world, be galvanised by the same vital emotional forces.

Such a doctrine will of course be anathema to the 'liberal' and left-wing intellectual, who fancy that they have in their brains the prescription for a more enlightened organisation of the world. Later we will examine in greater detail the mind and soul of this type of the species. Suffice it for me to state my belief here that at the bottom of this 'liberal' and leftist rejection of country and race and the rough arena of history into which they have been cast is a basic condition of physical and mental ill-health, which makes the type unfit to face the demands of survival in the real world. Just as the weakling will do all he can to keep away from the school playing field, so will the spiritual cripple wish to escape from a world of manly endeavour, in which the strong are victorious, to an ivory tower populated by his own kind, where his sick and puny values are the accepted wisdom.

This would not suffice to explain, however, the degree to which all contemporary political opinion has been mobilised against the national idea and every powerful institution commanded by those who oppose it. How is it that that political faith which alone offers a lifeline to Britain in her present hour of desperate crisis has become everywhere, in politics, in the press, in the academic community and in the church, the number-one heresy of our times? How have the nation's political leaders, at every stage of recent history, steered Britain with a consistency that defies all sense and all logic, along a course of national disaster? It is the time to enquire into the question of whether our decline as a nation is the result merely of muddle combined with ill fortune or the product of a malevolent design.

Chapter 5
Is there a conspiracy?

Earlier in this book I recounted the time at which I first began to entertain the idea that some of the major political events of the modern world might be explicable in terms of a conspiracy at work. This was of course my initial aquaintance with a subject that has been the focus of a vast amount of speculation and comment during the present century.

At first sight, the conspiracy theory is something that imposes a considerable strain on one's powers of digestion. Small plots involving very limited numbers of people are easy enough to believe in. But something as gigantic in scope as a conspiracy to direct the major events of a whole epoch of world history, involving the major decisions of the leading nations and enlisting, as such a thing must do, the participation of vast numbers of agents — that stretches human credulity to the utmost. And it was with considerable scepticism that I first undertook a study of this topic.

Nevertheless, against this cautionary thought was a counter-thought: if this theory of conspiracy was entirely groundless, the invention of paranoiacs and cranks, by what other means were certain important events to be explained?

Supposing we take the case of a highly successful man who has reached, say, his fortieth year. By the use of his intelligence, common sense and practical knowledge, he has undertaken one profitable business operation after another, to build for himself a considerable fortune and a highly respected place in society.

Then he makes one investment that turns out to be an unwise one and loses a lot of money. On the strength of that one mishap, we may conclude that, for once in his life, he has been a trifle careless or otherwise just unlucky, and, assuming that he is still the man we know him to be, he will learn from his error and not make the same mistake again.

Even if he does again take a tumble here and there and make a loss, so long as these are outbalanced by a far larger number of wisely conceived and successful ventures we can assume that this man remains one guided by a sound business instinct and we can continue to put confidence in him.

But if, on the other hand, that same man from his fortieth year proceeds to make a series of disastrous business decisions, resulting in mounting losses, until he reaches the point of losing almost everything he ever had, we are entitled to suspect that some strange and malignant force has taken hold of him, some evil influence not previously evident in his life, which is steering him again and again in directions catastrophic to his own interest.

By this time the meaning of the metaphor will be obvious: what rule holds good for such an individual will hold good for a formerly highly successful nation.

As a youngster first engaged in the job of trying to make some sense out of the successive turns of British politics in the 1950s, I was mystified, as I can today vividly recall, by the series of decisions of state by which our country seemed to be wilfully digging the grave, not only of its Empire, but of its very self. One act of national policy after another pointed in the same direction: the undermining of the British national interest and the advancement of the interests of our enemies. In previous ages of our history errors of policy had been made, but these had been overwhelmingly outweighed by the good decisions, with the result of continuous national success and the advancement of national wealth and power. Now it was all error, all retreat and all decline.

The official reasons for these retrograde acts of policy did not stand up to a moment's intelligent examination. We went to war with Germany in 1939 because she invaded Poland — not Britain, mark you, nor any part of the British Empire, but Poland. Yet a short time later Russia invaded Poland from the opposite side but that was not regarded as a reason for going to war with her; on the contrary, Russia was soon to become our valued ally in war for four years.

Russia was our ally up to May 1945. Then almost immediately afterwards we were being told that Russia had aggressive designs on Western Europe, including Britain, and we had to arm ourselves against her!

We were told during 1939-45 that, apart from fighting to defend the Poles and the Czechs and others, we were fighting to defend our own empire — and this certainly would have been the only logical purpose for resisting Japan in the Far East. Yet as soon as the war was over our leaders set about dismantling the very Empire we were supposed to have been defending!

This was all explained to us at the time in terms of the right of the colonial territories to self-government, but it was perfectly clear to any rational person that these colonies were utterly unfit for self-government and that if they were granted it they would sink into poverty and chaos.

But even if it is accepted that we were right, on these grounds, in letting these colonies go, what on earth was the purpose in the preceding years of expending vast sums of money and many human lives of our servicemen in order to keep them?

The left in politics particularly applauded the process of imperial surrender, saying that it was wrong for one nation to rule others. Yet the left did not object to Russia still acting as an imperial power and ruling, not just backward peoples, but European nations in many respects more advanced and civilised than itself.

These points of view, which became the approved 'line' in the post-war period, were utterly incomprehensible to me as a young student of the political scene. Everything was being done, and with the greatest possible haste, to eliminate British power, wealth and resources around the world, not by Britain's external enemies (though they no doubt rejoiced at the process), but by British Government! And this after our nearly bleeding ourselves to death in a world war supposedly in defence of the very things we were now throwing away.

And not only was the political left supporting this abdication to the hilt, but so were **Conservatives** doing everything possible to bring it about too, the same Conservatives who had for decades proclaimed themselves the party of 'patriotism' and 'Empire'!

The list of these developments could be added to endlessly in what has happened since: the integration of Europe proceeding parallel to the disintegration of Empire (entirely contradictory developments); the flooding of an overcrowded Britain with immigrants, making for racial disharmony while being promoted by the very people who always preached racial harmony; the insanity of our middle-eastern policy, which alienated many nations whom we had every reason to keep as friends and for the sake of one nation whom we owed nothing; the squalid onslaught on, and eventual destruction of, White Rhodesia, our kith and kin, in order to set up a marxist tyranny in that country; the similar onslaught against South Africa today, which is wholly contrary to every British interest; the making of almost the whole of Black Africa a sphere of interest of the Soviet Union, despite the fact that we are supposed to stand on opposite sides to the Soviets in a 'cold war'. All these insane policies have been carried out by successive governments and by general consensus of agreement between the major political parties.

Why indeed has British Conservatism, which has constantly railed against the menace of Soviet expansionism and invites American forces to occupy our country in supposed defence against that menace, done everything that could possibly be done to aid the spread of Soviet influence over the continent of Africa?

At the same time as these things have been happening we have witnessed what could only be described as the systematic destruction of British manufacturing industry, with not a finger raised to help it, and the lunacy of the EEC farming policy, resulting in the piling up of huge food surpluses, which have either been left to rot or have been sold off at knock down prices to — believe it or not, Soviet Russia!

There has been the post-war paradox of international communism supposedly being our rival in a global power struggle while at every turn we have been at pains to help it. We spend many thousands of millions every year maintaining our armed services, primarily in anticipation, we are told, of a Soviet threat, while we assist the Soviets in taking over Africa and help regularly to rescue them from their food shortages. Sheer insanity — or is it something else?

Can it seriously be contested, in the light of these phenomena, that there is some hidden and sinister force that has taken over the direction of British politics in modern times and is guiding us to national self-destruction? That such a force exists may strain the powers of human belief — that I will admit. But what must strain these powers even more is the proposition that these things have come about by some normal, logical and rationally explicable process, that they are in fact to be accounted for in just the way that we have been told by our politicians and by our mass media. If we use the language of Sherlock Holmes, we must say of these things: "Once, my dear Watson, that we have eliminated the impossible, what remains, however improbable, must be the truth!"

Studying events up to the 1950s, and without the further evidence of numerous events since, I was driven to accept that the case for the theory of conspiracy was a strong one — indeed

before long I came to the conclusion that it was overwhelming —
and for the reasons I have stated. What kind of conspiracy then
was it? And who were the conspirators?

To answer these questions for myself, I turned, as always, to
study, and began a comprehensive examination of whatever
literature I could get on the subject. What was noteworthy from
the beginning was that none of this literature was obtainable from
the normal sources, such as retail bookshops and public libraries.
When one went into these places and asked for the books in
question, one received blank looks that might have suggested one
was asking for publications printed on another planet! I was only
able to get hold of the reading matter I sought by means of contacts
I had established among the small patriotic political groups with
which I had become involved or acquainted, one of which was the
Britons Publishing Company. I soon learned from older hands
than myself that all possible efforts had been made in the past to
get these books sold through the normal distributive network and
stocked by libraries, and that all these efforts had failed. Some
strange power of censorship existed throughout the book trade,
even in those quarters where pride was taken in the 'broad-
minded' approach of the proprietors and every conceivable form
of filth and obscenity was to be seen regularly stocked on the
shelves. In one case I was told of the chief buyer of a medium-
sized bookstore chain who, when offered supplies of this literature
on a sale-or-return basis, replied that if he took up the offer his
firm would be put out of business within less than a year. Put out
of business? By whom? For what reason?

Bit by bit, from an extensive perusal of certain books and
pamphlets on the subject, I began to form a picture of the conspiracy theory, which I put to the test at every stage of study by
comparing it with my own observations of national and international politics. Much of this literature had the weakness that it
was badly written, the authors obviously not being professional
journalists or writers but simply ordinary folk who had been
driven to an examination of the subject by much the same process
as I had been — people who, in any other situation than the one in
which the world found itself in the 20th century, would very
probably have kept out of political controversy and just minded
their own business. One of the symptoms of this unprofessional
approach was a tendency, at times, to absurd oversimplification,
while another was the presentation of mere supposition and hypothesis as if it were substantiated fact beyond dispute. One had to

resist the inclination to be put off by this often unscientific level of argument, which was something rather like a guilty man in court being made to sound innocent by reason of the very poor case being put by prosecuting counsel.

As I have indicated earlier, the writings on this subject of A.K. Chesterton definitely did not fall into the category I have described, Chesterton being a trained journalist and author of considerable experience and with a healthy scepticism towards wild and unproven allegations of fact. I followed his regular commentaries on political events in *Candour* newsletter and in addition read a number of pamphlets written by the same author. Everything that I read of Chesterton's seemed eminently sane and almost completely in accordance with my own picture of events, both before and after I had come into contact with the conspiracy theory.

What then is the nature of this theory? Allowing for some variations between the interpretations of one exponent and another, and concentrating on the broad outline rather than being immersed in small details, it is that there is a power behind the scenes in modern politics dedicated to the destruction of the existing nation-states of the world, and of the distinct races that make up those states, and their replacement by an international order, eventually to become a world government; that this power works almost entirely in secret, aiming to obtain manipulation of the affairs of nations by exerting pressure over their governments by means of control of key strategic points of political influence, such as finance and banking, press and broadcasting and other areas of the mass media; that most of the subversive movements of the modern world, including particularly communism, are the creation of this power; that in fact the power of which we are speaking has had a greater influence in the shaping of modern history than any other agency, including the world's leading nations.

In what then does such a power consist? Merely to say that it is a group of people unified together in a common objective does not get us very far. Some more cohesive factor than this is surely needed to blend such people together in the carrying out of a single policy on a worldwide scale, and often at great hazard to themselves. Of what people then are we speaking when we talk of this power?

On this matter the literature I studied was almost, though not wholly, unanimous. At the centre of the network stood a group of

Jews — not all the Jews, not even most of the Jews, but the most powerful and influential sections of Jewry, comprising its leaders in politics, in business, in journalism and in the cultural and intellectual world. The idea inspiring the majority of these people was **Zionism** — not just the obvious and self-acknowledged Zionism aimed at the setting up of a Jewish national home in what was once Palestine, but a greater Zionism directed to bringing all the world's nations and resources under the control of Jewry and giving that race effective world leadership.

On first impressions, this theory seemed almost too fantastic for me to swallow, notwithstanding that I had become convinced that **some** conspiratorial forces were at work, at least in Britain, and certainly had sufficient power to wield decisive influence on a number of major events. But as I pursued the further study of this subject I found it difficult to come to any conclusions other than to give credence to the view that persons of Jewish race were a major factor, if not **the** major one, among these forces. In the course of time practical experience, as well as much reading, brought home to me the immense power of organised Jewry in Britain, and the way it could be mobilised against anyone and anything which incurred its displeasure.

Perhaps one stumbling block in the way of the theory of conspiracy behind current world events is the idea that, to be proved to exist, such a conspiracy must be shown to be able to make happen everything that it wants to happen. Of course no power in politics, however great, can ever achieve quite this total omnipotence. Enormous power, however, can undoubtedly be wielded in public affairs by any group of people in a position to determine what shall **not** happen, and, perhaps even more to the point, what things may not be **said**. State censors in Soviet Russia, for instance, cannot possibly direct to order every word of every sentence written by every journalist or author in the whole of that country; the way that censorship operates is that it is decreed what such journalists or authors may **not** write. In time of course such censorship becomes a largely self-regulating process: it is barely necessary for everything to be actually proof-read, because everyone in the business of writing comes to know what he may get away with and what he may not. In this way the ideological route to be followed under the Soviet system is pretty well controlled: once the turnings one may not take are eliminated from the map, one's actual options of travel become tightly limited.

As I proceeded to study and become active in politics in Britain, I learned in time what might not be done and what might not be said. I do not mean by this that there were actually state laws which forbade people to do or say these things (such laws came later) but that, to all practical intents and purposes, one simply was not allowed to gain access to the facilities necessary to say or do such things effectively. What, for instance, is the use of being 'free' to write a book or a pamphlet putting forward a particular viewpoint if such a book or pamphlet is only going to be read by a tiny number of people — and most of them people already largely converted to that viewpoint already?

Freedom of the press, or freedom of authorship, means little unless it incorporates the freedom to have widely distributed, through the appropriate mass-circulation networks, the products of one's writings. Freedom of speech, likewise, means little if it is confined to the soapbox orator on the street corner or the guest-speaker at a house party. It only comes to mean something if it includes the right of access to large public halls and possession of the means of advertising whereby one can fill a hall with an audience. Today, increasingly, it only means something if it includes access to radio and television.

If any group of people operating as a closely co-ordinated force and together knowing exactly what they want, can find means of ensuring that certain views do not get into the mass-circulation newspapers or the books that are to be found for sale on the shelves of every high street bookseller, that group can be said to exercise something near to a dictatorship over the public mind — not by regulating what people will read but by determining what they will **not** read. When this happens, what we have is effective **ideological control**. I had already come up against this fact of life when I attempted to obtain certain books from bookshops and libraries, as I have already related. Eventually, some of these books could be obtained — if one ordered them and was prepared to have a long wait. In that sense they were not exactly 'banned'. But it did mean that only the special enthusiast would ever obtain and read such material; to the masses it simply did not exist.

Earlier, when speaking of my discovery that booksellers could be put out of business for stocking and displaying certain books, I asked the rhetorical question: by whom? Before long I was to know by whom. My researches established that, invariably, it was pressure from certain **Jewish** quarters that led to this blackballing of the books in question. The same researches led to my learning that an identical form of pressure could be, and at times was, applied against the owners and editors of newspapers, and with the same result: while these newspapers might, on *prima facie* evidence, expound diverse views and exhibit diverse political party loyalties, **all of them** steered clear of certain distinct 'no go' areas of public controversy that had been declared out of bounds by these secret forces of censorship. Later I will return to this subject in some more detail, but I mention these revelations now to underline my growing awareness of the immense power wielded in Britain by certain Jewish interests by means of this monitoring role they seemed to be able to exercise in the way of what view may or may not be written or otherwise communicated to a mass audience.

It was only after becoming properly conscious of these powers at work that I was able to see in full perspective the nature of Hitler's revolution in Germany and the campaign of hatred and venom whipped up against him by the press in Britain during that period. Previously I had seen the anti-German policy of the British political establishment of the 1930s as wrong-headed from the British point of view — as I had also, needless to say, seen our involvement against Germany in World War II. Now I began to understand that something much more than mere wrong-headed-ness had prompted these policies. Forces had been at work that were determined to smash Hitler, quite irrespective of whether it was in the British interest to do so. Why? For guidance, I turned again to reading. Some years previously I had made an effort to get through *Mein Kampf* but had not got very far with it. Now I read it again — after, I might say, experiencing no small difficulty in getting hold of a copy. This time I was older and more know-ledgeable and found the book less heavy reading. It was a revelat-ion! Here described in the language, not of a professional author, but of a highly intelligent and observant man who clearly loved his country with a passion, was everything that I could recall seeing myself in the way of what was wrong with my own country. These, I immediately thought, were not the words of a madman or psychopath but those of a seer and prophet. I did not agree with everything in the book, and some parts related to specifically German matters of which I had no knowledge so as to be able to form an opinion of the merits of the case presented. But one thing undoubtedly did accord with my own experience and thoughts: the descriptions of the workings of certain Jewish forces in Germany, which seemed uncannily similar to what I had observed of the same kinds of forces in Britain.

I learned in due course that advertising boycotts were the standard Jewish practice for maintaining press control. This method was in fact used in the 1930s to gag the Rothermere Press, which beforehand had advocated a policy of peace and friendship towards Hitler's Germany. Likewise it has been used in more recent times to bring into line any newspapers who dared to speak too strongly of Jewish power in Britain or criticise too scathingly the actions of the state of Israel. The power capable of 'arranging' this kind of advertising boycott is known to all newspaper-owners in Fleet Street, and such knowledge is quite sufficient to keep the press in line without such a boycott actually having to be put into practice.

Newspapers cannot possibly survive on sales alone; about half of their income comes from advertising. It is doubtful that advertising from Jewish companies represents anything more than a minority portion of total advertising revenue, but it is a large enough portion to make all the difference between a paper's profitability and unprofitability. If any group of advertisers is prepared to act as a bloc — and rapidly, it can, by withdrawing adverts deliver a newspaper to ruin with equal rapidity — the cash reserves of such papers not generally being high. Possibly, new sources of advertising revenue could be found, but this would take time and in the meantime the paper would be likely to cease publication.

It must also be remembered that a direct boycott of a paper is not the only means that Jewish interests have of putting pressure upon it; it is also quite possible for a business boycott to be organised against non-Jewish businesses which place adverts with such a paper, with exactly the same effect.

Some writers on the conspiracy theory undermine their credibility by speaking of "Jewish press control" in just those simplified terms. Such a statement, taken at its face value, can easily be refuted by pointing to the large portion of the press that is not under Jewish ownership. If we are going to use such phrases as "Jewish press control," we must be specific as to what we mean. Seen in the context of their power to prevent the publication of certain items of news or opinion, by the means of a threatened advertising boycott, certain Jewish interests most definitely do exercise a form of control over the press in Britain that is formidable indeed.

Returning to the subject of *Mein Kampf*, I was particularly struck by the passages in the book in which the author proclaimed a desire for peace and friendship with Britain and admiration for her Empire. It must be remembered that these words were written in 1924, many years before the writer was leader of Germany and engaging in international diplomacy, so there is no reason to suppose that they were uttered with a view to putting Britain off her guard. Also, putting these declarations together with Hitler's outline, given in the same book, of what he saw as the most suitable field for German expansion — that is to say Eastern Europe — such a pro-British policy fitted obviously into the logic of that strategy.

Recognising now the full scale of the lunacy of World War II when seen from the British standpoint, together with the non-stop flood of vituperation in the 'British' media against Germany before, during and since that calamitous event, I had to acknowledge to myself fresh evidence of the existence of sinister forces within our country, goading, inciting and steering us towards policies and attitudes certain to be conducive to our own downfall. If this was not a conspiracy, then the word had lost its meaning.

For the purpose of consideration of this subject, we may leave aside for a moment the question of whether the type of society created by Hitler in Germany was one in which **we** would wish to live; there are many societies all around the world whose ways may seem strange and alien to us — that of Soviet Russia being the first example that comes to mind — but that is no criterion by which to shape our foreign policy. Just two facts about Hitler's Germany are relevant here: firstly, that it represented no threat at all to Britain or her interests; secondly, that it most certainly did represent a threat to Jewish interests — the interests, at least, of that section of Jewry holding decisive power over Jewish policy. Hitler saw Jewish power exercising a nationally harmful influence within Germany and he was determined to break it, which he most certainly did do in the years between 1933 and the outbreak of war by a series of measures which eliminated the Jewish hold on the political, economic and cultural life of the German nation.

The world Jewish leadership therefore had every cause to want to bring Hitler down; Great Britain herself had none. And yet within seven years of Hitler's assumption of power in Germany Britain declared war on him. Let us then ask ourselves the question: was it the British interest or the Jewish interest that was the decisive factor in shaping British policy during this period?

The answer to this question, which will scarcely need spelling out, goes, along with many other answers to many other questions, to substantiate the view that there have been powerful forces, not evident to the public eye, that have shaped the course of British politics during the present century and in a direction diametrically opposite to our own national good. There is abundant evidence that within these forces certain Jewish elements play a powerful role, although this does not mean that such Jewish elements are the only ones present.

I have said earlier that the drift of the conspiracy theory is that the forces central to it have as their object the destruction of the world's nation-states and the setting up of an international order, eventually to become a world government. Can this be proven? In terms that would satisfy a court of law beyond all reasonable doubt, perhaps not at this stage. But what scarcely needs proving, because the evidence of it is overwhelming and there for all to see, is that internationalism has become the dominating idea and policy of the modern age, particularly in Britain, where it rules the thinking of all the established political parties and indeed also the mass media. The proposition that today in Britain all political roads lead to 'one world' is a proposition exceedingly hard to contradict. Without exception, every political party of the 'establishment' has declared itself in principle in favour of an increasing surrender of national sovereignty to international authorities. We have seen, for instance, the common commitment of all these parties to the European Community, notwithstanding the overwhelming evidence that membership of this community has been harmful to the British economy to a catastrophic degree. If we turn to our press, we cannot find one major newspaper which takes a contrary position.

The same drive to one-world can be seen in the attempt to integrate all the defence forces of the Western nations, both in terms of their command and their supplies of weapons and equipment. The rationale for this is provided by the alleged threat of a Soviet invasion westwards of which there is not the slightest evidence — a theme to which I will return later. This 'threat' has nevertheless been built up by all the powers of an orchestrated mass media so as to create an atmosphere in which public opinion will consent to the international pooling of military power.

The pooling of economic sovereignty, and to an increasing degree political sovereignty also, in an integrated Europe are ideas parallelled by a more general philosophy of economic and political internationalism. Britain, at the time that these words are written, has nearly 3 million out of work. This 3 million could without great difficulty be put back into work by the simple policy of protecting the manufacturing industries that are being ruined by foreign competition. Any of the major parties that adopted such a policy would be assured of great popularity and increased votes. Yet the policy is rejected by all the established political parties and all of Fleet Street. Clearly, there is some power with a hold on these parties and journalists that is greater than the power exercised by their desire to win popular support — and, taking into account the average politician's thirst for votes and the average newspaper-owner's preoccuption with circulation figures, that must be a formidable power indeed. What power is it then that directs the course of politics in a supposed 'democracy' far more decisively than 'public opinion' — and which at the same time is not permitted ever to be a subject for public discussion? That there is such a power — whether you subscribe to the theory that it is Jewish or otherwise — can hardly be disputed in the light of the evidence. And if it exists, can it then be disputed that British political life is firmly in the grip of forces operating by the methods of **conspiracy**?

Along with the onslaught on national sovereignty in the economic, political and military fields, there is the equally one-sided onslaught against the idea of the British people remaining a racially homogeneous community. For many centuries we in this country remained nearly free of racially-engendered communal strife, due to the sensible policy of only attempting to assimilate compatible ethnic groups. In the past 40 years there has been a complete abandonment of this policy, as everyone knows, and in its place a policy of making Britain a racial melting pot. This new policy, like every other of an internationalist nature, has become elevated into something akin to a public 'holy writ', with every leading party, almost every leading politician and the whole of the press and broadcasting services bowing deferentially to it — while anyone daring to oppose it publicly can be certain of becoming the target of a campaign of the most vituperative character assassination and public ostracism, if indeed he is lucky enough to keep out of jail!

If I may at this point summarise what has been said, there is an overwhelmingly dominant trend in British politics today towards internationalism, and that same trend is supported and energetically promoted by all the leading organs of mass-communication. It is equally true that certain strange, almost esoteric, pressures exist to prevent any contrary trend being publicly aired, or indeed espoused by any public figure, except at great risk to his position and career. In addition, it is true that certain facts and opinions are deliberately censored out of the newspapers, despite the fact that British people are told every day of their lives that they are lucky to live in a 'free' country. This itself is evidence that certain big lies are put across on the public, beginning with this lie that we live under 'free' institutions where no political debate is suppressed. If there are powerful forces lying to us, while at the same time directing national affairs along lines entirely different to those we are led to suppose, then I submit that there exists a **conspiracy**. There just is no other construction that one can put upon these phenomena. Is it a **Jewish** conspiracy? I will not try to answer that question conclusively here, because the subject, for it to be done true justice, requires a book all on its own, whereas here it forms only a part of a much more general analysis of the harmful trends in British life and their remedy. Certain facts, however, need to be borne in mind in ascertaining the Jewish role in the politics of our century.

With one fact I have already dealt and that is the undoubted power of Jewry in Britain to influence what may be and may not be put into print, and the fact that the threat of Jewish boycott can be, and has been, used to bring the press into line. Another fact of which I am in no doubt as a result of having given close study to the political scene for over 30 years is that leading Jews are to be found, almost always, on the side of the internationalist causes that have dominated British politics during this time.

It is not denied, even by the Jews themselves, that Jewish activists formed the chief cadres of those subversive forces that brought about the revolution in Russia in 1917 as well as the short-lived red revolutions in Hungary and Bavaria almost immediately following, and that communist doctrine, beginning with Karl Marx and Ferdinand Lassalle, probably owes more to Jewish intellectuals than to any others. Bearing in mind that communism is an essential prong of the worldwide drive to internationalism, we can say that certain Jews have, through this movement, made an enormous contribution to the internationalist cause and to those trends making for the destruction of nations.

The same Jewish muscle that was to be seen in the setting up of the first Soviet state in Russia in 1917 was likewise revealed in the pressures that were applied, at exactly the same time in history, to induce the British and US governments to sponsor the setting up of the state of Israel. It is no secret that the support by Britain of the Balfour Declaration in favour of this Jewish national home was the major factor in bringing America into World War I, as in return for this British pledge the powerful Jews in the United States exerted all the influence they could on the American President, Mr. Woodrow Wilson, to persuade him and Congress to opt for war.

I have then described how Jewry used the same kind of influence and power in the 1930s to steer Britain towards war with Hitler's Germany, despite the fact that every British interest dictated a contrary policy. A short time later Jewry in America, this time putting pressure on President Roosevelt, again were a major factor in bringing the United States into the same war. Today it is well known that the Jewish lobby in that same country is able practically to determine America's middle eastern policy by the fact that it can mobilise sufficient muscle at every presidential election to be able to determine which candidate wins.

And, as I shall relate later, it is Britain's and the United States' support of Israel — contrary to both nations' true interests — that is the major cause of all the unrest in the Middle East today.

So we have here established three definite strands of fact: firstly the fact that internationalism is today the overwhelmingly dominant national and world ideology, in the case of Britain crowding every contrary ideology out of all public debate; secondly, we have the fact that there are undoubtedly conspiratorial forces operating in British life and with the power to exercise a profound influence on opinion and events; thirdly, there is the fact of undoubted **Jewish power** — of which I have related just a few examples. Are these facts then conclusive proof that a Jewish conspiracy exists? In terms of the kind of evidence that would be needed to convict a suspected person in a court of law, probably not. In terms of circumstantial evidence pointing to the role of certain Jewish elements in both the drive to internationalism and in the influencing of nations along paths detrimental to their national interests, I would suggest that there is a great deal.

I must also mention one other factor that must be taken into account, and this is the essentially dual attitude maintained by most of Jewry towards the questions of nationalism and internationalism, racial exclusiveness and racial integration.

My experience as a campaigner against the multi-racial idea in Britain and in favour of the retention of our country's centuries-old tradition of racial homogeneity has brought home to me beyond any doubt the fact that Jews are to be found in the forefront of opposition to British racial self-preservation. Just the briefest perusal through a few issues of their main organ, *The Jewish Chronicle*, will bear this out.

And yet within the pages of the same paper one will find regularly expressed the fears of Jews against 'assimilation' of their own kind into other races and their opposition to inter-marriage with Gentiles. And if there is any example needed of a 'racist' state in the world today Israel provides that example. Even the political left, which generally favours Jews and abominates 'racism', is forced to admit this.

People aware of this paradox in Jewish thinking are forced inevitably to the question: is it the policy of Jewry to regard 'multi-racialism' as a commodity essentially for export, as something to encourage in non-Jewish peoples but never to practise among Jewry itself? And, if so, why is there this inconsistency, if it is not for the reason that multi-racialism is seen as a method of weakening other races while Jewry, by adherence to the very opposite policy, strengthens itself?

Exactly the same kind of paradox can be seen in the fact that Jews will be found ceaselessly championing internationalist causes all over the world and denigrating nationalism as out of date and even 'evil', while in Israel what holds the whole state and community together is the most intense nationalism to be found anywhere on earth today!

These facts being indisputable, the question must be asked: why do so many Jews preach to other races and nations what their own people do not practise themselves? What lies behind this desire to strengthen Jewry while weakening non-Jewish peoples?

One thing that we must take into account concerning the theory of a Jewish international conspiracy and that is that it cannot, by any stretch of imagination, be regarded as an obscure subject. It lies at the heart of that doctrine that the Jews call 'anti-semitism', and it has been acknowledged by writers on the so-called 'holocaust' as being the theory that underlay the anti-Jewish doctrines of Hitler and the Nazis.

And we are never allowed to forget 'anti-semitism'. It is hurled at us almost every day of our lives by means of the television screen, newspapers and book trade. If two weeks of TV programmes and films go by without a reference to it, the guardians of the semitic interest begin to become greatly worried that the public may be in the process of being permitted to forget this the world's most important issue!

Considering all this, might it not reasonably be argued that the theory of a Jewish conspiracy must be one of sufficient public interest for it to be subjected to a thorough public enquiry, to an even-sided public debate in which someone is permitted to speak for those many people of historical importance who might be classed as 'anti-semites' — from Luther to Hitler, from Shakespeare to Belloc and G.K. Chesterton, from Richard Wagner to Henry Ford?

Surely, if the theory of a Jewish conspiracy underlining 'anti-semitism' has caused so much misery in the world, the proper way to avoid future misery of the same kind is knock the theory thoroughly on the head by having an open debate about it and once and for all demolishing it by the power of arguments and facts! Yet it seems that those who control the channels of communication whereby such a debate may be staged are strangely reluctant to do this. Why?

It would appear that those who are always raising the 'anti-semitic' bogey want it both ways: they want to ensure that the subject is never kept out of the spotlight but they want to ensure, equally, that two points of view on it are never presented. Cast your eyes about the historical section of any large bookshop and you are almost certain to see an ample selection of books dealing with the sufferings of the Jews, including of course books about World War II and about life in Germany under National Socialism. Do the same thing in a public library and you will have the same experience. Yet ask for any book putting forth the point of view of those accused of 'anti-semitism' and you will be told that such books are not in stock! Why they are not in stock was a question I asked myself when I first began this study as a youngster years ago. Today I put the same question for the consideration of the reader: why?

It is not as if people have not made any efforts to get such books into bookshops and libraries. I have related the efforts to get bookshops to stock these publications. I know personally people who have volunteered to make gifts of such books to public libraries and I know that their offers have always been turned down. I also know of cases where isolated copies of these books have found their way onto the shelves of the odd public library but have subsequently 'disappeared', either being quietly removed when no-one was looking or being withdrawn after a loud protest by local Jews.

In just the same way, there is a total censorship on the subject on radio and TV and in the press, as far as any attempt to present the reverse side of the 'anti-semitism' issue is concerned — while the Jewish side is rammed down our throats almost to the point of mental and emotional indigestion.

Surely, those who would deny indignantly that they are engaged in a conspiracy have the onus placed upon them to demonstrate that they would like things out in the open, just as an innocent person accused of a dastardly crime should welcome a fair trial in order that his innocence may be proved. When, on the other hand, the accused party would seem to want anything **but** an open enquiry into the case, that would indicate, to most people, a guilty conscience.

Coming up against this question of 'anti-semitism' as a young man in the 1950s and early 1960s, I straightaway thought it right to investigate it from both sides. When eventually I was able to get my hands on literature which tackled the subject from the side of those accused of this 'crime' — and that was not easy, as I have shown — I was able to see clearly what 'anti-semitism' was in most cases: it was simply a defence mechanism on the part of peoples of many nations (and not just Germany) against Jewish power. It struck me then as a matter of interest that, time and time again and in one country after another throughout history, this phenomenon of 'anti-semitism' had appeared: in England in the period prior to the expulsion of the Jews by Edward I, in Spain at the time of the Inquisition, in Russia both before and after the coming of Communism, in France and America with regularity over the ages, and of course in Germany long before Hitler.

No parallel exists anywhere of movements of opposition to any other race or religious group that have manifested themselves with the same intensity, the same universality and the same repetitiveness as these movements against Jewry. Are we to believe that the people involved in such movements were all lunatics, beasts or sadists, intent on persecuting a racial group just out of the malevolence of their natures? Was William Shakespeare, Britain's, and perhaps the world's, greatest dramatist, so wrong in his manner of dealing with this subject, as in *The Merchant of Venice*, while he was considered so right in his observations of practically every other human problem under the sun?

Or did all these people perhaps have a reason for their attitudes towards Jewry? We are surely entitled, if we live in a society in which intellectual freedom is allowed, to debate the matter in a spirit of open enquiry by hearing both sides of the argument. Yet in fact we are only allowed to hear one side. Again I put the question: **why?**

I have said already that at the heart of 'anti-semitic' doctrine, at least in its modern version, is the theory of a conspiracy by certain Jewish interests to bring the nations under their power and set up an international order controlled by Jewry. This is a very serious allegation that should rightly concern those Jews who stand thus accused. It might indeed be described as a kind of collective libel.

In the laws of all civilised countries there are provisions for any person who believes himself to be the target of a public allegation of a libellous or slanderous nature to take his accusers to court and obtain a retraction and damages by establishing the groundlessness of such attacks, and it is the normal reaction of any person thus defamed to do just that — for if he does not he is liable to give rise to the suspicion that the accusations against him may have some substance.

I have used the word 'defamed', and it is here perhaps pertinent to point out that the Jews themselves have an organisation which they call the 'Anti-Defamation League', whose special function it is to deal with what they regard as 'defamatory' propaganda against them. This 'Anti-Defamation League' is extremely active; let any TV or radio programme anywhere allow something to be said that is not entirely flattering to the Jews, and the makers of that programme are liable to receive a very prompt telephone call from someone on behalf of the League protesting about the matter.

Surely, in view of this, the leaders of Jewry must regard as 'defamatory', i.e. libellous and slanderous, the supposition that they are engaged in a conspiracy to gain control of the world by the process alleged in the standard textbooks on the subject. This presumably being so, the obvious thing to do would be to have a public enquiry on the matter along the lines that I have suggested here, in which all evidence produced by their opponents could be examined in the clear light of day and answered by their own spokesmen. It seems, however, that while there is more than a willingness to attack 'anti-semites', there is not a corresponding willingness to allow people to hear the point of view giving rise to this 'anti-semitism'. The whole subject has today become completely taboo in the press and on TV and radio. No film is ever allowed to be shown which expounds the conspiracy theory or the 'anti-semitic' viewpoint, while thousands are being shown all around the world all of the time expounding the view that the Jews are just a defenceless minority whose 'persecution' has no rational basis. No book is allowed to be sold to the general public through the mass distribution network which attracts Jewish disapproval — at least not up to the present time — while millions of books of the opposite kind are sold every week.

If the Jewish conspiracy theory is groundless, if it is rubbish churned out by paranoiacs, cranks and hatemongers and not worthy of a moment's consideration by intelligent and civilised people, then why are certain interests so anxious to ban all open discussion of the subject? Why can it not be properly debated and members of the public left to make up their own minds?

I have said earlier that I shall not try to answer conclusively the question of whether the forces of conspiracy that shape our national life today are Jewish or not. As I have indicated, to prove that they are is far beyond the scope of this chapter, which is intended merely to be a synopsis of my own personal observations on the matter and some of the experiences that led me to give credence to the theory. Other authors have covered the subject much more comprehensively in books in which that subject is central. Examples are: A.K. Chesterton in *The New Unhappy Lords*; Douglas Reed in *The Controversy of Zion*; Ivor Benson in *The Zionist Factor*; and Alfred Lilienthal in *The Zionist Connection*. Lilienthal's book should be of particular interest because the author himself is Jewish, and it relates the ruthless pressures applied by certain sections of Jewry in the United States to regiment American public opinion in support of that country's continuing pro-Israel policy.

My purpose here might be likened to that of a magistrate whose job it is, not to pronounce a defendant guilty and sentence him, but to determine whether there is, on *prima facie* evidence, a case for him to answer whereby he may be sent to a higher court where that case may be examined in the fullest detail and with all the available evidence submitted to the closest scrutiny. I am convinced beyond all reasonable doubt that the evidence of conspiratorial forces operating in British politics, and to the great detriment of the national interest, is overwhelming, and I have tried, within the very limited space available in this chapter, to explain how I have come to that conclusion. I am furthermore convinced that evidence of Jewish participation within these forces has been established beyond doubt. As to the final question, that of whether the ultimate directing power behind such forces is Jewish, I do not find a case as yet proven but I certainly do find that there is a case to answer; and not the least of the factors that influence me in this direction is the frantic reluctance of the leaders of Jewry to have that case examined in the open. Precisely to what degree the conspiracy is Jewish-controlled I leave to the reader to decide after a comprehensive study of this and other evidence on the subject.

On the latter question by no means all conspiracy theorists are agreed. The American author W. Cleon Skousen in *The Naked Capitalist* gives an excellently argued case for the existence of an international conspiracy directing 20th century affairs. Skousen takes as his cue a series of admissions to this effect made by Professor Carroll Quigley in another book *Tragedy and Hope*. Quigley's admissions carry special weight because he was, by his own acknowledgement, in sympathy with the aims of the conspiracy to which his book refers. It is an interesting sequel that *Tragedy and Hope* has since been completely withdrawn from circulation and copies are extremely difficult to come by. Despite his convictions as to the workings of the conspiracy, however, Skousen denies any special Jewish role in the process — whether from genuine conviction, or merely the desire to escape being labelled an 'anti-semite', one cannot know.

At the other extreme, the works of such authors as Arnold Leese tend to over-state the Jewish role to the point, at times, of absurdity, suggesting for instance that Chinese communism is Jewish because Jews were behind the opium trade which was one of the factors giving rise to the revolutionary conditions in China which led to the Maoist victory in 1949!

Between these opposites is the view of A.K. Chesterton (not to be confused with the more famous G.K., his second cousin) and which is stated succinctly in *The New Unhappy Lords*:-

> "...Whether or not One World is the secret final objective of Zionism, World Jewry is the most powerful single force on earth and it follows that all the major policies which have been ruthlessly pursued through the last several decades must have had the stamp of Jewish approval. Indeed, common sense applied to such facts as have come to light must lead to the conclusion that the policies, directed against the most cherished Gentile Values, were incubated by adroit Jewish brains and fulfilled, or carried to the verge of fulfilment, by the dynamism of the Jewish spirit. At the same time, so many Gentiles are associated with the conspiracy, both directly and through the formation of fronts, there are so many Gentile agents and

agencies, and so many Gentile governments which have
acquiesced in the conspiracy by falling into line with policies
inimical to their own national interests, that it would be ludicrous to offload upon Jewish shoulders responsibility for the
destruction, or near destruction, of Christendom and the
Western World. Nevertheless, it would be equally ludicrous to
deny the Jewish part, especially where it is admitted...

"Had we of the Gentile nations stood firm in defence of our own
traditions and values, instead of cravenly capitulating, the Jews
would have remained what they ought to be — a small sect
living contentedly and at peace with their neighbours, exercising neither national nor international power and entertaining no
inordinate ambitions. That, as I wrote at the outset, is how most
of them actually do live. That a minority of them has been able
to mount such a stupendous drive for world power is not their
fault but ours alone, and it is we who must put things to rights —
or perish. The way to put things right is not to engage in 'hate
campaigns' (which in any event more often than not play into
Jewish hands) but to make a determined stand for our own
legitimate and distinctive interests."

Chesterton's view, which is at the same time both the most
factual and the most balanced, is the one to which I myself
subscribe, and I endorse particularly the contention that it is the
weakness of Gentile society that we must blame for whatever
power in the world the Jews currently enjoy.

Why have we Gentiles, as Chesterton says, cravenly capitulated? It is, in my submission, because we have got our politics
and our values all wrong. No human tribe that succumbs so easily
to the domination of another — whatever the argument may be
about the extent of that domination — can be healthy within itself.

A conspiracy to subvert, undermine and destroy a nation from
the inside could never in a thousand years succeed as long as that
nation remained vigorous in its national spirit, its intelligence, its
resolve, its sense of direction and its instinct for survival. It is only
when a nation loses these faculties that conspiratorial forces
working against it can operate with any real effectiveness. Just as
the individual of sound constitution will naturally produce the
anti-bodies that will protect him against most disease germs, so
will a nation of sound organisation and outlook and inner vitality
resist, by natural reaction, any such infectious and destructive
tendencies the moment they appear.

Unhappily, the British Nation of today is in the very worst
condition to do this. The conspiratorial forces threatening her on

every side, far from encountering a vigorous resistance, have found many allies among the native population falling over themselves in their haste to help these forces accomplish their work of destruction. And this has been the most marked of all in the upper echelons of society.

The American writer Professor Revilo P. Oliver has touched upon this question in his book *Conspiracy or Degeneracy?* which commented on the situation in his own country but is equally applicable to ours. He said:-

> "There undoubtedly is a conspiracy, and a powerful one. We know there is a bolshevik conspiracy at work. Our difficulty is that we need something more than a conspiracy, however cunning and subtle you suppose it to be, to explain our decline. So let us look a little at biology..."

Oliver went on to explain how certain species, such as the dinosaurs and the dodos, became extinct because they lost the basic will to survive, and he drew the parallel between these species and certain white nations of today, like the US and Britain, saying:-

> "If we intend to survive ourselves and have a posterity, we shall have to toughen ourselves intellectually by facing some very unpleasant facts. I know they are unpleasant, and that it would be ever so much nicer if we could pretend that those facts just didn't exist..."

The facts Professor Oliver had in mind were simply those involving the unavoidable struggle between the human races for control of the resources of our planet and the reality that in that struggle someone has to win and someone has to lose. Those races that had lost even the desire to win, let alone the will to do so, must be considered to have become degenerate, and would as surely perish as did these earlier species that became extinct.

Sometimes it is my feeling that too many conspiracy theorists get their subject out of perspective, regarding the present forces of conspiracy as some kind of diabolical aberration from the historical norm. Could we not view the existence of conspiracy in politics as being as natural as the art of deception in wartime? Clausewitz, when he said that war amounted to politics by other means, certainly meant that war and politics were merely the violent and non-violent phases of the same process. If we expect a commander on the battlefield to conceal his objectives from his enemy and, in pursuit of that aim, to feed the enemy with all manner of false intelligence whereby the latter will be misled as to his plans, should we not then expect those engaged in the power contest of politics to operate by precisely the same rules? If so, we should not be surprised, least of all outraged, to find ourselves in danger of political conquest at the hands of adversaries who have simply extended to the field of political warfare the same techniques of deception as are considered perfectly normal to the soldier.

Conspiracies are not recent phenomena in politics but are as old as the political art itself. Ancient Rome was rife with them, and Shakespeare caught the mood perfectly in *Julius Caesar* with the words of Brutus shortly before he cut his emperor down:-

> "Grant that, and then is death a benefit:
> So we are Caesar's friends, that have abridg'd
> His time of fearing death. Stoop, Romans, stoop,
> And let us bathe our hands in Caesar's blood
> Up to the elbows, and besmear our swords:
> Then walk we forth even to the market place,
> And, waving our red weapons o'er our heads,
> Let's all cry, **Peace! Freedom and Liberty!**"

Today, just as when those words were written, and as at the time they described, politics is a struggle for power concealed almost invariably behind high-sounding slogans. When we hear that somewhere in the world the forces of 'democracy' are being mobilised to bring down some 'autocratic' ruler, we should not be deluded into thinking that this is a conflict of principles; all that is happening is that someone has power and someone else is trying to take it away from them. Such phrases as 'democracy' and 'autocracy' are merely the verbiage of political conflict whereby the would-be usurpers of power clothe their objectives with the appearance of noble intent.

Our own weakness has lain in the quite staggeringly credulous way in which we are prepared to accept such verbiage as representing the hard substance of a matter rather than the mere shadow that it is. The minds of so many of our people seem to have been thoroughly tutored so as not even to understand the first basics of politics as being about **power**, and the need to possess power before anything can be done. From this comes the inability to discern behind such slogans as 'democracy', 'freedom' and 'human rights' the reality is that a power-struggle is taking place and that we will lose it if we do not wake up in time.

It is no use whatever us vaporising about conspiracy in politics being 'evil', for conspiracy in politics is a simple fact of life; all that distinguishes the gigantic modern conspiracy facing us from much more ancient conspiracies aimed at winning power is the infinitely greater sophistication of the weapons now available to those engaged in the practice: television, radio, the cinema, video-tapes, etc. — this and the fact that the rules of the game, instead of being understood by both sides in the conflict, are today only understood properly by our enemies, and that all effective conspiracy in our contemporary world is directed, not to our defence as a nation and race, but to our destruction as such.

In fact conspiracy is not in itself evil; the evil or otherwise lies entirely in the **objective** towards which the methods of conspiracy are used. Any nation or race, faced with evidence of a conspiracy to destroy it, should recognise such a conspiracy as wholly evil from its own point of view, and should thereupon fight back against it with all means in its power — where necessary using itself the weapons of conspiracy (i.e. deception) in the course of its struggle for survival. It is when a people does not possess this will to fight back, but on the contrary makes a positive virtue out of its acceptance of defeat, and instead of recognising its enemies' weapons of deception for what they are, enthusiastically offers itself up for destruction by those weapons as if they were bounteous gifts, that we must regard that people as afflicted by **degeneracy**: a degeneracy of the intellect, of the body, of the will, of the spirit, and above all of the instinct to survive.

Such a sickness has without any doubt now afflicted a portion of the people of our country, and it is that portion that predominates today among the 'educated' classes who occupy the positions of decisive influence in national affairs. The next few years will tell whether it has similarly afflicted the remainder of the British people or whether, from out of the ranks of the latter, there are sufficient reserves of vitality for a fight-back to be organised.

This degenerative sickness that paralyses nations has in modern times acquired the status of a clearly recognised political doctrine which, while it is rife throughout the Western World, has taken on a particularly virulent form in our own country. It is vital that we should understand it if we are to arm ourselves to take the necessary remedial measures, and I hope to contribute something to this understanding in the coming chapter.

Chapter 6
The cancer of liberalism

"One symptom of the decline of a ruling class is its inability to tell its friends from its enemies — when it does not actually prefer its enemies." Those words, written by Malcolm Muggeridge in *The Sunday Telegraph Magazine*, are an apt introduction to a study of the values and psychology of liberalism, which is the dominant thought-form of our times.

Straightaway, in discussing liberalism we must learn to distinguish between the modern kind and its ancestors of the 18th and 19th centuries. The genealogical link is undoubtedly there, but the species, as with every other, has evolved today into one not entirely identical with its parent and grandparent. We all know that the word 'liberal' comes from the Latin word meaning 'free', and that to older liberals the freedom of the individual stood as the highest aim of politics. From an early age, it seemed to me that this evaluation showed a very shallow understanding of the essential interdependence between the individual and society and the balance of rights and duties that arise from it. Liberals grudgingly accepted the need for some mechanism of law and state but that mechanism was never seen as anything other than one made to serve individual ends. The obligation was almost all a one-way process: on the part of the state and towards the individual and almost never the other way round, thus ignoring the truth that everything the state may offer to the individual in the way of rights, benefits, security and protection must depend on what the individual is prepared to render back to the state so as to give it the means to fulfil this providing role. This imbalance of obligation encouraged a solipsist and selfish attitude on the part of the citizen and provided the worst possible conditions for the attainment of national cohesion and teamwork, essential to group survival in an always competitive world.

Along with the worship of 'freedom', the older liberals paid much credence to the assertion of Jeremy Bentham, one of their high priests, that the aim of society should be "the greatest happiness of the greatest number." — a philosophy which seemed to see its highest ideal in the picture of human populations as herds of contented cattle. Liberals saw life as "the pursuit of happiness," as enshrined in the American Declaration of Independence, perhaps forgetting that happiness in its highest form is found, not in its own pursuit as a conscious objective, but — at least in the case of the major western races — in the quest for growth and expansion in the fields of human knowledge, discovery, achievement and spirit, happiness becoming a secondary by-product of this Faustian process.

On the global plane, the older liberalism believed in the ultimate ideal of an international community of nations, dealing with each other in accordance with a set of universally accepted laws. Yet it did at least have the wisdom to recognise the limits to which this ideal was immediately attainable, so that it did not exclude entirely from its mind the need for the use of national power — albeit that it rated that factor much lower in importance than it should have done. Liberals, though they clung to the prospect of their dream world, did not entirely lose contact with the world as it was.

This international ideal found its expression in the liberal view of economics, which was heavily biased towards the principle of free trade. There was at the same time, in the case of British liberals, some rational basis of self-interest in this, as the formulation of the philosophy coincided with an era of almost unrivalled British industrial supremacy. What was weak in the idea was that it was short-sighted, failing to understand that this favoured British position was only transitory, and to anticipate that it would in due course pass away, forcing the British economy to rely on its own national resources, not only of manufacturing and commercial expertise, but also of primary produce and consumer markets. This outlook was perhaps natural because economic liberalism was essentially a rationalisation of the will-to-profit, being the pragmatically conceived doctrine of the mercantile classes on whose cheque books was established the Whig tradition in British politics. The laws of profit propel enterprise into those markets where costs are lowest and sales income highest — measured of course in immediate terms. Free trade was the system that offered the best returns to British capitalism in the early industrial era, and from it liberalism took its economic wisdom.

In the longer term, of course, this policy was to have disastrous consequences. Liberal free trade doctrines stood in the way of the unification of the Empire just at the time when, politically, the best opportunity existed to fulfil that task. The liberal cheap food policy, put into effect through the repeal of the Corn Laws in 1846, ruined much of British farming, drove millions into the cities and put an end to Britain's self-sufficiency in food — an asset that could not have been sustained in its entirety in any circumstances but need not have been thrown away to anything like the extent that it was.

The cheap food policy was of course necessary to the achievement of the maximum profits for industry and the financial interests which, already then, had obtained much sway over industry. This, however, was not its only rationale. To expand Britain's export trade in manufactured products, it was necessary to give to the importing countries the purchasing power to buy these products. This power was supplied by loans from the international banks which, of course, had to be repaid. The only way that the latter could be done was by the exporting of food. The lowering of the protective barriers formerly operated in defence of British farming would clear the way for this massive new trade. The cheap food policy, made possible by these imports, only slightly reduced, but did not prevent, that appalling poverty that was to be the lot of the British industrial working classes — thus providing fertile ground for the future growth of marxism.

The entire bottom was of course knocked out of the old liberal economic system when those countries possessing similar manufacturing aptitude to Britain built their own manufacturing industries, first cutting down the demand for British goods in their own markets — often with the aid of tariff walls — and then later competing with British goods on the remaining world markets. From the moment that that age dawned, the liberal economic system was in fact effectively finished. It was just a question of how long it would take for political thought to catch up with this reality and devise alternative methods for organising our economic life.

This process of coming to terms with new economic facts has taken much longer in Britain than in most other countries, and in fact is far from being completed even today. This we owe mostly to the fact that the full effects of our continuing to work with an obsolete system were long delayed. British living standards were, until quite recently, kept up to a fairly high level by world comparisons, not because of any merits in the British economic system itself, but because for a long time after the system outlived its usefulness we were able to shelter behind the immense accumulated assets of our Empire, our overseas investments and our hidden earnings made possible by the financial expertise of the City of London. We were also aided by the two world wars of this century, which in the first case temporarily knocked out Germany as an international competitor and in the second case knocked out, not only Germany again, but also Japan, as trade rivals. These factors gave a stay of execution to the old system in Britain but they did not prevent the sentence of death being carried out eventually.

It may therefore be seen that the old liberalism bequeathed an appalling legacy to us in economic terms. But it left us a legacy equally appalling in political terms, if not more so. As the need to adapt economics to a new era became increasingly evident, the political will and organisation necessary to this task were wholly lacking. The new era demanded, not nations consisting merely of the aggregates of so many millions of individuals, each following his own bent, and linked together only by common laws devised to curb the more extreme exercises in self-interested activity, but nations bound together as closely unified and co-ordinated communities, with the interest of the individual being identified with the interest of the whole. Such an undertaking was not only beyond the capacity of liberal political institutions but entirely outside the compass of the liberal mind. It required the systematic organisation of the nation's life so as to enable it to exploit to the absolute maximum all the resources, human and otherwise, with which fortune and history had favoured it, and for the purpose of best fitting it for survival in a world that was itself entirely out of harmony with liberal suppositions and ideals, a world of fierce power rivalries that would forever prohibit realisation of any kind of international order except that imposed by the strongest upon the weakest.

The other prominent characteristic of the old liberalism, at least in its British form, was its sermonising moral sanctimoniousness. To British liberal leaders the world was regarded as some kind of gigantic parish and themselves the parish priests. Some foreign ruler only had to act towards his subjects, or towards another foreign state, in a manner that did not fit comfortably with British public school and high church conceptions of 'fair play', and a loud campaign of moral indignation would be let loose against him — even if no British national interest was in the remotest way affected by his actions. The British acquired the unedifying reputation of meddling like fussy governesses in the affairs of other nations, and British foreign policy became more and more a series of postures, absurd to all except ourselves, of the righteous knight errant on his white horse slaying morally unacceptable dragons, instead of being what it should have been: a coolly conceived business based on strategy. Not for nothing did Lord Macaulay say of his countrymen that "There is no sight more ridiculous than the English in one of their periodic fits of morality."

This older liberalism met is nemesis on the beaches of Dunkirk, where, battered and bemused, the army of what was supposed still to be the world's leading imperial power took to the small boats after having been thoroughly routed by the soldiers of a nation which, though no greater than our own in the way of resources, was immeasurably superior in organisation, morale, unity, industry, leadership and will. Only to the blind and the ignorant did the fiasco come as a surprise. For some time previously, the liberal conscience in this country had been pontificating, breast-beating and fist-shaking over what had been happening on the European continent, goading the British people to war while taking care to leave them almost wholly naked in terms of the means to fight such a war. In the end, the combined armies of the Empires of Britain and France lasted just five weeks against an adversary whose state and system we had done nothing but denigrate for the past seven years and whose leadership we had delighted in ridiculing in the cartoons of our moronic press. If liberalism wanted its monument, perhaps that monument should have been situated in one of those cemeteries containing the interred bones of the legions of British Tommies who fell in France and Belgium, the victims of their politicians' ineptitude, cynicism and folly.

In modern liberalism are reproduced all the vices of the old liberalism but with some additional features making for an even more nationally destructive philosophy. The old liberal faith in 'freedom' as an absolute good has been replaced by a valuation of freedom that is entirely selective. Putting it briefly, freedom is fine as long as it is extended only to liberals and those to the left of them. Perhaps this is because the paths of liberals and marxists, having for decades followed increasingly converging courses, have now met, and the difference between them is often hard to discern. Most certainly, today's liberal has taken into his baggage the marxist-leninist idea that all political expressions can be made to mean what one wants them to mean and taken up or rejected according to how it suits the tactical imperative of the moment. Thus left-wing militants should be allowed to promote their activities uninterrupted because to stop them would be a 'violation of freedom'; on the other hand, militants of the so-called 'extreme right' should be banned from speaking or doing or saying anything because their activities constitute an 'abuse of freedom'. The liberal of yesteryear, while taking second place to no-one in his talent for hypocrisy, would probably have thought this double-standard to be taking things a little too far; but the liberal of today feels quite comfortable in such totalitarian clothes, providing that it is always the totalitarianism that acts in suppression of right-wing, and never left-wing, opposition.

But of course to the liberal of our own times the whole world of friends and enemies has been turned upside down, perhaps inspiring the quoted observation with which this chapter began. The liberal of today really does prefer his enemies to his friends because his dominant impulse is the will to self-extinction.

I have related earlier my experience in arguing with liberals in the youthful stage of my study of politics and how, when I tried appealing to such sentiments as national pride and patriotism, I found I was completely wasting my time, as those sentiments just weren't there. This was a startling introduction to the liberal psyche which took some time coming to terms with. As I have indicated, I formed then the view that the modern liberal is an animal who has somehow been deprived of all capacity for independent thought — relieved of his brain, as it were, and had another brain, much more powerful, planted in its place, which directs his reactions to situations as if he were a robot. It was as if one of the belligerents in a war had devised an extraordinary new weapon in the form of some kind of computerised machine which took over both the minds and the bodies of the enemy soldiers and directed them by remote control, inducing them to fire, not at their adversary, but at their own side.

For today's liberal is certainly the product of a similar technique. He has been induced to hate his own people and 'love' all others, not only including his people's enemies but **particularly** those enemies. Not only has his own mind been taken away but so have almost all of his instincts as well, certainly, as all healthy masculine faculties needed for the maintenance of a vigorous national spirit.

Something of the zombie quality of the liberal mind can be seen today in the way that it is reacting to events in South Africa. Just supposing for a moment that we accept (which I certainly do not) that the South African Government is a brutal tyranny that oppresses and ill treats large numbers of people, depriving them of their so-called rights and freedoms and all human dignity. In that case South Africa would simply join the list of a great number of states all around the world, and including most of Africa itself, which belong to that category.

But do we find liberals fluttering and squawking in protest against all of these states? Oh no! Their venom is concentrated almost entirely on South Africa, whereas elsewhere it is a case of "see no evil, hear no evil, speak no evil." Many hundreds of thousands, possibly millions, may be rotting in slave-labour camps in Soviet Russia and the rest of the Communist World and this barely receives more than half a minute's attention beyond just a resigned shrug. Yet let the South African Government make half a dozen arrests of political dissidents and a shriek of wrath goes forth from liberals everywhere, accompanied by a fresh round of demands for more punitive measures, such as sanctions, to be taken against that state.

Why this inconsistency? The self-righteous indignation of Gladstonian liberals, comic though it often was, was at least to some extent distributed around the world, condemning 'evil' in many places and under many regimes and flags. The indignation of today is pure concentrated fire, aimed at one target and ignoring the others. Why?

Of course we know the reason. The South African situation is one in which white people, Europeans of our own stock, are defending themselves and their country against a threat from those of another race. To the mind of the liberal, no more dastardly act could be conceived. It offends against the whole liberal catechism, which says that your friends are your enemies and your enemies are your friends, that any cause in defence of your own race is a bad cause and any cause for the advancement(?) of another race at the expense of your own is a good one — provided of course that you are **white**; 'racism' is perfectly acceptable if you belong to any other of the world's numerous ethnic groups. Communists who take oppressive measures to protect their political system from those who challenge it are acting within the bounds of permissible behaviour. Black dictators elsewhere in Africa who starve their people are merely looking after their own countries' business and should not be interfered with — on the contrary, they should if possible be supplied with economic aid. But **white** folk taking measures to protect their civilisation and way of life against those who would destroy it simply cannot be tolerated within the international community!

In the midst of the South African emergency in 1986 those British people with some sense of national dignity and honour had to choke back their disposition to vomit as they watched their own Foreign Secretary go on a mission to Zambia, one of those comic-opera black African states where nothing runs and nothing works and whose masses live under conditions besides which the lot of South Africa's Blacks is one of the utmost luxury. For what purpose was our Foreign Secretary going to Zambia? Why, to plead — and I ask the reader to note that word: **plead** — with the President of that country to show patience with the British Government (which gives it a handsome annual subsidy) in the matter of tightening the trade and financial screws against South Africa. The British Government agreed with him (the President) that these white people daring to hold onto control in South Africa were very awful and must be brought down; the only difference of opinion lay in the matter of how this should be done. The British Government could not quite bring itself to go along with the demands of Zambia for all-out sanctions against the South African Whites. Why? Because of course that would hurt South Africa's **Blacks**! In other words, if only Whites would be hurt that would be perfectly alright, but if the Blacks were liable to get hurt we ought to proceed very cautiously! Would the Zambian President please bear with HM Government just a little longer and allow it to proceed in the task of smashing White South Africa at its own speed and in its own way — he could rest assured that that task, over which we are all in complete accord, will be accomplished in the end!

In the course of this visit the Foreign Secretary was subjected to an angry lecture by the Zambian President, which he accepted deferentially in the manner of an erring schoolboy who had been summoned to the headmaster's study. Not content with this wigging, the FS of Her Britannic Majesty proceeded on to neighbouring 'Zimbabwe' (also heavily subsidised by Britain), where he got another, this time from the local boss, who a short while previously had been the leader of the ZANU terrorist organisation which carried out scores of murderous atrocities against innocent people, including little children, in the country that had formerly been Rhodesia but which Britain eventually destroyed because, like South Africa, it committed the unforgivable sin of being ruled by Whites.

Once again Sir Geoffrey purred his explanations and excuses as to why the process of wrecking white civilisation in South Africa was not being carried out to quite the schedule that his dusky host wanted, while dutifully affirming HMG's absolute commitment to that objective in the fullness of time. Like a whipped cur, he then made his exit and got on the plane home.

We do not have a transcript of the entire conversations conducted on these occasions but I am quite sure that our travelling doormat of a diplomat did not think to commit such a disrespectful *faux pas* as to remind the chiefs of Zambia and 'Zimbabwe' that practically all the useful amenities their countries have today, such as railways, roads, public buildings, factories and man-made sources of fuel and power, were built for them either by the British or by other Whites (including, to no small degree, South Africans), and that it ill became gentlemen who relied for the very shirts on their backs on white charity and expertise to be hectoring the representative of a white nation as to what it should do or not do. Oh no! Sir Geoffrey pleaded and grovelled as befits an appropriately chastised white 'liberal', doing penance for the crime of his ancestors of being great.

And was our Foreign Secretary's obsequious performance in Zambia and 'Zimbabwe' condemned in the press at home for the fact that it had humiliated Britain? Perish the thought! In the Tory press it was praised as an act of statesmanship, while in left-wing papers and among politicians of that ilk the only criticism was that Sir Geoffrey had not conceded or been apologetic enough! His ticking off had been thoroughly deserved in view of the way that the government was dragging its feet over sanctions, and it should be taken as a warning that the job of pulling down white civilsation in South Africa should be stepped up to a much faster tempo!

All this of course was just one minor cameo in a much bigger repertoire, but the story illustrates perfectly the state of lunacy and abjectness induced in a people who have thoroughly succumbed to the liberal disease. The rest of mankind, beholding such whimpering antics on the part of the representative of what was not very long ago a great power, and taking into account the overall policy of his government towards its fellow Whites in South Africa, could be forgiven the observation that the British had become utterly effete — that observation most certainly being true in respect of those classes in Britain holding the reins of political leadership.

Almost 1 million of the white South Africans are of British stock and belong to a community which throughout its history has identified itself strongly with the Mother Country and been only too ready to send its sons to fight for it. The remainder of the white South Africans are our fellow Europeans. They and we have had our differences in the past but those differences should now long have been buried. It should be our deepest instinct to side with them in any conflict in which they are engaged with the other races of their part of the world, even to give them practical help in that conflict if we can. Yet this is not the way the liberal conscience sees it; on the contrary, to the liberal the very fact that the race in control of South Africa is white, and that those trying to wrest control from it are non-white, is quite enough to ensure that all sympathies and support are for the latter, irrespective of any other issues involved.

In the previous chapter I have given some attention to the forces of conspiracy within Britain, and considered how far empowered they are to direct national affairs. But it suffices to reduce a population to the state of mind exemplified in our modern-day 'liberals' for there to be little need to do any directing at all; like lemmings headed for the precipice of racial suicide, liberals will do all that is asked of them of their own accord!

This instinct guiding white liberals is one of pure racial self-hate, leading to a racial death-wish — an absolute perversion of the natural instincts with which most people on this planet are endowed. Such a perversion can be given no other name but **decadence**.

The very same decadence is indicated by the dispatch around the globe to represent Britain of creatures who from every pore of their skins exude a weak and cringing attitude towards other nations, and particularly towards other races, treating with them in the manner that our Foreign Secretary did with the tin-pot mandarins of the two African joke regimes that I have described. Our country's chief representative abroad — its Ambassador to the World, so to speak — should be a man with a personality of strength. He should possess diplomacy and tact, certainly, and, where warranted, should display courtesy to those with whom he has to deal, but none of these rules of the trade require that a British Foreign Secretary should sit and listen to the kinds of tirades against his country as those coming from these two upstarts. But of course Sir Geoffrey and the people who sent him on his mission are liberals — not the large 'L' Liberals of the Liberal Party but the small 'l' liberals who dominate all the leading parties — and to the liberal any national self-abasement is quite in order; indeed it is today's established norm.

Of course we can see exactly the same mentality at work in the manner in which liberaldom has completely capitulated to the immigrant invasion of Britain. 'Capitulated' might indeed be a euphemism, for liberals have in fact been falling over themselves in their eagerness to. promote this influx. Liberals seem quite impervious to the fact that the influx, bearing in mind the origins of most of the immigrants, will, if not stemmed and reversed, lead to a permanent alteration in the composition and character of the British people. Does this prospect trouble liberals? Goodness, no! They positively welcome it. Utterly lacking themselves any pride in national identity, they cannot see that they have anything to lose!

As could have been predicted by anyone with a grain of sense, the coloured influx has led to a serious race problem and the inevitable tensions that occur when peoples of wholly different types are thrown together, these tensions exploding into the ferocious riots of the 1980s. Responsibility for the riots was inescapable; it lay with gangs of thugs from the inner cities who were, beyond any dispute, mainly black. Their riotous behaviour was compounded of two main elements: pure criminality, directed towards looting premises, particularly shops; and black racism, directed against white society in general and white police in particular. This very same black racism can be seen in the public pronouncements against white society and police by a whole legion of self-appointed 'spokesmen' for the ethnic minority communities in our country, which are heard on TV and radio and in the press every week. Yet liberals, when confronted by this racism, which runs against all their supposed principles, do not condemn it but rush to appease it — by hamstringing the police in their battle against black crime, by rewarding the black racists with financial grants to set up 'community centres', which just become the breeding grounds for more black racism and serve as command posts in times of rioting and mayhem, and by attributing all such black racist attitudes to the 'injustices' of white society in which Blacks live — conveniently ignoring the fact that those Blacks were never forced to live in such a society but have chosen themselves to do so.

Yet this conciliatory attitude towards racism immediately disappears when it is **white** racism that is involved. Let any white British native protest against the behaviour I have just described, or object in general terms to the turning of his country into an ethnic Babylon after centuries of internal peace and unity bestowed by its former homogeneous character, and that person is not considered fit to have his voice heard where decent people gather.

And if such a person uses particularly strong and forthright language in voicing these objections, he is liable to be prosecuted and maybe flung into jail under the new 'race hate' laws which liberals have devised for white 'racists' but never administer against non-white racists. I should know, for as I write these very words I sit in a prison cell, to which domicile I have been sent, along with a political colleague, for committing the crime of writing the truth, as we see it, about the racial situation in Britain.

Liberals were confronted with a particular dilemma in the Falklands conflict. For some time previously, liberaldom in Britain had been squealing in outraged protest against the Government of Argentina because that government had taken some particularly vigorous measures to curb the activities of political subversives within its own borders. This is always an unpardonable sin in the liberal mind, which sees no greater evil than the evil of a country defending itself against its enemies (again provided always that that country is white). The Argentine Government, for doing this awful thing, was promptly designated 'fascist', and as such was placed in the familiar chamber of horrors that liberals reserve for regimes to which they attach that label. Protest against Argentina became a part of the diet to be served on the same menu as protest against South Africa.

Imagine the consternation of liberals in Britain when Argentina invaded the Falkland Islands — British territory! Here it was Britain that was forced into a position of having to defend what was its own against its enemies. Just what were good liberals to do in that situation? If they supported General Galtieri they would be supporting a fascist monster. If they supported the British task force that was being dispatched to the South Atlantic to deal with the occupiers of the Falklands, they would actually be championing a patriotic war — even an imperialist one! One's sympathy almost went out to the little pets in their quandary. By sanctioning the use of armed force in a national cause, they would be committing a heresy of which there is none greater in the liberals' big black book of diabolism. We all waited to see how our liberal friends would get themselves out of this conundrum.

The gyrations and twitchings of liberal consciences in the newspapers in the ensuing weeks were fascinating to behold. In the end, unable, for the most part, to support one side or the other, liberals contented themselves with a few spluttering platitudes about the need for a 'peaceful solution', which no doubt sounded to their own ears like the loftiest proclamations of wisdom and mature statesmanship but were in fact nothing other than pure, infantile drivel. What kind of 'peaceful solution'? Were the Argentine fascists to be allowed to keep the islands? Well, no! Were they then to be handed back to Britain? Oh, definitely not — that would be imperialism, wouldn't it? Well what? Well, er, um — there has to be a peaceful solution!

Pressed a little further, our liberals came up with various formulae. One was that the Falklands should be under 'joint sovereignty' — a sort of half-British imperialism and half-fascism. But not many liberals liked that idea when they thought about it. Another suggestion was a 'lease-back'. Argentina keep ownership of the islands but Britain run them for a specific period of time. You mean give the Argentine fascists what they have taken by force, only give it on the instalment plan? Well, no...and so it went on. One particular liberal moraliser and verbaliser excelled even the high standards of his own creed in the art of inanity. This was Mr. Frank Giles, at the time Editor of *The Sunday Times*. Faced with the same predicament as his fellow liberals, he wrote: "The simple restoration of British sovereignty cannot be the final outcome of the war in the South Atlantic." Then writing about this in *The Sunday Telegraph* four years later he later he said that his attitude at that time had been that "force should only be used as a last resort but when it was used we sanctioned its use."

Only a liberal of course could say that force should be supported, albeit as a "last resort," in pursuit of a policy that should not be the restoration of sovereignty, when that sovereignty had in the first place been taken away by force. For what purpose then should the use of force be supported? To the rational man, there could be no purpose in such a situation other than the restoration of the lost sovereignty — unless it was to risk the sacrifice of British lives in a mere gesture of futility. But to the mind of the liberal the simple mental discipline of having to choose between the two sole, though harsh, alternatives that are on offer — either using force or capitulating to force — is too much. Escape has to be sought in pretty abstractions which leave the question entirely unresolved.

As if realising himself guilty of this, the same writer continued his recollection in *The Sunday Telegraph* by saying that, though with reluctance he had in the end to support the use of force by Britain in the Falklands dispute, what he would not let *The Sunday Times* do was "glory in war as a sign of national virility."

So now taking military action to recover a piece of your territory that has been invaded by an aggressor amounts to "glorying in war as a sign of national virility" — or so the erstwhile Editor of *The Sunday Times* thinks it may do if he does not insert his sanctimonious rider on the subject, which, stripped of all its verbosity, amounts to an insult to the intelligence of his readers.

Not that all liberals engaged in the moral acrobatics of Mr. Giles. Some of them, impatient with all this prevarication, came down solidly and unequivocally on the side of Argentina. Thus we saw the dedicated opponents of fascism actually championing the cause of a fascist regime. And what had been the extraordinary circumstance that brought about this U-turn? Why, the cause had been an anti-British one, and that of course attained priority over every other consideration!

One is reminded of Robert Frost's little satirical poem: "I am a liberal — I mean, so altruistically moral — I never take my own side in a quarrel!" For that is the truth about the liberal of today: he is always to be found lined up against his own side and on the side of its enemies, even when that means taking a position contrary, from the ideological point of view, to everything he has stood for all his life. The liberal is always the fifth columnist in the enemy's employ: he knows no other instinct than to kick through his own team's goal.

The government, at the time of the Falklands crisis, although itself moved by the same liberal slush underneath the surface, ultimately was forced by the pressure of public opinion to do the right thing and take the islands back. Yet throughout the operation it was still hankering after 'compromise solutions' that in the end were not adopted only because the Argentine Government refused to consider them. And prior to this the same government had for some time been negotiating with Argentina over the future of the

Falklands knowing very well that nothing less than a surrender of sovereignty over the islands was acceptable to the other side. Almost certainly, the military action to retake the Falklands was a political decision, and not one made on the basis of any firm principle concerning British sovereignty. Politicians who have been prepared happily to surrender sovereignty over our own country to the Common Market bureaucracy are not going to be averse, if they can get away with it, to doing the same thing with a collection of far off islands containing less than 2,000 people.

Observing the liberal, as I have done over many years, I have come to the conclusion that he represents much more than just a person holding to a particular set of beliefs; he constitutes a biological type. I am here of course referring to the truly committed crusader for liberalism and not the ordinary apolitical individual who, for want of having given much thought to politics, has adopted some of the popular liberal attitudes.

Seeking a brief refuge from the writing of this book, I chanced to turn to a potted history of the 20th century in which was featured a photograph of a group of 'peace' campaigners in the 1920s, and was struck with how, in physical features and bearing, they so closely resembled their heirs of today. Those of them one would presume to be 'male', if only from their hair-length and clothing, are distinguished by skinny bodies, sandals or plimsolls on the feet, a wetness of features and an indisposition to stand upright. On the faces of the women there are smiles indicative of a certain scattiness that is instantly familiar. Above them is a banner proclaiming "No more war," and from their expressions one would assume that they believed themselves to be the ingenious inventors of this idea, while the rest of mankind was positively itching again to be bombed and machine-gunned day and night.

The species has changed little over 60 years, indicating, as I would suspect, the correctness of my thesis. Assemble any group of liberals together on one side of any room and then assemble on the other side a group of equal number and sexual composition but of outlook fundamentally opposed to liberalism. Most of us then entering the room would immediately be able to tell which group was which after the most cursory glance. Liberals, generally speaking, constitute the most unimpressive specimens of the white race — and, interestingly enough, it is almost only among the white race that real liberals (as distinct from those who just chant liberal slogans for tactical reasons) are to be found.

The South African writer S.E.D. Brown had liberals well

summed up when he said: "...having severed themselves from
their own society and all the sources of social vigour and health,
they cannot imagine themselves happy until they have made
everyone equally sick."

The references of the writer here to health and sickness recall to
me my own thoughts when in my youth I first encountered the
liberal phenomenon in my arguments with my young contemporaries. Those exact words occurred to me then as descriptive of all
that liberals seemed to hate and cherish respectively. All that was
strong, manly, radiant, vital and proud was repellent to them,
while everything that was crippled, diseased, stunted, tired and
wretched had, in their eyes, virtue. This outlook seemed to me
what Nietzsche once described as "the rebellion of all that crawls
along the ground against that which has height." As their bodies
and faces exuded human decay, the outpourings of their minds
revealed a veneration of softness.

Looking at the young wimps who prance and screech at the
conferences of the parties of liberalism, the same bacteria can be
observed. They are all look-alikes and the slogans which drip
from their mouths in those whining 'unisex' voices amount to all
the same pap. Let us listen again to S.E.D. Brown as he speaks of
those people:-

> "...who flee from reality into the safe little dream-worlds they
> create with words. Inherent in their attitude is a rejection of life
> with all its intense significance and all its necessary dangers.
> They reject Man as he is and always will be; and they substitute
> an abstraction...in the pallid world of pure intellection they
> project a picture of Man as they would have him be, something
> tame, harmless, ahulic, passive — a two-dimensional being, a
> mere shadow in the real world." (The Anatomy of Liberalism)

Intrinsic in liberals and liberalism is a flabbiness of person and
outlook. Liberals simply cannot bear the world of nature that is all
around'them, the world in which the strong prevail over the weak
— whether this be at the level of individual intercourse or that
involving nations. Weak themselves, but with more than their
share of conceit and vanity, they construct in their minds an
alternative world where people of their kind, instead of being
serfs, are kings — looked up to for their wisdom instead of
despised for their puniness. Their ideology is one gigantic
rationale of the contemptible elements in their own character, the
elevation into a creed of moral rectitude of the values of the
coward, the sneak, the liar, the crawler and the parasite. Whole

nations must then conform to this creed if they are to earn the liberal's approbation. They must embody, writ large, his own miserable being.

For everything that fails to conform to our liberal's little universe of fantasy — everything that identifies with the forces of life and health, instead of death and sickness, everything that seeks to build and strengthen rather than to wither and decompose, the liberal has an adjective — a catchword that immediately damns it out of court: it is the adjective 'fascist'. If this adjective had not been brought into the language by a political movement in Italy earlier in this century, from the liberal point of view it would surely have had to be invented. For it suffices in the liberal's mind to act as a guillotine on every critical examination of his system of values. If you do not rejoice in the new utopia that liberals are planning for you, you are a fascist. Patriotic feeling is designated as fascism. Parental authority over children is fascism. Punishment of criminals is fascism. Self-defence against an enemy is fascism. Polarity of the sexes is fascism. Preference for the company of your own kind, your own race, is fascism. In this way the liberal is absolved from any obligation to defend in honest and forthright debate his cherished structure of ideas and ethics. A state of emergency has arisen: the fascist is at the door. All further argument is suspended forthwith.

My friends and I have seen this tendency at work whenever we have thrown down the challenge to liberals to meet us in open public debate on the issues over which they are so often condemning us. According to their own theory, they should welcome such a debate more than anyone else, for are they not the people who most strongly believe that issues should be resolved through discussion and 'reason'? But no! Whenever this proposition is put forward, the liberals go scampering for refuge, crying that they refuse to give people like us 'a platform'. Discussion and reason, you see, are only in order so long as out of them comes a verdict favourable to liberals!

In this, the liberal reveals that, aside from all his other pernicious characteristics, he is a hypocrite and a coward. Intellectually, he is like the school bully who goes strutting around bragging about his prowess in combat and, as if to underline it, pushing around people he knows to be no match for him. But when he finds himself confronted by an adversary he suspects may give him a real fight he backs away.

Why will the liberal, whose philosophy is supposedly founded on 'reason', not submit himself to the basic test of the 'reasonable-ness' of that philosophy? The answer is predictable: 'fascism' again! One never debates, you see, with 'fascists' (meaning all non-liberals). The mere mention of this word 'fascist' is enough to bring into being a state of intellectual martial law.

Thus does the liberal, whose entire literature whines with protests against 'totalitarianism', reveal himself, when the crunch comes, to be the worst type of totalitarian. As in so many other things, the liberal loves to accuse his opponents of the things of which he is the most guilty himself.

While certain words exist in bold type in the liberal dictionary, one word that never seems to exist is the word **honour**. It does not exist because such a sentiment is utterly alien to the liberal: neither personal honour nor national honour are comprehensible to him. The former deficiency leads him, not only to funk any honest argument against his beliefs, but to sustain the edifice of these beliefs with a structure of **lies** that becomes bigger and more ludicrous the more the world of facts contradicts it. As for national honour, those who believe in such a thing are, in the liberal's eyes, plain silly and worthy only of parody. Thus does the use of armed force to reclaim a stolen national possession become, as we have seen, a "glorification of war as a sign of national virility." The liberal compensates for his inability to win an honest argument by setting up a bogus one and winning that, hands down!

The liberal's attitude to national honour is well illustrated by James Burnham in his scathing exposure of liberalism, *Suicide of the West*:-

> "It does not grieve him that his country should lose a colony or strategic base, or be humiliated by a vote in the United Nations; if his is an advanced nation of the West, he may rather rejoice thereat (as he may have contributed actively to the result) because it will seem a step towards the global justice and peace that he seeks. He will not feel uneasy, certainly not indignant, when sitting in conference or conversation with citizens of countries other than his own — writers or scientists or aspiring politicians, perhaps — and they rake his country and his civilis-ation fore and aft with bitter words; he is as likely to join in with them in the criticism as to protest it. It does not seem to him an anomaly that his own nation's communications industry should on a massive scale print the books, produce the plays and movies, present the television scripts of those who hate his nation and his civilisation, and seek, often avowedly, the

destruction of both.''

On face value, the liberal explains his lack of any sense of national honour as being rooted in his belief in internationalism and his conviction that the preoccupation with honour on the part of nations is detrimental, even dangerous, to international goals of 'peace' and 'brotherhood'. In reality, the liberal positively enjoys the dishonouring of his own nation, as Burnham has indicated. This can be seen from an examination of the profusion of literature by liberal and leftist intellectuals describing Britain's loss of Empire and her fall from world power status. Appearing, only very thinly veiled, between the lines is a perverse pleasure at every phase of national retreat and humiliation. Liberals are at the same time far from applying the same rule to nations other than their own. Any kind of 'nationalism' or 'patriotism' that can be used to undermine the interests of Britain is often ethusiastically supported. Liberals have always been infatuated with 'nationalist' leaders like Gandhi, whose particular brands of 'nationalism' lent themselves, in the circumstances in which they were placed, to attacks on Britain — just as liberals positively love 'nationalists' like Nelson Mandela, even to the point of building statues to him and naming streets and parks after him in the cities of Britain. Why? Because his is a 'nationalism' that can be used against the white race. Liberals are also sympathetic to Scots, Welsh and Irish 'nationalism', as they are useful in breaking up the unity of the British Isles and race. When 'nationalism' in that kind of context is discussed, the liberal suddenly does an about-turn away from his previously professed convictions. It is not any longer contrary to his ideal of a one-world international community to support 'national honour' or 'national freedom'. One moment the liberal is saying that these things are out of date; the next moment he is excusing the gunmen and the bombers of the IRA on the grounds that they are fighting for them!

This paradox is of course explained by the fact that everything to which the liberal gives his hand in politics is fired by an essentially destructive impulse. Where the 'nationalism' of small nations or non-nations is of use in breaking up great nations, it is to be championed; where it provides the cement with which to build and strengthen the same great nations, it is to be opposed.

But the paradox has another logic. We have seen how the liberal mind is in reality merely the transplanted mind of others who know, much more than he knows, what they are doing. To these others, who constitute the true brains behind the idiot yappings o the liberal tongue, such inconsistencies as we have examined here are merely part of the well established dialectic of political warfare. Liberalism is, in effect, dancing to the tune called by marxism. To marxists, all political ideas have but one criterion of evaluation: their use as tactical weapons in advancing the cause of marxist world-revolution. Thus can a marxist this week be heard championing a particular cause and then next week championing another cause which, on intelligent examination, can be found to be completely contradictory. The marxist sees nothing wrong in this, for in the course of this short time there has been, for him, a change in the tactical situation, obliging him to attack that which only a week ago he was to be found stoutly defending.

Modern liberals, whether consciously or unconsciously, think, talk and act in accordance with the French revolutionary slogan: *"Il n'ya pas d'ennemi a gauche."* Their whole world picture today is one conceived, designed and built in the marxist thought-factory, and their conditioned-reflex reaction to issues is the reaction of performing dogs taught by marxist trainers. To quote S.E.D. Brown again:-

> "Contemporary liberalism and communism are, in effect, forces of the same revolutionary movement. The only significant difference is that the 'liberal' may not know where he is going; the communist does."

I have mentioned already the liberal's love of the sick and the diseased and his hatred of the strong and healthy. This of course he will be in haste to explain as arising out of his 'compassion' — another word that figures prominently in his vocabulary, and most of all when his nostrils scent the imminence of an election where there are votes to be picked up. Such compassion, the liberal would have us believe, emanates from nothing more than his noble nature. But does it? Anthony Ludovici, in his *The Specious Origins of Liberalism*, sheds some interesting light on the matter:-

> "It is the intimate relation which, in most ordinary people's minds — I speak of people not accustomed to be lucid concerning the nature of their feelings and the motivations of their conduct — exists between pity and envy. Because, wherever envy is widespread, people's peace of mind is naturally disturbed by the spectre of any marked superiority — whether of health, wealth, personal gifts or merely situation — in a neighbour...But what brings most relief to the ache of envy? — Obviously the spectre of any inferior plight, any misfortune in a neighbour! Every calamity assailing a human being necess-

arily appeases the ache of envy. Nor is this all there is to it. For the whole gamut of this feeling of relief does not end there. In people not too clear about their mental processes, the sense of relief from envy may insensibly prompt spontaneous feelings of gratification which incite to acts of generosity, and it often does so. They are ready, if not eager, to display this half-conscious gratification by indulging in various kinds of indiscriminate and therefore often mischievous benevolence. The fact that the contemplation of a criminal in the dock, even if he happens to be a murderer, may in some people afford them such relief from envy as to provoke obscure feelings of benevolence for him and make them forget his victim or victims, shows how unreasoning this kind of charity can be.''

It is important here to distinguish between pity and compassion, in the personalised sense, shown in particular cases towards individuals in genuine misfortune, particularly loved ones, and the kind of pity and compassion of the liberal, which is directed towards the whole of mankind whose lot, whether deservedly or not, is one of misery, and which becomes elevated into a doctrine that rules all judgement in matters of state.

The former sentiment is a perfectly normal and proper one, without which we would not be civilised beings.

The latter, on the other hand, is a recipe for social and world chaos, amounting to an attempt to bring about a reversal of the entire natural order of life on this planet. The liberal, in pursuit of this sentiment, tends to turn the greater part of the resources of society towards the goal of improving the lot of the wretched, the botched, the criminal and the socially inadequate — to the point of dragging down the superior, the healthy, the strong and the useful. Society, if the liberal had his way, would become one gigantic hospital in which illness and weakness would be the norm and healthy people excluded except where they had a function in tending the sick.

The liberal's ideal is shown in his promotion of the 'anti-hero' in literature, the theatre and the cinema where at the end of the story the seven-stone weakling who is also a failure, a loser and a coward comes out as the one on top. This is life exactly as the liberal would love to see it. How do the words of the liberal protest song go? ''Those who are last shall one day be first...''

Some liberals in Britain have recently exceeded even their own notable tradition of sick imbecility by agitating for the banning of competitive sports in schools. The idea of this is that in such competitive sports not all can be winners; some must be losers. To the liberal mind, it simply is not right that there should ever be losers in anything. A world with no winners would of course belong to the losers (except that they would not be **called** losers) and that sort of world is naturally one in which the liberal would be in his element.

What Mr. Ludovici has said about liberal pity being the child of liberal envy leads us to a related observation, and this is of the disposition of the liberal towards 'missionary' work, whether it be a life of looking after the wretched in some remote corner of the 'Third World' or doing the same thing in places nearer home. Studying the kinds of people who get irresistibly drawn to this kind of occupation, I have come to the conclusion that their motives in the matter are not nearly so pure as they would like to have us believe. In every liberal that I have known — and I stress here again that I am referring to the dedicated zealot for liberal causes — I have detected a deep sense of inadequacy. It is a strong instinct of the inadequate to seek an escape from that world where he is confronted by his hated superiors and into a world where he is surrounded by people inferior to himself. There he can win a respect, even deference, that he would obtain nowhere else and strut around like a little lord.

No field of missionary activity attracts liberals as irresistibly as the cause of 'anti-racism'. In that direction they flock like wasps to a picnic table at the smell of jam. In all the 'anti-racist' crusades in which they vaporise and posture with such sustained monotony there is very little, if any, real love for the coloured man, least of all concern for his welfare. Were it otherwise, liberals would rejoice at the fact that in South Africa the lot of non-white people is far better than anywhere else on the African continent, and they would do all they could to support and encourage the development of the segregated social system in South Africa that has achieved this result. Instead, they dedicate themselves to bringing that system down — with the certainty that, if they succeed, living conditions for that country's non-Whites will plummet to the level of the rest of Africa — possibly in time even to that of Ethiopia, over which country's condition liberals the world over are now busily regimenting our consciences towards the relief of a catastrophe which liberals themselves, in the blueprint for Africa that they drew up in the wake of World War II, did more than anyone else to create.

So what is the dominating impulse behind the liberals' great 'anti-racist' drive? Above all, it is their hatred of their fellow Whites and their desire to see white society, everywhere in the world where it has implanted itself, wither and die. This racial self-hate stands out in everything the liberal says and does in connection with racial affairs. At the end of the liberal's chosen path of destiny is national and racial death. The death-wish is his strongest instinct. I was struck by this thought in my first conversations with liberals many years ago, and everything that I have seen and heard of them since confirms it.

At root, the liberal has a sense that he is a poor specimen of his own race, and in the company of his co-racials this is acutely felt. In a 'raceless' world, on the other hand, the liberal feels entirely at home. A miniature of that raceless world of his dreams he manages to achieve in the 'anti-racist' movement, where he can enjoy the self-gratifying sensation of patronising members of other ethnic groups in a kind of perverse racism of his own. Surrounded on all sides by the 'oppressed' and the 'disadvantaged', he feels a proper little aristocrat by comparison with his position in the natural order of things among his own people.

In the previous chapter I asked the question: is there a conspiracy? The manner in which I approached the question made it clear that what I had in mind was a conspiracy to destroy our own and the other great nations of the Western World, and ultimately Western Civilisation itself. I should have made it abundantly clear in this examination that I believe such conspiratorial forces to exist. This, however, would not in itself be an adequate explanation of their spectacular success. For every knave who manages to deceive, there has to be a fool who is willing to be deceived. For every successful swindler, there has to be a victim whose guard is down. For a scheme of subversion to eat its way into the very heart of a nation, with its agents commanding high positions of influence and power over the institutions of that nation and able to play a decisive role in shaping state policy, there has to be a fundamental weakness in that nation in the first place, a flaw in its defences that leaves it dangerously disarmed against its foes.

Professor Revilo P. Oliver addressed himself to this truth in *Conspiracy or Degeneracy?* when he asked of his own country the question that is equally applicable to ours:-

> "Have our minds become so befuddled by the hypocritical gibbering of invaders and the babbling of our own fools that we have lost even the instinct of self-preservation? If indeed we have, then by the irrevocable law of nature we have become,

like the dinosaurs, the dodos and the mountain gorillas, biolog-
ically obsolete and the world will soon know us no more.''

It is liberalism that is the eternal weakener of nations, by
atrophying their national spirit, their powers of common sense and
their instincts of survival, so as to render them ripe for conquest —
whether by armed force from without or by subversion and
conspiracy within. It is liberalism that, by its influence, brings
about a progressive degeneration of the mind, body and soul of a
people by its unceasing war against everything in that people that
is vibrant and healthy.

I have in this chapter tried to draw a picture of the archetypal
liberal: the way he looks, thinks, talks and behaves. Some
generalisation is inevitable, and in many an individual case there
is bound to be some feature that is an exception to the rule. In the
ranks of 'conservatism' in Britain (to which subject I shall come
later in this book) there are here and there, at least on the surface,
some variations of the type in which not all the most obvious
liberal characteristics are displayed. British conservatism,
nevertheless, today belongs firmly to the liberal family and is
rooted in the liberal outlook on the world. Generally speaking, it
remains true that there is in the liberal character a remarkable
predictability which permits us to regard liberals as a distinct
species — perhaps even genetically determined.

Of course, throughout the history of the white race (as I have
indicated, the breed is extremely rare in other races) this species
has been with us. But in times of health and sanity it has been
possible to leave those of the species to dribble their effete
doctrines from their ivory towers, without too much danger that
they would infect the mainstream of society. Today, however,
these towers have become the commanding heights of national
morality and thought, and liberalism is now the state religion,
while opposition to it is, for many, dangerous heresy.

The series of disastrous turns in the British history of our
century are the inevitable outcome of this shift of power. There is
a cancer in the body of the nation and liberalism is that cancer. Its
consequence will be terminal unless rapid surgery is used to
remove it. We are at the 11th hour: we have not got long left.

Chapter 7
The left

As Britain's established state religion, liberalism is the common ancestor of every creed and faction that enjoys acceptance within the pale of contemporary British politics. Like every ancestor, it has produced offspring which show some diversity of characteristics and have come to pursue their own separate lives. Frequently, the offspring will bitterly quarrel, but it is always essentially a family quarrel; the common blood that flows through their veins is always recognisable to the outsider in certain common behaviour patterns; and when confronted by any outside threat the family always forgets its quarrels and closes ranks.

Of the major factions that dominate the British political scene today, the one which is nearest to inheriting the mantle of liberalism as described in the last chapter is the recently formed 'Social and Liberal Democratic Party', known for short as the 'Democrats'. This party, together with the remaining rump of the Owenite 'Social Democratic Party', occupies what might be regarded as the 'centre ground' in current debate. The term 'centre' is of course entirely relative. It does not, as some suppose, represent 'moderation' in politics but is merely a location drawn by those who design the political map and likewise determine the positions of 'right' and 'left'. No extra chapter is needed to discourse further on this faction.

In the case of the other two offspring, some additional comment is called for. For each has come to represent a distinct brand of the *genus*, marked by certain external features which differentiate it from the others. It is important that we look at these in turn, particularly as, at the time of writing, they still command between them by far the largest portion of the seats in parliament.

The first of these is the Labour Party. It might be queried by some whether this party should today be described as an offshoot of liberalism, as so many of the actions of its members would strike the observer as 'illiberal'. This, however, would be a superficial observation; in essence, the contemporary Labour Party does not differ from the family strain, in as much as it is inspired by the same spirit of woolly internationalism and racial suicide. It inherits all of liberalism's ongoing love affair with the scum of society, whose 'rights' it defends with religious fervour; it is only 'illiberal' towards those who oppose it politically.

If a satirical writer against liberalism — like, say, Peter Simple of *The Daily Telegraph* — wanted to lampoon it by exaggerating all its idiocies to the point of caricature, he need go no further than report the antics of the Labour Party as they occur today in reality. They are all there: Mrs. Dutt-Pauker, Arthur Grudge MP, Duke Len of Erdington, Dr. Heinz Kiosk, Ken Slabb and the Bishop of Bevindon — existing in real life, with the difference that we can no longer afford to laugh at them because they are actually doing in the real world the things they do in the fantasy world of the Simple column, and getting away with it! They comprise probably the majority of the parliamentary Labour Party. They dominate several major local authorities. They are running riot in the world of education. They are a power to be reckoned with in our cultural life.

In the present Labour Party the tendency is to carry to the stage of nutty lunacy all the fashionable liberal fetishes of our times. 'Anti-racism' is of course very high on the list of these. One practice in pursuit of this is to ransack all public libraries to discover whether there are any books remaining in such places that were written and printed before the 'race equality' madness gripped our society and which depict negroes or other non-Whites in positions of social or occupational inferiority. Not even children's nursery stories are allowed to escape this censorship. If any such books are discovered, they are promptly removed.

The 'anti-racist' frenzy extends to the most vicious victimisation of any public employee thought to offend against its code. One headmistress in a London school was recently suspended from duty because she was alleged to have made what was construed as a 'racist' remark to a colleague — notwithstanding that she had previously, apparently, had an impeccable record in the cause of anti-racism! In another case, a headmaster in Bradford was hounded out of his job for daring to write a magazine article pointing out the difficulties experienced by white children in mainly coloured schools. Again, he was not much helped by the fact that he had been a loyal servant of the new multi-racial order.

But things can go even further towards the totally farcical. One woman in the council offices of a London borough was suspended from duty because she introduced into her office a ballpoint pen made in the shape of a banana. This was regarded as an insult to black employees in the same office. It is understood that this lady was later reinstated after an enquiry, though it must be assumed that the offending pen was not.

Hard on the heels of 'anti-racism' as a left-wing crusade is 'anti-sexism'. The heresy here is to say, write or do anything that suggest that men and women are different. As with race, libraries are combed in order to weed out books containing such subversive sentiments, and of course the same operation is conducted with textbooks used in schools controlled by left-wing local authorities. As one instance, a textbook was judged unsuitable because it contained illustrations of a little girl helping her mother in the kitchen while her brother was helping his father in the garage. This, according to the adjudicating authorities, portrayed youngsters in the roles of 'sexual stereotypes' and therefore had to be withdrawn from use.

It is of course only a short journey from 'anti-sexism' to 'homosexual equality', and, knowing the left, we are not surprised to find this to be an area of the most intense activity. The Inner London Education Authority recently caused a big stir by approving for use in schools a textbook which showed a picture of a little girl in bed with a couple of male queers, the accompanying message being that this is a perfectly normal family situation and children should not be afraid of it! Schools in Labour-controlled areas are now frequently visited by 'gay' lecturers, who deliver talks with basically the same message. Considerable public money is of course allocated to pay for these supplements to our children's education, as it is also to the setting up of 'gay switch-boards' in various localities through which homos can enquire after prospective bed partners. It seems not to occur to anyone concerned that such facilities set aside for the exclusive use of certain minorities should be paid for by those minorities; on the contrary, all the ratepayers in the neighbourhoods in question, though most may detest such establishments, must contribute to their upkeep.

Vast sums out of public funds are also allocated to the provision of 'community centres' for various ethnic groups to meet and enjoy leisure facilities - provided of course that these ethnic groups are non-white. Some years ago some friends of mine made an application to their local council for a grant to set up a community centre for white Britons. Needless to say, this was abruptly turned down.

The authorities responsible for these projects would of course claim that the 'community centres' in question are not for exclusive use by ethnic minorities but may be used by anyone. In practice, however, when they are located in areas of high immigrant concentration (as most of them are) the clientele becomes so predominantly non-white that Whites attend and use them at considerable risk to their personal safety. The result is that they become black clubs, to all intents and purposes, even if they are not so in name.

The list goes on. One Labour council in South Wales banned the armed forces from carrying out a local recruiting drive — on the grounds that this was glorifying war and 'militarism'. The logic of such an act was of course that Britain should have no armed forces whatsoever, for that would be the obvious consequence if the forces were not allowed to recruit anywhere. All this of course is part of the theory of the left that getting rid of all Britain's means of self-defence is going to lead to the world banishing war! Another manifestation of this lunacy is the series of notices that have gone up in public places in certain Labour-dominated areas proclaiming that these areas are 'nuclear-free zones'. Just like that! Presumably, any future enemy of this country, when he sends his planes over our towns to drop their H bombs, will issue instructions to the pilots to keep an eye out for such signs and ensure not to bomb any areas where they see them!

One of the most distinguishing features of the left is its love of terrorists — always as long as their terrorism is carried out against British people or against other members of the white race. A short time ago the leader of the now defunct Greater London Council invited over to be wined and dined as his guests a delegation from Sinn Fein, the party in Ulster which openly supports the IRA. The same individual, more recently, caused a furore in the House of Commons when, having just been elected an MP, he named as an 'assassin' a member of the armed forces whose job he alleged it was to hunt down and eliminate IRA personnel. Whether the man ever was given such an assignment or not, the fact is that, had he been, it would have been no more than a perfectly legitimate act of war. To the likes of this particular left-winger, however, such a man is an 'assassin', while of course IRA men who set off bombs that kill scores of civilians are not assassins.

Recently, a number of Labour councils have, as mentioned in the last chapter, adopted the practice of naming public places after well known, and not so well known, terrorists. 'Nelson Mandela

Park' in Leicester is just one example. It is frequently said that one man's terrorist is another man's freedom-fighter. The distinction between the two is always perfectly easy for people of the left. 'Freedom-fighters' are those who use violence, as has been indicated earlier, against any British or white racial interest. Loyalist paramilitary groups in Northern Ireland, on the other hand, have been known to use force in order to defend their British heritage, and they, naturally, are termed 'terrorists'.

The catalogue is endless, and a whole book could be written about the crackpot schemes introduced by Labour governing bodies in municipal areas in pursuit of their warped ideological obsessions.

What Labour believes in today is pure communism — but without the hard realism of the Soviet version. In a kind of way, British Labourites are at a similar stage of thinking to that of the new rulers of Russia in the years immediately following the Revolution of 1917 and before the dawning of any awareness of the necessity of getting down to building a country from out of the rubble of the one they had just wrecked. It is no accident, in this regard, that Trotsky (real name Bronstein) is to many current Labour zealots something of a doctrinal guru. Trotsky and his kind made a highly developed science of red revolution, a revolution with a wholly destructive urge. I differ from conservatives in their belief that revolutions are always bad; they can be good or bad entirely according to the impulses governing them, and of course the people behind them. There is the type of revolution that is conceived with wholly positive political aims in view, aims directed towards the reconstruction of a nation. Some destructive process has to precede that development, just as some process of demolition of a decayed urban area has to precede the task of renewal. Such destruction, however, is not wholesale and indiscriminate; that which is sound in the old scheme of things is preserved and utilised in the building of the new. On the other hand, there is the revolution that is entirely destructive from beginning to end, which aims to pull down everything and has the capacity to build nothing.

Marxist revolution comes into this second category, and what distinguishes it is yet another paradox: in the business of subverting and destroying societies it displays the thinking of clear and logical minds. There is indeed a kind of almost uncanny brilliance in the techniques by which marxists set about insinuating themselves into positions of power in the institutions of the society they have marked down for annihilation, a brilliance indicating that somewhere in the process formidable brains are at work. And yet when we examine the 'ideology' in the name of which all this activity is carried out, the marxist vision of the utopia that is to follow the revolution and become the pattern for the new world order, it bears all the hallmarks of being hatched in the minds of retarded children. So ridiculous are its propositions that no society could put them into practice without descending into chaos. Mrs. Nesta Webster, in *World Revolution*, details numerous attempts to set up 'perfect societies' in accordance with the precepts of communism, all of which came to nothing. One example of these was the 'New Harmony Community of Equality' established in America by the British philanthropist Robert Owen in 1824. Says Mrs. Webster:-

> "...Owen had calculated without taking human nature into account; the difficulty of eradicating the sense of property amongst the colonists proved to be an insuperable difficulty, and the noble desire to work for the common good with no thought of personal profit failed signally as an incentive. Human passions had a strange way of springing to the surface even in the minds of the enthusiastic communists who comprised Owen's following; thus the organ of the community, *The Co-operative Magazine*, relates that one fine evening a member in the full flow of a discourse to an open-air meeting, on the theory that all forms of punishment shall be replaced by kindness, happened to perceive in the distance a small boy helping himself to the plums in the speaker's orchard, and instantly abandoning oratory hurried towards the offender and administered a sound thrashing.
>
> "Various attempts were made to organise the community on different socialist principles. For a time the system known today as guild socialism was practised in the town of New Harmony, whilst communism was banished to the country. But in all these experiments human nature still remained the insuperable obstacle, and in 1827 Owen in despair resigned the management. The cause of his failure was attributed by convinced communists to his own management. By Owen it was attributed to the character of the people who made up the community. His experience, he acknowledged, 'had shown one thing: the necessity of great caution in selecting members. No societies with common property and equality could prosper, if composed of persons unfit for their peculiar duties. In order to succeed it was needful to exclude the intemperate, the idle, the careless, the quarrelsome, the avaricious, the selfish...' In other words,

communist settlements must be composed only of perfect human beings. But as Owen's biographer observes: 'One wonders whether for a society so weeded, any peculiar organisation would be necessary. It is just the selfish and the intemperate who constitute the difficulty of our present arrangements.' "

If those comprising the population of Owen's New Harmony settlement could not make it work, one wonders what hope there is of any society conceived along present left-wing lines being made to work, with the kind of people now being encouraged to breed and multiply by socialist prophets in the Britain of the 1980s!

In the real world, every nation that has undergone a revolution along marxist lines has before long had to dispense with much, if not all, of the ballast of marxist ideology if it wants to achieve any kind of stability and undertake constructive works, let alone make itself defensible against its external enemies. Russia itself is a vivid example of this. In the years following 1917 marxist internationalism gradually became a principle to be honoured much more in theory than in practice and today is to be found placed among those ideological goods marked 'for export only'. For some years during the early career of the Soviet state the Lysenko doctrines denying the influence of genetics and heredity were applied to farming, with the predictably disastrous results, until they were, with admirable pragmatism, dropped and forgotten. Soldiers' councils, the marxist prescription for running the armed forces — where armed forces are permitted at all — soon disappeared to be replaced by the old hierarchical forms of military organisation. Hierarchy indeed came to prevail throughout the whole structure of government, with the babble of parliaments duly giving way to the rule of the strong man — modified only when the necessary individual to fit the role could not be found. Two important relics of the old revolution remain: the elimination of economic competition and the theory of sexual equality, with its recruitment of women to do men's work. The signs are that the first is now being scrapped, with the recognition that a degree of private enterprise is essential to make economic activity efficient. And it is probable that the alarming decline in the birthrate among European Russians will eventually induce the authorities to reconsider the sex-equality rule that has clearly undermined motherhood.

Yet, despite this evidence, infantile leftism is still alive and kicking here in Britain and taking ever more absurd forms with the passing of time. All this leads to the question: how genuinely and seriously does the left believe its own propaganda?

Are we to suppose that people intelligent and clever enough to have made such a spectacular success of the science of revolutionary unrest could be taken in for five minutes by the mindless drivel that comprises the motions passed at the conferences of left-wing organisations and litters the columns of left-wing magazines and newspapers, while constituting the apparent doctrines underlying the policies of numerous left-wing councils?

Undoubtedly, a number of left-wing activists do quite honestly believe in the nonsense they spout. A look at some of them — which my associates and I regularly obtain at the frequent demonstrations they mount against us — is enough to explain why: quite clearly, a large portion of these 'comrades' are specimens of humanity some thousands of years behind normal people in the scheme of evolution — freaks and half-wits whom sane societies put in padded cells, or at least in occupations where they can be rendered harmless, but whom our own society of today has graciously honoured with positions of influence and power.

But behind these raving loonies there simply must be other forces at work, brains shrewd enough to have brought great states and civilisations crashing down in ruins by the skill and professionalism of their subversive activity, and therefore with an obviously cynical inner disbelief in the hugger-mugger of fairy tales that they parade before the world as political doctrines. To such people, this claptrap can only have one purpose: to unhinge the minds of the masses of society to a degree that they are quite incapable of realising that they are being attacked by an insidious enemy whose interest is in society's liquidation.

As I related earlier, I began to perceive this gigantic fraud in left-wing politics in the 1950s, when it started to become evident to me that the left was built on a mountain of lies. I was able to see this by examining reports in left-wing publications of events to which I had myself been a first-hand witness and in some of which I had personally participated. When my friends and I read these reports a few days later, we simply could not recognise the printed version of what had happened as relating to the same event in which we had been involved.

Left-wing mobs would come to our meetings with the obvious intention of smashing them up and not permitting a word to be heard by the audience. As soon as the first speaker took the platform a barrage of organised chanting would begin, making it an obvious waste of breath for the speaker to continue as long as it lasted. We would ask these mobs to stop and give the speaker a hearing, making it clear that if our requests were not heeded the noise-makers would be required to leave. Of course these requests were ignored and our men were compelled to eject those responsible. Those being ejected resisted violently and at that point made their move to break the meeting up by force. They were always defeated and eventually thrown out.

Yet the next week they would give their version of what had happened. Needless to say, this version did not remotely correspond to the true facts as we knew them. According to the left-wing press, the comrades had gone there with perfectly peaceful intentions and were brutally assaulted as soon as one or two of them — **one or two**, mark you — made points of objection to the speeches!

I remember reading similar reports of events I had witnessed where the left had turned up with the obvious intention of causing disorder and had been dealt with by the police. On these occasions I had often felt that the police action was extremely mild and restrained — too mild and restrained at times — and had only been taken as an absolute last resort when all reason had failed. Yet in left-wing reports that followed all the talk was of the 'police brutality' in attacking, without provocation, people who had only come along to demonstrate peacefully!

I remembered marvelling at the gall of these 'reporters' in the size of the lies that they manufactured in order to give support to their co-leftists. Bit by bit, I learned that in the left-wing press whatever was presented as true could be relied upon with at least 80 per-cent certainty to be untrue.

It is a constant claim of the left that it represents the cause of 'the workers'. Observing the berserk mobs that we have encountered in our clashes with the left over many years, I would comment that the majority of them certainly are not 'workers' in anything like the sense they intend to mean by the word. They are mainly middle-class. A large portion of them are currently attending some university or other, and most of the remainder are ex-university people. A good number are permanently living on social security, as our investigations have established when we have monitored their court appearances after disturbances. Most of the causes that they take up have nothing remotely to do with any 'workers' ' interest, and their claim to represent this section of the community is therefore just another piece of blatant dishonesty.

I came to realise years ago that behind the political left, just as with all factions of the old party spectrum, there lies the controlling hand of **money power**. The purpose of exercising this control through a plurality of parties is elementary if one thinks about it a little. Our controllers know that their policies will always provoke discontent and protest. What better way to contain and neutralise that protest than to give it a safety valve? As soon as there is a sign that any large number of the masses are disenchanted with the policies of one party, you give them another party into which their anger and opposition can be corralled, and then regulated within bounds determined by those who in the background still retain ultimate power. Communism is no exception to this; it merely represents the most extreme form of what might be called 'controlled opposition'. A programme is devised that will appeal to the most anti-social, imbecilic and indeed criminal elements of the community by offering to them as a sacred right all the benefits made possible by the labour of honest and hard-working people. The whole doctrine is devised for life's natural 'losers', and is intended to provide comfort to them in the idea that their unfavourable position in society is the result, not of any inadequacies on their own part, but of the injustices in society itself, which has been 'hard' to them by denying them what is due to them as members of a community in which all are 'equal' in talent and worth.

It is a well established fact that the type of human material recruited by this hogwash, whatever its natural shortcomings, is well suited to movements of subversion and revolt. It includes a lot of people brim-full of resentments and with plenty of time on their hands: that section of the unemployed that is unemployable, the socially and sexually frustrated, all ideal material for mobilisation for disruptive activity. W.B. Yeats told us that our century was one in which "the best lack all conviction while the worst are full of passionate intensity," and the latter truth is certainly one on which the left has been quick to capitalise. As part of the debris of the rotting civilisation of western 'democracy', there is a huge pool of cannon-fodder available to subversive organisations. This consists of social drop-outs and misfits of all classes, including, in no small part, the pampered offspring of well heeled families, allowed in our discipline-free society to drift into squats, drugs, idleness and dirt. While in properly ordered societies this refuse is taken by the scruff of the neck and obliged to earn its keep by useful work (either outside or inside penal institutions), in a society in which all leadership has abdicated and government has collapsed, such elements are courted as a valuable section of the community (after all, they have votes!) and are at the disposal of any group of unscrupulous agitators who may wish to organise them into 'movements' dedicated to mayhem and destruction.

The point always to remember, of course, is that those who devise the vapid slogans about 'workers' revolution', and so on *ad-nauseam*, attach no more seriousness to these slogans than the rest of us. They are not interested in 'ideals', whether sound or unsound ones; they are only interested in **power** — and power, as history records in all cases of social and political breakdown, lies with those who can control the mob.

I should remind the reader: these movements of the far left, whether in the Labour Party or outside it, are not short of money, or sponsors in the world where money rules. They have a well-financed press. They have generously oiled facilities of publishing. The works of their playwrights, critical though they may appear to be of 'capitalism', are screened regularly on commercial TV networks sponsored by capitalist interests. It does not seem to occur to those interests to organise boycotts of the companies that promote such productions — as they undoubtedly would anyone who promoted productions with a message of nationalism or 'racism'. The truth is that the political left, far from being a revolt of ordinary working people against the great interests of wealth, is in fact the creature of those very same interests — which have seized hold of the 'workers' ' movement in order to conduct and lead it themselves — an aim that presents very little difficulty when the power of money is in their hands and when the entire climate of politics is at the level of the most moronic.

In truth, money-capitalism (which should not be confused with productive private enterprise) is merely the opposite side of the same coin as represented by the leftism of the Labour Party. The Money Power, by the manner in which it submits the economy to the slavery of interest, perverts the capitalist system and creates manifold injustices which cry out for remedy. Then, with brazen cunning, the Money Power creates, in the political left, its own instrument for the supposed supply of that remedy. Left-wing agitation inflames the workers, not against their real exploiters, who are the sharks of loan capital, but against the management and ownership of industry, who are as much victims of the system as they are. In this way the nation is held in a vice: control by money from above, and subversion by left-wing socialism from below.

Always it is the factory-owner, or other types of supplier of useful services to the economy, who is the victim of strikes and other kinds of industrial disruption — never the Money Power itself. How often has the reader heard of a strike of bank employees? Always it is the useful entrepreneur that is the target of the hatred of socialist pamphlets, which drip with poison in their efforts to whip up antagonism between the two vital wings of productive industry: ownership/management/industrial capital, on the one hand, and labour on the other.

At the same time as this campaign of hatred is being stoked up against the leaders of industry, so does the same Money Power, in its 'conservative' press, encourage a similar hatred among the proprietorial and middle classes against the workers who participate in strikes, though on occasions the reality is that the workings of the system offer those workers no alternative action. 'Workers' are blamed for industrial inefficiency, while 'bosses' are blamed for low wages and unfavourable conditions on the shop floor. Few people understand that, at the end of the day, it is the same master who controls both sectors of the nation's life, albeit by different methods.

On the global level, we have the supposed conflict between western 'capitalism' and Soviet 'socialism'. This conflict too is more apparent than real — if it were otherwise, why would western governments and western capitalists have been financing the Soviet system ever since New York bankers payrolled the bolsheviks who took over Russia in 1917? Why also would the two systems have combined in World War II against Hitler? Of course it pays the masters who control both systems to have the functionaries of those systems spitting and snarling against each other across the world stage, so as to maintain the illusion of a 'cold war' and mislead the masses as to where the real sources of international trouble reside, but when the crunch comes — as when one or another system seems in danger of collapse — its so-called 'adversary' will always be sure to come to its aid.

When we look at the record of 'socialism' in government in Britain, when measured against all the promises of left-wing pamphlets and manifestos, we find that it is abysmal. It has signally failed to find answers to the problems of poverty, unemployment, slums, inflation and social injustice — precisely because it is not founded on any genuine recognition of the causes

of these evils. It is tied to the same system of economic internationalism and deficit-financing as its Tory opponent, while both
are similarly tied to a political system that has long been obsolete
in relation to the nation's needs.

The best that Labour manifestos can do at election times is
croak the worn-out slogans of 'soak the rich', which they seek to
do by a policy of escalating rates of taxation. By this manoeuvre,
Labour is able to kill two birds with one stone: it can find more
money to subsidise its own incompetence, while at the same time
maintaining its posture as the champion of the deprived and the
downtrodden. Needless to say, such a policy in no way threatens
the really powerful moneyed interests which finance the left, as
these interests control international business networks through
which money can be shifted about the world in such a way as to
escape the highest levels of taxation. The people most hard hit are
the hardest-working and most productive members of the
community: the medium-sized and small manufacturer, the most
highly qualified professional man, the highly skilled worker and
the prudent saver and investor. We should also not forget the
home-owner and ratepayer, who increasingly has to bear the
burden of the extravagant programme of social engineering and
political stunts engaged in by leftist-controlled local governments. Today's 'socialists' have developed to a fine art the
practice of fleecing the very people who represent the backbone of
the economy while leaving the really big financial parasites alone.

Much of what has been said in this chapter about the antics of
the political left in Britain will be familiar to the reader, and will
indeed strike a chord among many conservatives, who doubtless
have been making the same observations of the species for some
years. I certainly make no claim to any startling revelation or
novelty in what has been examined here; such exposures are a
regular feature of the Tory press. Millions know about the mini-
police states set up by local Labour councils, about the shameful
handling of public servants, about the barmy schemes of
'education' and the profligate spending of public money on ever
crazier political hobby-horses of left-wing fancy. The whole issue
is, quite understandably, a matter of widespread national outrage.

But at the end of it all one question remains unanswered by the
great majority of those who would join in the chorus of condemnation of the so-called 'loony left'.

It is simply the question of how the left gets away with it.

What indeed must be our verdict on a society, on a political system, in which such things are allowed to happen? Just by what process have these subversives and wreckers been able to worm their way into positions of influence and power — in our institutions of parliament, local government, education, industry, the press, broadcasting and others? Should we not be putting that process itself under the microscope and considering its alarming implications for the future of our country just as much as we should do the symptoms it produces?

When the inhabitants of a zoo escape from the cages, overpower their keepers and take control of the establishment, running amok and smashing everything in sight, about what phenomenon should we be asking ourselves the most searching questions?

Should it be the behaviour of the animals in their wild rampage, wrecking property and endangering public safety?

Or should it be the running of the zoo itself, the competence of its staff, the soundness of its system of rules and security?

In other words, what kind of institution could it be in which such a thing was ever permitted?

The truth is that today's 'liberal' establishment and consensus provide the soil on which the virulent plant of left-wing militancy is able to flourish and grow to a stage at which it constitutes a mortal danger to society, country, people and civilisation. **Liberalism** is in the first place, as stated before, the spiritual parent of far leftism and marxism, and then liberalism sets the rules of society under which its obnoxious offspring has the licence to run riot and reduce that same society to chaos and eventual collapse.

We will not be successful in the fight against the hard left unless we extend that fight to a war against liberalism in all its manifestations and all its products — for both are part and parcel of the same forces that today combine in malignant alliance to destroy us.

Chapter 8

Conservatism in surrender

A short time ago a lecturer at the University of Bristol was forced to resign his post as a result of a series of violent demonstrations against him staged by young red campus rowdies as he entered university premises. This man, Mr. John Vincent, in addition to his academic duties, wrote a regular column in *The Sun* newspaper, and something appearing in this column had, whether rightly or wrongly, been designated by these student censors as 'racist'. This, in their eyes, disqualified him to hold his university job, and accordingly they set about employing physical intimidation to prevent him doing it.

In the end they succeeded. Mr. Vincent was forced to quit. And the student mobsters? Not one of them was given any disciplinary punishment. The university authorities simply capitulated to violence. One of their colleagues was deprived of a part of his livelihood, while the young red mafia got off scot-free.

Doubtless, one or two of the university hierarchy who were responsible for this shameful capitulation were left-wing radicals who welcomed such a development — we know that these sorts of people are rife in in the centres of higher education and it would be no surprise to us to learn that they were into the woodwork at Bristol, just as they are at most other universities.

A few more no doubt were moderate Labourites or supporters of one of the parties of the 'Alliance', and, while they may not have exactly approved of the methods used to get rid of their fellow academic, they were glad to be shot of anyone who might be suspected of 'racism'.

But it is reasonable to suppose that at least some number of the seniors involved were Conservatives. We must presume that, even if they disliked what their colleague had written in his paper, they believed in his right to write it and not be deprived of his post at the university on account of it. Even more must they have been appalled at the methods used to bring this about, and at the fact that none of the culprits had been punished. We must presume all this, if only on the basis of the pronouncements that have continually been made by leading Conservative spokesmen in condemnation of this very kind of student hooliganism.

Yet what did these dons of Conservative disposition actually **do** to prevent this outrage? Beyond perhaps a few muted murmurings of disapproval, apparently **nothing**. There was no loud public protest. There was no walk-out. There was no strike. The whole thing was passively accepted. Nor was there any intervention by the Tory Prime Minister and her government — not that we should be surprised at this, in view of their silence over the hounding of Ray Honeyford, the Bradford headmaster, out of his job in almost exactly similar circumstances.

Supposing that Mr. Vincent and Mr. Honeyford had been radical leftists and had been deprived of their employment as a result of writing articles, say, in praise of the IRA or in support of freedom for paedophiles. In that case, you can bet that the reaction would have been very different. The political left would have mobilised itself into action. Left-wing members of the academic staff would have made loud public denunciations and perhaps would have suspended their classes. An outcry would have gone up from Labour Party HQ. There would have been big demonstrations against the university and school authorities. Labour MPs would most certainly have made a rumpus in parliament.

And, most probably, under these pressures the two men would have been reinstated.

Here is illustrated the difference between the left and right of mainstream British politics today. The former is continually on the offensive. It is aggressive, noisy, demanding. It will not take what it sees as injustices lying down. It plays hard for its own side. If one of its own is harmed, it makes a fuss — in fact it raises hell — until the harm is undone.

The right, by contrast, is continually on the retreat. It is passive. It is cowardly. It declines to battle for anything. Before an angry mob it will always give in.

This is British Conservatism today — a tepid, pallid, anaemic political creed, led by people of the same description. It has developed surrender to a fine art, for it has been surrendering for a long time. It has surrendered an empire. It has surrendered national freedom and honour. It has surrendered public order in Britain. It is in the process of surrendering Northern Ireland. In the battle of ideas, it is in a constant state of surrender, conceding ground to its enemies at every turn. And of course it has surrendered in the schools and universities a long time ago.

Perhaps a glance around at the delegates at a Tory annual conference will suffice to explain why. They are not, in the main part, people who look as if they will fight for anything. Their faces have an aspect that is a mixture of softness and resignation. And not too many of them exude great intelligence. The platform contingent have the look of people whose main aim in life is to keep their jobs. The speeches remind one of nothing so much as the Peter Sellers recording of years ago lampooning a Tory MP whose address to his flock consisted of naught more than elegant waffle.

When an election is on, it is almost always possible to tell who is the Tory candidate at a quick glance, even if he has left his rosette in his car. He is usually the bright executive — well groomed, suave, a salesman's smile, a personal interest in everybody that is so transparently phoney it can be seen through a mile off. He has stood before a party selection board and obviously won top marks for tameness. His answers to every question are those of a well-programmed computer. If he has a mind of his own about anything, it is about golf, gardening and choice of table wines. There is a near to 50 per-cent chance that he works in the City, most likely as stockbroker or merchant banker.

The creed of British Conservatism today, whatever the party's distant origins, is no less an offshoot of the one liberal ancestor than its Labour counterpart. It is in fact very largely a rehash of 19th century liberalism under another name. It is the instrument much more of mercantile classes than of the landed aristocracy, which has long ago surrendered practically all power and exists today only as a factor of antique value. To the Conservative, the nation is no more than a gigantic business, to be run for profit. He is not in the slightest bit disconcerted at the prospect that substantial slices of it should be owned by foreigners; on the contrary, if these foreigners can help to increase profits their ownership of the nation's industry and resources is welcome, indeed sought after. This attitude typifies the difference between the old aristocratic view of land, property and resources as a heritage which must at all costs be kept in the family as something of sacred trust and the purely commercial concept of such things as commodities to be bought and sold in the market place.

The Conservative speaks much of the 'British sickness' but when he does so he means only **economic** sickness, i.e. lack of profitability, cost-effectiveness, industrial competitiveness, managerial proficiency and factory performance. He can drive through our cities and see moral, spiritual, cultural and human degeneration all around him — without being in the least bit affected by it. He can read his newspapers and swallow a daily diet of lies without questioning the integrity of their authors. He can partake in an evening's TV viewing and not feel anger at the hour-by-hour procession of pigswill passing off as 'entertainment'. He can see Britain made a doormat by every nation in the world, without the slightest dent to national pride (of which he has very little or none at all). It is only when he hears of a group of workers going on strike, or of productivity rates in some national industry being lower than in its counterparts abroad, that he shows the slightest flicker of discontent — but even then he is incapable of placing the blame where it really lies: with government (particularly if it is a Tory government).

It never seems to occur to the Tory mind that the economic sickness in Britain which so much preoccupies him is merely a product of a much greater and deeper sickness of the national will — for which all governments, and indeed the entire political system, are collectively responsible.

At the time of UDI in what was formerly Rhodesia, and when the Whites in that country were fighting for their survival against practically the whole world, one Rhodesian said of British politicians: ''A Labour man is always preferable because you are never in doubt that he is an enemy: he will come rushing at you with dagger raised. The Tory is different: he will smile and shake hands with you, and then, when your guard is down, he will stab you in the back!''

This aptly sums up the spirit and intent of modern Toryism. It is the most insidious of all the corrosive forces currently gripping Britain because it is the least honest in the declaration of its objectives. For a long time the Conservative Party has posed as the 'patriotic' party, while working for aims that are in fact the absolute opposite of everything that is meant by true patriotism. More than any of the other parties, it has been responsible for the scuttle from Empire. More than any of the others, it carved out the way for Britain's entry into the Common Market and the concessions of political and economic sovereignty that have been a part of membership of that association. At least as much as any of the other parties, it has encouraged the immigrant flood into Britain while hiding behind constant avowals that it was 'controlling' this flood.

Real patriotism must not be confused with the shallow, synthetic Tory product. Real patriotism lies in a dedication to homeland and soil, to national freedom and sovereignty, to the native culture and above all to race. Real patriotism is at one with **nationalism**, and is meaningless without it. It is essentially national, folkish, **tribal**.

Tory 'patriotism' is merely an attachment to certain external symbols and accoutrements that are identified with the ruling establishment: Royalty, the National Anthem (which in Britain's case is a eulogy to the monarch, not the nation), Parliament, Flag and 'liberal' ideology. The latter is particularly in prominence: abstractions like 'freedom' (for some of course but not for others) are depicted as the things that men go to war and die for. To be 'patriotic' is to have an infinite faith in ancient and established British institutions — and purely because they are ancient and established, not because they contribute effectively to national strength or success.

In the fantasy world in which Britain has increasingly immersed herself in the present century, events like a royal wedding or a state opening of parliament are deliberately boosted up by the mass media and made occasions for this *ersatz* 'patriotism'. Children are given little paper Union Jacks to wave (probably made in Hong Kong). The BBC's senior commentator is wheeled on to give solemnity to the proceedings, and regal dresses and hats become the main national topic for the week in question. All this of course conveniently distracts the attention of the masses from unemployment, slums, race riots and the sale to Americans of another great manufacturing company. The whole show is one gigantic soporific designed to divert national ardour into channels where it will not threaten those who rule but will allow them to get quietly on with the job of destroying every element of real nationhood.

I am not against monarchy but, on the contrary, strongly support it. Precisely for this reason, I detest seeing it exploited to bolster institutions and interests that are no good to Britain and to induce a false national euphoria in the midst of national catastrophe. I am not against pomp and pageantry but would like to see more of it; but it should be pomp and pageantry behind which there is the genuine substance of national power, not merely the pathetic enactment of ancient rites when all the glory giving rise to them has departed.

And if is pageantry we want, would not the disciplined marching of thousands of youth at the peak of physical well-being be a sight far more apt to stir the blood than the shuffle of elderly dignitaries, adorned with robes and gaiters, amid the scenery of twilight?

By some strange chemistry of the mind, patriotism to the Tory requires a reverence for everything which he cares to stamp with the label 'British', quite regardless of its worth, while any strong criticism of the state of Britain is thought 'unpatriotic'. 'Patriotism' is not rocking the boat but putting our limitless faith in established institutions to 'see us through'.

In my book, the real patriot must be a person capable of subjecting his country to the most exacting critical scrutiny, recognising its weaknesses and cursing it for failure to live up to high standards. The relation of patriot to nation must be that of parent to child: it must incorporate the capacity for the most intense anger when behaviour does not live up to the requirements of true love. A patriot must be capable of hating and waging war against everything in his country that is rotten, diseased, base and decadent.

If truth be known, we British have been hoodwinked into accepting an alien definition of what it is we should be proud of in our own nation. We have been induced to see as national virtues what in reality are our worst national shortcomings: tolerance of subversion, contentedness with the second-rate, lack of national discipline, our tendency to be a soft touch for every imported carpet-bagger. This smug national self-righteousness which we mistake for patriotic feeling admirably suits our enemies, external and internal, who are pleased to continue in the business of destroying us while we sit sipping our tea from little plastic mugs bearing the portrait of Her Majesty The Queen.

Right at this moment, the Tories are exploiting their well practised talent for projecting a bogus 'patriotism' in a campaign designed to foster the illusion that some mythical national renaissance is coming about as a result of their policies in the economic and other fields. They speak of industrial recovery when there is no industrial recovery. They speak of a drive to restore the rule of law when there is only an abdication of the rule of law. They speak of a restoration of standards in education when there is only a headlong flight from standards in education. They talk of the recapture of Britain's power and prestige in the world when those things are in fact at their lowest ebb ever.

But that is not all.

By means of the party game of which they are a part, Tories are experts in the trick of making a thoroughly bad policy seem a good one by pointing to the fact that the policy adopted by their opponents to deal with the same issue is even worse. The trick goes hand-in-hand with that of conducting an impassioned debate with opponents about some detail on the periphery of an issue while over the essentials the two sides are of one mind and one policy. Over the ditching of the white Rhodesians, all the mainstream parties shared a common purpose, but this did not prevent them having the effrontery to engage in heated controversy with each other over the Rhodesian issue — which, when all the steam had cleared away, was merely about the method and timing of the hand-over of Rhodesia to black rule. The Tories shrewdly perceived that there was a great deal of support on the part of British public opinion for the white Rhodesian cause, and particularly in the ranks of their own party and voters. They therefore cunningly shifted the argument on Rhodesia from what it was really about — the question of white rule or black rule — to entirely subsidiary and, in reality, scarcely relevant arguments revolving around the procedure by which 'progress' towards black rule was to be negotiated — and, when that was complete, what sort of black rulers would take over. As part of this, they would pick on particularly outrageous attacks made on white Rhodesia by left-wing politicians and press and vehemently rebut them, thus giving the quite erroneous impression that the Tories were the champions of the Whites, which they never were.

Exactly the same bogus argument between right and left is now going on concerning the question of race in Britain. Mindful again of the strong public feeling there is against the attempt to make Britain a multi-racial society, the Tories and their press have contrived to present themselves in an entirely false position on this issue by picking on some of the more ludicrous statements and actions of their opponents and loudly condemning them. One technique here is to attack some of the more blatantly intolerant manifestations of 'anti-racism', such as I have described in the previous chapter. Such attacks are of course guaranteed to win public applause, while at the same time being calculated to shift public attention away from the central issue — which is whether Britain should be a multi-racial country or a white one — and onto a side issue, which is the method by which multi-racial Britain should be promoted and enforced.

As these very words are being written, there is an impassioned debate going on following a public statement by the leader of the Labour Party attacking present Tory government 'controls' over immigration, saying that they are unfair to would-be immigrants and promising a relaxation of such 'controls' when Labour gets elected. Tories have loudly counter-attacked and defended their 'controls' as absolutely necessary to prevent the country being 'flooded' with immigrants — all of course to rapturous applause from grass-roots Tories everywhere! The whole argument conveniently glosses over the fact that these alleged 'controls' are not working in the slightest and are indeed not really controls at all, the immigrant flood still continuing at a rate officially acknowledged as being between 50,000 and 60,000 a year (and, unofficially, probably much higher — when illegal immigrants are taken into account). Yet the Tory policy of 'controls' is made, by this argument, to seem firm and resolute compared with what would happen under Labour, in which case the entry of immigrants would be even greater!

This deceitful practice of shifting the argument from the issue that represents its core and onto one which exists only on the sidelines of it is accompanied by another, equally deceitful, one. This is the practice of making policies which in reality are wholly wrong and unacceptable seem to be the epitome of 'reasonableness' and 'moderation'.

This is done by changing the location of what is regarded as the 'centre ground' of an issue by moving it, subtly and almost imperceptibly, to a new position (usually to the left of the original one) and then condemning all those who stand a long way from that position as 'extreme'. In fact, the whole strategy of reducing political debate in Britain to a battle between so-called 'moderation' and 'extremism' conveniently absolves those who contrive this arrangement from the onerous burden of having to argue the actual issues. The effect of this on the public should not be underestimated. Time and time again, I have had people say to me: "I agree with many of your policies but I think you are too extreme." To this I have replied by asking the critic to tell me which particular policy he regards as **wrong** — and **why** it is wrong. Invariably, there is a failure to do so, and in the end it boils down to the critic admitting that he has no basis for describing such policies as 'extreme' other than just some vague feeling that they are, induced entirely by the influence of those who determine the fashionable political attitudes of the moment.

Such fashionable attitudes designate as 'extreme' any argument which cuts through the mush and the slush to the very inner guts of an issue and demands that it be decided according to two straight and clear alternatives. The Northern Ireland issue is just one such case.

Ever since the current phase of the troubles in Northern Ireland began in 1968, there has been a concerted attempt by the political establishment, and particularly by the Tories, to blur the issue at stake, which quite plainly and simply is one of whether the province remains British or does not. Its loyal citizens, who are very much in the majority, are entitled to ask of British politicians that they should give a firm commitment to the first of these two alternatives. The politicians, almost without exception, have not done so in any meaningful terms, but have constantly tried to strike postures of compromise between the demands of Loyalists to stay British and those of Republicans for a United Ireland. Now while there are some issues that can be settled by a compromise solution this is not one of them. Northern Ireland cannot belong to two countries at the same time; it must be part of one or the other. The Tory response to this situation, however, has been to give a purely nominal, equivocal and obviously grudging commitment that Northern Ireland will remain within the United Kingdom "for as long as the majority wants it," while at the same time feeding to the Republican element a series of concessions which quite clearly would be out of the question if this commitment was to be worth anything. The latest of these is the infamous Anglo-Irish Agreement, which gives to a body appointed by the government of the Irish Republic the right to play a consultative role in the administration of this British province.

This is quite clearly a step — and a big one — in the direction of surrender of British sovereignty, just the latest of many made by Conservatism in recent years. It is seen as such by the majority of Ulster people and, in consequence, is vigorously opposed by them. For this opposition, they have been designated by politicians and media on the mainland as 'extremists' and therefore to be shunned by all reasonable-minded, civilised and 'moderate' people.

Here we have a classic example of the old and familiar manoeuvre. A policy of surrender is decided upon, which represents the end of the road. A point in that direction but some way short of it is then arbitrarily selected as representing the 'middle ground', to which all rational and respectable people are expected to adhere. Those who want to go the whole way to surrender in one quick jump are designated as 'extremists' on one side (although in fact they are only favouring the policy that has been decided upon anyway) while those who oppose any step at all in the direction of surrender, because they see it for what it is, become the 'extremists' on the other side. 'Moderation', in other words, represents the position between these two poles which favours surrender by a series of sly, gradual steps, each wrapped up in such dressings of cotton wool that it permits official spokesmen to stand up in public and proclaim, with perfectly straight faces, that it is not surrender at all!

The Empire was given away by the use of just such a technique. Large areas of mainland Britain are being delivered up to coloured immigrants in a similar way. Political and economic sovereignty are being sacrificed to the EEC in a manner no different. The scuttle from Northern Ireland is merely part of a well established pattern.

Is this to say that the whole of British Conservatism is a party to a gigantic conspiracy to surrender and sell out everything that Britain possesses, being fully conscious of the ultimate objectives to which all policies are leading and endorsing those objectives inwardly while denying them in public? Is every Conservative, in other words, a conscious traitor?

If only it were so simple! In fact, probably only a minority of Conservatives, albeit a highly placed one, knows exactly what is being done and willingly endorses the grand strategy. This consists of a select group of people wholly committed to the achievement of an internationalist world order and who regard the sacrifice of everything making for their country's nationhood as a necessary condition of that aim. They are, for whatever motive — ambition, money or a warped sense of principle — traitors.

But the vast majority cannot be placed in this category. They are simply people caught up in the spirit of their times and without either the intelligence to see where it is leading or the force of character to resist it effectively. In many cases they are people who have built political careers on their subservience to the policy of this inner 'establishment'. In the odd moments when they experience unease at the trend things are taking they remind themselves that their mortgages, their sons' or daughters' school fees and their next scheduled holidays in the sun depend on their willingness not to 'rock the boat'. And then of course they can, in all sorts of ways, get their consciences to back them up. Family, rather than self, is the first justification. Then there is the thought that if they want to influence things for the better they had best stay 'inside' rather than be cast 'outside'. Finally, there is the ultimate rationale that never fails: party unity must be maintained — if there is disunity and the next election is lost, things would be far worse!

All these things are of course the characteristic features of an army in headlong retreat in war. There is going to be defeat anyway, so why risk getting killed for nothing? Better the orderly and dignified withdrawal, with the minimum of casualties, than the hopeless fight against overwhelming odds! This is the mood of which all great capitulations are made, and it is the dominating spirit of modern Conservatism.

Nowhere is this craven and cowardly mentality displayed more than in the Tory reaction to far-left militancy, of which we might include black racial militancy as a division of the species. I cited an example of this cowardice at the beginning of this chapter, and it is fairly typical. The hooligan left can be regarded as having more or less taken over as the referee of what is going to be permissible debate at our centres of advanced learning up and down the country — in the sense that any would-be speaker at any meeting of whom the left disapproves will be denied a hearing — by the threat, and where necessary by the implementation, of physical violence. The second is seldom necessary, however, as the first usually suffices.

Yet left militants are never more than a minority at the universities and colleges they rule. In practically all these places there are Tory groups who have given way to them simply because they are terrified of them, as well as dons — some at least of whom, as at Bristol, must be Conservative in sympathies — who just do not have the will to maintain order in the institutions for which they are responsible, and are too frightened or timid to discipline those students who cause the trouble. Many are the times that my colleagues and I have provisionally been invited to appear as guest speakers before university audiences, this type of invitation usually coming from Tory student groups. After our initial acceptance, the meeting has been advertised. Once this has happened, the campus left militants have got to work with threats of mayhem if the meeting is allowed to proceed.

We have then been contacted again by the Tories organising the intended meeting and informed of certain 'difficulties', due to this intimidation by the opposition. Our first reaction has been to say to them: ''Very well, if there are those difficulties, you can surely deal with them — you must have some able-bodied young men there who can act as stewards and control the trouble-makers if they start.'' On being given a negative reply, we have then said that in that case our speaker will bring with him a body of his own supporters who will guarantee to keep order. This offer has in turn been declined. The plea has been: ''We cannot guarantee the speaker's safety.'' Our speaker has invariably replied that he is willing to take a chance with his own safety. All this, however, has been to no avail. The meeting has been cancelled and the left has won another victory.

Again and again, we have been struck by the utterly pathetic lack of gumption on the part of these Tories in the face of red intimidation. Of course, when they have spoken about being concerned for the safety of the speaker we have always known that what they have really been thinking about has been their own safety, which is more precious to them than any principle of free speech.

They are just feeble, yellow-bellied wimps — a fact that is confirmed when you actually meet them, or even when you hear their voices on the telephone. And yet this is the generation that is tomorrow's Tory leadership! Clearly that leadership is going to represent no change from the present one.

The flabby reaction of Tory students and dons aside, we should have a right to expect that government — especially when it is a Tory one — would intervene to ensure that this campus hooliganism was firmly stamped upon and free debate maintained. Contemporary Tories are after all regularly making speeches about the need to defend our freedoms in the face of those who would destroy them. Yet what have they done in the face of this elimination of free speech in the universities and colleges? Precisely nothing!

Just the same petrified response can be seen in the face of street violence in the large urban areas now mainly occupied by Blacks. This violence increases in direct ratio to the demonstration of weakness displayed in dealing with it, and this weakness has been clearly manifest in the directions given by the Home Office to chief constables all around the country in the way of guidance on how to avoid race conflict.

After the Brixton rioting in 1981, the Tory government commissioned Lord Chief Justice Scarman to produce a report, afterwards known as the Scarman Report, dealing with the causes of the riot and making recommendations as to how such trouble may be prevented in the future. As everyone knows, the Scarman Report was a dripping wet 'liberal' apology for the rioters, and its recommendations included proposals of 'softly-softly' policing of black areas which virtually amounted to no policing at all. Whenever police received information about criminal activity in these areas, such as drug-peddling, any action the police took should put the considerations of 'community relations' (i.e. not upsetting the black population) before those of law-enforcement (i.e. apprehending and charging the criminals). If by a police operation in any such area a riot was likely to result, the operation should not take place — or at least it should be carried out in such a 'low-profile' manner as greatly to impair its effectiveness.

Quite clearly, the government made the decision to put the recommendations of the Scarman Report into practice, as following its publication complaints began to come in from police officers everywhere that they were being hamstrung in the fight against crime in black areas by directives from above that were obviously influenced by considerations of politics. The government was determined at all costs to avoid rioting: it was petrified of violence on the streets, particularly violence by Blacks (which, among other things, would reflect yet further discredit on the policy of multi-racialism). To avoid such violence, the government was in effect telling the police to turn a blind eye, at times, to crime, including drug-pushing — and at the very time when Tory politicians were making public speeches about the urgency of tackling the drug problem!

All this, it must be remembered, happened under a **Conservative** government. The question must be asked: why did this government, which must have known what sort of a person Lord Scarman was, appoint him of all people to prepare the report and recommendations on the rioting — if not because the government knew that Scarman could be relied upon to produce exactly the kind of report it wanted, a report which would give the sanction of one of the nation's top legal figures to the policy of abdication from law-enforcement against Blacks, on which the government was set?

When the rioting occurred in 1980, 1981 and again in 1985, innocent people, including many old folk, lived in terror of the rioters. The protection of these people and their property should have been the government's first concern. With this in mind, it should have given the police the equipment and instructions to go in and deal with the trouble in the manner of an operation of war. This should have included the issue of firearms and the sanction to use them if necessary, in order to clear the streets and protect innocent lives. The government shirked this responsibility out of pure funk.

I have implied earlier that the Conservatives are the least honest among the established parties of today, and that is saying quite a lot! I say the least honest, not because Conservatives necessarily tell more lies day-to-day than their opponents, but because with Conservatism there is the biggest gulf between what the party is to its masses of supporters and what it is in its real political object-ives. Undoubtedly, a great many of the best elements of the British population, of all classes, vote Conservative at election times, year in, year out. What makes them do so? Can we put it down to the Tory art of bamboozlement? To a great extent we can, but that does not explain all. We need to go a little more deeply into the philosophy of modern Conservatism to study its political appeal.

To begin with, there is probably something of the natural conservative (note the small 'c') in most of us. I can certainly feel it in myself, although I have always had the deepest contempt for the Tory Party. We see change in the world all about us, and nearly all of it is for the worse. It is all too easy to deduce from this — if we are not given to thinking deeply about political questions — that radical reform is undesirable, that we should seek to make what improvements are needed in society by making better use of existing institutions rather than replacing those with new instit-utions. That feeling is strengthened when we see that all political forces on the immediate horizon which postulate great and radical reform, i.e. the forces of the left, represent a concept of the world that is repulsive to us in almost every aspect. That our society should be defended against these forces is a quite natural reaction, and this only too often sends people scurrying into the arms of those who seem to offer the most readily available line of defence, in other words Conservatives.

Yet the truth is that Conservatism offers no effective line of defence at all. It is a line of defence that has been in continual retreat for many decades. Seemingly in accord with the idea that, if you can't beat them, join them, the only response of Conservat-ism to the rampages of the left has been to fall in with much of the left's own thinking and adopt, under suitable guises, many of its ideological positions.

The French and Russian revolutions were undoubtedly retrograde steps in history, as was the English Revolution which preceded them. But this cannot hide the fact that in all the societies existing before these revolutions there were monumental weaknesses, all the product of ruling classes that were without vigour and were destined, by inexorable historical laws, to be overthown and replaced. Indeed the very fact that all those revolutions became possible is a testimony to the state of national decay that preceded them. In the cases of the French and Russian revolutions particularly, some massive intellectual disorder had to exist among large portions of the 'educated' sections of the population for the infantile doctrines of jacobinism and bolshevism to have such a strong appeal. That those disorders came about is a testimony to the truth that the old societies in those countries were exhausted and their rulers no longer fit for leadership.

In just the same way, the almost continual drift leftwards in British affairs over the past three-quarters of a century (a drift leftwards that has not abated in the times of 'Conservative' governments) could not have occurred unless the old society was rotten and ripe for extinction, and unless those who represented the forces of tradition in politics had clearly failed to address themselves effectively to the great problems that the 20th century has thrown up.

When I speak of the old society being 'rotten', I should hasten to add that that does not mean rotten in every aspect, that none of the old institutions and traditions are worth preserving, that every single vestige of the old order needs to be swept away; I mean rotten in the sense that the essential ingredients of effective rule have disappeared: a vigorous and intelligent ruling *elite*; political institutions that would enable such an *elite* to rule properly; a healthy cultural and intellectual climate, giving rise to a firm consensus among the educated classes conducive to the policies necessary for national success and power. If any or all of these things are lacking in a nation, that nation is headed for trouble.

In the Imperial Russia preceding the revolution of 1917, by no means all the institutions of the state were bad. National finances were on a sound footing. Fast progress in industrial development had been made in the previous two decades (in fact much faster than in the following two decades of communism). Positions of rank in politics, the professions and the forces were no longer denied to people of humble birth but, on the contrary, were being awarded increasingly on the basis of merit. Education was being extended universally by leaps and bounds.

The thing that was most glaringly lacking was a strong ruling class with an adequate sense of the duty of its position and with a firm will-to-power. The ruling class that existed was small (in relation to the size of the country) and far too great a portion of it was sunk in excessive luxury, decadence and the pursuit of pleasure. Contrary to popular supposition, it was far too indulgent with its enemies, dispatching them to a comfortable exile in Siberia from where they could continue to organise their revolutionary forces by proxy and from which they could far too easily escape. Czarism in fact fell, not by being too ruthless, but by being nowhere near ruthless enough. At the same time it failed to prevent a large portion of its intellectual classes being radicalised because it offered no dynamic alternative to the subversive doctrines of the left.

It finally collapsed when, as has happened to exhausted ruling regimes before and since, it embarked on a disastrous war declared in pursuit of no vital national interest and fought with armed forces hopelessly inadequate to the task.

Britain's ruling classes reveal all the symptoms of exhaustion shown by those of pre-revolutionary Russia, while her political institutions are far more diseased than those of the latter. Both are bound to give way to new forces; the only question to be decided is: which forces?

The conservative position is a tenable one when the ruling class, institutions and national consensus of a country are basically sound and that country is, notwithstanding occasional difficulties — even crises, set on a healthy course of development. But when difficulties and crises come in unending succession, irrespective of regular changes of government and the personages presiding over government, and where there is no forward pattern of national development but only continual national contraction and retreat, and when furthermore there is not even a vigorous national consensus favourable to enlightened reform through existing institutions, such a conservative position becomes quite impossible to hold. The state has become like a rotten apple, riddled with maggots and impossible to save. All patriotic endeavour must be concentrated, not on preventing the death of the existing state, but on ensuring that when that inevitable death comes the new state to emerge out of it is of the right kind and in the right hands.

In America today, a fashionable theme with conservatives is the 'defence of the constitution', a cause which on face value might have some merit when it is seen that all recent and current attacks on that constitution come from the left. The question, however, must be asked: how can anything be defended which cannot defend itself, as the US constitution quite clearly cannot — since the attacks on it have been overwhelmingly successful? If that constitution were adequate, a national condition would have been created which would render impossible the subversion that has occurred. Indeed it might be argued that the very weakness of such a constitution is the main ally of those bent on subversion of the state.

Although the word 'constitution' is not so much in vogue in Britain as to form part of a political slogan, the situation is not far different. Conservatives want to defend established institutions against subversion from the left, but they have completely failed to do so, partially because of their lack of will to defend anything, but also partly because those very institutions are themselves hopelessly indefensible. If it were otherwise, the left would not have made the inroads into them that it has.

Tories rail against the lunatic leftism that now manifests itself on numerous city and borough councils, a few examples of which have been given in the previous chapter, but they defend the political system that has allowed the lunatics to get a foothold. It is exactly the same with the red take-over of the universities and schools.

As these words are prepared for the printer, Britain has experienced nine years of Tory government. During that time much has happened in the country giving rise to Tory anger. But at the end of the day it has to be said to these indignant Conservatives: Your party is the party of government — what has that government done about it?

In fact, Conservatism as it is in Britain today, far from doing anything to halt the march of the left, is the left's best recruiting officer. By its hopeless failure to offer millions of our people the prospect of work, economic improvement and, above all, any great and dynamic vision of the nation's future worth striving for, it drives millions into the arms of socialism and the political mafia that controls it. Indeed, for a party that seems only capable of understanding national sickness in economic terms, the Tories have made a spectacular failure of every prescription they have offered for economic recovery.

It is therefore a totally unrealistic proposition to suggest that

Britain can be rescued from her present plight by the purely defensive and rearguard measure of 'conserving' our society from the marauding onslaughts of the radical left. It is far too late for that. The reality is that there is little left to conserve, and nothing at all to conserve in respect of workable political institutions. All of those have been discredited by their manifest failure and by the fact that they have given way, one-by-one, before the rampages of their enemies.

Indeed it is pertinent to ask: can the left really regard itself as being the enemy of our ancient institutions at all, seeing that it has found those institutions so easy to conquer — just as it has found the nation likewise?

If we are to find one more feature of Conservatism that is attractive to many, it is the Tory concept of individual independence and self-reliance, which is often contrasted with that of a state which looks after the individual from the cradle to the grave and thus absolves him from the responsibility to help himself. Certainly, if we judge this issue by the kind of state that has come about as a result of the influence of left-wing ideology, there would seem to be some substance in this belief. Beyond any doubt, there has been a marked decline in the national character as a result of the increasing softening of life in Britain in recent times. To the extent that this softening is a product of an over-indulgent welfare state, the Tory appeal to the spirit of self-reliance strikes a sympathetic chord with many.

There is a danger, however, that we can get carried away with this idea to the point of gross over-simplification. No rational person would dispute that self-reliance is a fine ideal. But there are certain practical limits to its application which Tories are unwilling to recognise. When a quarter of the population in a given area is unemployed, due to the closure of that area's most basic industry, and little alternative work is in the offing, it is no good going to the redundant workers in that area and telling them that they should survive just by being 'self-reliant'. Just a few may be able to do so by going into business on their own, and I have earlier given one example of this. A few more may be able to obtain alternative employment by making exceptional efforts to acquire the tiny number of other jobs going in the area. Then a few more may get work by moving to another area. But there is no possibility whatever that the mass of the unemployed population can, just through 'self-reliance', get by.

The Tory mentality seems to be that it is a fine thing to make of the nation a place where there are large stretches of economic wasteland, and then preach to people that they should demonstrate their 'self-reliance' by negotiating their way through that wasteland to survival. That doctrine will not produce a sturdy population, only an embittered and chronically divided one.

As I shall outline in detail in a later chapter, the first priority is to ensure, by sound economic policies, that in every area there are work opportunities for all who wish to work. Then, and only then, will be the time to speak of the virtues of self-reliance, and to set about penalising those who seek to milk the welfare system by 'dodging the column'.

Even that, however, is not the whole solution to the problem. The spirit of self-reliance comes with **pride**, and pride comes with a healthy moral outlook. Contemporary Britain is hopelessly lacking in any kind of moral leadership — and I do not just mean in the religious sense of the term or indeed in observance of the 'Ten Commandments'. We have entirely lost sight of the principle that it is the duty of a nation's rulers to set a moral tone in the way of promoting the virtues of good citizenship — in the first place by personal example. Political leaders today seem frightened of venturing into the realm of individual morality and private behaviour, no doubt in large part because their own lives in many cases would not stand up well to any kind of scrutiny. The result is complete moral anarchy.

The 'free market' society favoured by the Tories is very largely contributive to this. The principle of this society is that 'market forces' should be allowed to rule. If these market forces establish a large demand for any kind of product, no matter how trashy and worthless, whoever can supply that product will make an easy million. As a result of this, we have a situation in which a homosexual pop-singer who is also a drug-addict can be earning a great deal more money than a leading heart surgeon, an outstanding inventor or the managing director of a highly successful manufacturing company. Into the bargain, our junkie pervert will very likely find himself co-opted onto the new year's honours list on the grounds that he is helping the nation's export trade! Alternatively, some utterly worthless individual may make many thousands selling his or her story to some sensation-mongering newspaper. The only qualification here is that the story is sufficiently spiced with salacious details of the writer's or someone else's sex life. Indeed the more despicable worm the writer is, the more likely the public is to pay to read what has been written.

Again, the 'market' can make fortunes for the trash of society —
they have something to sell, and there are more than enough mugs
who will buy it!

When human flotsam of this kind can so easily find their way to
riches, and far worthier contributers to society have to work
extremely hard for a fraction of the same reward, is it any wonder
that there are a great many people in the country who feel bound
by no ethics whatsoever in the rush to grab what they can for
themselves and in any way they can? Why should Joe Blow,
unemployed refrigerator salesman, put himself to great trouble to
get another job when fortunes can be made by the kinds of people I
have just described? If the state has to keep people like him in
idleness, that is no more wrong than for those social parasites to be
driving about in Rolls Royces and living in stately homes!

Conservatism, like socialism, has completely failed to build a
society in Britain in which financial reward is in some way
commensurate with the value of the contribution that the individual makes towards the nation's life. Yet only when such a society
is achieved can we hope to have a social and moral order that can
command popular respect.

To summarise, a community of self-reliant people is an
admirable ideal, but two essential preconditions must exist before
we can achieve it. Firstly, we must make work available for all
who want it, for only then can we sift out the truly workshy and
penalise them accordingly. Secondly, we must build a society
governed by certain firm moral principles, of which personal
pride is among the most important. Conservatism offers no
prospect of either of these things, and indeed its market place
philosophy ensures that society's rewards will continue to go
largely to society's most worthless elements. Conservatism talks
of a 'meritocracy' but can only achieve an undeserving pluto-
cracy.

Notwithstanding the barrenness of Conservatism as a political
creed, and notwithstanding the gigantic yellow streak that distinguishes the party and most of its leading representatives, there is
nonetheless one factor remaining that still exercises a pull towards
it upon some people with good intentions. This is the belief that
the Conservative Party, with all its weaknesses, may through the
endeavours of folk of the right kind be turned into something
better. To this purpose, a very large portion of those individuals
needed to form the vanguard of a movement of national resurgence remain with the Tories and are thus effectively neutralised,

though they themselves may be unaware of the fact.

The reasons for this choice of strategy are not difficult to ascertain, and some of them may be found in the experiences related in this book. The struggle to promote and build the movement to which my friends and I are dedicated is an immense one, and cannot be won without great sacrifices, punctuated by hard setbacks, and sustained over a considerable period of time. The might of an entire establishment is against us, placing continual obstacles in our path which can only be overcome with patience and by titanic effort.

Great is the temptation, then, to grasp at more facile solutions, affording to the individual the eased conscience that comes of 'doing something', while not subjecting him to the rigorous battle conditions of active nationalism.

Allied to this attraction is the one of being close to the scene of 'power'. By keeping his nose clean, the Tory Party worker may get himself adopted as a candidate for his local council, even for parliament. If he can get elected, he hopes, he may be able to exert some influence, however limited, on the course of events — all of which seems to him more rewarding than the long fight in the cold wilderness for much more distant political goals.

I should not need to say that this approach to politics is based on a pathetic delusion. For many decades people have been staying in the Tory Party, though thoroughly disenchanted with its leadership and policies, in the hope that they might set it in a different direction. They have continually failed. They seem incapable of understanding that they are up against an establishment far too strongly entrenched for them to have a hope of defeating it by those means. This establishment indeed only tolerates them in the party as long as their efforts to reform it are totally ineffectual. The moment that there appears any possibility that an organised group within the party may begin to influence any significant number of members away from the soggy, liberal, internationalist doctrines that have ruled it for at least the past half-century, that group will immediately be neutralised by pressure from Central Office — pressure which indeed seldom has to be exerted very much, such is the spirit of cowardice that reigns throughout. This happened with the Monday Club in the 1970s, as soon as it began to look as if it was recruiting a body of people with genuinely patriotic intentions.

Of course it is to the advantage of the Tory Party to retain at all times some sort of 'right-wing' pressure group. This keeps in the party fold numerous people who would otherwise desert it and work against it from the outside. If such a pressure group did not form of its own accord, it would have to invented by Central Office — and almost certainly at times has been! A safety valve must exist in the party, and it is always in the party rulers' interest to tolerate it, or indeed provide it themselves if need be. It is useful so long as it keeps people comforted in the illusion that they may one day see their influence prevail. It must be stamped on the moment there appears a possibility that this may happen.

The spirit of cowardice in the party that I have indicated before always guarantees that this task will not be too difficult. Few Tories, even of the more sensible kind, are made of the stuff of which great movements of historical change are formed. They are generally a soft lot, and can with little difficulty be brought into line with threats of media exposure, combined with hints of career promotion if they knuckle under.

One TV investigative programme made in 1983 referred to some of these Tory 'right-wingers' as 'Maggie's Militant Tendency'. The appellation was laughable: these people could not be militant if they had sticks of dynamite tied to their backs.

In the programme, allegations were made against a number of Tories, including some MPs, that they had had connections with 'racist' organisations and that in fact they themselves harboured 'racist' inclinations. Had the individuals in question been **men** with an ounce of backbone to their characters, they would have turned on the programme-makers and said: "Yes, if wanting to protect our country from a foreign invasion and to preserve its traditional ethnic character means being 'racist', then you can call us racist if you like." But no! Instead of such a forthright defence, there was a series of cringing disavowals and *mea non culpas*, culminating in a court action against the BBC programme team in which one MP actually broke down and cried — yes, **cried**! — in the witness box on account of the accusations that had been made against him.

The whole strategy of working for improvement in national affairs within the Tory Party is anyway a completely inadequate one. It does not range beyond the application of mere local anaesthetics to our national ills, Nothing is more futile than small groups of people trying, by softly-softly methods, to slow down (for that is all it is) the process of national disintegration wrought by a political system that is diseased and rotten from head to toe. They may as well stand on the beach and, with the aid of teacups, attempt to throw the tide back.

And even in the event of the thousand-to-one chance that such people could capture the Conservative Party, where would that leave them with regard to capturing the nation? If we draw an imaginary line from the Severn to the Wash, and look at the huge portion of the United Kingdom north and west of that line, we will find that we are beholding what has become a desert in terms of Tory support. There are tens of millions of people in that area who will never vote for that party, whatever forms of persuasion may be employed to induce them to do so. And yet those millions are vitally needed in any movement that is going to succeed in bringing about real national recovery.

This national recovery, far from being possible by means of any reform of Conservatism, can only come about through the political demise of Conservatism. The Conservative Party ties up in a dead end many of the people whose support is so necessary to the patriotic cause. If it went into oblivion, these elements could be harnessed together with the healthy elements from the ranks of socialism (and there are plenty of them) in a true union of the British people dedicated to the building of a new nation.

But Toryism, far from being a movement of national union, is capable only of fostering national division. In addition to this, it is totally lacking in any great or inspiring ideals. Its product — as I sensed as a politically green teenager many years ago and have seen amply confirmed ever since — is a mean, selfish and materialistic society, dedicated only to the pursuit of individual gain.

Tories ceaselessly protest about the barminess of the left. But they defend the political system that has been the left's gateway to power. They drive people towards the left by the poverty of their own economics and the shoddiness of their own politics. And they run like petrified rabbits from the anger of any leftist mob.

Conservatism is the last gasp of a world that is dying. It has surrendered every bastion of defence of that world, to the stage at which there are no more left. All that it has succeeded in conserving is putrid and decayed. All that it might usefully have conserved it has sold off. We leave it, floating like a rotting corpse on the stagnant waters of an historical epoch that has come to the end of its time.

178

Chapter 9
Years of political apprenticeship

In a previous chapter, I have described how I reached the
decision to devote my life to political work. I started, as I have
related, by enlisting as a member of the League of Empire·
Loyalists. This was the beginning of a period of activity lasting
about 10 years during which I made many mistakes and at the end
of which I had to acknowledge to myself that little had been
achieved by all this effort, apart from a series of lessons in the do's
and don'ts of politics, as a result of which I had become something
of a wiser person and therefore better able to put the future years to
good effect. At the same time, I was able during this period to
develop certain capabilities which were to stand me in good stead
later. I have mentioned public speaking. There was also writing,
which combined, as I went on, with experience in the techniques
of production of printed material. During these years I founded
my own small publishing concern and launched the journal
Spearhead, which became possibly the most successful patriotic
periodical in post-war Britain. I also gained practice at organising
and personnel management. I became thoroughly acquainted with
the multitude of practical problems involved in building and
promoting patriotic organisations on the proverbial shoestring
budget, as was always our lot.

Indeed, it was a revelation to me during these years how poorly
financed the patriotic cause always was, by comparison with its
opponents on the left. It is a popular myth among left-wingers that
'our side' is heavily subsidised by big business, while its own
cause draws its support primarily from the ranks of the poor and
the downtrodden. My experience soon told me that the very
reverse is the case. Those who control the main sources from
which money is channelled into political organisations are solidly
opposed to our movement and all it represents, while at the same
time they are far from averse to bestowing generous benefactions
on the so-called 'radical' left.

Among the many lessons that I learned in these years was the futility of splintering — and in the best way possible: by being involved in that practice myself. One of the characteristic features of those years was the bewildering succession of organisations that came and went, due to the tendency of their chief operatives frequently to fall out, and then feel bound to formalise their quarrels by fragmenting their already tiny organisations into even tinier ones. All this was the product of a certain immaturity of character, combined with an inability to see the greater picture and take what I might describe as the 'big view'. I will freely acknowledge that I was not without guilt myself in this respect during those earlier years. I was young and headstrong and had an awful lot to learn.

It seems to me that there is no crime in going through these foolish phases in one's youthful years. The crime lies in not growing out of them at the age when one might properly be expected to do so. Some people never seem capable of this, but continue as political adolescents till the time comes to collect their pension.

Some of my mistakes during this time were made partly as a result of the persuasion of others. In stating this, however, I should make it clear that in each such case the responsibility was mine and mine alone. I was not forced to act as I did; I was a free agent. Mine was the error. If I listened to unwise counsel, I had only myself to blame.

It was also during these years that I came to know something of the human resources available to the patriotic movement. In that movement I met some very fine people whom I became proud to call my friends. It would also only be honest to say that I met some others of much less admirable character. I learned in time that an unfortunately high proportion of those who push themselves forward to senior positions in political organisations are motivated by nothing as strongly as personal egotism. To many of these people, a position in a political group (however tin-pot it may be) was compensation for personal failure in the big wide world outside and an opportunity to obtain station and rank that they could never achieve in any normal occupation. I learned eventually to recognise those in whom these drives were uppermost and to tell them apart from those moved by a genuine sense of vocation and responsibility. I also developed the faculty — vitally important in any great endeavour — of distinguishing those who will enter into argument and controversy out of sincere conviction and those who do so merely because they have axes to grind, and are interested in creating divisions out of which they may themselves profit by removing from the scene those whom they see as rivals. The former will always express their disagreements with you honestly and face-to-face, so that then there can be a constructive discussion of the subject, usually ending in an amicable solution. The latter will never act in this way, but are only happy in an atmosphere of intrigue and plotting in which frank argument is always avoided. It was very necessary for me to learn to identify these characters, as I did in those years of apprenticeship, so as to prepare myself for those contingencies in the future when I found myself embroiled in political warfare.

Eventually I became convinced that much of this warfare between people who are supposed to serve the same cause is generated by our opponents, who are not above placing their agents in our ranks specifically with the purpose of promoting quarrels and splits in pursuit of the strategy of 'divide-and-conquer'.

I entered the political fray in the middle-to-late 1950s, being confident that there would be a fully adequate supply of people of outstanding ability to give leadership to the patriotic movement. It was not long before I realised that this expectation had been, to say the least, naive, and that the number of those of the calibre for this task was extremely small. It was not until this realisation dawned that I began to consider any role for myself in the movement beyond that of rank-and-file disciple and follower.

It is very rarely in this world that we encounter people of truly outstanding talent who are at the same time totally indifferent to questions of personal reward or the approval and applause of their contemporaries, and who are prepared to apply their great capabilities to working for aims that may take many years to come to fruition, during which time they are likely to be condemned to a position on the outer fringes of society — prophets without honour, as it were, until some destined cataclysm, which they among very few have foreseen, arrives and justifies their warnings, at the same time turning upside down the criteria by which human worth is judged and thereby transforming them from pariahs into popular heroes.

So it will happen that the brightest talents of any age will usually direct themselves along very conventional paths, where the greatest accolades and rewards may be won. For this reason, a reforming movement which hurls its challenge against the contemporary world long before that world is ready to understand it is doomed, at least in its growing stages, to attract only a very small number of people of exceptional ability. Later of course, when that movement has gathered momentum and can offer lucrative posts and careers, the pool of talent placed at its disposal will greatly increase, as the bright stars in the national galaxy will feel ready to jump onto the train that other, more intrepid, spirits have set into motion. Of course it would be impractical not to welcome these latecomers, but it is important while harnessing their gifts not to give them the power that belongs by natural right to those who gave birth to the idea and whose pioneer work nursed it through infancy until it was strong enough to generate its own development. Later I will return to this theme because it is vitally important. Suffice it to mention it here because it is part of a fundamental law of selection that I discovered early on in my introduction to politics. At first it caused me concern, but later I came to accept it as sound and natural.

At any rate, it was on discovering how few were qualified for leadership of the movement I had joined that I first began to see my own political involvement as a true vocation. It was then that I thoroughly set about educating and training myself with a view to taking, in the years ahead, a major share of responsibility in the struggle.

I have said that I joined the LEL with the idea that out of it something better might come. I was impatient and I wanted the League to assume the role of a fully-fledged political party. In its function as a mere pressure group I saw little future, because it was quite clear that the opinion it sought to change — which basically was Conservative opinion — would not be changed. I did not see eye-to-eye with A.K. Chesterton on this matter, much though I respected him as a writer and observer of national and international affairs. A clash was inevitable.

In the course of my activities with the League, I came to meet John Bean, who was nearer to my generation although a few years older than me. Our talks established that we had much in common, particularly the idea that a political party should be formed. JB had a number of contacts from which he believed that a circle of people could be formed that would render such a venture possible, and I was persuaded by him to support it. Very naively, I did not believe that such a party would be in conflict with the League and that, by participating in it and urging others to do likewise, I would be guilty of an act of disloyalty to the group to which I already belonged. Of course, I was wrong, and at the first sign of moves on my part in the direction of the new venture I was quite rightly expelled from the League by A.K. Chesterton. Upon this, I partook, with John Bean and others, in the formation of the National Labour Party, with Bean as leader.

The thinking behind this choice of name was mainly Bean's, but I did not oppose it. We had despaired of trying to appeal to people of Tory bent and there was a feeling that the message should now be pitched in another direction. A vast number of people support Labour who are not natural leftists. Bean's reasoning was that we should break new ground in trying to reach these people with an image and a programme that were radical in scope, combining nationalism with a kind of popular socialism, shorn of left-wing ideology.

The National Labour Party, beginning in 1958, had a career of two years, during which it recruited about 500-600 members. I was active on its behalf, while preferring not to occupy a major position. I did not consider I was yet qualified for the latter and beside my activities wished to have time to continue my political education with much private reading. I realised then that the NLP was before its time and that what it could achieve in a period like the 1950s was limited. I nevertheless thought it a step in the right direction and was willing to be associated with it, though not in the way of too heavy a commitment.

At about the same time another organisation had come into being. This was the White Defence League. The WDL was not a party but a pressure group, like the LEL, and had been formed solely for the purpose of opposing coloured immigration, by the late 1950s beginning to become a very real national problem. The WDL was headed by Colin Jordan. It was smaller in size than the National Labour Party but had the advantage over the latter of possessing a headquarters building, a shop premises in Princedale Road, London W.11. In 1960 the two organisations, recognising that they were on parallel paths, began discussions towards a merger of forces, which took place during that year with the formation of the British National Party, under Jordan as leader and Bean as his deputy. This party had no connection with the party of the same name that I now lead, except that it might be numbered among the several ancestors of the latter. The identity of title is purely coincidental.

I gave my support to the new formation with the same reservations as I had done with the NLP earlier, and became a fairly active member. During this and the NLP phase preceding it I had continued to do quite a lot of public speaking, mainly out of doors and at impromptu meetings of the 'soapbox' variety. One meeting, however, did become a fixture: this was in a street adjoining London's Earls Court Road, where we appeared every Wednesday evening for a time. As our political opponents got to know about our scheduled appearances, they regularly turned up to heckle and chant abuse. This all provided good training for the speakers, including myself. But sometimes the opposition went beyond the merely vocal, and there were scuffles. It was out of this that there began the series of encounters with the law that have punctuated my political life and out of which my opponents have done their best to make capital. When our meetings were attacked, we defended them. That may seem a highly peculiar, not to say provocative, reaction to people accustomed to the idea that the best response to left-wing rowdyism is to run away from it. But defend our meetings was what we did. We knew that these meetings were effectively under attack the moment that chanting by our opponents reached the point at which the speaker's voice was drowned, for thereafter the meeting could not effectively continue. This was my introduction to a familiar technique of the political left, of which I will have more to say later.

On one occasion at Earls Court a colleague of mine was trying to speak and I was among those surrounding the platform protecting him. An aggressive individual at the front of the crowd was one of several who were trying to shout him down, and he was having great difficulty being heard. I went up to this fellow and asked him to keep quiet. After he had refused, I repeated the request, this time in a less polite tone. Upon this, he became even more aggressive and took a lunge at me. In self-defence, I went to hit him back and was immediately seized by two large police constables and carted away to a police van. On the way I was held by a grip on my collar which was causing a feeling of strangulation. While not attempting in any way to resist arrest, I tried to ease this grip so as to avoid the discomfort to my neck. As I did so, my arm — so I was later told — caught one of the constables. In the event, I was charged, not only with disorderly conduct in connection with the encounter with the opponent, but also with assault on a police officer!

In court I pleaded that, if my arm struck the officer, it was not intentional, and I explained the circumstances. The magistrate seemed to accept this and to understand that the 'assault' had been purely technical, for he let me off with a very light fine. The conviction stood, however, and has remained on my record. In view of the small size of the fine, I did not appeal. I should have done, of course. I have always preached, and tried to practise, the rule that political activists should not try to prevent the police doing their job, and it goes against the grain that I still have this conviction against me for something that is contrary to my whole approach to politics. Had I been a little older and wiser, I would have seen the good sense in trying to get this conviction quashed, whatever the cost. Later when that thought occurred to me it was of course too late.

As our small movement began to make a bit of an impact, opposition to it built up and started to become more unpleasant. This opposition never came from the ordinary British public, which reacted to us at our meetings with much sympathy although with a great deal of apathy. Our opponents consisted of members of left-wing political groups and also organised Jewish bodies, such as Mosley had encountered earlier. In fact up to that time we had said very little on the Jewish question but had concentrated mainly on opposing the new presence in Britain of West Indian and Asian immigrants. What we learned from this was that, as soon as anyone takes a stand against the intrusion of these new arrivals, the Jewish community — or at least its most politically active members — will tend to line up on the side of the latter. I have remarked earlier that many Jews take an ambiguous position on 'racism', condemning it in others but being only too willing to practise it themselves.

Against this build-up of violent opposition, some of us began to feel that we would need to take firmer measures to ensure our own defence and safety, and the idea began to form of a disciplined body of men who would undertake this task as a special function within the party. Upon the decision of Colin Jordan, this body was formed. I was one of those who endorsed the decision and I indicated my willingness to take part in the project.

We were aware of course of the provisions of the Public Order Act of 1936, which made it a punishable offence to take part in any body of people which was "organised, trained or equipped to use physical force in the promotion of a political object." We believed at the time, however, that this law was only applicable to the use of physical force in the **offensive** sense, and that it would not be used against us as long as our activities could be seen as only a preparation for self-defence against offensive action by others. We were to prove wrong, and in the process I learned something as to the real purpose of this legislation, introduced in the 1930s on the pretext of preserving public order, and later updated in 1986. But more of that anon.

The development of this self-defence force caused a great deal of dissension in the BNP. Jordan was for it and he was leader. Bean was against it and so was the party's president Andrew Fountaine. A not inconsiderable body of members backed Bean and Fountaine on the matter.

I came to see later in retrospect that it would have been better if this special group had not been formed. Regardless of its theoretical merits, if it had a strongly divisive effect within the party this was good enough reason for abandoning it. I could not admire, however, the methods used by its opponents in the internal feud that ensued.

What they should have done was call a meeting of all concerned persons on both sides and thrash the issue out in the open, stating frankly that this project for the formation of the defence body was unacceptable, and that they would feel obliged to part company with us if we were insistent on continuing with it. In this case, I would have regretted their attitude but accepted the shelving of the project as being preferable to a party split. The party could then have carried on, albeit with a few ruffled feathers here and there which we all have to put up with from time to time.

But this was not what was done. Instead of an open confrontation, there was a sly little plot hatched by means of which a meeting of the party's council was convened without Jordan, its leader, even being informed about it! At the meeting the decision was taken to 'expel' Jordan, me and other members prominently associated with the defence group. The members' files were stolen and removed to a place outside Jordan's reach, and the members were then circularised with a bulletin explaining what had happened, but without Jordan and his supporters being able to reach those members on their own behalf and give their version of events. Jordan, I and others were 'expelled' from the party without even being given the chance to testify in our own defence. This was in the spring of 1962.

I relate this little episode, not because it is itself of any great importance — it features only minutely in the history of the patriotic movement in the time that I have been connected with it — but because it was indicative of a tendency that I have described earlier in this chapter and which was to repeat itself in later years:

the unwillingness to thrash out differences in honest argument and the preference for shady plotting and secret meetings, to which those who might disagree are conveniently not invited. This tendency has been a curse to our movement over the past two or three decades.

In fairness to those responsible for this particular plot, it should be said that perhaps they sincerely thought that what they were doing was in the best interests of the cause, just as I had thought that way a few years earlier when, unbeknown to A.K. Chesterton, I had tried to persuade members of the LEL to support what would have been, in effect, a rival organisation. I was wrong then, and this BNP faction was wrong later. Distrust and division are always sown when things are not done completely in the open.

Colin Jordan and his followers, including me, considered whether to contest this act of 'expulsion' — which we would have been in a strong position to do in a court of law, had we tried — or to accept it as a *fait accomplit* and begin anew. On Jordan's recommendation, we did the latter. Discussions then began on the setting up of an entirely new political organisation, with a name that would distinguish it clearly from the one with which we had just parted company. It was at this point that another decision was made which I later came to recognise as a profound mistake. It was proposed by Colin Jordan that we call our new group the 'National Socialist Movement', taking that name directly from the Hitler party in Germany, together with a programme that in all essential respects was the same.

I have already made it clear earlier in this book that some years before this time I had come to view Hitler and his movement in a vastly different light to that in which they had been portrayed by orthodox historians and propagandists, having satisfied myself that many of the claims made against them were based on fabrication, put out in an attempt to justify a disastrous war in which Britain was the loser to a degree equal to Germany. Having made a thorough study of the forces dedicated to destroying my own country, and knowing that Hitler faced very similar forces in his, I have come to believe that many of his intentions were good ones and many of his achievements admirable. I do not propose to budge from that point of view, because to do so would be to be guilty of a dishonesty which I thoroughly despise in politicians. Of this dishonesty we have had far too much. If truth be known, there are probably millions of people in the world today, including many who gave their best years fighting Hitler, who now feel in their bones that in a great many respects he was right; they simply believe (and not without good reason) that it is not yet expedient or safe to state such views openly. But times will change, and yesterday's heresy will become tomorrow's truth.

But that does not mean that it is right for a British movement belonging to an entirely different phase of history to model itself on the movement of Hitler to the extent of adopting identical nomenclature and symbolism and acknowledging itself as being in direct line of descent. We are a different country, with our own proud past and traditions, and these — not the traditions of foreigners — should be our source of inspiration. We may indeed study reforming movements in all parts of the world and at all junctures of history, and learn something from their achievements as well as from their mistakes. But nothing in history ever repeats itself exactly. There was only one Hitler and only one National Socialism. They belonged to Germany between 1919 and 1945. Our task in this age is to build a 100 per-cent British movement that is its own original, not a photo-copy of another.

I had something of this feeling at the time that the events of 1962 took place, but with nothing like the strength and certainty that I later came to have it. I had just lived through a split and did not want a further one. I submerged my misgivings and went along with the scheme. I should not have done, and the decision to do so was my fault. As I have said earlier, I was a free agent; no-one forced me. My opponents of today of course like to make a big meal out of this episode in my political life. Well, let them. I have a clear conscience about it, and I would put the question to those who hold the episode against me: can you name any man who has undertaken any big task in this world who has not made some mistakes on the way? I was 28 years old at the time and still had a lot to learn. One of the things I had not yet learned was: follow your instinct. My instinct told me that the step might prove to be unwise. I did not obey that instinct and, along with those others involved, I came a cropper. To this day, however, I maintain that when one sees one's nation and people in danger there is less dishonour in acting and acting wrongly than in not acting at all.

The National Socialist Movement enjoyed a career of about two years, during which it won national and world publicity out of all proportion to its size and importance. No doubt this was partly because to the press it had a certain 'horror' value, which is always good for circulation in an age when people buy newspapers more to be entertained than to inform themselves about important public matters. The movement attracted some people of serious political intent but it also recruited a good many oddballs of the kind who enjoy being unconventional for its own sake, and who in due course become just an embarrassment. We were portrayed as freaks, and to some extent it was freaks who became drawn to us, fascinated by our image as it was put across in the sensationalist newspapers rather than interested in us for what we were in reality.

During this period I had two further brushes with the law, and both were highly instructive. The first occurred as a result of a public meeting held by the NSM in Trafalgar Square in July 1962. One of the Jewish organisations referred to earlier sent along a large mob, whose intention clearly was to stop the meeting being held, and if possible to administer some physical injury to us in the process. This was one of my early lessons on the tendency of certain elements in the Jewish community to set themselves up as the arbiters of who may and who may not hold a political meeting in Great Britain. With our tiny number, there was no chance whatever that we could have resisted any attack by this mob had it not been for a very large police presence on the occasion.

At a certain point in the meeting the mob made their attempt to smash it up, and a large riot ensued. The police handled things with admirable efficiency and the peace was restored, allowing the meeting to proceed to its conclusion.

Following the meeting, prosecutions were taken out under the Public Order Act. And, believe it or not, the people prosecuted were not the instigators of the riot but **ourselves!** Colin Jordan and I were both charged with using words in our speeches that were construed as 'provoking' the disorder. We appeared in court and were given prison sentences, which in my case was later reduced on appeal to a fine.

No such prosecutions were taken out, as I have said, against the organisers of the riot, although a few arrested on the spot were given token fines for specific acts of disorder. We, in other words, were treated as the villains of the piece.

This episode led me to a serious study of the Public Order Act and to a realisation of what an infamous piece of legislation it is, both in its original conception and its subsequent application. The Act was introduced, as I have mentioned earlier, in 1936, and to deal with disorder of the kind attending the meetings and demonstrations held by Sir Oswald Mosley's British Union. These disorders were, on the admission of the police involved at the time, caused, without exception, by Mosley's opponents. Yet the principal thrust of the act was to penalise, not those who planned and promoted the disorder, but those who were its intended victims. Part of the Act forbids the wearing of uniforms in public places by any political organisation, this arising out of the use of such uniforms by Mosley's defence squads for the simple purpose of telling colleagues from opponents. The uniform had no part whatever in causing disorder but it did have some usefulness in enabling stewards at an event to thwart attempts at disorder, as it made them more of a disciplined and co-ordinated body. It has been claimed that the uniform caused disorder because it was a 'provocation', but this is nonsense; all the riots that led to the introduction of the Public Order Act were planned well in advance and would have taken place if those opposed by the rioters had been dressed as choirboys. The law against uniforms did nothing whatever to stop rioting but just made it more difficult for the would-be victims of rioting to organise themselves in effectively co-ordinated bodies for self-defence.

Another part of the Act I have referred to earlier. This contained the clause I have mentioned concerning groups "organised, trained or equipped for the use of physical force in the promotion of a political object." But in addition to this there was a supplementary clause stating that it would also be an offence if a body of people were "organised, trained or equipped **so as to cause reasonable apprehension** that it might use physical force in the promotion of a political object."

This meant of course that if they could not catch you doing a thing they could still prosecute and convict you just for looking as if you **might** be about to do it! The possibilities for abuse of such a law as this should hardly need spelling out. People can be convicted and punished, not for doing anything wrong at all, but merely on the supposition that they may in future **intend** doing it. Such a supposition, in cases where political undertones are involved, is bound to call into play pure personal prejudices based on people's political leanings and their views about the likely intentions of a defendant as these have been portrayed by propaganda.

What anyway constitutes "using physical force"? If a man discovers a burglar in his house and physically overpowers him, that is a use of force to which no reasonable person can object. The only reasonable context in which the law can be applied against people using force in a situation in which politics are involved is

where that force is used, as I have indicated before, offensively —
that is to say force is used to prevent someone exercising their
lawful political freedoms or rights. The law becomes an utter ass
when it is applied against those who are only defending their own
exercise of political freedoms or rights, or preparing themselves to
do so. This also makes a nonsense of a law which renders it illegal
to act "so as to cause reasonable apprehension" that one is going
to use physical force in the promotion of a political object, unless
it can be firmly established that that force will be of an offensive
nature.

Of course, if a political organisation is found in possession of a
store of guns or bombs it is reasonable to suppose that its intention
is to use force in the promotion of its political objectives —
certainly in the case of bombs anyway — but in that case there are
provisions of the law quite adequate to convict the people
concerned without it being necessary to invoke the Public Order
Act. If, on the other hand, a political group only gives evidence
that it is organised, trained or equipped so as to enable it to act in
self-defence in the event of an attack on its members or activities it
is surely monstrous to penalise it on that account. Reverting to the
case of the man who overpowers the burglar in his house, you may
as well say that it should be made an offence to keep in the house
any implement, such as a walking stick or fire poker, that may
assist him to do so — or even to partake in exercise so as to make
himself physically fit and thus more capable of dealing with such
an intruder! We are now of course into the realm of the utterly
ridiculous, but that is where things lead us once we adopt the
reasoning involved in the Public Order Act as it relates to such
situations.

The other main part of the Public Order Act deals with public
events, and here it makes it an offence to use words (whether from
the speaker's platform or elsewhere) that are "threatening,
abusive or insulting" in circumstances where a breach of the
peace might be occasioned. In effect, it has come to mean that if
those who are opposed to a public meeting organise a mob to go to
it to smash it up, anyone speaking at that meeting is banned by law
from saying anything that might be strongly displeasing to the
mob in question — and on the grounds that this may 'provoke' the
mob into some disorderly action. This reasoning is of course
thoroughly fallacious; as anyone knows who has the most
elementary knowledge of the mechanics of political violence, no
serious act of disorder at a political meeting is ever spontaneous; it

is always planned in advance, and is in no way 'provoked' by the sight of a uniform or banner or the sound of something said in a speech. Only the odd individual on such an occasion is stung into a violent reaction in these ways, never a mob.

The effect of this use of the law under the Public Order Act has been invariably to penalise people holding lawful meetings for trouble that other people create. If the purpose of the Public Order Act was to reduce disorder at political events, it has had precisely the opposite effect. If you know that by your going to a meeting of your opponents and causing a riot there is a very good chance that they, and not you, will be punished for what happens, there is obviously all the more inducement to you to do just that. This Act, introduced supposedly in the interests of public order, has in fact given the green light to those bent on public disorder.

This tendency is increased by another section of the Act, under which, in the event of an organisation planning to hold a march or public demonstration, and in the subsequent event of its opponents threatening an outbreak of disorder against it, that march or demonstration may be banned from taking place. Again, this legislation says to those who have no respect for the law: "Go ahead and threaten a riot against people you dislike, and the law will then oblige you by having their activity banned, even though it may be perfectly peaceful and lawful in intent!" Naturally, the mobsters of the far left have welcomed this anomaly of the law with open arms and have exploited it for all they are worth. I know of great numbers of perfectly lawful marches and other kinds of public demonstration which have been banned in this country merely on account of the threat by those opposed to them to turn up and attack them.

In fact, in Britain over the past half-century since the passing of the 1936 Public Order Act, many times more breaches of public order have been committed by left-wing organisations against patriotic groups than has happened in reverse. In fact the left has openly and insolently proclaimed, again and again, that the activities of the 'fascists' and 'nazis' (i.e. anyone who believes that Britons have a right to a country of their own) must be smashed by force, while no evidence exists of those who are opposed to the left making any such proclamation about the activities of the latter, or indeed putting such a policy into practice on any substantial scale. In at least 95 per-cent of cases where left-wing and patriotic groups have physically clashed it has been the result of the left attacking the patriots and not the other way round.

And yet, while there have been numerous cases of the leaders of patriotic groups being prosecuted under the Public Order Act, there has not, to my knowledge, been one single case of any leader of a left-wing group being hauled into court for planning or organising acts of disorder or even ''giving reasonable apprehension'' that they may be doing so. All prosecutions of left-wingers have been against those individuals caught in the act of disorder, never against those who have put them up to it.

The overwhelming impression that one gains of the Public Order Act is that it was introduced, and has subsequently been implemented, essentially with a view to curbing the rights of patriotic organisations, and not to the preserving of the public peace — something in which it has manifestly failed.

Shortly after penalising us in 1962 for a riot that our opponents caused, the powers-that-be struck again. This time we were prosecuted under the same Public Order Act for taking part in the special formation that we had organised for the purpose of our own physical self-defence — notwithstanding the evidence of the recent Trafalgar Square meeting that we had every good reason to anticipate situations in which such self-defence would be necessary! Colin Jordan and I were charged, along with two others, Denis Pirie and Roland Kerr-Ritchie. We four added up to not far short of half the entire strength of the organisation in which we were being prosecuted for taking part — which shows something of the laughable nature of the suggestions, made throughout the following trial, that we were a menace to public safety.

The trial took place at the Old Bailey and received big publicity. The jury threw out the first charge, that we were organised, trained or equipped for the purpose of using physical force in the promotion of a political object — it could hardly do otherwise, for the prosecution failed to produce a shred of evidence that we had used any such force. We were found guilty on the second charge, which was that our activties had been such as to cause ''reasonable apprehension'' that this might be our purpose. In other words, we were convicted, not on the basis of any proven facts, but purely on someone's supposition of what someone else might think!

People who are familiar with the forces at work in Britain which are described throughout this book will not be surprised to hear that there was no prosecution of the leaders of the Jewish organisation, by this time known openly as the '62 Group, which had promoted the riot in Trafalgar Square a short time earlier. India has its sacred cows, on which no hand of harm must ever be laid.

Britain is no different!

We all went to jail, Colin Jordan, as arch-villain, getting nine months, I, as villain number-two, getting six months and our two colleagues getting three months each. So in October 1962 I found myself on the wrong side of the high wall that surrounds Wormwood Scrubs Prison in West London. CJ was with me for about a month, after which we were split up, my being sent to Stafford Prison in the West Midlands and he to Springhill Open Prison in Buckinghamshire.

My stay at Stafford was not a long one. Our case had received, as I have said, a lot of publicity, and of course there were people on the inside of prison who were only too eager to inflict harm on us. At Wormwood Scrubs we had always walked the exercise yard together, and this safety of numbers, combined with the fact that neither of us was a seven-stone weakling, seemed to be sufficient to discourage trouble. At Stafford I was on my own. Soon after I arrived, someone approached me from the rear on exercise and delivered me a blow on the head. It was not hard and I suffered no injury, but I lost my bearings for just long enough for my assailant to disappear into the crowd before I could identify him — the fellow being such a big, brave warrior of course that he took great care to approach me from a position where I did not see him coming.

Within a day of this incident I was lying on my bed in my cell with the door temporarily open due to it being 'slop-out' time. I had completed my own operations in this regard and was waiting for the officer on duty to lock me up. A black prisoner suddenly appeared and emptied a bucket of dirty water over me and was then gone in a flash. Again, I was not hurt, although hardly pleased. However, this incident, coming so shortly on top of the other, made me think hard about my new situation. I was, as I have always been, in good physical condition and well able to look after myself. The problem was that if I got into a fight the prison authorities were likely to punish both parties to such an enounter, without too much regard to who started it; and this would probably mean loss of some of my remission. I was resolved to get my freedom not a single day later than it was due to me, which was two-thirds of the way through sentence. It had not taken me long to decide that my new place of abode was not the most congenial environment a man could wish for, and I was not anxious to remain in it any longer than I had to. My worry was that, knowing my own nature, I would not be able to take this kind of aggravation very long before hitting back (no doubt a legacy of my Irish ancestry!). Then of course I would be in trouble.

I approached the Wing Governor and requested protection. Prison rules allow an inmate this facility on request, and I got it. It was not necessary for long, however, for the prison authorities decided to solve the problem by transferring me to an open prison, Sudbury in Derbyshire. In these establishments all inmates are serving relatively short sentences and are not usually of the violent type. Conditions at Sudbury were much better, and so in the end I was indebted to my two attackers at Stafford for putting me in a situation where I was able to obtain this transfer.

I saw out the remainder of my sentence at Sudbury, with little trouble. The nearest I got to injury was a somewhat fierce tackle in a football match, which up-ended me for a moment but broke no bones. Life in the place was not too bad. In the long off-duty hours I was able to retire to the library and listen to music and play chess. There was also a table-tennis room which I frequented quite often, and I finished runner up in the prison knock-out competition. There were plenty of books to read, and I was even able to write an article for the prison magazine, which caused a minor stir.

Just a few people — a minority — were noticeably hostile to me when I arrived. They knew nothing whatever about me as an individual but had been appropriately conditioned by the horror comics that passed as newspapers and assumed, from what they had read of my politics, that I must eat new-born babies for breakfast. I made it a policy to treat this hostility with patience and understanding until it evaporated, which it usually did. At the end of my time a number were coming up to me and telling me I was a much better fellow than they had expected me to be. One little incident was amusing as an indication of the incredible ideas that some people can get from their daily press. This was when a fellow, after talking to me for a few minutes, complimented me on the fact I spoke such good English! For a moment I inclined to the temptation to click my heels and tell him: "I voss for two years at Oxford." I resisted this, however, and informed him that my facility in the native tongue was due to nothing more remarkable than that I had been born in Devonshire, had lived in the London area for most of my life and was in fact as British as roast beef!

In order to help pass the time, I enlisted for evening classes. It will not surprise anyone to hear that I chose Current Affairs. I remember the lecturer as a youngish Tory type, who looked and spoke like a thousand others at the Brighton or Scarborough conferences. He had been used to a rather easy ride until I joined his class. After listening a little while to his standardised, sanitised Central Office version of all things and being struck with how pathetic it was, I entered into debate with him. It was not long before this debate occupied the main part of the lessons, leaving little time for anything else. I knew of course that I would never convert him — these types are so well programmed that trying to establish a meeting of minds with them is like trying to get blood out of a stone — but it all helped to relieve the boredom and pass the time, while keeping me in regular practice in the thing I did best.

Another character I remember from these sessions was a little chap whose name was, I think, McLaverty. I was told when I first enrolled for the classes that this fellow was an ardent left-winger, and that when we encountered each other we might come to blows, so opposed were our views. The latter proved to be true but the former did not. He was by no means an unpleasant fellow and had a good sense of humour. We actually got on quite well, although disagreeing about nearly everything.

This point is worthy of a further word. I have always thought it the silliest thing, and a sign of immaturity, to be personally hostile to an individual because you detest his opinions. I have never had that attitude, but have taken people exactly as I have found them. My antagonist in these arguments was rare among leftists in thinking the same way. Most of his kind, together with priggishly moralistic 'liberals', attribute to you devil's horns and a pointed tail immediately they know you are diametrically opposed to their outlook, so that you cannot carry on a normal conversation with them, whether it be about music, travel or a hundred other subjects unconnected with politics, without their hostility being apparent throughout. They seem to be saying all the time to the world: "This fellow is so frightful that I'm determined not to be seen behaving towards him as if I actually **like** him!" Basically, this attitude is an effeminate one, a sad product of the unchivalrous age in which we live. Liberalism, and its cousin leftism, seem to produce an abundance of this type, to whom anyone with opinions strongly opposite to their own cannot possibly be 'decent' and therefore must be kept at arms' length. Let us hope that we will grow out of this mean-spirited way of thinking; we must do if we are to become again a nation of adult men and women.

Eventually my time for release came and I resumed my activities. A short while later Colin Jordan was also freed and things reverted to normal.

Our little enterprise was not to last for more than another year. Before I conclude the account of it, however, I should mention just two further events, both related, which took place in 1963. The first occurred when three or four members of the National Socialist Movement were walking down Kensington High Street off duty from party activities one evening. By a strange stroke of misfortune, they must have been spotted shortly before by someone in contact with the Jewish '62 Group to which I have referred. By whatever means I do not know, but a number of members of this group were tipped off and sped quickly to the scene. A mob of about 20 of them set on our men out of the blue and completely without provocation. One of our people, a Newfoundlander named Charlie Thompson, was very badly beaten up and subsequently hospitalised for several weeks. After that we never saw him again.

Shortly after this incident and with it still very fresh in our minds, the NSM held a general party conference at London's Caxton Hall. As an indication of how small the organisation was, there were no more than about 30 in attendance.

The '62 Group had got to hear about the conference through an informer they had placed in our ranks and they sent a mob along to attack it. Small though our numbers on the occasion were, our opponents had obviously expected them to be even smaller, for when the mob turned up it was no more than about equal in number to our own members present.

They came in shortly before the meeting was about to start. It is my usual preference, when trouble-makers come along to disrupt meetings, to favour the minimum use of force to remove them. Quite apart from the ethics of the matter, this is political common sense, since, if more than the necessary force is employed, potential supporters might be alienated.

On this occasion, however, as soon as we saw who the intruders were, the thought of our friend in hospital leapt immediately to our minds. It would be telling a lie if I said that in the ensuing fight our adversaries were ejected in a spirit of gentleness. I saw one thrown over the banisters to the floor about 30 feet below. The mob were given a pasting that I suspect none of them ever forgot, and it is more than probable that local hospital staff had to put in some overtime later that day.

I recount this occasion, not to glorify violence, but to give the reader some indication of the circumstances in which much of our struggle is carried on. With normal opponents — and by this I mean people who may disagree with us but whose minds are open to reason and who at least respect our right to our own views — we would much rather talk to them than fight them. Our whole purpose is to make friends, not enemies, and you do not make a friend of a person by inflicting injury on him.

But there is on the left fringe of politics in Britain — and in much greater numbers today than in the Sixties — an element consisting of pure sadistic thugs and would-be assassins, with whom no normal dialogue is possible. The belief of people like these is that those such as ourselves have no rights whatever but should be obliterated from the face of the earth. With specimens of this kind, you cannot argue or reason; the only thing you can do to keep them off your back is scare the living daylights out of them. This was very much in our minds at Caxton Hall on that day in 1963. After that occasion we did not see or hear anything more of the '62 Group for some time.

Our whole politial climate in Britain today is one of paralysis on the part of law-abiding people in the face of mob terror. 'Liberalism' has emasculated our proper instincts when it comes to dealing with those who use violence and intimidation to gain their ends, and we shirk the duty to respond to them in the only language they understand and the only language that will ever work. It is of course shockingly unconventional to state this view, but I state it nevertheless — with all due respect to the Archbishop of Canterbury and others who would urge us to "turn the other cheek."

Shortly afterwards, the splintering tendency of which I have spoken revealed itself again, and internal differences brought things to a point, in the Spring of 1964, when the National Socialist Movement fell apart. I think it would only be boring to the reader for me to recount this process in detail, for the events themselves are not of great importance. I came to find myself in increasing disagreement with Colin Jordan. The disagreement was solely over political and organisational matters and was in no way influenced, as some have claimed, by any personal quarrels. Years later CJ and I met again, shook hands and buried any antagonisms that had arisen during this period of conflict, and so there is not anyway any useful point in raking over matters here. Probably there was some right and wrong on both sides. We were two strong-minded individuals and had our own distinctive and different ideas on the kind of organisation needed to further our common cause of race and nation. To some extent, we still do have, but these differences are no longer a cause for conflict. We now each work in the spheres to which our talents and temperaments are best suited, while being in friendly collaboration where and when we find ourselves pursuing the same things. I respect Colin Jordan as a man who has devoted a major part of his life to the service of his beliefs, at times at considerable personal sacrifice. At this distance of time, this seems much more important than the matters over which we fought a long time ago.

At the time of this conflict I had it in mind to discontinue political activity for a while and concentrate on getting some of my personal affairs in order. I had impoverished myself financially by my years of almost total political involvement, and had had to borrow money from a family source to meet my personal expenses, which, modest though they were, could not be covered anything like adequately from the equally modest funds of the political groups for which I had been working. I needed to concentrate for a time on some work outside politics which would bring me enough money to repay the debt I had incurred and leave something in balance as security for the future. Eventually I did this, but it was not to be possible immediately.

In addition to this consideration, I wanted time to think out my next political moves. The organisations with which I had been connected had not been successful. This did not persuade me in the slightest way that their principles had been wrong, but it did call for a fresh look at the methods, organisation, strategy and tactics that had been used. I was bound to acknowledge that the idea of the National Socialist Movement had been a mistake, and for the reasons I have stated. Yet my association with that group for the previous two years had isolated me from many others who had during that time pursued different political paths. No possibility of working with them seemed to be in the offing for the time being. All these factors pointed to the idea of a temporary rest from active politics. Had I been an entirely free agent in this matter, this is the course I would probably have taken.

But events forced my hand. Along with me were others who had taken the same position as I in the recent internal division in the NSM, and they made it clear that they looked to me for leadership. They wanted to continue in some kind of political activity and I did not want to lose them as collaborators. Instead of going into the temporary retirement that I had considered, I agreed in concert with them that we would set up an alternative organisation. This came in due course to be known as the Greater Britain Movement, thus adding just one more chapter to the bewildering story of regroupings and name-changings that have been an unfortunate feature of the history of the patriotic movement in Britain.

With the formation of the GBM I found myself for the first time in the position of leader of a political group instead of just a lieutenant to someone else. This was not a role that I had sought at that stage. I was then just turned 30. To say that the thought of assuming a leadership role had never occurred to me would be to state an untruth. I had by this time developed considerable confidence in my own powers. I had over the preceding years worked with various others and had found them lacking in the necessary qualities of mind and character for leadership — or, in cases where someone did have these qualities, he was set on a course with which I could not agree. In the latter category I placed A.K. Chesterton, Colin Jordan and Sir Oswald Mosley, all gifted men but men who, at the time, did not share my very firm ideas about the correct way forward.

I was convinced — and you can call it arrogance if you like — that I did know the correct way forward. By this time, I had developed a set of absolutely cast-iron and unshakeable beliefs as to the necessary programme for the salvation and rebuilding of Britain. I was utterly certain that I was politically right, that I knew the correct road.

Over 20 years later, I find that I have had no reason to change any of these beliefs, except in the minutest detail.

But at that time, in 1964, I was prepared to believe that there could be someone, somewhere, who understood the road to be taken as well as I did and who, moreover, was better qualified to lead. I hoped I might find him. At the same time, I did not exclude from my mind the possibility of my having to assume leadership myself at some date in the future. At that particular moment, however, I did not think I was yet ready for that task.

I formed the Greater Britain Movement as a stop-gap measure. I wanted to keep together the little circle around me and in a state of some active readiness. They on their part wanted to remain politically active and I did not want to let them down. In the longer term, I saw the best hope for progress forward as lying in a linking up with other factions from which I had become estranged some years before. There was no possibility of this at that moment, however, and I saw our most practical course as being to build up a unit of some strength and fighting capability, and with some assets, so that we would then have something tangible with which to negotiate terms with others in a wider unification of nationalists that might become possible in two or three years' time. I did not see the Greater Britain Movement, in other words, as being the final answer, and certainly did not envisage its being able to develop into anything as grand in concept as a political party. In view of this, the choice of name was probably an over-pretentious one, as well as being a little theatrical.

Looking back on the seven or eight years in which I had been politically active, I was bound to admit to myself that I had made a number of errors and that I had not worked to any kind of clearly-thought-out design. Rather had I tended to make decisions impulsively and as a reaction to the exigencies of the moment, never looking very far ahead. I resolved thenceforward to rectify these errors and bring much more planning and method into my approach to political work.

One of the decisions I made at this time was to found my own small publishing firm and to launch the magazine *Spearhead*, which ever since has occupied a major part of my time. This publishing concern and magazine were established as privately-owned enterprises, though they were run in close conjunction with the Greater Britain Movement. Long after the GBM was disbanded, they were kept in being and are still in being today.

I have here used the term 'privately-owned' and I should clarify this in case there are any misunderstandings. Not all the capital that I drew upon to set up the two ventures was my own, nor has it been since; I have received donations from other people who supported these ventures, and I could not have done without them. I use the term 'privately-owned' to establish a distinction between these concerns and any political group with which I may be connected. Within those terms of reference, I regard it as my prerogative, and indeed duty, to exercise **control** — and that is the sole purpose of giving them this status. I certainly do not regard them as my personal property, to dispose of in the pursuit of any personal interest. I have learned the necessity for this practice: political organisations may come and go, and there is always the possibility that they may get into the wrong hands, as many have done, and finally end up on the scrapheap. I was not prepared to place any publishing firm or publication I may build up in that position, where others might get their hands on them and wreck them. Had I ever taken the step of making these concerns the property of any political group or party, and thus removed from my control, they almost certainly would not exist today but would have gone into oblivion along with the many other bright schemes launched by political dilettantes over the years, whose liking for personal publicity was never equalled by their staying power.

This is a vitally important lesson that I learned during those years. I have mentioned the people who were connected with me in the setting up of the Greater Britain Movement. When I recall their names now, I am struck by the fact that none of them is today any longer active politically. Their disposition to political activity was a passing phase in their lives; eventually it ran its course, and they discovered other interests and other priorities. Perhaps they still have the same opinions, but their resolve to translate these opinions into action has long disappeared. I wish them no ill, and if I were to meet them again today I would in most cases react to them in a friendly manner. But I recognise them for what they are: followers and not leaders. To the follower belongs the luxury of retiring from the struggle when the mood takes him; to the leader, such a luxury is not permitted; he must fight the good fight to the absolute end — otherwise he is no leader.

The various political groups that have come and gone in this country in pursuit of our aims have witnessed plenty of people of this dilettante nature rise to top positions, only to have those people flit away into the wilderness and perhaps to more personally rewarding pursuits when it suited them to do so. In no way was I prepared to put in the toil and sweat to establish something, then to see it come under the sway of people of this kind and duly go into oblivion.

I had to start these publishing activities, however, on an extremely tiny budget, notwithstanding the help I received from some others, which was in some cases very generous in relation to their means. I soon found myself exploring ways and means to produce printed material with the maximum economy. I became acquainted with offset printing methods, which seemed to offer the best possibilities in this regard. I obtained a cheap typewriter, with a type-face bolder than with the usual office model and consequently with a certain 'printed' look. I had always been fairly proficient in the use of this species of instrument, having started practising on one at the age of 12. I also had as a helper the wife of a colleague, who was more proficient than I because professionally trained. This was Mrs. Valerie Trevelyan, to whom I will always be grateful for the work done in those early

years. She would set the final type from my original copy, placing
the last letter of each line in exact alignment with those of other
lines so as to achieve what in the printing world is called 'justification'. She would return the typeset galleys, which were then cut
out and pasted onto a paper surface with lines drawn in light pencil
to denote pages and their columns. Headings were then done by
use of the Letraset method, which is probably known to most
readers. The whole process was long and laborious, and needed
good eyesight!

This job completed, we then presented the copy to the printer,
who from it made lithographic plates by a photocopying process
and then did the print runs. In this way, printing bills were cut
down to a minimum.

The magazine at first appeared spasmodically. Not until five
years later was I able to stabilise it on a monthly basis. By that
time I had managed to obtain further financial support, including a
loan from one quarter which made possible the purchase of
improved typesetting equipment.

Mainly by means of *Spearhead*, I was able slowly to extend the
influence of my ideas beyond the tiny circle of my immediate
friends and colleagues, and I like to think that the magazine was in
some way instrumental in creating a climate of opinion among the
adherents to the British nationalist idea which made possible the
unification of forces which occurred later in the 1960s.

In 1966 I reached the point at which I could no longer survive
personally while devoting the whole of my time to political work.
Extra finance was needed to develop *Spearhead* and my other
publishing enterprises, modest though these were, and I felt that I
would need to supply most of that finance myself. At the same
time I had to keep body and soul together. I was single at the time
and my living needs were very modest. I did, however, require a
motor car if I was to operate at reasonable proficiency. All these
things pointed to the need to find more money without imposing
yet further on the generosity of loyal supporters.

I looked for some additional means of employment and found a
company with which I negotiated a position as manufacturer's
agent, working in an entirely independent and self-employed
capacity and being paid on a commission-only basis. For the next
11 years I sold hundreds of the products of this company with only
a small number of hours each week allocated to the work in
question. This helped me clear my debts, to buy and run for the
first time a decent and reliable car and to finance the expansion of

my publishing activities. I only ceased this work when it had become impossible any longer to find the time for it and when my face had started to become more widely known, thus risking embarrassment to the company whose products I handled. For obvious reasons, I will not name that company here, but I have much reason to be grateful to those running it; they knew of my politics but took the entirely fair and sensible view that they were my own concern so long as I kept them absolutely separate from my company work.

From 1964, my dedication was increasingly directed to the achievement of unification among nationalist political groups. I had seen clearly the damage caused by splintering, in which process I had myself played some part, having been a supporter of one split, a willy-nilly participant in a second and the leader of a third. I kept the Greater Britain Movement alive only with a view to its making a contribution to unity as soon as that became possible. If people merge previously smaller companies into one larger company, the influence that each will exert in that larger company will obviously be related to the capital he brings into the merger, and this was what was in my mind in the efforts I made to strengthen the small group that I led.

In 1966 I began to enter into consultations with people belonging to other groups who shared my sentiments on the matter of unity, and after a while a good friendly relationship was established. It was clear to me from the start that I could campaign and negotiate for unity much more effectively if I did not attempt to make any terms concerning my own position in the scheme of things but, on the contrary, volunteered to take a background seat. By this time, as I may have indicated, I did not regard myself as inferior in capability to any of the other would-be leaders on the scene. I could see, however, that if I pushed for any leadership position it would be counter-productive to what I was trying to achieve. Such a practice was contrary to my nature anyway: leadership does not establish itself through such 'deals', but does so in the field of action and achievement. I was quite content to let others be the front-runners, knowing that in the course of events the natural order would sort itself out.

There were then five organisations of any note in the field of nationalist politics in Britain. Apart from the GBM, there was the League of Empire Loyalists, still led by A.K. Chesterton. There was the British National Party under John Bean and Andrew Fountaine. There was the group headed by Colin Jordan, which by that time had reformed under the name of 'British Movement'. Finally, there was the Racial Preservation Society, a group similar to the one-time White Defence League: not a party but a pressure group concentrating solely on the immigration issue.

I could not see any prospect of British Movement agreeing to link up with, or being accepted by, the others. It therefore had to be left out of the reckoning for the time being.

There was obviously some usefulness in the Racial Preservation Society continuing its own existence, although it was to be hoped that, if it did, it would co-ordinate its efforts more closely with the other groups than previously.

Between the other three groups what was obviously desirable was a straight amalgamation. I believed that the best man to lead this combination was A.K. Chesterton, provided he could be persuaded to venture into the political party field — his not doing so in the past being my main point of difference with him.

My first discussions were with the representatives of the British National Party. Out of these I hoped to be able to progress towards agreement to a merger between the BNP and the GBM, then when this agreement had been reached to present our plans to Chesterton and invite him to bring in the LEL too, with him as leader of the whole.

The name that I favoured as the one to be adopted by the new amalgamated body was 'National Front'. This idea was not mine in the original but had been taken from a small party led by Andrew Fountaine in the early 1950s, which enjoyed a short career. I did not know much about that organisation but thought its name a good one, coming quickly and easily off the tongue.

This was the essence of the formula that I had in mind and which I put to those with whom I was in negotiation. Things would have progressed rapidly towards an achievement of this project had it not been for the depressing small-mindedness and obstruction of certain people in the BNP. Here I saw at work a tendency which has been a constant hindrance to constructive effort in our field of politics.

A familiar figure to everyone in this world is the man who likes to be a big fish in a small pond. If the pond is enlarged and additional fish are brought in, he may find himself with rivals and lose some status, and this is something he could not bear. This type is very common in political groups and a constant barrier to the achievement of more effective combinations.

Going hand-in-hand with this mentality, and usually combined in the same person, is a terror of entering what might be called, to use an Americanism, the 'big time'. These people feel comfortable only in the atmosphere of cosy little clubs. Though they pay lip service to the theoretical idea of growth and the eventual winning of power, in practice their minds are set against these things, and their instinct is to resist any development likely to bring them nearer. Graduating from the tiny nucleus and entering the real political arena where one is playing for much higher stakes requires a certain mental adjustment. The challenges and responsibilities become immeasurably increased, and the men are then sorted out from the boys. Public exposure is much greater and the political charlatan and hobbyist is shown up in a much more glaring light. The fellow at home in a little clique will very often find this environment frightening and so prefers to avoid it.

I had to sit back and wait patiently in 1966 and 1967 while my fellow negotiators contended with people in their own ranks of this type. It was duly reported back to me that no progress had been made and it seemed then that negotiations towards unity had broken down. Disappointed, I directed my mind back to my own small field of activity, resigned to the likelihood that fragmentation would for the time being continue.

Imagine my amazement when a little while later I heard that my unity formula had been adopted to the letter — with the one exception that our own group was to be excluded! Agreement had been reached for a merger between the British National Party and League of Empire Loyalists, with A.K. Chesterton as leader and for the new organisation to be called the National Front. The Racial Preservation Society would remain in existence but would narrow the range of its independent operations and devote the resources saved to helping the NF — exactly what I had conceived and advocated!

I had to laugh at the nerve of these people. Receive a friendly approach from someone — reject it — steal his idea — and then put it into operation yourself, freezing him out and claiming the credit as if the idea were your own! Such were the types of people with whom we were dealing. But never mind! The object of the exercise was bigger than they. I resolved that this object would still be achieved. It simply meant a change of tactics.

I let things rest for a little while, the National Front in the meantime being founded. I decided that in a few months I would make a direct approach to A.K. Chesterton, whom I should incidently like to say I entirely exclude from the type of petty-mindedness and plagiarism that I have just related; I am sure that none of it was his doing. I would make the offer to AKC to disband the Greater Britain Movement and place all its members and assets at his disposal unconditionally. If he wished me to join the NF, I would do so gladly but if he preferred not I would accept this and work in support of it from the outside, chiefly through the medium of *Spearhead*.

I eventually did meet Chesterton some time in the Spring of 1967 and made the offer to him exactly as described. His first words to me in response were: "What is the *quid-pro-quo?*" I replied that there was none. This seemed as if it was something of a novelty to him after the other people he had been dealing with. We shook hands and put our past conflict behind us. By mutual agreement, I stayed out of the NF for the time being. A few months later, AKC invited me to enrol as a member, which I did. This process met with the predictable obstruction from the sources I have described, but this was duly overcome. A new chapter had opened up in my political life. It was to be much more fruitful than those in the past.

There are some today who accuse me of an excess of egotism and the coveting of power for its own sake. The actual record shows that I have been more than prepared to do the very reverse when the situation has demanded it. I was the only one among the leaders of those groups which merged into the National Front in the middle-to-late 1960s who made no attempt to negotiate a position for himself as part of the merger arrangement. I think I have a fairly good past record of being prepared to place myself under other leaders. I did so in all cases because I believed they were men better qualified then to do the job than I was. If I ask others to place themselves under my leadership today, it is precisely for the same reason in reverse. All this, however, belongs to a later chapter.

The National Front was to become one of the most important developments in the history of our nationalist movement, and was to dominate the next 12 years of my life. Everything previous to it was an apprenticeship for politics. Now we had a viable organisation, and could begin to engage in activities on a scale that would enable us to break through and appeal to a real national audience.

As I shall relate in the coming chapter, the National Front recorded some considerable achievements, introducing many thousands of new people to the nationalist idea. As a result of its work in the late 1960s and 1970s, the patriotic movement made enormous progress forward. At the same time, the NF developed as it went along certain fatal weaknesses. It is time to examine those fascinating years of its heyday, and draw from this examination the important lessons those years offer for our guidance in the future. In the end the NF, for all its achievement and promise, proved not to be the final answer to Britain's need. I hope in the coming pages to explain why.

Chapter 10
The National Front

The National Front represented the first serious attempt in the post-war period to take British Nationalism out of the arena of 'back street' politics and the foolish and petty factional quarrels that are part of that tradition and make it a potentially revelant national political force. The forming of the NF in 1967 was certainly a development profoundly unsettling to the entrenched defenders of the 'liberal establishment', and they undoubtedly resolved at its outset to place a close watch on it, from within and without, and oppose it with all means within their considerable power.

Nothing is easier than infiltrating a young, fledgeling movement, small in numbers and anxious for recruits. A few well-chosen agents, able to demonstrate above-average ability and keenness, can without difficulty become part of such an organisation to the extent of being regarded as amongst its most valued activists and functionaries. If, in addition to this, they act cohesively as one body to build up their influence within, they become the embryo of a devastatingly destructive force once a situation is created which works to their advantage.

In its first stages, the National Front was wisely organised so as to counter this possibility by the adoption of an internal structure which placed great powers in the hands of its leader, whose *bona fides* as a genuine patriot were beyond question and whose practical experience in the political arena was unsurpassed. A.K. Chesterton had occupied a senior position in Mosley's pre-war British Union, and had had a taste of the reality of battle conditions in the seven-year period of that party's challenge against the old world forces. He was a strong personality and character who would not flinch from the decisions necessary to keep the new movement on the rails. That his judgement, both of people and situations, could at times be faulty I considered to be of less importance than these positive qualities that I have mentioned.

Amenable to sensible argument from people able to earn his respect, he could be induced sometimes to change his mind. Infallibility was not therefore one of the things I sought in him. What was essential was that he should have impeccable credentials as a crusader for our ideals, that he should have the natural gift of command and that he should be the absolute opposite of the cowardly, self-seeking, principle-trading 'politician'.

AK, as he came to be known by his friends, presided over a governing body called the 'Directorate'. The latter was instituted for consultative purposes but also, to some extent, for cosmetic ones — the *realpolitik* involved in welding together the previously separate factions that had formed the Front necessitated some sops to them in the way of senior positions for their leading officials on the senior councils of the new body. What was important, however, was that power of decision on this Directorate should lie with AKC himself, an arrangement with which I wholeheartedly concurred, both in the first stage of my involvement with the new party, when I had no position on this Directorate or indeed any other kind of party office, and at the subsequent stage, when I was a Directorate member. Everyone's position on this body was determined by AK's appointment and could be terminated by AK's dismissal. Whatever vigorous exchange of views might precede a decision, the decision itself was, as I have said, in the end his and one for which he took full responsibility.

To stunted minds, this was a system devised to ensure the promotion of favourites and 'yes-men' and to emasculate criticism of the leadership, but in fact it was a thoroughly sensible procedure, occasioned by the reality that the movement we were creating was in the position of an army in war, needing to maintain unity and internal discipline as an essential condition of survival, and in which mutual loyalty and trust between leader and led were ingredients no less indispensable. What was vital was that no faction should form on the ruling body which could overthrow the established leadership by engendering a situation of mutiny. Most certainly this could have happened had places on that body been obtained by election from below and had those holding them been then empowered to overrule the leadership by means of 'majority vote'. Such a procedure would have been a sure recipe for the hijacking of the movement, at the best by ordinary political adventurers and opportunists of unproven competence, and at the worst by agents of the movement's hidden enemies.

Unhappily, this stable system of leadership did not endure for long. After a promising rate of progress over the first three years or so, there occurred an internal crisis in the winter of 1970-71, as a result of which the movement became set on a new course that was to have devastating consequences a decade later.

I have indicated my belief in the NF's initial governing system, with its emphasis on a strong individual leader, as providing the best guarantee against internal schism. Such a system on its own, however, cannot give such a guarantee that is absolute. It requires, in addition, the regular presence of the leader on the scene of events and, in cases where this is not possible, that he has a deputy acting for him who is fully capable of keeping things under control on his behalf. If these conditions are not present, even the best system of leadership is vulnerable.

A.K. Chesterton, by this stage of his life, had for reasons of health to spend five of the winter months in South Africa, the land of his birth. It was his custom when away to appoint as his deputy Aidan Mackey, a schoolmaster who, although totally loyal and trustworthy as a colleague, was not able, for reasons of working commitments, to be in the front line of party activity and thus make himself known to the general membership sufficiently for him to be able to establish any great personal authority in the party. The months of AK's sojourn abroad, therefore, constituted a period of some precariousness with regard to the party's ability to withstand any serious process of internal disruption. Naturally it was assumed that any such disruption would be avoided by means of the availability of the party's annual general meeting as a safety-valve for the airing of any contentious issues as may threaten to divide the party, so that these may be settled before AK's departure overseas.

By now, however, a squalid little faction had insinuated itself into the party which was bent on disruption at the first available opportunity. If its representatives had nurtured honest grievances, the opportunity to voice these grievances was provided at the AGM of October 1970.

That meeting, however, passed without any such demonstration of dissent. AKC was given an overwhelming mandate to continue as leader, and no person present at the meeting demurred against this.

Immediately AK was out of the country following the meeting, however, and there was absent in the party a strongly established authority able to act as a rallying point of unity and a firm agent of discipline, the faction made its move. Its first action was to hold a secret meeting clearly designed to be a 'council of war'. Were this meeting to have been held for the purpose of an honest discussion of problems in the party, all interested personnel would have been invited to it, including myself — for by this time I had attained a fairly prominent position in the party and a place on its Directorate. Neither I nor numerous others of similar status were invited, however, for the simple reason that we were known to be loyal to AKC and likely to be unfavourably disposed towards whatever it was the faction was plotting.

As a result of the meeting, the faction, arrogating to itself the title of 'Action Committee', drew up a petition of alleged grievances which it then sent by post to A.K. Chesterton in South Africa. As indicated before, none of these grievances had been brought up at the AGM a short time previously, where their merits or demerits might have been assessed by the members present and where AKC or his supporters might have had the opportunity of replying to them. From this it may safely be assumed that the supposed grievances were conceived, not in any constructive spirit of trying to improve the party, but entirely for the purpose of disrupting and subverting it. I later saw a copy of the petition and could see immediately that it was worded deliberately in the most impertinent and provocative language possible, so as to induce in its receiver a reaction of anger and intransigence.

This was exactly the reaction it got. AKC communicated immediately with his deputy and urged that all the signitaries to the document be suspended from membership pending disciplinary proceedings.

This was, from the human point of view, a perfectly understandable reaction but not an entirely practical one. In the first place, AK's deputy Aidan Mackey lacked, as I have said, the kind of personal authority in the party necessary to carry out such a far-reaching disciplinary action without seriously endangering party unity. Secondly, by no means all the signatories to the Action Committee petition were of ill intent — as I could see from a glance at the names. It was quite clear that a poisonous and malignant 'hard core' had simply manipulated a larger outer circle of rather naive folk whose only crime was their credulity. The correct procedure, therefore, was to deal with the petition with a little more subtlety, working to separate the fools from the knaves before applying the hatchet to the latter. I counselled this policy in a letter to Chesterton.

From several thousands of miles away, however, he saw things differently and, quite mistakenly, interpreted such counsels of moderation as indicative of something less than complete loyalty to himself. Feeling his position in the party to be much weaker than in fact it was, and feeling let down by a number of those he had regarded as his allies and friends, he resigned from the NF leadership and from the party altogether.

Had AKC been a younger man and in better health, he might have been induced to stay and fight, in which case he most certainly could have won. He was by now over 70, however, and suffering from the legacy of gassing in World War I, which had grown worse over the years, and he was of a mind to call it a day. He still continued publishing *Candour* and revived the old LEL under the name of the Candour League, taking with him into this group his close circle of old friends and associates. His days in party politics, however, were at an end.

I have related the story of A.K. Chesterton's exit from the National Front mindful that there may be a good many readers to whom it will not be of great interest. As with another story earlier, I include it in this book because of the lessons it provides in the kinds of problems we encounter in our struggle. The people who conspired against AKC are in no cases of any importance in themselves; what is important is the tendency in politics that they represent. It is a tendency against which it behoves us always to be vigilant.

By this time I had become deeply involved in the National Front myself and had overcome most of the obstruction that I had encountered earlier. Indeed, shortly before his departure for South Africa in 1970 AK had confided in me that he saw me as his most likely successor as leader of the NF. My response was to say to him that, if this were the case, I hoped such a contingency would not come too soon, as I did not then consider that I yet enjoyed sufficiently widespread confidence and support among the membership to be able to perform such a job properly. I have said that I had overcome most of the obstruction to my participation in the party as an ordinary member and activist, but my assumption of the party leadership was a different matter. This remained my position after Chesterton's resignation, and there was therefore a leadership vacuum, as no-one else remotely capable of stepping into AK's shoes was available. This was no doubt just what had been anticipated and hoped for by those who had engineered his exit. The stage was set for some kind of 'collective leadership', the formula always beloved of the levellers of politics, as it means that, in the event of their having a part in leadershp councils, no-one stands above them and thus delivers that agonising wound to their egos entailed by such an order of things. Under 'collective leadership', responsiblity rests in theory with everyone and in practice with no-one. Again, this is a state of affairs admirably suited to the mentality of the kind of people who coalesced in their shady little tunnels and back alleys to bring A.K. Chesterton down.

A working party was set up to devise a new constitution for the NF. As soon as I saw it, I did not like it, but I did not at the time feel in a strong enough position within the party to oppose it without a great deal of support from other leading elements, and this was not visible. I therefore acquiesced in the adoption of the new constitution but with considerable reservations. Years later, looking back on this episode with hindsight, I wondered whether I should not have made a stronger stand against this nonsense than I did. It was a difficult time, making decisions difficult. One wrong step and the whole precarious structure of the NF as it then was could have collapsed like a pack of cards. I felt that the first priority was to prevent this, and therefore I persuaded myself to leave arguments about the constitution till later.

The new constitution totally emasculated the office of party chairman and placed all power over party affairs in the hands of the Directorate, which thenceforth would be of fixed number (20) and elected by the general membership of the party. The Directorate would then itself elect a Chairman, who would preside over its meetings and have a casting vote in the event of a tie of votes; beyond that he would exercise no more power than any other Directorate member. All vital party decisions would be determined by a Directorate vote. The system was later changed so as to allow the Directorate Chairman, who would be the senior official of the party, to be elected by the whole party membership, but this made very little difference in substance, since power still remained with whomever was able to command a Directorate majority.

The system was wrong at very first base. It may well work for golf clubs and beekeepers' societies, since those bodies are not engaged in a political war and prone to infiltration by enemies in such a war. In the kind of struggle in which we are engaged, it is a truly disastrous formula. The system adopted for the NF at that time was founded on the false premise that decisions should be made by the counting of heads, with the idea being that the content of every head was worth the same — an absurdity that belongs to the doctrine of liberalism that has wreaked havoc with the Western World. Here we were trying to build a political movement that would challenge the whole liberal structure of ideas, yet we were ourselves embracing one of the central pillars of that very structure.

The system we were adopting was at the same time a perfect recipe for infiltration, and even possible take-over, by our movement's foes. The Communists have been known to proclaim: ''Give us one third of the places on any committee, and we will guarantee to control that committee.'' If we are to take these people at their word, it would mean that the enemies of the National Front needed to insinuate themselves into the position of having seven of their number voted onto its Directorate and they would be in effective command of the party's ruling body, and thus able to neutralise the party as a political force, irrespective of who was its official leader.

I do not suggest that the enemies of the National Front were quite in this position following the overthrow of A.K. Chesterton, but I certainly do believe that those acting as their agents had some part in this overthrow and that the same people enjoyed some positions on the Front's ruling body in the subsequent period.

The man who took Chesterton's place as NF leader in early 1971 was John O'Brien, who had previously served as head of the party's administration. I believed then, and believe now, that John O'Brien was an honest and sincere patriot, albeit with definite limitations in the way of leadership qualities. He was something of a compromise choice, selected to heal the divisions in the party that had arisen out of its recent bout of internal warfare; his chief qualification was that he was acceptable to those standing on both sides of that divide. By this time, I had broadened the support I had in the party and I was voted in as O'Brien's deputy.

It was not long, however, before the disrupters in the party were at work again. Though John O'Brien and I had hit it off fairly well together and managed to work amicably for a year or so, a group of these disrupters managed to turn him against me and others regarded as being allied to me. The thing came to a head with a vote on the Directorate over an internal matter which did not in any way affect O'Brien's position as party Chairman but which, when he was outvoted, angered him greatly. Immediately following, O'Brien and his supporters left the party to set up a splinter group, which they called the 'National Independence Party', making an appeal to all NF members to follow them, having beforehand abused their positions of trust by secretly copying out those members' names and addresses for the purpose.

The 'National Independence Party', needless to say, enjoyed a short life and soon went into oblivion, having failed to recruit anything more than a small fraction of the NF membership. What its promoters did succeed in doing, however — and no doubt this was their chief objective — was cause much disruption and demoralisation in the Front among party supporters, now growing thoroughly tired of internal splits.

It was in this somewhat unpromising situation that I now assumed the National Front leadership. I made it clear to all at the outset that, whatever the 'book of rules' might say, I intended to lead. I had not sought the office — certainly not at that time — but had had it thrust upon me by circumstances not of my making. As the party's head, I would be expected to take responsibility for its fortunes, and I therefore expected that whatever the course along which I judged it right to take the party my colleagues who wished me to shoulder the responsibility would comply. In everyday routine matters I would abide by the terms of the constitution that decisions would be taken in accordance with the vote of the Directorate majority, though I made clear my reservations about that system. In matters of major decision, however, where I judged the party's interest to be vitally at stake, I expected the support of my colleagues for the course that I judged to be the right one; if I did not get this support, the Directorate, and party, would find themselves in the position of looking for a new leader. I asked that anyone who objected to these conditions make their objections known there and then. Barring a few hums and hahs, no-one did object.

I soon found that the National Front was in an unholy mess in the way of administration, organisation and morale — indeed I had had inkling of this already but, on investigating things more deeply than previously, I found that it was even worse than I had realised. The chaotic administration was due partly to the incompetence of those who had previously run the headquarters office but also partly due to outright sabotage. And of course the low morale was hardly suprising in view of the two recent bouts of internal warfare, coming as they did one so shortly after the other.

I did a personal count of the membership, assessing first the number of members in each filing tray and then multiplying this by the number of trays. The estimated total was about 2,400. This, however, did not take into account the state of members' subscriptions; a large portion of the 2,400 had not paid their dues for one year and a not negligible number had failed to renew for two years. A realistic estimate of membership numbers, based on those paid up to date — plus the proportion of those unpaid who would be likely to pay on receiving reminders — was no more than about 1,500 at the most.

Together we set about rebuilding the party from the wreckage. I had some good and loyal collaborators, together with a number who were to prove in the course of time not to be loyal; but more of that anon.

A big drive was undertaken to bring the message of the party to the public, using what methods of publicity were available to us in the circumstances. We soon found by our experience that these were restricted, as I had realised in the course of activity with previous groups. By this time it had become obvious that there was a widespread ban on the hire of meeting halls. Opportunities to sell our publications by means of the normal commercial retail outlets were almost nil. We found that our ability to make our existence known and get our message over depended overwhelmingly on free leaflet distribution, which was undertaken systematically in the residential areas of the towns and cities around the country where we were able to establish active branches. Our local activists would obtain street maps of these areas and then make it their target to deliver a leaflet to every dwelling in every street therein, posted through the letter-boxes by keen party activists willing to walk many miles in all weathers. The leaflets covered all the main political issues on which the party fought. On the back of each one was a reply coupon on which the recipient was invited to write his or her name and address and send for further information about the party — or, if they were already convinced by the leaflet that they belonged with us, to apply to join straightaway.

Party head office would post the enquirers what was termed an 'information pack', giving all the details about the party likely to be required; but this was not the end of the recruiting exercise; where competent party representatives were available in the areas from which enquiries came, those enquiries were sent on to them for the purpose of a personal visit, which would be made upon the enquirer as soon as possible. When this procedure was carried out, we found the likelihood of the enquirer being persuaded to join was greatly increased.

Along with this practice, we stepped up the sale of party periodicals. *Spearhead* magazine had now become well established as a major party organ, although I took care to retain the magazine under my own personal control (a policy that was to be more than amply justified by subsequent events). In addition, we founded a tabloid that was designed for a mass readership, that is to say people uninitiated into the nationalist argument. Having no hope of getting these periodicals handled by the major newspaper and magazine distributers, we organised ourselves to sell them on the streets and, as a technique adopted at a later date, by calls on people's homes. The latter method was especially effective, as one successful call could be noted down and the same householder then called on again the following month with a very good likelihood of a sale.

Along with a vast increase in the output and distribution of literature, the party committed itself to a target, hitherto undreamt of, of contesting 50 or more seats at the next general election, which, as it turned out, was to take place in February 1974. I cannot claim to be the main initiator of this policy; the impetus to adopt it came from other members of the Directorate. Confronted with their enthusiasm for the project, I found myself uncertain whether it was at that stage a good one or not, but I decided to give my colleagues the benefit of the doubt and not to oppose it. From that day to this, I have felt that the arguments for and against this strategy are evenly balanced. I will explain why.

It is a rule in Britain that any political party fighting 50 or more seats in a general election qualifies to be given broadcasting time, to be precise, five minutes on TV and five minutes on radio. For any political party, this broadcasting time is important; for a party such as we were, it was doubly so, since it constituted one of the very few opportunities given to us to break into TV or radio that were available. Quite apart from having the time to express our viewpoint on the main issues of the day, there was the chance to get ourselves over as individuals — thus offsetting the gruesome image of ourselves projected by the mass media. In addition, we could use these occasions to inform the public about our address, something of which many were in ignorance. Altogether, these two broadcasts were of enormous value to us.

In addition to this, it has to be said that fighting elections are the ultimate means by which our movement has to win political power in Britain and, this being so, it seems logical that we start the way we intend to carry on. Even if we cannot win seats immediately, we will never do so unless we enter the electoral arena some time and make a beginning.

On the adverse side, the contesting of 50 of more seats in a parliamentary election costs money. In the 1970s it cost £150 for a deposit to field every candidate (now it costs £500). As well as this, there are campaign expenses which involve several more hundreds of pounds in the case of each seat — there is no use in putting up a candidate unless you advertise that candidate to the electorate, and this involves big printing bills. In the 1970s it was impractical to fight a seat with any hope of our candidate winning a respectable vote without investing at least £500.

In the election of February 1974 we spent what must have amounted to at least £25,000 on our campaign — probably more. For this sort of expenditure, the party might have acquired other assets which would stand it in good stead when the election had come and gone: property, printing equipment, etc. There certainly was an argument for saving our money that went towards the election and investing it in other areas of development.

This argument obtained extra impetus when the election results were announced. Nowhere did we succeed even in retaining our deposit. We were up against the big party machines and all the massed weight of propaganda of press and broadcasting, against which our two five-minute efforts were but flea-bites. It was not so much that the mass media persuaded the electorate we were awful people and should not be supported at the polls; it was more that the voters were persuaded that we simply didn't count, and that a vote for one of our candidates would be a wasted vote. To counter this kind of climate requires a nationwide machinery of party publicity and campaigning resources far in excess of what we had at that time. Our voice at the election was a tiny whimper by comparison with the massive blasts of publicity for the other parties. Our small vote was not entirely surprising. I am convinced that many more electors favoured our policies than actually put their crosses beside our candidates. We were beaten out of sight by the belief that such crosses, since they could not get our people elected, would be better cast for one of those they could.

The head of a party contesting an election in circumstances like these is in something of a no-win situation. He cannot afford to discourage his followers from making the very maximum effort possible, and this he would certainly do if he were not to radiate to them some spirit of optimism. On the other hand, when the election takes place the size of the vote obtained is bound to be small. This results in a discrepancy between the result hoped for and that actually achieved. In such circumstances, demoralisation can set in and this in turn can give way to post-mortems leading to internal quarrelling. Some party supporters can be persuaded that the results might have been much better had the leadership been different or had the campaign been conducted in a different way, especially when many of them are comparatively new to the political struggle and not yet conditioned to understand the situation in which they are fighting.

It will remain a matter for debate whether our decision to go for 50-plus seats in the general election of 1974 was the best one or not. It was clear to me when the decision was made, however, that there was an overwhelming consensus within the NF in favour of it. On the other hand, while not being sure that this consensus was correct, I was not convinced either that it was incorrect. Having no definite opinion of my own on the matter, I went along with the tide.

This target of 50-plus seats was, however, a highly ambitious one for a party at the stage we were at in 1972, and there were many who felt that it could not be reached, particularly if the next election was held before the scheduled time of Summer 1975. Once the decision had been made that we should pursue that target, I was determined that we would succeed in doing so, and to this purpose, along with the others the party had set itself, we threw ourselves into work with gusto.

In the one and a half years from the time that I assumed the NF leadership in July 1972, the growth of the National Front was in fact nothing less than remarkable. Its membership forged ahead by leaps and bounds. The scope and scale of its activities increased spectacularly. And, inch-by-inch, it edged its way forward to the target we had set ourselves. In the event, the general election for which we had been planning was called some considerable time ahead of schedule. Nevertheless, with a stupendous effort we managed to mobilise ourselves to contest 54 seats, the four in excess of requirements being necessary as a precaution against errors resulting in one or more candidatures being invalidated because of some technicality or other.

Such a big effort necessitated dispersal of campaigning strength, and this was one further reason for us not to expect a high vote anywhere. As I have indicated, our vote in the final outcome was not high. What we did succeed in doing, however, was get our message into many millions of homes all over the country by way of our TV and radio broadcasts. This resulted in a huge flood of enquiries about the party, with many of the enquirers duly becoming members. The party thereby continued to grow rapidly. In doing so, it became the focus of considerable attention from the mass media. Needless to say, the slant of this reporting was not favourable; neither did we expect it to be, knowing as we did the nature of media ownership and control. What mattered, however, was that we were becoming known and talked about. Those who heard of our existence and were open-minded in their attitude would make their own enquiries and form their own judgement on the basis of what they saw.

The February 1974 election resulted in a hung parliament, and this made a further election inevitable in a short time. In the event, it was held only eight months later, in October of the same year. Despite the huge effort that we had recently made, and the inevitable state of exhaustion, financial and otherwise, that followed this, we quickly recuperated and resolved to make an even bigger effort in the coming contest.

We did. By October we were in a position to fight no less than **90 seats**. Again our vote was not large but again we achieved our aim of making two more broadcasts. More new members flooded in. By this time, the National Front was becoming a household name in Britain and was starting to get known throughout the world.

I was the very last one to seek to take sole credit for this remarkable spell of success. It was the work of a team comprising numerous talents, without the help of which I could not possibly have done the job. Nevertheless, I felt that I had reason not to be dissatisfied at the outcome of this, the first phase of my term as party leader. As I have already said, I did not seek the office, and when it fell to me I had in fact not been certain that I could perform the duties involved to my own satisfaction. After 27 months of unbroken success, I felt reassured on this point: I had not failed the party and I was ready to carry on. It did not at that time occur to me that in these circumstances there would be anyone in the party demanding my head, and I took no special precautions to watch my rear in the internal party elections that had become due.

This proved to be a costly piece of complacency and naivety that I was soon to regret. In the course of its very rapid growth since the summer of 1972, the Front had attracted a large diversity of new recruits. Most of them comprised the very best elements in the British population, but they did include a certain quota of opportunists, egotists, careerists and political adventurers — plus of course an additional complement of infiltrators, placed in the party by its opponents for the purposes I have described earlier. Absolute proof of the existence of the latter is, needless to say, impossible to establish, except in the doubtful event of their providing irrefutable evidence of their affiliations and connections. One can only assume, from knowledge of the political process, that the placing of such agents in our ranks would be an elementary exercise undertaken both by the government itself and by political groups outside it but equally hostile to our aims. There are things that I have seen happen in nationalist organisations that could have no logical explanation other than that they were the work of saboteurs and subversives, and this serves to confirm the assumption to which I have referred. Again, the theory cannot be **proved**; it is simply that all common sense points to it.

Nor is it always easy to decide, to one's complete satisfaction, which person is the disrupter for motives of deliberate sabotage and which one disrupts just as a natural product of the inner character. The two types of course perfectly complement each other in any process of disruption, though with the former always knowing exactly what he is doing while the latter may not.

In any event, by the Autumn of 1974 — and due of course to the 'democratic' process introduced into the party after the exit of A.K. Chesterton — a number of disruptive elements had infiltrated the party to the stage of being strongly represented on its Directorate. At the first Directorate meeting following the October general election I was voted out as party Chairman and my place was taken by Mr. Kingsley Read, a relative newcomer to the movement. I soon learned that this operation had been carefully planned by means of the usual secret meetings with which I had become familiar some four years earlier, and all at a time when I myself had been strenuously occupied with the recent general election campaign. That certain 'colleagues' had had time to divert their attentions from this campaign to plot and plan my downfall was an interesting commentary on their scale of priorities.

I do not propose to go into any great detail over this development in the party beyond what has already been said. Suffice it to say that it bore all the same marks as the conspiracy to unseat Chesterton four years earlier and involved exactly the same types of people, in some cases precisely the same people, as then. My dismissal was followed by a year or so of chaos and disintegration in the party similar to what had occurred after Chesterton's departure at the end of 1970, with the result that a great deal of what had been built up in the years of 1972-74 was allowed to fall to pieces. Eventually the 'new guard' that had taken over the party overreached themselves in an attempt to get me and my supporters excommunicated from the ranks altogether, and found themselves the defendants in a civil action in the High Court. The court ruled against them and the tables were turned. It was they, and not we, who made an ignominious exit from the party. True to tradition, they tried to launch their splinter group using stolen members' records. This group duly went into oblivion, as had its predecessor in 1972.

As an interesting sequel, Kingsley Read was years later revealed as an agent of the far left-wing Jewish anti-nationalist magazine *Searchlight*, a scurrilous little lie sheet, on no less an admission than that of *Searchlight* itself. This was following Read's premature death at the age of 50 in 1985.

Our victory over the usurpers had not been achieved without a fight. It would of course have been the gentlemanly thing to do to accept the take-over of the party by this faction and work with it in good grace, and there were a number of people among my collaborators who, no doubt with the best of intentions, advised me to do just that. I knew, however, from an intuition and instinct that had been developed over a decade and a half of involvement in the struggle, that such an acceptance would have been the wrong course to take. I had by this time come to hold the absolute conviction that it was only under my own leadership and control that the party could progress forward, or even survive. There will of course be those who will attribute this to vanity and conceit. As far as I was concerned, it was based simply on a recognition of reality, and of the sense of duty that comes of that recognition. I knew all the people who comprised the rival faction, from Read downwards. It was clear to me that not one single one of them was fit for the power that they had inherited. At the best, they possessed none of the intelligence, character or commitment for the task; at the worst, they were enemy infiltrators in disguise, and something told me that Read was one of these — years ahead of the proof that I have mentioned. I simply had to do battle to recover control, no matter what misunderstandings this may create among some of the members and no matter if it lost me, temporarily at least, some of my best friends. When you are in

the arena of real politics where the nation's future is at stake —
and in the 1970s the NF constituted the sole possibility to do
something for the nation's future — you are not engaged in a
game of cricket on the village green, where the ethics of good
sportsmanship might be regarded as paramount; you are involved
in a bloody war. And in such a war there is only one crime, and
that is to be defeated. It was in this spirit that I reacted to this
'palace revolution' that had taken place in the Front, and all
subsequent developments confirm that I was right.

It is symptomatic of the state of stupefaction affecting the minds
of so many in British politics today that they imagine themselves
to be involved in some sort of sporting contest, to be entered into
in the spirit of the noble amateur, who sees it as the first requirement to play the game and who regards winning as secondary to
this purpose. If only the condition of our political life was such
that we could afford to think and act in accordance with this
olympian ideal! But the harsh truth is that today our politics are
plagued with people of subversive intent who are governed by a
code of utter ruthlessness which sanctifies any brutal act if it
contributes to victory. Broadly speaking, those on the left know
that they are in a war and fight according to the rules of war; those
who would oppose the left, on the other hand, tend to live in a
cloud-cuckoo world where getting their hands dirty in defence or
pursuit of their principles is beneath dignity. When things are seen
in this light, it is not difficult to understand why the left is winning
on all fronts.

I resumed the NF leadership in February 1976, and once again
the process began of rebuilding the party from out of the wreckage
that others had left behind. Again we were outstandingly successful. The party leapt ahead in membership growth. In a series of
parliamentary by-elections and elections to local government we
showed our potential with results which, although they fell short
of what was needed to win, indicated a definite upward trend
which seriously worried our opponents. In elections to Leicester
City Council in the Spring of 1976 the party polled a total of
43,000 votes, won by 48 candidates fighting all the city's wards
and with one candidate coming within only 63 votes of getting
elected. Then in elections to the Greater London Council the
following year the party won over 119,000 votes, in many areas
beating the Liberals. Our turn-out on major activities increased
steadily and in November 1977 we mobilised a number variously
estimated at between 5,000 and 6,000 for a march through

London in recognition of Remembrance Day. Nothing like this progress had been seen since the war.

From a figure of approximately 1,500 members in mid-1972, our membership climbed to somewhere around 12,000—13,000 in 1977. In 1976 we set ourselves what seemed to many an impossible target of contesting 300 parliamentary seats in the next general election, but in 1979 this target was in fact achieved, a total of 301 seats being fought throughout the United Kingdom.

It was during this period that the NF began in earnest the practice of staging marches through the towns and cities of Britain. Marches were held in London, Birmingham, West Bromwich, Leicester, Manchester, Bradford, Rotherham, Thurrock, Bristol, Blackburn, Winchester, Huddersfield, Walsall and Coventry. In a number of cases these big public demonstrations were attended by violence, in every single instance the product of counter-demonstrations by the left. A great deal of nonsense has been written in the press about these events and, as a result, there has been much misunderstanding surrounding them.

Why did we take to the streets marching? Very simply because this was one of the few forms by which we could manifest our presence in Britain and publicise our aims. Routine door-to-door leafletting and paper-sales are all very well, but they do not give any impression of a movement of substantial strength and, in the case of leafletting, are wholly impersonal. Every political movement, to get itself over to the public with real impact, requires from time to time to bring out its supporters in large numbers so as to form a massed gathering. This can take the shape of a large public meeting, a march or a combination of the two, with one ending in the other. These events have been a time-honoured tradition in Britain for centuries, and no-one has ever thought of outlawing them nor designated them a public nuisance; on the contrary, the right of a political or any other movement to publicise itself by such means has always been considered one of our most basic freedoms.

In the case of the Labour movement there have for many years been such traditional events as the Durham Miners' Gala. The Campaign for nuclear Disarmament, in the 1960s and again in the 1980s, has regularly taken to the streets in huge, theatrically staged marches that have caused no end of disruption to traffic and tied down great numbers of police, at big public expense, who might otherwise have been occupied dealing with the mounting crime rate. Yet few have ever seriously suggested that such marches as these are an obnoxious phenomenon, least of all that they should be banned. Yet it had not been very long after the start of the National Front's marches of the 1970s that a huge national campaign against them was being whipped up by the media in which they were alleged to be a menace to the public peace.

Why was this? On what grounds was such an allegation deemed to be justified? Solely because these marches became the target for violent attacks by political opponents. The attacks were not, as some claimed, 'spontaneous' reactions to provocation by the marchers; they were deliberately and carefully organised in advance as part of a campaign of intimidation by the opponents of the Front. We soon had evidence that gangs of left-wing militants were being transported from the far ends of the country for these confrontations, the expense of such transport being borne by mysterious personages whose identities were seldom revealed. The purpose was clear: either to smash the NF physically so that it would never be capable of staging such marches again, or to create a degree of public disorder which would earn widespread national condemnation, part of which it was anticipated would rub off on the NF itself.

This latter object would not of course have been achieved had there been a reasonable measure of factual and honest reporting of these disturbances by the mass media. Had they been portrayed for what they were, violent and unlawful attacks, planned well in advance, against perfectly peaceful public demonstrations, and had the entire weight of media condemnation come down, as it should have done, on the opponents of the Front for this vicious behaviour, the public would have understood perfectly well where the blame for the disorders lay, and this would in the end have had the effect of signalling to the left that its violence was entirely counter-productive, winning for the Front a great deal of publicity and public sympathy while bringing widespread opprobrium upon the left itself — apart from costing its supporters a great deal of money in court fines. By such truthful and responsible reporting, the media could have hastened the day when these violent counter-demonstrations were called off, and thus rendered a valuable public service.

But the media did nothing of the kind. Instead they reported these affrays in language which suggested that they amounted to 'six of one, half a dozen of the other', i.e. that the National Front was at least as responsible for the trouble as its opponents, if not more so. Again and again, we heard in broadcasts following riots at our marches that ''there was a clash between the National Front and its opponents'' and that ''police kept the two factions apart.'' Not a word about who started the clashes or who were the intended victims of the attacks! By their wholly misleading reporting of these disturbances, the media positively encouraged the left-militants to believe that their violence paid off and to continue that strategy in the future.

For my part, I am content to leave comment to Metropolitan Police Commissioner McNee, who, after the bloodiest and most highly publicised of these clashes, in Lewisham (South East London) in 1977, said that the trouble was caused entirely by the National Front's opponents and was in no way the fault of the Front itself. A very similar summary was given by the Chief Constable of Leicestershire following a similar fracas involving the NF in Leicester in 1979. Police officers, whose business it was to know the origins of the violence and who had by far the best opportunity to assess where lay the blame, were always more reliable witnesses to what happened than the scribblers of Fleet Street and the lefties of the BBC, a number of whom, but for the sake of appearances, would themselves have been only too happy to be in the ranks of the rioters.

One viewpoint which did gain some currency at this time was that, even accepting that the National Front did not itself initiate the disorder, its very policy of staging such marches was itself provocative and bound to invite trouble; it should therefore have abandoned the marches as soon as their consequences became evident.

I cannot accept this argument. The truth is that what was 'provocative' to the Front's opponents was the very fact that it existed as a political movement at all. The only way not to 'provoke' these people was simply to shut up shop and retire from the political scene. We were a 'provocation' to them by the very fact that we lived and breathed and had thoughts entirely contrary to their own.

If a man happens to be walking down the street going about his ordinary business and is suddenly stung into committing an act of wilful violence, it is reasonable to consider that something may have happened to provoke him into such an act — although that would not necessarily in all events be an excuse for such an action. When, however, busloads of people, all with definitely preconceived political opinions against a particular event are taken to the location of that event from as far as 400-500 miles away and thereupon proceed to stage a riot, the very idea that their violence can be explained by the event being a 'provocation' is obviously preposterous. The fact is that, as I have indicated earlier in a different context, were our marchers to consist of choirboys in white habits parading down the street behind banners proclaiming brotherly love towards all mankind, the very fact that they were known to harbour inside themselves political sentiments diametrically opposed to those of the left would have been a guarantee that they would be attacked with at least equal viciousness.

What was our 'provocation' at Lewisham? We simply marched under our national flag and the theme of our march was that of opposition to muggers — **all** muggers, regardless of race. Can it seriously be deemed a 'provocation' to march through an area of London where muggings of decent, law-abiding people are rife, and therefore, presumably, opposition to this kind of crime ought to win wide approval from all sections of the population? Or have we now reached a stage in Great Britain where one must not condemn muggers for fear of 'provoking' the practitioners of that profession?

I was regularly asked, when we went to an area to stage a march: "Why here? Why have you picked this locality?" My invariable reply was: "Because this locality is part of our country!" The very idea that there should be sectors of our own land 'out of bounds' to us because our presence in such places might be resented by certain parts of the local population — to wit, those parts with the least in the way of roots in the country — was offensive to our whole creed and philosophy of 'Britain for the British'. In fact our popularity or otherwise with the locals in any area never had anything to do with the question of whether our appearance there was likely to result in disorder, for the largest element among those causing the disorder was always imported from outside, and by the method of massed transportation that I have described.

No-one regretted more than we did the inconvenience to ordinary law-abiding people caused by a riot, or the likelihood of one, in an area where we had elected to march, but there just was no way in which we could have allowed this factor to induce us to call off the marches; to do so would have been pure capitulation to violence and thuggery, a tendency for which we often enough despised and condemned established authority; it would hardly have been consistent with the views we had, again and again, expressed on the subject if we had allowed ourselves to become infected with the same spirit of surrender.

It must be remembered that the politicans who regularly deprecated our practice of holding marches and other types of large public demonstration were people whose parties, without exception, had easy access to television and radio and whose leaders' speeches, though they were usually delivered to selected audiences in closed meetings, would be reported faithfully in the press the next day, and often broadcast as well. To such people, the need for activities of the kind in which we were engaged was almost zero. We did not enjoy the same favourable position; the streets of our country's towns and cities were among the very few places open to us to make our presence felt and our name known. I have no apologies to make to anyone for the fact that we availed ourselves of the right to take to those streets, notwithstanding the regret that I have already indicated for the trouble caused to ordinary folk by the vicious antics of the left which attended our marches. All political movements in history, and particularly those which have risen to throw a radical challenge against the prevailing orthodoxy of their times, have been bound by the simple laws of survival. When certain channels of activity have been barred to them, they have had to use whatever other channels have been available.

Responsibility for the violence that attended National Front marches in the 1970s and any nationalist events of similar kind since can be said to lie in three quarters, namely:-

(1) With the people who organised these violent counter-demonstrations, in all cases the opponents of nationalism.

(2) With the reporters of the mass media, who for the most part failed to make clear from what quarter the violence came, often giving the impression that the victims were at least as much to blame as the culprits, thus encouraging the latter in the view that their thuggery was paying off.

(3) With the nation's political leadership, which likewise failed to condemn, unequivocally, the perpetrators of the violence and make clear their sole responsibility for it, and which also failed in its duty to bring the strong arm of the law down on those who repeatedly could be seen to be organising these breaches of the peace.

In the face of these attacks, the self-discipline and restraint of our own people was admirable. Cases of disorderly response to the provocation of the left were very few in proportion to the scale of the disorder coming from the other side. Of course our members, when attacked, had the right to defend themselves, which they did in those incidents where the police were not on hand to take charge of the situation. On the other hand, cases of disorderly behaviour by our own members on such occasions were, as I have said, very small in number. I am speaking of course of the time when I was head of the National Front in the 1970s; I cannot speak of the subsequent period when I and many others had severed all our links with that organisation.

I have made mention of our inability to obtain the hire of meeting halls, and something more should be said about this. The pattern of left-wing violence that attended our activities always made it probable that privately owned halls would be closed to us on account of the owners' fear of damage to their property. In the case of those halls owned by local authorities, one would suppose that it would be a statutory rule that these should be available to political organisations of all complexions, as the halls are paid for by the local ratepayers and are a public amenity to which all such ratepayers should have equal right. One would also suppose that in Britain, which is theoretically held to be a 'democracy', it would be ensured that there would be no violation of this right. In fact the right was withheld from us on practically all occasions where we were not able to assert it by law — something I shall in due course explain.

When we applied for the hire of halls owned by Labour-controlled local authorities, we were refused outright, and on the grounds that these halls would not be made available to 'racists'. This rule was adhered to whether or not the proposed meeting we had in mind had anything to do with race. On the other hand, when we made application to Conservative-controlled councils, the language of refusal was different but the end result was just the same. Usually, we were refused hire on the pretext of a fear of damage to premises. Sometimes, however, acceptance of the application would go ahead, only for it to be cancelled later after threats from opposition groups. Here we saw, again and again, the yellow streak that is a central part of modern British Conservatism and which I have described in an earlier chapter. I suspect, however, that more than just fear of trouble from the left lay behind these refusals, Tory councils, no less than Labour ones, were only too anxious to deny us a hearing, and they were grateful for any pretext that would allow them to do this. In one or two cases when we applied for a hall to a Tory council, we were told that: yes, we could have the hall — if we were willing to pay a huge insurance premium to cover damage to the premises in the event of a disturbance. As the premium was always fixed at a figure far above any likely expense involved in replacing or repairing damaged property, it was clear to us that this was just a perfectly cynical get-out by the council aimed at making sure we could not make a booking.

One council, however, did give a thoroughly typical display of Tory cowardice. This was Hillingdon, in North West London. This council actually did give us a booking of a local hall for a public meeting without the condition of an insurance premium. Then the left-wing opposition got to work. All manner of threats were made against Conservative councillors who supported the granting of the hire, one of them having excreta dropped through the letter-box of his home. In due course, the brave Tory warriors of this council buckled under the pressure and the booking was withdrawn.

In only one kind of event were we able to force local authorities to grant us the hire of meeting halls and this was when we were fighting an election in the area concerned. In that case, a clause of the Representation of the People Act makes it obligatory for local authorities to make halls available to all candidates taking part. Here, and here alone, we were able to get meeting halls, but even in these cases we sometimes had to obtain court injunctions against the councils in order to assert our rights.

From the state of affairs that I have described, it should not be difficult for the reader to understand why I have little respect for 'democracy' as it is represented in the Britain of our times. As I have made clear in the foreword to this book, the whole thing is of course a fraud. I shall examine this matter in some more detail in the next chapter. I should make it clear here, however, that I do not object to democracy as an ideal — in as much as it means government by consent rather than by coercion, and entails the right of people to free discussion of public matters. What is wrong is not the ideal but the way in which, in the name of that ideal, things have been translated into reality in the Britain of the 20th century. I believe that there are better ways in which the ideal can be realised, and on that point I shall later have something to say.

As I have also related, we met just the same kind of barrier when it came to expounding our views on television and radio, the former being by far the most important medium of communication today. Right from the start, we recognised that, as a minority party, we could not expect the same degree of representation on television as the major parties. All we asked was that we be given TV time in keeping with our status as a minority group among other minority groups — and this claim was particularly valid at times when we were a considerable public talking point. After all, it is the habit, when any organisation or individual become 'news', for them to be given the opportunity of speaking for themselves on the issue of newsworthiness surrounding them. We were continually the subject of media controversy throughout the 1970s, and often of the most vehement media attacks, yet hardly ever were we given the chance to reply to the attacks made against us.

It was interesting to note that on radio and TV current affairs discussion programmes representatives of small organisations outside the mainstream political parties were frequently invited to take part — our own representatives never. In the 1970s we scored appreciably higher votes in elections than, for instance, the Socialist Workers' Party and the Ecology Party. Yet their spokesmen were more than once invited onto current affairs discussion panels. This invitation was never extended to myself or any of my colleagues.

The BBC, a body about which I shall have some more to say later, is always preening itself on the generosity with which it gives time to 'minority groups'. What it means of course is **certain** minority groups but not others. Aside from the two organisations I have mentioned, all manner of other groups regularly seemed to get spots on television during that period, with their leaders invited to take part in studio interviews during which they had the opportunity to explain their case. These included black and other racial minority organisations, homosexual and lesbian groups and just about every other minority under the sun — except, as I have said, nationalists. The same has been the trend since. In the 1980s Britain has seen some of the most appalling racial disturbances, which have forced race and immigration right into the foreground of public consciousness and provoked much earnest discussion of the implications of the rioting. Yet never during any of this debate has the opportunity been given by broadcasters to nationalist groups to come on TV and state the case for a ban on immigration and a policy of repatriaton of immigrant groups. As I stated at the beginning of this book, it is quite clear that an invisible censorship exists in this country where the views of people like ourselves are concerned.

These facts simply underline the necessity for us to stage the large public marches and demonstrations that we staged in the 1970s: very little other means to advertise ourselves were available to us. The 'establishment' ensured that we were banned from the use of public meeting halls and almost excluded from TV and radio. Then the very next moment its spokesmen, with a humbug that almost left one spellbound, were popping up everywhere and making loud condemnations against us for our taking to the streets!

Notwithstanding all these difficulties we encountered, by about late-1977 the National Front had made a public impact that was seriously worrying the forces of the establishment of politics and the media. It was noticeable to us at the time that our enemies who controlled these institutions were mobilising themselves for a series of counter-attacks designed to halt our progress.

Up to this time, notwithstanding the conditions I have mentioned, occasional reports and articles about us had appeared in the press which, though unfavourably slanted, had at least given some coverage of our point of view, while being in the main truthful and factual. After 1977 this almost wholly ceased, due no doubt to the action of the National Union of Journalists, which applied intense pressure on its members not to report on the National Front in any shape or form except where it could be connected with some unsavoury event, such as an outbreak of disorder and violence. After this time, newspaper articles on the NF almost dried up, with exceptions of the type mentioned. On television, a whole Labour Party political broadcast in the Summer of 1978 was devoted to an attack on the NF, containing a number of quite scurrilous allegations to which we were never given the right of reply. About the same time, a *World in Action* programme on ITV dealing with the NF was viciously slanted against the party, featuring a list of cases of criminal attacks by white people on ethnic minorities with the insinuation that the culprits were NF members, something which we found on detailed investigation to be untrue in all except one of the cases mentioned (and in that one case the member in question had some time previously been expelled). Needless to say, we were not allowed the right to reply to these vile smears.

Parallel with these developments, our opponents formed a group called the 'Anti-Nazi League', dedicated solely to opposing patriotic organisations, naturally dubbed 'Nazi' because they happened to be devoted to the cause of the British nation and race. The ANAL in its first stages managed to attract supporters from all across the spectrum, including the usual complement of political priests of the type who salivate like Pavlov's dogs at the very whiff of an 'anti-racist' cause. The ANAL also obtained the endorsement of a number of public celebrities of show business and sport. Its driving force and ultimate source of control, however, was the Socialist Workers' Party, for whom, in the last analysis, it was nothing more than a front. The SWP was a group in which there were concentrated some of the worst criminal scum of the political underworld. That this group of rabid left-wing militants and gangsters managed to hoodwink large numbers of total political innocents into joining forces with it in its campaign against the NF and other patriots was a measure of the madness that can grip people in the many thousands whenever the phrases of 'anti-nazism' and 'anti-fascism' are conjured up. At the mere mention of these trigger-words, masses of people throw all reason to the winds and hurl themselves into a kind of collective frenzy of foaming hate. The process is also instructive as to how genteel 'liberals' and red revolutionary thugs seem to see only a thin dividing line between each other when it comes to the imperative of fighting nationalism.

Probably the high point in the career of the 'Anti-Nazi League' was the gigantic carnival-style demonstration it staged in London in 1978, when probably over 100,000 were present. It achieved this by the method of offering a big jamboree of 'pop' music to those in attendance, rather as small children have to be offered lollipops to win their support for an event they might otherwise find tedious. Anyway, the political children of all ages flocked to the capital in droves for this spectacular festival of degeneracy during which, I am given to understand, an effigy of Yours Truly was wheeled through the streets to an accompanying cacophony of screaming hate. We saw them in all their finery in the TV reports of the event: teenage morons 'high' on mind-bending drugs; student floozies with heads stuffed with 'universal brotherhood' and ready to promote it in the most practical possible way; perverts and queers of every conceivable stripe; dotty clerics frantic for self-advertisement as compensation for their empty pews; every little Labour Party jerk in search of a constituency to adopt him or a paid joyride with his local union; every freak and every misfit; every bleeding heart and racial masochist; every modern miss and every liberal trendy; they were all there, in this crazed, gibbering mob — the perfect cast for a filming of the Decline and Fall of the British Empire. And who got them there?

Again, those mysterious gentlemen with bottomless wallets who have appeared before in this story. One youth in attendance, when asked what he had paid to get to London from somewhere in the provinces, said "10p." 10p indeed!

As I have said, we watched this pantomime on our television screens later in the day. I think that we were all unanimous in our conclusions afterwards, which were that, if these are the people who are so passionately against us, we must surely be doing something right!

In due course the various 'celebrities' who lent prestige to the ANAL in most cases discovered the kind of bedfellows they had become associated with and dropped out, quite possibly due in part to a well-documented pamphlet which we produced at the time exposing the latter's far-left and criminal connections, and which was mailed to many of the public figures who had aligned themselves with the 'anti-nazi' cause. In any event, the ANAL did not hold onto its mass following for long and eventually dwindled to a much smaller 'hard-core' of left-wing nasties. A few years afterwards no-one heard of it any more.

All these pressures from without created a situation in which, from about the beginning of 1978, the National Front found itself under heavy enemy fire and hindered in its progress forward by numerous obstacles that were not encountered by any ordinary political party. These kinds of obstacles had always been there, of course, but from the time mentioned they increased in the difficulties they presented for us. Of all these difficulties, the 'silent treatment' of press and broadcasting were the greatest.

We had absolutely no means with which to fight back against the increasingly vicious media treatment to which we were being subjected. We possessed no mass-circulation newspaper of our own, nor any TV or radio channels. In the propaganda war we were like an army equipped with bows and arrows facing an adversary using heavy artillery, bombers, missiles and all the other accoutrements of modern fire-power. We had to rely simply on our own publications of very limited circulation, which were wholly inadequate to combat the barrage of lies and hate hurled at us by the established press and broadcasting networks — plus whatever powers of discernment the British public possessed whereby it could be immune to the proaganda against us and exercise its own independent judgement. In the climate of our time this, as we learned, is a fragile entity.

Much of the hostile media treatment consisted, as I have said, of boycott, and in accordance with the NUJ directive to which I have referred. Party events that would have been treated as 'news' in any other context became non-events as far as the media were concerned. Hardly ever were we reported unless some riotous situation surrounded the activity concerned, and then the question of who was responsible for the riot was dealt with with, to say the least, considerable ambiguity. There was quite clearly an orchestrated campaign to implant in the public mind an association between the National Front and violence and disorder, although the reality was that the violence and disorder were, without exception, of the making of our opponents.

Elsewhere in this book I shall have more to say about the mass media. The fact is that this massive and overwhelmingly powerful institution — indeed in some respects one with more power than governments — can, if in irresponsible and dishonest hands, completely poison the whole atmosphere in which a nation's politics are conducted. It is a popular illusion of the British that their press and other resources of mass-communication are 'free'. We know this not to be so from our own bitter experience. Until this 'Fourth Estate' is restored to responsible, honest and, above all, patriotic hands, British public opinion is going to continue to be led blindly on to endorse policies of national self-destruction, as has been the case for at least the last half-century.

In any quality army, one vital feature is the ability of the troops to remain cool under heavy fire. This is partly a matter of battle experience, partly of leadership and training, and partly of the basic human calibre of the men themselves. The membership of the National Front by the late 1970s was a mixture of many sorts. There were the hardened veterans of the political struggle against the old world forces, and these never lost their resolve despite the increased difficulty of battle conditions. Then there were the many newcomers we had recruited in our rapid growth of the preceding years. Many of these, after the initial shock at the severity of the enemy bombardment, came to terms with the reality of the war conditions in which they found themselves and, with a little nursing, became good fighting 'soldiers'. But there were some who, to say the least, were of rather brittle material. This was especially noticeable with recent recruits from the old and established political parties. At the first sign of real flak, they would be inclined, either to turn and run, or start blubbing and wailing within the ranks in a way guaranteed to lower morale, undermine discipline and spread defeatism and mutiny. Instead of accepting the shells and bullets as an inevitable hazard of war when the name of the game is to engage the enemy, they clung to the naive belief that such a contest could somehow be waged in the spirit of a game of croquet on the vicarage lawn, and when they found themselves in the firing line they liked to imagine it was because their commanders had somehow given a wrong order resulting in an error of navigation which had placed them in the battle zone instead of in cosy billets behind the lines. Get rid of those commanders and change the marching orders, the reasoning went, and we can have a comfortable war, ending in the sure defeat of the enemy without any of us even getting his feet wet!

In time, this tendency to look for the political 'soft option' acquired a name. It was its own exponents who referred to it as 'populism', and the term caught on. These self-styled geniuses in political strategy discovered a truth that it would seem had never occurred to the rest of us: that it should be the wish and aim of our movement to be 'popular'! If we were not popular, it was simply because we did not put ourselves over as 'nice' enough. How should we appear 'nice'? Why, by eliminating all the people, tendencies and ideas from our party that the enemy media attacked. Then, presumably, those who today were lambasting us with the vitriol of their reporting would tomorrow cast upon us the friendly smile of their approval. This, largely, was the *leitmotif* of those who staged the rebellion in the NF in 1974-75, to which I have referred earlier, and after its unsuccessful conclusion left us and set up a rival political organisation, which I have also mentioned. The very brief career of that rival organisation was, I think, ample testimony to the theories upon which it was founded.

Every possible effort was made by me and my seasoned colleagues in the party leadership to counter this type of thinking. Right from the start, we endeavoured to counsel all new recruits that they had entered a battle that would be long and hard, and that there were no facile ways to mass popularity and mass support. Our task in this regard would have been less difficult in circumstances of steady, but not overly rapid, recruitment. New members in the 1970s, however, were for much of the time coming in in a flood, and bringing with them all the problems of training and conditioning a fast-growing army to a war situation to which most of its number were not accustomed.

The tendency to mutiny under fire of which I have spoken provided, of course, an ideal opportunity to those who saw our movement primarily as a vehicle for their own egos and personal political ambitions. Some of these people defected to us from the Tory and other parties for no loftier reason than that they found the path to promotion in those parties too slow for their liking. In a young and new party looking eagerly for new talent, they no doubt thought that their progress up the ladder would be speedy by comparison. Some of them even had the cheek to imagine that their record of having held some position in the party of their previous affiliation would be an automatic credential for quick elevation in the NF! When such assumptions were dashed, they were in haste to join the ranks of the mutinous, the disaffected and the disruptive.

From all this it will be seen that we had the constant problem in the National Front of reconciling the obvious need to grow and expand with the equally important need to prevent the party we had built falling into the wrong hands and going off course. It was never easy to strike a balance between these requirements.

Generally speaking, it is right that those who have been the pioneers of a new movement in politics should retain control of the reins of that movement through all the periods of its subsequent growth and development. They, after all, were the first to conceive the need for the movement in the beginning, and if they were the ones to surmount the first hurdle in lifting it from complete obscurity to a level at which it was large enough to attract widespread public interest and support, they will furthermore have proved that, in addition to having the initiative to get the movement started, they have shown the necessary competence to bring it successfully through the first stage of its development.

If new people subsequently enter the movement and claim that they have greater qualifications to lead it than those who were in at the start and guided it through its most difficult phase, it may be asked of those people why they were not there at the start themselves, why they were not among the first initiators and pioneers. The fact that they were not so, but left to others this, the hardest of all the phases of the movement's progress forward — the most important of which was the conception of the basic political idea giving rise to it, indicates a natural status of subordination to those responsible for that achievement. The simple question to these newer adherents is: Where were you when we began it all? Why were you not with us?

To this question there may of course be in some cases a perfectly valid answer. At the time the newcomer may not yet have crossed the boundary line between youth and maturity but may subsequently have become much more mature. Or he may have harboured in his mind a similar political idea but not had any contact with the kind of people who could have helped him found an organisation to give expression to it. There could be any number of perfectly acceptable reasons for such a newcomer not to have been present at the birth of the movement, and the fact that he was not should not necessarily be regarded as a permanent reason for his exclusion from the leadership circle.

But the fact nevertheless remains that the movement's pioneers have, by being pioneers, established a very strong claim to primacy, which they would be extremely unwise to relinquish, presuming that their intention is not to allow their movement to be hi-jacked and then deflected from the purposes for which it was originally brought into being. Where new blood enters the movement which they perceive to be of the best quality, they can induct that new blood into their leadership circle at their own discretion and their own speed, ensuring at every step, and by careful judgement, that it meets their requirements in terms, not only of talent, but in sincerity of conviction and in depth of commitment to the movement's aims. Even here they can be capable of error, but if the process is gradual the likelihood of error is not great, and it can usually be discovered in time for it to be remedied by the casting out of the erroneously promoted recruit.

There is another truth that should be taken into account, and this is that in such a movement any newcomer who enters the ranks after the initial formative period but nevertheless has the qualities to be admitted to the leadership circle, will commend himself and establish his credentials, not by setting himself up as a rival to the established leadership, but by joining forces with it and helping it. Indeed, any Johnny-come-lately who has to establish his claims to leadership by forming a rival faction against the leadership-in-being and then conducting a power-struggle within the movement for the latter's place proves in that very act his manifest unfitness for the position he has coveted — quite apart from the already proven fact that the leadership he seeks to challenge showed superior judgement to his in the first place in respect of its much earlier recognition of the political truths giving rise to the movement and the need then for that movement to be formed.

I should again stress here that I am speaking of movements which progress beyond tiny back street status and thereby give some indication of their founders' capability to promote their growth, and also of circumstances in which there is no evidence of any decline in those pioneers' commitment or capabilities from the time they founded the movement and saw it successfully through its earlier stages. Obviously, if these conditions do not apply, there can be justification in an attempt to supplant the established leadership by internal challenge — assuming that that leadership does not relinquish its position voluntarily.

It should also be said that the rules I have outlined here do not apply to today's established political parties, for in those bodies leadership contests are one long ongoing rat-race and those who challenge the established leadership by the deployment of factions are only using the same methods as those used by the latter to win that leadership from previous rivals.

In a healthy political organism therefore (which of course the established parties are not), change-overs of leadership should not be brought about by party in-fighting but by a smooth transition, usually at such time as the established leadership has come to the end of its natural active span and has selected and trained the person (or persons) best fitted for the succession, and these will always be the ones who have given evidence of putting cause above selves and worked at all times to help the leadership in power rather than hinder it by fomenting rivalry and division.

This sure process of direction, however, depends on one vital condition: that the movement is constituted in its internal structure so as to make the control of its pioneers legitimate and unquestioned; if things are otherwise, immediately it begins to expand into anything approaching a large membership, it is headed for certain trouble.

This principle whereby expansion is successfully pursued while basic direction is preserved means one thing above all: that the movement cannot admit into its constitution any of the normal procedures that we understand by the word 'democracy'.

The existence of such a democratic structure within a movement engaged in a life-or-death struggle for the survival of a nation carries with it the virtual certainty that, sooner or later, those who were its founding pioneers, together with their natural heirs, will be in danger of becoming dispossessed of control and the movement of passing into hands which, in the natural scheme of things, are less fit for power — the people concerned being merely the followers of a trend rather than the setters of it.

It is no argument against this to say that such newcomers may be slicker in their practice of the political process by reason of their greater ability to garner votes in party elections. If this were a justification of their claim to leadership, it would likewise be a justification of the whole game of mass bribery, trickery and lying by which our contemporary politicians have obtained and held on to the reins of national office while presiding over recurrent national catastrophe. The whole purpose of those who founded the National Front in 1967 and took part in its early battles to gain recognition was that it should become a revolutionary challenge to that system, not a pale copy of it.

But the internal revolution which took place in 1970-71 ensured that the party would incorporate into its organisation all the worst features of the disease it was supposed to be fighting. From that time, the way lay open to any chancer and political confidence-trickster to insinuate his way into the senior councils, in which then his voice and his vote were assumed to be as good as those who had undertaken the pioneer work of getting the party off the ground. If he and his type could do this in sufficient numbers, they could effectively take control. In addition to this, the practice of making the party leader merely a chairman of meetings and limiting his effective power to one vote in 20 made a mockery of the principle of leadership.

The chief official of a party always becomes, in the eyes of its membership, the one responsible for the party's fortunes. If bad decisions are made, they are assumed to be his decisions; if the party fails to progress, he is assumed to be to blame. In view of this, it is perfectly ridiculous that the leader should not be given decision-making powers commensurate to his responsibilities. The latter are a hundred times greater than those of any other committee member; yet in the NF after 1970 decision-making powers were divided equally between 20 people.

This system, apart from making proper leadership exceedingly difficult, ensured that the collective leadership body would be an almost permanently divided entity, with a generous complement of members who were there with no other purpose than to promote the tendency to faction and to embarrass, hinder and undermine leadership rather than assist it.

For several years as NF leader I lived uneasily with this system, never liking it and always intending, at the first suitable opportunity, to alter it. During my years of tenure of the post, however, circumstances constantly intruded to postpone this time of opportunity. Until after the general election of 1979, there never was a time when the next election was far away. I wanted to do nothing to risk a division in the party with a general election imminent, and I could see that, inevitably, a drastic change in the party's internal constitution would become a matter for bitter argument and conflict with those who had a vested interest in preserving that *status quo*. It was only after the election of 1979 that the way become clear to grasp this nettle. When finally it was grasped, as events proved, the internal rot in the party's leading councils that had been brought about by this adherence to 'democratic' procedure had become so great that the move turned out to be too late.

Throughout the whole period of my leadership of the National Front the party was being regularly torn asunder by recurring bouts of factional strife, made inevitable by its monstrosity of a constitution. It became a microcosm of British politics as a whole, a battleground of warring interests and position-seeking rivalries, instead of a disciplined organisation dedicated to a common constructive purpose. And in case my detractors should wish to suggest that this might somehow have had something to do with the fact that I was leader at the time — implying that I might have been a divisive influence, I need only point to the state of affairs that has existed in that party since my withdrawal from it in 1980. In fact, since that time the tendency to factionalism and internal strife has greatly increased.

Notwithstanding these difficulties, I am able to point to the fact that in my time the Front emerged from the obscure fringe of politics to become a household name and a real potential national force. It was most certainly the most successful by far of all the post-war patriotic organisations in Britain up to its time, and among the two or three most successful in the world during the same period. I say this, not for the purpose of an exercise in self-congratulation — credit for this achievement, as I have already said, should not go to me alone — but only as my answer to the numerous people who during this period set themselves up as rivals to me for the leadership of British Nationalism and at every turn sought to undermine my position instead of collaborating with me in the great endeavour to which we should all have been mutually dedicated.

But having spoken of the petty careerists, self-seekers and disrupters with whom I had constantly to contend, I should not leave the subject without speaking of the truly fine people with whom I also came to work and at the head of whom it was an honour to serve. Side by side with the dross who caused nothing but trouble, there were some magnificent nationalists and patriots whom I was proud to know and who became my lifelong friends, people who at every stage were helpful and loyal and without whom our success would have been impossible. Some of these are now gone, but many are still with me, and from them a new team has been built to meet a new phase of the nationalist struggle, which belongs to a later chapter.

We succeeded in standing 301 candidates in the general election of 1979, despite all the immense difficulties of the preceding years of party development when, as I have stated, our enemies became mobilised against us with a much greater thoroughness and intensity than ever before. This was a mammoth achievement for a movement as young as we were and with the meagre resources at our disposal. In the political climate of the time that election build-up should have been regarded as a triumph for our party, regardless of the actual number of votes we were able to obtain. Votes in fact never were the main object of the exercise; if they had been, we would have fought a vastly reduced number of seats and thereby been able much more to concentrate our limited forces. We set ourselves the highly ambitious target of 300 in order to make the greatest possible nationwide publicity impact, with the hope that this would result in a further big wave of recruitment in the period that was to follow.

In view of the fact that in February 1974 we had, by fighting 54 seats, qualified for five minutes' broadcasting time on TV and radio, it was not unreasonable to hope that, under a fair system for the allocation of broadcasts, we would obtain a commensurately greater amount of time when fighting over 300 seats in 1979, or, if not that, at least substantially more time than in 1974. In the event, we were allocated only the same two five-minute broadcasts — a telling reflection of the BBC's standards of fairness. In other areas of publicity we reckoned that in fact we received **less** coverage in the run-up to the 1979 election than in the two elections five years previously, when our challenge had been only a fraction as strong. This was, without any doubt, a consequence, at least in part, of the NUJ policy towards us, determined a year or so earlier, which influenced broadcasters and newspaper-writers equally.

To all this, a further factor affecting our fortunes was added. The Conservatives, as part of a 'new look' programme introduced with the accession of Mrs. Thatcher to the leadership, deliberately projected the image of a 'shift to the right' in the policies it presented to the electorate. Sensing that the people were growing tired of soggy 'liberal' prescriptions for the solutions to our national problems and wanted to see a more resolute approach to such issues as law and order and immigration, as well as a generally more patriotic stance in national and world affairs, the Tories deliberately, though quite falsely, cultivated a line of electioneering propaganda designed to give the impression that they were moving in the direction desired by public opinion. On the immigration issue particularly, they were at pains to project this illusion, with Mrs. Thatcher coming on television and speaking of the concern of the British people lest they may be 'swamped' by coloured aliens. This, and the vitriolic reaction to it by the left-wing press (which gave it further publicity) was probably worth millions of votes to the Tories.

We knew from the start that the Tory Party had not the slightest intention of putting into practice, when in office, any of the policies they were hoodwinking the electorate into believing they had adopted. We knew from the start that this was just Mrs. Thatcher's way of heading off the nationalist challenge, which in view of the number of marginal seats the NF was fighting must have scared Conservative Central Office considerably. Nevertheless, with the bulk of the press and much of the rest of the media on their side, and with the entire media against the NF, the Tories had the means to make most of the people believe their lies, while we were almost wholly lacking in the means to rebut and expose them.

In the event, the Tories, as might have been expected, stole many votes from the National Front by the simple device of stealing — at least as far as appearances were concerned — a large part of its platform. The NF vote was a disappointment by comparison with what many of us had hoped for, although I myself was never one to entertain the wildly optimistic expectations that gripped some of our party members.

I believe that in the general election of 1979 the National Front did as well as any party in its position could possibly have expected to do, taking into account three factors in particular, namely:-

(1) The dispersal of its campaigning strength over more than 300 constituencies.

(2) Its treatment by the media during and preceding the election.

(3) The poaching of much of its traditional support, by entirely dishonest means, by the Tories generally and Mrs. Thatcher in

particular.

Needless to say, however, there were those in the Front who were only too ready to turn this mammoth party achievement of fighting over 300 seats upside down and present it as a catastrophe, blaming the party leadership for the fact that the votes were not higher and using this grumble as the pretext for yet another internal power struggle involving yet more fratricidal war. Indeed, just how sincere was the use of the votes issue as a weapon against the leadership may be gleaned from the fact that, as I later realised, the disrupters were busy plotting their move **during** the run-up to the election and obviously **before** anyone had any idea what vote we would get. To these gentlemen, this occupation evidently seemed more important than the election campaign itself and thus deserving of priority in the allocation of their time. As I was working almost round the clock, together with other party loyalists, in the performance of election campaign duties, these people seemed to find the time to engage in long and expensive telephone calls, letter-writing and secret meetings, all directed to the one purpose of mobilising other party members in the promotion of yet another party split at the first moment when the opportunity presented itself when the election was over. An outstanding case of *deja vu*, needless to say.

This treacherous coterie comprised the usual combination of political weaklings and shell-shock victims, grasping egotists and enemy agents that had promoted previous divisions, with the latter — as always — the dominant and directing force. Long before the 1979 election took place, they had manoeuvred themselves into control of certain vital party assets, including most importantly a large building we had obtained close to Central London — this again making a mockery of the claim that the election results were the reason for their rebellion.

Again I prefer not to bore the reader with all the extensive and sordid details of this affair, which themselves would occupy a whole book on their own were such a task to be attempted. In all essentials, the revolt followed a similar pattern to the previous ones in 1970-71, 1972 and 1974-75. An attempt was made by forces outside, exploiting weaknesses inside, to smash the NF by means of contrived civil war.

Even without the intricacy of detail that I have omitted, some readers of this book may be wondering whether I have not devoted excessive attention to these sordid internal divisions in a book whose purpose is, after all, to signpost the way to the future recovery of Britain and ought properly to be devoted mainly to matters of national and international importance. It might also be conjectured whether this is a case of personal emotions engendered by bitter past conflicts being allowed to overflow beyond proper proportions when the correct policy might be to regard such matters as dead and buried.

I can perfectly understand such a reaction, but I must hasten to stress that there is a deliberate purpose in mentioning these matters. Even within the wide consensus of support for the broad political aims of our movement, there has always been, and will continue to be, much debate as to what are the correct means to be adopted in the promotion of these aims and the type of political movement that we must build as the vehicle for this endeavour. I feel it is right that I should give some explanation of the factors that have led me to adopt the methods of leadership and organisation that I presently employ in this regard, and to help others to avoid the pitfalls to which I have sometimes myself become a victim in the past. In many respects, the nationalist movement in Britain has in past years been its own worst enemy, sabotaging its future by internal splits just at a time when opportunities for progress were bright. Nothing is more important than that we should avoid, so far as is possible, a future repetition of these acts of suicide. Therein, and therein alone, lies my purpose in raking over past conflicts. As I have stated before, the people responsible for them are not themselves important; but their habitual attitudes and practices are so. If we are on our guard against a re-emergence of these things, we will be vastly better equipped for the struggles ahead.

I come back to where I left off: the internal conflict in the National Front in 1979. Despite the similarities with past conflicts, there was in this case the difference that the conflict was a little less simple than in the past; in this later case there were not quite the same neat divisions between the loyal and the disloyal. Certain people who sided with me in the first phase of the conflict, which took place in the late Summer and early Autumn of that year, were found later to be about as loyal and reliable as allies as many of those who in this first phase had opposed me. The challenge in the first phase of the conflict came from a group oddly terming themselves the 'National Front Constitutional Movement', and was eventually defeated — though not without great damage to the party, including long and costly litigation in the courts. In the true tradition of former rebels, the promoters of the

NFCM took themselves out of the party, once beaten, and tried to set up their own separate nationalist organisation. This went the way of all its predecessors.

The victory over this faction, however, did not mean, by any stretch of imagination, that all was again well in the party. The rumblings of further divisions were becoming ominously loud. One of the running sores which the NFCM faction had exploited with no little success was one that had been festering for some time, and to my increasing concern.

Our party had always attempted to immunise itself against the moral decline rampant in modern Britain and to encourage, in the personal behaviour of its members, the idea that it was a force for moral regeneration.

Of the many unwholesome habits opposed by the vast majority in the party, homosexuality was one that featured prominently on the list. It was therefore with considerable alarm that I had in the last year or so become aware that the National Front was itself by no means immune to this sickening cult. Bit by bit, I had come to realise that there existed within the party a network of homosexuals which extended right through the organisation and even into its higher councils.

To be aware of this network, however, was not quite the same thing as being empowered to take the appropriate measures against it. In the first place, such measures had to be based on concrete proof and not just on gossip. Secondly, even if proof could be obtained, the 'democratic' internal organisation of the party made it by no means certain that the necessary disciplinary action would be forthcoming. I could take no such action by my own decision; I could only do so by the vote of the Directorate, and it was clear that by no means all those on the Directorate shared my view that homosexuality was something we should take pains to exclude from the party — indeed some would have a positive vested interest in seeing that it was not excluded!

In October of 1979 some information came into my possession which constituted about as solid evidence as we were ever likely to obtain of homosexual activities within the party, and it involved not an ordinary member but an extremely highly placed party officer and member of the Directorate. I placed this evidence before the Directorate and demanded action. By an overwhelming majority, action was rejected.

I knew, when this evidence was brought to light, that the affair to which it related had incensed party members in the Midlands, where it occurred, and that widespread resignations in that area were probable if action was not taken against the offending officer — and so it was duly proved. All this, however, had about as much effect on the Directorate as water on a duck's back; those whom fortune (and votes) had selected to be my colleagues seemed to live in a little dream-world of their own, almost wholly insulated from events and from feeling in the party for whose destiny they were responsible.

In the ensuing weeks much of my time was spent making contact with members in various parts of the country urging them to hold back any plans they had to leave the party until I had formulated in my mind some definite steps that could be taken to bring my fellow Directorate members to their senses over this and other issues that were threatening to tear the party to pieces.

In the meantime yet another mutiny had broken out in the party, this time involving mainly members and units in the Midlands. The prime mover in this rebellion was a man who had taken part in the previous one in 1974-75 but had wormed his way back into the party in its aftermath by means of an attitude of apparent contrition. He had clearly planned his move a long time in advance and was in no way influenced by the homosexual affair. Nevertheless, that affair certainly did have the effect of providing him with a great many willing accomplices who might otherwise have stayed loyal.

This faction broke away from the NF and set up a new party of their own. As with others before them, their watchword was 'respectability'. The NF had acquired too much of an 'extreme' image. They were going to win over the legions of 'moderate' people in Britain whom we had alienated, and so on *ad nauseam*.

A short time later, something of the credentials of this group in the way of respectability and moderation was demonstrated when their leader was exposed in the papers for gun-running and forced to hot-foot it to Ireland, which is where he was last heard of. His party of course duly fizzled out. Later on two of his leading collaborators, who had been misled rather than filled with bad intentions, joined forces with me again and took their place among my most valued colleagues and friends. By no means all those who get caught up in these splits are bad people; some simply find themselves borne along by a tide of events beyond their control, set off in the first place by cunning and dishonest manipulators who know how to exploit human credulity to the uppermost.

As the year 1979 drew to its close, I found myself having to take urgent and decisive stock of my position in the movement of British Nationalism. I had given many of the best years of my life to that movement. I was prepared to go on doing so, labouring anew to reconstruct everything that had been wrecked in the turmoil of the past few months. I knew that there were others in the party of like mind to myself, willing, in the words of Kipling, "to see the things you gave your life for broken, and stoop to build them up with worn-out tools."

But what I was not prepared to do, and knew these others were not prepared to do either, was give more years to the patient work of reconstruction only with the probability that **again** what we built would be wrecked by an alliance of saboteurs, egotists and political weaklings, in just the same way as had happened constantly in the preceding decade.

If we were to begin work again with reasonable hope that what we built would endure and withstand the destructive attempts of future wreckers, what would be needed was an entirely different kind of organisation to that in which we had worked in the past: an organisaton which would simply prohibit the infiltration of the subversive and the wrecker, at least to the degree at which he could do real damage.

This did not necessarily mean a new party; on the contrary, we were at that time firmly against the formation of any such body. We had seen the disastrous consequences of people trying to form splinter-groups from the National Front and we did not want to follow that path. It was in the National Front itself, appropriately reformed and reorganised on the inside, that we wished to continue the struggle.

In most respects the National Front was basically sound. Its political objectives, as they stood, needed no alteration. The vast majority of its members consisted of sound people, albeit people in some cases needing further political education.

What was wrong with the party was a minority of members who were a harmful influence, and, above all, its internal constitution and organisational structure, which permitted the continuous infiltration of bad blood into the ranks and thereafter the rising of much of that bad blood to the top. The party most certainly had no future unless it could be immunised against this tendency, and this immunisation had to start with an alteration of the rules by which the party was run.

The first requirement was the adoption of an organisation that was essentially hierarchical. Democracy could be practised in the election by the whole membership of a party leader. While even in this system there are dangers, I was confident of our ability to guard against them. No internal rebellion in the party had ever succeeded in the way of the Chairman being toppled by a general members' vote; the trouble had always lain in the composition of the Directorate, and then — at least since 1971 — in the Directorate's power to make decisions contrary to the will of the Chairman, thus relegating him to little better than a figurehead.

The proper procedure was for the Chairman, once elected, to have full executive power over the party, including powers of appointment of all subordinate officials, power of discipline and indeed power over all other matters of party business. Though the vulnerability of the party to infiltration would not by this process be reduced to zero, the scope for the infiltrator would be reduced practically to zero, for he would be unable to use his vote in leading councils even if he obtained a place on them. At the same time, the moment that there were any signs of any faction emerging in the party that was bent on some subversive action or policy, that faction could be neutralised by its members' immediate expulsion.

Of course, the party leader would, as in the past, need people to advise him and bring to the making of decisions the fertility of brainpower of numerous minds. But the procedure would be for the leader to select such people by the exercise of his own judgement of their ability, character and — not least — motivation. Then, notwithstanding that he should listen to their opinions, final decision should be his and his alone.

This would mean great personal power being placed in the leader's hands, but it would also mean great personal responsibility going with it. If the leader's decisions proved wrong, no-one but he would be to blame. With added prerogatives also come added burdens — the leader could not hide behind a committee when making a difficult decision or facing the consequences of his own error.

The protest of the opponents of this procedure can immediately be anticipated. They will say that it places enormous powers in the party leader's hands, and that it could result in the abuse of such powers, in personal favouritism, in the formation of leadership cliques, in manipulation of power for personal ends, and so on.

And of course the answer must be: yes, it **could** result in all of these things! But equally, just these same abuses: favouritism, cliquishness and personal self-serving can result from power being placed in the hands of committees, and indeed I have witnessed just such tendencies manifesting themselves as a consequence of committee rule.

Ultimately of course, natural forces have a way of redressing things should such misuse of power by an individual leader occur. If this happens in the way feared, this will in time have its effects in the form of the failure of the party and the widespread discontent within it that is certain to result from that failure, and the leader's eventual downfall would be in that consequence certain. He simply cannot run the party effectively if his most valued colleagues walk out on him. And in the final analysis, a leader can only be leader if he has a party to lead. As no-one is conscripted into the party by compulsion, everyone has in the last resort the option of voting against the leader with his feet. It is hardly likely that anyone able to obtain the leadership in the first place would fail to understand this.

It is a matter of common sense that in the event of an individual leader of the party manifestly failing in his job there is all manner of practical measures that his colleagues can employ that would make his position no longer tenable, without any need for a formal written document existing to give sanction to their action.

And indeed the fact that all party members, the vast majority of whom are unpaid, can walk out at any time they please always provides a brake on any leader's inclination to use his powers tyrannically, corruptly or self-interestedly. He stands or falls by his ability to show success, and he will reduce his chances of doing this to the exact extent to which he allows his decisions to be influenced by any considerations other than the party's good.

In a party where all decisions and appointments are by committee vote, this natural law cannot operate to anything like the same degree, because the blurring of the lines of responsibility does not enable any but a few to see and know who is to blame for the committee's abuse of power and who not.

As the decade of the 1970s drew to its close, I became resolved that the time had come to take the bull by the horns and force through the constitutional changes necessary to set our movement on a sound course for the new decade soon to begin.

At the first meeting of the NF Directorate in 1980 I put my cards squarely on the table. I told the assembled company that I was not prepared to continue leading the party and taking responsibility for its fortunes unless I was invested with proper leadership powers. I said that I required the calling of an extraordinary general meeting of party members at which I intended to present to them a set of proposals for changes in the party constitution which would give me the powers I needed. If the Directorate declined to agree to such a meeting, it would have my resignation as party Chairman by the last day of the month (January 31st). If the demand for such a meeting was accepted and then that meeting turned down my proposals, likewise I would resign. I was determined on this course of action and was prepared to go to the bitter end to force it through. Whether the Directorate properly understood my determination was a question yet to be answered.

In the discussion that followed this ultimatum it was proposed by one of those present that a decision be postponed until January 31st, when there should be a further meeting. To this I agreed.

At the meeting on January 31st the Directorate rejected my proposal and I duly handed in my resignation.

It was not my intention at that time to leave the National Front, and for the reasons I have explained earlier, I and those who shared my view about the need for changes resolved that we would pursue these changes within the party rather than have it break up, the next opportunity to do so being the internal party elections later in the year. I retained my seat on the Directorate and continued to support the party through the pages of *Spearhead*.

What then followed I do not want to risk boring the readers of this book by relating in detail, for the whole episode was a tedious one and has anyway been more than adequately chronicled in *Spearhead* stage by stage. Suffice it to say that a squalid little war was unleashed against me and my supporters by the faction now in control of the Directorate in the weeks following my resignation from the NF leadership. This war made it abundantly clear that no possibility existed of our carrying out the changes we sought by the constitutional process originally intended, or indeed of exercising, in the short term, any reasoned persuasion of the Directorate to take a more sensible attitude. In June 1980 we decided by unilateral action to disengage ourselves from the official National Front party organisation and function for the time being as an independent body. Even at this late hour of the proceedings, we still hoped for some eventual reconciliation of differences within the orbit of the National Front and with that party name, now well established throughout the country, still preserved. We therefore chose to identify ourselves by a name which retained the NF link. We called ourselves the 'New National Front'. We saw our break with the official Front as one that it should be hoped would be only temporary, and we made this clear to all those in the Front to whom we announced our decision. It was our hope that, if reasonable counsels could not for the moment prevail on the Directorate, they might, by our action, be brought to prevail in the party, and that pressure on the Directorate from the wider membership would bring about a restoration of sanity, and a reconciliation of the two warring factions be achieved.

It was not due to any kind of *hubris* but only to cold realism that I knew that the National Front could not survive as any kind of effective political force under any leadership other than my own. The people left behind either were simply too young and immature or did not have the necessary capability or character to do the job adequately, let alone put themselves over with the necessary credibility to the British public. It was naturally hoped that this reality would dawn on them as time went on, but of course the facing of reality was not something at which so far they had proved themselves very adept. The Front might indeed survive in name for an indefinite time but its survival as a serious challenge to the forces of national betrayal in Britain was a clear non-starter — unless there was a reconciliation of our divisions and the reconstitution of the party along the lines we had laid down.

The New National Front was constituted from the beginning along these lines, with the head of the organisation having complete executive power. The procedure worked smoothly and effectively and, bit by bit, we began building up a solid organisation — small by comparison with the NF a year or two earlier but soundly based.

Meanwhile, in the old National Front things went from bad to worse, with every development in the party vindicating our analysis and predictions. Internal discipline fast deteriorated, with a moronic, loutish element coming increasingly to the fore and seeming to be especially in prominence on public activities. Enemy propaganda against the Front began for the first time to contain a note of truth, what with the antics of some of the people now under the spotlight within it. Its widely known name, up till then an undoubted political asset, started to become a liability.

By the end of 1981, a year and a half after our break, we had to take cold stock of the situation and recognise two unhappy but inescapable facts: firstly, that no sign whatever existed that events had persuaded those on the NF Directorate of the necessity to sit down with us and work out a formula for the reunification of the party; secondly, that, even should this now happen, it was highly doubtful that anything was left that was worth uniting with — if such a unification were to take place under the name of 'National Front'. Previous to 1980, the party of that name had certainly not enjoyed 'respectability' in the conventional sense — the media treatment of it ensured that this would never happen — but it did earn a certain **respect** among many British people for the courage and honesty of its political stand; after 1980, the human dross that its leaders were prepared to take into the party ranks, and the unedifying public antics of the party that were largely a consequence of this, effectively ruined the Front as a credible force for the eventual revival of Britain.

In the meantime, the existence of two 'National Fronts', each now with increasingly divergent political ideas, created a situation that was at the same time bizarre and confusing. The old Front had for some time been moving away from us, not just in methods of organisation and tactics, but also increasingly in its basic political philosophy, adopting more and more a set of attitudes that can only be described as left-wing.

By now something had become clear to us which perhaps we ought to have recognised at the beginning of the dispute: that in fact the majority of the NF Directorate positively **wanted** and **welcomed** a permanent split in the party, as it would enable them to mould the NF in accordance with a new and entirely different set of beliefs to those for which we fought in the 1970s. This thought first began to occur to me in the early part of 1980. Starting from the supposition that my adversaries in the party, though they disagreed with me as to how the party should be run, at least were with me in wanting to keep it united, I came to realise that in the case of some of them placed in key positions this simply was not so, and that these people positively desired a permanent parting of the ways. In the ensuing two years this became more and more evident and strengthened my suspicion that certain personages on the Front Directorate were in fact 'sleepers' working in the service of our political opponents.

At any rate, by 1982 we had to recognise the remoteness of the prospect of the National Front ever again becoming united under its old name, with its traditional policies intact and its dynamic public appeal restored. The time had come to think the unthinkable, to contemplate a complete break with the past and the formation of an entirely new political movement.

Such a step ran contrary to all the beliefs I had come to hold about the futility of splitting; but we had to acknowledge now that this step had become inevitable. For no-one was this harder to come to terms with than myself. I had put 13 years of my life into the National Front, about half of those as its leader. My name was identified with that party probably more than was any other. To abandon the thing that was the focus of one's strivings and dreams for all those years was no easy decision.

The decision had to be made, however, and plans for the forming of a new party were laid. It would be based on the same political ideals as those for which we had fought in the National Front up to 1980 and had continued to fight in the New National Front thereafter, together with the constitutional structure adopted since the 1980 split. It would discard the old party name and old party habits of internal organisation. Its structure would be hierarchical, with authority proceeding downwards and responsibility proceeding upwards, though at the highest level of national leadership responsibility would be regarded as operating both ways: on the part of members towards the leader and he towards them.

In the new party the pursuit of a mass membership, though essential in the longer term, would for immediate purposes be regarded as of lesser priority than the building of a tightly-knit, rock-hard, highly disciplined organisation, with undesirable elements kept out and a careful selection of party officers of character and quality. Over these years of internal strife, I had gathered around me a circle of collaborators who at the same time had become my very valued personal friends, people who were on the same wavelength with me and with each other, and who shared together a common view of the type of organisation needed to see us through the coming phase of the struggle. The skeleton of the sort of party organisation we needed was already in being, moulded by natural forces.

It now just required a name being put to it, and this was done at a meeting in London in April 1982, attended by officials of the New National Front along with those of a number of smaller political groups with which we had by then come into contact. At the meeting there was formed the British National Party. By unanimous decision of those present, I was chosen to head this party and given the powers to lead it as had been contained in the New National Front constitution. A new era thus began in the story of British Nationalism, and one which belongs to a later part of this book.

I have considered it right to discourse at some length and in some detail upon the story of the National Front because it forms, for good or ill, an important strand in the history and tradition of the patriotic movement in Britain, and also because from it valuable lessons were learned which were taken to heart in planning the later political enterprise in which I became engaged and which help to explain our thinking in our approach to the future.

In this chapter I have laid great stress on the mistakes and faulty thinking of numerous people with whom I became involved in my years in the National Front. I do not wish the reader, however, to assume that I regard my own record as faultless and without error. In the course of performing an extremely difficult task, I made some mistakes too — perhaps most of all in the selection of some of those who became my principal colleagues during the period, although it must be understood that a good deal of this selection was done for me by the votes of the committee with which I was saddled. This does not mean, however, that I had no say in such matters or that my judgement in these regards was always flawless. In fact I would say that, in the earlier phase of my leadership of the National Front, one of my weaknesses was my failure to judge character in people, a failure which came from my willingness to take them too much on the value of what they were currently saying and doing and not to give nearly enough attention to a study of their personalities. This led me to elevate, or encourage to be elevated, to positions of importance many people who in the final outcome turned out to be brittle and unreliable and, at worst, thoroughly treacherous. As a result of these unhappy experiences, I subsequently came to give much more attention to a study of the personalities of the people with whom I became closely involved politically, and I like to think that today my ability to pick personnel is much better developed than formerly. I can still make mistakes here of course, but in recent years I have made far fewer than in the past.

In addition to this, I sometimes lost the support of good people by my failure to cultivate a sufficiently close personal relationship with them. Here I plead some mitigation in the fact that, continually throughout those years, I was stretched to the limit with my work schedule. I never at any time had adequate secretarial help, and for far too many hours I was imprisoned at my desk. This made getting about and getting to know people a difficult assignment. There were no doubt many in the party who felt that I did not pay sufficient attention to them, and when things are seen from their point of view the feeling is understandable. In the end, whatever mitigation may be pleaded for lapses in this exercise of personal relations, the exercise must be seen as an essential part of the tasks of leadership of a party. I should have made more time to get to know people and I did not; I can blame circumstances up to a point, but after that I must blame myself.

No doubt there were other areas in which I sometimes erred. Again, the heavy load of my duties might be pleaded as an excuse for the fact that I did not pay the attention to some matters that I should have done, but since all leadership is faced with the same problem I cannot plead my own case as exceptional. As in matters of personal relations, it is a case of having to make time or suffering the consequences.

In my time of leading the National Front in the 1970s, I never claimed infallibility nor absence of personal faults. At the end of the day, however, I ask only to be judged on the basis of overall results, and overall the record shows that for nearly all of the time of my tenure of the leadership the party was progressing forward, at some times very rapidly forward. By comparison, all those who set themselves up as rivals against me presided only over failure and regression, whether this be in the course of leading the Front itself or in the numerous splinter groups that they led after having left it. There my case on my behalf, and against them, rests.

One very happy legacy remains from the National Front period as far as I am concerned. My deep and passionate immersion in political work from my early twenties onwards had led me into something of a monk-like private existence, married, as it were, to the cause to which I had given myself. By the time I had reached my 40th birthday in 1974, I was still a bachelor and that status did not seem likely to change. Then a year later, better late than never, the lady came into my life whom I had long hoped to find but so far had not done. I met my wife-to-be Valerie. Her father and mother, Charles and Violet Parker, had recently joined the party and had become very active on its behalf — and for some years afterwards were to render to me very much valued help in my political work. Valerie followed them into the party a short time afterwards. I knew very soon after meeting her that she was the one for whom I had waited. Apart from much else, we found that we felt the same about most things, and this naturally helped bind us together — my life is of a kind that it would be perhaps too much to expect any conventional woman to share. We married in November 1977 and

I have never regretted the step. A year and a half later, Valerie presented me with a beautiful daughter, whom we named Marina. Since then the love of these two dear ones has been a constant refuge and comfort to me in the often stormy times of my political struggle. My political enemies like to depict me with horns protruding from the front of my head; I like to think that these horns have become a little blunted through the love of my family, which at one time I wondered if I would ever have. I cannot pretend a state of happiness at the condition of my country, but in recent years I have experienced the greatest possible personal happiness as consolation for the heartache induced by national events.

Chapter 11

Roots of the British sickness: the political system

Grumbling about conditions in present-day Britain is a popular national pastime. The facts of our decline as a nation and the chronic condition of many of our national institutions are so self-evident that scarcely a word needs to be said in corroboration of them.

However, the fault of so much of the discussion of these topics is that it revolves around symptoms rather than causes. Seldom is there any effort to get to the very roots of what is wrong, and then the examination is at best shallow and superficial.

Conservatives like to tell us, as I have observed in a previous chapter, that our future national welfare lies in individuals taking initiative to help themselves, rather than looking to government and state to do things for them. But this is a superficial argument from the beginning. It is the government and the state that create, or fail to create, the conditions that determine just how much a nation's reserves of individual enterprise and ability are properly put to use, also whether these resources are employed purely for selfish ends or serve the whole national community.

This stress laid by Conservatism on the responsibility of the individual is something more: it is an attempt to absolve government and state from being answerable for the appalling state of our national fortunes in the present age. It is a cop-out. It is tantamount to army generals who, by a series of disastrous tactical errors, have got their men into a near hopeless position in battle, telling those men: "Don't look to us to get you out of this; you must use your own individual initiative to do so!" Of course, in such a situation the soldier who has initiative and other individual qualities will have a better chance of surviving than the one who does not. But this does not alter the basic truth that wars are won or lost primarily through the decisions of commanders — together of course with the military resources they have at their disposal. Given that the resources of two combatants are roughly the same, it is the side that has the better generalship that is going to win.

On the left of politics there is an absurdity opposite to that of Conservatism but equally fallacious: that if the decisions of state are right, national success and prosperity can be assured, irrespective of the types of human beings of which the nation is comprised, that every individual and every group of individuals have the same potential for achievement, and only differences in the constitution and decisions of government and state determine differing national fortunes.

The truth lies in between. The quality of individuals and nations is a vital factor in human affairs, but so also is the way in which those qualities are brought out, mobilised, organised and directed. By good leadership, the individual can be enabled to realise close to the maximum of his potential and in ways that enrich the community as a whole. Without such leadership, individual energies, where they are released at all, are likely for much of the time to be directed to ends which advance the individual only at the expense of that community and society.

Years of observation and study of the British scene have convinced me that our whole political system militates against the possibility of good national leadership except in the very rarest of circumstances. The abysmal quality of most of the public figures we have produced within living memory testifies to this. The system also results in a fragmented and divided national community, incapable of being geared to any great constructive effort on the nation's behalf. Only in the two world wars of this century has there been any change from this pattern, and even there the slowness of transformation from a slack, splintered and weakly led nation to an organised, united and firmly led one was such that 'victory', if it can be called that, would not have been possible had we not been part of coalitions overwhelmingly superior to their adversaries in numbers and materiel.

In almost every department of our national life it is normal to stress the value of 'team spirit': in the forces, in industry and on the playing field — just to quote three prominent examples.

Yet in the most important area of all, that of national politics, our affairs are organised so as to make team spirit impossible. The body politic is a battleground of warring factions and interests, busy tearing each other, and the nation, apart.

This ongoing civil war, our masters tell us, is part of our heritage of 'freedom'; in other words, we cannot consider ourselves 'free' men and women except when living under a political system which ensures that the energies of political leaders are turned against each other in a never ending party fight, instead of harnessed together in constructive national works.

A moment's adult thought will dismiss this proposition as ludicrous.

Let us examine the workings of the party game they call 'democracy' and see to what extent it really has anything to do with the 'freedom' that is supposed to form the basis of it, and whether in fact any such 'freedom', in meaningful terms, exists at all.

I have related how in my younger days I observed the party candidates and their supporters coming round to homes at election times begging for the people's votes, never of course having time to tell the electors why they should vote for the candidate in question but only to give a smarmy smile before passing on to the next house. This act may of course be subject to slight variations. If the voter happens to have a very young child to hand, it is possible that the candidate will pick it up and kiss it on the forehead, and such an event becomes a veritable certainty if a press or TV camera happens to be nearby. Everyone is familiar with the silly gimmicks used by electioneering folk to ingratiate themselves with the people whose support they are after. On the rare occasions when political discussion comes into the act at all, it is at such a juvenile level that the mind boggles at the thought of the destinies of great nations being decided on such a basis. And should the elector have the temerity to raise any real issue of importance giving rise to embarrassment on the part of the party represented by the canvasser, the latter will take a sudden glance at his watch and find a reason for an urgent departure with the most. hasty of farewells.

The elector of course has a choice between one or another of these door-to-door salesmen, between one or another political party — or so we are told — so that if he doesn't care too much for Smith's doorstep smile he can vote for Jones. It all boils down to which one engages in these one-minute pleasantries with the greatest tact, charm and expertise; but the outcome could be influenced by factors of pure chance, such as whether the caller rang when the family were watching *Coronation Street* or the semi-final of the European Cup; in either of those cases the average elector's order of priorities would probably result in the door being slammed in the face of the canvasser before he had even had the chance to get his first word out!

I am not of course speaking here of **every** case in which an elector's choice is made, merely a great many. Sometimes there is a genuine attempt to examine and consider the state of the country and vote accordingly. But how exactly does such an examination proceed?

The voter, unless he is one in several thousands, cannot possibly have any comprehensive knowledge of the really important national issues at stake, and less still of the problems faced by those whose task it is to deal with such issues. Supposing he is, for instance, a worker in a motor factory. He may in that case have some knowledge of the mechanics of motor vehicles, although the degree of such knowledge is likely to differ profoundly depending on whether he is a senior engineer supervising large operations of production or merely a very minor operative on the factory floor. If he takes a higher-than-average interest in the workings of his industry, he may perhaps have some informed view on matters affecting that particular industry.

But on the rest of the vast range of economic, social and political issues affecting the nation he is likely to have only the sketchiest understanding, if any understanding at all — unless he happens to be one of those exceptional people who make a deep study of public affairs — not too easy a task if he has a job to do in the daytime and a home and family to look after in his off-work hours.

But just supposing our motor factory worker is one of those people who do have some real understanding of politics, his one vote in an election counts for just the same as the one vote possessed by every other person of 18 or over who is not (a) a foreign tourist, (b) in jail, or (c) certified as insane. Clearly, in any elections to national or local government the tiny few voices of knowledge and wisdom are going to be swamped by those of the massed battalions of ignorance.

So what means, then, do those who wish to use their votes intelligently have of overcoming this ignorance if they do not possess the time or the means to be students of politics? Clearly, they have to rely on the information and views communicated to them by the mass media — particularly the press, television and radio.

Here straightaway we can see the nonsense of the theory that under our 'democracy' the ordinary man in the street, the voter, is politically speaking a 'free agent', able to make a 'democratic' choice. For this to be the case, the mass media on which he relies for news and advice in forming his opinion would have to be under popular control, the property of the common people and theirs in which to express any opinion they chose — each and every one of them! Of course this is so far from reality as to make the supposition preposterous. The vast majority of newspapers in Britain, national and local, are owned by huge press combines controlled by people who comprise only a minute fraction of the population and placed there only by virtue of their access to enormous funds. If there is any brake on the power of the mighty press magnates, it certainly does not come from the ordinary people themselves who read their papers; it comes from the large companies which place advertisements in those papers and who may withdraw their advertisements from any paper that prints articles or items of news disagreeable to them — or else from the 'godfathers' of the journalists' or print unions who can bring the papers to a stop in the same circumstances.

Anyone who has worked in Fleet Street will know, as an elementary fact of life, that the idea that we have a 'free press' in Britain, in the sense that the ordinary person understands it, is pure fiction. Our press is **controlled**, as completely as if it were the mouthpiece of the government of a totalitarian state; it is controlled, in the case of Britain, by minorities representing powerful interests of politics and money. The ordinary citizen has about as much say in what is printed in his 'free press' as does the average Russian in what is printed in *Pravda*.

It is not basically different with the broadcasting services. These are controlled with equal thoroughness by powerful oligarchies and *elites* in no way responsible to the average voter. The BBC, for instance, is run by a Board of Governors appointed by the government of the day. The commercial networks are owned, as is the case with the press, by powerful moneyed interests and rely for most of their income on advertisements placed with them by similar big moneyed interests. As with the press, effective control is always in the hands of small minorities.

It is not my purpose at this point to argue whether this media control is exercised in a good way or a bad way, in a way beneficial to the nation or detrimental to the nation; to that question I will come later. Here I am only dealing with the supposition that these institutions are subject to the rules of 'democracy' — in the sense that they permit a true freedom of debate on the great public issues. In fact the only 'freedom' that exists within them is the freedom of powerful minorities to impose their own political and other opinions on the rest of us.

Yet it is upon this supposition of a 'free' and 'democratic' media that we must base the concomitant supposition that the average voter has a 'free' choice at election times, since that voter's range of choice, as he sees it, is tightly circumscribed by the range of facts, views, politicians and parties permitted coverage in the media. If the latter are proved — as I believe I have proved them — to operate according to principles that are not in any way democratic, the whole process of elections conducted according to those same principles of 'democracy' is revealed as a fraud.

As I have already acknowledged, the voter can choose between one or another party — or so the theory has it. But just what is this choice worth to him if, for all practical purposes, on particular issues about which he feels strongly there is no party standing in his constituency committed to policies he can support? Just how much freedom of choice, for instance, has a voter who wishes Britain to withdraw from the Common Market or wants us to become again a mono-racial society, if the candidates competing for his vote represent the Conservative, Labour, Democratic or Social Democratic parties — all pledged to policies opposite to those in which he believes.

It is no answer to this question to say that there is nothing to stop another party, or individual candidate, standing in that same constituency in support of withdrawal from the Common Market or a mono-racial Britain, or that the voter himself can stand on such policies. Every realist knows that matters are not so simple as that. Should our voter stand as a candidate himself, he would first have to raise at least £1,000 to cover his deposit and the expense of printing campaign literature — quite apart from his problem of getting that literature distributed when printed. And even if he should overcome all these problems he would be campaigning in a political climate created by the mass media, which never tire of telling the electorate that, as candidates not backed by the big party machines have no chance whatever of winning, there is no point in voting for them anyway!

Just the same situation is faced by organised parties outside the favoured pale of the 'establishment', i.e. backed by the media and enjoying the seal of their approval. With the media smearing or slandering such parties, or dismissing their challenge as irrelevant, the public can without difficulty be induced not to vote for them, even though their policies may find favour with a great many electors.

The parties with which I have been involved have faced exactly this situation: our efforts to bid for public support at the polls have brought us face to face with the crippling handicaps involved in campaigning without mass media sanction, and we have learned from this experience that elections in this country — whatever the pretensions of 'democracy' — are simply media-rigged. It is possible to defeat the racket, but only after many years of patient spade work in building up a nationwide organisation with the resources to meet the media on equal terms — and the coming of times of total breakdown and crisis which will render all the old and 'orthodox' prescriptions discredited. We know that time will come and we are now preparing for it, but this does not invalidate our contention that a racket is what the present system is; we can apply no other description to the present party game, the rules of which are carefully designed to exclude any contender who does not carry 'establishment' blessing.

Here we have, then, a political system that amounts in effect to a monopoly. Those who control the media of communication decide who are the 'approved' parties and who are not, by the simple device of treating the parties they favour as the only 'relevant' and 'credible' ones and killing any others stone-dead, either by mentioning them in the most unsavoury terms or not mentioning them at all. Elections become simply a charade, little different to those conducted in Soviet Russia, where the people's 'choice' is between candidates all selected and vetted by the ruling power.

Apart from the two issues I have mentioned — the Common Market and Race — large numbers of voters are effectively disenfranchised on a number of other vital matters of public concern, such as Capital Punishment, Homosexuality and Abortion, just to mention three. These millions who favour policies on these matters opposite to those laid down by the 'liberal establishment' have not the slightest chance of seeing their views adequately represented in parliament, let alone translated into government policy. Again, the idea that elected politicians carry out the will of the people on these issues is a total sham.

I have indicated the obstacles in the way of anyone who may try to found a new political party with policies in keeping with the desires of this huge unenfranchised section of the electorate. What will also be an obstacle is the fact that vast resources of money are needed to keep in operation any party able to be even an outside challenger for power. Ordinary members' subscriptions are quite inadequate for this purpose; large funding from powerful moneyed institutions is also needed, be these trade unions or large private or public companies. 'Democracy' thereby becomes, not government of the people, by the people and for the people, but government of the people by the servants of the big financial interests and specifically for those interests.

Elections take place under conditions in which the public are induced to believe that they only have a limited number of candidates (in England usually three and elsewhere perhaps four) for whom it is even worth bothering to vote, and it is ensured that all these candidates are thoroughly 'vetted' by their parties and by the mass media so as to guarantee their acceptability to the ruling establishment — the one exception to this rule being in Northern Ireland, where it is still possible for a candidate not in this category to be a serious contender (one of the reasons why the establishment in London is currently doing everything possible to expel Northern Ireland from the Kingdom). Over all but one small corner of the country, therefore, the voter's choice is in effective terms strictly limited.

The vast majority of voters, through no fault of their own, are only very dimly aware of the important political issues, and such awareness as does exist is one for which they have to depend almost entirely on what they are allowed to know by the media. Elections are inevitably fought, therefore, not on serious arguments, but on mere empty slogans, the parties competing with one another to appeal to the lowest common denominator of political intelligence.

And what of the candidates who covet the people's votes? Are they required to have established any proven competence in politics, administration and government? Not a bit of it! The successful candidate who gets elected to parliament can be a total ignoramus in such matters; all that he needs is, first to be a good party man, loyal to the prevailing party line and thereby to get adopted by his local constituency organisation, then — so as to prevail over his rivals in the election itself — perhaps to be photogenic, perhaps to show prodigious energy in shaking hands and kissing babies, but above all to be a representative of the party with its nose currently in front in the see-sawing national popularity contest.

The prospect, if we think about it for a moment, is frightening. If we want the brakes of our car repaired, we go to a qualified motor mechanic — otherwise we could meet a premature death on the road. If we require a complicated throat operation, we put ourselves in the hands of a trained surgeon who is a specialist in that field. If we have to fight an intricate court action, we hire a professional lawyer. Yet in the most complex field of all — and the most serious in its consequences for the greatest numbers of people, we put our trust in unknown amateurs; in the administration of the nation's political affairs, competence in which should require many more years' training than in any of these trades or professions, and in which the results of failure are far more grave because they affect the entire nation and its millions of inhabitants, we choose men or women who, for all we know, have no capability in the profession whatsoever.

After this big pantomime is over, the lucky candidates — at the present count, 635 of them —assemble in parliament. Or at least that is the idea. But in fact they don't have to be there at all! One successful candidate in an election for a Northern Ireland constituency has proudly boasted that in the whole time he has been his people's representative he has never been near the place! The elected MPs choose which debates in the House they will attend and which not — which of course they cannot personally be blamed for doing, as, what with all their other duties, they could not possibly be present at every sitting, some of which go on till the small hours of the morning. That the members cannot be present at all of these sittings is a reflection, not on them, but on the absurdity of the system, which requires them to represent their constituents and indeed pays them to do so but conducts affairs according to a schedule which makes it inevitable that they are absent from the scene for much of the time.

Parliament is supposed to be the law-making body of the land, and the legislation passed there — if it is to justify the claim that it is 'democratic' — should reflect the will of the people to whom such laws will apply. Anything further from reality could not be imagined. A great number of laws are passed at sittings at which nowhere near the full complement of MPs is present. And even when such MPs are present the way they vote bears little relation to the views of their constituents, as the Capital Punishment issue has again and again shown. Each time the issue has come up in parliament since Capital Punishment was abolished in the 1960s, the motion that it should be restored has been defeated. Yet opinion polls to this day show that an overwhelming majority of electors are in favour of its restoration.

The other absurdity of course is that parliament is expected to contend with a great deal of legislation on subjects so specialised that they can only be properly understood by specialists in the fields concerned, which of course none but a very few parliamentarians can possibly be. Again: amateurs and ignoramuses doing the job of experts!

We owe our democratic institutions, so we are told, partly to the cultural legacy handed down to us from the city-state of Athens, and partly to the 'Age of the Enlightenment', mainly coinciding with the 18th century, which laid the foundations of modern liberalism. But in fact such ancestry has little connection with the way our political system operates today. The Athenians who determined the great public issues of their time constituted an *elite* of the population, distinguished from other inhabitants by intelligence and education and rigidly separated from them by a social system not dissimilar to the *apartheid* system in South Africa today. They were, in addition, a leisured class with little else to do but immerse themselves in the study and conduct of public affairs, for which they were firmly schooled by family tradition. In a word, they were an **aristocracy**.

As for the 18th century 'Enlightenment', this was, as I have indicated earlier in this book, supposed to be a development in which the sunlight of 'reason' shone down on a Europe previously engulfed in the darkness of superstition.

Just what correspondence to the aristocratic tradition of Athenian democracy, and just what atmosphere of 'reason', can be found in contemporary Westminster may be gleaned from listening to the early morning radio programme *Yesterday in Parliament*. What will be heard is not a debate conducted between people of superior intelligence, least of all one taking place in an atmosphere of 'reason', but an orgy of hysterical noise more appropriate to feeding time at the zoo, an almost non-stop bedlam as the party warriors on each side of the House bawl abuse at each other — sometimes punctuated by vain cries for "order" from the Speaker's chair, whose occupant would have an easier job, one thinks, if he had to supervise a class of delinquent children.

But all we would in fact be hearing would be modern 'democracy' at work. The nation goes out to the polling booths to elect political leaders to go to parliament to govern its affairs, and thereafter pays them well to do so. Yet immediately they get into this parliament the men and women thus elected and paid proceed, not to get on with the task of running the nation's business, but to engage in an everyday slanging match against each other which consumes a major part of their working time — and all in pursuit of the never-ending party war. The admission of radio recording equipment into the House has done the nation a considerable favour in revealing the level at which this party war is conducted; we might be done an even greater favour if, in addition to this, television cameras were admitted too, for then we would see in the flesh and in all their daily ravings and tantrums the ludicrous figures who, by the device of the 'democratic' system, find their way into the country's most hallowed political institution, where they are then allowed to preside over our destinies.

Of course, the ongoing party war makes wise and provident government of the nation quite impossible, as might be gathered by contrasting it with the conduct of a sound family business. In the first place, those running the business are not in the positions they occupy through election by the whole of the workforce; they are in charge because they have been **trained**, and in some cases **bred**, to exercise responsibility. They may consist of those members of the family who have shown an interest in the business and have served some time gathering experience in the lower echelons of the concern, but also probably people from outside the family who have attained qualifications in business competence.

Decisions made on behalf of the business are not made in response to the baying of the mob; they are made according to the considerations of company interests, both long-term and short-term. Resources are not squandered with a view solely to instant profits and fat bonuses; they are carefully apportioned, with part of them set aside for investment in projects not likely to pay off for many years. Allowance is made for the eventual need to replace worn-out or obsolete equipment. Attention is paid to likely changes in market trends five years, ten years and even 20 years hence. If the business is connected with any kind of farming, fruit-growing or forestry, works will have to be undertaken which will only pay dividends many years after; in the case of forestry in particular, sometimes more than a generation can elapse between the planting of new trees and their attainment of full growth.

And if the business is a family one, as in our example, those running it are bound to make provisions for future generations who will inherit the business when they are retired or dead. The whole operation has to be conceived as a carefully planned development extending indefinitely into the future, with decisions made accordingly.

The science of politics should be based on similar principles, differing only in so far as matters to be dealt with are a thousand times more complex. The nation should be seen as one huge family concern, and all political decisions considered carefully with a view to its long-term development and interest. Those engaged in the running of the concern should be a team, united in a common cause and policy. Of course there will be arguments as to the implementation of such a policy; that is only to be expected. But given that there is unanimity in the broad policy objective itself, based on recognition of a common national interest, such argument should be capable of reconciliation by the reaching of common consensus, and once an agreed course of action has been thrashed out all co-operate together in pursuing it forward to maximum effectiveness.

Yet none of these conditions prevails in the madhouse of party politics we call 'democracy'. Those entrusted to govern our affairs, apart from being, for the main part, wholly unqualified in intelligence, character and training, are, right from the first moment they occupy their seats at Westminster, in a state of war with each other and are expected by their party bosses to place the requirements of that war in a position of paramountcy over everything else. The war is not merely an argument about ways and means to carry out policies but a basic conflict over the very nature of the policies themselves, a conflict made absolutely inevitable by the fact that such people begin by possessing wholly different and conflicting loyalties. They are not playing for the same team; they want things that, in the last analysis, are utterly irreconcilable; there is never, therefore, the slightest hope that their differences can be resolved by consensus and they can then be induced to work together for a common end, for it is that end itself that is a matter of complete polarisation between the warring party forces. They believe in what are, to them, wholly opposite societies; each is dedicated to the pursuit of his or her idea of the right society to the exclusion of the other. The only possible outcome is war.

Of course, seen from a truly adult perspective, there is not really that fundamental difference in conceptions of society held by the parties of liberalism that there would appear to be from the intensity of this conflict. Looking at their squalid little party war as we do, we might be left wondering why they hate and oppose each other so passionately, since the values they all have in common are much greater than the things that divide them — a fact fully understood by those much more intelligent personages who manipulate them like puppets and ensure always that they serve the same transcendent interests.

But we must understand that this is not the way that things are seen by the participants in the party dogfight. To them, the truly adult approach to politics is foreign. They are people with painfully small and limited horizons, and they simply cannot see beyond the bounds of their own minuscule world, a world in which the creeds of 'Socialism', 'Conservatism', 'Liberalism' (of the Liberal Party, that is) and 'Social Democracy' are actually genuinely contending ideologies. We must also understand that caught up in these 'ideological' rivalries are conflicts of personal interest and ambition. Once Mr., Mrs. or Miss Parliamentarian has hitched his or her career to a particular party bandwaggon, the success of that career is inextricably bound up with the success of the chosen party in the ongoing political party game. We are dealing here, we must remember, with people who love power — or at least the trappings of power — for their own sake. Party fortunes are bound up with personal fortunes; hence the intensity of the struggle.

We thus have a situation, at the opening of every new parliament, in which one group of people has been elected to govern and the other group elected to stop them governing! Can there possibly be, in such a situation, any purposeful application of minds and energies to the solving of national problems?

Of course, this polarisation between the objectives of the conflicting parties — a polarisation which, as I have indicated, seems absurd to us from where we stand — is itself a symptom of the muddle-headed thinking of those who are the architects of the 'ideologies' of those parties. 'Socialism', 'Conservatism', 'Liberalism', 'Social Democracy', etc. are made into ends in themselves rather than mere means to an end; they take on the aspect of religious dogmas, to be pursued with a fanaticism and bigotry that permit no possible compromise between one and another. In no case can they be reconciled in a deeper commitment to the cause of the **nation** because to all of their adherents they assume an importance that takes overwhelming priority over that cause. To the committed Tory, Conservatism is his motherland, his flag and the entity for which he will fight, while Conservatives are regarded as his race of people. To the Socialist, it is no different: nor is it to the partisans of the other parties and creeds that predominate at Westminster.

Were these people to take a truly **national** view of politics, their varying opinions on social and economic questions would become capable of reconciliation through **synthesis** and thereby topics, perhaps for argument, but never for all-out **warfare** of the kind that now prevails at the centre of our political affairs. But with the topsy-turvy scale of priorities and values now prevailing this cannot be so.

Quite apart from the time and energies they expend in the party fight, our politicians are never able to apply themselves to the carrying out of wise and far-sighted policies of national development for the very obvious reason that such tasks must always take second place to that of furthering the party interest.

To every party politician, all policies and all endeavours are geared to one object which overrides everything: the winning of the next election; it cannot be otherwise; even where there is a quite sincere and genuine desire to serve the national good, the mind of the party politician simply cannot conceive of such a good being served except by means of his own party being in office. The keeping of that party in office — or, as the case may be, the winning of office if it is at present in opposition — must take priority over everything. The very nature of the system decrees that the party interest must come first.

This means of course that no party dare incorporate in its programme any policy, no matter how beneficial — indeed essential — from the nation's point of view, which might not immediately be appreciated by the electorate or, more to the point, by the mass media which condition the electorate. Tory leader Stanley Baldwin was once on record as saying that he did not dare go beyond a certain point of expenditure on armaments (at a time when nations abroad were arming to the teeth) because it would be electorally unpopular. No doubt he would have been able to provide a rationale for such cowardice by saying that, had national affairs been in the hands of his opponents, the nation's defences would have suffered even more dangerously. The story is of course more of a comment on the system than upon Baldwin himself.

But indeed should any party in office decide, in an unusual fit of courage and wisdom, to embark upon a number of public works of great national benefit there is always the likelihood that, with a subsequent change of government, the whole programme will be scrapped. To revert to our analogy of a business, no such concern could ever launch out on any provident forward planning or development if every five years the management was liable to undergo a complete changeover and new management be installed which had completely different ideas on the whole purpose of the enterprise. No business could survive for long in such conditions.

And yet these are exactly the conditions under which government is carried on in Britain through our party system. Everything is unsettled; nothing is of permanence. And every policy has to be evaluated in terms of its vote-winning potential and its potential to please the powerful pressure groups on which the survival of government and parties largely depends.

It should, from all that has been said, be abundantly clear that in Britain today the worst possible conditions exist for the realisation of strong, resolute and intelligent government, dedicated to the defence and furtherance of the national interest and the purposeful direction of national affairs. In the first place, those recruited to politics largely comprise the very elements least fitted to rule. The process by which they are required to claw their way up to the highest offices in the land requires that they be experts in mass bribery, mass flattery, empty talk and, very often, lies. The national debate that precedes this acquisition of power is one that takes place at little higher than a kindergarten level of politics, with the subject matter for that debate chosen, not by the people (who are supposed to be the arbiters of everything) but by the oligarchies who control the organs of 'public opinion', and from which all issues which those oligarchies wish to suppress are rigorously excluded. Most of the people go blindly out to the polling booths completely ignorant of the true forces regulating the nation's political life, and cast their crosses by the names of candidates carefully selected for them and with hardly a moment's serious consideration of the real national issues at stake. They cast their votes with all the frivolity of an amateur punter at the races, moved by nothing more than momentary fancy or whim, or perhaps the last tipster's forecast that they have read. If any deviate from this rule, it is simply to vote for the party for whom they, and usually their fathers and grandfathers, have always voted — without the slightest attempt to examine seriously the programme on which that party presently campaigns, or indeed its recent record when in power.

Then the victorious candidates, once they get into parliament, proceed to spend most of their time there administering a verbal bashing to each other in an unceasing party squabble that has been going on for the lifetimes of all of us living today, while the nation has been suffering from a slow, drawn-out death.

In effect, what we have in Britain is an ongoing state of national disunity and civil war, chaos, inefficiency and weak and flabby government — without, at the end of it all, even the free choice and sovereignty of the people that are supposed to justify these things.

For government in Britain is not democratic government; it is oligarchic government, operating within a purely nominal and overt framework of democratic institutions and procedures; nor is it oligarchic government of the type that might be justified: an oligarchy bound in devotion to nation and people and the guardian of their welfare; it is oligarchy which, at least in modern times, has been consistent in its betrayal of nation and people at every juncture of affairs.

In the hands of this oligarchy of power, the politicians and their parties have become nothing better than marionettes, to be paraded before the people each at his appointed hour and then withdrawn from the stage as soon as he has served his purpose, to be replaced by new performers with a new act, though of course manipulated by the same puppet-masters behind the stage.

Year in, year out, the swindle continues. One gang is given a spell of government; it may be five years, it may be more. That government fails miserably to grapple with the nation's problems, and in the course of time inevitably the people lose confidence in it and itch for a change. And who is on hand to offer them that change? Why, the other gang — controlled, if only the people knew it, by exactly the same forces! Gang Two does its stint, and before too long can be seen to have made just as big a mess of things as Gang One. The time has come, therefore, to wheel Gang One back again. The people's memories are short — but not quite that short. Some of them may recall that Gang One, the last time it was given a chance, did no better than Gang Two has done; and so something has to be done to convince the people that this time things with Gang One will be different. Usually this involves a revamping of the party image, with a change of leader (i.e. chief puppet) included in the face-lift. A big publicity exercise is launched in which a programme of 'exciting' new policies is announced. Only to the perceptive observer who is able to tell the wood from the trees is it evident that these new policies of tomorrow are only the old (and failed) policies of yesterday dressed up in new packaging. The wheel turns full circle again and Gang One is back in office, to continue the old mismanagement where it left off.

Every so often of course, the natives get a little more restless than usual and decline to be as enchanted as they are expected to be by this game of musical chairs. They look a little further back in time and recall that the two main gangs have had more than just one chance and have muffed things each time. They are willing to consider that behind all the talk of 'change' there is not really any change at all. At such moments, a dangerous number of these natives are inclined to say: "A plague on both your houses!"

But our puppet-masters are ready for this too, for they always have in reserve a third gang — and even, if necessary, a fourth one — available to parade before the people to pick up the votes that some of them are no longer disposed, at least for the time being, to give to the first two gangs. This is of course the reason why the Liberals, for long after they had ceased to be contenders for power in their own right, were kept on ice by the establishment and accorded a certain level of 'credibility'. They provided a useful safety-valve for those voters who might grow disillusioned with both Tories and Labour. By courtesy of *The Guardian* newspaper, it was ensured that the Liberal Party did not fade into total oblivion but, on the contrary, was always there at election time to soak up the protest vote just in case that vote rose to unmanageable proportions. This of course happened at Orpington in 1961 and has happened on a number of occasions since, thus corralling safely into the establishment pen any maverick steers that might be so bold as to break loose from the general herd.

More lately, a similar device has been employed in the creation of the Social Democratic Party. Again, the establishment has astutely judged the public mood: sensing that a larger than usual number of voters and members were deserting Labour, and realising that not all of these could be relied upon to drift into the Liberal camp, our real rulers did everything possible to encourage and nurture the infant SDP, giving it a rousing send-off in the press and thereafter generously publicising the daily utterances of its leaders and the *pastiche* of old-gang cliches that it tries to pass off as 'policies'. In consequence, the voter who has grown tired of the Tory/Labour cycle of misgovernment of the past half-century now has, not one alternative, but two! Well, almost: as will be known, the two parties of the 'centre' did for a time form an alliance between them, as part of which they undertook not to stand candidates against each other at elections. At the present time of going to press, this alliance is in disarray, with part of the SDP joining the Liberals and the remaining part carrying on as a separate party though with an ideology barely distinguishable from that of the others. We know not what the future holds for this collection of political oddities, but one thing we do know: stripped of all the trimmings, the policies of both of these 'centre' factions consist of just the same soggy *pot-pourri* of internationalism, free trade, racial suicide and 'wet' prescriptions for social problems that form the bases of the manifestos of their rivals. Whatever way the poor voter tries to turn, he ends up down the same blind alley.

This is the reality of the political system under which the people are deluded that they have a 'free choice' and under which every symptom of governmental weakness and ineptitude is glossed over by the consoling cry that Britons are favoured by the benign smile of providence to live in a 'democracy'.

No meaningful effort to grapple with our immense national problems will be possible until this ludicrous and wholly unworkable system is done away with and we institute an effective system of government capable of bringing to the fore a high calibre of national leadership and then properly equipping that leadership with the necessary powers of action.

There will be those who will ask if such a change will threaten the framework of 'democracy' and the 'freedom' of the people that is supposed to lie at the centre of that ideal. To them, let us straightaway reply that at present no such framework of 'democracy' exists which can be threatened and no freedom exists for the people to control the processes by which they are governed. Indeed, it is virtually impossible to put the ordinary people of this country in a position of having less power over national affairs and less freedom to choose how they will be governed than they have today. An alternative system of government designed to produce leadership of the quality for which I have called, and which empowers it to act effectively, is by no means incompatible with the objective of giving the people greater freedom and a more influential voice in national affairs. On the contrary, the establishment of such conditions of government would, without question, meet a need that is yearned for by millions of Britons as never before.

It is quite ridiculous to place a man who has never had a driving lesson in the seat of a motor car and then tell him: "You are now free to drive this car anywhere you like!" Ridiculous and also dishonest. The dishonesty is then compounded if the lay-out of the streets in the area is such that, whichever one he takes, he is bound to end up at the same destination.

It is equally dishonest to tell a man that he has the freedom to determine what government he wants by exercising his vote at election time if he is completely lacking in the information needed to use that vote intelligently and discriminately and if, furthermore, his effective range of choice is limited to candidates and parties whose policies, at the end of the route, land him in the same place!

And there is no less idiocy and dishonesty in telling a group of people that they are all free to drive motor cars if only a small portion of them actually wish to do so. The majority of them may only wish to get to the destination of their choice and prefer to be taken there by a driver competent to handle the vehicle and negotiate the route. Likewise, in politics it is true to say that the vast majority of people are much more interested simply in getting **good government** than in having a say in government.

If the freedom of the individual to influence the course of politics — supposedly the first foundation-stone of 'democracy' — is to have any meaning, it must be in the context of that individual, first having sufficient interest and desire to exercise that freedom, and then of his having the capability to do so by understanding the political issues. Without these things, 'democracy' and 'freedom' are a fraud. That is a cardinal truth which must be taken into account in any effort to formulate an alternative political system for the achievement of sound government.

The next truth which must be accepted is that it is futile a government being elected to carry out policies approved by a majority of the people if, from the moment it takes office, it is engaged in a non-stop civil war in parliament in which every possible device is used to sabotage its effective operation.

Likewise, the will of the people, just supposing that we have a way of clearly ascertaining what that is, cannot be carried out by any government effectively if its power of action is hampered at every turn by the need to appease various vested interests and bend to the pressures of the various lobbies, invariably representing organised minorities, which bay at government's heels. Here we come back to the truth recognised by Mosley in the 1930s and dealt with in an earlier chapter. Under the old system, as Mosley said, the power of finance "can affect the lives of the mass of people more closely and more terribly in the decision of one afternoon than can parliament, with puny labour and the mock heroics of sham battles, in the course of a decade." No government that is not prepared and equipped to subordinate the power of money, among others, to the nation's political will can with any honesty claim to be representative of the people, let alone act in the people's name.

These stipulations are all necessary to clear the dense fog in which discussion in Britain about methods of government is customarily conducted. Lest the call for strong and effective government be interpreted as threatening a violation of the principles of 'democracy' and the 'rights' and 'freedoms' of the people, it is just as well that we start by establishing a realistic definition of such 'democracy' and of 'rights' and 'freedoms' in terms of their usefulness to the ordinary citizen. A mechanism must certainly be preserved, indeed improved, for giving the people a say in the matters of state — but just to the extent that people want such a say and are capable of exercising it from a properly informed position; otherwise it is totally useless, both from the nation's point of view and that of the individual also.

I have suggested earlier that, while only a minority of people take a serious interest in general national affairs, a great many more people are likely to take an interest in the affairs of their own occupational groups, and to have at least some knowledge of matters affecting those groups. I have also suggested that that knowledge is likely to be the greater the more highly placed in the group the individual becomes.

It will therefore follow that the franchise can be much more fairly and effectively exercised if it is organised on occupational lines, allowing the ordinary individual a say in that department of national affairs in which he or she has genuine experience and knowledge. In this way the likelihood is greatly reduced of the individual being unscrupulously exploited and led blindfolded by the media in the process of voting — as is the case when the individual votes on affairs of which he or she has little knowledge or understanding.

By means of an occupational franchise, parliament would be changed from its present form into a chamber comprised of the elected leaders of the various occupational groups. In the case of groups in the population which cannot be defined in terms of any official occupation, such as, for instance, housewives, these people should have the option of registering on the electoral roll of any occupation in which they have previously served or, alternatively, of voting as houswives, and in most cases also as mothers, for representatives of that section of the community.

But such a franchise should not be based on the assumption that every member of an occupational group has the same level of understanding of the affairs of that group. The franchise should be ordered in such way as to place greater voting power in the hands of those more qualified and with greater achievement to their credit. For instance, the head of a large engineering company should possess substantially more votes than his most lowly placed employee. We must dispense once and for all with the idea that, when it comes to exercising judgement over affairs, everyone's judgement is worth the same.

The actual schedule of this parliament should be limited and its role confined to discussion of issues which transcend occupational lines but do call for varied occupational knowledge. Most of the parliamentary work of the leaders of these occupational groups should be carried out in departments connected with the various ministries responsible for their own areas of national affairs. Elected representatives of the medical profession, for instance, would assist in the running of the Ministry of Health, representatives of farmers in the running of the Ministry of Agriculture, and so on.

I have said that the process of legislation by parliament is a ridiculous one in so far as only a tiny minority in each area of legislation can have any expert knowledge of the matters to be legislated upon. The process is also painfully slow, as it depends on a single legislative assembly to debate and pass all the laws coming onto the statute book.

Far more rapid, while at the same time more enlightened, legislation would be possible if the function were divided into two categories: in the first place, that relating to matters of general national concern in which the whole of the population was likely to have an interest; secondly, legislation concerning special areas of national affairs calling for specialist knowledge.

In the first category might be placed legislation on Capital Punishment, Abortion, Drug Laws, Decimalisation, etc. The national parliament would concern itself solely with this category.

Responsibility for specialist legislation, on the other hand, should be devolved onto sub-parliaments comprised of the representatives of the various occupational groups, enabling such legislative matters to be approached from the standpoint of professional knowledge and thus debated at a much more informed level.

In dealing with the question of legislation, it is important that we should distinguish between issues involving informed political judgement on the one hand and, on the other hand, 'gut' issues involving simple questions of right and wrong. While I have cast doubt on the ability of the average member of the public to understand the first, in the case of the second the instinct of that member of the public can often be more sound than that of the so-called 'experts'. There is therefore a strong argument for such 'gut' issues being put to popular referendum. In Capital Punishment, Abortion, Drug Laws and Decimalisation, I have given a few examples. Here the national parliament, if it votes on such matters, would be well advised to pay careful heed to public opinion as expressed in such popular polls; and in a few cases those polls should indeed decide the issue. Here we have a chance to put true democracy into practice — a process of which 'liberals' are always scared.

It is at this point that something should be said about the House of Lords, a matter which must be dealt with in any consideration of reforms in our political system.

I have indicated earlier in this book that I am in favour of aristocracy — provided that it is aristocracy of a type which represents a genuinely superior caste in the way of ability and character and provided that its special privileges are balanced by its assumption of special duties. Unhappily, this is not the kind of aristocracy we now have in Britain; our aristocracy today consists mainly of the very distant descendants of those earlier breeds of men who raised Britain to greatness; and in some cases even the first of the line owed his position, not to merit or achievement, but only to some chance circumstance whereby he was able to perform a favour to the monarch of the time and was in turn given his title as a measure of royal gratitude.

But even in the case of the dynasties which began with leaders of quality, the centuries have gradually brought about a dilution of the noble strains. Through unwise marriages, often contracted simply for reasons of financial expediency, a dysgenic process has taken place that has left the heirs of today totally unfit for the role in society to which they are born. Britain's titled families, throughout modern times, have been conspicuous for their almost total lack of resistance to the policies of national betrayal that have reduced this nation to the status of a third-rate power.

Observe the faces and carriages of a great number of the young scions of this class today and you will see, not aristocrats in any meaningful sense of the term, only vacuous drips of a kind of which their ancestors would certainly be ashamed. The very idea that these specimens should be placed by inheritance in positions where they have an especially privileged influence over national affairs by way of being able to delay legislation and, furthermore, have their House of Lords speeches broadcast to the nation on television and extensively quoted in the press, is offensive to every healthy public instinct.

The fact that the Upper House is also filled with persons not there by any hereditary right, such as bishops, venerable judges and life peers, does not today contribute one jot to its usefulness, as these persons are in fact no more than the appointees of the very liberal establishment that is mainly responsible for our low national fortunes. Indeed, the fact that our life peers are mainly mere political has-beens who have been kicked upstairs as a token of their faithful service to the old-gang political parties, or alternatively rewarded for their financial donations to those same parties, is hardly a recommendation to us to accord them any special awe or respect, let alone power.

All that can be said for the House of Lords today is that its occupants are probably no worse than those of the House of Commons and that, for that reason, there are occasions on which some of the more idiotic legislation approved by the latter chamber may be modified as a result of suggestions from the former. It is for this reason that the proposition that the Lords be abolished, while the Commons be preserved as it is, does not make much sense.

However, we must here view the House of Lords, not in terms of its credit or debit rating under the present system, but of whether it can be useful under a new system. My own view of this question is that it depends entirely on the type of titled class existing in Britain at the time. Before we can again say that we have an aristocracy, there needs to be a massive 'weeding out' of the useless elements among the existing titled families and their replacement by families of sound quality from the ordinary ranks of the population, selected on the basis of outstanding achievement and public service over at least two generations. If such a renewed aristocracy can be established, then it would be prudent to bring it into the circle of those holding political power. Then a reconstituted House of Lords could have a useful role in the political life of the nation. For the moment, the House should be left — if it is left at all — merely as an ornament. Its upkeep should not be paid for out of public funds; nor should it have the prerogative of blocking legislation.

One other change is essential to bring an atmosphere of sanity and reason to elections to parliament, and this is that candidates should stand as individuals and not on 'party' tickets. In this way, the focus will be concentrated on their qualities as individuals and on the soundness or otherwise of their ideas, which of course they would be free to formulate and espouse in accordance with their own consciences and independently of the dictates of party machines. Issues could at the same time be debated on their own merits and without the intrusion of party labels, which reduce all public discussion to a silly and destructive dogfight.

Entirely separate from this process must be that of national government. Here we face the ancient dilemma of how to achieve government that is on the one hand strong and stable while on the other hand remaining government by consent. It is my view that in Britain today we get the worst of both worlds by having to put up with government that is neither, that is continually weak and cowardly while not being able to claim that it exists by 'consent' in any realistic sense of the term — and for reasons which should be clear from everything I have said previously on this subject.

Britain's first need in the new age is to produce national leaders of an altogether higher order than those thrown up by the old party system, and it may straightaway be said with certainty that that system provides the worst possible arena for the recruitment of such leadership — as we have surely seen.

The first requirement is that politics be given the status of a profession, which should indeed stand as the highest of all professions. As I have stated before, we hire trained professionals to attend to the specialised tasks that we need to get done for us, whether they be doctors, dentists, lawyers, motor mechanics or builders. This does not mean that the professionals will **always** do the job properly but only that we have never discovered, and can never discover, any better way of ordering human affairs, It therefore follows that those to whom we entrust the most important of all tasks, that of government, should be people of long training and proven competence in that field.

In a properly organised state, a thorough system of graduation through a many-tiered administrative structure, combined with examinations of competence at every stage, would sift out those best fitted for the immense responsibilities of statesmanship, so as to provide solid cadres of national leaders for the future. Such a system would aim to establish a true meritocracy based on achievement and not in any way reliant on the candidates' talents as television-performers or on instant popularity contests of the type which today are the test of fitness for office.

The majority of government leaders and administrators should attain their posts by such a system. In every department of state calling for specialisation there should be specialists. The Minister of Defence, for instance, should be an experienced professional serviceman who has attained high rank. The Minister of Education should be one with a solid career background in that field who has demonstrated high achievement in such a capacity. Large publicly owned industries should be run by men who have been successful themselves as heads of industry.

At the top of this pyramid should stand the head of government, on whose authority all major leaders of government should be appointed. The procedure for the selection of this head of government, and the subsequent terms on which he would continue to occupy his office, would constitute the most important aspect of the whole political system.

I should by now have made clear my belief that no head of government can carry out his duties adequately and responsibly if he is subject, as at present, to the demands of a party system based on the quest for mob popularity at every turn, and the need constantly to appease powerful sectional pressure groups. It is necessary for our head of government to have firm and rapid powers of action, and those powers must range over the whole field of executive matters concerning the nation. He would be expected to give weight to the recommendations of parliament and the various occupational assemblies but in the final analysis decisions would be in his hands. He would have an executive role more closely similar to that of an American president than of a British prime minister under the present system, though I do not advocate the adoption of the former title — which would be particularly unsuitable in a monarchical state. Prime minister our head of government would remain, but his powers would be vastly stronger and more sweeping than those of any prime minister as we now understand them.

To make such power effective, our head of government needs to be given, I believe, an indefinite period of office — subject to the right of parliament to terminate that period of office in special circumstances and by a no-confidence vote requiring a two-thirds majority. In that event, the prime minister would need to seek a new period of office by obtaining a mandate from the whole nation, which would be based on a straight vote of Yes or No. If the verdict was Yes, he would be empowered to continue in office irrespective of the endorsement of parliament, which would be required to wait a period of at least three years before being able to vote on another no-confidence motion. If the verdict were No, a national election would take place to elect an alternative head of government.

All the candidates in such an election would require to be people of proven record in public affairs and to have undergone thorough training in politics. They would be selected as the nominees of groups in parliament, and would first compete in an eliminator. If no one candidate won an absolute majority over all the others in this eliminator, the two most successful would then run against each other in a final contest.

In such an election, no special advantage would be given to any candidate on the basis of backing from moneyed interests. All would be given an equal sum of money as a grant to finance their campaigns and would be required to submit their campaigning expenses to an audit to establish that they had not exceeded this sum. All newspapers and TV and radio networks would be required to give equal space and time to every candidate to advertise himself and his policies, and to make no editorial comment, and permit no article, at any time for or against any candidate. In this way, we would achieve something entirely unknown on the British political scene: a scrupulously fair system of election to public office.

In order also to achieve a scrupulously honest election, it would also be necessary to insist that any statement made by any candidate in support of his candidature that he knew to be false would render that candidature null and void, and, in the event of this being serious, may render him liable to prosecution.

What is vital in this election — as also with elections to parliament, as I have stated earlier — is that such elections should not be conducted on a party basis: candidates should not carry party labels. This is not to prohibit the existence of political parties, or public officials belonging to such parties; it is only to ensure that party warfare be taken out of all contests for public office. Such warfare must be consigned to the dustbin of history, for it completely rules out the possibility of any united national effort to solve the country's problems. If it be asked what then would be the role of the political party in the new system, the simple answer is that it should be permissible to form political parties to promote certain political ideas just as it should be permissible to form organisations to promote specific theories on religion, education, science, medicine or anything else — subject to the rule that such organisations do not engage in subversion, preach sedition or otherwise break the law.

But this does not mean that the political resources of the nation should be dissipated in warfare between political parties any more than they should be dissipated in warfare between Jehovah's Witnesses or Plymouth Brethren, advocates or opponents of comprehensive schools or those who accept and those who repudiate Einstein's relativity theory. The question of what party a candidate for public office belongs to should be of no greater relevance than the question of whether he is a Methodist or a Presbyterian. It can be mentioned in his campaign — certainly, but he should be judged in that campaign essentially on his merits as an individual and on the policies he advocates for the nation, which should be his own policies and not the policies of any party whips.

The proposals that our head of government should have strong powers of the kind described, and that party warfare should be taken out of politics, with national destinies determined by other means than elections governed by mass ignorance and hysteria, will of course invite from our opponents the usual chorus of angry squawking parading as 'thought'. They will say that we are proposing the setting up of a 'dictatorship' in Britain that will crush opposition and disfranchise and 'oppress' the people. I hope that I have given sufficient evidence that this is nonsense, but a few more words may be said to underline the point.

To 'dictate' to people is generally understood to mean compelling them to do something against their will. Well, there is always going to be some will, somewhere, that is opposed to the policies that are necessary for the beneficial government of the country: the will of certain pressure groups and sectional interests, if nothing else. Therefore, to speak of a political system being a 'dictatorship', we must mean that it acts against the will of the majority; there can be no other valid definition.

Straightaway we may see here that the phrase 'dictatorship' becomes meaningless in a political context, for there are numerous examples of men who have been recorded by history as 'dictators' who in fact have governed much more in accordance with the will of the majority of their countrymen and -women than have many parliamentarians and so-called 'democrats' — including, notably, those of Britain in modern times.

A government can hardly be said to have majority consent merely by virtue of the fact that it has been formed by a political party that has won the last election — particularly if, as in Britain, such a party can be victorious while gaining a minority of the votes cast and if, along with the other parties that are serious contenders in that election, it shares in common a number of policies for which there is not the slightest evidence of majority approval.

And, to repeat myself at the risk of tedium, a government cannot in honesty claim to have majority consent when it is elected with the backing of a mass media controlled by minority interests.

The truth is of course that these terms 'dictatorship' and 'democracy' are simply inventions of the well-known class of political verbalisers who set themselves up as the guardians of the public's conscience and thoughts. They are nothing more than slogans, emotive catchwords designed to free their users from the burden of engaging in a reasoned argument in support of their case. The purpose is that immediately these words are brought into the debate all further objective discussion becomes impossible and the audience is neatly herded, like unthinking cattle, into whatever pen is designed to accommodate it. The words have the same obfuscating and mesmeric function as 'fascist', which I analysed in a previous chapter. They are intended as a substitute for an honest examination of the issues.

Then what about crushing opposition? Exactly what is meant by the term? If it is intended to mean the silencing of all criticism of government, the allegation is rubbish. Every facility for such criticism would be given both to the parliament and the various assemblies representing the occupational groups — with the difference that such criticism would be based on a non-partisan judgement of the issues rather than being shots fired in the party war. What most certainly would not be permitted in the system advocated here is a body politic given up to the pastime of two or more factions tearing each other, and the nation, apart. People who deem the elimination of this pastime as 'crushing opposition' show either that they do not know the meaning of words, or that they are just plain liars.

That the people would be neither disfranchised nor oppressed I have, I think, clearly shown; on the contrary, their effective political freedom and their ability to have their say in national affairs would be positively increased by the provision for them to use their votes in a way that would enable them to bring to those votes practical knowledge of the issues on which they were voting, and therefore for them not to have to rely on second-hand information from the media.

"Ah," the sceptic would say, "but what would be the position in society of those people and creeds fundamentally opposed to your point of view?" My answer is: "By all means, let them speak!" I have never at any time had the slightest doubt of my own ability, and the ability of my collaborators, to defeat in argument any and all comers — providing that the debate is under conditions where there has been a fair presentation of all viewpoints over an extended period of time. Such conditions do not exist, and for a long time have not existed, in Britain. An artificially large consensus of opinion in favour of the leftish-liberal-internationalist viewpoint has been created solely by the growing monopoly by people holding to that viewpoint over the communications media and the institutions of education, and the parallel suppression by those people of viewpoints opposite to their own. If this monopoly and suppression are broken, along with the power of the hidden forces that have brought truly free debate to an end in Britain, I am fully confident that within a short time we can win the millions of our fellow-countrymen and -women to our side by the merits of our arguments in a completely free forum of political ideas.

What today makes the message of marxism, and its twin sister liberalism, so formidable and dangerous is the complete absence of any firm and well informed counter-argument which exposes these creeds as the exercises in lunacy that they are, as well as exposing the subversive and destructive forces behind them. With the facility for such counter-arguments provided, these poisons can be wiped off the face of the earth — not by suppression (for that is not necessary) but simply by stripping them naked in the battle of ideas, so that their appeal will be limited to a tiny minority of cranks, whom we can afford to ignore.

Let no-one, therefore, fall for the ridiculous lie that we aim at the silencing of people who oppose our viewpoint. On the contrary, we aim to bring to an end the silencing treatment long used by our opponents against us, so that we can then engage them in open argument, with no topics forbidden, and let reason and common sense decide the issue. It is our opponents who have everything to lose by an open and unfettered public debate, not we.

Another reason for asserting that the mass of the people would not be disfranchised lies in the fact that, apart from their right to elect the leading representatives of their occupational groups, they would, in the last resort, have the power to dismiss the head of government in a national poll should the emergency arise where that head of government had clearly lost the confidence of parliament. In case this may seem contradictory to the principle that the people should not vote over matters beyond their understanding, it should be said that such an election would not be a normal or regular occurrence but would only take place in a situation of some exceptional crisis. There is a world of difference between the present pantomime of regular general elections and a condition of emergency of this kind. Notwithstanding the fact that the choice of national leadership should be based on politically educated and informed opinion — which is impossible under our present electoral system — it is still a fact that leadership which has overwhelmingly lost the confidence of the led cannot effectively carry on. The device of a no-confidence vote in parliament followed by a national poll of all qualified electors is a safety valve made available to deal with conditions of rare occurrence; it cannot be compared with the ongoing mass popularity contest with which we are saddled today and which reduces every would-be leader to a slavish stage performer, forever having to tailor his or her political stance to the demands of the multitude.

And quite apart from this device, there are all manner of practical measures that can be used to make the position of a leader or a government untenable once it becomes universally detested. I have quoted in an earlier chapter Sir Oswald Mosley's proposition that the people simply stay away from work, and compel the country to come to a standstill. It is not even necessary for the whole population to do this; it would suffice that it is done by those engaged in the daily administration of government and the civil service. It does not require a mind of genius level to think of many other ways in which the practical conduct of government can be made impossible in such a situation. The truth is that in a modern western state — as distinct from a banana republic — 'dictatorship' of the kind envisaged by those who trade in the word is beyond the bounds of possibility.

But certainly our head of government would be strong, as he must be. I have suggested certain procedures which would give him that strength, but a word more on the matter might be said. One vital need, as I have stated, is for the government to be freed from the stranglehold of pressure groups and sectional interests which today dominate politics in Britain, and the main ones of which are the interests of **money**. Mosley in *Tomorrow We Live* has pinpointed the power of finance (in that context international finance) to exercise a far greater influence on conditions than the decisions of parliament or government. To counter this power, new measures are needed in the economic field which will form the subject of a later chapter but which may be briefly stated here as involving the liberation of the British economy from the present world economic system. The power of money over politics, however, has an additional source, and this lies in the nature of the present division of the body politic into warring parties. As long as the party fight constitutes the process by which governments come to power, money will play a dominating role by its ability to play off one party interest against another. To stay in the party game, politicians need vast sums of money to keep their party machines going, and they become beholden to moneyed interests, which can easily transfer their support to other politicians and parties if those they have supported in the past do not show sufficient gratitude. The present system also places enormous power in the hands of the media, as I have repeatedly pointed out, and this again strengthens the hand of big money.

Oswald Spengler, one of the greatest minds of the present century, put the spotlight on our problem of leadership in the West when he said that it is essential that we establish a power in the state that is above economics, clearly meaning that a nation's political will should be the master of economic forces rather than the reverse. Economic forces will never be totally without influence in the political process — the world is not perfect enough for that; but with the party war taken out of political life that influence will be cut to the lowest practical minimum. Only therein lies the possibility of strong government.

While we are dealing with the powers necessary to national leadership, there is a further power that should be mentioned which is hardly ever discussed: this is very simply the power that comes from having time to observe, to study and above all to **think**. What is to me one of the most obvious wrongs of our present political system is the working schedule that that system imposes upon the average member of government. In addition to attending to all the tasks of his or her ministry, that member is also a parliamentarian, which involves regular attendance at parliamentary sittings **and** the constituency duties that are normally necessary for the retention of parliamentary seats. People who elect candidates to parliament for their constituency expect those who are elected to look after their local constituency interests. This can involve an extremely time-consuming range of duties, from presiding over weekly 'surgeries' to following up complaints about uneven paving stones and badly maintained country footpaths. The average elector expects to be able to write a letter to his local MP about the most trivial of personal problems and receive a courteous answer together with an assurance that the problem will be carefully investigated. Quite apart from any questions of principle involved here, the MP in his turn knows that, if he fails to give satisfaction in such matters, he will soon lose votes and his whole position in politics will be in danger.

Of course, there is nothing whatever wrong with this rule that the people should be able to vote for a public official to attend to their problems and then be able to throw him out if he fails to do so; such a system is one of the essentials in making the country a decent place to live in. But what is badly wrong is that the officials who have to attend to these matters are the same officials who have to attend regular sittings of parliament and, in the case of government ministers, also deal with the affairs of government itself. Not only is it unreasonable to impose all these burdens on the same people, it is highly damaging from the standpoint of the national interest.

National leaders who have to attend to matters of state at the highest level need to have reasonable time to relax and to reflect. Decisions of great weight require this process of unhurried contemplation, enforced by reading and study that keep one abreast of all the facts relevant to the task. In times gone by, when the whole business of politics was much less rushed, this facility was available to our leaders, and the greater wisdom that they brought to the decisions of state was a testimony to better working conditions. I have said that we must again produce **statesmen**. But we must do more than just that: we must create the conditions under which statesmanlike judgement is possible. The present political rat-race to shake enough hands, kiss enough babies and arrange the repair of enough drains to stay in office gives us no hope of realising this possibility.

What our new system must therefore do is separate these various functions so that those who are responsible for national government are able to give their whole time, attention and mental and spiritual energies to that task, leaving others to the more mundane chores of administration such as now occupy a great deal of the schedule of every parliamentary member. If those in government do not have the opportunity to think, others are going to do their thinking for them, and that is no healthy thing from the nation's point of view!

In this chapter, I have attempted to point to the unworkability of our established system of government, which in reality scarcely qualifies to be called a system at all. If there is anything systematic about it, it is the unscrupulous exploitation of the credulity of the people by those in power, deluding the people that they control government whereas in fact government is wholly outside their control. From the standpoint of governing the affairs of the nation, and of the good of the nation, nothing is system; everything is chaos. And the chaos is, of course, an inevitable product of the party war. The whole thing is a squalid political racket, designed to keep certain interests in power for perpetuity while misleading the masses into thinking they have a 'free choice'. In the direction of national affairs, the racket produces only weakness and muddle.

In an earlier chapter I spoke at length about certain subterranean forces that exercise overwhelming power over British affairs while keeping themselves away from the spotlight of public gaze and thereby from accountability to the nation. From an early age of my life I have been dedicated to the task of breaking these forces, for I am convinced that until they are broken our nation is going to be without unity, without strength, without purpose, without direction and without hope. The preservation of the existing political confidence trick that is misnamed 'democracy' is essential to these forces, for it is their principal weapon. Only when that weapon is eliminated will their power be broken.

The procedure for government that I have advocated in the place of this racket is an attempted formula for giving the nation dynamic, while responsible, leadership, and at the same time to preserve the meaningful human freedoms that are part of our national heritage. It is now time to look much more widely and deeply into these questions of freedom and the balance that must be struck between the rights and duties of citizenship if we are to build a stronger, healthier and more cohesive British society.

Chapter 12
Freedom: the illusion and the reality

In the preceding chapter, I have proposed certain reforms for achieving a higher quality of government. Here I want to look at the question of nation and society as a whole. What kind of nation do we want to be? What kind of nation **must** we be to regain our strength and a position of respect in the world? What is the place of the individual within the national community? What are the rights and the duties of citizenship? For a long time, I am convinced, our thinking on these matters has been awry — due, more than anything else, to the stupefying influence of the shamans of 'liberal democracy'.

Nowhere in the ideology of liberal-democracy is so much nonsense spoken and written as in that area concerning the relationship of the individual towards society, state and nation. The two entities, the individual and the community, are conceived as two mutually exclusive and antagonistic ones in terms of interests, rights and freedoms; for one to be protected, there must be a weakening of the other. The only circumstances in which the liberal will admit that the individual can retain his dignity are those in which there is a weak community, a weak state and a weak government.

In fact this is a monumental idiocy. From the first moment that individuals discovered that they were not alone on this planet, they have found the need to combine together in communities for common survival, with the good of the individual and that of the community being seen as complementary to one another. The safety and security of the individual have depended at all times on the efficiency of the community's services of law-enforcement and, in times of outside threat, on the effectiveness of the community's military defences. The prosperity of the individual has depended on the community's aggregate resources of wealth and its organisation of the forces of production. The very freedom of the individual has depended on the community's power to prevent anti-social elements endangering that freedom.

These truths are so obvious and elementary that a small child should be able to understand them. Yet everything that liberalism has to say about the relationship between individual and community is an implicit rejection of them. Liberals deprecate the idea of a strong state and government on the grounds that these will violate the rights of the individual and oppress him. Yet what are a strong state and government other than simply expressions of an effective communal organisation and will? Liberals fail to recognise that where state and government are weak it is not the individual who is thereby strengthened; what happens is that a vacuum of power is created into which will step other forces which, unrestrained, are much more liable to violate the rights, and threaten the interests, of the individual than any state power. In the American Wild West frontier days, a weak sheriff was the surest guarantee that outlaws would control the town. In contemporary Britain, a weak governmental hand on the machinery of industrial relations increases, rather than reduces, the probablity that trade union power will come down on the head of the worker who wishes to exercise his individual right not to join a strike. In a hundred different ways, individual freedom and welfare can be put at risk, not by government being too strong, but by its being not strong enough.

A perfect example of this rule can be seen in the present workings of local government in Britain. The powers extended to town halls, and the right of local citizens to choose who will run these town halls on their behalf, are popularly regarded as an ideal expression of liberal-democracy at work — contrasted as this is with the authoritarian administration of a centralised state. Yet what has this done for the local citizen today? It has simply placed him, in many areas, in a position of subjection to petty soviet tyrannies, run by miniature Stalins ready to lavish ratepayers' money on all manner of projects in no way desired or approved by local townspeople. Lack of strong central governmental authority over local administrators, and not the imposition of such an authority, has been the factor that has made for these tyrannies.

Liberalism claims to set great store on economic freedom as a prerequisite of other freedoms, but when we delve into the actual working of economic freedom as it turns out in nations governed by liberal theory we find that it is the freedom, not of the ordinary wage-earner or even the ordinary small businessman, but that of the huge multi-national industrial and commercial empires — specifically the freedom to move their capital about the world and buy and sell as they like, that is permitted. In a liberal economic system, economic freedom is commensurate with economic power, and of this the ordinary citizen has little; that ordinary citizen can, however, greatly suffer from the workings of such power by being deprived of his livelihood through international movements of capital that weak governments do not possess the will to stop.

For the average British person, economic freedom means having a job to go to and the opportunity to change to another job if the original one is not to his liking. If he lacks any chance to get a job, his only freedom is the freedom of the dole and the social security office — which in effect erode his independence and make him less free rather than more so. If he has a job but knows that if he loses it he cannot get another, he becomes in effect a slave at his place of employment — perhaps to his employer, perhaps to his trade union.

As for the small businessman, freedom to him means a prosperous local community with the money to spend on his goods or services, and that in turn means a high level of local employment.

Yet the liberal economic system is the very system under which these conditions, and therefore these freedoms, are the least likely to be secure.

From these few examples it will be seen that the claim of liberal democracy to bestow upon man the highest freedom that he can attain is pure fraud. When the liberal shouts, as he continually does, about 'freedom', he really has in mind freedoms entirely different from those that are of interest to the average citizen. But of course the average citizen's freedoms and rights never have figured highly among liberal priorities.

Aside from the economic freedom to which I have referred, there is the freedom from **fear**: fear of harm to person, family and property, fear of the late-night attack in the dark street, fear of every kind of lawlessness that might menace the life of the respectable citizen. Is this fear greater or less in a society governed by liberal doctrines? I would suggest that it is much greater, and for the reason of the wholly inadequate protection given in such a society to the law-abiding and against the criminal.

The average man wants the freedom to do a decently paid job and to be able to change it if he wishes. He wants the freedom that comes of owning his own home within reasonable time of his first acquiring it. He wants the freedom to send his children to a decent school of his own choice. He wants the freedom for himself and his family to be able to walk the streets and parks of his neighbourhood at any hour of the day or night in peace and safety. He wants the freedom to be able to spend his leisure time as he would wish and facilities to do so that are within his means. He wants the freedom to choose his friends and, if he is in business, to decide with whom he will trade and whom he will hire or fire. Last but not least, he wants freedom from financial debt.

Only a small minority seeks the freedom to take part or have a say in politics, and this is particularly so with the British, who are not by nature a highly politicised people. The average Briton, when the subject of politics comes up, declares that he simply is not interested and tries, as soon as possible, to switch the conversation to football, television or the merits of the various holiday resorts or local restaurants. Political freedom to him is almost valueless, as he does not have the slightest disposition to use it; and, when he does, he seldom knows how. He just wants to live his own life in peace and concern himself with his own family, his job and his club. In so far as he cares about government at all, all he wants is good government — as has been said earlier — good government, able to create a society that satisfies these basic desires that I have listed. The only reason why he even stirs himself to go out and vote at election times is because every government he ever gets is a bad one and he just goes on hoping, year in, year out, that the next one might be better — or, if not that, he takes a look at the Opposition and decides that that would be even worse, so he puts his cross beside the government in office because he sees it as the lesser evil.

Am I not right in this diagnosis? Of course, the truth will come uncomfortably to the liberal-democrat, who has in his mind's eye a picture of the mass of people passionately concerned with public issues and using their collective will and wisdom to decide the nation's destiny. But anyone with a grain of understanding of the real workings of politics in Britain knows this liberal idea to be sheer fantasy.

In stating this apathy and uninterest in politics that is characteristic of the average Briton today, I do not acknowledge that it is either natural or healthy. Although in any community it will be a

minority that is intensely politically motivated, it is nevertheless a
fact that the British of today are much less motivated in politics
than they should be: apathy and lack of interest in political
matters, in other words, goes deeper in this country at the present
time than is normal or should be desired.

But for this liberals must take the major share of the blame, for
it is they who have created a nation with so little to inspire or
enthuse the ordinary citizen into caring about it; and it is they who,
by their control and operation of the mass media, have done more
than anyone to induce this comatose state among our citizenry
where matters of public concern are involved.

Lest anyone think here that by stating the average man's
uninterest in political freedom I am denigrating that freedom and
proposing that it be done away with, I should hasten to affirm that
I am doing neither; I am merely placing political freedom in what I
believe is the correct perspective and position in the order of
priorities. To some people it occupies a very high priority; to most
it has a relatively low one besides others that I have mentioned.

I do not want to withhold political freedom from those who
genuinely desire it and understand how to use it intelligently and
responsibly; I merely want to do away with the deception that this
means everyone, and to propose that to most of the population
there are other freedoms that are much more important.

It is a very old adage that for every freedom extended to one
person there has to be a restriction of the freedom of another
person. Extending this principle nationwide, it is true to say that
the extension of freedom in one area is not possible without a
contraction of freedom in another area. Freedom for the law-
abiding depends on withdrawal of freedom from the criminal.
Economic freedom for the ordinary worker or small trader
depends, as shown earlier, on the restriction of the freedom of the
international business tycoon. Freedom to live in a country that is
safe from attack by a hostile foreign power entails the reduction of
freedom that is involved in the organisation of the nation's
defence, and in the military disciplines that are essential to that
defence — including, if necessary, conscription of men into the
armed forces in order to provide the manpower for defence needs.

Freedom is not an infinite resource; it has to be conserved
carefully and then distributed where it is most needed and has the
most beneficial use.

Political freedom is no exception to this rule: extended without
limit, and in quarters where there is neither the disposition,

wisdom or knowledge to use it sensibly, it can end only in anarchy. And when that occurs, hundreds of other freedoms, precious to far greater numbers of people, become endangered and in the end inevitably disappear.

Having spent many years observing and talking to people, I have become convinced that those freedoms that are valuable to the majority depend first and foremost on a stable, prosperous, efficiently governed society, backed up by formidable national strength in all fields, including, when necessary, the field of war. For those conditions to be present, it is necessary that a nation has government prepared and able to organise it for such purposes, that such a government does not have to bend hither and thither to every pressure and whim of self-centred interest groups and that it can get on with governing with the co-operation of a united body politic rather than one torn apart by party conflict. For a government to be able to fulfil this role, not only must it extend to the individual certain rights and freedoms but it must also be able to demand from that same individual certain duties and obligations.

The Briton of the 20th century has grown up in an environment in which there has been little disposition to recognise this simple truth. He has been brought up to believe in two great illusions where his own life is concerned. The first is that he is in the real sense 'free'. The second is that it is alien to his tradition and his nature to be in any way **organised**. Neither supposition has any foundation of reality. I hope that what I have said so far has put this question of individual freedom in some kind of rational perspective and shown that, in the things that really matter to most of us, we have much less freedom than many think. What then of the question of organisation?

The truth is that the Briton of today is much more organised, indeed regimented, than he imagines himself to be in his wildest nightmares. His life is lived day-to-day, and year in, year out, in a straightjacket of opinions, values, tastes, habits and petty regulations imposed upon him by the keepers of the liberal-democratic national conscience, who control, not only the nation's laws, but the whole of its thought-forms — by means of their monopoly of the goggle-box, the cinema screen and the reading matter on everyone's breakfast table and bookshelf. Just let us take the younger generation as an example. It only requires that the czars of the media and the advertising world decide that a particular fashion in clothes or hairstyles should become the norm and millions immediately follow that fashion like conditioned zombies. If the 'pop' music industry finds a neurotic, bi-sexual freak, with a castrated voice and a predilection for female clothes, and publicises him as the great male singer of the age, with his name in large coloured lights in one city centre after another throughout the world, he will in no time have a vast fan club and a whole legion of prospective emulators.

The same mind-benders only have to create a 'new' political trend — which in all probablity is just an old trend in new clothes — and in no time it will have a following, not because anyone has seriously thought it through and found it has genuine merit but only because it has been presented, with all the power of mass suggestion, as the 'in thing'. No, the people of today have been trained to respond like obedient robots to the command of their master's voice as it comes into their living rooms every day and every evening. And yet these are the people who liberals will claim are 'free' and are averse to being organised and regimented!

Real freedom, of the kind valued by our ancestors, comes from a liberation of the mind and spirit. The truly free man is the one who is master of his own instinct for what is right and wrong, who is his own judge of what is beautiful and ugly — in literature, in art, in music and all else. Freedom is the independent faculty for formulating values, loves and loyalties. Such a person as has these attributes does not then become less free by submitting himself to certain restraints and disciplines devised for the maintenance of a strong and cohesive community, nor by acknowledging the necessity in every community for leadership and by respecting and following leadership when it manifests itself.

Reverting again to this matter of organisation, do we not see organisation — of the worst kind — in the miasma of laws and restrictions we live under today which do nothing to make our nation more efficient but simply provide more jobs for the desk-wallahs who administer them? We cannot buy a drink outside certain limited licensing hours, though alcoholism is not one iota less of a problem in this country than in others where the same laws do not exist. We dare not cane disobedient children in our schools because a gang of trendy educationalists sitting in an ivory tower somewhere across the Channel say we cannot. We must wear a seat-belt when we drive a motor car, even if it is only our own life we are risking by not doing so. We dare not fire a black man from our company because he is likely to bring us to court for 'racism'; nor may we give a job to a male instead of a female because that would be 'sexism'. Now the business has gone from the sublime to the ridiculous, with the banning of children's story books on the grounds that some of the stories and pictures are 'racist' or 'sexist'.

Every business in this country, large or small, has to devote a considerable amount of time and expense to keeping records and submitting returns of Value-Added Tax, much of the money involved here simply travelling round in a circle and ending up where it started, and with the nation not a penny better off. Yet should any business fail to comply with this rule it is likely to be for the high jump. Reverting to racial matters, I am, as I have previously said, currently in prison because I have dared to publish an honest and frank opinion on the respective merits of Whites and Negroes.

Digest these facts and then come back and try to tell me that the British of today are a 'free' people and that they are not organised and regimented, not to say coerced, in all manner of ways affecting their daily lives!

But this is not an organisation of the people directed by responsible national leadership for great national purposes; it is the fussy bossing and scolding of the nanny state, treating the people as children requiring supervision in the nursery. This is autocracy, liberal-democratic style — the dictatorship of the governess, the despotism of the kindergarten teacher.

And if any further evidence of this should be required, may I remind the reader of what has been said earlier in this book: that today the movement that I represent is effectively banned from the use of meeting halls around the country, as well as from TV and radio — for no apparent reason other than that the people of Britain are regarded as so immature that they should not be allowed to listen to what we say and make up their own minds as to whether we are right or wrong!

In place of regulation of people's lives by petty tyrants for small purposes, we need a national mobilisation of the people by true leadership for great purposes — in a nutshell, for the purposes of the regeneration of Great Britain and the British Race. We need the systematic organisation of every national resource, human and otherwise, in the task of national reconstruction and the regaining of national strength and vigour.

Beginning with the institution of a system of government able to unite the nation to these ends, which has already been discussed, we must proceed to the next need, which is a thorough overhaul of society from top to bottom, incorporating a new code of citizenship, new values and new goals.

I have already spoken of the need to reject the liberal concept of society, with its one-sided emphasis on 'rights', and to replace it with an alternative concept which establishes an equal balance between rights and duties. A few examples here should suffice:-

Along with the right of the currently unemployed person to receive state welfare benefit, there should be the duty of that person to perform work in return for that benefit, always provided that he or she is not in some way disabled.

Along with the right of the people to be defended against the threat of attack and invasion in war, there should go the duty of all able-bodied males to take part in that defence.

Along with the right of every person to receive free medical services in the event of illness, there should go the duty to minimise the national cost of these services by the practice of a way of life conducive to good health and fitness.

Along with the right of people to local public services for the maintenance of tidiness and cleanliness in their neighbourhoods, there should go the duty to contribute to that tidiness and cleanliness by the practice of tidy and clean habits in public places — in particular by desisting from throwing litter about.

Along with the right of people to have persons and property protected by agencies of law-enforcement, there should go the duty to give to those responsible for law-enforcement the fullest co-operation at all times.

Along with the right of people to have their country care for them, there should go the duty to care for their country — in a word, patriotism.

Britain today is afflicted with an all-too-large segment of the population consisting of parasitic and useless slobs who contribute nothing whatever to society but who are the first to expect that society will look after them, help them when they are in trouble, grant them every kind of 'right' and afford them every kind of protection. Indeed it seems sometimes that the whole of our society's amenities, welfare, compassion and help are directed towards making life as easy as possible for this sediment of the populace, and at the expense of useful and responsible citizens. This is of course a natural consequence of 'liberal' values in operation. First, liberalism, by its lack of firm leadership and direction, particularly in people's early and formative years, breeds legions of these misfits; then, by the softness of the social order under which we live, it keeps them in comfort and security for the rest of their lives.

The British public is well used to picking up its daily papers and reading of drunken mobs of football fans disgracing our country's name by their oafish behaviour abroad; but in fact these specimens are only the natural product of a society which fails, from the very beginning, to instil into many of its young people the virtues of national pride, discipline, tidiness, temperate habits and responsible civic conduct.

Our first priority in creating a population fit for a respected place in the world must indeed be with the young. It is not within the scope of this book to enter into the debate over methods of academic teaching. What can be done, however, is the laying down of certain basic principles and procedures that should govern **all** education. It should not be the purpose of schooling merely to fill the heads of pupils with book-knowledge; it should be the aim to train them to become useful, responsible and loyal citizens of a great nation, prepared at all times to carry out their duties to that nation as well as expect their rights from it. Patriotism and national pride should in fact be the first civic virtue that is taught, and this should occupy a major role in the school curriculum. History in particular should be presented to the young in a way that places heavy emphasis on Britain's achievement in all fields — but not to the point of glossing over national weaknesses and mistakes. The young should be thoroughly imbued with a national view of the world, and taught the eternal laws that govern the success and failure, the strength and weakness, the rise and fall, of nations and empires. The overall purpose must be to instil an unshakeable national pride, together with an intelligent appreciation of what contributes to the national weal. Youth should also be taught something that is sadly lacking in Britain today, incredible though this may sound: that is a simple understanding of what their nation is, where its borders begin and end. One of the common products of this shortcoming is that people go through their lives, at least in the English part of our kingdom, talking of their nationality as 'English' and their country as 'England' — a wholly unjustified, albeit mostly unintended, insult to the Scots, Welsh and Irish who have contributed so much to Britain's greatness. We should ensure to rectify this error by bringing up our young to feel themselves part of a **British** nation, while this need in no way exclude a pride of identity with its component lands and peoples.

Likewise, education should emphasise the all-important link

between the peoples of the British isles and their ethnic kinfolk overseas, indeed to the point of instilling a sense of loyalty towards the latter that is every bit as strong as towards the native occupants of these islands. We should see the British Race as one people, with one destiny, whatever geographical or political barriers may at the moment separate its members.

Educating young people to understand race does not mean the promotion of hatred for other races, and indeed the latter tendency should be firmly excluded from any school teaching. We should encourage the young to respect the ethnic diversity of the world's peoples and to wish to preserve it. They should be encouraged likewise to recognise the special qualities and attributes of the respective races while not imagining those qualities and attributes to be the same. It must be firmly inculcated into the young that we British belong to the European family of races and cultures, and that for them, when they come of age, marriage and the procreation of children outside that family is harmful and wrong — to all races concerned. This must — and I repeat — be taught without hatred, and we must always remember that racial hatred is part of a caricature of nationalism created by its opponents and does not correspond to the reality of our outlook. On the other hand, we must not fall into the opposite error of believing that we can force people by legislation to 'love' other races; the individual should be left to form his or her personal feelings on such matters in accordance with the inner preference and conscience.

Next in importance among the young — indeed of equal importance — is to build the foundations of a healthier and fitter British Race, and this aim must be linked with that of establishing a firm polarity between the sexes, with young males being imbued with the qualities of **manhood** and young girls with those of **womanhood**.

Physical education in most schools in Britain today is appallingly inadequate, and this can be seen in the depressingly large numbers of people in this country of very poor physique, as well as the high rate of sickness. Regular vigorous body exercise must be a vital part of the school curriculum everywhere, with PE periods increased both in frequency and in the toughness of the schedule, particularly for boys. For these youngsters, in place of the soft-option jumping about and arm-flapping in the manner of third-rate ballet-dancers, I am in favour of the introduction, under careful supervision, of weight-training and other resistance exercises, which not only aid muscular development but also build will-power.

All young boys should, in addition, be obliged to take part in vigorous competitive sports, including at least one sport where hard physical contact is involved, such as rugby, boxing, wrestling or one or another of the martial arts. Every young lad should grow up with the experience of fighting and be capable of defending himself if attacked. Aside from other advantages, this breeds personal confidence and a manly approach to life.

The nation should be prepared to undertake a vast increase in expenditure to provide adequate school and after-school facilities for all the young to use in the drive for fitness and strength. Such facilities must be installed in every area of the country where today they are lacking.

In addition to body-training, there must also be education in the subject of diet. It is a pity that today a certain MP with an obvious taste for exhibitionism and personal publicity has taken it upon herself to become the principal advocate among politicians of healthy eating and living. While some of her methods may be nauseating, we should not allow ourselves to be led by these into discounting the totality of her message. Political leaders **should** set an example in these matters and occasionally run the risk of appearing to 'preach' to others, for the issue is an important one. It is only regrettable that at present such a cause does not have a convincing and credible public spokesman or spokeswoman. Putting it in basic terms, much of the food that many of us British eat is pure junk. We probably have the worst standards of nutrition of any of the more advanced nations. Not only should there be an ongoing national campaign of education in these matters — and I mean here education of **all** age-groups — but there should also be a firm policy of eliminating these junk-foods from our shops and substituting natural and wholesome products.

Coming back to the matter of polarity of the sexes, school-teachers should have it drummed into them at all teacher-training colleges that they must use all the influence within their power to combat any sign of effeminate tendencies in young boys, just as they must encourage to the utmost the development of femininity in the girls under their care. The first, of course, is largely comple-mentary to the second. I am convinced that much of the rampant 'feminism' of our times, represented as it is mainly by the most repulsive harridans, is due to the general decline among the White Race (and particularly in Britain) of real manhood. The 'liberal' spirit of our modern civilisation has, in a hundred different ways, led to the emasculation of a large part of the male species, and this is the most noticeable the higher one looks in the social and educational scale. The real man brings out the best in woman; where manhood is in short supply, woman begins to try to ape man and become a substitute for him.

As part of the fulfilment of this need, every schoolboy should undergo some rudimentary military training, as an apprenticeship for more thorough training later. This may be obtained by means of school cadet units or through a national youth organisation, which should be formed to provide educational and recreational facilities of all kinds for youngsters, supplementing the school curriculum in areas where it is lacking and replacing it in the case of those who have left school. This youth organisation should be, like the schools, strongly permeated with a patriotic outlook and should work in close collaboration with educational authorities. The purpose must be to ensure that all young people obtain, whether through school or through the national youth movement, the desired training in mind, body and character necessary for good citizenship and are thoroughly imbued with patriotic attitudes. Part of the aim of this training should be to instil into the young a sense of the value of service to the community above self.

Apart from the normal academic education and the background of military training and hard sports, the young man should take part in regular adventure courses which expose him to rough living and, within certain limits, physical danger. Courage and initiative should be put to the test at an early age, and supervisors should be constantly on the look-out to spot and foster qualities of leadership. It should be our aim to identify potential leaders of society early in life and in the process of these stages of youthful upbringing, and then to mark them down and further train them for responsibility in national affairs at a later stage. Just look at our 'leaders' of today! How have they established their positions? Merely by coming first past the post in the huge organised fraud to which we give the title 'elections'. Usually, in terms of the true qualities required to lead — manhood, personality, toughness, courage, initiative, command and sound, cool judgement — they are totally lacking.

Finally, there should be the institution of national military service, which Britain abolished in 1960 to her great cost. This should be restored again, but with some changes from the regime of former days so as to put the time to better use. There are some objections to national service that are heard regularly from military chiefs, and with these I shall deal later in this book where the matter will be looked at in more detail. Suffice it to say here that I regard national service as essential, not only from the standpoint of national defence, but also equally so from that of training for citizenship.

I have given attention to these needs because it is my conviction that the first requirement of a better society is a better population. Every influence of modern society has the opposite effect. Liberalism, with all its nationally and racially weakening tendencies, is an outlook which appeals, as I have made clear earlier in this book, essentially to the unhealthy and sickly in body, mind and spirit; and in turn liberalism breeds a society of yet more people with these afflictions, as if in a vicious circle. To reverse the process, and to produce a population healthy in constitution and outlook, we must start with the young.

In many older societies, and before the liberal world-view began to make its influence felt, citizenship was regarded as something of value and something to be earned. Under liberal-democracy, a person is regarded as being a fully fledged citizen immediately he or she comes of a certain age — in most matters at 18. No qualification whatever is needed for this status. At such an age, the individual straightaway becomes vested with numerous 'rights', first and foremost of which is the right to vote for the Tweedledum or the Tweedledee among the candidates in the political party charade. Added to this are numerous other rights, which may come slightly before or slightly after one's 18th birthday: the right to drive a motor vehicle, to open a bank-account, to buy alcoholic drinks, to take out a mortgage on a house, and so on. The whole emphasis, as I have indicated, is on 'rights'; nothing is ever asked of the citizen in return for these rights. Anyone and everyone inherits them as they pass from adolescence into what is supposed to be adulthood.

But it was not always so. In ancient Sparta, young boys, before they could be recognised as men, had to undergo certain tests to prove their fitness to be granted manhood and the rights of citizenship that went with it. Even in some African and Red Indian tribes, which we might call 'primitive', the same rule has been followed — indicating, in these respects at least, a greater wisdom than in the softened society of the modern West. I am one of those old-fashioned folk who believe that citizenship, at whatever age we decide young people should qualify for it, should be something to be earned by proof of fitness, and not a god-given right' that is bestowed on everyone, regardless of worth. The fields of training that I have outlined should constitute a part of this process of qualification.

This education and training should set the pattern for a new social order that will grip and transform every aspect of British life so as to bring it into step with the needs of national survival in the modern world. In two later chapters I shall outline how the firm hand of national leadership should give guidance in two vital spheres: the informing of public opinion and the direction of the economy. A brief word or two, however, should be said about these things here.

Of public opinion, it must be stated that there never was a time in history when this was not shaped by the influence of a numerically small and powerful *elite*. The idea that individuals in the majority make their own choice in a 'free market' of ideas belongs to pure make-believe. They are guided towards one or another outlook by those controlling the forces that are dominant in education and, today, also in the organs of mass communication. The only questions to be resolved are: which *elite*? And: what kind of forces and to what sort of outlook?

It is surely preferable that such forces should be ones identified with the nation and its vital interests rather than those serving internal and external enemies, and the outlook they promote should be a patriotic one rather than an unpatriotic one. It should be our resolve that in the future the guiding hands that mould public opinion, whatever the diversity in debate over the current issues, should be wielded by powers dedicated to the overall cause of the British nation and people, and to no other.

When we come to the economy, we find in Britain again the dire need for national leadership that will direct all economic resources, energies and skills to real national purposes. In my twenties, and after much study of economic forces, I came to realise that the debate between the respective theories of capitalism and socialism was a shallow and sterile one, and had anyway been completely overtaken by the facts of the new world of economics, which had rendered both these concepts in their old forms utterly obsolete. The big question of the modern age was one of whether national leadership would lead and direct economic forces or whether it would be swept along by them, their slave rather than their master.

What is needed today, as I have quoted Spengler as saying, is a power in the state that will be above economics and will regulate economics to national purposes. When this reality is grasped, we will see that capitalism and socialism are merely utilities, to be employed alternatively, or in combination, in accordance with their usefulness in tackling each particular economic task — always with the proviso that where capitalism is applied it is government that directs the capitalist and not the capitalist that directs government.

Class war should have no place in a truly national community, but rather than merely utter that sentiment as a platitude we must take positive action to organise and direct national affairs so as to remove the causes of this particularly pernicious form of conflict. Part of this task lies in education but part also in putting an end to the abuses that generate attitudes of class antagonism.

I have never been impressed by the arguments of those who claim that it is possible to achieve a society without classes. Such classes will always form as the natural consequences of profound differences in aptitude and skills between different sections of the population, and this is just as true in Soviet Russia today — a society that, while theoretically classless, is in practice deeply impregnated with social barriers — as in Britain.

What is important is that class divisions should never be allowed to reflect separate, and ultimately antagonistic, group interests, as has happened in this country — resulting in the two leading political parties representing a polarity of classes in which each one's commitment to what it perceives as the interest of its own social group leads it *ipso facto* into the assumption that this interest must be furthered at the expense of the other social group. By this attitude, a kind of 'class patriotism' has pervaded British life, and in the course of doing so has largely superseded national patriotism.

And of course this state of affairs is tailor-made for those who would wish to divide the British people in order to conquer them. One class is played off against another by the presentation of politics as being a 'class struggle', while the real enemy of all classes tightens his grip.

In my life I have mixed a great deal with all classes, and much more with the so-called 'working class' than have most people of middle-class background. I have found on both sides a fairly equal quota of stupid attitudes of the kind that lead to class conflict. I am in no doubt that these attitudes are rooted in the lack of an adequate sense of national consciousness in the British people; such a national consciousness would transcend class sentiments and relegate them to the background. But also to blame are a bad economic system, which creates much unjustified poverty at one end of the scale and much undeserved opulence at the other, and the steady drip of class-war propaganda, which of course exploits these two other factors for all it is worth.

Having said that this stupidity is to be found on both sides of the social divide, I have to say that in the final analysis it is the 'educated' classes that must bear most of the responsibility, for it is they who have done more than anyone to shape the conditions and climate of the society in which we live and they who, because of their education, should know better.

In a great part of today's middle classes there is a depressing lack of comprehension of the problems experienced by large numbers of people at the other end of the social scale — problems that are complacently dismissed as the product of idleness and lack of initiative, whereas this is in most cases wholly untrue. The middle classes, through their almost dog-like loyalty to Toryism, have maintained an economic system that, consistently throughout this century, has condemned to lasting inactivity millions who genuinely want to work. This attitude has in turn given rise to an intense class resentment among many of those affected which, when taken to extremes, can become equally socially damaging, and is only too welcome as inflammable material for political fire-raisers of the left, who work to polarise society yet further.

I have indicated in the previous chapter that aristocracy can be a nationally beneficial asset, and I would here go further and state that inherited wealth, far from being a social evil, can be a great social good. Quite apart from that institution providing an incentive to one generation of a family to work for the interests of the next, inherited wealth, and the social rank that often goes with it, increases the probability that such assets will come into the hands of those best fitted to use them wisely by virtue of genetic advantages (I have deliberately said 'probability', for the matter is never a certainty).

We should not need reminding of the advantage to society of a breed of public servants born of families of the best stock, with the financial security to be able to devote their time to such service without regard for monetary gain (thus reducing the likelihood that they may be 'bought'), and with access to the best possible educational facilities in early life to prepare them for their tasks. Disinterested service to the nation may well be said to be more likely to come from a man born to power than one who has had to elbow his way up to obtain it.

At the same time, the potential weaknesses of aristocracy are obvious. The high racial level that should in theory be maintained is often not maintained in practice. Anthony Ludovici, whom I have quoted earlier in another context, put it succinctly in *The Specious Origins of Liberalism*:-

> "Other influences apart, the matrimonial policies of our aristocracy alone would have sufficed to undermine the nation's faith in their ability to govern.
>
> "However rare the occurrence may have been, we know that for centuries, especially in France and England, the nobility of Europe produced personalities who, had they maintained their family qualities, might have bred a race of rulers capable of kindling an unquenchable faith in the reality, advantage and indispensability of a class of thoroughbreds in the seat of government. For, as J.B. Rice truly observed, 'an aristocracy of blood is eternally right, because it is natural.'
>
> "But from the earliest times, alas!, owing to the absence of any controlling body within their Order, they not only violated every precept of sound rulership, but also every measure which might have ensured a continuance of ability, dignity and even ordinary health in their family lines.
>
> "In vain, as early as the sixteenth century, sages arose who inveighed against the notion that infatuation alone was to be trusted as the motive for a sound marriage, because the privileges of a Ruler Caste involved corresponding sacrifices incompatible with the irresponsible self-indulgence which was one of the few luxuries of the masses..."

Ludovici went on to cite the aristocracy of Venice as an exception to this tendency to permit the adulteration of noble blood through unwise marriages, quoting the historian Lecky as describing it as "the most enduring aristocratic government that the modern world has known." Continued Ludovici:-

> "And what was the secret of this exceptionally successful aristocratic achievement? Simply that the Venetian aristocrats, being more realistic and more intellectually gifted and upright than those of other European States, first of all knew that they must allow for the natural iniquity of Man, even when it is clothed in ermine and silks; and secondly that, if they wished to survive as a ruling minority, they must devise a system of internal control and discipline designed to maintain a high standard of quality among the members of their Order and punish, if necessary with degradation, any one of them who fell below a certain level of decency and

efficiency.''

For aristocracy to be socially useful in the Britain of the future, it must be regulated along similar lines to the Venetian ruling caste that Ludovici has mentioned, with special emphasis on the need to maintain the quality of its blood-lines through prudent marriages. A way must be found to eliminate from it all those elements that have demonstrated beyond doubt the absence of true aristocratic qualities. I have said in the previous chapter that these elements should be replaced by families of outstanding merit from the ordinary ranks of the population, and I would add that outstanding service in the armed forces should be regarded as a major qualification in this regard.

In addition to this, we should be ready to reconsider our laws of primogeniture whereby a family title is inherited by the eldest son. As Ludovici has pointed out in the same study, there are very many cases in the history of aristocracies in Europe where younger sons displayed more of the ancestral qualities of the line than their seniors. Such a system of internal regulation as Ludovici quoted from the noble families of Venice might do well to change this rule and permit the heir to each title and estate to be appointed on merit rather than succeed by right of being the first-born.

An institution of aristocracy in which wealth and privilege are directly related to the performance of public duty would be one of the guarantors against the insidious disease of class warfare that now poisons our country.

We hear much talk in Britain today about the need for a 'caring' society, and so much so that many of us have become accustomed to wincing at the very sound of these words! I have made it a rule to deduce that every politician who lays stress in public on how 'caring' he or she is is likely to care most of all about the votes to be won by such language. Of course, the wider the section of society you 'care' about, the more votes you will expect to get! It has become an occupational habit today for the party leaders to 'care' not only about those people in the population who genuinely need care but also the professional loafers, spongers, drop-outs, parasites and misfits as well, even the criminal element — as is witnessed by the generous allocation of state 'care' to those who riot, loot and burn in our inner cities. In the rat-race for electoral advantage, the original concept of a state which looks after the welfare of its people has been hideously perverted.

Care in social services should be primarily dedicated to the very young, the very old and the genuinely sick and disabled. For the rest of the population those services should be available to cope with cases of real misfortune but should never be seen as a substitute for self-reliance. I have dealt with this question of self-reliance in my chapter on Conservatism, and from this it should be clear that I do not regard individual possession of that attribute as a substitute for the opportunity to work. Nevertheless, these writings are anticipating an age in the future when such opportunities are present in every part of the country through enlightened economic policies. In that happy situation, it will be permissible to say to the able-bodied man who is hard up because he has no job: "Go out and get one!" Then self-reliance can come into its own again as a necessary attribute in a responsible citizen.

Our social service ethic should be based on the time-honoured dictum that you do not help the weak by discouraging or undermining the strong. The first ideal of social welfare should be a strong population, and we should recognise the truth that such a national asset, and the resources it creates, must be the main basis on which we are able to take care of the genuinely weak and the genuinely needy.

We come back here to the question of the promotion of national health. I do not claim to be unique in believing that, where illness is concerned, prevention is better than cure. The practice of healthy eating habits, combined with vigorous exercise, and the avoidance of excess in things like smoking and drinking, are the best way to reduce visits to the doctor to the minimum. As for drug-taking, it is barely conceivable to me that young people should even think of attempting this. When I was in my teens, health and physical fitness were to me a religion, and they have remained so since. That any young person should entertain drug-taking in even the mildest doses is an indication of the low priority that exists in his mind regarding care of the body, and this is the fault of our national leaders and educators for having failed to create a national climate stressing the urgency of good health.

Of course, we now see moves to warn people against drug-taking by the use of TV propaganda films. This is better than nothing but, like most of the few useful things done by those in power today, it is too little, and in the cases of many, too late. Half-measures such as these will not have much effect on a population which for many decades has been left to go to seed.

A population dedicated to fitness will reduce to a fraction the cost of health and other social services, as well as providing a greater fund of energy for all kinds of endeavour in work and leisure. With health and fitness also comes greater pride — a commodity we are short of in Britain at both national and personal level. A proud individual will prefer not to avail himself of social welfare unless it cannot possibly be avoided. And a proud individual will be unlikely to follow a way of life that will lead to the need for social welfare in the first place.

One of the most vital needs in the pursuit of a strong and healthy population is to reverse the alarming decline in the nation's birthrate. It is noteworthy that not one of the established political parties of Westminster has shown any real concern over this, let alone done anything about it. Instead, we have complacently sat back and watched with equanimity a process which in effect amounts to a slow national death.

It should not require a professional mathematician to work out that a drastically declining birthrate means inevitably that the average age of the community is gradually going to increase and that in consequence, year by year, we are going to have a diminishing portion of young, able-bodied and active supporting a growing portion of elderly and, in large part, inactive. If we are concerned, as many are, about the present strain on the resources of the health and social services, we should see that this strain is only going to increase as long as this tendency of national infertility remains. That such a prospect should not alarm our present leaders is a token of their unconcern for the nation's future.

Needless to say, it is also significant that nations and races which restrict their births in a world where other nations and races are fast increasing theirs will in time suffer a relative decline in strength which could be disastrous. One of the factors that most profoundly affected the international balance of power between the end of the Napoleonic Wars and the start of the First World War was that, while France sustained a very modest birthrate for much of that period, those of the Anglo-Saxon and German races were comparatively high. Today the British Race has become sterile while the coloured world is increasing at an alarming rate. This would be bad enough in itself were it not for the fact that it is made ten times worse by the liberals and bleeding hearts amongst us who, with every 10 million that is added to the coloured world's population, intensify their demands on us Britons and other Whites to hand over part of our own hard-earned wealth to feed and clothe these extra millions!

It is no argument in defence of a low birthrate to say that Britain is overcrowded and cannot take more people — and indeed such a proposition comes oddly from mouths that at the very same time seek to justify coloured immigration! I would certainly agree to the assertion that we should not wish to bring about any substantial increase in the population size of the United Kingdom but I would not agree to the suggestion that we should seek to reduce it (except by the resettlement overseas of unassimilable races presently in this country). It is preferable that the population size of Britain become stabilised at approximately its present level. A vigorous birth-rate at home should be balanced by a high rate of emigration to other parts of the White Commonwealth, where there are abundant open spaces waiting to be filled up and which should far preferably be filled up by Anglo-Saxons and Celts than by other races.

I am not one of those who believe that the state should put pressure on people to have large families who, perhaps for very good reasons, find it impractical to do so. At the same time, I am passionately against the present policy of the state of positively **discouraging** such families, by the numerous devices now employed. What the state should certainly do is remove all such discouragements, while at the same time providing inducements to large families in the form of increased family benefits. I believe, however, that in offering the latter we should not make the mistake made in the past, which resulted in encouragement to breed being given to some of the least fit and desirable elements of the population. We want to encourage quantity, but not at the expense of quality.

I leave it to specialists to devise the specific methods whereby we can encourage the best types of families to have plenty of children while discouraging the others. Income-related benefits might be one course, but I make no hard or fast stipulations in favour of these. Here I only state what should be the basic **aim** of the policy; I leave others to formulate the means.

One important step towards countering the catastrophic fall in the British birthrate should be the repeal of the law permitting abortion — though I hasten to add that that is far from being the only reason that I advocate such a step. I believe that abortion is a crime from every point of view, except in those cases where, on the advice of doctors, it is necessary to protect the mother's life. Apart from anything else, it encourages a totally irresponsible attitude towards sexual relations, which is part of the general pattern of promiscuity, permissiveness and plummeting moral standards for which we have to thank the liberals who have run riot in our society over the past few decades.

Legislation against abortion is just one item in a series that will be needed to reverse the trend to moral anarchy that has rotted the fibre of Britain in recent times. Another is a repeal of the law permitting acts of homosexuality. This is just one more piece of rulemaking that our political masters have sprung upon us without the slightest indication that it ever had the endorsement of the people. It has proved a wholly regressive step which has now rebounded against its promoters with the recent spread of the AIDS disease.

I am the first to acknowledge that banning homosexual acts will not stop them; least of all will it alter the perverted nature of those who wish to engage in them; but this is not, and never has been, the main issue.

By forcing this perversion back into the closet, society limits its growth and influence to the minimum. By legalising it and allowing it out into the open, it unlocks the floodgates through which pours a poison that utterly corrupts the community and infects many in it who, under conditions where it was illegal, would have stayed uninfected. The unleashing of homosexuality has also given rise to the emergence of a whole mafia of queers that has eaten its way into the fabric of our cultural and intellectual life, impregnating that life with its values and philosophy. When the homosexual community shouts for 'gay rights', what it really means and wants is **gay power**. Like certain other minorities, the poofters call for 'emancipation' as a euphemism for an aggressive imperialism all of their own, in which they work to promote their brethren and expand their life-style everywhere. In my own experience of political groups, I have seen this process at work. It exists also in journalism, broadcasting and the academic world, where these creatures are rife and proliferating. The gay mafia is also, needless to say, into government, particularly local government, where it has spent other people's money on promoting products designed to spread the virus to young schoolchildren. And I do not have to tell the reader that it is now running amok in the Church.

One thing that one learns about these people after some experience with them is the way in which they are bound to each other in a kind of mystical brotherhood. The author E.M. Forster, one of their number, put it in a nutshell when he said: "If I were faced with the choice between betraying my country and betraying my friends, I hope I would have the courage to betray my country.'' The traitor Anthony Blunt has said much the same.

Quite apart from the moral — and indeed now also the medical — considerations involved in the fight against homosexuality, that fight must be seen as a token of our pursuit of the ideals of true manhood and womanhood, which we must recover if our nation is to recover. The literary and artistic products of the homosexual mind can only flourish in a society where heterosexual values have been gravely weakened; and that very simply is a society that has become degenerate. Legislation alone will not drive this perversion into the catacombs where it belongs; that must be accompanied by a total change in national philosophy, aiming at a national cultural, moral and spiritual renaissance. Again, to reduce matters to the simplest terms, the fight is against decadence.

In this fight against decadence, we come, inevitably, up against our old adversary whose name has been mentioned often enough in these pages but cannot be forgotten because he will not lie down: yes, the liberal. We come up against him because it is the hypnotic influence of his values and philosophy that has paralysed our governing classes again and again when faced with the need to clean out the augean stables. When we tackle the liberal on these questions of national morality and standards, and of the role of authority in the lives of people, he will offer a defence which, on a moment's examination, will be revealed as resting on foundations of the grossest humbug. Of course, it is the defence of 'freedom' — the rallying cry of liberal mischief-makers and sowers of chaos across the ages. People should be 'free' to practise their own sexual preference. They should be 'free' to indulge in drug-taking. They should be 'free' to partake in a diet of porn and smut. They should be 'free' to contract out of the obligation to fight for their country in war. And why should they be endowed with this 'freedom'? Why, because it is the proper thing in a mature society to leave individuals to make up their own minds about what they want to do with their lives and about what is good and bad in literature, art and human behaviour.

But is it not this very same liberal who is the foremost opponent of the principle that people should be 'free' to listen to political doctrines offensive to the liberal conscience and make up their own minds on the rights and wrongs thereof? In fact, the liberal, with breathtaking composure, has done a 180-degree turn and expects us not to notice it. The pompous moral autocrat in suppressing those tendencies in society he sees as a threat to him, he becomes the benign democrat in defending everything that is to his taste. This is the animal that we have put under the microscope in an earlier chapter of this book, and here he is again — unchanged and untouched by the evidence of his own inconsistencies!

Nevertheless, while we may now have the liberal with his back against the ropes, we must not presume that the fight has gone out of him. He has one punch left which he relies upon to turn the tide of the contest, and this is one that merits our close examination, because on it so much of the case for liberalism rests.

The liberal will defend the individual's right to engage in any degenerate behaviour of his choice — on the important condition that that behaviour does not do harm to others. For a long time the doctrine of liberalism has had us paralysed in the face of this argument, and it is time that we buried the argument once and for all.

Of course the liberal is right when he speaks of behaviour that is not harmful to others — so long as we consent to look at things within his own limited concept of time and circumstance. Here we are close to the core of the liberal-democratic outlook.

Liberal-democracy, as an ideology, seems completely incapable of seeing the present day except in terms of isolation from all history that has has preceded it and all posterity that will follow it. It is as if life for all of us in this world were static, the past and future being only of academic and speculative interest respectively. That we are what we are, and where we are, because of what our fathers did and their fathers did seems never to intrude on the liberal mind And from this it follows that what we do today has no bearing whatever on the kind of world that our children and their children inherit. The liberal simply cannot see the individual as a link in a chain of biological evolution, indebted to the past and with obligations to the future; on the contrary, the individual is a mere atom, surrounded by his little fence within which he may do as he likes so long as he does not cross that fence in a way that interferes with the life of the atom next door. That such atoms might have an origin is an idea alien to him, as is the idea that some atom yet unborn might have an origin in one now living. From this, he is unable to conceive of a continuity of duties and obligations between the successive generations of a race, or even a family.

The liberal is all too pleased to avail himself of the benefits of a technology and a civilisation that exist only because those going before us made it possible for them to exist. They made it possible because they conducted their lives in accordance with a spirit of **order** and **purpose**, obeying certain rules and submitting to certain disciplines — not all of them, mind you, but at least that portion of them that created something of value to hand down to us today. From this it follows that we have a duty to posterity to conduct **our** lives according to some order and purpose in order to preserve that which we have inherited and, if possible, to build further upon it so as to hand on something of value to those coming after us.

Again, I am running the risk of couching in pedantic terms a concept that a child should be able to understand. But in fact the whole of the liberal ethos is a denial of it. When a potentially valuable member of the community drinks himself to death or kills himself by use of drugs, he is not 'harming no-one else'; he is taking from out of his community someone who was pleased to inherit worthwhile things from those who preceded him but to leave nothing to anyone coming after him — even if it is only the life of a future member of value to the community whom he could have fathered but for his premature demise.

As another illustration of the point, we live in one of the best endowed countries in the world because in the past men have been prepared to **fight** for it. Had they not been thus prepared to fight, this land might have been laid waste or subjected to conquest by barbarians or savages — thereby bequeathing to the present an environment a hundred times more harsh than that in which the present generation lives.

Yet the liberal will protest indignantly that no-one living today in this country has the obligation to fight for it if he does not want to; whether he does or not is a matter of his own sovereign choice. Of course, if that became the rule and all followed it, not a great span of history would have to follow before the occupants of this land would be born into a life as bleak as would exist today had that liberal ethic prevailed among former generations.

It is upon this fundamental truth that we of today's generation are not sovereign in terms of our debts and our obligations but are merely the contemporary links in a chain of past, present and future — of destiny — that the whole liberal-democratic case for free conduct and free morality collapses.

But there is another consideration here which we should not ignore. It is that in the ages when liberalism first took root in

Europe the vast majority of people lived in a much tougher and more natural environment than at present. To a great extent, natural conditions of living imposed upon individuals the disciplines of an orderly, prudent and creative existence — and by the simple pressure of the needs of survival. If a person became ill, he did not have a national health service to look after him, nor could he, in the case of the majority of the populace, afford a doctor. If he became very ill, he was liable to die, as many did at no great age. These circumstances provided as good incentive as can be for people not to engage in living habits harmful to health. The rule is given added force when we realise that there was no such thing as insurance against loss of pay through non-attendance at work. If a sick man was fortunate enough not to succumb to his sickness, the chances were that he would go broke and be unable to feed his family.

Add to this the fact that man then lived in an age of only infant technology. There simply were not the labour-saving devices that we all take for granted today, whether at work or in the home. Both the manual worker (the majority) and the housewife obtained quite enough physical exercise in the course of day-to-day tasks.

In the very much shorter leisure hours that were available to folk, there did not exist the modern facility of obtaining instant entertainment by the push of a button. People had to devise their own forms of amusement. One of these was simply conversation, which can be an excellent exercise for the mind. Another was the reading of good books — which most books were before the age of mass printing and publishing. Alternatively, there was the pursuit of some useful and creative hobby — such as knitting for women or carpentry for men.

If people wanted music, they usually had to supply their own, and this involved the development of musical talents. Even in the days of my father's boyhood, spent in a small provincial town in Ireland in the first two decades of the present century, it was the custom of the family to hold musical evenings, with one member playing the piano, another the violin and another providing the vocal contribution. The evening out to hear a professional instrumental group was a once-yearly treat. The gramophone was only just making its entry into drawing rooms, and a minority possessed one.

If not these amusements, there was a walk — engaged in not only for leisure but for work as well, for there was no such thing as motor transport. The healthy exercise that people obtained in the course of working was supplemented in the task of getting there and then back home in the evening. It was the same with children getting to and from school.

Under these conditions of living, it was possible for *laissez-faire* principles to operate in people's daily lives without the likelihood that they would lead to decadence and degeneration — quite apart from the fact that the agencies which profit from these things today simply were not then present. The nation could be left to take care of itself with the assurance that natural forces present in the environment of the vast majority would provide their own regulating machinery.

The high priests of 'total freedom' who lived in those days could not have anticipated the conditions prevailing in the western civilisation of the late 20th century, where man, through his advanced technology, has created a Frankenstein monster that is likely to destroy him if he does not find, from somewhere, a means of controlling it. Now the natural pressures upon us to lead healthy and ordered lives, conducted in accordance with moral rules, have mostly disappeared. We now have an environment which brings with it a totally different danger: the danger that, cossetted by it day and night, we will grow soft — in body, mind and will. How is this terrifying danger to be averted?

I can see no means of averting it except by our preparedness to welcome what Spengler called the **'resurgence of authority'**. We must discover a form of leadership with the wisdom to perceive the immense degenerative dangers that modern technology presents for us and then the will to bring that technology under control so that it is used not to retard Man but to advance him. When I speak of bringing this technology under control, I ought perhaps to say that what needs controlling is not the technology itself but society's response to it. To say that the machine is what we make it is to mouth a well-worn platitude, but it is clear that in practice liberal-democracy has failed to make the machine a boon but has succeeded only in making it a curse.

We cannot put the clock back. We cannot cancel the coming of the machine-age; we are stuck with it and must make the best of it. It will not go away.

But if it is not to undermine, as it so obviously is today undermining, the quality of human life, we must find a way of re-regulating that human life so that the machine is kept in check.

I am convinced that this can only be done by the emergence of a power and authority within the community that is prepared, as our leaders in the past were prepared, to introduce **order** into society by establishing **standards** of public and private behaviour and employing all the vast means at their disposal to impress the value of those standards upon the nation.

We face a need, in other words, that runs entirely contrary to the liberal-democratic idea that is in vogue today whereby values and standards, as well as forms of human behaviour, are regarded as articles to be accepted or rejected in a kind of 'free market' of morality. This might have been practicable in the earliest days of liberalism, and for reasons that I have examined, but it is no longer practicable in the 1980s and 1990s.

I have spoken here of natural forces and the way in which, at the level of ordinary people's lives, these have been largely tamed by modern technology. But at a higher level, the level of global politics and the struggles for power that form part of them, these natural forces remain lords over us all — and over technology too. In the end, the brutal laws of survival assert themselves in the affairs of mankind, as in those of the animal world: tribes and societies with the attributes of health, strength and cohesion which come from living by disciplines and rules will conquer and drive from the face of the earth those which have become just aggregates of individual units, each following his own selfish whim and desire. We may rationalise until kingdom-come in favour of the 'freedom' for every vile and obscene tendency in our cultural life; such rationalising will not avail us when we have been driven out of existence or into servitude by stronger, more disciplined cultures which, so long as we continue in our present ways, will be destined by the unalterable laws of nature to supersede us and consign us to the dustbin of perished civilisations.

In this chapter I have touched upon just a few of the many areas of British life where fundamental changes are going to be needed to transform our nation from a mere aggregate of individuals and self-centred sectional interests into a genuine community dedicated to a common national purpose. That purpose may be summed up in one word: **regeneration**.

Twice in this century, by the blindness, weakness and folly of our political leaders, our nation has been placed in a position in which she has been fighting desperately with her back against the wall for her survival — against forces of immense efficiency and power.

On each occasion, she has only survived by a supreme effort of will, along with a total mobilisation of all national resources towards the common goal of victory. In those hours of crisis there were but one interest and one loyalty. It was a case of: "All for the nation; none outside the nation; none against the nation."

I am convinced that in our present national crisis nothing less than a similar effort and mobilisation will suffice for us to win through. That we are not this time engaged in a shooting war against a clearly identifiable foreign adversary does not in any way detract from the desperateness of our position. The reality of a war situation is none the less present and the threat to our survival as a nation undoubtedly much more real — if only that to many it is less obvious in its presence, and the resolve to face it and overcome it still needs to be created.

There has been all too clear a pattern in modern British history. In the years of peace, we have muddled aimlessly along, tackling every national problem with half-measures, when we have even bothered to tackle it at all, contenting ourselves with being ruled by a succession of weak and mediocre politicians and within antiquated political institutions, while looking on such words as 'efficiency' and 'discipline' as alien to our tradition, and always failing by lack of national organisation to exploit the immense reservoir of human skill and genius that lies within our people and our race.

Then, finding ourselves, in 1914 and again in 1939, largely through this lethargy and slackness, in a situation of desperate national emergency, we have shaken ourselves out of our slumber and found the national unity, organisation, discipline and purpose necessary to come through supreme crisis. Industry and commerce have been subordinated to government and made to serve national needs. Patriotism has been taken out of mothballs and used to galvanise the population to effort and sacrifice. People have been encouraged to face up to duties instead of ever yammering about 'rights'. We have suddenly discovered, as if by surprise, that manhood is a quality to be nurtured and trained. The nation has become a community with pride and with a goal, instead of a disjointed and dispirited rabble.

But after the immediate emergency has passed, we have sunk again back into the bad old ways. There has been no national organisation, except in the petty and negative sense described earlier, no direction, no great goal — just drift. The economy has again become a free-for-all. Politics have degenerated again into party warfare. Patriotism has again been abandoned. Defences have been dismantled. The return to the self-centred society has proceeded at breakneck speed. In short, nothing has been learned.

Such is the sick condition of Britain today that no measures can save it short of those amounting to an operation of war, a radical transformation of politics accompanied by an equally radical transformation of society from top to bottom, aimed at the harnessing of every resource, every talent and every last drop of human energy to the task of national salvation and then reconstruction. And if this is to be done effectively it must be undertaken as something intended to have permanence, not to be a massive outpouring of effort only later to be followed by a lapse into the sloppy ways of thinking and acting so familiar in the past.

This transformation is the mighty mission with which our generation has been entrusted. If we fail, the outcome is likely to be permanent national eclipse.

Chapter 13
The role of the media

Two generations ago, the allocation in a book such as this of an entire chapter to the communications media might have been considered as placing an undue importance on the subject. That could not be said today. The media have assumed such a crucial position in the direction of national affairs that no programme for national recovery can be put forward without taking them into account.

We British are brought up to regard our press, broadcasting services and other organs of public opinion as being different from those of 'totalitarian' countries in so far as the latter exist to promote one single point of view: the ideology of the established state and government, while our own are free of state interference and therefore, by some *ipso facto* presumption, at liberty to give voice to a wide range of opinions — in fact any and every opinion that people care to hold.

The reality is that this picture is grossly misleading.

It would be much more accurate to say that in Britain the media constitute a 'state within the state', or perhaps more accurately a 'state **above** the state', so that the question of whether they are independent of the existing government of the day is really an irrelevant one. Perhaps much more to the point would be the question of whether **any** government is in fact independent of the media, or of that tightly knit circle of privileged people who control and operate this all-powerful institution.

Let us take, to begin with, the BBC, the sole body with influence over public opinion that anyone tries to claim is publicly owned, i.e not in private hands. The theory has it that this corporation is not state-controlled. That in fact is legally not the case; the Board of Governors that presides over all the affairs of the corporation is appointed by the government of the day and can be dismissed by the government of the day, and is therefore within the control of any government that wishes to exercise control.

Even if this were not so, however, and the BBC was genuinely outside any such government control as manifest in this power of appointment, where would that leave us? It would leave us with a vast and all-pervasive institution with power over millions of minds that was responsible to nobody! Just why should the people presiding over that institution have such special privileges that are not enjoyed by anyone else in the population? They are not elected by the people. The people have not the slightest say in the composition of the programmes that are put out under their authority. So the presentation of the BBC to the public as some sort of body constituted in accordance with the principles of 'democracy' is sheer humbug. It is in fact no more responsible to the people, and no more within the power of the people to regulate or restrain, than the officially state-controlled broadcasting services of Soviet Russia.

The question of what the BBC's relationship is to the government therefore becomes, so far as the people are concerned, a purely academic one. Whether the government controls the BBC or the BBC controls the government is neither here nor there: in no sense is it a democratic institution.

I state this, not to approve or disapprove of it, but only to establish it as a fact, thereby cutting through the mass of mythology and cant that surround the 'official' presentation of the status of the BBC to the millions of those who finance it by the payment of their licence fees.

Reverting back to the matter of the power of the government to determine the appointment of BBC governors, this is in fact of much less significance than it may appear, for the reality is that both members of the government and governors of the BBC belong to the same 'club' of well-vetted establishment servants who can be thoroughly relied upon to uphold all the standard 'establishment' values. They are men and women of the same basic outlook, notwithstanding that they may have differing political party allegiances and may take differing stands on **some** of the public issues. We therefore have a situation in which the government, in a loose kind of way, has control of the BBC Board of Governors, who in turn have control over the appointment of programme producers (and therefore over the content of programmes) — which in effect means that they regulate the political climate within which works both government and opposition — thus completing a circle of mutual patronage that may be likened to a merry-go-round that rotates on its axis but always ends up in the same place.

Independent television and radio, on the other hand, serve, by their very names, to sustain the illusion that there is some kind of alternative 'choice' to the viewers who get tired of tuning into the BBC. So there is — as long as we are talking about variations in the non-stop diet of daily drivel consisting of soap-operas, chat-shows, parlour games, third-rate movies and 'pop' music. When, however, it comes to choice over the true fundamentals, i.e. the basic cultural and political norms and values that these programmes represent, there is no real choice at all, as I shall shortly explain.

For there is a definite limit to the independence of the 'independents'. The various private TV and radio companies, like the newspapers, cannot survive without advertisements and, as stated in a previous chapter when mention was made of the press, any closely knit community commanding a sizeable portion of advertising contracts can hold the whip-hand over 'independent' broadcasters, in the sense of being able to veto any programmes, or parts thereof, that they deem threatening to their interests. In addition to this, the 'independent' companies rely at the end of the day on franchises to operate within certain areas that are granted (and can be refused) by the Independent Broadcasting Authority, which is of course a public body and over which the ordinary electorate has no more control than it has over the BBC.

A lot is said of the fact that, in respect of the BBC, the government does not have the power to exercise day-to-day supervision over programmes, and an occasion highlighting this issue occurred in 1986, when the Home Secretary tried to intervene concerning certain parts of a programme, *At the Edge of the Union*, dealing with the troubles in Northern Ireland — to the great resentment of certain BBC personnel. This controversy, however, tended to obscure the true relationship between the two respective bodies of government and corporation. Of course there are going to be arguments about specific presentation of individual programmes, just as there will be between producer and co-producer of the same programme. These arguments, however, are no more than family tiffs, over matters of detail, and should not blind us to the reality that both parties to the argument are basically on the same side and champions of the same cause.

As to what is this cause, the *Daily Telegraph* columnist Peter Simple came near to the truth when, in some personal memoirs of a period in which he worked in broadcasting, he said that he found that "voicing a non-socialist thought in BBC circles was like blaspheming in church." Certainly, the political loyalties of the personnel working for the BBC and for the 'independent' broadcasting companies are overwhelmingly left of centre — as indeed very few of them would even try to deny. That, however, is not the whole of the story. The terms 'left' and 'right' can be misleading, as they tend to lure us into the trap of thinking in terms of Labour and Conservative party labels. If it means very much, I am quite prepared to believe that there are people working for the BBC who vote Tory at election time. What we are really speaking of here is an overwhelming consensus of minds and spirits favourable to the leftist-liberal world outlook, with its concomitant loyalties towards internationalism and multi-racialism and its aversion to anything suggestive of informed and intelligent patriotic sentiment. When we know that this outlook and aversion thoroughly permeate today's Tory Party, we realise that little meaning should be attached to the voting proclivities of BBC personnel.

I have said that Mr. Simple was 'near' to the truth. The only respect in which he might have chosen his words differently is where he used the description 'socialist'. In pursuit of absolute pinpoint accuracy, he might have said that any thought is blasphemous which is not in tune with the establishment-liberal consensus of one-worldism and 'anti-racism'. This is a bit of a mouthful for the middle of a sentence, and so we will accept Mr. Simple's description as the best shorthand that was probably available.

The true reality is that the whole of our broadcasting services are firmly under the control of those committed to this one-worlder liberal consensus — though only in the sense that the same establishment controls nearly every other nerve-centre of British life. For instance, with the universities and other places of higher education dominated by the same forces, it is a mathematical certainty that a very large portion, if not all, of the graduates applying for jobs in broadcasting are likely to be people of a similar way of thinking. The leftist-liberal-internationalist complexion of broadcasting is therefore, like that of the press, largely self-regulating. We need be in no doubt, however, that should anyone harbouring different sentiments think of trying to get into this 'inner sanctum', the vetting procedure employed with all applicants is likely to ensure his failure. My associates and I have occasionally talked and had correspondence with people who work merely as cameramen and technicians with the broadcasting networks — in other words, having no influence whatever on the content of broadcast material — and they have testified again and again that if their employers knew they even had this loose contact with us they would be instantly fired.

We therefore have a situation in which our whole daily diet of television and radio is as thoroughly controlled by the liberal-internationalist establishment as that of Soviet Russia is controlled by the Communist Party and the radio and other media of Nazi Germany were controlled by the ministry of the late Dr. Goebbels. Only the structure and methods of control are different. Whereas the latter two regimes are and were comparatively open and frank in their acknowledgement of their regulation of these amenities, never making any bones about the fact that they are and were there to be used for the defence of the established state ideology, our own system of public mind-control is shrouded in a haze of hypocrisy and soothing jargon designed to maintain the pretence that it is 'free'.

In order to make the pretence credible, of course, it is necessary to preserve some element of 'controversy' in the presentation of current affairs programmes. This is easily done by selecting the debates so as to limit them to 'safe' issues, on which our masters can, from the graciousness of their hearts, happily permit more than one viewpoint to be voiced, without the slightest danger that any of the real sacred cows will even so much as be exposed to discussion, let alone violated. At the same time, great care is taken to invite to these debates only people who can, by reputation, be relied upon to steer clear of all of the supreme taboos and heresies.

A typical example of this procedure at work is Sir Robin Day's *Question Time* programme on BBC1. Just to maintain the image of 'impartiality', a Conservative and a Labour MP are almost always a part of the four-member panel. It is only very rarely that the former is other than a spokesman for the 'orthodox' section of the party, or else a thoroughgoing 'wet'. Of the other two panel members, one usually represents the SDP or Liberals, while the fourth is by custom selected from outside the ranks of parliament: perhaps a trade unionist, perhaps an educationalist, perhaps a journalist, perhaps a spokesman for industry or the City. It is therefore certain from the start: (1) that consensus of the panel will be centre-left or, if not that, further left; and (2) that no-one will deviate from the 'approved' limits of debate on whatever subject is raised.

What subjects are raised depends, at least in part, on the audience. Simple people believe that this audience is a cross-section of the ordinary public. It is nothing of the sort; its members are the selected representatives of local bodies, political and otherwise, which beforehand have been invited to send them — in ones, twos or threes, depending on their status and size. In the forefront of these will of course be the local branches of the established political parties. It is almost always a cast-iron certainty that these people will represent, again, a consensus well to the left of ordinary public opinion as a whole — we well know the technique of the left in forming a myriad of 'front' organisations in every locality to campaign on every conceivable local issue. These organisations are given recognition locally even if they only comprise a husband and wife and their dog, and they somehow manage to wangle for themselves invitations to be represented at any and every local forum that is held. It is therefore always the case that these 'audiences' consist predominantly of leftists, some of them extremely noisy and aggressive ones, together of course with a disproportionately high number of members of ethnic minority groups, who never fail to have their local organisations to give voice to their interests and grievances.

This ensuring of a predominantly leftist-inclined audience is an important psychological trick, being intended, along with many similar tricks, to give the impression that the leftish attitudes shown by most audience members are the 'normal' attitudes of the great majority of British people.

Of course, not every member of the audience gets the chance to put a question; only a very few do, and these are selected by the compere of the programme. No prizes will be offered for guessing which types of questioner generally get a hearing!

Whatever the question, however, the manner in which it will be treated is equally predictable. Supposing, for instance, the question is about South Africa. Here we are near to 'dangerous' ground, i.e. we are dealing with one of the 'sensitive' issues on which discussion must be carefully regulated. The response of the panel, of course, can be vouched for because all precautions concerning it have been taken in advance. Not one single panel member, the Tory included, will have a good word to say about the South African political and social system and the principle of white leadership; all will condemn these things vehemently. The whole discussion will centre on the question of what is the best way to bring the white South Africans down. One part of the panel (probably the majority) will argue for sanctions against South Africa and the other (probably including the Tory) will argue for bringing the South African Whites down by other means.

Then when the members of the audience are allowed their say we can expect a similar range of opinions with, if anything, probably an even more vehemently hostile attitude to the South African Whites predominating. Here there is just the possibility that one intrepid audience member may have a word to say in defence of the white South African but it is certain that, if he does, he will be loudly shouted down by others in the audience and shown to be one of a very tiny and despised minority, thus making his voice of dissent seem almost pathetic.

In this way, what we end up with is a debate that is not really a debate at all but a carefully stage-managed performance in which the argument, such as it is, is merely one of detail about a matter on the periphery of the main issue — the main issue, in the case of South Africa, being that of whether the Whites survive or go under. This issue is of course never properly discussed — all are unanimous about it!

Thus has 'democracy' been vindicated: we have had a discussion, and there was plenty of disagreement! The millions watching the programme — whom the BBC mind-benders of course hold in total contempt — will, it is hoped, be satisfied with their evening's entertainment and reassured in their faith that free debate is alive and well.

Exactly the same type of 'rigged' debate takes place whenever there has been a major race riot in one of our inner cities. To exclude such a discussion completely might be revealing more about the BBC's bias than it wants to reveal, so the discussion is allowed but carefully steered in a direction whereby the argument is between two different points of view as to how we can make the multi-racial society work. Strictly forbidden is any point of view to the effect that that multi-racial society itself may not be a good thing and that we should consider putting an end to it. Such a suggestion is excluded because, of course, it represents the central issue involved in the racial controversy.

Indeed, it is on topics connected with race that our broadcasters reveal most glaringly their dishonest techniques of presentation. Of course, the treatment of the issue is always blatantly one-sided, with an unending stream of multi-racialist propaganda churned out daily, not only in current affairs programmes but in religious talks and discussions, to say nothing of films, plays, soaps, 'pop' music programmes and the rest. Just occasionally, however, to demonstrate their respect for the principles of free debate, our media masters permit the opposite viewpoint to be heard. Usually the show is entirely set up so as to present 'racism' in the most unfavourable light possible.

One technique that has been used on a number of occasions is to invite as studio guests a white 'racist' to debate with a Black. They go out of their way to select as the former the most moronic specimen they can find — a yobbo from the football terraces is ideal for the purpose. Against him, they pick a well educated and articulate member of one of the ethnic minorities who is experienced in argument on the topic and has all the glib tongue of the trained politician. The result is of course quite predictable.

Our mind-controllers lose no opportunity to exploit the successes of black sportsmen and sportswomen to popularise the multi-racial cause. Of course, no reasonable person would wish to take away the credit due to outstanding black athletes, save to say that their athletic merit is entirely irrelevant to the racial controversy itself. Sometimes, however, the practice of boosting black sportsmen is blatant even to the least experienced observer. On one occasion I recall watching a TV news bulletin when suddenly the face of what was evidently a black footballer was flashed on the screen. The announcer reported that he had scored the winning goal for his team in one of the day's league matches and was thus the hero of the moment with his club. A subsequent look at the newspaper revealed that in football league games that day there had been 29 victories and therefore, presumably, 29 winning goals. In four cases there had been hat-tricks (three goals scored by a single player). Knowing a little bit about the game of soccer, I was able to identify three of the hat-trick scorers as white, while not knowing anything of the fourth. The player whose face had been pictured in the TV news earlier had only scored the one goal mentioned, and furthermore this had not been in one of the most important matches of the day. Why then was he thought to deserve the five-star publicity treatment? Of course, we know why.

On three occasions afterwards, I witnessed exactly similar news reporting in similar circumstances.

I make no apologies for returning again to the South African issue, because it perfectly illustrates the mentality of those who control our news. During the emergency in South Africa in 1986, the news media became totally obsessed with events there, reporting all the troubles with a blatant bias and selectivity, and always in such a way as to show the South African government and security forces in the most unfavourable light. In many evening bulletins the issue occupied the first five to ten minutes' coverage, leading one to wonder whether in fact anything had happened in Britain during the day that was of the slightest public interest. Of course it had, but here again another aspect of the propaganda technique of the broadcasters was being demonstrated. This is the technique of choosing the order of importance and priority of news items in a manner which bears no relation whatever to their true and correct order. Focussing upon some disturbance in a far-off country, of course, has the very convenient effect of taking people's minds off troubles much nearer home and of much greater consequence to themselves.

Sometimes, indeed, items of news of importance in Britain are not just given less than their due attention; they are excluded completely. This technique is not new; it was common as long ago as when Spengler wrote his *Decline of the West* — well before the advent of television. Speaking of the press, the writer said:-

"And the other side of this belated freedom — it is permitted to everyone to say what he pleases, **but** the press is free to take notice of what he says or not. It can condemn any 'truth' to death simply by not undertaking its communication to the world — a terrible censorship of silence, which is all the more potent in that the masses of newspaper readers are absolutely unaware that it exists..."

Notwithstanding all that has been said about current affairs and news programmes, we should not imagine that the diet of TV and radio brainwashing ends there; I have mentioned some of the other fields in which it is served up. In fact it extends into every nook and cranny of broadcast output. 'Educational' programmes are used for the same purpose, as are religious ones, as has been said. One of the favourite techniques is first to make a programme popular by associating it in the public mind with pleasant music and agreeable surroundings — plus, if possible, the impress of a well-known and highly regarded public personality. There is little or no attempt at first to introduce any propaganda into it; this comes later when the programme has established good ratings and is assured of a large viewing public. Then the poison starts, drip by little drip. One such programme was a Sunday evening feature introduced by a well-known and popular comedian and singer with a pleasant, though at times a little over-ingratiating, manner. The programme went each week to a different part of the country, where its introducer met and talked with local people, pointed out some interesting local scenes, interspersing all this with music and poetry, including a song or two of his own. Running through the programme, though not laid on too heavily, was a religious theme.

In due course, needless to say, when the programme had become well established, it started to become a vehicle for propaganda, with one week's instalment, filmed in Bradford, given up largely to gushing tributes to the Asian community there. From there on it became just part of the standard fare.

Many other types of programme are fair game for the brain-washers, who just cannot keep their fingers out of anything. Full-length feature films consist, in no small part, of imports from Hollywood, mostly old and second-rate. Hollywood of course has been an almost exclusively Jewish preserve for a long time, and the contents of its products very much reflects the ethnic bias of its producers. There is an unending series of films about World War II, despite the fact that that war has now been over for more than 40 years. The pattern is always the same: Germans, and particularly 'Nazis', are always the bad guys and Jews, wherever they appear, are the angels. A farcical element has crept in here with the frequent use of some of the best-looking non-Jewish actors and actresses to play Jewish parts and the equally frequent portrayal by Jewish actors of Nazi villains. The very question of why this happens is a dangerous one, as it may lead him who asks it into the murky waters of racial controversy from which, in this country at least, he may not emerge a free man!

The Second World War, as I have said, is long gone and Nazi Germany is no more. Soviet Communism, on the other hand, is very much alive and kicking. Yet the films that we see portraying this regime in a brutal and unpleasant light are few and far between. Why, it might be asked, is Hollywood so soft on Communism while obsessed, four decades on, with National Socialism? Perhaps the late Senator McCarthy, were he alive today, might be able to supply the answer!

The Senator of course will be known for his courageous invest-igations of the 1950s, which showed that Hollywood was riddled with communists and fellow-travellers. It still is today, having survived, with help from some strange and esoteric forces, the expulsions of the McCarthy era. Communism is not, as a general rule, shown as anything more than a limited evil — when it is shown as evil at all — because communism and the film industry are on the same side. For his efforts to point this out to the American public, McCarthy has ever since been reviled by the industry, and by the media generally — both in America and over here, as a figure of horror on a par with the German 'monsters' of 1939-45.

If there is one thing that the Czars of the media are determined to crush, it is the spirit of awakened nationalism and race-consciousness.

For the national spirit to be crushed, one important tactic is to make people ashamed of their national history — and in the case of the British people this must of course include imperial history. A typical product devoted to this pernicious purpose was *Gandhi*, that vast extravaganza produced in the early 1980s by Sir Richard Attenborough. *Gandhi* glorified the Indian resistance movement against British rule (nationalism is only out of order if it is **white** nationalism; coloured nationalism is quite acceptable), while depicting India's British colonial overlords as a combination of brutality and cretinism, with a particularly vicious and defamatory (and factually untrue) portrayal of that fine soldier and patriot General Dyer.

But of course this film was merely one of hundreds, perhaps thousands, of its kind to be produced on the never-halting conveyor belt of propaganda showpieces of the silver screen aimed at undermining the White Race and the great nations of which it is comprised.

'Pop' music is of course one of the major weapons in the assault on white civilisation in which the barons of the media are engaged. Here, in order to avoid misunderstanding, let me stress that I am referring to popular music **in the form that most of it has taken in modern times**, not to the concept of popular music itself, which, in ages before the present diseased one in which we live, was an essential part of our native culture and often the inspiration for the most sublime achievements of musical genius. Brahms, Beethoven, Dvorak and our own Vaughan-Williams are examples that immediately come to mind of composers indebted to the folk melodies of their own and other European nations for many of their most famous works. Then, unlike today, popular and serious music did not belong to two separate and mutually antagonistic traditions but were simply the rudimentary and advanced forms of the same tradition, a happy circumstance which brought music-lovers together in a transcending of class barriers — as when Londoners of all social groups mingled in their enjoyment of the Royal Fireworks music of Handel in the 18th century — a masterpiece which perfectly bridges the narrow divide between orchestral music and good popular music. It is our modern culture-distorters who have used music to fragment societies by promoting an *ersatz* 'popular' music that commends itself mainly to the mentally and spiritually atrophied, or at least the extremely immature. In healthier times, the latter could be induced by stages in the development of their musical ears to find their way upward from the very simplest forms to the much more sophisticated and complex — for all represented component parts of the national and European musical art. Today, immature minds are prone to be exploited at a very early stage by the promoters of chaotic and barbarous noise entirely alien to the native musical soul, and thereafter led in a direction in which they lose all contact with their own true heritage.

Here, the style of the music itself is only a part of the general assault on the minds of its intended victims. Together with it go a number of additional features all conducive to the same end. Modern 'disco' music is played at a volume many decibels above that required to reach even the deafest of ears — suggesting immediately that the purpose is to reduce the hearer to a state of emotional shock, if not insanity. This is accompanied, at concerts, by the incessant flashing on and off of coloured lights, suggestive of the practice of KGB interrogators breaking down the resistance of their victim as a prelude to getting him completely under their power. In fact, the alternate switching on and off of prison-cell lights is one of the standard methods used against prisoners of the Soviet regime prior to the interrogation process.

'Pop' music stars are deliberately built up by the media to become heroes in the eyes of the young, in a manner that contrasts vividly with the treatment of the real heroes of British history, most of whom have become forgotten names. And of what calibre are these modern celebrities? Most of them look, dress, sing and talk like pansies — and many are just that. A great number of them are into drugs and most of them have an outlook that is left-wing. They constitute just about the sorriest specimens of humanity to be found anywhere. Yet it is these freaks to whom our youth are encouraged to look up as models. Look at the bedroom wall of today's average 17-year-old and you are likely to find a large colour picture, not of some young soldier who risked his life for his comrades and his country in the Falklands War, but of a prancing transvestite with a diet of heroin and a seven-figure bank balance whom our 'culture' kings have picked up from out of the sewers and made into a teenage idol.

Mention has been made of drugs but of course this kind of 'musical' entertainment has now itself been turned into a drug, with its addicts no more able to endure a few hours of life without it than are the addicts of the whisky bottle and the hypodermic needle. Many of them are incapable of walking down a street without this electronic noise dinning into their ears; and, with this fact in mind, the makers of transistor radios and tape-recorders are now equipping them with earphones so as to enable pedestrians in public places to continue to get their musical 'fix' as they proceed along their way. To normal and well-adjusted human beings, the joy of music would be completely lost if it were on every minute of waking hours, but not so those who have become hooked on 'pop'; to them, the sound of their preference has become like the very air they breathe: a non-stop living necessity.

Day in, day out, through the use of television, radio, the 'pop' concert hall, the record business, films, newspapers, magazines, books and now the lucrative video trade, this vast industry works to obtain a monopoly over our brains and our emotions — and all with an object that should be apparent to any rational observer: to bring about the degeneration of Western Mankind.

The use of the press differs only slightly from that of these other media. We may divide the newspapers into roughly three categories: at one end are the 'prestige' papers, which employ a lofty tone and language of reporting, which are produced mainly for an educated readership, which eschew big headlines and gaudy sensationalism and which pride themselves on the 'moderation' with which they deal with public issues; at the opposite end, there are the 'penny dreadfuls': the papers that specialise in front-page sex scandals, in nudes, in sensation and in trivia, which are all designed to appeal to the most moronic level among the reading public. The purpose of these papers is of course not to inform but to entertain; and any story, no matter how far it is removed from the truth, is gladly to be used if it accomplishes that aim.

Finally, there are the papers in between these two extremes, which employ a somewhat higher and more serious tone than the very trashiest, and which seek to provide a combination of news and titillation to suit a wide variety of tastes.

So these papers appear on the surface. But when we look

beneath this surface and analyse the heart of the content of the respective categories we see the differences between them narrowing the further our examination proceeds. In the end, our investigation brings us to the stage of complete convergence of outlook and policy. They are all basically organs of the same 'establishment'. They all serve the common cause of keeping that establishment in power and promoting the same goals of internationalism, racial integration and 'liberal-democracy'. The fact that they support different political parties is of scarcely any relevance because all the parties in question, as we have already seen, are obedient to the same masters and dedicated to the same worldly goals. The supposition, therefore, that they offer the reading public some kind of genuine choice, therefore, is pure fantasy. They merely administer the same poisons, marketed in different-coloured bottles and to suit different individual palates and levels of literacy.

The 'quality' papers are worth a particular study in this regard, for when the haughty prose of their reports, articles and comment are examined in terms of their true meaning they become exposed as just the same leftish-liberalistic claptrap as the content of the 'lower-class' papers their editors and writers profess to despise. Most of it is pure parlour bolshevism dressed up in the finery of 'moderate' opinion.

These papers lay great emphasis on the principle that the issues of the day should be discussed in an atmosphere of calm 'reason' and they tut-tut pompously at any public incident involving the attempt of people of one political persuasion to silence those of another persuasion by use of force or intimidation, invoking the famed remark of Voltaire that "though I may detest what you say, I should defend to the death your right to say it." They back up this pretence of rational debate by avoidance of inflammatory or emotive phrases, or language suggestive of any kind of militancy.

Yet beneath the surface it can be found that the 'quality' press no more desires rational debate than the 'extremists' it condemns. On the contrary, it defends the established superstitions of politics with all the bigotry and intolerance of a medieval priesthood. It steadfastly refuses to permit a word to be uttered in suggestion of the idea that conspiracy is at work in national and international affairs. It imposes a rigid censorship on news reflecting the political role of international finance. It regards articles supporting any kind of genuine nationalism, political or economic, as tantamount to sedition. It outlaws critical comment of any racial group (except of course white British). It particularly prohibits any in-depth examination of the activities of Zionist Jews.

A classical example of this humbug characteristic of the 'quality' press was provided in an article written in *The Times* on the 18th February 1978, at the time when I was leader of the National Front, and which commented on the then current NF campaign in schools. Said the writer:-

"...head teachers and teachers should be on their guard against allowing the Front any presence inside the schools...Such activities should not be tolerated...In general...school authorities should not see attempts at National Front recruitment in the same tolerant light as they regard the formation, say, of Labour or Conservative societies in the schools..."

Then a little further on the article comments on the NF problem in hiring meeting halls, saying:-

"...When the National Front wishes to hire a hall for a public meeting, there is nothing discreditable in taking into account the message it is likely to disseminate from that public platform before deciding whether or not to grant it permission to use the hall. Those local authorities or other bodies which have refused to allow the Front to use their facilities, because in conscience, and after considering broad aspects of public policy, they have come to the conclusion that it would be contrary to public order and good race relations to permit the meeting, should not be the subject of reproach."

It will be observed that throughout all of these two quoted passages there is an avoidance of crude language or any violent expressions, such as "smash them." The overall message, however, amounts just to that — that methods which *The Times* would in any other context dismiss as 'totalitarian' should, with perfect justification, be used to deny the voice of nationalism a public hearing. This is, I must remind the reader, the press which purports to stand for the loftiest ideals of 'democracy' and for the principle that all public issues of import should be subjected to free and reasoned debate!

The role of this so-called 'quality' press is of enormous importance in another field of the mass media: publishing. Upon the book reviews printed on the literary pages of papers like *The Times*, *The Guardian*, *The Observer* and *The Daily Telegraph* and *Sunday Telegraph* depends the survival or ruin of most of the publishing industry. Such reviews can kill any important book that appears, either by dismissing it as not worth buying or, better still, by refusing even to mention it. This fact is well known throughout the publishing industry and knowledge of it is sufficient to deter publishers from investing any money in the printing of a book that might violate any of the established taboos, some of which I have listed a short way back. An example of this kind of censorship at work can be found in the fate suffered by the historian David Irving. Irving was for years one of the best-selling authors, and his books were almost guaranteed a good circulation and handsome profits to their publishers. But Irving, as time went on, was getting ever closer to the minefield awaiting those writers whose works displeased the ruling establishment. In *Uprising*, a book dealing with the Hungarian revolt in 1956, Irving sent out certain danger signals by daring to point out that a large portion of the communist rulers against whom the insurgents had rebelled were Jewish. At about the same time, he attended as guest speaker a meeting in the United States promoted by an institute which questioned the veracity of some of the 'holocaust' propaganda surrounding World War II and which in consequence has been put on the international Zionist 'hit list'. Irving, by treading on these sacred toes, set in motion his own blackballing by the publishing industry to which he had previously been a most lucrative asset. When he completed his latest book, *Churchill's War*, which told many uncomfortable home truths about Britain's wartime prime minister which contradicted the popular picture of him portrayed over the years by 'establishment' writers and propagandists, he found that none of the well established publishers would touch the book. Eventually, the book was published by a small non-establishment publishing firm in Australia. When launched in Britain, it was subjected to the silent treatment by most of the media. We are here reminded again of Spengler's point about condemning a truth to death!

We may see from such facts that the book-publishing trade is not exempt from the rules of control and censorship that affect the rest of the mass media but is itself an integral part of that same massive empire of propaganda that is maintained to keep the people in intellectual, cultural and spiritual servitude. The component parts of the empire are, as has been demonstrated, interlocking: book-publishing is very much dependent upon the press; television and the cinema are mutually dependent on each other; the press, television and radio are dependent on advertising, which itself is just a branch of the same industry; and all, to some degree, are dependent on the patronage of the political establishment, which, as we have seen, cuts across parties and embraces that community of the high and the mighty thoroughly imbued with the liberal-internationalist world outlook.

I cannot emphasise strongly enough what has already been said before: that here we are dealing with a form of control that exists largely by means of a **negative** coercive power: it is concentrated on stopping the broadcasting of ideas it is against more than it is with promoting the ideas it favours — although the latter is always ensured in generous measure by reason of the types of people who are appointed to the positions of management throughout.

The controllers of the media are able to maintain some pretence of respecting the idea of 'freedom' by pointing to numerous areas of public debate in which they allow the unfettered expression of diverse views. What is not always apparent is that these are not the really **key** areas that determine the course of national and international politics. When it comes to these key areas, we find that all news and opinion are carefully supervised so as to ensure that 'dangerous' facts and ideas almost never see the light of day, except occasionally in 'set-up' scenarios where they can be depicted as no more than the ravings of despised minorities, cranks, villains and idiots. If, for example, a man in a TV film is allowed to voice a 'racist' sentiment, we can be sure that before the story's end he will become exposed as the criminal of the piece — or else will recant, after having a black doctor save his life by brilliant surgery, or some such traumatic experience.

When it is recognised what power the mass media have in the way of controlling news and opinion, it may be seen how illusory is the idea that in a 'democracy' there is necessarily any genuine political freedom. In law, of course, an individual or an organisation are entitled to hire a public hall and hold a meeting (unless they happen to be nationalists, as has been seen!). But of what value is that right today if only the people in actual attendance at the meeting (seldom a large number) hear what is said? Free speech these days only means something if what is spoken is relayed to a larger audience by way of being reported in the papers and on TV and radio — for no-one is going to influence the course of national politics unless what he says reaches millions. Every political speaker today therefore pitches what he has to say at meetings, not at the audience immediately to hand, but at the much larger media audience who he expects will read of or hear his speech the following morning or evening. If, on the other hand, the speech is not reported in this way, it is as effectively suppressed as if it had been banned by law in the first place — or at least almost so.

We have noticed this at our own meetings. While we are not yet a party big enough to have these meetings treated as national news, at least we are entitled to claim that they are local news — that is to say events worthy of reporting in the local newspaper and on the local radio in the area in which the meeting is being held. In practice, however, we find that this very rarely happens, except in the event of some disturbance at the meeting; in that case it is always the disturbance that is reported and hardly ever a word spoken from the platform.

This censorship has not crushed us and will not stop us. It has, however, compelled us to resort to other methods to bring our message to the public, while it has demonstrated clearly what has been stressed again and again in this book: that 'democracy' does not exist in reality but is just a fraud and a racket behind which a concealed autocracy rules.

Daily, the media feed the people with a diet of degeneracy, combined with censored news and comment, all with the purpose of reducing them to a herd of cattle lacking in either the wit or the will to resist the 'brave new world' that their masters have planned for them, and which world is now in an advanced stage of construction. Daily, there is the constant stream of poison directed to undermining all the finer human qualities that go to the building and preservation of successful nations. Along with non-stop political propaganda, in its direct and indirect forms, there is an unending avalanche of products encouraging moral and sexual license, homosexuality and every other imaginable depravity and perversion, while the same methods are used to denigrate morality, manliness, loyalty, patriotism, pride of race and the soldier qualities. A nation subject to this conditioning over the period of one or two generations becomes a nation ripe for conquest and enslavement, whether these are achieved by military or political means. The media are worth 100 divisions to any would-be enemy in war — so long as they are controlled and directed in the manner that operates in contemporary Britain.

I have referred previously to the brainwashing procedures prior to interrogation used by the KGB and similar bodies, and the parallel exists beyond the particular example stated. The victim is subjected to a systematic process of psychological warfare, so as to reduce him to a state in which he is completely subservient to the command of his captors. The lights flashing on and off in the cell; the constant noise, making rest impossible; the gradual undermining of the nerves and the reduction of the will; the sowing of the idea that resistance is hopeless because of the omnipotence of those in control; the alternating techniques of persuasion to capitulate: one moment the truncheon, the next moment the soft voice, the cigarette and the cup of tea. They are all there, figuratively speaking, in the fare meted out to us by those who control our news, opinions and 'entertainment'. When we understand the language in which they are communicated to us, we can recognise them by the hour and by the minute. In the acquisition of this faculty there lies the attainment of true freedom; without it, the constitutional 'freedoms' we are supposed to possess are entirely meaningless and useless.

Some very well meaning people in Britain, appalled at the flood of decadence pouring out from television, formed themselves some years ago into an association for the purpose of sounding a voice of protest, and, by means of their activities as a pressure group, applying some brake against this flood. I do not want to denigrate their efforts, for without them surely the national rot induced by the output of TV would be one or two degrees yet further advanced. Such efforts, however, represent little more than the resistance of pea-shooters against an army employing nuclear missiles and poison gas.

It is the ultimate in naivety to suppose that an estate of such massive and entrenched power as the mass media will be deflected in any substantial way from its course by such representations — except in the way of one or two tiny concessions which only slightly slow down the process of national corruption.

Nothing less than a revolution in our entire structure of state will halt this juggernaut, and that is something which probably very few of the very decent ladies and gentlemen of whom we are speaking here would be prepared to countenance for a moment. They want to restore broadcasting to 'respectability' (in the best sense of the word). That aim, however, is pure pie in the sky unless we are prepared to take up a position in support of political change which, in the present climate, is definitely not 'respectable'.

It is a noteworthy fact that those people who have caused most of the havoc in the modern world have the unbounded nerve to accuse those opposed to them of the very vices of which they themselves are the most guilty, and typical of this tendency is the attitude of the controllers of the mass media. Themselves the most expert practitioners of the business of censorship, they are the first to raise the shriek of 'censorship' against anyone who dares to suggest that their power and influence be curbed. These monopolists are always singing the praise of a 'free' mass media, but of course when they do so only a few well informed people understand the language in which they are speaking. When they talk about 'freedom', they mean precisely and solely their own freedom to hold onto their privileges and to continue to fulfil their role as the guardians of the nation's thought.

They feed us with a constant diet of vituperative propaganda against 'totalitarian' regimes, while they themselves practise the most advanced and sophisticated form of totalitarianism: a totalitarianism that is by far the most effective by reason of its being invisible to the vast majority of the population.

Notwithstanding all this hysterical talk about 'totalitarianism' and 'censorship', at the end of the day the government of a nation has a firm and inescapable duty concerning institutions of this kind. If any such institution becomes a monopoly of an interest group not identified with the nation and the broader public and national interest, and uses the power of that monopoly again and again in a way positively detrimental, indeed dangerous, to the national good, it is the clear responsibility of government to put an end to that state of affairs by whatever means are necessary.

British government has shirked this responsibility continually throughout the years in which the mass media have grown into that 'state above the state' that I described earlier in this chapter, now exercising almost certainly more power than government itself. Perhaps this is not surprising, in view of the fact that the nationally degenerative purposes to which the media have directed their output are wholly in harmony with those purposes to which our politicians have also been applying themselves within the same period of time. Basically, as I have said, they are members of the same club.

In considering the question of what is now to be done with the media, we must first of all free ourselves from the fetters of certain suppositions concerning how this power is constituted, the most important one of which is the assumption — indeed the illusion — that **any** institution like the mass media in a nation of over 50 million people ever can be 'democratic' in the sense that is generally understood by the term. There just is no way that the owners of newspapers and broadcasting companies, or indeed a corporation like the BBC, can be elected by popular vote and thereafter regulated in accordance with the popular will. In the field of privately owned mass communications, which is easily the larger field, power and control lies with the few who have the money to obtain it and hold on to it. In the case of the BBC, it resides in people chosen by a different process but one nevertheless equally removed from any kind of 'democratic' or popular mandate. The institutions of the mass media are, for better or for worse, *elitist* institutions controlled by oligarchies; indeed they cannot, in the nature of things, be anything else. They constitute, inevitably, a form of authoritarianism, with values, tastes and opinions handed down from above rather than received from below.

If, therefore, the media are to be regulated by an autocracy, the only question that becomes relevant is: which autocracy? If they are going to be the transmitters, rather than the receivers, of public values, tastes and opinions, the only question remaining is: which values, tastes and opinions?

To the latter question, the answer must be: those values, tastes and opinions that are conducive to the building of a strong, healthy, vigorous, stable and united national community.

And to the question of what power should control the media, the answer must be: whatever power is necessary to ensure that the media are put to that purpose.

At the end of the day, the fact must be accepted that the mass media constitute a vital national resource — like our railways, our road system, our sources of energy, our land, our armed forces, our civil service and our universities and schools. The very idea that these resources should be in the hands of interests empowered to use them quite independently of the nation and for purposes other than the service of the nation is too fantastic to entertain seriously for one second. Though some of these resources may indeed function under private ownership and be independent in respect of their day-to-day management and administration, it does not alter in the slightest the rule that they cannot be allowed to be used in any way by which the national interest is damaged. And yet that is precisely the position enjoyed by the mass media at the present time. They are, in fact, in many ways more powerful than government. Yet they are answerable to no-one!

Most certainly, the regulation of the mass media by the hand of government does not in itself provide any cast-iron guarantee that as a national resource they will be used responsibly and in the service of the nation. Indeed, in the hands of any government of the present type it can safely be guaranteed that they will not!

But for the purposes of this discussion we must assume the existence of a government that is truly patriotic and national, entirely committed to the country's interests and to the service of its people. I would submit that such a government would have, not just the right, but indeed the duty, to bring the media into line with the other national resources that I have mentioned and oblige them, for the first time in modern history, to serve the British Nation.

This does not mean that all of the media need be directly government-owned or controlled, although this would of course apply to the BBC. There could still be much scope for private enterprise and private ownership.

But it would mean that the media, public and private, would be required to operate in accordance with certain definite rules and standards, which would be laid down by government — rules and standards generally recognised as necessary in the case of any institutions enjoying vast influence and power. The government at this very time is engaged in setting out certain rules and standards to be followed by those responsible for our children's education. Why should there not be, then, equally stringent rules and standards observed by the media?

Neither does the proposal mean that there should not be room within the media for abundant free debate on the issues of the moment: indeed, these proposals are intended to ensure that there would be much more free debate than at the present time — in fact truly free debate **for the first time** in the case of many organs of the media of which I am speaking.

The one condition would be that such free debate would be expected to take place within the general framework of a common and shared loyalty to Britain and her people. There should be room for every idea and every opinion within this framework. But there should not be room for anyone to use the media for the purpose of attacking or subverting Britain.

One vital need would be for government to act to prevent particular interest groups not identified with the nation placing pressure upon the media by means of boycott, or the threat of boycott. The remedy to this is of course to ensure that within the British community of the future no such interest groups in fact exist.

My own opinion is that, once this stranglehold on the media, exercised by such interest groups by means of the boycott method, is finally broken, the media will become a largely self-regulating institution that can be relied upon to uphold the necessary standards and serve the national interest with the minimum interference from government. The firm hand of government will be needed most of all in the process of transition to that happy state of affairs.

As part of this transformation of the media, a whole series of new and desirable influences should be brought to bear. We must encourage films and documentaries which promote national pride and patriotic sentiment, and most of these films should be British-made rather than imported. Particularly desirable are films dealing with outstanding historical events in which the heroism of our ancestors, in peace and in war, is given special emphasis: films dealing with great victories won in battle, great exploits of imperial expansion, of discovery and of outstanding creative works by members of the British Race. The content of our cultural programmes should be European, with the accent more heavily than in the past on home-grown British products. As one example, we should do much more to publicise the works of little-known British composers of quality, such as George Lloyd. Everything possible should be done to preserve and nurture the national heritage in music, art, the theatre, literature and all other creative fields. At the same time, the media should become a bastion of sound and healthy moral and family values, rather than an instrument for the destruction of those values.

Above all, the media should be an instrument for the promotion of **truth**. It is an extraordinary anomaly, in a land where companies can be taken to court and heavily fined for making fraudulent claims in the course of advertising their products, that journalists and broadcasters are left free to lie knowingly almost every day of their working lives. If the media are to be made to use their power responsibly, one of the first requirements is that those working in them are rendered liable to prosecution for knowingly concealing the truth, particularly in the promotion of some viewpoint on public matters.

To these proposals, the cry is no doubt going to be raised that I am advocating censorship. Yes, I am! But it is the honest and open censorship of those responsible and accountable to the nation, rather than the invisible censorship of dark and subterranean forces that are never exposed to the public eye and which most of the public do not even know exist. It is a censorship to defend standards and safeguard the nation rather than one to protect just the interests of special self-interested groups. It is censorship of the type that has existed in every great and creative age of European culture and civilisation, and must always exist as a bulwark against moral corruption, subversion and decadence.

But such censorship would in fact not require to be anything like as great in degree as that by which we are ruled today. As I have said in an earlier chapter, we are not afraid of an absolutely open public debate in which the truth is allowed to come out; our opponents are! We are not afraid of those who differ from us being allowed to express their opinions freely, for we are quite confident of our ability to reduce those opinions to objects of ridicule by honest argument. I would far rather that the marxist point of view, for instance, be allowed a free airing on television than that it be gagged; for if it were gagged some might believe that we were frightened of something it contained. Let it be aired! But let also be aired the views of those who are properly informed on the true origins and nature of marxism and who will expose it in the way that, for a long time, it has not been exposed.

Neither am I in favour of any attempt to 'ban' the excrescences of 'art' and 'sculpture' produced by those of the so-called *avant-garde* schools in these departments, the hideous and mis-shapen objects of a Moore or an Epstein. What gives this rubbish its great influence today is not its intrinsic merit but simply the fact that it has a powerful and well-entrenched mafia of promoters working for it in the corridors of the cultural establishment and in the art-critic pages of the major newspapers and artistic house journals. Destroy the stranglehold of that mafia over our artistic life, and these products will find their natural level of popularity and support — they will in fact be laughed into oblivion by the great majority of art lovers among the people.

In conclusion to this chapter dealing with the mass media, there is one final thing left to be said. When all has been debated, we are left with the truth that there is no higher right belonging to a nation and a people than the right of self-preservation. If the leadership of any people is faced with the existence of an influence within the national body that is serving as nothing short of a fifth column eating away at the very vitals of that body and promising with certainty to destroy it if not checked, then that leadership, by failing to root out that influence, is showing, not 'moderation', 'restraint', 'tolerance' or 'broad-mindedness' but sheer craven cowardice, irresponsibility and lack of will to govern. This is the principle upon which we must base our policy to rescue the mass media from the hands of the liars, seducers and corrupters who now control them — to restore them to the property of the nation to which they rightly belong.

Postscript: After the original text of this chapter was written, but before it was submitted to the printer, an incident occurred which typified the outlook and behaviour of many operatives of today's mass media. One of the author's leading colleagues, Richard Edmonds, gave an interview to two journalists of *The Sunday Times* newspaper concerning a literature distribution project in which he had been engaged. The journalists, Jon Craig and Jo Revell, asked him before leaving him to give them a telephone number at which they could contact him during weekdays in case any further matter arose in connection with the subject of the interview. When they requested this number, they undertook to treat it in strict confidence.

Mr. Edmonds gave the two journalists his business number in good faith. Subsequently they rang the number and ascertained, from the switchboard operator at the other end, the name of the company for which Mr. Edmonds worked. In their report in *The Sunday Times* the following weekend, they publicised the name of this company — though it had no relevance whatsoever to the matter being reported.

The very next day, Mr. Edmonds was summoned to the office of his superior in the company and informed he would have to leave.

Richard Edmonds was thus deprived of his livelihood because of this piece of spite and viciousness on the part of the two reporters. Because they did not like his politics, they decided that they would cause embarrassment to him in his job, in the hope that through this he would be dismissed.

They succeeded in their objective. Such are the practices of the 'free press' which the British people are taught to regard as one of their most valued institutions.

These are of course the tactics of the gutter, and it is at that level that the so-called 'quality' newspapers operate, no less than do their more crudely presented counterparts.

This point has been made in the preceding chapter, and this little story underlines it.

Chapter 14

Beyond capitalism and socialism

When we look at today's economic scene, two facts stand out above all others; and, as I shall attempt to establish, both these facts are inextricably related.

The first is that that entity popularly described as the 'world economy' is in a state of total chaos. Every week sees an escalation of the trade war. The neat and pretty rules devised by the pioneers of the post-1945 economic era to govern the trading relations between nations lie in tatters, either disregarded with contempt or the subject of heated arguments in the interminable international conferences held to thrash out an agreed formula for the continuation of the world trade system. Even more chaotic still is the state of world finance, with many nations sunk in a trap of completely unpayable debt, and the world's leading bankers making the ominous prediction of a financial collapse on a scale that would make that of 1929 seem like a minor hiccup.

The second fact is the deep-rooted nature of Britain's economic decline — for this is not merely the kind of decline that can be depicted as the normal downward turn in an economic cycle; the decline has proceeded almost uninterruptedly for the past hundred years, though in the most recent decade it has accelerated to the point of facing us with the imminent threat of extinction as a manufacturing nation.

The British economic system has, for as long as any of us can remember, been the subject of deep national introspection. Britain has had, after all, more of the ingredients of economic success than almost any nation. Her lead in the first Industrial Revolution was aided by the existence of a population with an unsurpassed talent for economic activity, including an exceptionally high level of manufacturing inventiveness and skill, combined with abundant reserves of the most vital energy source of that time: coal. Together with these assets, we had, then, access to an Empire of boundless resources and wealth, able to provide us with

almost every raw material we needed, and with a huge internal
market for our manufactured produce.

At the dawn of this first industrial era, therefore, it would have
been correct to say that our success was not some shaky
phenomenon, based on purely ephemeral conditions, but
something which had no reason not to be permanent — always so
long as our economic development was guided by people of
wisdom and foresight who could recognise changing conditions
when faced with them and make the required adjustments to meet
them as they came — in other words, so long as, over its economic
affairs, the nation had **leadership** and a **policy**.

Of course, we could not expect to maintain indefinitely the
domination of the world market for manufactures that we had up
to about the middle of the 19th century; but that fact should in no
way have brought about an inevitable decline, only an adjustment
of trade practices. With this adjustment, we would have had no
less advantages than Germany and France, and later Japan, and in
fact much greater advantages than any of those nations — for as
long as we held on to our imperial power.

Today, notwithstanding the scuttle from Empire, we remain in
a more favourable position than any of these three rivals with
regard to total resources, when our oil and coal are taken into
account.

And yet our economic performance is a good way inferior to
that of France and many, many miles inferior to those of Germany
and Japan.

And this descent into inferiority is something that has been
continuing, almost without pause, for the past century.

If this decline is not the product of any disadvantage in the way
of resources, either human or natural, it has to be the product of
bad leadership, organisation and policy — indeed of the fact that,
for the whole of the time in question, we have simply not had
anything that could qualify to be called a policy.

The very phrase 'economic policy' must imply, if it is to mean
anything, that a nation's economic affairs have a direction, and
that that direction is chosen and implemented by government. An
aggregate of industrial and commercial units, each pursuing its
own path to profit, does not constitute a policy in the national
sense of the term, only a collection of many policies, separate
from, and largely in contradiction to, each other. There is only a
single policy if there is a government in control, prepared and able
to co-ordinate economic forces and direct them towards a single

national goal.

This much was recognised by the pioneers of socialism. At the time of their entry onto the British scene, they were presented with an opportunity unparallelled in history. The old capitalist economics had manifestly failed, bringing with them millionfold human misery and social injustice, a hideous living environment for a huge part of the population, and a wholly unstable industrial system subject to cycles of boom and slump. Yet along with this legacy there was an inventive, skilled and — at least at that time — diligent workforce and a productive national soil, backed up by the vast natural resources of an Empire on which the sun never set. The failure of capitalism had spoken louder than any words could do of the obvious need for radical economic reform, while the tools needed to make that reform effective in Britain were all there, only waiting to be used. Socialism had in its possession a ready-made case, and together with it the means to achieve as near as mankind could ever achieve to an earthly paradise.

But socialism failed utterly to meet this immense challenge and exploit this immense opportunity. It failed because right at the start it made three cardinal errors that were at the root of the failure of its predecessor, each of these errors originating in the legacy of liberal institutions and ideology that our socialist pioneers took into their baggage.

The first was that, while these socialists called, in principle, for government regulation of economic forces in the service of the general good, they never understood or accepted the need for political institutions that would make that regulation effective. While proclaiming their 'radicalism' in respect of the economic and social change for which they stood, they showed themselves to be dyed-in-the-wool reactionaries in their reverence for the old, and failed, political party system. Indeed they incorporated into their doctrine and practice all the most hopeless features of that system writ large. Everything was to be done through committees and voting majorities. No individual was to have authority within socialism itself; nor was socialism to have authority over national affairs. A proper mechanism for action was utterly rejected. All was to be talk, talk and more talk. While socialism spoke in theory of dynamic reform, in practice it brought to the top men incapable of dynamism in anything, and it saddled them with a system that stifled all dynamic impulse even in the unlikely event of anyone emerging who possessed it.

The one sole example of the latter was Sir Oswald Mosley, to whom I have already referred. Early in the 1930s and when a remarkably young man, Mosley produced a programme for dealing with unemployment that incorporated a bold call for the mobilisation of all national resources in a policy of economic development that represented the first ever effort to get to grips with reality in a Labour Party previously lost in woolly and impractical dreams. Socialism rejected Mosley, and with him the one supreme opportunity to overcome the crisis of that age. Instead, it preferred the dreary cavalcade of cowardice, inertia, stunted thinking and empty wind — as represented by MacDonald, Thomas, Snowden, Lansbury and the rest of the feeble figures who shuffled across the socialist scene in the inexorable procession to slump, poverty, war and — in 1940 — defeat.

The second cardinal error committed by our socialist pioneers was their embrace of internationalism. Failing to see that it was that very internationalism that had been the main factor in making the capitalist economy unworkable, they set out on the same disastrous road. British economic prosperity and progress were to be pursued, not through reliance on national resources and national effort, together with — as was then fully possible — the immeasurable assets of Empire, but through fatuous dreams and abstractions expressed in such phrases as "the brotherhood of man" and "Workers of the world, unite!"

Finally, socialism utterly failed to get to grips with the other evil that had attended the career of the capitalist system: the tyranny of finance — not finance as the necessary handmaiden of productive economic activity, but finance as the economy's master, placing all the productive forces into the grip of the bankers and usurers and making money the arbiter of all that is possible for industry, rather than materials, machines, skills and work. Socialism, while breaking much rhetorical wind over the diabolism of the big bankers and financiers, produced nothing whatever that was practical to free the economy from their thrall, and eventually settled down to a routine of economics which left the powers of finance every bit as much in control as before.

Socialism thus became, behind all its brave slogans, just another tool of the forces of economic reaction — incorporating all the worst features of the capitalist disorder, but without its dynamism, its enterprise and its incentive to effort.

To this nonsense, socialism added another piece of similar folly: the idea that all men were created equal in their inherent capabilities and only differed in their performance on account of inequalities in economic status and education — followed later, of course, by the attempt to extend this equality mania to the world s widely contrasting racial groups, resulting in the misery we now see throughout the length and breadth of Africa and elsewhere where the decolonising process — eagerly promoted by all 'progressive' opinion — was carried out in the wake of World War II.

Thus has Britain been governed since the Industrial Revolution, whether by parties of the 'left' or the 'right', by approaches to economy which reject the very first basics, and which, therefore, at no point could be dignified by the description of a 'policy'. At one moment, economic forces have been fighting it out with one another in accordance with the laws of the jungle — while government, far from intervening to institute order between them, has sat back radiant with satisfaction and actually proclaimed that this free-for-all was in accordance with the most enlightened economic laws, out of which, if they were allowed to operate in a free market, the greatest good for all the people would result. Then, at the next moment, there has been a token attempt to bring order to the business by a measure of control and planning; but the control and planning have been totally inadequate, the levers being in the hands of the wrong kinds of people, with the wrong machinery to back them up, and within an economic area where control and planning are impossible anyway.

The capitalists of the 19th and early 20th century periods have taken a great deal of punishment from historians and from political ideologues, and no doubt in many individual cases this has been deserved. What is not often enough taken into account, however, is that they had to operate within a system which imposed upon them two vital disadvantages in the way of raising the pay and conditions of their employees to a decent living level.

The first of these was a banking and financial system which, since the setting up of the Bank of England in 1694, had given the bankers the power to create the nation's money by means of the fractional reserve regulation under which bank loans could be made to a total several times in excess of real monetary assets. By this process, the new money needed to fuel an expanding economy came into existence, to ever increasing degrees, as a debt owing, with interest, to the banks.

This practice gave the banks increasing power over the economy, with a growing portion of the wealth created being yielded to them as tribute — and for no essential service to the economy that could not better be undertaken by other means. Industry, inevitably, got into increasing debt, with an ever greater portion of its income going to service this debt (as was also the case with government).

The second disadvantage suffered by industry was the necessity for it to survive in world markets by means of competitive prices. The raising of wages to the desired level would have resulted in British goods being priced out of these markets. This tendency was further accentuated when the Orient began to become industralised, largely with the aid of finance from the City of London — which knew then, as it knows now, no national boundaries or patriotic loyalties. From that time on, cheap coolie labour enabled Orientals to dump goods around the world at prices with which British manufacturers could not possibly compete, except by keeping wages down at a level well below that required for the barest living standards. Added to this, British goods were also faced in foreign markets with tariff barriers erected by foreign governments, quite understandably and justifiably from their own point of view, to protect indigenous industries. These goods had to be artificially lowly priced to be subject to the tariff and still be competitive. Another practice was that of foreign governments helping their own industries by means of subsidies — never a profitable practice in the permanent sense but useful in the short term to get those industries off the ground and enable them to steal the markets of their competitors.

Had Britain had anything resembling an economic policy, our reaction to these developments would have been simple and obvious. From the moment that it became clear that our easy and unquestioned world manufacturing supremacy was at an end, and that thenceforward we would face in world markets stiff competition, often of a kind impossible to match, we should have elected for a nationalist policy, shutting foreign manufactured goods out from the British and imperial markets and giving a monopoly of those markets to British industry and to the young industries of the Dominions as they developed. Wages could then have been steadily raised, as would have been possible in an industrial system geared mainly to the domestic and imperial markets where cut-price competition would have been absent. With this rise in wages would have come an immense rise in domestic and imperial purchasing power, thereby aiding the further expansion of industry in a market that would have been assured.

Industry then, by means of its immense profits in the home and imperial markets, could have afforded to sell its goods at much lower profit margins in foreign markets and still, in many areas of trade, maintain a competitive price; and this process would have been assisted by the huge increases in production resulting from booming trade at home, making possible ever greater economies of scale.

Parallel with this policy, government should have assumed full command over the nation's financial institutions, curtailed their international role and put them to work in the British interest, directing their profits to investment in domestic and, where required, Dominion industries instead of into the building up of Britain's foreign competitors.

All this was entirely possible in the later 19th and early 20th centuries, when the British Empire was a single unit in terms of national loyalties and could have been made, without difficulty, a single unit in economics as well — for it would not have been hard to obtain the co-operation of the Dominions in the carrying out of a policy which was manifestly favourable to their interests, as part of that policy would have been to give preferential terms of entry into the UK to their minerals and food products, as well as preference to their manufactures over those of foreigners; indeed, the Dominions were in many cases ahead of Britain in **asking** for just such a policy.

But none of this was done. It was not done because British economic affairs were the slave to liberalism and international-ism. There was never a policy, only drift. There was never leadership by government, only the continued deference of government towards economic forces. And these economic forces, in large part, stood to lose by such a policy. City of London finance, which had invested enormously in foreign economies, could only obtain its dividends by allowing those countries in which it had invested to export their goods to Britain, at the expense, if necessary, of home and Dominion producers. And City of London finance always seemed to have the necessary pull over every government, of whatever party complexion, so that no government was prepared to intervene to protect the industries that were our life's blood.

The chance to show leadership, renounce drift and adopt a firm policy came with the presentation of Joseph Chamberlain's Tariff Reform proposals in the first decade of the present century, and to which I have referred earlier. But these proposals were rejected. The power of commerce and finance triumphed, not for the first or last time, over statesmanship and national good sense. Most certainly, had Britain had a mechanism of government that enabled political leadership to prevail over economic forces, the Tariff Reform proposals would have been adopted. Precisely the same fate as befell Tariff Reform also befell the proposals put forward in the Mosley Memorandum presented nearly three decades later. Again, liberalism and internationalism held sway.

Within such a national system as would have been developed through these reforming movements, the worst abuses of the capitalist system could have been eliminated by the adoption of a high-wage economy geared to home and Dominion markets — an economy which the great leviathans of industry could have sustained while remaining profitable and viable. In other words, within a national system a measure of capitalism could have worked, and to the benefit of all sections of the population. But within the international system capitalism was, and is, doomed to go on manifesting the same fundamental weaknesses and abuses — its present legacy to Britain being a massive increase in the legions of the jobless.

A partial adoption of a national policy did indeed occur in 1933, when, as a result of the Ottawa Conference of that year, some measures of imperial preference were put into effect by the then National Government by the adoption of tariffs within the Empire against foreign produce. These were not accompanied by any firm measures to regulate the economy at home, to reform the money system and to control investment. Nevertheless, they did lead to some improvement in the economic situation and gave promise of what might have been achieved had the process been extended further and a full-scale programme of nationalist economics adopted.

This never happened, however, and in the aftermath of World War II and in consequence of the Bretton Woods Agreement, our imperial preferences were not given the necessary upgrading and eventually were dropped altogether with the infamous and disastrous act whereby Britain entered the European Common Market in 1973.

The decision to join the Common Market was one made wholly in accordance with the internationalism which, by the post-1945 era, had come to dominate British politics even more completely than previously. The decision was presented to the public by the politicians as being a measure necessitated by the fact that, by then, the Empire and Commonwealth had ceased to exist as a viable unit and its members, including the Dominions, could no longer be relied upon to regard themselves in any kind of special relationship to Britain. This bland assertion conveniently overlooked the fact that it had been Britain's politicians and their parties which, for many years previously, had done everything possible to undermine imperial unity and break the special relationship between Britain and her overseas kin — a very important part of this process being the protracted series of negotiations to join Europe that had dragged on for many years before entry finally took place. If the Dominions no longer regarded the special relationship as existing, this was primarily in the nature of a response to a state of affairs that had been brought about by many years of neglect and snub by Britain. As one Australian put it succinctly: "We did not leave Britain; Britain left us!"

The other excuse for this debacle was that, with Britain reduced in size and stature by the disintegration of Empire (which our own leaders, as will surely have been indicated, brought about), there was need for us to be part of a larger economic area so as to be able to 'stand up' to the 'super-powers'.

That there is a need for a large area is partially true, in as much as such an area is an asset — providing that within it there is a genuine homogeneity of loyalties and interests. At the same time, nations like Norway, Sweden and Switzerland (minute by comparison with Britain) have shown themselves able to build highly successful and prosperous economies without belonging to huge trading blocs.

If these nations can survive on their own, the idea that Britain is not big enough to do so is laughable; in fact that idea is merely part of the elaborate mythology created to lead us blindly into the spider's parlour of internationalism.

In summary, we have seen over the past century the decline of what was once the 'workshop of the world' into what is now a second-rate, almost third-rate, industrial power — despite the existence, all along the line, of every national advantage conducive to continued economic success. This decline testifies to the total failure of all the old and tried nostrums of political economy, of international socialism just as much as of international capitalism. It underlines the need for an entirely new economic creed and system, as revolutionary in relation to what has gone before as was the first age of industrialism in Britain.

But before any new economic creed and system can work at all we first need to establish new political institutions and an entirely new national climate to set the scene for action. In earlier chapters, I have given some attention to the changes necessary to achieve this end. These changes are directed, as will have been made clear, to the establishment of government with the strength to make itself master of all the forces determining the operation of our economic life. Parallel with this, I have called for a society animated by a spirit of national unity and national discipline — without which nothing, whatever the good intentions of government, can ever be done. Likewise, the institutions that shape public opinion must be mobilised to give guidance in this. new organisation of the nation's life, a guidance which will concentrate the nation's mind on the tasks to be accomplished.

It has often been said that the British inventive genius time and time again goes to waste due to the fact that there is lacking the organisation of industry to exploit it properly — with the result that foreigners seize upon the invented product and, by superior organisation, put it to much more profitable use. No doubt this has something to do with the weird national superstition that organisation is an alien idea — despite the fact that, as I have said when speaking previously on the subject, the British are organised and regimented in so many different ways — and with their hardly knowing it — for all manner of much less urgent and worthy purposes.

We must certainly overcome this absurd superstition if we are to effect any kind of real national recovery.

In a pamphlet I wrote in the 1970s calling for a revolutionary new creed to regenerate the British economy, I chose as the title theme: *Beyond Capitalism and Socialism*. This encapsulated, in a way on which I cannot improve, the direction in which our thinking must proceed. The old capitalism and the old socialism are outdated concepts — as is the struggle between them, which today only exists in the minds of those whose thinking remains imprisoned in the straightjacket of Victorian and Edwardian economics and whom the new facts of a new age have passed by as if they were standing still and with eyes blindfolded.

At the level of understanding that is needed to cope with the economics of the new world, the weaknesses in the old capitalism and the old socialism need not be a matter for argument, as both can be discarded as useless. As for the strengths, over these we need not argue either because these can be combined in synthesis.

I have mentioned the dynamics of capitalism, these consisting in the scope it gives for individual enterprise and the great spur of the profit incentive. Then there is in socialism the virtue that, at least in theory, it stands for the replacement of the economic free-for-all with a regulation of economic forces by the state and in the interests of the whole. These concepts are not irreconcilable, despite the attempts of our present day economic philosophers to make them so.

The antagonism towards profit on the part of the left of politics has always been an entirely juvenile sentiment. Profit is merely a variable wage which cannot be determined by any ethical yardstick but is at all times fixed at the level needed to attract the necessary investment of capital and the commitment of time, energy and proprietorial skill to an enterprise, and then maintain the efficiency with which that enterprise is run. Take away profit, and you have to replace it with some other financial reward that will accomplish all these purposes; and it is clear from the experience of Soviet Russia and similar economies that no-one has ever devised a way of doing this that is remotely as effective. Profit is one factor that undoubtedly must be left to be determined by market forces — though in other matters we cannot allow these forces free reign, as I shall duly explain.

Profit is directly related to that other useful component in capitalism: the enterprise of the imaginative, initiating, energetic and bold individual, willing to stake his all on a venture in which he has faith. Of course, such an individual has no respected place in socialist thought because that thought hates to acknowledge that any human being is superior to another or that there are such species within humanity as leaders and led. In fact, private enterprise, just so long as we know just where to place the limits to it, is the natural arena of life in which leaders of economic activity are selected. In effect, they select themselves by stepping forward and risking their capital, and sometimes their reputation, in the pursuit of an idea ahead of their fellows — which the latter, either have not thought of at all, or, if they have, have not had the boldness and initiative to translate into action.

It is entirely right that men of this kind should be the leaders of our economy, rather than state-appointed officials who mostly have given no such proof of their powers of leadership at all, and who anyway do not have the personal stake in their concerns that provides the incentive to them to give of their utmost. And this applies to the great large-scale enterprises just as much as to the smaller ones — indeed more so, as the qualifications needed to run the former successfully must usually be greater.

There are some quaint theorists around today who believe that when trading enterprises have grown to a certain size (i.e. when their owners have proved a certain competence) they should be taken away from those owners and placed in the hands of 'workers' co-operatives'. Such schemes totally ignore the question of those workers' financial commitment (if any) to the concern, the question of whether they have the necessary expertise to participate in its top-level decisions, and that of whether they even wish to be cast in this role and take this responsibility. The schemes also ignore the question of how the money is to be found to make such a transfer of ownership anything other than theft from the people whose investment and managerial ability built the concern up to the point at which it was to qualify for this take-over.

This is not to say that there is no room in any concern, large or small, for a sharing of profits. But this question should be left to the head (or heads) of each concern to decide according to their own discretion. If they judge that such profit-sharing will induce their workers to give better performance and thus increase the firm's overall profitability, they may well introduce such a scheme. But they are the best judges of the practicality of such an idea. Also, it must be conditional on two things: (1) that the workers accept a share of losses in bad times as well as of profits in good ones; (2) that, particularly in consequence of this rule, they **wish** to enter into such an arrangement, instead of having the security of a regular and guaranteed wage.

If all these conditions prevail, there is nothing to stop profit-sharing schemes being introduced. The important point is that they should not be imposed arbitrarily from above by politicians who have not the same knowledge of each individual concern thus affected, and also that control over the concern in question should remain in the hands of those whose leadership has built it up to what it is.

It is an entirely different matter if the concern is about to go into liquidation — a fact which might suggest that its existing ownership was not of the highest competence — and its workers are willing to form a co-operative and together invest their own money to keep it going and themselves in employment. In that case, let them try — and good luck to them! They may succeed, and, if they do, at least their ownership exists by right. If they do not succeed, the money lost has been theirs and the decision to risk it their own decision.

Capitalism has the virtue, as I have said, of providing an economic environment in which the most capable participants in the economy, and its natural leaders, can come to the fore by reason of their achievement. Where many capitalist systems fail — and certainly our own is here included — is in their indisposition to set limits on how far individual enterprise should be allowed to go. Such enterprise is, after all, a national asset — to be mobilised and organised for national purposes, not something carrying its own divine right. We must assume that the successful capitalist is a person driven on by a high endowment of individual ambition. If left entirely to himself, he may not necessarily regard national borders or national interests as imposing any boundaries to that ambition. If he can realise higher and quicker profits by investing his capital in a factory in Hong Kong rather than in one in Birmingham, that is what he will do — and too bad for the people in Birmingham who might have hoped to find work in his employ! If he can make more money importing cheaply produced Japanese radio sets and selling them in British shops than he could selling more expensive British products, that again is what he will do. In a cut-throat competitive world, he cannot afford the niceties of an over-zealous dedication to ethics, particularly the ethic of patriotism, for he knows that if he did he would soon be put out of business by other traders who had no such scruples.

It therefore falls to government to draw up rules circumscribing capitalist activity in accordance with national needs and to act as referee to ensure that that activity operates within the rules. Over and above every other consideration, British government has the duty to protect and nurture domestic British industries, and to create in Britain the conditions for maximum employment. This duty is completely inconsistent with allowing British money to be invested in the industries of Britain's international competitors or the goods of those competitors to flood the British market and take away the business of our own home producers.

To these assertions, the 'free market' economists will of course have their ready-made replies. The first is that international competition stimulates all producers to improve their products and prices just as does internal competition, and to an even greater degree than the latter. If foreigners have the chance to sell their goods in the British market, so do British industries have the chance to sell in foreign markets; the granting of success in every market to the best competitor will in the end work in the interests of all, and, in particular, of the consumer, who will have the greatest freedom of choice and will be able to buy what he wants at the cheapest possible price.

I well remember this issue being discussed when I visited an electrical goods shop a year or two ago to find a replacement for my clapped-out tape-recorder. On running my eyes along the shelves and seeing nothing but foreign (mainly Japanese) brand names on all the products available, I asked the shop manager if he had a British-made tape-recorder for sale. He replied that, much though he regretted it, he did not. Home-made products had simply been priced out of the market. To my observation that this was appalling, he replied: "Maybe so, but would you prefer to buy the machine you want at twice the cost?"

This is of course a seductive argument, but the matter goes much deeper. While cheaply priced foreign products of all kinds are coming into our shops in this way, Britons are being laid off work in droves. A vast army of compulsorily idle now languishes in our towns and cities up and down the country, and a vast amount of the nation's money is being spent on keeping them in that condition. If this army were working, at least a part of the extra expense of buying British-made tape-recorders and other products would be saved in terms of smaller contributions being necessary to pay national insurance against unemployment and a smaller sacrifice by the taxpayer would be required to pay for social security benefits.

But there are other considerations too. The only possible circumstances under which these foreign tape-recorders could enter the British market at the prices for which they were selling were that they were yielding to their producers very narrow profit-margins (if indeed any profit margins at all), which were compensated by the huge volume of sales worldwide (including sales, at much higher profit margins, in the home markets of the producing countries) and the resulting economies of production.

Putting back to work the near 3 million unemployed in Britain would result in the generating of an enormous new element of national wealth, which would be to the benefit of all — and not just the newly employed. This would certainly counterbalance the loss involved in paying higher prices for such products as the one I have mentioned. In addition, the economies of scale that would come within the reach of British industry as a result of this process, would most certainly enable that industry to produce at much lower costs than at present.

The truth is of course that we British are allowing ourselves to be made the complete suckers of the international trade system. The artificially deflated prices of these foreign products will only be maintained just for as long as their manufacturers feel they are necessary to eliminate all competition. Then the prices will be dramatically increased, so that even the dubious benefit the British consumer has of being able to obtain these products cheaply will disappear. We will be faced with highly priced foreign products in all our shops, and with a huge portion of our own population unemployed many will not have the money to get even a sniff at them.

Another practice employed abroad to enable foreign goods to flood world markets is of course the practice of government subsidy. This is particularly widely used in communist countries. It has the same effect of reducing prices to a level with which, in a free market, British products cannot possibly compete. This practice of subsidy, together with cheap sweated labour, makes a complete nonsense of the free-trade doctrine, with its supposition that if one nation's products compete successfully with another's it is always because of superior industrial performance.

If the government took measures to restore Britain's manufacturing in tape-recorders by the progressive exclusion of foreign products, firstly by tariffs and eventually, when our capacity had been expanded to supply the whole home market, by complete import embargo, we could be making these products in sufficient quantities to achieve far greater economies of scale than is now the case, thus bringing the price down. And if this procedure were applied throughout every sector of industry the millions now out of work would be back in work, increasing consumer purchasing power and thus the sale of all home products — and taking away the huge burden from the nation of having to support millions doing nothing.

These conditions would mean that, as fast as the prices of British products were coming down, the amount of money in our pockets to buy them would be going up.

All these factors would help our export trade. Combined with a resolution on the part of government to fix a fair and realistic rate of exchange with our foreign customers, they would mean that Britain would again be paying her way in the world, and under conditions that did not rely on oil exports, thereby having some permanence.

The free trader will immediately object to these proposals by saying that they will amount to protecting inefficiency. Let British products compete with these imports, he will say, by being better in quality and in price. The onus is on our manufacturers to put their houses in order and improve their methods of production; then we will win back markets without having to impose trade barriers. If the British worker finds himself out of a job as a result of lost trade, the argument continues, that is his own fault; it is up to him to become more productive and efficient and get that trade back in fair competition. One can just hear this line of talk echoing like a well-worn gramophone record down the smart avenues and over the garden hedges of Finchley and Orpington.

But the argument is full of flaws, being refuted by logic, common sense and, above all, facts. I am the first to agree that protective measures to shut out imports are not in themselves alone going to overcome our industrial problems, in particular the problems of inefficiency, obsolescence, bad labour relations, lack of enterprise and poor work discipline that have dogged British industry for a long time. Such measures must form merely part of a comprehensive range of policies, which would include action to tackle all these shortcomings.

But what is clear is that exposure to the open international market has not, as assumed in free trade doctrine, provided the gust of fresh air to British industry required to clear out the cobwebs and set it on the road to renewal; on the contrary, that exposure has very nearly killed British industry off, and bids well to complete the process before many more years are out. Very little of the things that are supposed to happen under the stimulus of foreign competition have in fact happened; indeed, the 'British sickness' of which we often speak has got, not better, but much worse. Inefficiency, obsolescence, bad labour relations, lack of enterprise and poor work discipline are still there. For every one branch of industry in which there has been some improvement in these respects, there are several that have gone yet further downhill; and even where improvement has taken place there is no particular evidence to show that it has been the result of foreign competition in the home market. It does not require such competition to tell us when the performance of our own industry is not measuring up to that of industries abroad; such facts can easily be ascertained by a simple study of production statistics and working methods of our foreign rivals. The knowledge of our poor performance has in fact been in the possession of British politicians, economists and businessmen for many decades; what has been lacking is the will to take the steps necessary to remedy it, together with the means to do so in terms of economic where-withal. These means have steadily diminished as British industry has become poorer and weaker under the onslaught of the invasion of our market. As for the will, this is something which, in the final analysis, must come from government. And from that quarter it has been continually lacking.

As one example of this, let me just mention the quite pathetic response by the Thatcher government that took office in 1979, and had its mandate renewed in 1983 and again in 1987, to the challenge to reform our system of industrial relations and grapple with trade union power. After much brave talk before coming to office, this government, when faced with the moment to act, adopted a series of spineless compromises which left union power practically undiminished. The government paraded as a show of 'strength' its refusal to give way to the demands of the NUM against pit closures which led to the miners' strike, and when that strike ended it engaged in an orgy of self-congratulation for the fact that it had "seen the thing out." But in fact the scenes of picket-line violence that accompanied the strike merely showed that the government had done precisely nothing to enforce the law properly against the picket-line thugs, as its leaders had loudly talked of doing for many years before.

In the meantime, after proclaiming loudly the need for the secret ballot to determine all decisions whether to strike, the government introduced that ballot under terms which left its enforcement to employers, telling them that if a strike was called not in accordance with the new rule, the onus was on them to sue for damages the union responsible. This was in fact a half-baked cop-out, just another passing of the buck.

As for blaming 'the British worker' for poor performance, this practice is about as contemptible as that of an incompetent and cowardly general in wartime blaming his troops for defeat. If those troops have fought badly, then whose fault is it that they have done so? First and foremost, it is the fault of the general himself — for failing to give the troops the leadership beforehand necessary to bring them up to scratch, and then subsequently in the conduct of the battle.

The British are not by nature an indolent race. Visitors from the Continent in the 18th and 19th centuries, such as the French authoress Madame de Stael, testified to our people's incredible energy and industry. If a great many Britons have fallen into ways of indolence and workshyness today, it is because our rulers over many years have created a society conducive to the spread of these vices and made it all too easy for people to get away with them. Just as bad generalship creates an unenthusiastic and undisciplined army, so does bad political leadership allow a naturally industrious and productive population to degenerate into one containing an undue portion of low performers and loafers.

In this regard, our rulers subjected Britain to the ultimate depths of degradation when recently they gave warm applause (and money) to the setting up of Japanese factories in this country in which supervisors flown over from the land of the rising sun were to organise the British labour force and teach it how to work properly. It did not seem to occur to our politicians that their action in importing Japs to show us how to run industry was a classic admission of their own lamentable failure of economic leadership.

As for saying that foreign exporters should be allowed to capture the markets of this country and deliver British industry to ruin by virtue of the former's superior performance, that is, when you really think about it, the most fantastic rationale for failure that could ever be imagined. The logic of such argument must surely be that, at every stage of our history when we were confronted with an enemy army more efficiently organised than our own, we should have let that enemy invade our shores and conquer us without our firing a shot to stop it!

I firmly believe that this attitude is rooted basically in the philosophical liberalism about which I have spoken in a previous chapter, and of which the Tory Party is today the main standard-bearer. In this outlook there seems to be a marked incapacity to see the nation as an integrated and interdependent community, in which no part has the right to be unconcerned with the fate of any other part, and over which government has the duty to be concerned with the fate of all. The preparedness to let Japanese businessmen steal the markets that should rightly belong to the producers of our own nation is perfectly logical and unexceptionable to those in whom a proper sense of national consciousness is totally lacking and whose loyalty to the successful entrepreneur (of whatever nationality) overrides loyalty to the members of their own race.

Reverting to the question of the performance of British industry, it is a fact that the measures necessary to improve that performance will rely in very large part on a policy of protection, albeit that that policy will not in itself suffice. Government, in order to put through the measures of rationalisation needed to increase the efficiency of industry, first needs to win the confidence of the labour force of that industry and its support in carrying out such measures. This it can hardly do in such a climate of mass redundancies and unemployment as the one existing at present. For government and the work force of industry to collaborate as a team to improve industrial performance, it requires the visible signs of unemployment coming down, not going up, and the prospect of more work opportunities for people rather than less. Such a happy partnership is out of the question with an embittered industrial work force of the kind which we see today throughout many regions of Britain. And who can blame these workers for being embittered, when we look at the appalling record of the Thatcher government in preserving jobs?

This whole situation argues, with added force, for the policies of protection that are shunned by the present government.

Protection will not itself immediately make British industry efficient, but it will create vast numbers of new jobs — in fact it could soon wipe out unemployment entirely. A government then having won the prestige and goodwill born of this achievement would be in the best possible position to enlist the co-operation of large parts of the trade union membership in the reform of the industrial relations mechanism necessary, among other things, to improve industrial performance.

So it is with another important task: that of streamlining industry by reducing manning levels. It is hardly surprising that there has been a great deal of resistance to recent efforts in this field, since those comprising the surplus labour in overmanned industries have known that the almost certain result, for them, of the streamlining process is going to be the dole. A classic example of this was the case of the planned pit closures leading to the miners' strike of 1984, which has been mentioned. The closures plan, while in some parts justified, faced thousands of working men with idleness, simply because there was no prospect for them of alternative employment unless they moved to other parts of the country. This led to the very justified contention that the closure plan would break up many local communities. This was what gave fuel to the strike, which dragged on for more than a year at appalling national and human cost.

Exactly the same tendency has been seen in resistance to

streamlining in the steel and other industries. You simply do not make the streamlining process attractive to a worker if he knows that, through it, he is going to be without a job — and probably for a long time.

The Thatcher remedy to this problem is that, where the traditional economic base of a region is destroyed by such a process — as has happened, for instance, over large areas of South Wales and North East England, just to mention two cases — the remedy lies in a movement of population away from such a region and into another region where, in accordance with the working of 'market forces', greater work opportunities exist. And what a depressing proposition that is! Such a development might be likened to the listing of a doomed ship to port and to stern, prior to sinking. In every section of the ship, people and furniture slide, by the force of gravity, to the rear left-hand corner — which only accentuates further the listing tendency and the imminence of the ship going down. 'Market forces' are in effect creating a few economic booms in selected areas, mainly in the South East of England; this is resulting in the moving of people to that corner of the country, to the even greater impoverishment of other regions. Open country is fast disappearing in the South East, as more and more land is needed for the extension of housing and industry. Meanwhile, other parts of the country, albeit with some isolated exceptions, are becoming economic and demographic deserts. The waste in resources involved in this process is catastrophic.

But none of this need be; there is an alternative. In a protected economy, immense numbers of new jobs are being created all the time to take the place of old ones being lost. In the case of steel, the domestic British demand for this product could easily have guaranteed continued employment for the whole workforce, even with the streamlining scheme that was undoubtedly needed — particularly if other sections of British industry were working to full capacity and therefore sustaining a regular high demand for steel. Where men had to be taken away from certain production lines in order to accommodate new techniques and make those lines more cost-effective, those men could have been transferred to other production lines in the same industry, in many cases in the very same steel plant. In other words, instead of rationalising by paying fewer men to produce the same amount of steel, we could have paid the same number of men to produce more steel.

As our government tried to justify the redundancies brought about in British Steel in the early 1980s by saying that the world demand for steel had fallen off in relation to steel-producing capacity, this country was being flooded with foreign steel and, moreover, with thousands of other foreign products possessing steel components. Motor vehicles were a prominent example, for by then more than half the family cars and heavy trucks on our roads were imported. Had those vehicles been made, as they should have been, in British factories, not only would jobs in the vitally important motor industry have been preserved but also a huge additional demand for British steel would have been created. The streamlining of the industry could have proceeded simply by expanding production to meet an expanded demand, and without the huge lay-offs that occurred.

Exactly the same policy could be adopted throughout the rest of industry where manning levels are excessive, simply by raising domestic demand by shutting out imports.

Then, as these industries became more cost-effective, without any appreciable loss of jobs, exports could rise — thus creating more jobs.

The plan to close coal pits came, not at a time when Britain was producing excess coal, but when she was importing coal. The plan, in projecting likely future demands for coal, presumed no great rise in British industrial production and therefore no great increase in the demand for coal as an energy source for industry. Had this been otherwise, and had industry been able to expand — as it could have done — through protection against imports, and were this protection to have included coal itself, the demand for home-produced coal could undoubtedly have been regarded as likely constantly to increase.

This is not to deny that at least some of the pits marked down for closure could not be made to continue operating at anything near an economic level and that, therefore, some redundancies were inevitable. However, in these cases such redundancies need never have led to the certainty of the dole and the destruction of local communities — had there been a parallel plan to establish new industries in the areas in question to provide alternative work opportunities for those affected. Here is where the liberal *laissez-faire* system of economics totally failed, and is continuing to fail, the test. Such a project would have needed a massive degree of enterprise from the state — something abhorrent to the Tory mind — to get it off the ground. Such new industries would preferably have been those in which the British market has hitherto relied upon imports, such as motor cycles, photographic and optical equipment, domestic electrical goods, office machinery, etc. These industries could have been nurtured behind protective walls exactly as happened with the same industries in Japan in the early post-war years, when they were being built up in preparation for future world conquest. Such new industries, had they been set up here, would probably not, in their initial phase, have brought their products to the British market at as low a price as the same products could have been obtained from abroad, but the process would have enabled Britain to have carried out the necessary reorganisation of industry, with the result of greater efficiency and competitiveness but without mass unemployment — which, as I have indicated, creates a hidden tax that we have to pay on every foreign product that we purchase at the expense of British jobs. In the longer term, and with the mass-production methods that would become possible in these new industries, the prices of these products would of course fall dramatically.

Confronted with these facts, the internationalist brigade will no doubt come forward with a further argument against protection: that it would invite retaliatory measures against British exports abroad, which would cost us a huge loss of trade. Here we come back to the popular supposition mentioned earlier: that in a world free-trade system British industries have the same chance to sell their goods in foreign markets as foreigners have to sell their goods here.

In fact, the latter supposition is far from true; British exporters face all kinds of barriers in markets overseas, and particularly in Japan, where the free-trade doctrine is regarded essentially as something for export, for foreigners to practise but not for the Japanese to do so. A great deal of publicity has been given to the covert discrimination against manufactured imports practised by the Japanese, so that it is not necessary for me to elaborate any further on the theme. We are, as I have said, the suckers of the international trade system: while our own leaders see that system in terms of the liberal ideal of a world economy in which everyone plays the game scrupulously in accordance with the rules, and where everywhere there is absolutely just and fair competition, many foreigners — and particularly our most formidable competitors, such as the Japanese — see it as merely a racket, open to themselves to exploit at our expense. In economics and trade, as in so many other fields, the world of facts is wildly out of step with liberal dreams and liberal theory.

As for the argument about retaliatory measures, the truth is that no conceivable loss of export trade could be great enough to outbalance the huge gain in business that would ensue to British industry in the home market. 100 per-cent retaliatory action against British exports would never materialise — anymore than Japan's customers have retaliated against her import barriers to anything like the degree that would wipe out the advantages of her huge internal trade. But even in the purely hypothetical case of this happening to Britain, it is still a fact that our trade would score a massive net gain. Just to take the year 1986 as an example, during that year foreign manufacturers exported to Britain ₤13,057 million's worth of goods in excess of what our manufacturers exported to their countries. This would be the gain in trade to our manufacturers in the most extreme contingency of retaliation. And that figure excludes the gains that our exports would enjoy in other, non-industrial, countries by virtue of more competitive prices made possible by the higher levels of production at which our factories would be able to operate.

Indeed, Japanese goods sell successfully abroad, not because of any reciprocal trade arrangements between Japan and other industrial nations, but because of the extremely high competitiveness of those Japanese products. And this competitiveness has been achieved, not by adherence to 'free market' economics, but by an industrial structure governed by a policy of state-paternalism that runs entirely contrary to the doctrines underlying present British economic practices. Japan indeed operates the very economic nationalism that is being proposed in this chapter as a formula for our own economy, and the practice has certainly not led to any kind of 'featherbedding', as is argued by free-traders, who would claim that it would reduce the efficiency of British industry. What the policy has done is give to Japanese industry the enormous profitability and power that are needed to undertake the most sweeping programmes of modernisation by which the Japs have kept ahead of their rivals in industrial technology. Again, the theory postulated by free-traders is not borne out by the facts.

British industrial revival must be pursued by methods not dissimilar to those governing the rise of Japanese industrial power — methods particularly appropriate since, like Japan, Britain is an island with a large population crowded into a comparatively restricted territory and needing to import most of its raw materials. Britain of course has the advantage over Japan of possessing huge coal reserves, plus her offshore resources of oil.

The first requirement is a declaration by government of a policy to make Britain self-supporting in all her vital requirements of manufactured goods, by the building up of a domestic industrial structure designed to supply all our needs in this field. In those industries where we have the capacity straightaway to supply all the needs of the home market, we should place an immediate embargo on foreign imports. Where this domestic capacity does not yet exist, we must set about building it by means of a declining import quota while British industries in the applicable fields are developed gradually to fill the vacuum. When these industries have been fully established, imports of the products in question should also cease completely.

Allowance should be made for a very small continuation of imports of curiosity and gift items of a highly specialised manufacture, which would never exceed more than 1 per-cent of manufactured goods sold in this country.

Parallel with this policy, a crash programme for the modernisation of Britain's entire industrial structure should be pursued in the manner of an operation of war. Government would need to establish from the outset that it intended to be the master of all economic forces within the nation and not their servant and tool. Private ownership would be regarded as the most desirable method for the running of the greater part of industry, and the profit reward for the enterprising and successful private entrepreneur would be high. On the other hand, 'privatisation' would not be allowed, as in Tory doctrine, to become a fetish. Where public concerns have shown that they can operate efficiently and cost-effectively, they should remain under the ownership of the nation. Our attitude to the constitution and organisation of every sector of industry and services would be based on the criterion of **national utility**. And every sector, private or public, would be regarded as a **national resource**, to be adapted to national needs. The freedom of private concerns to pursue their own paths of policy and development would not be absolute but would be confined within bounds laid down by government in accordance with the requirements of the nation.

One of the first tasks of government would be to ensure the organisation of all industries, and in particular the very large, capital-intensive ones, into units of a size necessary for viability in the modern world. Here it would be following the example of the Japanese Ministry for Trade and Industry (MITI), which has undertaken that operation very effectively in its own country.

Government must then reorganise the whole of the nation's financial institutions, turning them, as with the rest of the economy, into a national resource. Later I will give some attention to the question of the reform of banking so as to free British industry from the burden of usury and unpayable debt. Here it is sufficient just to mention the need to take a grip of investment policy — indeed it would be better to say introduce a proper policy for the first time, for the City of London and other financial institutions have never in the past had any policy at all that could remotely be called a national one, only the independent and self-interested policy of each financial concern. Money has always been invested in the most profitable market, quite regardless of whether it has benefited or harmed British industry. We should not attach too much blame for this to the financial concerns themselves, for they, as the guardians of the interests of their many millions of depositors and stockholders, have the obligation to invest their money in the most profitable way permitted; and under present conditions they would not be able to survive if they did otherwise. The blame lies, again, with government, which has always been too weak-willed to take the action necessary to bring these institutions within the orbit of a national policy, and put them to work to serve the productive sector of the British economy — which indeed is the sole justification for their existence.

It will of course be argued that these institutions are serving the British economy now, by using the considerable expertise they possess to make money for the nation by contributing to those 'invisible' earnings that have to be set against adverse trade balances; and this is the standard rationale of the spokesmen of the City itself. The argument does not wash, however; no policy that impoverishes the productive forces of the nation is ever, in the end, profitable from the national point of view; for every million of profit made in the way described, there is a many millionfold loss in terms of the huge trade imbalance in goods, and the need for the nation to pay for millions of its workers to be kept in idleness.

Another great fallacy of the internationalist school of economy is that the nation benefits from foreign investment in Britain. In support of this theory, huge slices of what is left of British industry have come under foreign ownership. At the time that I write these words, three out of the four mass-produced motor cars made in this country, namely those made by Ford, Vauxhall and Talbot, come out of factories that are owned by foreign capital.

And only recently an attempt was made, with all possible encouragement by the government, to turn the fourth manufacturer, Leyland, over to the Americans — this for the moment being shelved, although Leyland's truck division has been happily handed over to the Dutch manufacturer DAF. It is the same story throughout the rest of industry: when today we speak of 'British industry' we are speaking largely of the factories of the multinational conglomerates which just happen to be based in Britain but most of whose owners reside overseas.

In reality, any short-term financial benefit that is obtained through this process is overwhelmingly offset by the fact that, by means of it, our own industry simply passes out of our control, with the decisions affecting millions of our workforce made in foreign boardrooms and in accordance with the interests of the foreign owners concerned.

This has in a great many cases resulted in the closure of factories in Britain in order that production may be transferred elsewhere in the world where the owners expect to pick up fatter profits. Today, the Far East is providing an increasingly attractive proposition to the owners of the multi-nationals in this regard, with a ready pool of labour that is considerably cheaper than in western countries. As long as we see our industry as part of a 'world economy' in which free movements of capital are the norm, this process is going to accelerate, with catastrophic effects for working people in this country.

In the case of the recent would-be American take-over of Leyland, to which I have referred, it was suggested with perfect nonchalance by certain financial and industrial journalists in Britain that very likely the purpose of this intended take-over was to close Leyland, or parts of it, down. In this suggestion there was not the slightest note of outrage but only the resigned attitude that, in international big business, this was quite a routine development!

Even where ownership by the foreign multi-nationals does not result in the closure of factories and the consignment of their labour forces to the scrapheap, it is liable often to lead to a 'rationalisation' process in which factories in Britain, instead of turning out the whole product, produce only parts of it, with the remainder being produced in factories belonging to the same conglomerate but located overseas. This may, from the standpoint of the owners, be an expedient division of labour, but from the standpoint of British industry it simply further undermines self-sufficiency and increases vulnerability. The process has become advanced in the motor industry, of which I have spoken, and the results have not been to the benefit of British motor-manufacturing capacity. What happens if a strike abroad holds up the supply of parts needed here? What happens if we find ourselves in a war, and we cannot produce motor vehicles for war use without the co-operation of foreigners who may not be on our side?

This latter question is not put frivolously. The strategic dangers of an industrial machine that does not permit a self-sufficient military capacity has been amply demonstrated in both the major wars of this century. In each contingency, Britain found herself without a number of the essential components needed for arms manufacture and had to import these, mainly from America, before home production was organised to meet the need (and the latter never was accomplished totally). Correlli Barnett pinpointed this shortcoming in *The Collapse of British Power* when describing our dilemma in World War I:-

> "There were but few light engineering factories with lines of semi-automatic lathes and other machines to be converted to finishing shell-cases; few precision industries like mechanical toy and clock-making to switch to the mass manufacture of finely accurate shell fuses. Before the war Britain had imported German toys and clocks. Thus in 1915 and 1916 Britain was forced to create a light engineering industry. This attempt immediately uncovered another deficiency — there was no modern machine-tool industry capable of producing the sophisticated machines for the new production lines...Modern machine tools had been imported from Germany and the United States before the war. This deficiency was particularly appalling because a machine-tool industry was the key to every kind of modern large-scale production, in war as well as in peace — shells, fuses, aircraft, vehicles and all sorts of equipment and instrumentation. It was the purchase of American, Swedish and Swiss machine-tools that prevented a total breakdown of the British effort to create new industries between 1914 and 1916. Nevertheless, shortage of machine-tools exercised a pervasive throttling effect, not only on shell production, but also, for example, on engines and aircraft."

Government must act, not only to achieve self-sufficiency for Britain in all manufactured products, but to restore all industry in Britain to British ownership and control, for only within the framework of such a policy can there be any effective leadership and organisation of industry towards national recovery.

Not only is it essential that government take action to protect industry at national level, it is equally essential that action be taken to protect the economic structures of the nation's various regions and, where these have been undermined, to restore them again. In the regional economic imbalance that exists today in Britain we can see another appalling result of the *laissez-faire* approach. Left purely to the play of 'free-market' forces, economic units will tend to situate themselves in areas of the greatest convenience from the standpoint of immediate profits. And here, what is privately profitable will in no way be likely to correspond to what is nationally profitable.

A truly national view of the location of industry will place importance on a number of considerations, of which profitability is only one. The first consideration is to make the maximum use of national territory and resources of land. This is particularly important in the case of a country like Britain, where land is very limited in relation to the needs of the population. In these circumstances, the maximum dispersal of population is the thing to be desired, thus reducing as far as possible the tendency to excessive overcrowding in gigantic conurbations that make living barely tolerable.

Inequality of economic opportunity between regions hastens the tendency for some regions to become overcrowded and others deserted and impoverished, as population — usually comprising the youngest and most active — shifts to the former from the latter. The tendency, of course, has a snowballing effect: the more depopulated an area becomes and the poorer, relatively, become those who remain there; local business will slump yet further through declining purchasing power, and then yet more people will move away.

Travelling through the beautiful Scottish Highlands, it is difficult for one to remember that Britain is an overcrowded country. Of course, the latter is only true of certain parts which constitute quite a small proportion of the land area of the kingdom. The Highlands have become deserted, and in large part impoverished, by migration — to elsewhere in Britain and of course overseas — and all through the working of the 'free market' economic mechanism, which sucks people to currently booming districts at appalling cost to their native regions. The same is true of much of Ireland, Wales and even parts of England — all, sad to say, areas of the greatest scenic quality, the proudest local traditions, and therefore the places most congenial to a healthy life in every sense of the term.

Regional imbalance is also harmful from a strategic point of view in as much as it renders the country easier to attack by air. Bombers have a smaller area of targets, and civil defence becomes more difficult. Since the southern and eastern areas of Britain would be in the front line of any such attacks in any future war, it is all the more desirable that both industry and population should be dispersed so as to become located more in northern and western districts.

Finally, regional imbalance is politically harmful. It creates the 'two-nations' outlook; it is not conducive to national unity. In Scotland and Wales it fuels the fires of separatism, and all over it creates a spirit of resentment and envy on one hand and of falsely assumed superiority on the other.

One of the first tasks of the future must be to restore regional balance throughout Britain, both in economic development and population. Private enterprise is not likely to provide the main spur to do this; that spur must come from government, which must be prepared to channel vast investment into the country's impoverished regions by means of direct grants and incentives to industry to relocate in those areas. I am aware of course that some attempts in this direction have been made in the past and are still being made. They have failed mainly because of their meagreness of scale and because they have been pursued within the framework of an economic system that has left the international 'free market' structure entirely intact. Such schemes can only work within a reformed, national system as is being advocated here. The key to the success of such schemes can be summed up in two words: **assured markets**. It is no use whatsoever channelling massive amounts of money into 'development areas' unless the increased output of those areas which the money makes possible can be sold. Whether it can be sold abroad is always a matter of conjecture. We must start by ensuring that it can be sold at home.

As a vital part of regional renewal and economic balance, government must give all possible support to the revival of British farming. Farming in this country is most definitely not one of the industries that have suffered in consequence of inefficiency; on the contrary, it is one of the most efficient of its kind in the world. Parts of it, however, have undoubtedly suffered as a result of international agreements, mainly under the aegis of the EEC Common Agricultural Policy, by which foreign products have flooded into Britain. The lunacy of this policy is a subject deserving of a book all to itself. Suffice it to say here that Britain should opt out of it completely and adopt a policy aimed at the maximum possible self-sufficiency in food, consistent with the need to preserve part of the home market for White Commonwealth producers like New Zealand, to whom it is very much in our interests to give especially preferential terms of trade. I shall expand on this theme in a later chapter.

I am one of those who believe that a nation is not enriched when a disproportionately high part of its population moves from the land to the cities. This tendency has proceeded in Britain ever since the onset of the Industrial Revolution, and to the point at which we are now one of the most heavily urbanised nations in the world — and all without any effort on the part of government to curtail the process.

The advance in food production techniques have now rendered completely impractical the return of people to agriculture by the many millions; that occupation simply does not have the labour-intensiveness of former times. This, however, does not mean that it is impractical to envisage a very large resettlement of population in rural areas, close to, if not actually working on, the soil. New technology is making possible a widening variety of occupations that can be performed at home, such as office work by means of computer contact with central offices. These, along with the maximum revival of small cottage industries and crafts, render possible a great resurgence of rural communities.

It will not have escaped the reader that the proposals for the protection of British manufacturing and farming that I have made in this chapter are completely inconsistent with British membership of the European Common Market, the rules of which forbid such practices. It goes without saying, therefore, that I am proposing British withdrawal from the European Community as presently constituted — since no possibility exists of a changing of EEC rules to enable us to carry out such policies while remaining a member.

It must always be understood that when the architects of the EEC first conferred together to draw up plans for its formation the good of Europe and its nations were the very last things they had in mind. Later I shall give some more detailed attention to the question of our relations with our Continental European neighbours, but it should be stated clearly here that to oppose the institution of the EEC as it stands, and as it is certain to remain, is not to be 'anti-European'. Certainly, some mechanism for inter-European relations is called for which will give prospects that there will not be a repetition of the past century of bitter conflict, and I shall later propose the principles on which that mechanism might best be based. I should, however, say here that it should definitely **not** be based on the supposition that the European states have, or ever can have, absolutely identical economic interests or can ever be made successfully to conform to a common set of rules governing economic policy.

The one argument giving rise to the idea of an integrated European economy that, taken on its own, has some validity is the argument concerning the economies of scale that are possible in a very large economic area, and in this regard the United States is usually cited as the example that Europe should try to emulate.

The comparison, however, is not an acceptable one. The USA, whatever the diversity of its people's origins, is *de facto* a single national entity. Its states, it is true, have a certain tradition of local autonomy, and a conflict of interests between such states is not unheard of. No such conflict, however, seriously threatens to develop to the point at which it could override the broader American national interest. Some federal power and policies are commonly accepted as essential to the well-being of the whole. And even where state loyalties are strong they are not based, for the most part, on any distinct, uniform and exclusive ethnic heritage or language.

Furthermore, the component states and regions of America are economically complementary to each other, so as to make a natural economic unit. Texas does not compete with the Mid-West because the speciality of one is oil and cattle while that of the other is arable farming products. Southern cotton does not menace the economy of New England because the latter is not a cotton-producing area. Detroit produces most of the motor vehicles without any other district of the country feeling that it may be economically ruined by this arrangement.

No comparable situation exists in Europe. For better or for worse, and whether we like it or not, Britons, Frenchmen, Germans and Italians, etc., regard themselves primarily in terms of those nationalities and only secondly as Europeans, while some of them — particularly ourselves — feel more strongly identified with certain peoples thousands of miles from Europe than with near neighbours in Europe. There is not, in other words, a European Nation, no matter how sweet and wonderful that idea may appear to some Europeans as a hypothesis.

In consequence of this, most Europeans still look on such

institutions as the EEC as something to which their nations are joined (where this is the case) primarily out of national convenience, for the pursuit of national interests, and just for as long as membership is thought to serve those interests. European assemblies and conferences are gatherings to which delegates go primarily to extract from them the greatest possible advantages for the nation-states that they represent. Even where these delegates may themselves feel more as Europeans than as members of their respective nations, they nevertheless represent electorates at home which expect them to uphold national interests, and they are thus always strictly limited in the commitment they can give to any overall European perspective or policy.

At the same time, the economies of the European states are much more similar to each other, and therefore much more mutually competitive, than are those of the regions of the USA. Britain and West Germany, for instance, are two countries of almost identical size, population and resources — with the one difference that West Germany does not possess our offshore oil and gas reserves. Both depend very heavily on manufacturing and both have to import food.

France and Italy, while traditionally more agrarian and less industrialised, have in recent decades been developing in a direction which brings their economies into ever closer similarity with our own and the Germans'. And so it is also with Spain, albeit that she is perhaps 10-20 years behind France and Italy in the progress she is making along the same road.

Holland and Belgium are merely reproductions of Britain and West Germany on a smaller scale. Only Denmark, specialising in dairy farming, and Portugal and Greece, in fruits, wines and tourism, differ substantially in their economic structures, and they represent only about 7 per-cent of the Community in population and much less in economic statistics.

France, Italy, Spain, Portugal and Greece are important wine-producers, as is West Germany (though to a lesser portion of GNP), and will therefore compete with one another in this field — a competition which at times has escalated into great antagonism.

Thus it may be seen that between the nations of the EEC there is not, in economic terms, a concurrence of interests, but a substantial conflict of interests. They largely produce the same things and in a surplus that requires that much of what they produce has to be exported. The natural customers for their exports are expected to be their fellow EEC countries. Is it any wonder that this state of affairs has brought much more inter-European quarrelling than European unity?

Of course, the ultimate purpose of the Euro-planners is to rationalise the Community's industrial and farming production to the point at which much of this competition is eliminated. But this is wholly unacceptable, and quite rightly so, to the nation-states in question, which see as a consequence the dismantling of huge parts of their traditional economic bases and the throwing of millions of their workers into idleness. This process has gone further here in Britain than anywhere else — which is not unconnected with the fact that it is here in Britain that the EEC is the least popular.

None of this is to deny the point at which this dissertation began: that economies of large-scale production do have definite advantages in certain fields of industry. The decisive question, however, is whether an economic community of the Western European nations as constituted by the EEC is necessary to achieve that objective, or indeed provides, from Britain's point of view, the best area of co-operation for its achievement. To put it another way, if it is accepted that there are certain industrial and technological undertakings so large and expensive as to be beyond the resources of Britain alone (at least without intolerable strain and cost), why must we always necessarily look across the Channel to Europe to find the partners with whom we tackle such undertakings?

The truth is that we do so, not out of any particular economic logic, but essentially because the drive to European integration has always been first and foremost a **political** one, and it is a case of inventing economic reasons for justifying this political aim and idea rather than unifying Europe politically in order to achieve economic objectives.

The programme that I have outlined for industrial recovery in Britain will clearly be seen to involve an operation of reconstruction bigger than anything we have attempted in our history. This, needless to say, will invite the question: how is it all to be paid for? Private investment will of course account for a great deal of the money required to expand and modernise existing industries and build new industries. Past evidence, however, does not show that private enterprise always provides the needed elixir of economic vigour. I have mentioned how, in two world wars, state action was needed to create certain industries vital to arms production. Most certainly, state action on a massive scale will be required in this new undertaking, and that will need a vast investment of the nation's money. How is it to be done?

It must be done by our first of all ridding ourselves of certain well entrenched misconceptions about the nature and function of money. Money is not, as economists of the current orthodoxy would have it, a finite resource of which we can only obtain so much, and then, when it runs out, cease all operations that depend upon it until more comes along. Money is merely a token of our ability to produce. In this respect, it is in the same category as tickets printed for the purpose of enabling people to take holiday flights to the Continent. No-one ever suggests that such holiday flights must be suspended at such time as the supply of the tickets runs out. Our capacity to print the tickets is limitless. The only limit is on the number of people desirous and able to make the flights. We therefore do not fix the number of flights in accordance with the tickets available; we fix the number of tickets to be printed in accordance with the numbers of travellers.

It is basically the same with money — although this fact has been largely lost sight of. Money itself does not limit the possibilities of national economic expansion and construction; those possibilities are only limited by the optimum of human labour, skills and materials available. What can be done by these things, money can be printed to finance being done. Such a printing of money is not inflationary if, by the harnessing of labour, skills and materials, new quantities of real national wealth are created to an equivalent value.

Who can possibly say that with nearly three million people in Britain unemployed, and with a population of 57 million available to buy the goods and services they would be producing or rendering if only they were employed, Britain is today anywhere near the limits of its economic capacity when it is measured in these real terms? The materials are there. The labour is there. The skills are there. They are simply waiting to be put to productive use. It is no more inappropriate to print the money to finance this use than it is to print the tickets for a series of aeroplane flights for which we know there is ample demand!

But, contrary to all common sense, such printing of money has come to be regarded as one of the great iniquities by our modern politicians and economists. When new money is needed, their minds are capable of conceiving only one way of obtaining it: by borrowing! In borrowing such money, of course, they incur a debt on behalf of the nation, which has to be repaid with interest. This was just how such money was raised in the hyper-inflationary period of the 1970s, when there was plenty of it about but it was all the time rapidly decreasing in value. What we were never told was the real truth as to why it was inflationary.

The element making for inflation was not the fact that new money was being created; had that money been applied to the creation of real national wealth to an equivalent value, the process would never have been inflationary. What made for inflation was that the money was being brought into existence in the form of bank loans, repayable at the very high rate of interest that had then become the norm. This interest became an increasing burden on everyone who was borrowing money at the time: government, commerce and industry, and the individual citizen. But not only that, it became a burden also on everyone who was buying anything. As the cost of every item of goods or services for sale has to take into account every cost involved in bringing it to the customer, including the servicing of any debts owing by the supplier, it needs no mathematical genius to deduce that, with a rapidly rising burden of interest on debts owed by every sector of the economy to the banks, there would be a rapid rise in prices.

The Tory government that took office in 1979 promised loudly that it would bring down inflation; and so it has — but not in a way that has brought the slightest benefit to the economy. All that the Tories have done is reduce borrowing and therefore check the spiralling burden of debt-interest on the nation. The result of course is that what the nation has gained by the reduction of inflation it has lost by there being a chronic shortage of money — since the same government refuses to countenance any alternative method of creating money to that of borrowing it at interest.

But how, some readers may ask, is money 'created' by being lent by the banks? Surely, when money is lent it is money already in existence and is merely being transferred from one possessor to another, i.e. from possession of the bank to possession of the borrower?

This of course would be the case if the loan transaction was between Smith and his next-door neighbour, Jones. It is also the case when any goods are bought from a shop on credit. The shop is in effect lending the purchaser money to the value of the goods by transferring those goods to his possession without immediate payment. The shop does not conjure the goods out of the air; they are part of stock for which it has paid. No new element of wealth is being created by the transaction; location and custody of wealth already existing (i.e. the goods) are merely being changed.

But this is not what happens when money is lent by the banks. We all know that when we negotiate a bank loan for, say, £10,000, we do not normally have £10,000 handed to us by the bank in notes or coin; the bank simply authorises us to write out cheques to an amount of £10,000 in excess of the money we have in our account, in other words to overdraw by £10,000.

It is popularly assumed that a bank would not do this unless it had somewhere in its vaults notes, coin, gold or other items to the value of that £10,000 — and indeed every other sum of money that it lent to its account-holders — in other words, that if, currently, that bank's account-holders owed it a total of £1 billion, somewhere in the possession of the bank there would be actual cash or other items to the value of that £1 billion.

In reality, this does not happen in modern banking as practised in Britain. It does not happen because experience has taught the bankers that, except in very special emergencies, only a fraction of the money required by borrowers is ever asked for in cash; almost all of it is obtained by the writing of cheques. The banks need to keep cash in reserve only to the extent required to meet these customers' cash demands. They can therefore, almost at any time, allow their borrowers a total credit amounting to many times the actual money they have in their possession!

I ask the reader to ponder on this carefully and pause for a few moments to consider the implications of it. In fact it amounts to the counterfeiting of money by the banks on a massive scale, a scale amounting to inestimable billions. I ask the reader to suppose for a moment that he wrote out a cheque for £10,000 in payment for some transaction, while in fact he only had one tenth of that amount in his bank account, and had had no permission from his bank manager for an overdraft. He would of course be passing a 'dud cheque', and would be breaking the law. As soon as the cheque was returned to his bank, this would be discovered and the bank would stop payment on it. During the time, however, that elapsed between his writing the cheque and the bank stopping payment on it — and presuming that the payee accepted it on face value — a sum of £10,000 would have been brought into existence that was not in existence before. £10,000 would have been newly 'created'.

If then we take into account that, when banks create money in this way by the authorising of the writing of cheques, there does not exist at the other end of the cheques' journey that corrective mechanism resulting from the money to cover payment being there at the bank, we may quickly glean that the banks are all the time engaging in the practice of writing 'dud cheques', or at least authorising such cheques to be written on their-behalf, on a scale many millions of times that operated by the ordinary credit swindler.

For, of course, when the banks are paid back, with interest, for these 'loans', they are paid in **real money**. The money has to be earned by honest economic activity by the man who does the repaying. That money becomes added to the bank's financial resources as and when it is paid in. And yet that same money does not get subtracted from the bank's resources when it is originally 'lent'.

The banks, in doing this, cannot themselves be accused of criminality because they are not in fact breaking the law, amazing though this may seem. Indeed they are permitted by government to get away with the practice, which is recognised by the latter as monetary 'orthodoxy'! Why they are so allowed is a question which leads us once again back to a theme that has been repeated with recurring frequency throughout this book: that under our so-called 'democratic' party political system it is not government that is truly in control of affairs but the bankers that are in control of government!

The procedure is amply explained by the economist and financial journalist Robert Beckman in his book *The Downwave:-*

> "At the root of banking is the 'fractional reserve' system where money can be created by the banks. Banks in Britain (along with those in most other countries, supposedly under the watchful eye of the Bank of England, the Federal Reserve, or some other central bank) may not only lend the money they have on deposit, but may also lend several times that amount. How many times depends on the existing fractional reserve requirements...If the reserve requirement is 10 per-cent, the banks can lend £900 for every £100 on deposit. You can now begin to see how the system may have some built-in perils. But the fault is not with the system but the way it is operated."

From the last sentence, it will be clear that the writer of these words is not, as our movement is, an opponent of the basics of this banking procedure; he only believes that there are certain hazards in it if it is not applied carefully. When he speaks of the system having "some built-in perils," he is making what must be close to the understatement of the century. At least, however, it is gratifying to get an admission of how the system works from one of its own partisans. Mr. Beckman's diagnosis was in fact corroborated by no less a servant of the same system, The Hon, Reginald McKenna, Chairman of Midland Bank, who said in 1924:-

"The ordinary citizen will not like to be told that the banks can create and destroy money. The amount of money in existence varies only with the action of the banks in increasing or diminishing deposits. We know how this is effected. Every bank loan and every bank purchase of securities creates a deposit, and every repayment of a bank loan and every bank sale destroys one."

From these facts it will be seen that, as long as the system is preserved, inflation is inevitable. All new money now coming into the economy does so as interest-bearing debt. This means that if this debt is all to be repaid it would require a total repayment sum (taking into account the interest) far in excess of what the economy can supply, even if all the populace is sucked dry in the effort to repay it. It is therefore, in effect, unpayable. Scheduled repayments of loans can only be made by the contracting of new loans, thus all the time increasing the millstone of interest around the neck of the economy. And all the time the banks are sucking a regular tribute from the producing sectors of the economy in the manner of a latter-day 'Danegeld'. Even where the loans cannot be repaid, this is of small account to the banks, as such loans are not normally made without security. All the time, the banks are profiting in the form of a huge income by means of the interest paid on these 'loans' — which in the first place they only made by means of a book or computer entry. They are getting something for almost nothing. Their sole expenditure is the upkeep of their buildings, the payment of their staff and the fraction of obligations they have to meet in the form of hard cash. Compared with what they are taking in, this is, as the saying goes, 'small beer'.

The only interruption to this happy existence is when there is a panic, and account-holders seek to draw out their holdings in hard cash all or largely at one time. This can happen when confidence in the banks is shaken, and it creates what is known as a 'run on the banks'. It happened in 1929, and a number of banks, unable in that situation to meet their obligations, were ruined — along of course with vast numbers of their customers. The present chaos in the world financial system, with its mind-boggling scale of unrepayable debt, indicates that this could happen again before too long. We can be quite sure, however, that, if it does, those to suffer least will be the individuals controlling the international banking system, for they will be the first ones to know about the impending crash and will be able to transfer their assets to places where they will not be affected. The real losers will be, as in the past, the millions of ordinary honest businesses, as well as ordinary account-holders of other kinds, who will have all their reserves and savings swept away.

Inflation is inevitable under the system because, as has been said, the loans contracted by the economy can never be repaid, and therefore the element of interest is always increasing. All that is variable is the extent and pace of the increase. When government operates an 'easy money' policy, the pace is very fast — hence rapid inflation. When, and usually in consequence of this, the policy changes to one of a restriction of money, the level at which the element of interest is increasing slows down, and therefore inflation slows down with it. But the price that we pay for this easing of the rate of inflation is a starving of the economy of money, leading inevitably to a running down of the forces of production — just as if flight tickets for the air travel mentioned earlier were withdrawn and no-one would accept any substitutes for the tickets as tokens of people having paid for the flights. In this latter event, the flights would cease.

This factor, added to the invasion of imports with which I have dealt earlier, is the reason why we have chronic unemployment. The employment situation would be somewhat improved if the government were to return to an 'easy money' policy and thus create more consumer purchasing power. But that of course would, under the present system, restore things to the rampant inflation of the 1970s.

The only solution is to change the entire system, to reform the whole procedure by which money is created for the expansion of the economy. Private banks must be relieved of their privilege of creating money, and that privilege must become solely the prerogative of government. Government must exercise that prerogative by feeding new money into the economy, not as a loan repayable at interest, but as a free grant. The extent of the grant must be measured carefully in accordance with the estimated increase in national wealth that will become possible by means of the increased economic activity which the new money will generate. Obviously, in such estimates error is possible, and indeed, within certain limits, probable. A corrective mechanism can soon evolve, however. Should new money in any year not be matched by the expected increase in real wealth during that year, and should there be, as a result, a degree of inflation, in the next year there can be an adjustment downwards to remedy this. When such a system is working smoothly, as very soon it could do, we would be likely to suffer, at worst, an alternative inflation and deflation of no more than 1 per-cent a year. Over the longer term, money would retain its constant value.

It need hardly be stated that under these circumstances that element in prices representing the burden of interest borne by the economy would whittle eventually down to zero. Vast new financial resources, of a scale undreamt of under the old system, would become available for economic expansion. The only limits would be those mentioned earlier: the limits of labour, skills and materials. Our principle for economic development would be that what is physically possible is financially possible.

By what means would government effect this regular flow of money into the economy? There are alternative solutions, one of which is advanced by the Social Creditors: this is a regular free issue of money to every member of the population, to be known as a 'national dividend'. This would be calculated according to the yearly growth in the national economy just as dividends to a company's shareholders are calculated in accordance with yearly profit figures.

This system has some merits, and is vastly preferable to the present one of interest-slavery. I believe, however, that it is not the best available. Part, if not the whole, of the national dividend paid to the people by one hand would have to be taken away again by the other in the form of taxation to finance public services, thus requiring a huge bureaucracy to administer the operation.

Vastly preferable is that government, having ascertained from its economic advisers the rate at which new money can be created consistently with the growth of the economy, should allocate that money to meet the demands of public expenditure. Where those demands exceed the money that can be created in this way, the balance would of course have to be raised by taxation. At the most pessimistic estimate, however, taxation could be reduced to a fraction of its present level. We must not forget that a huge portion of taxation today goes to meet the servicing of the National Debt, that is to say the interest on all the monies that governments have borrowed in the past under the old and fraudulent system. With the methods advocated here, the National Debt could eventually be eliminated. Legitimate creditors, such as ordinary national savings bond-holders, could be paid off. On the other h͏   ͏ ͏ts incurred with the banks by means of the 'fractional reserve' system of lending should be repudiated. The same principle would of course apply to debts around the necks of local government.

The private banks should at the same time be prohibited from lending money in excess of that on deposit; in other words, they would be made subject to just the same rules of trading as any other commercial concerns. They could not lend or invest what they didn't have. This would of course force them to other practices to remain profitable. They would most certainly have to raise charges but not necessarily interest rates. We must not forget that in an inflation-free economy the rates paid to depositors would not need to be anything like as high. This would offset the loss of profits elsewhere, so that that loss would not have to be thrown, if at all, too heavily on borrowers in the form of increased borrowing rates. At the same time, however, companies and individuals who today have to borrow heavily from the banks would enjoy such immense relief in the way of reduced taxation that this would far more than offset the loan-interest rates and increased charges. With much faster capital accumulation through this tax relief, the need for borrowing would anyway be greatly less.

In effect, what is being proposed here is nothing less than a complete revolution in our whole financial system, which would form merely a part of a wider revolution in the entire system of economy. Account-holders at banks would have to pay a realistic price for the service of those banks of keeping their money in safe custody, a price which today is mainly hidden by being incorporated into the enormous profits made by the banks in exercising the privilege of manufacturing the nation's money and getting paid for doing it at the people's expense. On the other hand, the account-holder would be spared paying enormous taxes and rates to help fund government and municipal debts to the banking system, as well as paying, in respect of every item of goods and services he buys, a huge tribute owed by the supplier to the bankers. In the end, the whole people, other than the bankers, would be immeasurably better off.

Needless to say, much of the newly created money used by government to finance public expenditure would find its way into the pockets of the people, either directly by means of the wages paid to public employees or indirectly by means of wages paid by those companies with which the government would do business, thus further enhancing consumer purchasing power.

This revolution would go hand in hand with the revolution in our industrial and trading system. British industry would be organised to cater for an assured home market protected by trade barriers against imported produce. This home market would be boosted by full employment and high wages, making possible great purchasing power. The need to import would be reduced to raw materials and a portion (less than now) of our food and drink, creating a correspondingly reduced need to export.

Virtually all our necessary imports could be obtained from countries of the Old Commonwealth and South Africa, with whom, by offering trade preferences, we would be able to build good fraternal links quite independently of any political ties. In a later chapter I shall have something to say about the need to pursue a new form of association with Australia, New Zealand and Canada to replace the old Empire that our politicians have destroyed and the ludicrous and ineffectual Commonwealth structure they have erected in its place. In the meantime, however, it can safely be stated that such an association would not be necessary to a decision by Britain to increase her purchases from these countries to the maximum; that decision can be made at any time, Empire or no Empire, Commonwealth or no Commonwealth.

Cutting adrift from the old financial system at national level is not quite the same thing as cutting adrift from it at international level. We cannot do the latter with our present dependence on international trade, for that trade involves heavy recourse to international financial institutions for credit facilities both in buying and selling. With a vastly reduced international trade commitment, and that commitment mainly with the same regular customers, we should attempt as far as possible to carry out our trading transactions by the method of barter, which cuts out the international moneylender and strengthens our immunity to the storms and stresses of the increasingly unstable international financial system.

I have mentioned earlier the need to control the forces of private investment in Britain so as to direct them into channels needed for the reinvigoration of British industry. Such control, however, is also essential for another reason. In a free international money market, investment flows where interest rates are greatest. In effect, this has meant in recent times that world interest rates have been pegged to whatever is the current American rate, other borrowers of course having to raise their rates to a competitive level to attract investment away from the American market. To get interest rates down it is essential to break this tie with American rates, and that can only be done by denying British investors access to the international market except in specific cases allowed by government, and directing British investment into Britain.

This chapter would not be complete without a further look at one final area of vital importance to economic revival, and this is the area of industrial relations. I have spoken of the weakness of the Thatcher government in dealing with trade unionism, a weakness born of lack of resolve but also of the lack of an intelligent policy and strategy. In fact no hope whatever exists of achieving an effective system of industrial relations in Britain as long as the old Tory and Labourite mentalities remain in control of our destinies. The latter is financially, spiritually, and even physically, enslaved to reactionary trade unionism, while the former is dominated by attitudes which constantly allow the game of industrial relations to be played on ground of the choosing of its adversaries.

Get on any commuter train wending its way into London from the genteel suburbs, and if you hear any political conversation at all it is likely to include much cursing of the latest group of industrial workers demanding wage rises — with the comment that these rises, if granted, will only force up inflation by increasing the prices of the goods or services that those workers provide. Tory leadership is the captive of this very same outlook, as speeches from Tory platforms clearly bear out. When such pay demands are granted, it is only in a spirit of capitulation that this is done; the Tory conviction remains that the granting of them will lead prices to rise, and almost always it does — though for reasons that that same Tory mind can never comprehend. Pay rises in one sector cause prices to rise in the service rendered by that sector. In time this leads to a general inflation, with the result that pay rises are then demanded in other sectors — for the workers in those sectors have no alternative if they are not to see their living standards fall, perhaps to the extent of their mortgage payments not being met and their homes lost.

To the Tory mind, this refusal of groups of workers to forfeit their living standards, and sometimes their homes as well, is an utterly unreasonable attitude; far better that these workers should show themselves prepared to make such sacrifices, necessitated though they may be by economic forces far beyond those workers' control. That, in the Tory book, would be the 'patriotic' response;

when such a response is not forthcoming, the workers in question are eagerly designated 'unpatriotic'.

But of course the reality is that wage rises are not themselves the basic cause of inflation at all! Demands for them are merely the inevitable **consequence** of the inflationary process described earlier, a process brought about by the banking system and its debt-financing of the economy. In an economy freed from this debt- and interest-slavery, there would be a constantly enduring relationship between money in circulation and real wealth to buy. This would mean that a wage-rise in one sector of the economy not backed up by increased production and profits, and therefore followed by a corresponding price-rise in that sector, could not occur without a parallel price-reduction in some other sector (or sectors). General inflation would therefore be impossible; all that would be possible would be inflation in the prices of some goods or services parallelled by deflation in the prices of others — and in accordance with the laws of supply and demand.

But the point is that in a properly regulated monetary system, without the built-in inflationary tendency caused by the interest factor, the pressure for wage-rises as it now exists would no longer exist. With no wage-rises, living standards could be maintained at their existing level. Naturally then, if production and profits increased, there would be a good case for such rises, and they could be granted without a resulting rise in the price of the product or service in question. As it is now, with a wage-freeze (as attempted by the last Labour government) living standards must inevitably go down as prices go up.

No possibility whatever exists of bringing true industrial peace and order to Britain until these truths are grasped, and we abandon the illusion that inflation originates in wage-rises and tackle that inflation at its proper source: the bankers' 'Danegeld'.

This having been done, and full employment having been assured by the policies set out here, the conditions will be achieved for a whole new era of industrial co-operation in this country, an era which must be hastened in by revolutionary changes in our whole industrial relations system.

The old system, we must always remember, was born in the era of unbridled capitalism, and was made inevitable by that era and the conditions pertaining to it. Labour had to organise to defend itself against capital because no-one else would undertake that defence. With government having abdicated the task of regulating economic forces in a just balance of rights and duties between these two components of the wealth-creating process, and of protecting capital (and thus also labour) against cut-price foreign competition, labour was left with no alternative but to regard itself as an entity entirely separate from capital and with conflicting interests, instead of — as should have been the case — one of two complementary and interdependent elements of the same economic process, and with one single interest in the success of that process. So it has remained to this day.

The integration and co-ordination of industry in a single policy of national economic development will entirely remove the need for labour and capital to be seen as two competing and mutually antagonistic forces. With this, there will be removed the need for separate institutions to represent these two elements of industry; instead they can, and should, be merged into one single institution with a single purpose and aim: a just deal for **all** those who contribute to economic prosperity, whether by hand, brain or money.

Such an institution should be empowered to settle all industrial disputes, as it may be able to do with complete impartiality, being representative, not of capital or labour, but the entire nation.

To this, the question may be asked: would a worker still have the right to withdraw his labour if he found the terms of his employment unacceptable? The answer is that he would have that right in the only form in which it has any real meaning and can be effectively asserted: he can transfer his labour to another employer. Such a right is of small comfort or value in the present climate, where unemployment is at record level and alternative jobs are like gold dust in a deserted mine. But in a condition of full employment, and with a consequent seller's market for labour, the situation would be totally transformed. In those circumstances, business has the true spur to treat good labour as a priceless asset, not to be alienated by low wages or otherwise unsatisfactory conditions of work.

Nothing is more ludicrous, pathetic, and indeed dishonest, than for the defenders of the present system to claim that the British worker has 'freedom' merely because of the right to strike. Very often the reality is that he is not free **not** to strike — unless he wishes to get his home burned to the ground and himself, his wife and his family exposed to vicious physical attack. And if he does join a strike, to what can he look forward? Perhaps more than a year of constant shortages and privations, even sometimes hunger, together with the demoralisation of enforced idleness in his most active years — as befell many thousands of miners during the 1984 coal dispute that has been mentioned. Of course, for those who got fed up with the whole miserable ordeal, there was very little chance, in the areas in question, to go out and get alternative jobs. So where did this 'right to strike' get the miners in the end?

Despite this reality, there are still many people in British politics who insist upon the 'right' of large groups of workers to condemn themselves to a year or more of idle misery and semi-starvation as if this were one of the most sacred pillars of liberty and of a civilised order of life. People imprisoned in this habit of thinking simply show that their outlooks have failed to move forward one inch since the days of the Tolpuddle Martyrs.

The new system of industry will render these archaic practices completely unnecessary and superfluous — not in such a way as to leave workers with less rights, but indeed to leave them with far more. The rights and freedoms of the worker reach their highest level when there is abundant employment, the demand for labour is constant in every area of the country, and that labour therefore has real bargaining power. We can then dispense with much of the top-heavy, and entirely unproductive, machinery of industrial relations with which we are now encumbered and which, in the new era, will have about as much use as horse transport; and in the process we can put to useful employment, in many cases for the first time in their lives, the army of parasites, trouble-makers and professional windbags who today enjoy swank hotels and Jaguars on the workers' dues.

Our alternative industrial relations machinery would only require to be a fraction of the size, and cost only a fraction of the expense, of the present one — which of course is one reason why it will be fanatically opposed by all the tin-pot caesars who luxuriate in jobs under the present system. They see in the dragging of British trade unionism into the modern age the disappearance of the comfortable semi-sinecures they have long held as if by divine right, as well as the licence to mischief that they crave as compensation for their manifest personal inadequacies. No, Britain will be none the poorer for these people's disappearance from the scene!

There is another vital benefit to be obtained from full employment. Not until we have achieved that condition can we with justice tackle the problem of society's habitual shirkers. Today a large army of these individuals have battened onto our

welfare state, having made a thorough science out of the exploitation of our 'compassion' and our desire to help the unfortunate.
These are people without the slightest intention of settling down to
regular honest work, even if it were offered them. Far from their
merely obtaining from the state the bare means to survive, many
of them seem to be able to extract enough public charity to be able
to run up-to-date motor cars and even enjoy holidays abroad. In
many cases, of course, this is made possible by drawing dole and
social security cheques while continuing to do jobs 'on the side',
meaning in effect that such people are not 'unemployed' at all. It is
not surprising that these lead-swinging legions have become a
national scandal.

The response of the old parties to the problem, however, does
not give us any promise that it will ever be tackled satisfactorily.
The Labour Party knows that it has many voters among the shirker
brigade, and it has no intention of losing them by adopting a firm
policy for getting them off the nation's back. Labour leaders, who
always tend naturally anyway to identify with the dregs of society
(many of whom are their most active constituency members),
have continued, and probably will continue, to run away from this
national problem as they have run away from every other.

The Tory attitude is somewhat sterner, but here there is another
disadvantage. Placed alongside the professional idlers in the
claims for welfare benefits are great numbers of people who are
out of work through no fault of their own, who cannot get work,
and whose need of public assistance is therefore perfectly
genuine.

Tory spokesmen do no service to the problem by the extravagant over-generalisations they are apt to make about it,
designating everyone as a 'shirker' and a 'sponger' who happens
to need public help, and not discriminating between those who
rightly come into those categories and those who are simply the
unwilling victims of mass unemployment.

When, and only when, we have created an economic situation
in which there is ample work in every area for anyone who
seriously wants it, can we set about the task of getting the real
welfare loafers off the nation's back — for when people remain
out of work in such a situation of abundant work (assuming they
are not hindered by any disability) there is good reason to believe
they simply do not want work.

As a test of an unemployed person's willingness to work, I am
in favour of introducing a scheme similar to the 'Workfare'

system operated in certain states of the USA — and in fact a system that I was advocating in pamphlets and articles in the 1970s, before I and most others in this country had heard of its introduction anywhere else. The system is that all welfare benefits, except in the case of the old, sick or disabled, are given only in return for work. Claimants are employed in repairing or maintaining public amenities, or otherwise hired out by the welfare authority to local firms which need a bit of temporary labour. The scheme has two benefits: one is that it is good for the self-respect of those involved; the other is that it discourages welfare spongers by demonstrating to everyone that there is no 'free ride'; no-one can get 'something for nothing'.

In this chapter I have put forward a series of proposals for the economic regeneration of Britain. They are for the most part proposals for which I do not claim any originality. Most of them have been advocated in this country before in some form or another, but turned down because the interests opposing them had more political influence and power than those supporting them — or because they offended against ancient superstitions that ruled the minds of those in government at the time. In places overseas, they have been tried and found to work, and I am in no doubt that they will work in our own country if adopted.

They are proposals that take us far beyond the sterile conflict between capitalism and socialism, which is a conflict belonging to an age now past and one of no relevance to the problems of today or tomorrow — though this fact seems to have made no impression on the minds of our old-world politicians, who re-enact the same clapped-out debate in the interminable exchanges of the old-party bunfight.

I proposed the alternative doctrine in *Beyond Capitalism and Socialism*, the pamphlet that I wrote in the 1970s and to which I have referred. The facts and proposals set out in that work are valid today, simply being given extra force by a series of developments affecting the economy since. The alternative doctrine I called 'Economic Nationalism', and while this is a simplification it is the most appropriate description of short length that is available. The doctrine advocates the mobilisation and organising by national government of all the nation's economic resources public and private, in a co-ordinated national programme for the achievement of national prosperity, strength and power — and in pursuit of goals of economic development that are conceived, not four years or five years, but fifty years ahead of time. The doctrine strives to take the nation's economic future out of the arena of cheapjack party politics, with their daily jostling for momentary factional advantage, and elevate it to a level at which it commands the selfless dedication of a united people, working for aims which, though they do indeed include material betterment, do not make that a be-all-and-end-all, aims which include national security, freedom and honour, national and racial health and the preservation of the best of national tradition and culture.

In putting forward these aims, I have stressed, and I stress again, that no worthwhile economic policy can be carried out without there being present the requisite political power and will. Economic reform and political reform must therefore be seen as two vital components in a single policy of national regeneration.

Let there be no doubt about it: the new economics will not be achieved by means of the old politics. The necessary political instrument must be forged before the desired economic changes become possible. Politics must lead, and not be led by, economic forces.

Chapter 15
A new land and a new people

In the late 1950s and early 1960s I took three holidays on the European Continent in which I attempted to see as many countries as possible, each holiday being condensed into the space of a fortnight. In the first two cases I hitch-hiked and in the third case I took a car.

On my return, as I vividly remember, I always had the same impression. This was of the shabbiness and seediness of much of Britain — by comparison with the places where I had just been. The contrast was most noticeable in the cities and larger towns. My memory of the return journeys is of dilapidated railway stations staffed by scruffy looking porters, of ugly and badly planned town centres and squalid suburbs, all noticeable for an abundance of dirt and litter, of large numbers of unhealthy looking people whose faces, bearing and attire showed little signs of personal pride. It all had the aspect of a concern that was under bad management, thoroughly run-down and where no-one seemed to care.

This is of course something of a generalisation, and there were, and are, many places that are an exception to the rule. In the land of Britain there is a heritage of history and beauty, natural and man-made, that is unexcelled anywhere. There are many magnificent buildings. There are some towns — notably, York, Bath, Oxford, Norwich, Chester, Edinburgh and Aberdeen — that have some very fine views and are a delight to visit. There are places where the people look more alive than in others. None of this alters the fact, however, that much of our country needs a massive face-lift. It could be the finest-looking land in the world if we troubled to make it so, but the problem is that not enough of us do trouble. Least of all do we get a lead from government in the matter.

Over the past two decades there has been a huge outpouring of literature and talk about the 'environment', with a mushrooming of organisations, even a political party, supposedly dedicated to environmental improvement. Yet the more the fuss over the matter the worse things seem to become. Since the times of my return from Europe that I have mentioned, this has certainly been so. Brighton, near where I live, is an example: I remember thinking around 1960 that it was one of our better towns; since then it has sadly deteriorated.

While there is much in the way of good intentions in the environmentalist lobby, I am convinced that most who belong to this lobby approach the problem from entirely the wrong angle. In the first place, they suppose, quite wrongly, that a proper renewal of our environment can be achieved in a climate of liberalism and under our ancient and established political institutions. I am convinced that it cannot. Education and 'lobbying' are not alone sufficient to accomplish the task; these must be backed up by a strong element of national discipline that today is entirely lacking in this country and which is only going to come through radical political change of a nature which I suspect most environmentalists, conservationists and ecologists would be loath at this stage to accept. We British have become, in large part, a sloppy people. Until this changes, the surroundings in which we live are going to be a mess. In a previous chapter I have given some sketches of the requirements of such a change. Our starting point, as I have proposed, must be the young. A new generation must be bred which will practise a new code of citizenship, and in the training for this, both at school age and after, we should not be reluctant to bring military influences to bear on those concerned. Tidiness, cleanliness and a good appearance of neighbourhood and person are first of all matters of **pride** — and that is only inculcated in institutions that are the absolute opposite of 'liberal'.

Next, the appalling anarchy in urban design that has resulted in the disfigurement of so many of our towns and cities today, and which is surely the greatest environmental sore, is the product of the same 'liberal' spirit at municipal level. In the case of Britain, the phenomenon has deeper roots than almost anywhere else in Europe. The magnificent cities of the Continent, with their spaciousness, symmetry and overwhelming impression of **civic pride** and **planning**, have in almost all cases been the product of a political tradition in which strong public authority has prevailed over commercial forces dedicated only to utility and profit. In Britain, across the ages, the dominance of the public interest over the commercial one has been badly lacking, and nothing has been done to change this, despite the laws which in theory demand that local authority consent be given for all private building and development. On the contrary, town and city councils have everywhere formed an unholy alliance with the developers in the mutilation of the urban landscape. The calibre of individual that now sits on these local bodies makes this hardly surprising. Quite apart from the factor of bribery and corruption, as highlighted in the T. Dan Smith affair in Newcastle-upon-Tyne some years ago, there is the never-ending local party political game. The party in current control of a council is constantly cocking its eye to the next round of local government elections, and in this regard is looking for ways to finance its own vote-catching schemes without too much increase of the rates charged to local householders. Big office, shop and department store developments, together with multi-story car parks, right in the centre of town, bring in much revenue. To councillors not in the first place imbued with much in the way of civic pride or local tradition, this is a tempting prospect — and one to which, on present evidence, there is little resistance.

Local government in Britain must be removed from the 'market place' where it is just another business bent on making profits, and made subject to a firm national authority which obliges it to serve the community in the way that it should.

Here, as in so many other spheres, the ideals of those who care deeply about our environment simply cannot be realised effectively until we accept the need for a political **power** in the land enabled to prevail over all the many and varied interests that stand in the way of the necessary action.

And there is one more vital respect in which the environmentalists are lacking in an answer to the problems to which they devote so much ink and talk. They speak of conserving the quality of this and the quality of that, but never a word is heard from them about the most important conservation of all, which is that of the **British people** — in both their quantity and quality, but especially the latter. At the end of the day, even if — and it is a big 'if' — we create the right political conditions and attitudes for the attainment of a fine country to live in, our ability to achieve this depends most of all on the type of **people** we produce, not only in respect of their upbringing, education and training, but on the biological inheritance of intelligence, character and health with which they are born in the first place.

It is an astonishing anomaly that, in a society in which we acknowledge the need for **selective breeding** of almost every living species in order to improve the quality of the type, we are totally indifferent to these breeding laws when it comes to the most important species of all, and the one on which we most depend for the raising of the quality of everything: man himself. Among those who determine what is sometimes called 'public policy' in Britain are included farmers, racehorse-owners, dog-breeders, gardeners and horticulturalists, all of whom recognise as an elementary truth of life the importance of **race quality** and of the need to nurture the mating of the best. But these same people would in all likelihood raise their hands in horror at the proposition that such rules should be applied to the human species, stigmatising it as 'racism'. They seem not to recognise that if 'racism' were not applied in the process of food-production, for instance, the whole community would soon starve!

Obviously, this is not to suggest that human beings could be subject to the same clinical process of arbitrary selection as members of the animal and plant world, but what it does suggest is that we should preserve our country for those people of British and related European stocks who gave it its identity, character and high level of human achievement, so that these, by natural individual choice, would marry among, and reproduce, their own kind. It should also mean that society's scale of incentives and rewards should be such as to encourage, among our native stocks, the highest birthrates on the part of the best endowed and accomplished. 'Conservation' is nothing more than a meaningless piece of verbiage unless it includes this principle — and indeed starts with it.

In recent times, the nation has been horrified by the dramatic rise in the crime rate, and especially at certain particularly brutal crimes, involving child rape and murder, which indicate a nature which can only be described as sub-human. We hear frequently from those on the right of politics about the need for a greater element of deterrence to be introduced into our penal code and practice to combat this phenomenon, and I do not by any means disagree with this prescription — in fact, when we think that the British taxpayer will be obliged to keep such creatures as the 'Yorkshire Ripper' and the 'Stockwell Strangler', together with the bestial killers of little children, in food, warmth and clothing for the rest of their lives — instead of, as is right, these monsters being dispatched from this world with the greatest possible speed and efficiency — the idea is offensive to every normal human being's sense of natural justice. But the adoption of these proper penalties, necessary though it is, will by no means deal with the totality of the problem.

That society is today producing such unspeakable specimens, in far greater numbers than ever before, is indicative also of a regressive genetic process that should cause us even greater alarm than the softness with which they are dealt in the courts when they are caught and come to trial. It means simply that we are breeding more and more of the worst human garbage — just as we seem to be producing less and less people with the finest qualities of mind and character, who are so urgently needed.to provide the leadership required for the nation in all the many fields where it is lacking. 'Liberal' dogma forbids us, on pain of the worst conceivable ostracism (including the attachment of the well-worn epithet 'nazi') even to consider the introduction of a policy of genetic improvement as a means of eliminating the worst, and procreating the best. strains in our population. But it is my honest opinion that, if we are not prepared soon to stand up and defy the 'liberals' and accept the need for such a policy, the atrocities that make headlines in our newspapers now almost every week are going to increase without limit.

I do not propose that we oblige those of the 'liberal' and 'humanist' persuasion by indulging them in their love for caricature of everyone and every idea that meets their disapproval: I am not suggesting that we set about treating human beings as creatures to be conceived in laboratories. I advocate only that we strive to create once again the conditions for a healthy, uncontaminated and organic society where the best will tend to proliferate, and the worst not to proliferate, in the ordinary natural course of affairs, through the sensible and just provision of incentives and rewards at one end of the social scale and the correct imposition of penalties and deterrents at the other. As I have said previously, some readjustment of social welfare benefits will be a necessary part of this process. At the same time, I shall not shirk proposing that there are elements in the population which, if not deprived of life themselves, should most certainly be deprived of the faculty and right to give life to future generations in whom criminal tendencies of the very lowest kind might be reproduced.

As I have stated when dealing, in the previous chapter, with the need for an economic revolution, there is a vital urgency in Britain for a redistribution of population, both from the urban to the rural areas and from the more heavily populated regions to the underpopulated ones. In this process, considerations of pure profit-and-loss economics should take second place to that of building healthy and thriving communities, living in surroundings of beauty and with room to breathe. North and Central Wales, North West England, the Scottish Border Country and the Scottish Highlands are blessed with the most magnificent scenery and the healthiest environment in Britain; and yet these areas have been, over the centuries, tragically denuded of people. It must be our policy to attract people back to these areas and to revive them in every sense of the term. Here there is much scope for the mobilisation of the abundant idealism and energies of our young people.

As Britain has become more and more beset by social ills and tensions caused largely by the presence of great battalions of youth with time on their hands and nothing to do — an inevitable symptom of our *laissez-faire* way of life — there has been increasing talk among sociologists of the need for such youngsters to be organised into some form of 'community service'. I could not agree more, but it is important that in approaching such a question we get our priorities right.

In another chapter I have spoken of the need for young men to receive a period of military training. Supplementary to this, and possibly in combination with it, we could organise these same young men to take part in great public work projects connected with the revival of those very run-down and depopulated regions of which I have just spoken. Indeed the most suitable time to do this would be towards, or at, the end of their service in the armed forces but while they were still members of those forces and subject to their disciplinary rules and duties. In such formations, they could then be sent to the areas in question, and possibly even overseas to parts of the White Commonwealth, to provide a disciplined and organised labour force for schemes of development. A good rule of this service would be that every such young man should be obliged to undergo experience of tough manual work, irrespective of his social background or education, and thus come to understand the meaning of belonging to a true national community, undivided on grounds of class.

One possible side-benefit of introducing these young people to such underdeveloped regions is that they may be encouraged, when their service is over, to settle there. In that case it would be helpful to provide them with special grants to do so; indeed this system of inducement grants should be extended to all others desirous of such internal migration — provided of course that they met certain standards of qualification and character.

A great many of our young people are of course already engaged in community work, but all too often it is of a kind from which the British race receives no benefit. Let those who feel it is 'doing good' to perform services for Ethiopia or the Sudan be told that it would be doing much more good to plant forests in Inverness-shire, build roads in Gwynedd or — if they want to go overseas — to bring water to dry areas of Queensland or New South Wales.

With the revival of the countryside must come the ennoblement of the city and town, and here again there is scope for a labour force of the kind I have described. Such a force could be supplemented by the local unemployed under the 'Workfare' scheme spoken of earlier. The large cities of Britain, with one or two exceptions like Edinburgh, are the ugliest in Europe, and also very nearly the filthiest. Our object must be their complete transformation and regeneration.

A lot of claptrap is talked about 'inner city' revival and renewal, this usually envisaging solutions to be provided by the throwing of infinite money at the problem. The first truth to be recognised here is that a great many of the ills besetting our inner cities are the result of our importation into them of people who by character and temperament simply are not suited to that kind of environment. To state this is not to condemn the people themselves or to say that they are worse or better than we are, only that their proximity, in our inner cities, to the native British has led to tension and discord. In another chapter I shall deal with this matter in more thorough detail. Suffice it to say here that the resettlement overseas of Britain's coloured ethnic minorities is an essential requirement of our task of inner city regeneration — if only because, before any such regeneration is possible, those living in such areas must form united communities with a sense of common loyalty and identity.

I have spoken of the insidious axis of political weakness and commercial power that has permitted the gross disfigurement of our urban centres by excrescences of 'architecture' that affront the human eye. But this does not wholly explain the phenomenon.

Let it be admitted, our current fashions in building, sculpture, music, painting and other artistic fields have been arbitrarily determined by a seemingly omnipotent cultural 'establishment' that is as firmly entrenched as the political and financial establishments to which it is allied. The 'modernist' revolution has too thoroughly succeeded in imposing its styles on society, despite most of the latter's dislike of those styles, for this to be explained as a normal and natural artistic development. Today, no new composer can hope to gain national notice unless his 'music' consists of a series of discordant, jangling noises more appropriate to a metalworkers' shop than a concert hall. No painter can win recognition if his works bear any resemblance to the subject in question. And no major building will be commissioned which does not resemble a beer crate stood on its side.

It is as if some strange power, far removed from any public or popular censure, has decreed that henceforth the creation of beauty, whether of sight, sound or thought, will be outlawed. Those creations of former ages will have to be tolerated for just as long as the 'philistine' masses want to keep them; but nothing of the new age must bear their stamp. Art, music, literature, the theatre and every other cultural medium must be placed at the service of the reigning modern orthodoxy and subjected to the will of its proprietors and promoters.

Typically, the controllers of these new art forms turn truth on its head and insist that the hideous art world they have designed for us has been created in the name of 'freedom', and that behind all resistance to it lie the dark intentions of 'totalitarians' who would suppress the new spirit, given the chance.

In fact, as I have stated before, no such 'suppression' would ever be needed. In a natural order of things where artistic products were allowed to find their own level and where conventional 'taste' was not rigged by those who controlled the main channels of communication on artistic matters, the modernists would soon find themselves out on the despised fringe of the art world, putting on their own exhibitions to their own tiny audiences of cranks, weirdos and cultural charlatans, in their own galleries and paid for out of their own pockets.

For the fact is that the artistic 'totalitarianism' of which the modernists are always speaking is of the very opposite kind to that which they allege. It is their own totalitarianism that is today making the running in the art world, consigning by the methods of intellectual intimidation all products they disapprove to the cultural wilderness, while their tight control of the mass media relegates everything classical and traditional to almost total obscurity — by the simple method of never mentioning it!

For the fact that the modernists have been able to trample roughshod over all normal popular taste, they must be thankful that political muscle has been exerted on their behalf, together with massive financial endowments from strange private sources as well as vast allocations of public funds that have been made available to them by means of their having hi-jacked the institutions of state by which such funds are dispensed — the so-called 'Arts Council' being the most prominent example. In this way they have found the money to promote their sick products by courtesy of the taxpayers, most of whom would not give those products a second glance.

From the beginning, the left of politics has allied itself with this cult of degeneracy and ugliness, notwithstanding that the 'proletariat' over which it is always drooling is for the most part well capable of recognising its creations for the trash that they are.

Our revolution must be a revolution against modernism and back to classicism. It must be a revolution which aims to recreate for our people an environment of harmony and beauty as expressed down the ages in the immortal soul of our race and through the labours of those who stand in the pantheon of European genius. The concrete junk that deforms our town and city centres should be pulled down and replaced by spacious and noble designs which draw their inspiration from the Greco-Roman, Gothic, Baroque, Georgian and other great and healthy traditions. For this to be possible, the grip of Mammon must be removed from the necks of public authorities, and these authorities staffed by people who will build for town, city, region, nation, people and eternity.

Britain has not failed to produce the architectural talent necessary for the construction of noble cities; but we have failed again and again, through municipal meanness and paucity of vision, to give that talent its head. Wren, after the Great Fire, and Lutyens, after the 'Blitz', each produced designs for a new London city centre that would have rendered it one of the great showpieces of Europe, but these imaginative concepts were both turned down. Today, we have provincial cities with truly imposing buildings whose aspect is ruined by the erection of architectural eyesores in the immediate vicinity. The view of St. George's Hall in Liverpool is polluted by the presence of semi-skyscrapers nearby. The fine Guildhall in Portsmouth can no longer be seen frontally from a distance, because a shapeless cube has been put up virtually in its forecourt. The centre of Birmingham is not without buildings of architectural merit, but these can hardly be seen in any panorama of the city today, which is dominated by the cylindrical hulk of the revolting Rotunda.

It is time to halt this mutilation of our urban landscape and give a chance to beauty, space and order once again.

Just as our town and city centres should be places of architectural splendour, so should they be tidy and clean. Shortly before these words were written, we were informed that our Prime Minister had just 'discovered' what a litter-infested country Britain was — when most observers with eyes to see had known this for decades. The Premier, we are told, has set up a public body to undertake a clean-up. Well, that will do no harm; but it is nowhere near enough — there is no virtue in sweeping the streets if the very next week they are going to be filthy again! What is needed more than anything is a thorough change in people's attitudes, which must start at school. At the same time, we must introduce penalties for litter-louts that provide a real deterrent to their untidiness.

Side by side with the improvement of the appearance of our towns and cities, there must be a vast increase in the amenities offered by them for cultural and recreational pursuits of the kind calculated to assist the fullest development of our people in every sense of the term. Every large city should have a symphony orchestra and resident opera, as well as an art gallery of high quality; and these facilities should be subsidised so as to make them available to the people at a cost that is within the reach of everyone. Particular effort should be made to promote native British products in all fields.

Coming to the cinema, it is appalling that a nation which produces such a vast output of talent in this field should possess almost no film industry to call its own, being obliged again and again to call upon foreign finance to make large pictures and then to give them an international appeal to win a market for them. How often have we seen an American actor conscripted into a British war film, contrary to all historical fact, simply to boost viewing in the United States? The cinema today is one of the few art forms not yet at the limit of their possibilities of development. It is a fact that we in this country have the home-grown talent at our disposal to make us leaders of the world in this field, but we will not achieve this if we regard the film industry as just one more of those that must make their way in the international 'free market'. No art can be truly great, least of all truly national, if it is subject to such commercial considerations. We should regard our film-making talent as a national resource — to quote a term I have used much in this book — to be funded publicly to whatever extent is needed to render it capable of reaching the greatest possible heights of perfection, while at the same time retaining its national identity. British films should be made to boost national consciousness and to carry, like Italian Renaissance painting and German symphonic music, the stamp of national greatness. If foreigners like them and want to buy them, all well and good; but this should not be our first consideration.

Along with the best facilities for the arts, there should be the finest possible ones for sport and all forms of physical recreation. Every locality should have an amply equipped sports complex, staffed by properly qualified instructors. No person who wishes to succeed in a particular sport should lack the means of training or coaching to do so.

Britain lags far behind many countries in the world in the provision of these amenities — which is one reason for her poor performance in many branches of international sporting competition, as well as generally low standards of national fitness. That we see fit to invest so little in this field is a token of the low importance that we place, both on international sporting prestige and on the physical well-being of the population generally. I have said in a previous chapter that our national performance in every sphere depends on our ability to raise the level of health and fitness among our population. The lack of concern about this displayed by the majority of our political leaders is an appalling commentary on their sense of priorities.

Elsewhere I have spoken of the need to change the tone and quality of the daily fare served up by television, but in addition to this we should give urgent attention to the deeper question of just how much of our available hours should be taken up by this institution. In my opinion, we have far too much at present. TV in millions of homes has so taken over the household that it dominates family life, occupying endless hours watching that could be given up to much more useful pursuits, such as healthy physical exercise, the reading of good books and simple, old-fashioned conversation — all things that I cited earlier as being institutionalised in older societies before modern technology provided diversion at the press of a button. The constant diet of TV absolves people of the need to call on their own inner resources to occupy themselves. The result of this is that many are being turned into TV-addicted zombies, able by means of this medium to relieve themselves for the whole evening — and now most of the day and night as well — of the need to think.

Television is undoubtedly a boon to elderly people living alone, particularly if they find it difficult to get out and meet their neighbours, and no arbitrary decisions about the allocation of TV viewing hours should be made without careful consideration of this factor. I believe, however, that there are very strong grounds for making a reduction of those hours, and most probably the best time for cuts would be the early to mid-evenings, nights and weekends. Plenty of viewing on working weekdays would not affect the majority but would be welcome to the old and retired.

While we are on the subject of home life, something should be said about the kinds of homes in which people are going to live. I have spoken of the disfigurement of urban landscapes by office blocks and other eyesores cluttering town centres, but the same thing might be said of the high-rise flats which now comprise a large part of residential property in this country. It is becoming a generally accepted view that this experiment in housing has been, not only an aesthetic disaster, but a gigantic social failure as well. It is time to end it, at least as far as flats of great numbers of storeys are concerned. Our housing schemes for the future should be based on a return, so far as possible, to the old model of terraced or semi-detached dwellings, each with its own garden. We should make much greater efforts than in the past to renovate old properties rather than build new ones; but where the latter is necessary the building should be in a style that blends harmoniously with tradition.

In this chapter I have tried to illustrate a few of the changes needed for the building of an entirely new country. They must be seen in context along with the other changes proposed elsewhere in this book, and particularly in those sections dealing with political and economic reform and the redirection of our media of mass communication. It will surely now be clear to the reader that running through this whole work is the belief that British society has degenerated and needs renewal of the most radical kind. We talk glibly of the preservation of our 'way of life' but how good a way of life is this really? Probably, each person, when he speaks in those terms, is referring to some past memory of an ordered world in his own immediate vicinity and circle which he mistakenly confuses with the pattern of society as a whole. Increasingly, this pattern has become one of **disorder**, and of a large portion of our people living their lives in a condition barely worthy, if worthy at all, of their ancestors.

As I have pointed out in a previous chapter, we have been

overwhelmed by the impact of technology and industrialism, and have not devised forms of social organisation, or any adequate moral code, to cope with this impact. As I have said, in ages before the machine, nature regulated the lives of communities in accordance with sound natural laws which enabled those communities to survive the aberrations of politics. Even in earlier stages of the machine-age, this did not greatly alter. Liberals could babble about their utopias in their Jacobin clubs, but this did not change the season for the gathering of the harvest, nor the certainty of procreation, nor the call for manly strength in the wielding of the blacksmith's hammer, nor the need for self-reliance in village and hamlet for the filling of leisure time with talk, reading, contemplation, music and song. But now we have to contend with entirely different circumstances governing the lives we lead. The western genius for manufacture, more recently supplemented by that of the East for simulation of the western product, has put into the hands of all of us the power to obtain our sustenance with only a fraction of the old effort of body, mind and character. With this gift comes the frightening prospect that civilisation will book its passage to decline and extinction by the simple process of going soft.

For, together with the appliances that reduce the need for human labour, toughness and will-power, and the canned entertainment that can be brought into a drawing room at instant command, there is the additional life-killing agent of equally instant gratification and escape from the real world through the availability of drugs — a phenomenon that threatens to add the finishing touch to the degenerative process brought on by these other products of modern science.

And, perhaps worst of all, this same modern science has given us the means to gratify the sexual drive without the accompaniment of the natural product of the furtherance of life, with the result that today in Britain, as throughout the West, the race is not reproducing itself sufficiently even to guarantee survival, let alone expansion. The point has been made before, but it cannot be reiterated strongly enough.

In the face of this looming disaster, the genius of our race must again rise to the call of destiny and face its greatest challenge yet: that of devising a new form of political, social and moral order that will enable society to live with the products of technology and science — not to be destroyed by them but to harness them to the achievement of yet higher possibilities of human life.

I have long been convinced that 'liberal democracy', as we understand it today, is utterly inadequate to this task. It is a task that calls for a strength and wisdom of leadership that that system simply cannot produce; all the evidence of the past century proves this. The crisis demands, truly, a 'higher type' of man, of the kind foreseen by Nietzsche but rejected by most of his contemporaries and ours. It must be a type of man capable of rising above the solipsist clamour of the mob, and also above the temptations to ease and comfort offered by this push-button era. What we need, in effect, is a new species of aristocracy, possessing the will to live again in harmony with nature, and to direct society in accordance with that imperative.

Our people today have been conditioned to accept so much that is trashy and second-rate in their society and environment, as if it were the norm and nothing could be done to change it. We accept ugly and filthy cities. We accept drivel in the way of art, literature and entertainment. We accept low standards of human health and physique. We accept vaporing nonentities as national 'leaders' and we accept government after government that fails to bring any real improvement in the quality of our existence.

We accept these things because our standards have become so debased that we have an estimate of human possibilities far below that which is actually attainable. We take the truism that "nobody is perfect" and we turn it into a feeble excuse for a level of imperfection that is contemptible to anyone who understands history and knows the real heights of which humans are capable, given the right direction and the vision of a better order of life.

In the dream of liberalism the world of the future belongs to the 'ordinary man', and ordinariness has become our ideal in everything. We are encouraged to like our leaders to be 'ordinary', and those leaders compete with each other in the employment of gimmicks to demonstrate who is the most 'ordinary'. Now even royalty has joined in the game, with each member striving to appear as 'unroyal' as possible. Utterly rejected is the idea that there should be a leadership which summons the people to great tasks, setting standards for society higher than those that have become the accepted fashion, calling the nation to self-improvement.

And any political creed that aspires to goals above this level of comfortable mediocrity, and lifts the eyes of the people to horizons of nobility and heroism, is immediately stigmatised as 'dangerous' and its advocates as 'fanatics', whose voices should be silenced in the interests of public safety!

We reject this entire world-view, based as it is on contentment with the shoddy standards of a sick and decrepit age, and we proclaim unashamedly our aim of leading our countrymen and -women to an altogether higher level of civilisation. If that is 'dangerous', and we are 'fanatics' in pursuing it, then well and good — we are quite prepared to rejoice in such descriptions!

If I am asked to define our ideal in a few words, it is that of a noble race, attaining the highest possible standards of character, health, strength and beauty, living in a land cleansed of disease, dirt, ugliness and degeneracy and in complete harmony with the natural order. We want a nation dedicated to pride and honour — far above material ambitions, and surrounded by an environment of great art and culture which will provide continual nourishment for the national spirit.

In holding to these ideals, we are not utopians — for we recognise that absolute perfection in such things is not possible, but we believe that in the striving for such goals we can nevertheless realise the maximum potentialities for human development, which we hold are far in excess of those of our society of today. We believe in the principle of making our reach always exceed our grasp.

We are not 'world reformers', as the liberals are. The itch to 'save mankind' is absent from our armoury of ambitions and motives — because our common sense tells us that this is a goal that has eluded the most resourceful spirits across the centuries and will forever elude us. Our concern is to rescue our own particular section of mankind from degradation, aimlessness and chaos, and guide it to new peaks of quality and achievement. While liberals are forever international, we are essentially national.

While liberals place infinite faith in social schemes, disregarding the importance of the human worth of those involved in them, we set as the first priority the improvement of the quality of our people — without which no social scheme can succeed beyond the narrowest limits.

Through the attainment of a higher man will we build a higher civilisation. That is the ideal for which we fight.

Chapter 16
The racial controversy

The stranger within my gate,
He may be true or kind,
But he does not talk my talk —
I cannot feel his mind.
I see the face and the eyes and the mouth,
But not the soul behind.
RUDYARD KIPLING

Britain today, as everyone knows, is in the grip of a mania of 'anti-racism'. As each week passes, new heights of madness are scaled in the all-out drive to hound into silence every voice of nonconformity concerning the race issue — that is, every opinion that dissents from the view that the races of the world are exactly the same in their innate attributes and differ from one another only in skin colour.

I happen to be one of those dissenters, and for my sins I have joined the list of those who have been flung into jail under legislation devised to bring all public opinion into line with official policy and all frank and open public discussion of the issue to an end. As I write these very words, I sit in a cell in Wormwood Scrubs Prison, along with my colleague John Morse, found guilty of the same heresy. The fact that our incarceration has bestowed on me the advantage that I have had the time to write this book does not not lessen the enormity of the injustice of it. To those who for years have slept snugly in their beds safe in the thought that it could not happen here in Britain, I carry from this cell the news that it can — and it has! We are here, though we spoke for millions; that is a measure of the new inquisition.

Of what did they accuse us? The precise wording of the charges was that we published ''written matter which was threatening, abusive or insulting in cases where, having regard to all the circumstances, hatred was likely to be stirred up against racial groups, namely coloured people, Asians and Jews in Great

Britain.'' In other words, in the expression of our opinions about racial matters we used language that was likely to cause hatred. The inference from this is that such opinions are not themselves a crime; only certain words used in support of them are — words, that is to say, that are liable to cause racial hatred. If we had expressed the same opinions but had used words containing nothing that could be construed as hostile to any racial group, we would have retained our freedom. This was more or less implied in the prosecuting counsel's speech, when he stated that it was not for expressing our opinions *per se* that we were in the dock.

I am not of course able here to quote the passages in what we wrote and published that resulted in our being convicted, for that would lay this book open to risk of placing me back behind bars again for the same 'crime' as before. I can only say what was said in our defence in the trial: that we thought it necessary to speak vigorously and forcefully on the matters being dealt with because we believed them to be matters of desperate urgency to Britain, and that required the sounding of a loud alarm. What we said in criticism of some members of ethnic minority groups was not intended to apply to all members of those groups. The main thrust of our condemnation was not against any ethnic group as such but against multi-racialism as a policy, which we contended had manifestly proved a disaster.

In the end, the probable factor that sealed our fate was that in two places in our publications we used words which reflected on the respective capabilities of the different races for the building of civilisation. The words in question were strong and forthright, but they represented a perfectly sincere expression of our opinions. What our conviction established, however, was that anyone henceforth who ventures to suggest in public, either in speech or in writing, that one race may not be equal to another is on 'dangerous' ground. It is well that I should sound that warning as a guideline to those who wish to campaign in opposition to immigration and to the multi-racial experiment. You are not barred from doing these things — yet! But should you attempt to reinforce such opposition by using words that suggest that one race is better than another, you are in the danger zone!

The ludicrousness of this situation is obvious to anyone who gives the matter a moment's thought. In the course of my defence in the trial at which we were convicted, I went into the witness box, where I was asked what would be my reaction as a coloured person if I heard or read words which cast my race in an unfavourable light in relation to Whites. I replied that it would be no different from my reaction as a white Briton when I hear some of the capabilities of my own people compared unfavourably to those of other races — as I frequently do. I would ask myself first: is there any justification for such an unfavourable comparison? If I were able to answer to myself honestly that there was not, I could ignore it. If, on the other hand, there did seem to be some foundation of fact supporting the comparison, then if I did not like that I should do something about it, which would mean trying to persuade my fellow-countrymen to improve themselves. Either way, the most absurd reaction would be to demand that anyone making such a criticism should be silenced and locked up!

But of course, as we know, uncomplimentary things are said about the British people, or sections thereof, in the newspapers every day, and no-one suggests that the writers or editors are stirring up 'racial hatred' and should be sent to prison.

In fact, as I write these words, I know of not one single case of a prosecution being brought against any person for using words offensive to white people. Legislation of some sort governing this kind of thing has been on the statute book now for over 20 years, though additions have been made to it during that time. The legislation has always been used against Whites and in defence of the ethnic minorities, never against ethnic minorities and in defence of Whites.

This of course reflects the true — as distinct from the purely official — purpose of the legislation. The purpose is not to prevent 'racial hatred' — for this it quite clearly has not done, and cannot do — but to suppress all frank public discussion of racial differences. It has not fully reached that stage yet; so far it has only placed certain limits on the language that might be used in this discussion. Most certainly, the ultimate intention, however, is to extend these limits bit by bit, and to the point at which no-one feels safe to say anything on racial matters anywhere — unless of course he is a non-White, in which case he may say what he likes.

I underlined the absurdity of this whole concept of 'race hate' legislation in an article in *Spearhead* magazine in June 1987*, when I wrote:-

   "...Hatred can be justified or not justified in different situations, and in those situations where it is not justified there is a natural defence mechanism against it that is built into the average human

---

* This reference was added to the original text in the process of preparation of final copy for the printer, and after the author had been released from prison.

mind, with its faculties for fairness and common sense.

"Just supposing that I were to get up in a public place somewhere in this country and proclaim to a crowd there that all Manxmen, say, were psychopathic killers or that all Scots were stupid. The manifest absurdity of such statements would provide all the protection needed to Manxmen or Scots from any public opprobrium or contempt that might be thought to arise from my utterances. I would in fact be dismissed by such a crowd as an obvious nutter not worth listening to, so that any laws to defend those groups against the likes of me would be quite superfluous."

And so it has been across history. When new groups of people arrived in a country whom it was possible to assimilate peacefully, that was exactly what happened: they were peacefully assimilated, if not immediately then before very long, and no-one ever thought of introducing laws to enforce that assimilation.

By contrast, the very act of introducing these laws to suppress opposition to recent immigration to Britain is itself a confession that there is no natural basis for the immigrants' assimilation into our population and that, therefore, the attempt must be made to bring about this assimilation by coercion and police-state methods. And as for words used that are uncomplimentary to these groups, it seems strange that our political masters do not feel they can trust to people's instincts of fairness and common sense to repudiate those words if they are unjustified, as has always been the case in the past. Is not this legislation to outlaw 'racism' itself a piece of concealed 'racism', in as much as it acknowledges that certain groups living amongst us today require special protection, not only from hostile actions by others but even hostile words as well? Is it not, in fact, an acknowledgement that the multi-racial experiment has not worked?

At any rate, despite this overhanging threat of prosecution, I intend to go on speaking about racial matters in Britain because I believe them to be matters of the gravest public concern. Under the circumstances, however, I am obliged to exercise certain care in the words I use in so doing, lest I be jailed again and thereby silenced. As this will not help the movement for which I fight, it is obviously desirable that it should not happen.

One of the commonest arguments used by the promoters of today's multi-racial society is the claim that Britain has always been 'multi-racial', taking in new ethnic groups over the centuries. This is of course downright rubbish; all the migrations into Britain, up to those of the Jews from Eastern Europe in the last century, were peoples of similar racial type to ourselves and who were therefore easily assimilable within a generation or two (this is excepting the Jews who came over here in the wake of William the Conquerer and were subsequently expelled by Edward I, as mentioned earlier). In more recent years, we have taken in refugees from Poland, Hungary and the Baltic states, and these have caused little or no problems, again being Europeans sharing with us the same basic culture. These people have settled into our society and got ahead by their own efforts. They have not demanded, or needed, 'positive discrimination' to get them jobs in preference to native British people. Their presence here has not resulted in riots.

We nationalists have, from the start, opposed Asian and Afro-Caribbean immigration specifically because we have been convinced that the immigrants concerned, not being European and therefore not sharing our cultural heritage, could never be successfully integrated. I came to hold this view in the 1950s, when I saw with my own eyes what was happening in the inner cities where these people had begun to settle; and, with others, I spoke out against the policy. We warned of catastrophe if it was continued. Instead of being listened to by the politicians and being given a fair hearing by the media, we were treated with scorn, and given every unpleasant label that the political dictionary can supply: 'extremists', 'bigots', 'haters', 'troublemakers', 'racist fanatics', 'nazis' and so on. You name it, we were called it. No epithet was considered too abusive to describe those of us at that time and since who forecast that multi-racialism in Britain would not work.

Many of us sounded these warnings long before Mr. Enoch Powell made his entry into the racial controversy. By the time that Mr. Powell decided, in 1968, that the moment had come to speak out in protest against what was happening, I had been saying just the same things for more than 10 years — and I was 22 years younger than he and, not occupying any public office, had none of the facilities and information that were available to him whereby I could find out what was going on. And I was not unique or alone; men such as A.K. Chesterton, Sir Oswald Mosley, Colin Jordan and John Bean had been awakened to this situation before I was, and had used the very limited means available to them to warn people about it.

Naturally, we welcomed Mr. Powell's conversion to our viewpoint on immigration on the basis of 'better late than never'.

But we found it difficult to suppress a smile when we heard him described as the 'leader' of public protest on the issue. In this, as in many matters, the true lead in pointing forward to what had to be done came, not from parliament, but from men regarded as being on the despised 'fringe' of politics — a fact which surely says something about the political situation in post-war Britain.

Over the past two decades, as is common knowledge, the predictions made by Mr. Powell and by others long before him have of course all been more than amply vindicated. The appalling riots of the 1980s have served as a monument to the failure of the whole multi-racial policy that has had the backing, with only minor variations of commitment, of every government in Britain since 1945.

But with characteristic gall, those responsible for this disaster, instead of acknowledging honestly that events have proved them wrong and their opponents right, and setting to work to rectify what they have done by throwing the policy into reverse, have tried to shift the blame for the whole debacle onto the very people who warned correctly about the policy in the beginning. The promoters of the multi-racial fiasco do not indict and chastise themselves; they accuse and penalise those whom they call 'racists'. With every further piece of evidence that multi-racialism is not working, and that those who have opposed it have been right, they attempt to solve the problem by hounding, slandering, gagging and jailing those whom events have so decisively vindicated.

To back up this policy, our rulers and their acolytes of politics, the mass media and the Church have invented a phrase which conveniently sidetracks public attention from the core of the issue, and at the same time grossly misrepresents the motives of those who disagree with them: they have classified all opposition to the idea of a multi-ethnic Britain as 'racial hatred', and those who voice that opposition as 'hate-mongers'.

The truth is that hatred does not come into the issue at all. We simply love our own race and want to preserve it. We have no hostile feelings towards members of other races; different individuals among those races are agreeable or disagreeable, just as is the case with our own white people. Our whole position on the race issue is based on a recognition of **differences**. With those Asians or Blacks who recognise these differences as we do and wish to co-operate with us in bringing about the peaceful separation of the races that is the only solution to the problem, we have no quarrel, and we will be prepared to enter into amicable negotiation with them at any time. I well recall an occasion when I witnessed on television several years ago a discussion between an American Negro who was a well known champion boxer and a white British TV personality known as a compere of 'chat shows'. The former was a supporter of racial segregation and the latter, predictably, a multi-racialist. The boxer spoke of his being proud of being black and of wanting his children to be black like him. This shocked the TV man, who had no such sentiments concerning his own offspring. Listening to this discussion, I found myself far more in sympathy with the black man than with my fellow White, whose attitude filled me with loathing and contempt.

These feelings, I would say, are roughly representative of the attitudes of the overwhelming majority of us who oppose racial mixing. We cannot possibly 'hate' the likes of the negro boxer of whom I have spoken but, on the contrary, respect him and those like him. The way they feel is exactly the way we would feel if we were black.

Some years previous to that, I made the acquaintance of an Asian from Kashmir who had exactly the same views as I did concerning the mixture of the races. He wished his people to keep their racial purity and identity. We got on extremely well; there was no question of hatred.

And I have met Arabs, Chinese, Japanese and others with the same feelings. Indeed, the majority of Japanese are much more racially minded than today's British. Japan is by comparison with present-day Britain an extremely homogeneous country, and this, on the recent admission of a Japanese prime minister, is a major reason for her success. Homogeneity also would appear to have a lot to do with the maintenance of a low crime rate. According to recent statistics, there is currently one armed robbery yearly for every 10,000 people in the city of Tokyo, while in New York, possibly the most polyglot city in the world, the figure is **286** for every 10,000!

While I have no hostility to coloured people generally, I have no time whatever for those particular individuals among the coloured communities who choose of their own free will to come to Britain because they see it as being to their advantage to do so, and then, having got here, spend their lives complaining about everything in sight. And I have even less time for those Whites who are always ready to support them in their complaints, indeed even prepared to go looking for complaints that are not there. The presence of a large coloured population in this country has brought out from under the stones a particularly detestable species of white native, the type that makes a profession and a career out of exploiting the tensions of a multi-racial society in order to undermine his own people. Like a hungry cur attending the dinner table, he keeps an eager watch for any crumb of information concerning a coloured grievance, and immediately on receiving it gets to work like a termite to turn it to good account on his own behalf, and in the process knock away just a few more chips in the edifice of the white society he hates. These people come in various attire. Some of them get jobs as 'community relations' officers employed by local authorities, for which they are paid extremely generous salaries to make mischief all round, invariably mischief against the white population, however. Others wear the clothes of clergymen, politicians, broadcasters, social workers, schoolteachers, trade union shop-stewards and so on. In the squalid souls of these people, the driving forces are usually a combination of racial masochism, personal exhibitionism and an eye for the main chance. Very little, if any, part of them is touched by a genuine desire to do anything for the cause of the non-Whites for whom they are always banging the drum. If they were, and they used their brains a little, they would be able to see that the coloured man must ultimately be the loser in a divided multi-racial society just as much as the White. The very same people are of course usually to be found agitating against *apartheid* in South Africa, though that system has provided the only opportunity anywhere on the African Continent for Blacks to earn a reasonable wage and live under conditions of comparative peace, order and security.

Across the centuries, we in Britain have had a word for the action of a man who works against his people and in the service of their enemies. The word is **treason**, and for that crime we have sent people to the gallows. I cannot feel, however, that any who have met this end in such circumstances were more contemptible specimens of citizens than those busybodies who now labour night and day to turn Britain from a European society into a mulatto one. They serve the nation's enemies equally — and I do not here mean the coloured people but those shady characters behind the scenes who use the coloured people as mere pawns in the war to bring about Britain's destruction.

For, make no mistake about it, the darkening of our country is not taking place by accident. I have spoken in an earlier chapter of the existence of conspiratorial forces behind recent national and international events. Nowhere is the circumstantial evidence of this greater than in the case of the drive to eliminate the traditional racial character of the British Nation. Those governing this nation in the post-1945 period have had clearly before them the long and unhappy historical panorama of the negro problem in America, and all the obvious warnings that it offers to any other nations that might be contemplating setting out on the same road. To believe that the decision to open the gates of Britain to mass coloured immigration was made in ignorance of, and with eyes closed to, this tragic example is to extend the frontiers of human credulity beyond all logic.

And even if, by some fantastic circumstance, Britain's drawbridge had thus been let down out of folly and neglect rather than by design, would it not have been raised up again, and the influx stopped, as soon as the obvious error had been spotted and the consequences started to become apparent? And would there not have been a frank, free and open national debate about the matter, with every politician and every journalist feeling able to air his opinions without fear of the loss of his job, to say nothing of prosecution and imprisonment?

But, as we know, the error has not been rectified in the face of all the evidence of the disaster resulting from it. There has not been any truly free national debate on the subject; on the contrary, every public figure and communicator walks in terror of what will happen to his career, and perhaps his freedom, if he dares to protest with any real conviction and strength against the multi-racial juggernaut.

Concerning the post-war trend in which Britain, and other countries of the western world, had been thrown open to massed non-white immigration, the penetrative South African journalist Ivor Benson, writing in his newsletter *Behind the News*, had this to say:-

> "...Commencing almost immediately after the end of World War II, hordes of alien immigrants were deliberately brought in by the plane-load from the West Indies, India, Pakistan, Nigeria, etc., and delivered to all the main population centres — London, Liverpool, Birmingham, Leicester, Bristol, etc. — where they were immediately placed on full public assistance and provided with housing."

This represented, in Mr. Benson's words, the first phase of the plan. Then describing the second phase he said:-

"The continued importation of alien population elements into Europe and North America can now be clearly recognised as a gigantic, well planned and costly para-military operation, much of it routed through East Germany, the main staging post for bogus refugees flown in Soviet airliners from the Far East and elsewhere; from East Germany they are pushed out in busloads into West Germany, Denmark, Holland and Switzerland, and in boat-loads across the Baltic into Sweden and Norway, to be further distributed by all kinds of illegal means into Britain and across the Atlantic to Canada and the United States of America. Anyone who believes that all this could be the result of an exercise of personal initiative by the migrants, and all that at their own expense, would have to be naive to the point of weak-mindedness.''

This puts, in a nutshell, the reality that the massive invasion of Britain and other western countries that we have witnessed over recent years, involving peoples belonging to cultures hopelessly incapable of proper assimilation with those of the West, is no haphazard development; it has been deliberately **planned**. Mr. Benson might also have mentioned Australia, where precisely the same planned invasion is taking place, and with the object of destroying that country's traditional British culture which, over many generations, has bound it in fraternal association with our own.

Equally deliberate has been the campaign — amounting, I would claim, to nothing less than a conspiracy — to silence protest by the natives of these countries against the scheme. As I have said, in Britain Mr. Enoch Powell entered into the controversy and spoke his mind about it rather late in the day. But thenceforth his prospects of promotion in the political world were at an end. He was sacked from Edward Heath's Conservative shadow cabinet, and he ended his days on the parliamentary back benches.

A few years ago, the Fleet Street journalist Andrew Alexander, writing in *The Daily Mail*, produced an article frankly sympathetic to 'racialism', and in the course of it went so far as to cite the Jews as an example of a people with a decidedly racist attitude. In a short time, his column was shunted to the financial page, and thenceforth he has not been known to write anything about race.

In an earlier chapter I spoke of the witch-hunt conducted against schoolteachers, university lecturers and other public employees who have been suspected of being 'racists'. I might add to these the case of a colleague of my own (whom, for his sake, I will not name here) who was deprived of his job as a librarian on the payroll of one of the London boroughs, after many years of impeccable and loyal service, because he was found to be, in his spare time, the manager of our party's mail order book business, a 'racist' concern.

All these facts add up to overwhelming evidence of dark, subterranean forces at work beneath the surface of British society, dedicated to imposing multi-racialism on this country by lies, deception, intimidation and terror, while applying almost unseen pressures to prevent there taking place any proper public debate on the wisdom of such a policy. Am I being extravagant in describing this as a conspiracy? If the reader feels I am, the onus is on him or her to provide some other explanation of these developments.

A conspiracy is at work when there is an organised and deliberate attempt to conceal even a part of the truth. From the beginning, this has been the case with race in Britain. For years, the people were told that the numbers of immigrants coming in were not at a level to give rise to any justified concern. This plainly was not true, and now scarcely anyone any longer even tries to pretend that it was true. Next, it was admitted that the initial influx had been too high and that thenceforth 'controls' would be needed and were being applied. In other words, the numbers coming in in the past had, after all, been justified cause for concern, but this was not the case any longer. This also was untrue. The much heralded 'controls' that we were assured were in operation were just an illusion; while they existed on paper, they were having little effect in stemming the flood in practice. Where some would-be entrants were being prevented from getting in by rules that applied to them, others were pouring in because they were able to get round those rules. Yet more were pouring in illegally. As I write these words, official figures acknowledge that we are still receiving over 60,000 Third World immigrants every year. When the 'illegals' and other unaccounted-for ones are taken into consideration, the true level of influx is anyone's guess. The 'controls' are in effect a farce and a lie.

When the last national census was being prepared, it was at first proposed, very properly, to ask those filling in the census forms their ethnic origins, so as to enable government statisticians to make an estimate of the numbers of the coloured population in Britain. But after certain 'pressures' had been applied, this plan was dropped and the census went ahead without it. We still do not know what the true numbers are because there are no figures available for the offspring of coloured parents who themselves were born in this country. Most estimates that get into print still give the total of non-Whites as still not more than 2½ million, but these exclude the youngest category that I have mentioned, as well as the inestimable numbers of 'illegals'. Few people who have travelled around the main urban areas of this country and used their own eyes take this official figure with the slightest seriousness.

Such is the atmosphere of hysteria about race engendered by the 'anti-racist' lobby, it is quite impossible today to have a reasoned debate about the racial differences distinguishing coloured immigrants and their offspring from native Britons. And there is the additional veto on discussion imposed by the draconian race laws, which severely limit what one may say regarding such differences anyway. Suffice it to say here that an abundance of evidence reveals that these differences are profound, and have not been to any significant extent modified by the changes in the environmental factors usually cited as reason for such differences in the past. Children born and brought up in Britain belonging to Asian and West Indian families are still Asian and West Indian in practically every respect, apart from minor and superficial changes, such as the tendency of some young Asians to be bigger than their elders due to their being fed largely on a British diet.

As one example, there is a very substantial difference in scholastic achievement between young Blacks and young Whites, which is a matter of common knowledge among all educationalists, including those committed to the support of multiracialism.

The theory that attributes this to factors of family and cultural background falls flat on its face when it is realised that the backgrounds of Asian schoolchildren differ at least as much from those of Whites as do those of West Indians — with the additional factor of different languages. Yet Asian children's school performance is much nearer to the white level.

It will be appreciated from what has been said earlier that we are prevented by law from discussing here whether this difference of school achievement is due to any innate differences in mental ability. I might only remark that mental ability is something that cannot be measured by a single yardstick. The aptitude for learning and reasoning in the European tradition is but one criterion of mental powers. Another, which may strike some as equally important, is that mental faculty that might be described as the 'survival instinct': that mechanism of the mind that prompts the individual to think and act in accordance with his own interest and that of the group of which he is part — the life-wish, as opposed to the death-wish.

Europeans of today, and Anglo-Saxons in particular, whatever their intellectual powers with regard to art, science, technology and political organisation, display an extremely weak survival instinct, in as much as all too many of them are wholly indifferent to the future of their own species, its defence against internal threats to it, its collective well-being and sustenance, and its honour and pride. Were this not so, we would not see such a large section of our own race — and the largest of all among the most 'educated' — fall victim to the self-destroying ideology of liberalism, which has been extensively examined in a previous chapter of this book.

In this question of tribal survival instinct, modern Europeans certainly cannot be considered superior to Asians or Blacks, both of whom have it to a very pronounced degree — as can be seen by their growing political assertiveness on behalf of their own communities, an assertiveness which cannot be criticised if things are looked at from their own point of view.

Ultimately, the question of which races are superior and which inferior will be decided by which survive and which do not, rather than by any comparisons of aptitude in specific skills, whether academic, athletic or otherwise. And so arguments as to superiority and inferiority become a rather pointless exercise. All that can be established at the present time is that the differences between Whites and non-Whites in mental outlook, character, temperament and cultural tradition are vast, and, in my submission, insurmountable — therefore pointing to the impossibility of ever integrating them into a single harmonious society.

A further instance of incompatibility between the races can be seen in the fundamentally differing attitudes towards the requirements of law-enforcement, which spring largely from the strong tribal sense in some non-Whites that I have described. In several localities where police have had cause to arrest a member of one of the ethnic minorities for some suspected crime, that arrest is regarded by many of the latter's kin as an attack on the whole ethnic community, and one that obliges them to organise themselves in massed resistance. This kind of situation, as will be known, has led to the worst urban riots witnessed in Britain for centuries. We will of course all have our own strong opinions on the rights and wrongs of this tendency, and the vast majority of

Britons will agree with me here that such opposition to the process of law-enforcement and justice, by whatever race, is appalling. This is not, however, how things are seen by at least a portion of the coloured communities, which regard the police as being in a state of war with them — from which it follows that, in their minds, they must defend themselves in that war.

Again, rather than sermonise on the rights and wrongs of this attitude, would it not be best simply to recognise as a fact the vast difference that it shows between the native British and some of the ethnic minorities — this difference simply further underlining the need for racial separation?

It is a common assertion of the racial integrators that the ethnic minority groups living in Britain are, by that token, of British nationality; and if this is not wholly believed of those who were born abroad it certainly is so in the case of their children and grandchildren born and brought up in this country. Yet, while on the one hand ever repeating this claim, the integrators are, on the other hand, denying it in what they do. In every locality where such ethnic groups are concentrated, there are extensive provisions made by local authorities of cultural amenities guaranteed to emphasise the differences between them and the host population. Large sums of public money are ever being allocated to services bearing the names 'West Indian', 'Indian', 'Pakistani', 'Bengali', 'Islamic', etc. The supposition of all this is that a person can belong to two nationalities at the same time, which is of course nonsense — either he is one or the other. If the members of these groups were indeed British, they would have to be treated the same as the rest of us in all respects, and not regarded as having their own distinctive cultures or special links with their ancestral homelands. If, on the other hand, they are to have these things, let us do away with the pretence that they are part of our nation, and let us treat them as aliens.

Do these groups indeed regard themselves as British? All the evidence is that most of them do not. In dress, in language or dialect, in customs, in political alignments and even in such things as loyalties to cricket teams in test matches, they identify themselves with their own ethnic communities and the homelands from which those communities originate. There is of course nothing wrong in this; it is the way we should like people of British stock to feel and act when they leave these shores and settle overseas. I cannot condemn the members of the coloured communities for it; I can only condemn those who, in face of this evidence, maintain the pretence that the ethnic minorities are 'British', and who want to grant them all the rights and benefits of British nationality without demanding from them the reciprocal loyalties and obligations.

For all the reasons outlined here, I am convinced that we must now acknowledge the total failure of the multi-racial experiment in Britain and bring it to an end. This must entail, not only a complete stoppage of all further non-white immigration, but a comprehensive scheme of repatriation and resettlement which will remove from this country the non-white population we already have here.

To institute the first without also instituting the second would be to court certain failure in dealing with the problem. The number of additions to the coloured population caused by the entry of immigrants, large though it is, is now far exceeded by the addition brought about by births in this country. Even if a complete ban on further entry were effectively enforced, the non-white population would continue to grow alarmingly by natural increase, particularly in view of the far higher fertility rate among West Indians and, even more, Asians.

The categorisation of who should, and who should not, be admitted to Britain as an immigrant can only properly be determined on an ethnic basis. Use of any other criteria, such as place of birth of immigrants or parents, is quite unworkable. This has led in the past to the absurd situation of people who are British in every respect being denied entry and residence here merely through the accident of their fathers being on overseas service at the time they were born. It is also entirely counter-productive to what should be our policy of fostering fraternal links with people of British stock around the world, including those whose ancestors left these shores generations ago, to deny such people entry into their mother country should they wish to come.

Any white Australian, New Zealander, Canadian, South African, Rhodesian (I refuse to recognise such a country as 'Zimbabwe') or Falkland Islander, whether wholly of British descent or not, should be granted automatic entry into this country as if it were his own. Though this policy could of course result in the entry of a small number of undesirables, it is the only possible one that is consistent with the aim stated at the end of the last paragraph, and with which I shall deal in greater detail in a later chapter.

And the same rule should apply to white Americans who can

prove mainly British ancestry.

Applications from other Whites to settle in Britain should be dealt with each on its own individual merit and according to whether family or occupational circumstances give strong enough grounds for the granting of entry. Here, however, preference should be given to members of Northern European ethnic groups before others, as it is these people who are the most closely related to us and can most easily be absorbed.

Except where absolutely necessary for occupational purposes, no non-Whites should be granted entry into this country, and any allowed in in order to pursue an occupation should retain the status of aliens and have no permanent right of residence here.

Meanwhile, we must undertake the task of resettling overseas all members of the ethnic minority groups in this country, with the very few exceptions that I shall mention later. The question will immediately be asked: would this be voluntary or compulsory? The answer that I must give is that there is no alternative but for it to be, in the final resort, compulsory.

I have of course heard all the objections to this policy, but I am not impressed with them. Every one of them boils down in the end to the proposition that, if it is a choice between Britain's vital national interests and national future and our compassion towards the ethnic minority members affected, then it is our vital national interests and national future that must be sacrificed. No responsible government could make decisions on that basis.

A voluntary resettlement scheme simply would not have the effect of tackling the problem on the scale on which it must be tackled. If such a scheme were put into operation, presumably with financial inducements offered to back it up, some members of the racial minorities would no doubt take advantage of it, but a substantial number would not but would choose to remain here. In the countries likely to be made open to them, it is extremely unlikely that they would have the chance to earn the money and enjoy the standard of life that they do in Britain. Faced with this fact, there would be many — probably at least half — who would regard the financial inducements given them to leave as being outweighed by the long-term financial loss that they would inevitably suffer by going. We would then be forced either to try to integrate them completely into the British population or to maintain a system of political and social segregation similar to the *apartheid* system in South Africa.

If we decide on integration, we must be prepared to follow the

logic of our thinking to its final conclusion, and its final conclusion is that anything between one and three million non-Whites
would eventually have to be absorbed by intermarriage into the
British population, following which they would beget half-caste
children. Speaking as just one Briton, I am determined that this
will never happen and I suspect that the vast majority of my fellow
countrymen and -women would not wish it to happen either,
though they may be less explicit on the point than I am. I do
not want to see our population change; I prefer it the way it is — at
least in the innate sense, whatever changes we may wish to bring
about in the way of attitudes and living habits. When we think
about our children, it is our natural biological instinct to want to
see them resemble ourselves, and I believe that it is the instinct of
every healthy person to feel about his nation in the same way. We
want to preserve our own stock. It may have got into bad ways. It
may not at present be performing at its best. Some of its present
attitudes may be wrong. But it is still ours, and with it we are
identified and bound in fate.

The half-caste child born into this world is not born to a people
that can look on him or her in this way. He or she is neither part of
one community or another. Inside is a conflict of emotions and
loyalties; outside, in large part, is rejection.

I feel deeply sorry for the child of a mixed marriage, but I can
have no sympathy whatever for the parents who brought that child
into the world. Just to satisfy themselves in momentary terms,
they jeopardised the future. They produced an offspring that will
never wholly fit, and will undoubtedly face a life much harder
than the normal person born of pure race.

No-one can point out to me a single country in the world where
racial mixture has been a success. In almost all countries where it
has occurred, there has been internal instability and division, and
in most this has been accompanied by economic and other forms
of backwardness.

Racial mixture does not, as its advocates would like us to
believe, make for peace and harmony; it makes only for conflict.
There is conflict where white is made to live side by side with
black. And where interbreeding takes place and a mulatto
population is produced, there is even further conflict, because a
third group is brought into being that is not part of either of the
other two. The history of Haiti is an example of this. The
'Coloureds' (mixed breeds) also form a distinct and separate
group within South Africa that is neither black nor white.

But if we are not to have intermarriage, we must in fact have a South African-type system. In South Africa itself, this cannot be avoided; history has bequeathed the race problem to the present generation and the latter is only opting for the best of a selection of solutions, all very imperfect, that are available to it. But in Britain we are not confronted by the same circumstances: history has not bequeathed to us a situation like the South African one; we still have time to reverse the lunacy of the past three or four decades and avoid having to do what the South Africans have to do.

I repeat: a mixed-breed population or an *apartheid* system are the only two alternatives available to us if compulsory resettlement of non-Whites is not put into operation. Those who quake and quiver at such a policy should sit down for a moment and seriously think about the options open to us if it is not adopted. Whatever hardship may be caused to the present generation of non-Whites by such a policy, it is preferable to the endless hardship certain to be caused to both present and future generations of all races in Britain, through race antagonism and social division, if we shirk that policy.

In fact, resettlement can be carried out perfectly humanely and effectively if it is approached in a planned, phased and business-like way. The first principle should be that every person affected should be given all the necessary financial assistance. Their fares to the country of their destination should be paid, and they should in addition be given a resettlement grant to help them get established in that country. The second principle is that they should be given ample time: time to obtain a job and home to go to overseas, and time to sell their property and in other ways wind up their affairs in Britain.

In the case of each person or family to be resettled, the obviously preferable country is the one from which they or their family originally came. If this is not possible, then the attempt should be made to find an alternative country whose racial composition is as similar as can be.

Britain currently has a large programme of aid to Third World nations totalling more than £1,300 million a year. This gives us an extremely powerful leverage with which to negotiate agreements with some of those countries for the resettlement of our ethnic minorities. I believe it is right, eventually, to switch the whole of this aid to the helping of people in Britain. However, for as long as the aid is continued it is only sensible that we should use it to extract some reciprocal favours from the countries benefiting from it. The most obvious favour is the commitment of such countries to take quotas of our ethnic minorities in accordance with their size and resources and the composition of the host populations.

Government agencies should be set up here in collaboration with agencies in the countries concerned, with the object of finding jobs and homes for the migrants being resettled. No doubt, in addition to these, private agencies would spring up too, and these would be welcome. It was by this very process that, in the decades immediately after World War II, millions of British people were able to emigrate to the Dominions, particularly Australia, and there is no reason whatever why the same process should not be employed in the carrying out of this resettlement programme. In fact, the British migrants to Australia had to contribute £10 towards their fares at the time (a much larger sum of money than the same amount today) and they did not, except in a few special cases, get any additional grant to help them when they reached their destination. What we would offer the ethnic minority groups in the programme I am proposing would be considerably more generous.

No person or family involved in this programme would be obliged to leave Britain until they had a home and, where applicable, a job to go to in a country that had agreed to take them, and had also had the opportunity to dispose of their property in Britain at the going market price.

In the case of any elderly coloured folk settled in Britain, who would be long past child-bearing age and who might find resettlement a hardship, we should be prepared to consider, on application, the waiving of this rule and the allowing of such people to see out the remainder of their days in this country.

There is no doubt that the carrying out of this policy would cost a good deal of money, but in the end much more money would be saved by it. Today we bear the financial burden of a huge and expensive machinery of 'race relations', together with many more costs resulting indirectly from the presence of the ethnic minority communities in this country — in education, in law-enforcement, in inner city renewal and in repairing the damage caused by disturbances. To spare the nation these costs into eternity, it would be well worth while to invest for a few years in the programme that is here being put forward. The cost of the programme would be an investment in future national unity and social peace. The investment must be made.

Of all the important national and international issues, there is none today that generates the passion that is generated by race, and none at the same time that is discussed in an atmosphere of such unreason. This is unfortunate, because the racial question is of such profound importance that it, more than perhaps any other, demands that we apply our minds to it absolutely rationally, and make decisions about it that are based on clear and cool thinking rather than under the pressure of panic and hysteria.

Throughout this book I have been deeply critical of much in British life during this century, and no matter how much of our national woes may be laid at the door of our national leaders and institutions we, the British people as a whole, cannot entirely be absolved from responsibility. The fact that we have allowed our rulers to get away with so much, without our offering stiffer resistance to their schemes, is an indictment of us all. Too many of us have looked the other way, tended our gardens and concentrated on filling in our football pool coupons, while our national heritage has been sold. Altogether, this has not been one of the most distinguished centuries in the history of the British Nation.

Nevertheless, there remains the fact that, over the broader span of the human story, this nation and race of ours has a record of excellence of achievement in all fields that is probably unsurpassed by any other. Such an immense undertaking as the British Empire could not have been possible had that Empire not developed under the control of a people endowed with exceptional human qualities. Those very same qualities were to be found in the construction of the first modern industrial nation in the world, and can be seen right up to the present in the extraordinarily high proportion of mankind's most brilliant inventions that have been the work of British brains and ingenuity.

And when it comes to the smoke and blood of war, the world will not dispute that there is no more formidable foe on land, on sea or in the air, than the British fighting man — always providing he is given the right leadership, training and armament to do the job.

While we should be aware of our recent shortcomings and failures and spare no efforts to correct them, we have every reason to be proud of our past, and to look at the world with the level gaze of a people that has proved inferior to none.

It is our duty to ourselves — others too, but first and foremost ourselves — to resolve to preserve within us those racial attributes that made us a great people and may yet make us one again.

It is not hatred for others but only love for what is our own that should impel us to remain the same race that bred the bowmen of Agincourt, the victors over the Spanish Armada, the men who halted Napoleon, the breed that tamed most of three continents and exceeded the splendour that was Ancient Rome.

That today we need improving as a people is beyond doubt: improving in public-spiritedness, in discipline, in workmanship, in health, in morality, in pride, in social behaviour and in respect for the law.

But that improvement must come from a basis of preserved inner character, from the original model, from the traditional and proven national type. We must retain those natural attributes that lie in our blood — then we must bring them out under the stimulus of the great challenges that are to come.

It is no insult to others who do not share in our racial heritage to say to them that they should look to their own heritage — as many of them indeed wish to do — and build on that, developing along their own lines in their own homelands and bringing out of themselves the qualities that are natural to them, and through which they can make their similarly unique contribution to the infinite variety and richness of the human mosaic — something which I know very well many of them would prefer to do.

Our opponents will say that this is 'racism', and so it is! But it is a racism entirely different from that distorted representation of the idea that exists in their own squalid fantasies and is projected in their deliberately slanted propaganda.

What they call 'racism' in our attitude is simply a spirit of self-defence of our own people, and a wish to preserve and pass on that in our national character that our ancestors have handed down to us.

Today, we are being subjected to the most intense pressure from all sides to abandon this instinct and to consent to changes in our society that will make inevitable — whether it be in 50, 100 or 200 years — the permanent and irrevocable destruction of our nationality, thus rendering a total waste the centuries of endeavour that lie behind us.

Many are today willing to yield to this pressure, not because they are happy in their inner consciences to do so, but because they have been intellectually and psychologically terrorised — and to the point at which their rational faculties have deserted them and they bay with the herd or keep silent.

To give just one small illustration of the state of mind of those crusading against 'racism' (i.e. the instinct that I have just described), let me quote from a report that appeared in a newspaper of the court action to which I referred in a previous chapter, in which a Tory MP sued the producers of a BBC TV programme alleging links between him and other members of his party and 'extreme right-wingers' and 'racists'. The man's counsel, referring to the latter, told the court: "Into this stinking cesspit of unbelievable evil the BBC dropped a number of Conservative MPs..."

The stinking cesspit of unbelievable evil referred to here was of course that community of people in this country who wish to preserve the indigenous racial character of the British Nation, and along the lines that I have just described. This language, I remind the reader, was used by a barrister representing a **Conservative** MP, not a leftist. Whether the barrister's client would have endorsed that exact choice of words is unknown, but it certainly must be assumed that he endorsed the general tenor of the argument with which counsel presented his case, and that his feelings about being associated with 'racists' were ones of sufficient revulsion to make the words more or less representative of them — otherwise he would not have brought the action in the first place.

The customary reason why people sue for libel is that they regard their personal character to have been defamed, that they have been associated by some written public statement with some kind of criminality or moral turpitude. That this should now be considered an appropriate description of 'racism' by a Conservative MP and his lawyer is a measure of the mental dragooning to which some people have been subjected on this issue.

In fact, I saw myself the TV programme in question, and my abiding memory of it is of one Tory spokesman after another indignantly denying the charge of being 'racist' in a manner suggestive of someone who had been accused of being a carrier of AIDS or leprosy. The performance was pathetic, illustrating as it did the abject terror now induced in our elected representatives lest they be depicted as holding what is in fact a perfectly normal, natural and commonsense sentiment, i.e. a preference for their own kind.

Perhaps the most revealing remark in the programme came from Mr. John Selwyn Gummer MP, then Tory Party Chairman, who in reply to a question said: "A racist is just about the worst thing that anyone can be."

The worst thing? Worse than a mass-murderer? Worse than a child-molester? Worse than a batterer of old ladies? Worse than a pusher of drugs? Do I have to go through the entire catalogue of human depravity and ask of each category in this catalogue whether it is less morally reprehensible than the desire of people to maintain the character of their own stock? But this would seem to be the message that Mr. Selwyn Gummer had for us! Of course, if one had put him on the spot by asking him whether he actually **literally** meant that 'racists' were more evil than these other species he would no doubt reply: "No, that was not **literally** what I meant." No doubt he had got himself worked up into a state of such sweat that he was stung into an outburst which, when considered rationally, can be seen as quite ridiculous — in other words, his faculty for precision of thought and language left him. But is this not itself a commentary on the atmosphere in which the debate on the race issue is now being conducted? Here we have a leading political figure, not unaccustomed to expressing himself in public, getting in such a panic as to come out with absurdities of this kind. It would surely seem that our present-day rulers have been house-trained to react to words like 'race' and 'racism' as the legendary Count Dracula was supposed to react to the appearance of the crucifix.

I have seen this phenomenon at work many times and in many places. People of otherwise sound intelligence, and who are capable of rational discussion of almost any other subject, completely lose their reason the moment the topic turns to race, and descend to a silliness that would hardly be tolerated in a kindergarten class. Observing this process at work has been, to me, highly instructive in the study of how capable, but weak, minds can be reduced to a state similar to those of the dogs of Dr. Pavlov, which salivated at the mere sound of the ringing of a bell.

Why this paralysis of reason on race? Without doubt, the first explanation that comes to mind is the legacy of emotion produced by books, films and newspaper articles about Nazi Germany, indeed by the whole of what might be called the 'anti-nazi industry', an industry that thrives today long after Hitler's Reich went into oblivion. The Nazis were 'racists', the thinking goes, and in the end look what happened: their racism led to the gas chambers and the slaughter of six million Jews. The moral? Everyone who wants to preserve his own race is a Nazi, or at least an incipient one; and the end result of what he stands for will be mass-extermination!

There is a growing school of historians today that in fact challenges the accuracy of the allegation that the German Nazis ever had any intended extermination programme, and puts forward the counter-claim that the high death-rate in the German concentration camps towards the end of World War II was caused mainly by sickness, famine and the breakdown of food and medical supplies that was general in Germany at the time, and to which Allied bombing largely contributed.

But whether this revised view of that phase of history is correct or incorrect should not concern us here. Even if it could be proved beyond any possible doubt that the original and established view of what happened in Germany was factually correct, it would not have the slightest bearing on the validity or invalidity of 'racism'. It would merely confirm that certain people who happened to hold to that idea pursued it to an extreme and unjust end. If the argument for or against 'racism' is to rest on this question of the alleged 'holocaust', just where does that reasoning take us? It means that everyone who endorses modern liberalism must endorse the French Revolution that was carried out in the name of the same doctrine — this endorsement implying, by the same logic as applying to 'Nazism', endorsement also of the Terror that followed that Revolution. It means that everyone who endorses socialism must endorse the mass murders committed in the name of that creed in Stalin's Russia and countless other parts of the world under Soviet sway. It means that everyone who endorses Christianity must endorse the excesses of the Spanish Inquisition and the many other outbreaks of persecution and murder that have convulsed Europe in the process of our established church waging its many wars against declared 'infidels'. Need I go any further? The reader will surely by now be with me in accepting that we are going from the sublime to the ridiculous, but it is precisely this reasoning that has created the present climate in which racial differences, and the enormous political and social implications that spring from these differences, cannot be calmly and objectively discussed.

What people should today be asking themselves is: Why? Why the extremity of the pressure to which they are being subjected on this matter? Why is 'anti-racism' being pursued with the frantic urgency, and the crazy intolerance, that characterise its every move and gesture? What motives lie behind the frenzy that is now rampant everywhere in the drive to crush every act and expression of white racial self-defence?

In what cause and purpose is the world today being whipped up into a demented fury of hatred and aggression against South Africa, which threatens no-one and which is trying, by the most civilised methods possible, to cope with a situation of internal difficulty of which most of the rest of mankind is completely ignorant and could not possibly manage in any better way? How and why is this happening, while elsewhere in the world there is a daily routine of barbarism and inhumanity that passes almost without public comment and whose perpetrators are the targets of no comparable campaign of international opposition?

The answer can surely only be that behind this apparent lunacy there are shrewd calculation and method at work, that a deadly war is being conducted against the White Race, and that the greatest fear of those conducting this war is a proper awakening of race consciousness in the white nations.

To prevent that awakening, the term 'racism' has had to be invented. The word itself is new, but that which it describes is not. The latter has been the instinct of every healthy tribe and species on earth since life began, in the animal world as much as in the human. It means nothing more or less than our will to self-preservation as a group. It is, as I have said, an instinct that has nothing whatever to do with hate — for it is first and foremost positive, not negative. Those who have this instinct do not go about looking for enemies to attack, but prefer to devote their energies to building a better life for their own kind. If, however, their own kind is attacked, they recognise the attackers as enemies and deal with them accordingly. Hatred will inevitably come into the equation in this kind of situation, because the inability to hate one's enemy is the surest sign that one's survival instinct is exhausted.

Because we love our children, it does not mean that we hate everyone else's. But if someone else threatened to harm one of our children, they ought quickly to become an object of our hatred and be dealt with as an enemy. Then, and then only, would there be hate. Yet it is on the basis of the idea that someone who loves his own children must hate everyone else's children that our opponents try to depict 'racists' as necessarily hating every race other than their own.

What is intolerable to those who wish to destroy our race is that there should be some amongst us who wish to defend it against destruction. That, and that alone, is why 'racism' is under attack — by which I mean of course **white** racism, because it is the White Race that is being attacked today. Black, brown and yellow racism are not the objects of any opprobrium.

In warfare, it is elementary that when you are seeking to destroy your adversary you locate what is the most important weapon in his defence and you concentrate first of all on destroying that weapon. Our enemy knows that our most important weapon of defence is our racial consciousness and our will to racial survival. Destroy those things and thereby destroy us — that is our enemy's reasoning and strategy.

It is in this way that we must understand the frenzy of the current onslaught on white racial consciousness. The onslaught is a two-pronged one. One part of it is a drive to alienate us from the idea of racial consciousness by a complete distortion of its meaning — from a positive one of love to a negative one of hatred. The other part of the onslaught consists of psychological terror, aimed at intimidating away from racial consciousness anyone who may not be entirely persuaded that it is a bad thing. The strategy is simple: persuade as many as you can; and those you cannot persuade you frighten!

We have reached a point today at which this onslaught by our enemies has succeeded in effectively putting out of action all persons in Britain today holding any kind of public office or other positions of influence or power. Such people have been neutralised as defenders of our race by one or another of the two forms of attack of which I have spoken: their minds have been bent by the lies and distortions of the 'anti-racist' propaganda factory, or else their spirits have been cowed into submission by fear of the consequences if they resist.

We therefore have a situation in which the only ones able and willing to offer a defence of the British people against those who would destroy them are the ones who are prepared to stand up and be counted as 'racists'. And naturally it is against these ones — against **us** — that all the venom of the enemy is now concentrated. We of course are the ones who represent a "stinking cesspit of unbelievable evil" and similar such images!

In this war for the preservation and resurgence of Britain we fight battles on many fronts, some political, some spiritual, some economic, some concerned with social, intellectual and cultural questions. Every one of these battles is important, for all bear on the question of what kind of a nation this is to be in the future.

But the battle to save our race is the most important of all, for if that is lost we will have no nation in the future.

A nation can be led to disaster by a series of bad decisions in the political, economic or other fields. It can even lose a war and suffer conquest and occupation, with its assets plundered and its population reduced to servitude — for a time.

But it can recover and find again its unique greatness in new times, under new leadership and with a new direction. History offers abundant examples of this.

But if a race is destroyed, whether by genocide, failure to reproduce or genetic change, all is lost — and forever. Then no new leadership, even of the highest genius, no change, no new direction, no investment of money, can ever resurrect it. It disappears from history.

That is why the present battle to defend the British Race is the ultimate battle, and the one in which we **must** be the victors. For there will be no second chance.

Chapter 17
What is at stake in Ulster

I write about the Northern Ireland question, not in a spirit of objectivity, but as a partisan. Members of my family stood for the Union between Ireland and Britain, and I have inherited this tradition of thought and feeling. This is an appropriate theme with which to begin this chapter because the first lesson to learn about the Irish issue is that it can never be approached with anything other than a partisan attitude. The appalling mess made in Ireland by British policy is the direct result of politicians this side of the Irish Sea persisting in the idea that Ireland is a remote and separate country, in the affairs of which Britain has been cast by fate in the role of 'honest broker' in a war between local factions in which she has no interest. Nothing could be further from the truth. Ireland is a natural and inseparable part of that geopolitical, historical, economic, cultural and racial unit that is the British Isles. If Britain is today unaware of this fact, her enemies certainly are not. For the past century they have waged a war to separate the two islands, knowledgeable in the fact that every vital British interest demands that they be bound together.

The populations of the two Irelands are amalgams of the same stocks as those making up the population of mainland Britain. Of course, the proportions involved are different, just as they vary in different regions of the mainland; but this does not compromise the basic ethnic unity of the whole. Stand in a street in Dublin, and you would observe nothing in the passers by to indicate that you were not looking at British people walking about in a British city. That the same is true of Belfast hardly needs stating.

There is no such thing as an 'Irish Race'. At the time of the Viking invasions of Britain, those marauding Scandinavians crossed over to Ireland and settled there, mingling with the older Celtic elements just as they did in England and Scotland. Over subsequent centuries, Ireland was continually settled by English, Scottish and Welsh families. The mingling of these with the original Irish population produced some of the best stocks to be found anywhere in the British Isles, with an output of outstanding men far out of proportion to their modest numbers. The Anglo-Irish and Scots-Irish, for instance, have bred an extraordinary succession of magnificent soldiers — so much so that Ireland's role as a reservoir of military leadership for Britain has been compared with that of Prussia *vis-a-vis* Germany. In addition to this, a great number of famous writers, poets and musicians claimed as 'Irish' should in fact be given the correct designation of **British**, as they sprang from these same British-Irish stocks.

A part of the Irish population, north and south, is admirable testimony to the benefits of the mingling of closely related racial elements — which should not be confused with the admixture of entirely different and mutually incompatible races, such as white and black or white and Asian.

In Northern Ireland today, we have a community of people whose qualitative value to the British Nation is incomparably greater than that suggested by its size. Of all communities in the United Kingdom, it is the most patriotic — in the true meaning of the term. It is also the most politically aware. The academic standards obtained in its centres of learning are higher than anywhere on the mainland. And it has a fine heritage of skills in engineering and other industrial fields. The battlefields of four continents have been moistened by the blood of many tens of thousands of men from Ulster regiments, who have always been at the front of the enlistment queues at the times of Britain's greatest need.

Yet it is this community that the leaders of Britain are now showing more than willing to expel from the nation!

Of the main political factions at Westminster, two — Labour and the newly formed 'Social and Liberal Democrats' — are committed to work for the earliest possible absorption of Ulster by the Irish Republic. In the case of the Tories, this same purpose is clearly implicit — if not yet publicly acknowledged — in every action, gesture and attitude of Conservative governments and spokesmen of recent times.

Numerous theories have been advanced to explain this phenomenon. The politicians are tired of the strife that has racked Ulster for the past two decades and want to get the province off their hands in view of the commitment of military resources and money that is needed for its defence. External pressure, from Europe and even more from the United States, is being applied against Britain in favour of disengagement. British public opinion, sickened by the violence of the bombers and the gunmen, does not have its heart in the maintenance of the Union, and a withdrawal from Ulster would in that regard be electorally popular.

There is some truth in all these suppositions, but that should hardly be comforting to us — because none of them says much for Britain's present vigour or honour as a nation. Certainly, we have been under pressure internationally to withdraw from Northern Ireland, and in the case of the United States the pressure has been intense. But what kind of government can it be, in any country, that makes policy decisions on vital domestic matters in response to foreign demands? If every public issue in and concerning Britain were decided on that basis, we may as well renounce every claim to nationhood. The very idea that a British government should think and act according to such criteria is surely an indication that British politics have descended to a new low in contemptibility.

And if British public opinion (outside Ulster, that is) has no heart in the maintenance of the Union, what does that tell us? Only that this public opinion, over Ulster as over so many other issues, has become hopelessly misdirected and confused — due mainly to its reliance for facts on communications media which, as I have pointed out elsewhere, are today in the hands of people who do not want Britain to survive as a nation.

And if, in the face of this bemused state of public opinion, politicians can think of no better response than to tailor their policies to the purchase of votes, surely that again speaks volumes for the types of politician with which we have today become afflicted!

What, after all, is the source of the strife in Ulster? A neighbouring state, which for the purpose of present discussion must be accounted as foreign, wants to take from us a part of British territory, and in pursuit of that ambition has people situated in that territory who are prepared to work for it by every manner of criminal and subversive means. The majority living there, however, does not want to submit to this take-over, and many among that majority are prepared to resist it actively — some even at the risk of their lives.

To establish clarity on this matter, I ask the reader of this book to consider a hypothesis in which some region of the South East of England — say, Sussex — had become an area of contention concerning sovereignty between Britain and France. Let us suppose that the French had decided, on the basis of the landing of William of Normandy in 1066, that they had a claim on that county. Although the great majority of the people of the county wanted to remain British, there was an element there holding Francophile sympathies, and this element had embarked on a campaign of destruction and murder designed to intimidate the government into surrendering Sussex to France.

What would we then say if the most public-spirited members of the loyalist majority population in the county rose in fury against this Francophile element and organised themselves to resist, by all means necessary, the absorption of Sussex by the French? We would surely, if we were in our right minds, applaud their patriotism and give them all possible support.

Of course, as long as the hypothetical Francophiles in Sussex continued their campaign of destruction and murder there would be in the county a sustained atmosphere of strife. But would that be just reason for the rest of Britain to say that, because of this strife, holding onto Sussex was simply not worth all the unpleasantness and trouble, to say nothing of the loss of lives, and that therefore we should withdraw and let the county become a French *departement*?

Let us take the hypothesis further. Let us suppose — as would not be remarkable in view of recent history — that the government in London showed itself to be by no means wholehearted in its commitment to defend Sussex against foreign take-over but, on the contrary, indicated every sign of a willingness to consider the French claim, entering into talks with Paris about the county's future and inviting delegates from the French government to sit on a council set up to play a part in Sussex affairs; let us suppose, in addition to this, that for reasons of not wishing to upset the pro-French section of the Sussex population the government did not prosecute the campaign against the terrorists with all the force and vigour at its command but, on the contrary, gave the security forces there the order to act with kid gloves, and in every possible way gave sign of a lack of will to bring the war against terrorism in Sussex to a victorious conclusion; in such a situation, should we really be surprised if loyal Sussex people, feeling that their own government was not prepared to defend them adequately, began to organise their own local defence units and adopted towards those who had begun the terror campaign a policy of reprisals?

Yet this scenario, in which I have indulged in a little flight of fantasy, is not fantasy at all in Northern Ireland; the situation there exactly parallels it.

It may therefore be seen that, though all these cited reasons for withdrawal from Ulster may indeed exist in the minds of those favouring withdrawal, not one single one of them can be accounted a **good** reason; on the contrary, all of them are utterly pathetic.

I would, however, suggest another reason why the British community in Northern Ireland is under attack, and this goes more deeply to the heart of contemporary British politics than any of the reasons so far examined.

A recurring theme throughout this book has been the creeping take-over of Britain and the Western World by the forces of internationalism, liberalism and decadence, backed and controlled by money power. The attitude of these forces is proprietary and monopolistic: their masters cannot tolerate the existence of any community, any institutions or any square mile of territory anywhere where their writ does not run, where they do not have a thorough stranglehold — politically, economically, culturally, ideologically, spiritually. If anywhere among the white nations a pocket of resistance to this 'new world order', albeit only partial resistance, manifests itself, the rule is that that resistance must be crushed — and, pending the achievement of this, isolated out on a limb, so that its influence may not be contagious.

White South Africa is an example of just such a pocket of resistance: a community of white men and women that will not fall into line with the blueprint that 'Big Brother' has drawn up for us all, a community that dares to resist the destruction of its nationhood. That is precisely why South Africa is today under concerted international attack. Though even in South Africa there has been a degree of surrender to these world forces, the surrender has not gone far enough for the latter's satisfaction; it must be total. The onslaught against that country will continue until it is.

In a slightly different way, Northern Ireland is another case of a territory and community that will not conform. Due partially to a combination of the accidents of geography and history, and partially to a special spirit and quality in her people, Northern Ireland has, like South Africa, not wholly fallen captive to the *zeitgeist* of the 20th century. 'Liberalism' does not dominate her political institutions, nor her educational system, nor her church, nor her people. Though the liberal Trojan horse is present in Northern Ireland in the presence of British mainland newspapers, television and radio, and as a result the province cannot be regarded as entirely immune to such influences, the infection has not gone anything like as deep, or spread anything like as wide, as elsewhere.

Worst of all (from the standpoint of Britain's enemies), there is in the small population of Northern Ireland an uncomfortably large number of people who have not been lulled into political semi-consciousness by the soporifics, diversions and bread and circuses of our modern push-button civilisation, but who, on the contrary, care enough about the future of their community and its national heritage to lift themselves out of their armchairs and go out onto the streets and work — and if necessary fight — for that future and that heritage.

To the would-be makers of our 'brave new world' of comatose, uniform mankind, such a community is dangerous.

It is particularly dangerous to the liberal establishment of Britain as long as it lies within our territory and is part of our nation and state. Hence the strenuous effort to keep it at arms length, to deny it full participation in the national life (Ulster people are not allowed to join any of the established mainland political parties) and gradually, gently and by every available means of double-dealing and subterfuge, to force it out of the United Kingdom altogether.

This, above all, is the reason for the onslaught against Ulster — not Irish 'nationalism', which is an entirely synthetic product created to subvert our Kingdom and drive a wedge between British peoples. It is important that we should understand this if we are to arm ourselves with the knowledge to deal with the threat to Ulster and the wider threat to the whole British people of which it is part.

It is in this perspective that we must see the hooded IRA gunman and the smooth-talking Tory minister with the smart leather briefcase as twin daggers aimed at Ulster's heart — albeit that they are of entirely different appearance and are wielded from entirely different directions.

Elsewhere in this book I have described how anyone who is seen to stand in the way of the world juggernaut of liberalism and internationalism becomes the object of the most vituperative character assassination, at both the individual and collective level. In this way, in the drive to destroy White South Africa media propaganda has depicted the members of that community in a wholly distorted and unfavourable light, with the object of isolating them and inflaming the world against them. This technique has varied very little in the treatment of the loyalist community in Ulster, and with the same objective — particularly with regard to public opinion in mainland Britain. We should now look at the arguments used to discredit the Ulster loyalists, and see if they really stand up.

The first argument that is usually touted around is that the Protestant Ulsterman is a religious bigot and intolerant of anyone belonging to the Catholic faith. There probably are a few Ulster Protestants of whom this is true, just as there are a few Ulster Catholics of whom the same can be said. But this does not remotely represent the root of the divisions.

The loyalist Ulsterman is first and foremost a British patriot. As such, he is resistant to the idea of absorption into a state that has renounced its British connection. He is therefore naturally hostile to the republican movement in the province.

The republicans recruit their support predominantly from the Catholic section of the population. This does not by any means mean that every individual Catholic is a republican sympathiser; quite a significant number are not. It is nevertheless true that most politically active and committed Catholics are republicans, and virtually all Catholic organisations and institutions in Northern Ireland are, with varying vehemence, republican in outlook. It is also a fact that the hold of the IRA and other republican terrorist groups over the Catholic community in Ulster is such that members of that community openly aligned with the loyalist cause, or with the forces of the British State, live in constant danger. It is well known that Catholic members of the Royal Ulster Constabulary and Ulster Defence Regiment have frequently been the victims of republican murder gangs.

In consequence, the reality that every Ulster loyalist has to face is that the granting to Catholics of positions of power and influence in the province is more likely than not to lead to an increase in the power and influence of republicanism and a weakening of the province's British link.

If only the issue of republicanism became well and truly dead and buried in Northern Ireland and all members of the population fully accepted the province's status as a part of the United Kingdom and rejoiced in their British nationality, the way would be open to a proper integration of the two communities into one, where a person's religion was an entirely private matter and would be of no greater import in respect of his rights as a member of society than in England and Wales and most of Scotland.

But the republican issue is not dead and buried in Northern Ireland, and it is not so precisely because government in London has decided that it should not be so. Government in London has never given an unequivocal commitment that Northern Ireland shall forever remain British, only a half-hearted one that it shall do so ''for as long as the majority wishes it.'' This has been perceived by loyalists, and quite correctly, as being no more than a grudging acceptance of the present *status quo*, behind which there lurks the hope that this will one day change, and then Britain can wash its hands of Ulster with a clear conscience!

This conditional British guarantee, and the obvious inference it contains, has been the factor that has sustained the IRA and its allies in their will to continue the terrorist war and has ensured the maintenance of a state of instability in the province. Britain's enemies in Ulster know that the British — or at least their political leaders — want out, and are just looking for and hoping for the right circumstances to arrive for them to get out. This keeps all the hopes of republicans alive and gives the bombers and the gunmen the incentive to carry on.

London could end this state of affairs once and for all by asserting, with no ifs or buts, its determination to keep Northern Ireland British, telling the republicans, by word and by deed, that they have no hope ever of seeing their aims fulfilled, and saying to all who do not like living under British sovereignty that they should go and live somewhere else. By such a simple and forthright gesture, Britain could set Ulster on the road to stability and peace. But Britain refuses to make it.

Instead, Britain has instituted the infamous Anglo-Irish Agreement, which is in effect an open acknowledgement that she does not regard Northern Ireland as a wholly British concern and that she intends gradually to bring the Irish Republic into the province by a process of stealth, one little step at a time, until Ulster people wake up one morning and find that their British heritage has been bartered away.

London has continually reasserted its promise that the wish of the majority in Ulster over the question of sovereignty will always be observed; but how much are Ulster people expected to regard this promise as worth when London has completely failed to abide by the wishes of the majority on the question of the Anglo-Irish Agreement? First, the Agreement was declared government policy without any attempt to test public opinion on the matter by means of a referendum. Next, the Ulster Unionist MPs forced what, in effect, became a referendum by resigning their seats and compelling a series of by-elections, in which they stood again on the policy of opposition to the Agreement. They were all, with one exception, re-elected; and this proved that the Agreement did not have majority consent. But this did not prevent the government in London going ahead and implementing it. Once again, 'democracy' was shown to be the fraud that it is. So what is to prevent a British government in the future doing just the same again and ratting on its promise not to take Ulster into the Irish Republic without the consent of the majority?

For the fact that there is a very real threat of a republican take-over of Northern Ireland we have to thank the intervention of British government. And as long as such a threat exists, and the Catholic community in the province is seen as the breeding ground from which republicanism draws its fifth column in Ulster, it is natural that there is going to be a resistance among the loyalist majority to the idea of accepting Catholics as fully equal fellow-citizens, most of all against welcoming them into the circles of those holding power in the conduct of public affairs.

This leads us to a look at the next criticism that is made of many Ulster loyalists: that they have shown themselves incapable of a spirit of compromise and conciliation with the republican factions — the instransigent attitude of the loyalists towards the Anglo-Irish Agreement being just the latest symptom of this unwilling-ness to compromise. If the loyalists were British, as they claim to be, so the argument goes, they would embrace the British tradition of compromise; as they do not, this calls into question their Britishness.

Those who employ this argument clearly show that they have not the slightest ability to discern the limits within which compromise is possible, to distinguish between those issues that are soluble by compromise and those that are not. Compromise is possible, sometimes, between groups of people who have a common objective and a common allegiance. If the dividing factor is merely that of a difference of opinion as to ways to reach a common objective or pursue a common allegiance, then it is possible to conceive situations in which a compromise is workable and the best way out.

Likewise, compromise can be operable when it involves groups of people who, though they may differ, can live side by side in the same community — if not compromise, then at least mutual tolerance. An example is the differing attitudes between the adherents of grammar school and comprehensive education. A middle way in that dispute can be achieved by allowing both types of school to exist and letting the argument be resolved, if it is ever resolved, by which system gets the better results.

Likewise, a compromise between capitalistic and socialistic concepts of economy can be reached by having an economic system that includes elements of each and which in whole lies somewhere between the two. And it is possible to envisage the economic management of a nation being undertaken by a group of people including some who prefer one type of economy and some who favour the other.

But there cannot possibly be compromise between two groups of people who cling to two different and conflicting national allegiances, one of which wants its province to belong to one nation and the other to belong to another nation. Northern Ireland is either British or it is not British; it cannot be half British and half something else. And it is a complete nonsense to say that politicians in Northern Ireland whose allegiance is to the United Kingdom can be expected to sit down at the same table as politicians whose allegiance is to what is, by their own choice, a foreign state, and work out with them mutually acceptable solutions to the problems of that province when each side's conception of those solutions is at polar opposites to that of the other.

Loyalists in Ulster quite properly regard those on the republican side as **enemies**. That is the only term appropriate to those who wish to see sovereignty over a part of our national territory taken over by a foreign country. To revert to our earlier hypothesis, supposing that Britain and France were in conflict over the question of which nation had claim to the county of Sussex, what term other than **enemies** could British loyalists in that county be expected to apply to those who were working for the incorporation of the county into France? And how on earth could they be expected to sit down and form common council with them to work out common policies for the county when there was no common ground on which even to begin?

It is certainly true that in their attitude to this question Ulster loyalists are out of step with the probable consensus of thinking on the mainland — but only because thinking on the mainland over the whole matter dwells in a cloud-cuckooland that is utterly remote from the politics of the real world.

Ulster loyalists are in fact accused of being 'immoderate' men and women simply because, unlike the establishment mind in Westminster, they see no middle way between holding onto their national heritage and surrendering it. And neither can I!

If loyal Ulstermen appear to many people this side of the sea to be a strange breed of people whose ways of thinking are incomprehensible over here, I would suggest it is because the ways of thinking of many over here have become locked in a kind of mental paralysis in which reason and logic, and most of all instinct, have been placed under suspension. Liberalism, which rules on the mainland — at least among the 'educated' classes, has succeeded largely in reducing all issues to a kind of sponge-like substance, in which vapid sentiments are mistaken for policies and pious phrases as solutions to problems and conflicts. When Ulstermen speak in tones that cut through the mush and the slush to the core of an issue, they are talking a language that is strange to the liberal-conditioned mind, which prefers to escape from stark alternatives of reality into a dream world in which all such issues are blurred and in which reality is the enemy.

Liberals, when speaking of the Whites in South Africa, refer to them as having the 'laager mentality' — which translated into plain English means that when they see their country under attack their instinct is to defend it. Doubtless, liberals would use exactly the same phrase to describe the loyalists in Northern Ireland, who are guilty, in liberal eyes, of the unpardonable crime of being unwilling to compromise with those whose avowed intent is to take their province away from them and, in the process, destroy their nationhood.

One has the feeling about the liberal, the man of 'moderation', that if he were stopped in the street by a mugger who demanded his wallet his mind would immediately contemplate the alternatives of surrendering that possession or telling the mugger to get lost as representing two 'extremes' of the argument, and therefore options to be rejected. 'Moderation' would counsel that a compromise solution be sought: the mugger should be offered half the contents of the wallet in the hope that he would go away satisfied and a fight be avoided!

Or perhaps, in preference to the solution of dividing the contents of the wallet between the two, our liberal would suggest to the mugger that it thenceforth became joint property — neither solely the mugger's possession nor his! But before you laugh, consider that this little cameo is not far removed from what men of 'moderation' advocate we do with the republicans in respect of Northern Ireland!

Another count on which Ulster loyalists are put in the dock is their disinclination to accept the Anglo-Irish Agreement, notwithstanding that it was approved by parliament. "If they are as loyal to Britain as they claim to be," the argument runs, "they would abide by the decision of Britain's democratically elected sovereign body."

Here the politicians and press pundits reveal much about the thinking of the liberalist mind. To that mind, the 'nation' and its parliament are one. 'Patriotism' consists of being loyal to the institutions of parliament and government rather than to nationhood itself. The reality today is that parliament has approved so many policies and measures detrimental to the interests of the British people that it can no longer be considered a fit representative of this people. Are we all to sit back and regard it as the 'patriotic' thing to do to support the Africanisation of large areas of our great cities just because parliament in a majority approves it? Is it 'patriotic' to acquiesce in the surrender of British sovereignty to the EEC just because parliament has given its sanction to that policy? I could go on *ad infinitum* giving examples of policies obtaining majority endorsement at Westminster that in fact spell death to the British Nation. Yet it is considered the duty of the 'patriot' or 'loyalist' not to oppose them precisely because they carry that endorsement. No more feather-brained reasoning could be imagined.

What must be grasped today is that parliament as presently constituted, together with other established political institutions, is the **enemy** of the real British Nation, not its true representative. Patriotism and duty lie in **opposing** parliament, not in supporting it — opposing it within the law, of course, but opposing it nevertheless, and with all possible legal means.

And even the obligation to observe legality is not absolute. If the situation in Northern Ireland develops to a point, as it shows every indication of doing, at which parliament approved the transference of sovereignty to the Irish Republic, this would amount in effect to an act of **national treason** attaining the stamp of 'legality'. In that event, Ulster loyalists would face the choice between breaking the law and losing their nationhood. In my mind, they would, if forced to such a stage, be wholly justified in breaking the law. In fact, faced with an almost identical situation in 1912 they showed themselves ready to do precisely that, and warded off, if only for a time, the act of treason that has always been the ultimate intention of Westminster.

This brings us to another object of regular condemnation: the loyalist paramilitary groups. These are frequently described as consisting of 'thugs', 'bullyboys' and even 'stormtroops', and it is a regular pastime of the press to lump them together with the IRA and depict the two as being merely opposite sides of the same coin.

But in fact there can be no comparison. The IRA and its allies started the present terror in Northern Ireland, just as they started all previous phases of the same terror. The loyalist paramilitaries have been called into being solely as a defensive response to the violence from the republican side — and this only because, as indicated before, no government in London has shown the will, or even the wish, to win the war against republican terror. The official security forces in Ulster, though they comprise many very fine men, have been deployed, on the orders of government, in a manner which provides no hope that the IRA and its allies will be defeated and destroyed — indeed it is now conventional wisdom in the British 'establishment' that there can be no military victory over the IRA. What is really meant by this is that there can be no military victory over the IRA within the framework of present policy, which is to concede by political means everything that the IRA has been fighting for by means of armed force. It is also clear that there can be no military victory over the IRA by a state which is not prepared to use all the methods available that are necessary to obtain victory. An army in which each soldier is fighting with one hand tied behind his back is not going to triumph over an enemy that fights with no holds barred!

The reality is of course that Britain is at war in Northern Ireland, and the problem is that government does not recognise this reality. Official security forces in Ulster are hamstrung, not only by government policy of bending over backwards to appease the republican-leaning element in the population, but also by the fact that, a war situation not being acknowledged, the enemy must be dealt with in accordance with the ordinary rules of policing: he must be proven in a court of law to have broken the law before he can be punished.

This absurd situation was highlighted in the recent controversy involving the 'shoot-to-kill' policy said to have been adopted by certain RUC officers. In a climate of national sanity, such a policy would be accepted all round as an inevitable circumstance of war, and the men responsible should have been given commendations for carrying out their duty with courage and resolution; instead they are being regarded as little better than common criminals. The fact is of course that as long as the IRA operates a 'shoot-to-kill' policy against British police and servicemen, a reciprocal 'shoot-to-kill' policy on the part of the latter is the only rational response.

It is against this background that the loyalist paramilitaries have emerged. They recognise, if the government does not, that a state of war exists, and that in that situation the ethics and rules of war must apply. These are that you eliminate your enemy where you find him, and without the niceties of legal procedure. It is indeed unfortunate that we have come to such a situation in a part of the United Kingdom, and the sooner the situation is ended the better. But for this unhappy circumstance I blame the government and the whole 'softly-softly' strategy that it has adopted towards the men of terror and violence since the present phase of the trouble began in the late 1960s.

It must also be said in defence of the loyalist paramilitaries that nowhere at any time have they been guilty of the indiscriminate murder of innocent people by such practices as the placing of bombs in town centres. To draw parallels between them and the IRA or INLA is to bend the truth completely.

Above all, we cannot place the loyalist paramilitaries in the same category as the IRA or INLA because the former are on our side — the **British** side — while the latter are not. One group has resorted to the use of force to defend British sovereignty in Northern Ireland whereas the other has resorted to force to destroy it. That vast numbers of people on the mainland cannot recognise this crucial distinction is a measure of the stupor that has descended upon us where matters of our national interest and survival are concerned. We are here reminded of Muggeridge's homily about those who cannot tell their friends from their enemies...

This of course brings us to the crux of the issue. The handling of the Ulster question has been bedevilled from the start by the fact that Britain has maintained a neutral attitude between her own loyal subjects and her enemies — indeed, in a sense, something even worse than a neutral attitude in that, in ultimate policy, it is the intention to give those enemies what they are seeking. In the true tradition of 'liberalism', we seem in this matter, as in so many others, to have lost the instinct to play for our own side. As I stated at the beginning of this chapter, the only proper position that can ever be taken on Northern Ireland is a partisan one. The seemingly 'insoluble' nature of the problem lies only in the failure to recognise this truth and in persisting in chasing the phantom of a solution that will leave everybody happy.

But the whole matter has a much larger dimension. If, on the issue of Northern Ireland, we do not take our own side and support our own people, just where will we ever do so? As the world watches Britain play the role of the detached 'neutral' in a life-and-death struggle for a piece of her own territory and between those who are her most ardently patriotic citizens and those who passionately hate her, that world takes note that it is beholding a nation that has lost the faculty to tell friend from foe, together with the will to defend its own soil. Is that not surely an invitation to anyone, anywhere to wipe their feet on us with impunity?

Of course, present British policy in Ulster is consistent with our long record of retreat from Ireland. I have related earlier how my own grandfather gave the best years of his life to preventing that retreat, only to find at the end of it all that he and the staunch men who served under him had risked their lives, and in some cases sacrificed those lives, for nothing. The British establishment, then as now, was bent on surrender. Throughout this century, this establishment would fight for self-determination for Poles, Czechs and Jews in far off lands but would always surrender its own realm and abandon its own people. Ask White Rhodesians, for they know better than most!

The key to an ending of the troubles in Northern Ireland lies in a complete rejection of this non-partisan policy and the adoption of a policy of uncompromising defence of the province as a part of the United Kingdom, and of support for the people there who fight to defend their British heritage. This should involve the scrapping of the Anglo-Irish Agreement and all other schemes for the partic-ipation of republicans, whether local or imported from the South, in Northern Irish affairs. As for the government of the Irish Republic, it should be told curtly, as the rest of the world should be told, to mind its own business and leave Britain to mind hers — and Northern Ireland is exclusively Britain's business.

The declaration should be made that Northern Ireland will remain British for all time, and such a declaration should be made without qualification or equivocation.

Republicanism in Northern Ireland, in any shape or form, should be treated as what it is: not a legitimate wing of political opinion but subversion against the British Nation and State. And it should be dealt with accordingly.

We should regard religious non-discrimination in Northern Ireland as a desirable aim, though not one that can ever be enforced by legislation, as is presently being planned. But the freedom given to Roman Catholics should not include the freedom to impose the influence of a foreign religious head, or that of a foreign political power, on the policies of state. All Catholic organisations and institutions in Ulster should be required to drop their affiliations with Irish Republicanism, especially in the case of the schools and other places of learning. Therein lies, for the Catholics, the best chance of their eventually being treated as fully equal citizens.

We lament the fact that Northern Ireland is a divided community, and yet it has been our own weakness in the administration of the province that has ensured the maintenance of this division. If we allow the children of one section of the community to be taught allegiance to one state and those of the other section to be taught allegiance to another state, we are going to have division. Schools in the United Kingdom, of whatever religious affiliation, should instil into their pupils only one loyalty: a **British** loyalty. That is what they are there for.

The campaign against terrorism should be pursued with all the force and vigour at our command, and with no methods eschewed on the grounds that they might offend republican sympathisers. Security forces are in Northern Ireland to protect the British State, not as part of a goodwill mission to Britain's enemies.

The death penalty should be restored as an automatic punishment for those guilty of acts of terrorism, just as it should exist as an option for the courts in dealing with other categories of serious crime, including of course murder and treason.

We should accept that loyalist paramilitary groups are going to be necessary auxiliaries to the official security forces in Northern Ireland, just for as long as it takes for republican terrorism to be eliminated once and for all. While this emergency exists, the loyalist paramilitaries should be regarded as our allies, and there should be the closest co-operation between them and the official law-enforcement agencies. With a demonstration, however, of a firm resolve on the part of government to deploy the official security forces in the proper way, with no holds barred, and in pursuit of a consistent loyalist policy, the need for the paramilitaries will gradually recede.

I have spoken earlier of the patriotic spirit and heightened political awareness of the Ulster loyalists, and this must be counted as one of our greatest national assets — which is certainly the major reason why they are under attack. I would urge upon all Ulster loyalists, however, that their battle will inevitably be lost if they restrict their campaign to Northern Ireland alone. A British State which is dedicated to forcing them out of the Kingdom will most certainly succeed eventually in doing just that if it is opposed only by the Ulster loyalist movement itself and within the confines of the province of Ulster.

This fact aside, a British State that is dedicated to such an aim makes a nonsense of the whole cause and purpose of the Ulster loyalist movement. How can loyalty survive when it is for ever unrequited?

The victory of the cause of loyal Ulster can only be achieved within the framework of a United Kingdom entirely different from the one existing at present. And, furthermore, such a victory is only worthwhile if the Britain to which Ulster is loyal is deserving of that loyalty.

From this it follows that the Ulster loyalist movement must become allied to the cause of British Nationalism. The cause of Ulster cannot be victorious unless it prevails on the British mainland as well as in Ulster itself. And it is only the type of Britain to which we, as British Nationalists, aspire that can measure up to the ideals of those who have fought and died for a British Ulster.

Ulster loyalists must therefore, in the years ahead, undertake a fundamental change of strategy and of political vision. Instead of seeing themselves as a rearguard for the defence of an ancient order confined to Northern Ireland alone, they must assume the role of springboard and standard-bearer for the cause of a New Britain, fought for in alliance with mainland Nationalism — indeed as a leading element in that Nationalism.

For, just as the limbs of a body can no longer function if the heart and brain are dead, so Ulster will not survive if Britain is destroyed.

Before this chapter is closed, a final word should be said on what, in broader context, might be termed the 'Irish Question'. Indeed, our politicians have coined the phrase 'Irish Dimension', and so I will fall into line with that vocabulary and speak in the same terms.

Those many in Britain who obtain a thrill espousing any

national cause providing it is not their own are fond of giving voice to the concept of 'United Ireland' as a solution to the troubles in Ulster. This is of course shrewdly calculated because 'united' has a positive and agreeable ring while 'divided' does not. In our infatuation with pretty verbiage in preference to dealing with substance and reality, we are prone to be swayed by such slogans.

But the true reality is that those who shout for a 'United Ireland' today are the very political heirs of those who brought about Ireland's division. Ireland was split into two, not by the loyalist side, but by the republican side. Ireland was once united as a territory of the British Crown, and indeed this has been the **only** circumstance in which she has ever been properly and truly united.

Those who today shout for a 'United Ireland' mean, in the context in which they do so, that they want a divided British Isles; but of course the former terminology is preferred because it sounds so much better.

Britain, if she is to be true to herself, could only consent to a United Ireland if it were a **British Ireland** — if it were achieved, not by Ulster leaving the Kingdom and joining the Republic, but by that part of Ireland now known as the Republic abandoning her separate existence and rejoining the United Kingdom.

Personally, I hope that this one day happens. Indeed, I regard it as the only hopeful long-term solution to the Irish problem. Ireland is my ancestral homeland; I can never regard it as foreign. But until the day comes when Ireland as a whole finds its way 'home' we must at all costs hold on to that part of Ireland whose people, in the majority, wish to hold on to us. If we let it go, whether on account of external pressure or the sheer fatigue of sovereignty, we will have embarked on a course of national suicide to which there is no limit. This is what is at stake in Ulster. The sooner we understand it the better.

Chapter 18
The imperial imperative

For a nation that has known greatness and glory, there is no middle ground between the maintenance of its old prestige and complete impotence.

LUCIEN PREVOST-PARADOL

The British Empire in which our grandfathers grew up is now no more. By the 1960s it had faded into history following a process of dismantlement which, compressed within two decades at the most, was surely the most rapid ever. The process was all the more remarkable for the fact that it was attended by no military defeat. Our Empire was surrendered as part of a total collapse of political will by those officiating at its centre: a collapse which had no precedent in the long story of the rise and fall of great states.

But if that Empire no longer exists, the laws of the universe giving rise to it are still in force. Nature does not permit a vacuum: when power is laid down by one it is picked up by another. The imperial role abandoned by Britain and the other European colonising nations has been inherited by new imperialisms, faithful to the rules that we (not without encouragement from themselves) have forgotten. Two gigantic states today cast their shadow over the world. Both are, albeit in ways that may appear to be different, imperial. A third — China — shows the symptoms of a dawning imperialism of which we may see the full development in the 21st century. And it is not inconceivable that a fourth — Japan — could again take up the imperial role that she discarded only under the duress of military collapse in 1945.

This is all wholly contrary to the prognostications of the anti-imperial lobby that has dominated British politics and intellectual life, in the first case since 1945 and in the second since 1918. According to the theoreticians of this lobby, great empires were out of date: the world of the future would be governed by peace and not power, and where the European empires broke up they would be replaced by a new collection of sovereign states which, with colonial shackles thrown off, would bloom to prosperity and love us for granting them their freedom.

It will not need any spelling out from me to persuade the reader that none of this has happened. The territories in question now rot in poverty, maladministration and corruption, and are as dependent as ever before on outside agencies for their survival and what little development they are able to achieve. We are now pompously instructed by our leaders of opinion that it is still our solemn duty to subsidise these countries, even though power over them has been surrendered — though not of course to their own ludicrous presidents, prime ministers, parliaments and, in some cases, 'kings' (anyone who believes that believes in Santa Claus) but to the new imperia of Soviet and Dollar that have taken over where we have abdicated.

And, in addition to this burden on the British taxpayer, we have been required to perform another service: the service of accommodating, without complaint, whatever members of the populations of our ex-colonies grow disenchanted with living in their new 'free' countries and decide they would like to move to Britain.

In other words, while we have been expected to relinquish all the rights of an imperial power, we are still expected to fulfil all the obligations — and an extra one besides!

The exceptions to this rule of poverty are those former imperial countries that either are populated mainly by Whites or in which Whites remain the controlling group: the countries that we were accustomed to referring to as the 'Dominions'. Nevertheless, these countries, notwithstanding the loosening of their imperial ties with Britain, still have to live in the same world as before, where they need markets for their products and people for their empty spaces, and a world in which leadership still lies with the great powers. Whatever brave talk there may be of their new-found 'independence', their practical freedom of action is circumscribed in more than a hundred different ways by these unalterable facts.

The debunkers of the imperial idea are fond of dismissing the British Empire as nothing more than a gigantic status symbol, a kind of food for national vanity which we are now the better off for having shed, as it cuts us down to size. There is a kind of frivolity in fashion concerning the Empire, as if its disappearance was no more a thing to get concerned about than the passing of the

Gentlemen v. Players fixture at Lords or the end of steam locomotion — a topic of some mild nostalgia but that is all.

In fact the loss of the Empire was far and away the greatest catastrophe in British history.

By this I do not mean that it was ever practical, or indeed in our own interest, to preserve under the British flag and Crown every single territory, dependency and outpost that formed part of the Empire as it was when the final shot was fired in the war ending in August 1945. On the contrary, and as I shall explain in this chapter, in this enormous legacy of imperial responsibility that had been handed down to us by the middle of the present century there was much dead wood and much that was a source of weakness. In this Empire, we were far over-extended by the strain on our resources when measured in relation to the actual national benefits to be derived. There was certainly the need for a drastic stocktaking and reappraisal concerning the utility of each imperial possession, and a consequent reorganisation and streamlining of the imperial system to suit the practical needs of the British Race which owned and controlled it.

The catastrophe lay in the abandonment of Britain's imperial role in its entirety and her retreat to the position of small off-shore island.

Instead of giving up parts of the Empire, as we would have been right to do, because their upkeep was not worth the cost, we gave up the Empire lock, stock and barrel because we became afflicted with leaders who wanted to abdicate from greatness, from challenge, from duty and from history.

In the manner typical of everything that has been done in recent times, the surrender of the Empire was carried out with methods of lying and deceit. We were told, in the words of Prime Minister Macmillan, that the Empire was not breaking up; it was growing up. Something of what Macmillan had in mind when he spoke of this 'growing up' we have been able to see in the history of the last two decades in Black Africa. As a smokescreen for their work in disestablishing the Empire, the politicians invented a catchword: 'Commonwealth'. By the use of this dishonest verbiage, they hoped to mislead us into thinking that the Empire was not disappearing in substance but was merely changing in form. People in Britain with a sense of political reality were not deceived by this nonsense, but they were few in number; the majority most certainly were deceived, and nowhere did they fall for this deception more readily than in the ranks of the Tory Party. I was one of those who, in the Macmillan days, tried by a series of demonstrations to alert Tories to what was happening and stimulate some resistance amongst them to this betrayal of one of their party's foremost traditions. We might as well have been talking to the cows. This was my first real evidence — although I had long suspected it — of the climate of stupidity and apathy that dwells throughout Tory circles. The way in which the Tories, with a very small number of exceptions, tamely acquiesced in the imperial surrender of those times demonstrated, as early as 1960, that that party was rotten to the core. For generations, the Tories in Britain had proclaimed themselves the loyal guardians of the imperial inheritance and had made much political capital out of their opponents' indisposition to defend that inheritance. Yet here were the leaders of that party in the Fifties and Sixties engaging in a complete desertion of that tradition and winning rapturous applause at annual party conferences for so doing!

The great question facing our generation is: is there anything that can now be done to reverse the effects of this monumental act of cowardice and folly?

Certainly nothing can be done — or indeed should be done — to recreate the Empire that went into liquidation about a quarter of a century ago. We cannot, and should not, speak of restoring that Empire because that is out of the question.

But we can, and must, put our minds to the matter of creating an institution to **replace** that Empire — and for this very urgent and practical reason:-

The United Kingdom occupies an area of a little over 94,000 square miles and contains a population which at the last census numbered around 57 million. It has to live in a world of giant powers possessing territory and populations many times in excess of these figures. As I have indicated in another chapter, the people of Britain could be distributed over the country in a way that made for less crowding and much better use of resources than is now the case. But there is an obvious limit to this. Sooner or later, the strain of population on land and resources will become intolerable, and some way out will have to be found.

The current solution in vogue is population control by means of employing artificial practices to reduce the birthrate. As I have said elsewhere, I believe that this is, from the national point of view, a disastrous policy, and for the reasons stated. A nation that has lost the desire to produce abundant children is a nation that has opted to die. In the case of Britain, most (though not all) of our population consists of the very best human stock. It is surely detrimental, not only to ourselves, but to the whole world that this stock is barely reproducing itself while other races are breeding in profusion.

As I have said when dealing with this matter earlier, Britain should contain her overcrowding problem within tolerable limits, not by the adoption of a low birthrate, but by means of a high rate of emigration.

But the question then arises: emigration to where? If those people who emigrate go to settle in countries not bound by any special family ties to Britain, and thereby simply become citizens of foreign states, they become a loss to us. If we bear in mind that migrant peoples comprise, as a general rule, the most vigorous, energetic and go-ahead elements of the original stock, this means that with every wave of emigration from these shores we are making a present of our strongest people to our international competitors. Such a tendency amounts to national suicide. Emigration from Britain therefore can only be of value to us if it is to countries bound to us in a common national and racial destiny and which, along with us, act as a single and unified force in world affairs.

In another earlier chapter I have stated the undoubted advantage to a nation of economic self-sufficiency, with its virtue of relative immunity to the ups and downs of the international trading and financial system. I have also acknowledged the unquestionable benefits of the largest possible internal market for industry, and of economies of great scale in production, the example of America being a case in point. Such advantages and benefits in these regards would be of inestimable strength to Britain if she were part of an extended and expanding economic area, particularly if within that area she can obtain most of the goods that she cannot produce at home. My argument was with those who imagine that Europe can provide such an area, which it can quite clearly be seen not to do when the economic resources and structures of the European states are examined. However, the fact that Europe cannot provide us with this enlarged economic sphere does not invalidate the proposition that such a sphere is very desirable; that should be so self-evident as to be beyond dispute.

These facts about Britain's situation — facts that are the unalterable legacy of her geography and development, whatever political doctrines may happen currently to hold sway in the country — propel her **inevitably** towards external colonisation, to expansion across the seas. There are in the world today somewhere around 150 million people of British race (more still if all the Irish are taken into account). I ask the reader who is against territorial expansion by imperialistic methods, that is conquest followed by colonisation, to consider what life would be like today if all these 150 million-plus people had to be accommodated within the British Isles. Yet that is precisely the situation we would face had not we British been a people of imperialists and colonisers and created a whole huge world beyond these shores in which many millions could settle in surroundings of familiar language, culture, customs and institutions and among neighbours of familiar stock.

And this is not just a need relating to the past. As I have pointed out, we British in the future, unless we are going to become sterile and die out, as did the dinosaurs, the dodo and the mountain gorilla, must continue to be a migratory and colonising people. We have no choice.

It is no answer to this to say that Britons can continue to migrate but must be prepared to go to lands which to all intents and purposes are foreign, apart from the language they speak, and thereby assume — or at least pass on to their children — a foreign nationality. Apart from the consideration that I have just mentioned — that the process would, year by year, be impoverishing us of some of our best stocks, there is the additional fact that such a new environment would prove increasingly unattractive to Britons anyway, and that in that event the only likelihood of their migrating to such an environment would be if conditions and prospects here in Britain became so hopeless that anything would be better than staying here. These are hardly the right circumstances in which we would want to see people emigrating from this country!

Yet these would be the only two alternatives if present trends and policy continue: either we lose many of our best people, or they stay here in conditions of increasing overcrowding and urbanisation.

In the early post-war period, a boom in population in Britain was balanced by an extremely high rate of emigration, particularly to Australia. At that time that country was more British in composition and outlook than now, and was pleased to encourage British settlers. Many Britons in the 1950s and 1960s were anxious to go and live in countries like Australia and New Zealand, not only for the sunshine, open spaces and economic and career opportunities, but also because they saw their own neighbourhoods becoming increasingly alien through **immigration**, and looked upon the new environment as one that would be more British than at home. "More British than Britain" was indeed a description which New Zealanders were pleased to apply to their country.

Today, as a symptom of the weakening sense of kinship between our countries, both Australia and New Zealand are trying rapidly to become less British, and at the time these words are written it is less easy to get into Australia if you are British and white than if you are Asian and brown. Not entirely surprisingly, British emigration to the Antipodes has become greatly reduced.

These facts should enable us to understand that Britain is a country governed, inexorably, by what might be called the imperial imperative. Her whole survival rests on her capacity to maintain a large overseas sphere of influence within which she can dispense her surplus population and expand her trade. The Little England* philosophy that has underlain much of the retreat from Empire is based on a delusion, the delusion that we can retire to our island fortress and away from the responsibilities of world power while entertaining any kind of future as a nation.

In considering how the British Empire that expired in the 1960s can be replaced by a new form of organisation which will meet the needs of the future, we must first understand the weaknesses in the old Empire that led to its collapse, on the basis of the dictum that those who do not learn from the errors of history are doomed to go on repeating them.

The assertion that the British came into their Empire in a fit of absence of mind is one that has stuck in popular speech precisely because it contains more than a grain of truth. Never at any time in the early discovery and development of colonies did things proceed in accordance with any clearly conceived policy of state. Britons, best situated of all Europeans in their access to the high seas, and containing in their blood a very high degree of the spirit of maritime adventure, were bound to be in the forefront of that drive across the oceans that opened up the new world. Love of journeying into the unknown, and the prospect of riches — both essentially private impulses — were the driving forces in this

---

* Here the term 'Little England' is used in its original and correct sense: the concept of Britain which rejects an imperial destiny. This should not be confused with the currently employed, and wholly distorted, use of the same term whereby those resistant to internationalism are dubbed 'Little Englanders'.

outward thrust. But in time there came a recognition that much of this enterprise was nationally profitable as well as profitable to those individuals and companies engaged in it, and governments were prepared to back these sources of profit, where necessary, by armed force. Still, however, the economic motive predominated over all others; little thought was given to the idea that colonies might in time serve as a means of massive racial expansion and as additions to national power in anything beyond the strictly economic sense. At the time shortly prior to the American War of Independence the entire population of Britain was smaller than that of London today, and the demographic expansion that was to take place during the following century was something that had impinged upon the mental horizons only of very few. The means of communication that we were to enjoy in the present century were, moreoever, quite outside the imagination of that era. Hardly a thought was therefore given to the idea that these far-off colonies might provide the means for a massively expanded Greater Britain.

By slow degrees, however, the picture changed. By the mid-eighteenth century there was what was, by the standards of that time, a fairly substantial settlement of Britons in the North American colonies, and some forward-thinking people at home began to see the huge real estate of that continent and its predominantly Anglo-Saxon-Celtic stock as a national asset of tremendous potential.

But realisation of the vital importance of the American colonies was not sufficiently widespread, nor sufficiently ingrained, in circles of government, to make for the degree of wisdom needed to avert the revolt of the colonies in 1776, then, when it occurred, to ensure the victory of the loyalist forces. The scribblers who instruct public opinion in Britain today try to tell us that the American War of Independence was an event over which we in this country should rejoice because it brought into being a nation whose power now 'protects' the Western World. Leaving aside the question of whether this latter assertion is in fact true (and that is a question I shall take up in the next chapter) it should suffice to say here that the War of Independence had nothing whatever to do with the future development of American power, which would have occurred anyway quite irrespective of its result. The difference would have been that, if that war had not occurred or, after its having occurred, the loyalists had won and America remained within the Empire, its power would today have been a

British power, joined to Britain as if the two countries were one. In addition, the North American continent would not have been split in half through the trek of the defeated loyalists north to what became Canada, so that the whole of the immensity of the North American land mass would have become, with the federation that sooner or later would have occurred, one single unit under the control of the British Race.

The loss of the American colonies was by far the biggest catastrophe in the history of our people prior to the present century, for it divided our race in two — as it remains divided to this day, and with many of its very best elements on the other side of that divide. I am referring here to the very fine British stocks that are to be found in parts of the United States today, particularly the South, where they have remained largely uncontaminated by the cosmopolitanism of the giant cities.

I do not propose to enter here into a deep and extensive debate as to the rights and wrongs of the conflict leading to the revolt of the American colonies, for that is a study that lies outside this work. The point of overwhelming importance is that the conflict should have been resolved 'within the family', and not by the separation of the colonists, who were predominantly of British descent, from Crown and Empire. Such arrangements as were necessary should have been made to give the colonists the instit- utions of government that they required to meet their own local needs, but within the framework of a shared loyalty with the British in the Mother Country. Whatever the merits of the arguments for such political changes — and there certainly were merits — one argument which had no foundation whatever was that the colonists, by the fact of having crossed a stretch of water, had somehow assumed a nationality different from that of their kinsfolk whom they had left behind, and as such were destined by right to form a foreign state. As far as 'independence' was concerned, the colonists would in the course of time have acquired the only independence that mattered: the power not to have decisions made concerning their affairs that went against their will. That development would have become inevitable in the very nature of the growth of America that was to follow. That is a wholly different thing, however, from the assumption of a separate nationality and national destiny, which were never inevitable and certainly never desirable. It is to the eternal shame of British statecraft that it failed to produce a formula for the settlement of the colonists' grievances by which this parting of the ways could have been avoided.

Notwithstanding this major tragedy, something useful might have come of it had the appropriate lessons of it been learned, leading to an intelligent reassessment of the role of overseas colonies and the adoption, for the first time, of a clear-headed imperial policy. None of this happened, however. The development of colonies continued to proceed in an atmosphere of muddle, being compounded of a growing variety of motives and impulses, many of them not in the slightest way connected with what should have been the central purpose of imperialism: racial expansion.

It is the natural function of every healthy living organism on this planet to grow, spread, colonise and increase its power. When all the pretty rhetoric of ideology is swept away and we get down to first basics, history can be seen as a chronicle of the rise and fall of states, proceeding in accordance with nature's rule of the survival of the fittest. To acknowledge this is not to say that it should be the **only** ethical consideration governing our affairs; that would be to reduce man to the level of the animal world. We should, however, take care that our formulation of the complex ethical systems necessary to civilised society should proceed **within**, and not **against**, that fundamental biological truth. If might does not necessarily make for right, what is beyond dispute is that the former provides the indispensable condition for the reign of the latter. In the policies of all nations and states, therefore, nothing should be allowed precedence over the question of **power**, for without power all the ideals for the betterment of the human condition will remain mere pie in the sky.

To listen to the babbling of liberals, one would imagine that the Great Creator had somehow determined upon a legally fixed division of all the earth's territories and resources among its various races and in accordance with principles of 'fairness' and 'equality', and that the comparatively small homelands occupied by the European peoples for most of their history were their allocated lot, beyond which they had no right to expand if they were to remain within the pale of accepted decency.

Just half a minute's thought will reveal the utter absurdity of such a view. Every single square foot of territory that exists on this planet is the property of that particular nation and race that has been able to acquire it and defend it. Our own British Isles are no exception to this rule, having been conquered and colonised at various times in their earlier history by means of the sword and the axe. Whatever level of civilisation and peaceful existence we may enjoy today we owe, in the final analysis, to the fact that in the days of our early ancestors the strong prevailed over the weak by means of superior force.

Were any other law to be in operation, not only would the map of Europe be wholly different from what it is — indeed, no map of any kind, other than a purely physical one, would be possible — but the whole of North America would be the property of a small handful of Red Indians, Australia an even smaller handful of Aboriginals and the only New Zealanders we would know would be a dark-skinned people who painted their faces in a variety of colours, danced with spears and greeted each other by touching noses. However, even that is not strictly correct, beause even these races occupied the territories in which we found them at a comparatively recent time when measured in terms of the true age of the planet Earth.

It is this reality that reduces to preposterous nonsense all the pious blueprints drawn up for the maintenance of 'international law', as codified in the United Nations Charter and the Covenant of the League of Nations that preceded it. All that such 'international law' does is legitimise the map of the world that has been established by force while declaring illegal any attempt to change it by force. And, contrary to all the dreams of the international idealists who put their faith in these institutions, such institutions have not made the world one per-cent a more peaceful place. They, and the ideas underlying them, simply serve to immobilise the stupid and the naive among the nations, who believe in such fantasies, while the intelligent and the realistic get on with the job of pursuing their own interests in accordance with nature's laws — which grant territory, wealth and rights to the strong and the bold who are prepared and able to take them.

The Roman Empire established humane standards of justice for the people who lived under its rule, and it brought to its territories a quality of civilisation as high as any attainable at its time of history. None of this, however, alters the fact that that Empire was established, not by the Romans asking the permission of the international community to set it up, but by the scientific use of military power and the subsequent practice of an earlier form of Bismarckian *realpolitik*, aimed at sustaining that which had in the first place been acquired by military action. The same Empire collapsed, not when it became no longer 'right' to rule it, but when the will and the power to do so had evaporated.

So, it must be asserted again: **power** precedes and establishes every condition that is required for the achievement of the refinements of civilisation, culture, decency, humanity and order. These latter things, desirable though they are, must always be regarded as predicates of the first, never substitutes for it.

Vigorous and healthy races cannot indefinitely be confined within small territories; inevitably they will expand in numbers and economic needs so as to require new land for their sustenance. Probably some time before that point has been reached, the adventurous spirits of certain exceptional individuals among them — natural leaders — will have made for an advance guard in this outward movement, so that when the time of need arises the pioneer work has been begun and the new lands already acquired by whatever means necessary. These pioneers and those who shortly follow them are almost invariably of the hardiest stocks among the colonising race, being comprised of people with the courage and the initiative to uproot themselves in the quest for new opportunity, to move great distances into the unknown and to endure all the dangers inherent in living in frontier regions, often having to fight for their existence against those races which would dispute their ownership of the territory they have won. Some of course will not survive these trials and will die, either by the hand of their enemies or through sickness. In this way a process of natural selection takes place whereby the inheritors of the newly colonised lands will be those most fit to assume such rights.

Obviously there are two impulses involved in this colonisation process: the individual and the tribal. Both need each other. There has to be, in the individual, the desire for increased opportunity and the better life, for self and family. Equally, colonising individuals need to work as a group and have behind them national resources, political, economic and military, to back their enterprise.

But any such national effort to colonise new lands would be utterly pointless if the object, at the end of it all, was that the colonists would break with the original national body and form a foreign state, taking with them the very people whom the nation can least afford to lose, while rendering the entire sacrifice involved in the operation a waste of money, energy and — not least — lives.

Racial expansion by means of colonisation is therefore without logic if its aim is to set up new and separate states; it is only logical if it is directed to extending and enlarging the existing state.

This is not to deny the rule that where a territory is colonised a great distance from the original homeland some devolution of government to the colonists must eventually be granted — to the point at which they become, in fact, self-governing — in the sense that no policy can be imposed on them by the mother country that does not have their consent. This point effectively becomes reached when the colony has grown to a size and strength at which outside coercion from thousands of miles away is impossible, given the sheer logistics of bringing to bear the military force to give effect to it.

In the case of an empire of the dispersed nature of the British, and not comprising a contiguous land area, the imposition of a single sovereignty resting on force and compulsion is only possible in the very early stages of a colony. Thereafter, that sovereignty can only exist by consent, coming from a feeling of shared nationality and racial destiny. There was in fact never any conflict between the evolution of Britain's former colonies into self-governing units and the principle of their remaining in a single imperial union, speaking as a single entity to the other nations of the world. That such a conflict is thought to exist is due only to the muddled climate in which our ideas on the subject are formed — a climate largely shaped by the contrivance of those who have axes to grind in favour of the division of the British peoples.

If the British Empire was first acquired in a fit of absence of mind, presence of mind should certainly have taken over before the process of development had gone very far; and thereafter that development should have been directed in accordance with a clear policy and strategy for the growth of the British Race (together with such kindred and assimilable elements from other European races as formed part of home or colonial populations).

From this, certain basic rules should have been adopted, which ought to have governed all future development.

The first rule should have been the avoidance of over-extension. The taking on of an excessive imperial burden carries with it the danger of a commitment of money, people, administration and military power that is not justified, in many cases, by the dividends obtained. We can end up by being what Field Marshal Lord Montgomery called "weak everywhere and strong nowhere."

Proceeding from this principle, there should have been a sober and realistic stocktaking, carried out regularly, of all our imperial possessions, and a ruthless pruning in all cases where there was not a national benefit to be obtained — long-term as well as short-term — which justified the commitment required.

Right from early days, it should have been recognised that the primary purpose of empire, to which everything else should have been subordinated, was to acquire lands overseas for large-scale settlement by people of our own stock and under institutions which would ensure that they remained our people as firmly as if they had stayed at home in these islands.

The second purpose was economic: to acquire a self-sufficiency of necessary raw materials, energy sources and food products, as well as a large internal market for manufacturing industry.

The third purpose was strategic: to acquire facilities for military, naval (and more latterly air) bases such as were necessary for the defence of the Empire and its supply lines.

No purpose or justification for imperial possessions existed beyond these three essential ones mentioned. Yet Britain soon lost sight of this reality (if she ever had sight of it in the first place). To that large and influential section of our populace seized by the uncontrollable itch to 'do good', the Empire in due course became a vast experimental ground for the implementation of all the ideas beloved of 'liberal-democrats' and crusaders for evangelical Christianity. The notion gained currency that the purpose of Empire, predominating over everything else, was to bring to other races the assumed benefits of British civilisation — from which then grew the conviction, even more preposterous, that these other races could in time be moulded in our image and become citizens of the Empire on a par with the people who had built it.

Certainly, where our imperial expansion necessitated rule over other peoples we should have attempted to make that rule as humane as possible, not least because it was in our obvious interest to do so — a compliant native population being, self-evidently, preferable to a hostile one — but always providing that our humanity was balanced by complete ruthlessness in dealing with trouble-makers when they manifested themselves. Beyond this, no attempt whatever should have been made to interfere with local customs (with one or two extreme exceptions, such as *Suttee*) except where they affected our own people. Most important of all, we should never have attempted to **educate** our subject races. Practically all the trouble that Britain had in her Empire was from agitators to whom we had obligingly granted the benefits of our learning, mainly in our own schools and universities.

But looking at things in a longer-term perspective, we should in many cases have recognised, early on, the liability to ourselves of expensive colonial commitments where they involved ruling countries of which the majority populations would always be non-British. We British and our white overseas settlers of Empire simply did not have the human and economic resources adequately to develop, govern and defend our Dominions **and** all the multitude of other territories for which, by one circumstance or another, we had assumed ownership and responsibility.

Over-extension and over-commitment, together with our unpreparedness to maintain a sufficiently large army, resulted in inadequate forces available to deal with the revolt of the American colonists and ensure that, whatever the justice of their demands, these were met with the Empire preserved intact. After these colonies had been lost, this lesson should have been thoroughly learned. There and then, the decision should have been made to throw almost all resources into three main areas of settlement: Canada, Australia and New Zealand. The aim should have been to people these lands as far as possible with British migrants, certainly to the extent that people of British stock remained, in each of them, easily the controlling majority. No huge investment of people, money or armed force should have been made in any other areas where this might have detracted from the effort to populate, develop and defend these lands.

This need not have prevented our assuming control of at least some of our African colonies; for these could be defended, and order in them maintained, by comparatively small forces, always providing that our administration in those colonies was of genuinely firm will and made it clear to all would-be insurgents that any threat to order would be dealt with with the utmost ruthlessness. Some of these colonies had an undoubted economic value and were worth our trouble in holding onto them.

South Africa, however, was a different case. Here we encountered a population comprising some of the very best European stock but not one that wanted to be integrated into an imperial system. Our attempt to coerce the Afrikaners in this regard was a disastrous error and typical of the short-sightedness and folly which have characterised British policy towards South Africa from the very beginning.

In our relations with South Africa there have been two distinct phases: one preceding 1948, when Afrikaner Nationalism attained power for the first time; and the other from 1948 onwards.

In the earlier phase, Britain committed the cardinal error of getting the worst of both worlds: we imposed upon the Afrikaners enough to antagonise them and make enemies of them but not enough to subdue them. British retention of South Africa would only have been a realistic policy in the event of British settlement of the country attaining such large dimensions that the Afrikaners would be outnumbered in every part of it. When it was clear that this would not happen, the idea of incorporating the whole country within the Empire should have been abandoned. The Afrikaners should have been granted their independent republics of the Transvaal and Orange Free State, while we should have endeavoured to keep Natal. The Cape Province should have been divided up on an ethnic basis, with most of the inland areas going to the Afrikaners. In this way Britain might have protected the nationality of her own settlers in South Africa while minimising the friction with the Afrikaners. This would have been the policy by far best suited to the British interest.

The British interest, however, was not the main consideration in the minds of those responsible for the formulation of our policy in the years preceding the South African War of 1899-1902. The international money barons and gold and diamond interests — primarily Jewish — had their eyes on the gold and diamond mining reserves of the country, which were located in the Afrikaner lands, and they were not prepared to see these pass out of their clutches. Under the guise of an entirely bogus and artificially created 'patriotism' and 'jingoism', British public opinion was whipped up into support of an imperial 'crusade' to incorporate Afrikaner territory, as well as that occupied by our own settlers, into the Empire.

Thus there came about the conflict known to most as the 'Boer War', the result of which, whatever military decision was achieved, ensured that the Afrikaners would never be induced to be willing subjects of the Empire, while at the same time it sowed the seeds of a lasting bitterness between ourselves and a people whom we should have done everything possible to cultivate as friends.

From the moment of the victory of the National Party in the South African election of 1948, it was clear that it was just a matter of time before the whole of South Africa, and not just the Afrikaans-speaking part of it, would pass out of the imperial orbit. Had common sense prevailed in Britain, this could have become the starting point for a new era of friendly relations with South

Africa, with many benefits still accruing to us through the close trading relationships that had been built up between the two countries and by the retention of our naval base at Simonstown. But no! Even this opportunity was wasted; the political sermonisers who had taken over control of British politics and public opinion had by then found a new stick with which to beat the Afrikaners. The *apartheid* system, a wholly reasonable and justified political and social arrangement for the governing of South Africa and one which is the best that can be achieved taking into account that country's extremely complex ethnic pattern, did not meet with the approval of the British liberal establishment — imprisoned as the latter is in its obsession with setting up moralistic blueprints for solving every problem of every country in the world. Again, as in Victorian times, we have made of a people an enemy which could have been a friend — a particularly stupid policy in a world in which the latter species are in such short supply.

To the North, in what were the Rhodesias, Britain faced a different set of circumstances. There the majority of the ruling race was British. Everything should have been done to keep the Rhodesias in the Empire and on the basis of the maintenance of white leadership. Just as with South Africa, the policies of successive governments towards the Rhodesias right up to the hand-over of power to the Blacks in what was Southern Rhodesia in 1980 were a combination of criminal folly and outright race treason.

As far as the remainder of the Empire was concerned, the only other large territory which we should have considered holding was Malaya (now Malaysia) and solely for its production of tin and rubber.

These places apart, our remaining commitments should have been only to small territories useful as bases, such as Aden, Singapore and Malta, and of course the Falkland Islands for the additional fact that they are British in population.

Other colonies, notably the West Indian, West African and Central American ones, Burma, Hong Kong and Gibraltar, should have been dispensed with a long time ago, though some advantage would have remained in transferring Gibraltar to Spain on a lease-back arrangement. Above all, we should have abandoned India, which never had any value to us that came remotely near justifying the burden undertaken in administering and defending it.

India has been called 'The Jewel in the Imperial Crown'. In fact it was always much more a prestige symbol of Empire than an asset to it. The world was for two centuries mesmerised by the achievement of a few tens of thousands of British in maintaining their hold on this sub-continent, with its hundreds of millions of people, and no doubt this fact registered with Britain's rulers as a powerful psychological weapon of international diplomacy. But behind the dazzle and splendour of the rule of the British Raj lay the reality of an appalling wastage of many of our best engineers, administrators and soldiers, together with enormous sums of money, in the maintenance of an illusion: that India contributed one iota to actual British power. On the contrary, this huge white elephant soaked up resources over many generations that might otherwise have been allocated to the building up of the Dominions, where, in contrast to India, British people in great numbers had a future.

Typically, the decision to quit India, in 1947, was made at the very worst possible time and in the very worst possible circumstances: under conditions of revolution within and pressure without, when our abdication would be interpreted by the world as a collapse of power and will, instead of a sensible and self-interested rationalisation of resources.

In summary, Britain should have decided long ago — at least in the earlier part of the 19th century — to concentrate on building her imperial power on the huge areas of white settlement that had come into the possession of her people and did not need policing against large local alien populations — plus such other territories as yielded economic or strategic benefits that were high in relation to the military and financial commitment required in maintaining them. We should, early on, have relinquished territories that were little better than expensive luxuries, and we should have done so at the right time and at our own convenience, not in response to the clamour of our enemies.

Everything possible should then have been done to make of the Empire a single political and economic unit. Imperial Federation was the obvious solution, and this should have been pursued single-mindedly when the opportunity to achieve it was greatest, that is when feeling in the Dominions — at least in Australia and New Zealand — was highly favourable to such an arrangement. As with every other thoroughly worthwhile course beckoning British statesmanship over the past century or so, our political leaders were not up to the challenge but let the opportunity go by.

Here a word should be said about the principles involved in the issue of Imperial Federation — for nowhere has there been so much muddled thinking, most of it induced by that disorder of the mind known as liberalism, as on the question of the relationship between the people of Britain and their offspring who have settled the lands acquired through overseas colonisation.

As I have said before, there is no logical reason why those who partake in overseas colonising should suddenly assume a different nationality by virtue of crossing a stretch of water. Race, and not geographical location, is the cement that binds nations — as numerous examples throughout the world will bear out. Greeks, Italians, Poles, Ukrainians and numerous other ethnic groups that have settled in the USA, Canada, Australia and indeed Britain have retained the feeling of their old nationality rather than take on that of the country to which they have moved. And this applies to succeeding generations almost as much as to the first generation. In a television programme in 1986 featuring the communities of the Baltic nations settled in Britain, the sons and daughters of Latvians, Estonians and Lithuanians in this country proudly spoke of themselves as sharing the nationality of their fathers rather than feeling themselves to be British. No-one should condemn them for such sentiments. They only go to bear out what can be observed everywhere: that a person's ethnic inheritance is a much stronger determinant of national feeling than the accident of where they are born. Numerous Britons were of course born in Africa, India, the West Indies, Hong Kong or elsewhere in the Empire when their fathers were on colonial or military service in those parts of the world; this does not make them anything other than British.

But perhaps the most instructive example of all is that of the Jews, who are settled in every country of significance around the globe, and in considerable numbers in almost all western countries. This does not prevent these people feeling a bond towards each other that, on the admission of most of them, is stronger than any bond they feel towards the countries they have settled and the indigenous peoples of those countries. To point out this tendency is not to condemn it; indeed it is wholly commend-able, being in accordance with natural law. But it should not be ignored, for it offers the most striking instance of a people who remain unified in their dispersion. To Jews, Israel remains the Homeland, even though most of them have never been there or even thought of living there. If Israel is in trouble or danger, it is up to them to help. If Israel needs money, it is up to them to see that she gets it. If Israel is in conflict with any of her neighbours, it is their concern as much as if they were living there themselves, and any influence they are able to exert on the political leaders of their countries of adoption (which in the case of Britain and America is enormous) is directed towards a pro-Israeli foreign policy, regardless of whether such a policy is in that country's true national interest.

As I have said, this is entirely commendable. It should not be condemned, but it should be emulated, for it serves as a model as to how other ethnic groups should think, feel and act. We British, who are racially dispersed around the world in far greater numbers than any other people, most of all need to acquire the same kind of tribal solidarity as that possessed by the Jews. If we did so, we would be able to stand up to any enemy on earth.

But in fact, as our history has shown, our tribal sense is extremely weak. In America there are Greek-Americans, Polish-Americans, Ukrainian-Americans and above all Jewish-Americans, but those in that country of British descent are just 'Americans'. While the former groups stage their regular folk festivals to remind themselves and everyone else of their origins and their ties with the countries of those origins, the only folk festival that the Americans of British descent recognise is that of July 4th, when they celebrate the day when their ancestors **broke** with their tribal homeland. Quite a contrast!

The great difference of course is that people of British stock, wherever they have settled in the world, have carried with them the intellectual and cultural baggage of 'liberalism', in which nationhood is seen, not in tribal terms, but as something based purely on administrative convenience, arising from out of geographical situation. The result is the appalling fragmentation of the British Race and its consequent weakening everywhere — even in America, where it has gradually surrendered political, economic and cultural hegemony to *arriviste* ethnic groups.

As I have indicated, racial fragmentation should not be confused with the decentralisation of administrative functioning. Quite obviously, in the dispersal over huge distances that was involved in the overseas colonisation by the British peoples it was practical and sensible to grant to the colonists their own institutions of self-government, as no central power could possibly preside effectively over such a scattered selection of communities, knowing and judging the everyday needs of settlements thousands of miles away. This apart, the only ultimate sanction of centralised power, the use of armed force, was clearly out of the question where it might involve action against united communities of our own race to impose policies on them contrary to their own wish. Therefore, whatever formal political institutions governed colonies' and dominions' relationship with the Mother Country, they became effectively independent and self-governing from the moment they grew beyond the capability of a British government to coerce them.

Imperial Federation, therefore, never was, and never could be, an institution that made the lands of Empire less free and self-governing than they already were when it became an issue in the late 19th and early 20th centuries. It would have involved, at most, an agreement by common consent of all concerned to act as a co-ordinated body for the purpose of Foreign Relations, Trade and Economic Development and Defence, leaving local powers of administration entirely intact. Furthermore, even in those limited areas of common action any party to the arrangement could effectively have opted out at any time it chose — a prerogative inherent in the lack of any enforcing power, as mentioned earlier.

With typical dishonesty, those hostile to the imperial idea have always sought to create the idea of a conflict between the concept of imperial co-ordination, as implicit in the federal scheme, and that of the sovereignty and self-government of the participating members. In fact there never was any such conflict.

Today we see the very same forces at work in the effort to tear asunder what remain of the family ties between Britain and her overseas kin. We are told, with all the assumed authority that the controlled media can command, that our former Dominions must leave us because they have developed their own distinctive 'nationalism'. And yet the very next moment the same media are proclaiming that the world is moving away from nationalism and towards the idea of international order. As these words are written, Australia has a prime minister who shouts that his country must find its own 'national identity', and in pursuit of that dispense with its ancient links with Britain; but this very same prime minister is at the very same time doing everything in his power to destroy Australia's national identity by the import of vast numbers of immigrants from Asia, which if fully assimilated, will eliminate every vestige of the country's nationhood! What we must understand is that those who today have taken on the task of fashioning our thoughts on these matters have objectives and ideals entirely different from those that might be apparent from their daily utterances. An attempt is being made to destroy the Anglo-Saxon-Celtic peoples by the device of an entirely phony 'nationalism' which sets them against each other — while the object of those engaged in this exercise is, in the final analysis, the absolute antithesis of nationalism: the institution of a one-world state in which separate nations and races will not be allowed to exist.

The fact that the Imperial Federation idea was so readily dropped after encountering initial difficulties is typical of the tendency in British politics to abandon pursuit of a sound policy merely on account of evidence that it is not capable of immediate realisation. Here again we see characteristic lack of will. Federation should have remained the aim of HM Government, instead of being merely a short-lived kite flown to see if the weather was favourable, and then packed away in permanent mummification after encountering the first awkward gust of wind. A massive and sustained campaign should have been waged by British government to win acceptance for the idea all round, until success was eventually achieved; but this was never even seriously tried.

Exactly the same can be said of Joseph Chamberlain's campaign for tariff reform, which proposed the setting up of trading preferences within the Empire, and to which I have referred in an earlier chapter. This would have gone hand in hand with Imperial Federation, as quite obviously a politically unified area, in the sense that would have existed, would have needed to be an economically unified area at the same time. The movement for Tariff Reform, like that for Imperial Federation, was abandoned much too readily after its first setback at the general election of 1906.

Those who set themselves against these two vital policies and still continued to talk of a future for the British Empire were in fact adopting a position that was entirely self-contradictory, for the rejection of the former simply was not consistent with the espousal of the latter. What was called an Empire in name could not be regarded as an Empire in reality, unless within there was the political and economic organisation necessary to make it into an effective unit in world affairs, in the same sense as were the other empires of modern times, such as the Russian and German Empires — and indeed the United States, which though not imperial in name is certainly so in reality.

At the same time as our political leaders in Britain were letting slip by, through lack of determination and commitment, the opportunity to weld the Empire into a real instrument of national power, so were they failing utterly, both in Britain and overseas, to build up among the people what might properly be called an imperial spirit and outlook. Education up to World War I, and to a lesser extent up to World War II, paid lip service to the idea of Empire but was much too feeble in the way that it handled the subject. Prominent emphasis was placed on the value of the Empire as an instrument for the spread of 'democracy', on the wonderful things it was doing for its subject races, on its usefulness as a means of promoting 'international fraternity' and so on. To read these eulogies, one would imagine that the purpose of all the heroic endeavour of men like Cook, Clive and Wolfe was to bring the system of trial by jury to Bantu tribesmen or to teach Bengalis how to play cricket. Is it any wonder that in the generations subjected to this scholastic process there grew up many with little understanding of, let alone conviction in, what ought to have been our imperial mission, and as a result reacted with almost total apathy to the growing signs of imperial disintegration?

The practice of giving the idea of Empire all this silly and hypocritical sugar coating grossly weakened its position in intellectual debate, for it was easy for the young, clever-pants graduates being churned out by our universities in the 1920s and 1930s to demolish imperialism by suggesting that, to these races of Africa or Asia, there were perhaps some things more worth having than those institutions nourished in the classrooms and on the playing fields of Eton. The whole point of the debate was lost: that imperialism was — or at least should have been — a movement for the benefit, first and foremost, of **our own race**, that its purpose was not for us to play at being missionaries to other breeds — even if some individuals took it upon themselves to spend their lives in that pursuit, that our own race needed extra territory to expand and develop and achieve economic self-sufficiency, and finally that people of British stock around the world were of one blood and should belong to one community. This, stripped of all the cant, was what Empire was for; and the whole of the British people, of whatever class, should have embraced it and worked for it wholeheartedly.

But of course there was little or nothing of this in our school curriculum in the earlier part of the present century, and certainly none of it at all by the time that I was at school in the 1940s and early 1950s. This was no accident, because side by side with this omission there was a total lack of any effort to teach any concepts of pride of race or a sense of racial destiny. 'Patriotism', such as it came into the classroom at all, was a totally passive and anaemic sentiment — much more an attachment to institutions and symbols (many of them fit only for the breaker's yard) than to land and race, let alone Empire. In fact I well remember as a youngster being positively repelled at this first inculcation of 'patriotic' ideas, and as a result being by no means in a hurry to stand to attention when the national anthem was played at the end of cinema performances. As I have related in an earlier part of this book, I was fiercely patriotic according to my own understanding of that term. But when I heard this decrepit, snivelling present- ation of what patriotism was supposed to be I felt it enough to turn any healthy young lad's mind to thoughts of treason!

Along with the utterly feeble education in our schools in support of Empire, there arose a growing crescendo of hate, lies and distortion against the Empire in the left-wing press, in books, in films and in due course also in our schools and universities, as the teaching profession became increasingly riddled with reds and pinks of every description. I started to come into contact with this poison in my late teens, and I remember marvelling at the magnitude of falsehood to which its authors had the nerve to go. In the first place, the whole perspective of Empire that they presented was wrong, making it appear primarily as an institution enabling the British ruling classes and capitalists to 'exploit' coloured labour, instead of what it was: mainly a union of white peoples linked by common blood. Great emphasis was placed on the fact that coloured subjects of the Empire had a much lower standard of living than Whites — conveniently ignoring the much more relevant truth that most Coloureds under our rule lived a great deal better than those in countries elsewhere. Propaganda aimed at Britain's poorer classes focused attention on the latter's miserable condition and asked the rhetorical question: What has the Empire done for you? From this, the classes aimed at were expected to infer that imperialism itself had something to do with their poverty and lack of work, and that, *ipso facto*, if the Empire was given away they would suddenly find themselves, as if by the wave of a wand, in well-paid jobs! In an endless stream, this garbage poured forth from the left-wing lie factory to contaminate the minds of the British public and soften them up for the day when the great scuttle from Empire would begin.

Yet what was done to counteract this lying filth by our supposed guardians of the imperial heritage? What did the spokesmen of 'Conservatism' have to say in reply to it? Practically nothing! The mild-natured apathy with which they reacted to this polluting of the minds of the people was depressing to behold. And not only did they fail to respond to the propaganda of the left with the necessary force of expression, they opted to conduct the argument on ground of their adversary's choosing by putting emphasis on the great benefits that the Empire had brought to its subject races, instead of concentrating on reminding everyone that imperial possessions were essential to the sustenance and growth of the British people and that it was for that purpose, first and foremost, that the Empire had existed.

In the debate on the Empire that was conducted in Britain from the end of the First World War to the beginning of the 1960s the right lost the battle to the left by a landslide. It did so because of its own lamentable weakness, both in the soundness of the arguments it employed and in the lack of conviction and commitment with which it conducted them. The result of this was that by the time the retreat from Empire began to proceed in earnest British public opinion had been well softened up to accept it, at worst with positive glee, at best with apathy.

This of course was no surprise to those of us who had come to realise that imperial surrender, far from being a policy that British Conservatism was unable to stop, was one that it was actively promoting. While it soothed its followers to sleep with assurances that it was the protector of imperial interests, its leaders were already busily engaged in preparing the nails for the imperial coffin. This was clearly evident by the 1950s to anyone prepared to use the most elementary powers of observation and then make the logical deductions from what he had observed.

I became convinced from my studies of the political scene at that time that the British Empire was not dying a natural death; it was being deliberately murdered. All the portents of this murder were visible at the time to anyone with the eyes to see them. At that stage of affairs, Britain still had an enormous reservoir of goodwill in the Dominions, prompted in part by natural family sentiments and also in part by a widespread awareness of the bonds of common interest that united us with our overseas kinsfolk. What in the first place undermined this happy relationship was not any strong wave of separatism overseas but a series of measures taken here in the United Kingdom whose only possible object was to weaken imperial ties. One of these was the decision to embroil Britain in the European Free Trade Area, which had consequences immediately detrimental to trade with the Dominions, although nothing like as disastrously so as our later entry into the EEC. Long before the latter event was signed and sealed in January 1973, British leaders, with Tories in the forefront, had been making a series of statements and gestures which indicated that they saw our future as lying predominantly within an integrated Europe rather than in partnership with those countries of British pedigree — one of the most damaging of these being the merging of the Foreign Office and Commonwealth Office into what was thenceforth called the 'Foreign and Commonwealth Office', an order of wording that reflected chosen priorities. During the same years, measures were taken to place restrictions on the entry of Dominion citizens into the UK which as good as put them into the same category as foreigners. Then came the ultimate act of betrayal, when Britain formally entered the Common Market itself, an act which further eroded trading ties by imposing full-blooded discrimination against Dominion products entering this country — despite the fact that, in many cases, those products could be supplied to us at cheaper prices than those of their European competitors.

In the light of this series of snubs and betrayals, it would have been less than natural if our old Dominion partners had not felt that Britain was turning its back on them and that they would have to look elsewhere for allies, trading arrangements and, ultimately, migrants to populate their open spaces and develop their resources. If there has been a distinct cooling of pro-British feeling in these countries over the past decades, we have only ourselves — or, more specifically, our political leaders — to blame. If there is anything that is extraordinary, it is that there is today any residue of British sentiment remaining in these countries at all. The fact that there is — as can be seen by popular reactions to royal visits — is testimony to the strength of the bonds of common race that have survived such a succession of desertions by the Mother Country.

Yet, with the dishonesty that has typified the whole process of withdrawal from imperium, its advocates have claimed that Britain's change of policy has only come about as a result of her recognition that her former Dominions no longer wish to maintain their special relationship with her — a classic case of the cart being placed before the horse!

The collapse of the British Empire cannot be viewed as an event in isolation. It was the natural product of a general rot within Britain, which, unhappily, came in time to infect our kinsfolk overseas in almost equal measure. Canada and Australia have today in large part surrendered to the same disintegrating internal forces, with New Zealand in recent years not very far behind. This can be seen in the way that all of these countries have tolerated political leaders of the same treasonable stamp as those of the United Kingdom, and the manner in which their national borders, like ours, have been thrown open to the teeming millions of the 'Third World'. We are in fact, all of us, in the grip of a global disease that is casting its shadow over the entire compass of Western Civilisation. The disease, as I have indicated earlier, is **liberalism**, and the instant communications between continents that have become possible by means of modern technology have only served to make the infection yet more universal with every year that passes.

Even White Rhodesia, which seemed for a time to have resisted the contagion better than most, eventually showed itself to be no more immune than the rest of us when its people tamely voted in a referendum to sign their own national death warrant by sanctioning the 'majority rule' against which they had sent their young men to fight bravely in the bush for the previous decade and a half.

I return to the question asked in an earlier part of this chapter: can anything now be done to reverse what has happened? And I answer again: nothing can be done, or should be done, to restore the Empire that was; but something **must** be done to create an institution to replace it. What form then should that institution take, and how can it be created?

Answering the second of these questions first, there must be, before anything, a dramatic political change in the United Kingdom which, whatever the method used to bring it about, will amount to a revolution — in the sense that it will set this country on an entirely new course of political development. So far in this book I have sketched out some of the lines along which this change must proceed, and in the remainder I shall have some more to say on the subject.

Britain, as she is at the moment, is no use to anyone, whether as motherland, ally or trading partner. For us to commend ourselves to other countries, even racially kindred ones, as a worthwhile relation in any of these regards, we must become a nation very different from the present one. No possibility therefore exists of our taking on any effective world role until we have first put our own house thoroughly in order. National recovery and renaissance must begin in these islands, and with no assumption that we have any rights elsewhere in the world or that others in the world have any ties to us.

Any such rights and ties as we may establish we will have to win anew by our own national achievement and example. If we want to rekindle the loyalty of our kinsfolk overseas, we must first build something here to which they can, with self-respect, be loyal. If we want to appeal overseas to pride of British Race, we must first win back our own pride in that regard.

In the British people's present abysmal condition of servitude, weakness and decadence there is surely little to encourage those of our own stock elsewhere in the world to value their British roots and heritage, while there is so much to induce those people to wish to forget those roots and that heritage. But with the transformation of Britain from the land she presently is into the land that, with such changes, she could become, it cannot be predicted what possibilities might open up for a resurgence of British spirit and sentiment in those places overseas where presently such things are at a low ebb.

If such a national renaissance in this country can be accomplished — and I believe it most certainly can be accomplished — we should then seek, with the co-operation of others, a drastic reorganisation of what has now become almost a redundant institution: the 'Commonwealth'. I use that name, though I have never liked it for all the depressing associations that it has in modern times. Suffice it to say that the name will have to do until we can devise and agree upon a better one. I need hardly say that the Commonwealth in its present form has become, not merely almost redundant, but a positive liability to Britain, with its noisy chorus of 'Third World' ingrate chieftains who, by some weird reasoning of our own politicians, must constantly be flattered and appeased. We should disband the Commonwealth as it now stands and then we should attempt to form in its place a new global organisation around the nucleus of the United Kingdom, Australia, New Zealand and Canada. Whether this new grouping should also be called 'Commonwealth' or known by some other name is not a matter of first importance. As I have said, the name will do for the moment, and at least it provides a kind of 'shorthand' by which the community of countries of which we speak can be made instantly recognisable.

It must be understood straightaway that for such a new institution to become possible under the conditions envisaged here, not
only would great political changes be necessary in Britain, but
some substantial degree of change would also have to come about
in the other countries concerned; with the types of government
presently in office in those countries, it is a certainty that any
overtures from Britain to form such an association, consisting as it
would only of white members, would be instantly rejected.
Britain would therefore have to accept from the outset that the
achievement of such a goal would be a project to be worked for
over several years, with early discouragements not taken as
reasons to abandon the strategy.

What we must realise is that the people of the old Dominions,
having long ago achieved effective sovereignty over their own
affairs, in the sense of regulating their relations with Britain on an
entirely voluntary basis, have in more recent times surrendered
much of this sovereignty by their subservience to international
institutions and alien ideologies, as we have in Britain. We all
now have a common interest in helping each other throw off the
shackles of these institutions and ideologies, in order that we may
all again acquire the sovereignty that we have thrown away. These
are the realities that each of us must face.

An enormous factor making for modern political conditions
is that of the controlled mass media, to which I have given
attention in an earlier chapter. Today, mass media empires
operate over and above national boundaries and on a global scale;
for instance, the media tycoon Rupert Murdoch owns a huge slice
of the channels of public communication in Australia, the country
of his birth, just as he does in Britain, the United States and
elsewhere. I am firmly of the belief that this global media power
must be combated on a global scale — a case of nationalists
taking international action to counter a common enemy, by no
means a contradiction when the true spirit of nationalism is
properly understood. The key to the whole operation is **money** —
of vast dimensions, for that is the key to the power of the media
barons as it exists now. Against this background, there would be
no dishonour whatever in patriots in one country accepting the
financial help of patriots in another in the task of fighting the
common enemy of both, particularly if both countries are peopled
by kindred stocks, which, in the nature of things, are interdependent in a multitude of ways.

There is anyway, all over the world today, a common

movement of resistance to the internationalist forces that are enslaving us all. I have the absolute conviction that these forces will eventually be overthrown the world over, though the change is obviously going to come in some countries before it comes in others. Any projections that we make concerning Britain's relationship with her kindred peoples overseas can only be made upon the hypothesis of those peoples once again taking control over their own destinies and reasserting their own will. I believe that, when that happens, it will be the will and instinct of these peoples to recognise the value of their ancient ties with us and to welcome their renewal. Of course, under present conditions in these countries that is not possible, but neither is it possible under present conditions here, for it is as much the policy of the present rulers of Britain to reject our overseas kinsfolk as it is the policy of the latter's rulers to reject Britain. Again I must reiterate: the possibilities that are being discussed here are possibilities which would operate under fundamentally changed political conditions, and in a wholly different world. We have to live within the world that is, true — and that has been the whole tenor of this book's argument with liberalism — but, whereas the liberals speak of attaining a world that is, by its nature, unattainable, the changes in the world for which we work are changes that are well within the realms of possibility by means of human action, for in fact they involve the recreation of a world in keeping with the natural laws that have governed its evolution throughout most of history and from which it has only quite recently departed.

There is another vital way in which Britain could, under the right political conditions, use her influence to restore the former close relationship with the old Dominions, and that is by use of her considerable weight as a would-be buyer of Dominion goods. The fact that trading preferences within the Commonwealth have long ago been dropped does not present any barrier to our ability to restore them, even if that restoration begins by being a one-way process. Britain, despite her capacity for self-sufficiency in manufactures which I have outlined and advocated in an earlier chapter, will always be a large-scale importer of minerals and, to some extent at least, an importer of food. Nothing need stop our action in immediately granting to White Commonwealth farmers preferential entry into the British market for all imported meat and dairy products. This would be vastly advantageous to Canada, Australia and, particularly, New Zealand; and it would in one stroke provide a strong incentive for their governments to co-operate with us, if only for reasons of self-interest, while it could generate an enormous fund of goodwill among their peoples, whose prosperity would undoubtedly be enhanced by such a measure. Whilst New Zealand would be the greatest beneficiary in the way of food exports to us, Australia and Canada would gain enormously in their trade in minerals. Both countries are economically structured in such a way that their prosperity is based very largely on such mineral exports. They being sellers of minerals in a big way, and our being buyers of minerals in an equally big way, a natural basis for a huge trade exists between us, and it would be for Britain to initiate this trade by her own unilateral action of giving preferences to Canadian and Australian minerals in the British market — as well, of course, as the farming products of those same countries. Sheer self-interest would impel the producing countries to respond, quite irrespective of the current strength or weakness of other ties.

All these developments, utilising both trade and the organs which influence public opinion, would be intended to pave the way for the reform of the Commonwealth of which I have spoken. Into what kind of body should that Commonwealth then be reformed? Very simply, it should be a body comprised, as I have said, of white members; and its purpose should be simple and unambiguous: to serve the interests, development, mutual prosperity and security of the Anglo-Saxon-Celtic Race that would be its main component — plus such other European ethnic groups as constitute a part of its populations and which are sufficiently close to our own stock to make assimilation possible. Such a Commonwealth should seek to exclude members of non-European races within its borders — although this would in practice be a matter for the decision of each country concerned, and the rule would probably not apply to Aboriginals within Australia, Maoris within New Zealand or Canada's various Red Indian and Eskimo groups.

When I advocate such proposals, I am well aware of the very formidable barriers that today stand in the way of their realisation. In all the countries concerned at the present time, it would be true to say that only minorities would endorse such a vision of the future. The brains of the masses everywhere have been so completely scrambled by the incessant propaganda of many years that a thorough and prolonged 'unscrambling' process will be necessary before sufficient shafts of light begin to illuminate the horizon. Yet we should not be dismayed by the magnitude of the undertaking; we must always remember that the attitudes that stand in the way of our aims are attitudes that have been created over the past generation or two by use of human powers of persuasion; should we believe it beyond us to change those attitudes, as they have been changed before, by use of the same powers? I do not believe that we need take such a defeatist view.

When I was a young boy growing up in the London suburbs, the nations of Europe were locked in the bitterest struggle against each other, a struggle in which national divisions and mutual national hatreds reached a sharper pitch than ever before in the history of our continent. Yet within less than one and a half decades after that conflict had expired these same nations were joined together in a community for political and economic collaboration. What accomplished this transformation? Simply the power of human persuasion, exercised through a thousand different channels, all dedicated to changing, fundamentally, attitudes that had seemed entrenched beyond recall a short time before.

Yet we are now asked to believe that because contemporary 'trends' all point to a severing of the ties binding Britain with her overseas kin in the White Commonwealth those trends must necessarily be regarded as permanent and unalterable! And this despite the fact that the natural bonds uniting our peoples — bonds of common race, language, culture, tradition and history — are many times greater than those uniting the different peoples of the European Continent.

I believe that it was right to break down the barriers of hatred dividing the European peoples and leading them to war — although it is a strange paradox that those who were working to this end in the 1950s included people who, not so very long previously, had been striving with all their might to promote that very same hatred and division.

What was not right, and not natural, was the extension of this process of reconciliation to the point of economic and political union — things that have no natural basis of shared nationality, language and tradition. Nevertheless, the fact that a great many people in Europe have been persuaded to endorse such a development is testimony to what the force of propaganda can achieve when used with sufficient power and purpose.

I will not accept, therefore, that propaganda — in the right hands and properly applied to a great patriotic purpose — cannot achieve an equally effective result in changing opinions among masses of people in Britain and the White Commonwealth in such a way that what is now considered unacceptable can be made thoroughly acceptable.

Undoubtedly the principal obstacle standing in the way of an endeavour to consolidate the White Commonwealth and make it an effective unit in world affairs is the popular illusion fostered among our overseas kinsfolk that, with the loosening of imperial ties, they have somehow acquired a new strength of 'nationhood' of their own. Nothing, of course, could be further from the truth.

The idea that these peoples today are somehow 'sovereign' by having cast away their British heritage is as false as the idea that they were not sovereign when that heritage was firmly instituted and embraced. I have said earlier that these peoples became the masters of their own fate the moment that they grew to a strength at which no coercion of them from thousands of miles away would have been remotely possible — even in the unlikely event of anyone wanting to attempt it. From that time on, their attachment to their British heritage was entirely a voluntary thing, enthustically accepted because those peoples themselves willed it so and wished for nothing else. Therefore there never was, as I have said, any real conflict between the concept of a common destiny with other Britannic peoples and that of complete self-government and independence of action on the part of each component country.

By contrast, the notion that today these peoples are truly 'free' or 'sovereign', let alone that they enjoy anything amounting to real nationhood, is sheer fantasy. In a way, they are today almost under governments of 'occupation' — albeit ones staffed by their own nationals — and are having policies imposed upon them to which they have never consented. I have cited, as one such example, the flooding of all the former Dominions, as well as Britain, by Third World immigrants — in no single case with the desires of the people on the matter ever being ascertained. Running parallel to this is the drive, covertly supported by all White Commonwealth governments, towards the ultimate aim of **world** government, which would put an end even to the pretensions of sovereignty that are now maintained in each country. And I remind the reader again — these railroading moves towards internationalism are being promoted at the very same time as their promoters are proclaiming a new-found 'nationalism'. The reality is of course that Canadians, Australians and New Zealanders today possess much less in the way of genuine nationhood than they ever did at the time when they were loyal and proud members of the British Imperial family of peoples.

For this situation, the old Dominions must blame mainly the renegades among their own so-called 'leaders'. But the fact that these 'leaders' are so subservient to alien interests is partly a consequence of the profound alteration in the balance of power that has taken place in the world in the years since 1945. At the beginning of this chapter I spoke of the new imperia that have succeeded the old. Without any doubt, most of the world today dances to the tunes called by these new giants — in the case of the white countries of the British Commonwealth the tune being called by the Empire of the Dollar. It is with the latter that true sovereignty lies (though whether that sovereignty can accurately be called 'American' is open to question). As I said earlier, in such a world the practical freedom of action of all those countries once comprising the British Empire is circumscribed in more than a hundred ways by the fact that none of them, individually, has the resources to act as a power of anything more than the second or third rank — with all that this implies in the political, economic and military spheres.

Yet these countries, were they to be persuaded to find their way back to the close relationship with one another that they enjoyed in former times, could with their combined resources amount to a power of the very first rank, well able to plot its own course in the world without requiring the permission of anyone.

I have spoken of these peoples' common British heritage, and I know straightaway that this will invite the protest that such countries have already moved some way towards the goal of 'multi-cultural' societies, with mixed populations of considerable variety. All this is of course true — though we should not be stampeded into thinking that the process has gone so far as to make it irreversible. Here Canada and Australia, in particular, have made a fundamental and disastrous mistake. Possessed of enormous territory and requiring great population increases for their full development, they have opted to follow the American model, as described by the phrase 'melting pot', coined in the late 19th century, when the decision was made to take in immigrants of stocks widely different from those that had laid the foundations of the country and given it its identity. But all the faults of this 'melting pot' policy in the United States are glaringly visible to anyone with the eyes to see. Behind the facade of apparent omnipotence, as indicated by statistics of population size, industrial output and military might, there is the reality of appalling weakness, the product of the country's chaotic internal division — a weakness manifest in the low quality of many of the units of her armed services, the declining efficiency of her factories and, not least, the fact that few decisions of state can now be made without weighing in the balance their acceptability to the multitude of ethnic groups and lobbies, all of which have to be bribed and appeased by anyone seeking to win, or retain, political office.

In America's present population, estimated at over 220 million, there are a great many millions who feel themselves in no way identified with the country except in as much as it is a welcome source of welfare cheques and various other 'rights' which they would have difficulty in obtaining elsewhere in the world. Had America, at the time when she was still in the formative stages of her development as a nation, chosen instead to pursue a path of homogeneity, populating her spaces with British and other closely related stocks, she would today be perhaps two-thirds the size — but probably double the strength, and without the myriad of appalling social problems now tearing her apart.

The question of whether Canada and Australia will follow the same course is still an open one, as each country is, even today, only at the very early stages of its growth — given the optimum of population that its resources could accommodate. Each country will make its own decision as to where it will go from here — notwithstanding all that I have said about the desirability of a new Commonwealth partnership. I can only hope that the wise decision will be taken in each case, and that the American path will be rejected before the point of no return is reached. If this path of wisdom is followed, and the path to the 'melting pot' reversed, both countries have magnificent futures in which we ourselves can share by providing them with millions of migrant peoples, who will relieve the congestion of our own islands and populate and develop the abundant spaces calling to them overseas, where they may multiply and prosper almost without limit.

There is something quite pathetic in the delusion of many Canadians and Australians that, in their acceptance of all these diverse migrants from every part of the world, they are somehow building up 'nations' of their own, and in some of them there is an almost perverse satisfaction in the idea that, with every new mixture introduced into their populations, they are asserting their 'independence' from Mother Britain and the distinctiveness of their nationality. Nothing could be further from the truth; the fact is that, if this trend continues, they will have no nations left to call their own, and their countries will simply become mini-Americas, with all the USA's chronic internal tensions and contradictions but without its status as a world power.

It will be in the next decade or two that the battle will be won or lost which will decide whether these potentially great countries offer a future for our race or whether they become, effectively, lost to our race. That battle will be won or lost in the countries themselves. It will be a battle of ideas, but behind this it will be a battle of **money**, for money is today the artillery by which wars of ideology are waged. No great vision such as may be formulated for the future of our peoples can achieve fulfilment unless it is able to mobilise forces of monetary power in its cause, for without those forces it will remain a vision capable of communication to only a tiny number of people.

If we can win this mighty battle of ideas and economics out of which, by the force of persuasion, a climate can be created for the preservation of these great and spacious lands for our own kind, and thence for the achievement of a reformed Commonwealth of peoples along the lines that I have here advocated, it would follow that the interest and advantage of all would be served by the creation of a mechanism for common action in at least the major areas of policy. Most certainly, such a mechanism would bear little similarity to the present Common Market apparatus, in which a centralised bureaucracy aspires to impose a uniformity of policy on every member in the most piffling of details, such as road signs, traffic laws, internal taxation and even the retailing of milk. What is desirable is that between the members of such a Commonwealth there is a system of regular consultation between heads of government, augmented by a common secretariat operating on a permanent basis, with a view to the closest possible co-ordination of policies in the realms of Foreign Affairs, Defence, Migration, Trade and Economic Development. Needless to say, it would be entirely optional to every member whether it wished to follow a line of policy or not. However, when the respective situations of these countries are examined, the area of common interest is so vast that co-ordination in these fields offers infinitely greater possibilities than any presently offered in the European Community, where, as I have outlined in a previous chapter, the economic structures and interests of the member countries are far more conflicting than complementary.

Having initiated trading preferences on a unilateral basis,

Britain should seek eventually to negotiate reciprocal preferences as far as possible. She must at the same time recognise that the manufacturing capacities of the White Commonwealth countries overseas have increased considerably throughout the present century, so as to render out of the question any arrangement similar to that proposed in Chamberlain's Tariff Reform movement — an admirable concept for its time but now long outdated. Britain should certainly strive to obtain preferences for her manufactured exports over those of foreign producers, but she should be ready to accept that her partners may wish to give their own indigenous manufacturers preference over United Kingdom products. Nevertheless, the inherent nature of the Dominion economies as large-scale exporters of minerals and food would mean that there would always be in those countries a substantial market for imports of finished goods (for in what other way would their customers pay for their mineral and food purchases?). Here lies an enormous potential trade for British exports which we can use our considerable leverage as a buyer to obtain.

Much in fashion today is the practice of international collaboration on specific industrial and technological projects requiring very large resources for research and development, and in this regard Britain has in recent years entered into partnership with European countries in a great number of fields, notably civil and military aircraft, nuclear power, space exploration and a wide range of motor technology, not to forget several other fields connected with defence and weaponry. The rationale for all this is that such projects are beyond the resources of individual nations acting alone, and this policy has been put forward as an appropriate response to American dominance and threatened monopoly in these areas. There is much argument to support such co-operation, although we should beware of allowing it to become just another synonym for internationalism — particularly in respect of military hardware, where national self-sufficiency has an importance that cannot be measured in purely economic terms. However, what is extraordinary is that scarcely any voices have been heard in Britain in support of collaboration with other White Commonwealth countries in the same departments. Here I would suggest an extremely important function for those engaged in the kind of co-ordination of policy of which I spoke earlier. In fact, it is far preferable that in these fields requiring very large resources, and where therefore some pooling of effort is advantageous, Britain should look to her partners in the White Commonwealth rather than to those in Europe.

In the very early days of British overseas colonisation, we were handicapped all along the way by the remoteness of these settle-ments of our people from the Mother Country and from one another. Sea travel was the only form of communication and transport, and this would take several weeks. Yet despite these disadvantages our scattered peoples maintained a very strong unity.

Today we are aided by enormous leaps forward in commun-ications which have reduced these distances to small significance. Apart from supersonic air travel, there is satellite TV, which enables live broadcasts from the other side of the world to be shown in British homes. There is the ease, clarity, speed and cheapness of telephone communication, which in time will almost certainly become visual. In so many respects, today's and tomorrow's technology can bring together communities of peoples thousands of miles apart. New Zealand in these times is much less remote than Scotland was from the South of England a century ago. In our overseas relationships we should exploit these benefits to the maximum. All the time we are being urged that we must move closer to our neighbours in Europe on the grounds that this is what geography dictates; yet the barriers of geography which have separated us from the White Commonwealth are now being rapidly conquered by new technology. It is the time to use this technology to grow closer to our nearest kin.

Without any doubt, the full development of the resources of the White Commonwealth is a task of truly enormous dimensions. Conventional wisdom has it that both foreign peoples and foreign capital are required to meet this challenge. I repudiate that view utterly. In an earlier chapter, I spoke of the immense reservoir of youthful energy that is now lying redundant in Britain due to the incapacity, and indeed the indisposition, of the old world of 'democracy' to organise these young people in great constructive national works. To this army of the aimless and the drifting might be added legions of youth in the Commonwealth overseas, who waste away their time and strength in a similar nihilistic environ-ment. I spoke of the need to mobilise British youth in tasks of redevelopment and recolonisation of neglected regions of our own islands and I suggested that this might be extended to areas of the White Commonwealth. I can think of no better way to bring the youth of our scattered countries together, and provide a new impulse to emigration, than to organise schemes whereby

battalions of the young from Britain may join with their contemporaries overseas in such pioneering work of opening up the great
empty spaces of the White Commonwealth to development and
settlement — not as an undertaking pursued in worship of the god
of profit, in accordance with Thatcherite philosophy, but as a
corporate national and racial crusade, dedicated to a patriotic
purpose of growth and expansion. Israel has her *kibbutzim*; why
cannot the Anglo-Saxon-Celtic world have its programmes
organised along similar lines, where the ideal of service to land
and people calls forth the latent energies of youth, now mis-spent
in punch-ups at football grounds or sapped by drugs, booze and
tobacco? This is not to deride the role of private enterprise in
developing these untamed regions; it is only to say that some great
drive other than the merely profiteering one must be present as
well, and must in the final analysis determine all policy. The mind
of the 'liberal' intellectual world sneers at the vision of regiments
of young men, their bodies bronzed in the sun, toiling in the great
outdoors in disciplined endeavour to expand the frontiers of race
and nation and to build for posterity — such a vision evokes
associations with all that is hated and reviled by that sick world of
corrosive 'thinkers' that inhabits the salons of the great city from
whence it emits the polluted odours of western suicide. But to the
healthy in instinct no finer picture could uplift the spirit than this
prospect of strength, vitality and idealism harnessed to practical
schemes for the turning of resources to national benefit and for the
sustenance of future generations of the folk.

This chapter would not be complete without some attention
being given to the vast continent of Africa, most of which was, up
till two or three decades ago, ruled by Europeans but from which
those Europeans have since abdicated.

It hardly needs stating that decolonisation in Africa has been a
total failure — a result clearly foreseen by all those who knew
something of that continent from personal experience. South
Africa apart, Africa is now a patchwork of bankrupt states,
presided over by incompetent and mostly tyrannical governments
among whose functionaries corruption is the daily norm. But far
be it for 'liberal opinion', which initiated the decolonising process
in the first place, to acknowledge its error! Liberals can no longer
fall back on the excuse of imperial 'exploitation' for the African's
miserable condition; but not for one moment will they consider
that it might be their own crackpot doctrines of African 'freedom'
that are the cause of the present chaos. Right now they are

solemnly lecturing us from every TV studio, every newspaper editor's office and every church pulpit that it is our most pressing moral duty to relieve the massive starvation in Africa that their own policies and those of their predecessors have mainly created. At the very same time as they are delivering these unctuous sermons to us, they are agitating for the destruction of the one state in Africa where Africans do have the prospect of a regular square meal — so that, presumably, they can then add that country to the list of those on whose behalf they will be pushing around the begging bowls to the accompaniment of of heart-rending photographs and many tears. Of course, 'compassion' for the hungry of Africa and elsewhere has now become, like race relations, an expanding industry, with jobs for eager young graduate busybodies proliferating everywhere. Undoubtedly, with the downfall of *apartheid*, a new emergency area would be placed on the map which would become, like all the others, a subject for our 'concern' and a dagger thrust at our 'conscience'. Then fresh agencies would be opened up under the patronage of which new droves of relief workers would swarm like locusts to the scene of the catastrophe, each wound up in a paroxysm of missionary righteousness. Then once again the vast propaganda machine of these crusaders would rev up into top gear, with agony-provoking film shots of human skeletons from the Transvaal to the Cape, accompanied by whimpering voices telling us that it is "all our fault."

Sometime, of course, this nonsense has got to stop, and we have got to face up squarely and honestly to the problem of what to do with Africa, instead of tearing hither and thither trying to cope with an escalating series of disasters that are the product of our own illusions. We have got to admit that what has passed for holy writ on Africa in the post-colonial era has proved to be dangerous idiocy. We have got to run the liberals, the do-gooders and the dispensers of other people's charity off the scene, and devise a new policy for Africa which bears some relationship to the realities of the world we live in.

I suggest that here we have two simple alternatives.

One is to wash our hands of Africa entirely and leave it to the Africans, telling them that the price of their independence is that they must stand on their own feet, feed themselves and develop their own resources with their own capital, derived from the produce of their own labour and their own skills — in just the same way as we built Britain in times past. After all, if the African is as good as we are — which the liberals are always telling us he is — he should be perfectly capable of doing all these things.

Whatever the practical logic of such a policy, it is unlikely that that policy will be acceptable to many people in Britain or around the Western World in the foreseeable future. This therefore leads us to the second alternative.

This is that the White Man, in return for his aid, his technology, his know-how and his capability in administering and developing resources, should resume control of Africa, and thereby be in a position in which he can take responsibility for its fate. Africa should, in other words, be **recolonised**, and run, as in the past, by white governments and with Whites in positions of power over administration, economic life, law and order and security.

As these words are written, it does not need a lot of imagination to envisage the screams of protest that will sound forth from those who set themselves up as the guardians of 'approved' opinion. But in reply I would simply ask these people: Have you a better idea? All the evidence of the present and recent past is that there is not a better idea, and that the only other solution is to continue throwing good money after bad in an endlessly futile quest to rescue the African from a misery and hunger that will be his lot either way, whether aid is continued or withdrawn. Such a policy would amount in effect to making Africans the pensioners of the developed world for all eternity. What right has the bleeding-heart brigade got to impose this burden on limitless future generations of our own people?

On the other hand, Whites, by taking control in the rest of Black Africa as in South Africa, can offer the African, not a living standard as high as their own — for that would not be merited by the African contribution to the economy, but at least the prospect of relief from chronic hunger and of living in lands where order prevailed.

But there is one mistake we should not make — and here is where even South Africa has been at fault: we should not put ourselves under an obligation to keep the African properly fed while giving him the licence to breed without limit. Social services and subsidised housing should be made available to Africans only on condition of their acceptance of strict methods of birth control which would limit children to an absolute maximum of three per family.

I am quite aware that this may sound a contradiction of what has been said earlier concerning the desirability of a high birthrate in

Britain; but here we are dealing with a wholly different set of circumstances: no-one would be asking foreigners from outside to feed and clothe the British children that would be the result of this increase in national fertility; we would pay for them ourselves. Likewise, no-one would force the African to practise birth control if he did not want to; he should be perfectly free to breed as many children as he liked, providing he was prepared to pay to keep them and forego state welfare benefits in that regard.

In the event then of the Europeans recolonising Africa, how should this be organised? Here, I suggest, is a field for close European co-operation much more useful than the hare-brained schemes of the EEC. What we would not want is a disorganised 'scramble' for Africa of the kind that took place at the outset of the previous colonial era, with Europeans entering into rivalry with one another for colonies, and each coveting the lion's share. Here Britain, with ample other spheres of interest, should avoid being greedy. The territories previously known as Northern and Southern Rhodesia, together possibly with Kenya and Uganda, should be the limit of our claim. Other lands should be allocated by mutual agreement among European states and in accordance with need. Indeed, by a statesmanlike approach to this allocation of spheres of influence in Africa, Britain could make a positive contribution to future peace in Europe, for such a policy would provide new outlets for settlement of Europeans which would reduce the probability of wars for 'living room' — though of course I do not suggest that such a remedy would resolve **all** the grievances in Europe resulting from loss of national territory.

Aside from these areas of which I have spoken, Britain must give a firm commitment to defend and keep British the Falkland Islands. This territory differs from other small colonies in the fact that the people there are of British stock, and as such have a natural right to our protection. The position of the Falklands has anyway altered in consequence of recent history, and our abandonment of them now would, more than ever in the past, be taken by the world as indicative of a loss of national will. The Falklands have become a symbol of our determination to stand up for our kinsfolk wherever in the world they may be and whatever number of them may be involved. If we desert them for reasons of expediency, where would such a process stop? The Falklands must be retained, and by all means necessary.

These lands apart, that expensive and ridiculous anachronism that is the present 'Commonwealth' should be disbanded, its heads of government sent packing and Britain's responsibilities towards it terminated.

In this chapter I have attempted to sketch out a set of realistic proposals whereby Britain may rectify, so far as is possible, the appalling procession of errors and surrender by which she undertook the ignominious retreat from Empire. Lest it be suggested that this is a recipe for a step back into the past and a reversion to the age of Queen Victoria, let it be repeated: what is advocated here is an entirely new kind of association adapted to modern conditions and facts and based on a relationship of equals, in which no member could be coerced into acceptance of any policy that was against its interest or will. This would be a coalition of free peoples linked together across the ocean by ethnic ties, entering into collaboration with each other in specific areas of common interest. Any closer or more binding commitments that may emerge between these peoples over the years would come through mutual desire and not by compulsion; and that is a question which anyway is for the future to decide.

This then is the goal, perhaps the supreme mission, of our generation: to sound across the oceans and across the air waves the clarion call of racial kinship, bringing together the scattered elements of our wandering tribes in a mighty movement of regeneration through which we may combine as one to develop the great heritage handed down to us by our seafaring ancestors. Will this call be heeded? Will this heritage be claimed and passed on to our next of kin? Or will we duck the challenge, preferring instead the small and mean destiny of an effete people that has resigned from greatness? The next few years will resolve this question once and for all, because the British Race is now at its supreme hour of decision: to be or not to be, to live again in splendour — or to die the death of the senile and the exhausted. We must decide soon, for history will not wait!

Chapter 19
Britain and the world

Among the many disastrous areas of British policy over the past century, none ranks higher as a cause of national collapse than our handling of foreign affairs. As with the economy, it is doubtful indeed whether we can claim to have had a foreign policy at all. All that the record shows is a series of panic reactions to situations around the world which conform to no coherent system of logic and which in almost every case have been wholly mistaken. If international diplomacy might be likened to a game of chess, it is fair to say that nearly every major move undertaken by Britain over the past century has been a wrong one, allowing her enemies to manoeuvre her, bit by bit, into a corner in which her choice of options has been increasingly restricted.

Before we look at this record in detail, we should first achieve clarity on the question of what should be the basic rules underlying all foreign policy, for without this no decision on foreign affairs can be evaluated according to any firm yardstick.

This age of mass communication obliges political leaders to present their actions to their peoples and to the world in terms that can be understood and accepted by the simplest intelligence; and that seems, inevitably, to involve the invoking of high-sounding moral principles, such as 'justice', 'peace', 'humanity' and so on — to the point at which we are apt to forget that underpinning all international diplomacy is a competition of **interests**; and that is the only reality that really counts in world affairs.

True national leaders and statesmen know this and act in accordance with it, no matter in what way they may dress their actions up in the finery of ideology and morality in order to justify them to their public. To such men, the standard by which every international question is judged is that of how it affects their own nation's interest. From this line of reasoning is formed a science in which foreign affairs are viewed from the standpoint of a strategist, basing all thinking on military criteria — albeit that the means to carry the strategy out are for the most part non-military. This was certainly what Clausewitz had in mind when he said, as I quoted earlier, that war was the continuation of policy by other means. What 'policy' had as its objective, whether the means were those of war or peace, was **victory** — meaning, to be precise, the continued advancement of national interests, growth, development, resources and power. The conduct of foreign affairs that had any object other than this was, whatever else it may have been, not qualified to be described as 'policy'; hence the observation about Britain's handling of foreign affairs made earlier.

As these words are written, it is possible to envisage an itch in the mind of the reader who is a disciple of the current orthodoxies of liberalism and internationalism. He will no doubt be ready to jump from his seat and proclaim the other criteria which should, according to his convictions, govern our thinking on foreign relations. He will echo the words 'justice', 'peace' and 'humanity' to which I have recently alluded, no doubt adding a few more in similar vein — such as 'good' and 'evil', 'right' and 'wrong', and will talk of 'international law', and so on and so forth.

But he would be wrong in presuming that I exclude these considerations from all thinking on foreign affairs; I do not. I merely state that once such considerations are allowed to sway the leaders of nations away from the first principles of foreign policy that I have enunciated, and towards actions that, considered in the cold light of reason, are detrimental to national interests and policy, the road to national defeat and impotence has been taken, and at the end of that road is a national condition that will not allow for **any** effective role in world affairs, in defence of whatever righteous cause.

So we come back to these first principles again, which might best be expressed in General Douglas MacArthur's well-quoted axiom: "There is no substitute for victory." Indeed, there is not; and that applies to the competition between nations no less in peace than in war.

Because politicians are forced by circumstances to cloud this truth in rhetoric which appeals to other — and perhaps seemingly loftier — sentiments, it does not mean that they are entitled to lose sight of that truth, for the moment they do their nations are in danger.

The trouble with British leaders over the past century is that, not only have they made extravagant use of high-sounding moral verbosity to sanctify their international actions, but they have actually come themselves to believe in their own words and fall victim to their own propaganda! What was in previous ages a coherent and rational tradition of foreign policy, conceived in accordance with sound strategic considerations, degenerated into a succession of disjointed reactions to events around the world, fuelled much more by emotion than by rational judgement, and pursued in the service of pure abstractions which seldom bore any relation whatever to real national interests.

This does not mean that nowhere in recent policy have such national interests come into the equation; some consideration for these have remained in the minds of those in charge of affairs. But such has been the atmosphere of hysterics in which great issues of foreign affairs have been debated that even when the national interest has been given some thought the judgement of where it lay has usually turned out to be an appallingly bad one.

An example of this has been the application of the principle of the 'balance of power' in Europe. This was a perfectly sound principle for a number of centuries where England, and later Britain, were concerned. The error lay in failing to recognise when that principle had become out of date — which it had done by about the middle of the 19th century.

When England (Britain) was a comparatively small European nation, living on the edge of a continent dominated by a much more populous and powerful Spain or France, it made much sense for us to align ourselves with whatever state, or coalition of states, represented, at any one time, the main counterweight to whichever of these two powers was in the ascendancy. In this way the latter's power was curbed and the security of these islands was protected. Even in the earlier stages of the opening up of the new world, and when Britain had acquired extensive colonies, the principle still held good. France was still a formidable rival in North America and at the time a nation of considerably greater resources than ourselves. She was only prevented from bringing greater force to bear against us across the Atlantic by her heavy military commitments in Europe, such as in the War of the Spanish Succession (1701-14) and the War of the Austrian Succession (1744-48) — to which we ourselves added by siding with the anti-French coalitions in both cases — an entirely sound policy at the time.

In the Napoleonic era, our participation in the anti-Bonapartist coalitions was again undertaken in accordance with sound principles of *realpolitik*. Every indication existed that the First Napoleon could, and would, have invaded us had we not chosen this road and assisted thereby in tying his forces down elsewhere in Europe. A generation previously, French intervention on the side of the rebel colonists in America had been largely instrumental in bringing about the British defeat. Had Napoleon succeeded in defeating us in Europe, there is every likelihood that France would have sought to reverse her defeat at Quebec in 1759 and retake Canada.

But by the middle, and certainly by the end, of the 19th century the international situation had entirely changed, rendering obsolete the strategic considerations that had been perfectly valid at that century's beginning and before. France was no longer the leading power in Europe, having been overtaken both by Britain and Germany. German potential was formidable, but no more so than our own had we been prepared to organise properly the resources of our then immense Empire. In contrast to France previously, Germany was no threat to us in any of our overseas Dominions, even with the increased naval power that she had started to develop under Wilhelm II. Late in the rush for colonies, she had obtained territory in East and South West Africa, but the fear that she might wish to add to this by conquering our own African possessions was, at the most, speculative. It was true that she maintained the best army in Europe, but the briefest look at European geography and history should have sufficed to explain why. Confronted by a revanchist-minded and rapidly arming France on one side and a fast-industrialising Russia on the other, she had every reason to feel the need for powerful land forces, while her growing navy was no more than was necessary to safeguard her trading routes and her access to her colonies. That she might covet British possessions in Africa was not inconceivable but it certainly was not probable; with potential enemies enough, it was hardly likely that she should wish to add to these what was then the greatest empire in the world. In this situation, Britain should not have been complacent about German power but most certainly should not have regarded it as the greatest threat to her interests at the time. No nation can arm against everybody at once, and at every stage of international affairs there has to be a careful and balanced calculation as to what kind of foreign danger is the most probable and the most immediate. It is my view that, had there been such calculation in Britain in the late 19th and early 20th centuries, prudent policy would have pointed to a different attitude towards Germany than the one which in the outcome was adopted.

The strength of Germany had come primarily through sound internal development. There had been a steady growth of population, which had accelerated particularly rapidly since unification in 1871. That unification had mobilised into one single force the previously scattered, and often warring, German states (excluding of course Austria). With this unified Reich there had been a spectacular development of manufacturing industry, utilising the advantages of Bismarck's *zollverein* to achieve a large and expanding internal market. Finally, the Germans, under the impress of Prussian leadership, were a highly orderly and disciplined nation, practising a level of civic virtues probably higher than were to be found in any of the larger states in the Western World.

Britain's best assurance against eclipse by this new Germany always lay in precisely the same form of internal development by which the latter nation had grown powerful. Therefore, the absolutely top priority of British policy should have been to organise and develop the enormous resources of her Empire in a similar process of industrial expansion resting primarily on a national, rather than international, market. Imperial Federation, which I have mentioned in the previous chapter, should have been pursued in the same way as had German Federation. And we should not have been reluctant to emulate some of the Prussian virtues of citizenship, bearing in mind that these had been developed in a race much more closely related to ourselves in character and temperament than any other on the Continent. Finally, Britain should, as part of the same process, have adopted universal military service and training, bringing the armies of her Empire up to the same strength and standards of efficiency as the German.

From this position, Britain could have made herself virtually invulnerable to attack by Germany even in the extremely unlikely event of the latter country entertaining hostile designs against her or any part of her Empire — for the price of such an attack to the Germans would have been far too high.

Parallel with this, we should have sought to renew the ancient tradition of Anglo-German alliance rather than opt for the disastrous *Entente Cordiale*, which in the event drove Europe eventually to war and destruction. Racial affinity apart, this policy should have been based on the simple calculation that, of all the major powers in Europe, Germany was placed in the situation which made her our least likely enemy.

But Britain did none of these things. She remained weak internally by her unwillingness to adopt the political measures required for the consolidation and co-ordination of her Empire. She likewise did not adopt the necessary practices for the proper co-ordination of her economy. Finally, by a libertarian code of citizenship among her people, she encouraged a spirit of individualistic greed and selfishness instead of a firm sense of community, or *volk*. As for military power, the best comment on this was made by Bismarck when he said: ''If the British land an army on the coast of Germany. I shall send a policeman to arrest it.''

Being internally weak behind all the dazzle of her imperial panoply, Britain could see no better guarantee of her own security than to put her support behind whatever strength could be mobilised on the Continent **against** Germany. By joining the *Entente Cordiale*, she simply encouraged the French towards more aggressive posturing and thus heightened the tension in Europe to a point which inevitably had its effect in Germany, bringing about an escalation of mutual suspicion which eventually exploded in 1914.

Indeed, as far back as the end of the Franco-Prussian War the British outlook on international events had begun to be influenced by attitudes in which emotion was rapidly overtaking common sense as the main directing force. Typical was a speech made in the House of Commons in February 1871 by Mr. Auberon Herbert and for the source of which I am indebted to Dr. Peter Peel in his book *British Public Opinion and the Wars of German Unification: 1864-71*. Said the speaker to the House:-

''I must say that I look on the unification of Germany as a great peril to Europe; and for this reason — no-one will deny that the unification of Germany began with an essentially democratic movement. Since 1830. 15 sovereign princes have been removed from their thrones by their respective peoples. We have at this moment the unification of Germany under a military despotism...It cannot be for the good of Europe that there should be a great military despotism in Germany, built upon the ruin and destruction of France...''

Here we see two themes typical of the silliness of the doctrinaire 'liberal' moraliser. There is the implication that an authoritarian government standing at the head of a strong and efficient army is more likely to be a threat to the peace than a 'democratic' one —

a notion for which there is not a shred of historical evidence. Along with this, there is the assertion that the ruling regime in Germany was "built upon the ruin and destruction of France." This conveniently ignores the truth that it was French blustering and provocation that were at least as much a factor in bringing the war about as any actions by the Germans — indeed probably more so. That the Germans chose the moment of the French defeat to unite their formerly separate states into a single Empire was purely incidental; that unification would have come about sooner or later in any event, and almost certainly under the leadership of the House of Hohenzollern.

By the end of the 19th century, this strictly ideological view of international and political affairs had come to be the dominating feature in the British conduct of foreign relations, and under these conditions anything resembling a proper foreign policy disappeared. Feminine jealousy, rather than cool male reasoning, was the basis upon which issues were judged, and with this there developed the liberal's customary infatuation with the loser in a conflict and his assumption that in every international argument the weaker party must always be right.

This mentality led us to ditch the people who had been our allies for most of previous history, usually with great benefit to ourselves, and into the insanity of the *Entente Cordiale*, under which we would be aligned with a nation that bitterly resented being upstaged as the leading Continental power and was certain to do everything it could to provoke a future European war in which the German Empire that it hated would be vanquished and dismembered.

Thus were we led into the catastrophe of World War I. Almost equally catastrophic was that war's aftermath, when in a frenzy of hatred against their defeated adversary the Allied powers imposed upon her terms of 'peace' that made a further conflict inevitable. Though the bile of France was the principal factor in this spiteful act of revenge, the mood in Britain was not such as to induce us to do much to restrain our recent ally. It was left to a French soldier, the Supreme Allied Commander Marshal Foch, to cast a small nugget of wisdom into the proceedings when he said: "This is not peace; it is merely a cease-fire for 20 years."

Such was the insanity of the Versailles Treaty, which imposed terms on the defeated Germans that were certain later to be repudiated as soon as the means to do so were in Germany's hands. The Wilsonian principle of national 'self-determination' was supported by us as a pretext for the establishment of wholly unviable states like Czechoslovakia but, in the spirit of true humbug, was rejected in as much as it applied to Germany, which country was forced to accept the placing of millions of its nationals under the domination of foreign states, against those nationals' will.

Britain, having learned precisely nothing from the recent past, was back again playing the old game of the balance of power. The object was of course once more to deny Germany her natural place as the leading nation on the European mainland, and to that end weaken her as much as possible by means of reparations, the seizure of parts of her territory and people, the prohibition of her manufacture of certain vital weapons of self-defence and the confinement of the size of her army to 100,000 men — a quite ridiculous condition in view of Germany's situation *vis-a-vis* her neighbours. A simpleton ought to have seen that none of this could ever work, and that in the course of time the German national spirit would inevitably assert itself once again and all of these absurd fetters would be cast away like gnats from the wings of an awakened eagle. But such obvious facts did not impress themselves on the minds of the dwarfish figures who presided over Britain's destinies in the 1920s and 1930s.

As quickly as, with one hand, we were making ourselves a party to the imposition of peace terms that contained all the seeds of future war, with the other we were denuding ourselves of all the vital resources that had enabled us to be victorious in the previous one. As John Terraine remarks in *The Mighty Continent*:-

"Year by year, relying on 'collective security' through the League of Nations with general popular approval, British governments dismantled British power. In 1919 the Royal Navy had regained a supremacy unequalled since the Napoleonic Wars. In 1922, at the fatal Washington Conference, Britain accepted battleship parity with the United States; she agreed to scrap older battleships, stop current building, and build no more battleships for 10 years. So the Navy, once the nation's pride, was allowed to slide into numerical weakness and technical obsolescence. The Royal Air Force similarly: in 1919 the RAF was the most powerful in the world, with 22,000 operational aircraft; by 1922 it had sunk to one tenth the size of the French Air Force. As for the Army, it was not to be compared with the efficient and well equipped Expeditionary Force of 1914. But no-one seemed to mind (except the Chiefs of Staff, whose noses were increasingly rubbed into the consequences); Ramsay MacDonald expressed a widespread belief when he told the Fifth Assembly of the League of Nations:-

> 'Our interests for peace are far greater than our interests in creating a machinery of defence. A machinery of defence is easy to create, but beware lest in creating it you destroy the chance of peace.' ''

At the same time as this was happening, Britain was throwing away all the gains she had made on the industrial front under the stimulus of war. To quote Terraine again:-

> "Britain had inevitably suffered by the loss of shipping and overseas markets through the war. At the same time, however, she had profited by a long overdue industrial revival, an important step towards a second industrial revolution.
>
> "New industries had been created by the war, and were here to stay: chemicals, aircraft and aero-engines, the refining of non-ferrous metals. Electrical generating capacity had doubled. Electric bulb production had quadrupled. Ball-bearing production had doubled. Optical glass production had increased sixty times. All these were valuable gains, and with them had gone a great modernisation and reorganisation of existing industries, with large measures of state control. The question was whether these gains would be maintained and carried forward in peace; the answer, soon given, was that they would not. Orthodox economic theory, belief in free trade and *laissez-faire*, dislike of state control, lack of enterprise among industrialists, all these helped to account for a sense of poverty which was not entirely justified by fact. But justified or not, its consequences were far-reaching."

Britain was, in other words, doing exactly what she had been doing in the years preceding the World War: while her handling of foreign affairs was such as to make war increasingly likely, she was allowing herself to be weakened, militarily and industrially, so as to render her least ready to wage war effectively when it came.

In 1933 Hitler came to power in Germany and immediately began — as it was always predictable that someone would — redressing the grievances arising out of Versailles. Claims were made upon the lands and peoples that had been forcibly separated from Germany, while armed forces were built up to a level necessary to give backing to these claims. At the same time a revolution took place within Germany, giving rise to an extraordinary new surge of energy, dynamism and reconstruction. It is not my purpose here to argue the rights and wrongs of what happened inside Germany during that period because such matters are not crucial to the issue under discussion, which is that of British foreign policy — or lack of it. Even if we accept as gospel the very darkest picture of that revolution known as National Socialism and we concur with the orthodox historians that the Nazi leaders were evil men, this does not in the slightest way bear on the question of what should have been Britain's attitude to these events.

Our attitude should have been based, as it should in all such considerations of foreign affairs, on a cool assessment of what was in the British interest, and our policy should have been formulated in accordance with that assessment.

Hitler's plans were to lead, as was obvious, to Germany once again reasserting her natural position as the strongest power in Continental Europe. The whole point of the matter was: would Britain be threatened by this development? And from this a further question arises: even if it was perceived that Germany might represent some threat to us, could that threat be removed except by bringing into the balance forces that would comprise a much greater and more likely threat?

This latter question was the crucial one. No nation, least of all one with the commitments that Britain had at that time, can hope ever to enjoy a condition of **total** security. Wise statecraft, as I have hinted before, involves the careful weighing up of the various available security options, and deciding on the one that offers the greatest **probablity** of security in relation to the cost of achieving it.

If Britain was uneasy about the spectre of a powerful Germany bestriding Europe like a colossus, what options had she? In fact there were only two. One was to call into being a war to destroy Germany, which in view of Britain's own weakness at the time, could only be won with the help of much stronger allies which, as a price of such a victory, would most probably present a much greater threat to our security and interests than Germany was likely ever to do. This was the reality that stared British leaders in the face in the 1930s. To be specific, they should have realised that the new Germany could not be beaten except with the help of Russia or America or both, and that this help would have to be paid for in the form of the domination of the world by either or both of these powers in the peace that would follow.

The one alternative to this was to accept German power in Europe and learn to live with it — but, as the firmest possible guarantee against the threat of the use of that power against ourselves, to dedicate our energies to building up the strength of Britain and her Empire to such a peak that no power in the world could attack us except at a cost which would render the whole enterprise counter-productive.

This would have meant: firstly, the organisation of the Empire into a single unit, along the lines mentioned earlier, which would have presented Germany, even had she considered attacking us, with an adversary which in white population alone was equal to her in numbers and which in natural resources was considerably superior; secondly, the carrying out of an industrial revolution that would have brought British manufacturing output up to the level, if not in excess, of German output; thirdly, the mobilisation, by means of all the resources of Empire, of a military power equal to that of Germany; finally, the carrying out of a political and social revolution within Britain and her Empire that would have achieved the same high degree of organisation, efficiency, orderliness and national discipline as had been achieved by Germany herself — not necessarily with methods identical to those used in the latter country but at least with a view to the same effect.

All this of course would have been a gigantic undertaking, but no more so than World War II was to prove to be; and whereas the latter impoverished and ruined Britain the former would have made Britain stronger and more prosperous than at any previous time in her history. No greater effort would have been required in one than in the other, and the result in the first case would have been positive rather than negative: its effect would have been to **build** rather than to **destroy**.

This of course would have meant an entire reorientation of Britain's energies and preoccupations: instead of foreign adventures conceived with a view to meddling in everyone else's affairs, we would have turned our attention to the priority of internal development and got on with the long-neglected task of putting our own house in order.

One prominent public figure, and one alone, advocated this policy in the 1930s. I make no apologies for again quoting Sir Oswald Mosley. Speaking in October 1938, as the war clouds were gathering, he said:-

> "Supposing two lots of Englishmen wanted to join up and get together. What would you think of Germany if she said: 'No you can't, if you two lots of Englishmen get together we will declare war on you.' We would tell Germany or any other country that said two lots of Englishmen cannot get together, we would tell them to go to hell, and you know it. Supposing that Kent were occupied by

the Portugese and that in Kent the Portugese were insulting the British flag and bullying British womanhood. We in Britain would not stand for it. We would say those British people are coming home to Britain. What would we say to Germany if she tried to stop us? Yet that is what the Labour Party want to do to the Germans. "Each great nation has got to awake in its own great way. We, the British people, will never copy any other nation on earth, because we believe that with our own people we can make this the greatest nation in the world, that the whole world will look to Britain for an example. I want one day to be able to say to Hitler: 'I don't care what you do in the East of Europe — good luck to you. We are going to beat you in the race for higher wages; we are going to beat you in the race to build the fairest, noblest land the world has ever seen!' "

There will of course be those who will say to this that Britain could not stand idly by when atrocities were being committed by the Germans, both in their own country and in the lands they occupied. But to this claim Mosley made his reply in the columns of *Action* newspaper in December 1938, in which he said:-

"Supposing that every allegation were true…supposing it was a fact that a minority in Germany were being treated as the papers allege, was that any reason for millions in Britain to lose their lives in a war with Germany? How many minorities had been badly treated in how many countries since the war without any protest from press or politicians?…Why was it only when Jews were the people affected that we had any demand for war with the country concerned? There was only one answer…that today Jewish finance controlled the press and political system of Britain. If you criticise a Jew at home — then gaol threatens you. If others touch a Jew abroad — then war threatens them."

Here Mosley was touching upon another factor that came into the reckoning among those forces driving us to war with Germany and the act of national suicide that that involved, and I shall say something more on this matter shortly. Suffice it to comment here that Jewry in Britain could not possibly have persuaded our political leaders, whatever the methods of pressure used in that persuasion, to adopt an anti-German attitude were not such an attitude fundamentally in keeping with the view of the world that had developed in the minds of the British ruling class over the previous decades and which saw all great international issues, not in terms of a rational calculation of British interests, but in the 'goodie and baddie' perspectives of children's fiction.

The counsel of Mosley and those like him was of course

rejected, and the itch of Britain to interfere in the affairs of her neighbours became a positive St. Vitus Dance. The great obsession of the ruling orthodoxy in the 1930s was that of 'stopping fascism'. We witnessed the dreary procession of old-gang figures mounting the platforms to cluck-cluck their indignation, first against Mussolini for marching into Abyssinia (where no British interest was threatened), then against Franco for averting communism and chaos in Spain, and without cease against Hitler, first for proclaiming the outrageous doctrine that Germany should belong to Germans, then for marching into his own backyard in occupying the Rhineland, then for going to the rescue of his kinsfolk in Austria and Czechoslovakia. It made no impression at all that the German leader was only here doing exactly what we British would have done if we had marched into Norfolk or Kent.

While our leaders were delivering their strictures against Mussolini, Franco and Hitler, millions of Britons were out of work, millions more were suffering from malnutrition and stunted growth, and yet more were rotting in stinking slums. Britain's factory machinery was becoming ever more obsolete. The Empire that could have provided sustenance for all was going to waste and drifting into disunity. And as all this was happening our armed forces were being denied the manpower, training and equipment essential to fight the coming war these leaders were determined to have with the Fascist and Nazi powers. Well might we have said to them, in the words of Goethe: "Physician, heal thyself!"

These elements of course comprised only one of the two main factions of British politics of that period. The other we best know as the advocates of 'appeasement'. This faction represented a somewhat higher consensus of realism and common sense than did those it opposed. Its members had the wit to recognise that the path being signposted by the war lobby was one of national madness which would lead to national destruction. These people have been cast in a contemptible light by history; and Munich, the venue of Neville Chamberlain's last attempt to reach agreement with Hitler, has entered the dictionary as a word synonymous with national surrender. This is of course a wholly dishonest equation, since 'surrender', in the context used here, implies a craven sacrifice of some genuine national interest in an attempt to buy peace, whereas the view of the great majority of those who supported Chamberlain's efforts was that Britain's national interests were not served by a war against Germany. As subsequent events proved, this view was wholly right. It was in fact appalling that things reached a stage at which our premier of the time felt it was necessary to go to Munich, cutting a somewhat sorry figure as the leader of a great power, scuttling off to Germany for the third time in a few months to plead with Hitler over what he himself called "a far off country (Czechoslovakia) of which we know nothing." The very fact that a British head of government was busying himself over such a country at all when he had such mountainous problems to deal with back at home is a sorry commentary on the sense of priorities that prevailed in national affairs.

Chamberlain's efforts notwithstanding, the war lobby eventually won the day. Britain joined France in giving the ridiculous pledge to Poland that they would come to that country's aid in the event of a German invasion, a pledge that made the coming conflict inevitable.

Apologists for the war brigade will claim of course that much more was at stake in 1939 than the territorial integrity of Poland. Hitler, they will protest, had to be stopped. If he was not challenged at that point he would have proceeded to further conquests until he had the whole of Europe under his heel. Those who believe this claptrap have clearly not made the slightest effort to inform themselves about, least of all understand, the objectives of Hitler's expansionist policy. It was clear from a reading of *Mein Kampf* that Hitler did not believe in multi-national empires, as anyone will know who has bothered to study what he said about the Austro-Hungarian state in which he grew up. What Hitler did want was the incorporation of all ethnic Germans into a single state. Beyond that, he wanted new lands to accommodate Germany's surplus population, and in that regard favoured an expansion and colonisation **eastwards** in the manner that has been the custom of Germans since the Teutonic Knights. This policy, most certainly, was contrary to all conventional 'liberal' ethics of pacifism and 'international law', which saw the existing boundaries of nations as sacrosanct and fixed for all time. An argument can certainly be made against Hitler that he was violating the peace and the established order of Europe by such a policy, but the reply to such an argument would have been — and indeed was — that that peace and order had in the first place been established and imposed upon Germany by force, and that this was no more legitimate than Hitler's action in seeking to change it by force. It could have been, and was, argued that such nations as Britain and

France, which had annexed vast areas of the world by force themselves, could hardly protest if Germany was now using the same methods to acquire land in Europe of only a fraction of these dimensions.

Such arguments, of course, could not be refuted; and this rendered all the objections to German expansion on moral grounds pure hypocrisy. The only valid reason for going to war to prevent Hitler's expansion in Eastern Europe would have been the belief that afterwards he would have turned west and threatened us. As I have indicated here and in a previous chapter, all the evidence points to his not having the slightest intention of doing any such thing. This was to be further borne out in 1940 when, having pushed the British Expeditionary Force back to the Channel, he halted his armies to let it escape, largely intact, across the water.

This revealing moment in history was described by Captain Basil Liddell-Hart in *The Other Side of the Hill*. In Chapter 10 of this book, in which the author chronicles the German invasion of France down to Dunkirk, he mentions Hitler's telegram to General Von Kleist, instructing him to halt his forces at medium artillery range from Dunkirk, and then the German leader's subsequent conversation with Field Marshal von Rundstedt, in which he explained his decision. The author then quotes a report from one of those present at this conversation, thus:-

> "He (Hitler) then astonished us by speaking with admiration of the British Empire, of the necessity for its existence, and of the civilisation that Britain had brought into the world...He compared the British Empire with the Catholic Church — saying they were both essential elements of stability in the world. He said that all he wanted from Britain was that she should acknowledge Germany's position on the Continent. The return of Germany's lost colonies would be desirable, but not essential, and he would even offer to support Britain with troops, if she should be involved in any difficulties anywhere. He concluded by saying that his aim was to make peace with Britain, on a basis that she would regard compatible with her honour to accept."

Captain Liddell-Hart added his own comment to this quotation:-

> "If the British Army had been captured at Dunkirk, the British people might have felt that their honour had suffered a stain, which they must wipe out. By letting it escape, Hitler hoped to conciliate them."

The absurdity of the view that Hitler had to be opposed for marching into Poland, on the grounds of that nation's right to have her territorial integrity guaranteed, was of course doubly underlined when the Soviets shortly afterwards occupied the eastern part of that same country. Needless to say, we did not then hear screams that on that account Britain should go to war with Russia!

So, if there was no valid reason inherent in the British national interest to go to war with Hitler's Germany, why did we then do so? Some clue to this question may be provided by the headline on the front page of *The Daily Express* of March 24th 1933: "Judea declares war on Germany." This headline was followed by a report of united Jewish action all over the world to organise an economic boycott of German goods. Shortly afterwards, in the summer of the same year, the International Jewish Boycott Conference was assembled in Holland under the presidency of Mr. Samuel Untermeyer, of the USA, who was elected president of the World Jewish Economic Federation formed to combat the opposition to the Jews in Germany. On his return to the USA, Mr. Untermeyer gave an address over Station WABC, the text of which was printed in the *New York Times* of August 7th 1933. This quoted Mr. Untermeyer as saying:-

"Each of you, Jew and Gentile alike, who has not already enlisted in this sacred war (against Hitler's Germany) should do so now and here."

These sentiments were echoed by Vladimir Jabotinsky, writing in a Jewish publication *Natcha Retch* in January 1934:-

"The fight against Germany has been carried out for months by every Jewish community, conference, trade organisation, by every Jew in the world...we shall let loose a spiritual and a material war of the whole world against Germany.''*

It must be borne in mind that these Jewish responses to events in the new German state occurred when that state was no more than a year old, indeed in the first case when it was only two months old, before Hitler had properly consolidated his power and well in advance of any of the measures later alleged to have been taken against Jews, notably the incarceration of some of them, with many non-Jews, in concentration camps.

Along with this trade boycott, a flood of vituperation was let loose in the press against the new regime, quite obviously with the object of whipping up hatred against Germany among the British

---

* for this quotation and the previous one attributed to Samuel Untermeyer, the author is indebted to Captain A.H.M. Ramsay and his book *The Nameless War*.

public. In this regard, it is interesting to note the impressions recorded by a distinguished British sailor, Admiral Sir Barry Domvile, in his book *From Admiral to Cabin Boy*:-

> "I paid my first visit to Germany in 1935, and nobody with any powers of observation at all could have helped being struck by the gross discrepancy between the facts of daily life in Germany and their warped representation to the British public by their daily press...It was a great shock to me, and brought home, as nothing else could have done, the power of evil of the hidden forces which were at work to create a deterioration in the friendly relations between two great countries, upon whom the peace of the world depended, to say nothing of our own prosperity."

A great mass of documentation exists which bears out what Domvile was saying, and I need here only refer the reader to newspaper records of that period, which make it clear that certain powers in Britain and elsewhere, notably the United States, were doing their best to stoke up the enmity which was to lead to World War II. In a previous chapter I have drawn attention to one notable exception, which was the Rothermere Press, and spoken of the way in which that section of Fleet Street was eventually brought to heel.

It is not the place here to debate whether the vast flood of propaganda against National Socialist Germany was based on the truth or not — a point that I have made in a previous chapter and which I make again; that subject, as I have said, belongs to an entirely separate study. It is sufficient to assert, again, that no vital British national interest was served by a policy of hostility, followed by war, against Germany, and that every such interest dictated that war be avoided. The fact that war did eventually occur is something that we may put down to a variety of causes. Where there was an assessment of the national interest, it was a mistaken one based on a balance-of-power strategy which, as I have said, had long been obsolete, and an entirely erroneous view of Hitler's intentions in Western Europe based on ignorance. Added to this consideration, however, and probably far outweighing it, were clearly others. By the 1930s, the British view of world affairs had taken on such a childish perspective that millions of people actually believed that whole nations, as well as empires, should go to war, even when no threat or gain to themselves was involved, merely in defence of certain 'rights' against certain 'wrongs'. Allied to this factor, and most certainly a powerful cause of Britain's entry into World War II, was the fact that certain vested interests, some of them Jewish, wanted Hitler and his system destroyed at all costs — and not because of its brutalities, real or alleged; Soviet Russia had a record of brutality second to none, but that country was not marked down in the same way for destruction. The reason for this policy of bringing down Germany is something which, like other matters touched on in this book, really belongs to a separate study; and in this analysis of British conduct of foreign affairs for me to enquire in any further detail into that question would involve too much of a digression. It is pertinent, however, to cite one small clue to what was in the minds of the anti-Hitler forces around the world by mentioning the episode of the 'Venlo Incident', described in *The Schellenberg Memoirs*, written by Walter Schellenberg, a high-ranking official of the *Sicherheitsdienst* (SD), the security service of the SS. Schellenberg here describes how he met, in Holland, two British intelligence agents, Major Stevens and Captain Best, while himself posing as a representative of an anti-Hitler faction in Germany in the very early stages of the war, one of the purposes of this operation being to ascertain what kind of approaches were being made by the British to this faction. In his book, Schellenberg describes the terms carried by the British agents on behalf of their government, which would be offered to Germany in the event of the Germans overthrowing Hitler and agreeing to a cease-fire. To quote:-

> "The political overthrow of Hitler and his closest assistants was to be followed immediately by the conclusion of the peace with the Western Powers. The terms were to be the restoration of Austria, Czechoslovakia and Poland to their former status; the renunciation of Germany's economic policies and her return to the gold standard. The possibility of a return to Germany of the colonies she had held before the First World War was one of the most important subjects of our discussion..."

The key words in this passage are of course "the renunciation of Germany's economic policies and her return to the gold standard." These words make it abundantly clear that there were other motives at work on the part of the powers arrayed against Germany besides the stated ones that occupied the front of the stage of Allied war propaganda. Germany's economic policies and her rejection of the gold standard were measures that had long pre-dated the war and the apparent causes of the war. Who was determined to change these policies and restore Germany to the gold standard, and why? These are questions that, like many others here, belong to a separate study. Suffice it to mention them here as just one further indication that there were forces determined to bring Hitler down and eliminate National Socialism which existed far beneath the surface of current argument and debate. If we knew the answers to the questions just raised, we might have the answer to the more fundamental question of why it was deemed so urgent a matter to have a war to destroy Germany, and indeed to many other questions concerning British affairs in that period. What is certain is that pressures were being applied which had a decisive influence on the actions of the British government of that time, and that they were pressures that had nothing whatever to do with the normal considerations of state, which should be concerned, as I have said often enough, solely with sovereign national interests.

The outcome of World War II vindicated all those who had predicted catastrophe for Britain in consequence of her involvement in it. Germany could only be beaten by a coalition of the British Empire, the United States and Soviet Russia — a measure of the titanic strength of the state that Hitler had brought into being. Had the Germans been allowed to prevail in the East — as they most certainly would have done had Russia had to fight them alone — Soviet Communism would have been smashed, and we would have been spared the subversive and destabilising presence of this giant in the second half of the 20th century. Instead, Soviet Communism was saved by the intervention of British and American money and supplies, which sustained its war machine, and by British and American armour, which tied down in the war's western theatre German forces that could otherwise have been deployed against the Red Army, almost certainly with decisive results. And not only was Communism saved from destruction but it was brought right into the centre of Europe, where it has stood in occupation to this day.

That Soviet Communism has always been an inveterate enemy of Britain and her world interests is something that needs scarcely be stated here; and yet it was the decisions of British government, together with those of US government, concerning Germany and Europe that created this very Frankenstein monster in the dimensions in which it now exists.

The other result of this fiasco of a policy was that Britain herself could only survive the war by running to America for help and accepting her as the dominant partner in the Western Alliance against Germany. This very fact, quite apart from the consequences that flowed from it, revealed something of the British condition. Remember that Britain, with her Empire, had been the leading partner in the coalition that defeated Germany in 1918, and when the Germans had no significant forces tied down in other theatres of war and could concentrate almost their entire military effort in the West. Yet now, no more than a generation afterwards, and with the main part of the German forces deployed in Eastern Europe, Britain could not defeat that fragment of the German war machine facing her on the Western and Italian fronts except as the very junior partner to the United States, to whom she looked to supply the greater part of the forces engaged in Western Europe, as well as most of the tanks and much of the other war equipment used by British forces. This was a measure of our decline in the space of less than three decades.

American help in rescuing Britain from the catastrophe in which she landed herself in World War II was not bestowed in a spirit of Santa Claus; it was all forthcoming at a price. The price was a British bondage to the United States in the post-war world which has made our own Foreign Office, and indeed 10 Downing Street as well, mere local branches of the US government and the New York money power which provided the finance for Lend-Lease and subsequently for Marshall Aid.

One of the longest-lived myths of our century is the idea that the United States entered World War II out of a benign desire to preserve Britain and her Empire and that, in the post-war era, Britain's welfare has figured high on the list of priorities among America's leadership. The true reality underlying America's role in the war, and the attitude and intentions of her president to whom we are ever reminded of our debt of gratitude, was succinctly spelled out by David Irving in his penetrating book *Churchill's War*, in which he said:-

"Seen from the banks of the Potomac river, Roosevelt was the most illustrious American of the century. He gave his ragged nation a sense of empire. Ten millions were unemployed and his New Deal was in disarray, but by plugging into Churchill's war at the most judicious moment he would bring wealth and prosperity to his great nation. With eleven millions under arms, and by ruthless power politics and financial huckstering, he made it a great power. He blackjacked his allies into parting with their gold. Loaded with new richesse he contemplated taking over Britain's colonies, and offered cash on the nose for defeated France's two latest battle ships, *Jean Bart* and *Richelieu*.

"Twice by late 1940 contemporaries had benevolently applied the label 'gangster' to Mr. Churchill. But in a century of gangster statesmen, he and Roosevelt were not even in the same league. 'I never let my right hand know what my left hand does,' the president told his Treasury secretary as he settled into his third term. 'I may have one policy for Europe and one diametrically opposite for North and South America...And furthermore,' he bragged, unwittingly echoing Hitler's words, 'I am perfectly willing to mislead and tell untruths if it will help win the war.'

''He ran rings round the British and boasted that he was better at it than President Woodrow Wilson. He regarded Churchill as a pushover...

''This is not surprising. The survival of the British Empire did not figure high on Roosevelt's priorities. 'I would rather,' said Roosevelt in 1942, 'lose New Zealand, Australia or anything else than have the Russians collapse.' A few weeks later he repeated this. England was, he said, 'an old, tired power' and must take second place to the younger United States, Russia and China. Later this sly statesman conceded, 'When there are four people sitting in at a poker game and three of them are against the fourth, it is a little hard on the fourth.' Vice President Henry Wallace took this as an admission that Roosevelt, Stalin and Chiang Kai Shek were ganging up against Mr. Churchill.

''France's humiliating defeat and Britain's threatening bankruptcy gave Roosevelt the opportunity to clean up these old empires. At Teheran in 1943 he would confide to Joseph Stalin, 'I want to do away with the word *Reich*.' He added, 'In any language.' Stalin liked that. 'Not just the **word**,' he said. Roosevelt's policy was to pay out just enough to give the Empire support — the kind of support a rope gives a hanging man. When his Treasury secretary confirmed after visiting London in 1944 that Britain was penniless, the cynical man in the Oval Office would prick up his ears and snicker. 'I had no idea,' he said, 'I will go over there and make a couple of talks and take over the British Empire.' ''

There is about 90 per-cent truth in Irving's observation, the one bone I would pick with him being that Roosevelt's motives and actions were directed not so much to enriching America as to serving those subterranean interests of financial power that, by his time, had taken over control of America. However, in respect of his intentions towards Britain and her Empire — intentions which were at one with those of his masters behind the scenes — the analysis is absolutely correct. One of the disastrous errors of British statecraft in the 20th century has lain in the assumption that the United States and its leadership, both before, during and after World War II, were greater friends of Britain than was Hitler. We have paid a crippling price for this assumption, and we are continuing to pay it today.

When the day comes for British Toryism to be called to account, right at the top of the list of indictments against it will be its quite slavish adherence to the rule that Britain's and America's interests in the modern world are at one and that, in consequence, the Anglo-American 'special relationship' provides the cornerstone of British prosperity and security. This supposition has been contradicted by a succession of events too numerous to list here but which have done the gravest harm to our interests in a variety of areas, including imperial affairs, trade and industry, Europe, Northern Ireland and the defence of the realm. The phenomenon has roots which extend back to long before World War II and can be traced to a strangely myopic view on the part of Britain towards her one-time colony.

The parting of the ways between ourselves and our Trans-atlantic cousins in the 18th century was, as I have acknowledged earlier, a tragedy of the first magnitude. The trouble has been that the British political mind in the 200 years following has proved to be incapable of grasping that that tragedy ever happened. British politics generally, and British Conservatism particularly, have still continued to bask in the illusion that Americans really remain just British people living under a different flag and a different head of state, and at all times can be relied upon to see their interests and ours as being synonymous.

There are doubtless many Americans who do think this way, and on a visit to their country some years ago I was delighted to meet some of them and strike up friendships that I have ever since greatly valued. They consist of people of mainly British descent who share on most questions the attitudes of our movement. If all Americans thought and felt as they did, and if US policy reflected such sentiments, then such a comity of interests between our two countries would indeed be possible — even to the point of reversing the decision of 1776 and bringing these countries back into the same family of peoples.

But that is **not** the *de facto* situation that prevails today. A very long time ago, those holding the power in the United States took the view that their country's and Britain's interests were divergent, and this view has been reflected in American policy ever since.

Correlli Barnett, writing in *The Collapse of British Power*, put it well when he said:-

"The British governing classes in particular, aristocratic though they were in complexion, found the life of the rich Anglo-Saxon

East Coast oligarchy, which dominated American federal politics before the Great War, completely congenial and familiar. The myth of a common Anglo-Saxon destiny flowered on the lawns of the pseudo-European pseudo-manor houses of Long Island. The accord became more intimate in the warmth of London ballrooms where American heiresses were picked up by the sons of the English aristocracy...This connection by marriage between the then ruling American oligarchy and the English governing class supplied a further powerful and understandable stimulus to the notion of 'kinship' between the nations...

"That this myth of cousinhood and common interest was at least partly false to fact and in consequence misleading to British political judgement was not the least of its dangers. For necessarily underlying British belief in the myth was an assumption that the Americans too believed in it: that **they** for **their** part saw the **British** as less 'foreign' than other nations, to be judged according to special standards of charity and understanding; that they too felt there to be a natural harmony between British and American interests and policies. The assumption was mistaken...The special 'relationship' was a British fantasy. It was love in the perfect romantic style, unrequited and unencouraged, yet nevertheless pursued with a grovelling ardour. Although from time to time realistic observers warned the British that their feelings were not reciprocated, it was to no purpose."

Dr. Peter Peel, in British Public Opinion and the Wars of German Unification: 1864-1871, continues the same theme:-

"The economic and military dependence of Britain on the United States after World War II is a long and shameful record. It enabled the United States to put pressure on Britain to get out of India, and to go far beyond the stipulations even of the Balfour Declaration to permit the setting up of a sovereign Jewish state on Arab lands in Palestine. It enabled the United States to dictate the withdrawal of the British forces from Suez in 1956 after their successful operation to recover the Canal.

"Pathetically, the British talked for a while of their special relationship with the United States — even of 'partnership'. They would not see that partnership is only possible between those more or less equal in power or wealth. A Britain stripped of its Empire could only be a client-kingdom. It could no more be a partner of the United States than Athens — or perhaps Macedon — could be a partner of Rome. Modern Britain, sheltering under the supposed willingness of the United States to undertake a nuclear war in defence of what Yalta has left of Europe, has sent each prime minister, cap-in-hand, to Washington since World War II..."

Dr. Peel's reference to Yalta is pertinent, for it was at that conference, in 1945, that the Americans colluded with Stalin to bring the Soviets to the Elbe, to give them that portion of Europe now lying behind the 'Iron Curtain' and thereby to split our continent in two. Such actions would hardly have been undertaken by a United States which served as the leader of the 'free world' against Communism and a true friend of Britain!

The American attitude as pointed out by both Barnett and Peel is obviously not unconnected with the vast population change that has taken place in the United States over the last 100 years and the shifting of power away from the former Anglo-Saxon Ascendancy. To attribute it solely to that change, however, would be to over-simplify. The separating of national destinies that occurred through the War of Independence generated its own momentum as it proceeded along its way, fuelled by such questions as the future of Canada, which it would be a logical aim of American policy to see integrated into the US, and which aim is obviously enhanced by the weakening of Canada's ties with Britain. Had the revolt of those early colonists not gone the way it did, such conflicts of interest need not have arisen, but history turned out differently, and they have. No-one more than this writer would like to see a reconciliation between the two branches of the British Race that split in 1776, in which case such questions could become soluble. But it is difficult to see this happening other than through the dissolution of the United States as it presently stands, and the forming, from out of it, of an entirely new country populated just by Anglo-Saxons and closely kindred races, and imbued with an outlook radically different from that prevailing in America over most of the past two centuries. British policy cannot afford to be based on such remote projections, and must therefore take into account the reality of America as she now is: a foreign country that regards us as foreign in return, not being overmuch concerned with thoughts about the 'special relationship' over which Atlanticists in Britain wax so enthusiastically, and certainly not disposed to give British interests great consideration when formulating national policy. Perhaps if Anglo-Saxons had a position in contemporary America similar to that of the Jews it might be otherwise, but they do not.

British policy must proceed from a recognition of this reality, though that does not in any way mean that we should reject feelings of kinship towards those specific Americans with whom there is genuine kinship and who hold reciprocal feelings towards us.

The tendency of indecent haste to please America could be seen as far back as 1921, when at the Washington Naval Conference referred to earlier Britain announced its intention, which it finally carried out two years later, to terminate the Anglo-Japanese Alliance. This decision was made largely to placate the United States, which was hostile to that Alliance. It had a disastrous effect on Anglo-Japanese relations, the maintenance of which was of enormous importance to our Far Eastern interests. Writing of this action in *From Admiral to Cabin Boy*, Admiral Domvile said:-

"The Japanese had behaved loyally to the terms of the Alliance, and although it would have been put to a severe test by the acquisitive nature of the Japanese foreign policy, we could have kept a restraining hand on this policy with far greater effect than has been possible since the termination of the Treaty, and the consequent deterioration of our friendly relations. Our motives for abrogating the Treaty were never fully understood or trusted, and suspicion increased with the passage of the years, which showed our subservience to American policy to an ever increasing extent."

Domvile continued:-

"A foreign policy that rejects strategical conditions is bound to come to grief in the long run, and we shall see that our foreign policy during the period under consideration resulted in the estrangement of those countries whose friendship was essential to our own security, and in their ultimate combination against us, whereby they achieved a collective security far in advance of any attained by its sponsors at Geneva. Our anxiety to curry favour with our rich relations across the Atlantic was costing us dear."

The title of Admiral Domvile's book is interesting, for thereby hangs a story. In his choice of it he was referring to the demotion in his national status that occurred when he was incarcerated in prison without trial during World War II for the 'crime' of daring to oppose that war, predicting the awful results it would have for Britain. He was one of the numerous men of distinction in this country — Sir Oswald Mosley was another — who were not listened to in their analyses and prognostications. Instead, they were flung into vermin-invested concentration camps by a government that was calling upon the British people to fight for 'democracy' and 'freedom'. Today we erect statues to those who were responsible for the ruinous British policy of the times, while these men are forgotten and their writings and speeches hardly ever allowed to see the light of day, whereby they may be evaluated by the present generation in the light of history. One day this will change, and these prophets will be accorded the honour and respect that is their due.

Concerning Domvile's comments on the Alliance with Japan, there would have been no guarantee that its continuation at the time would have prevented war with that country two decades later, but its abrogation certainly made that war more likely. We had slighted a nation very sensitive to slights, and this was not forgotten. Under the Alliance the Japanese had loyally observed all their obligations to us. When in 1941 and 1942 we had our backs to the wall in Europe and the Middle East and could have done without a further enemy in the Far East, no such feeling of loyalty any longer prevailed.

Our foreign affairs 'experts', having entirely misread the world situation between the wars, continued to misread it after the termination of the Second War. I say 'misread' because this analysis has to be based on the hypothesis that they were men who genuinely believed that what they were doing was right for their country, and were not **willing** partners to the betrayal of its interests. This does not mean that the hypothesis must be assumed to be in all cases correct.

The orthodox reading of the post-1945 *status quo* was that the advanced nations of the world were now split into two mutually hostile camps, one — led by Soviet Russia — with aggressive designs of world military conquest in order to institute world communism, and the other — led by the United States — providing against this bloc a bulwark of 'democracy' and 'freedom'. The assumption in all this was that Britain's place lay, unalterably and naturally, with the latter camp, and that her interests and security lay in integrating her policies increasingly closely with those of America. If she and her neighbours in Europe did not do this, the argument ran, they would make themselves vulnerable to conquest and enslavement by Russia.

This scenario of world politics has persisted to this day, earning for itself the description of the 'cold war'. An endless series of US-Soviet confrontations has been enacted, alternating with gestures of 'reconciliation' and 'summit conferences', and all against the background of a continuing 'arms race' between the two blocs.

This, as I have said, is the orthodox view of the world scene as it has existed over the past four decades. But is it in fact the correct view?

The first observation that must be made is that it would be

extremely strange for two groups of powers to be allies, as the Soviet and Western powers were for the greater part of World War II, and in the service of this alliance for one to do everything possible to save the other from destruction, then to find, hardly more than five minutes later, that these two groups are mortal enemies, and that the state we strove to save with our aid and our 'Second Front' now threatens to conquer us!

If the last named supposition were true, this would render the Anglo-American Alliance with the Soviets against Hitler the most lunatic decision of any major powers in world history. But is it true?

Did our leaders pursue the Western-Soviet collaboration in World War II in ignorance of the fact that Soviet actions in the aftermath of that war would be such as to present a menace to the safety of the world? Or were they in fact aware of what these actions would be, and did they endorse them as thoroughly consistent with western policy?

If the latter is true, it would indeed indicate that the kind of post-war world envisaged by those who controlled the war from 'our side' was very different in reality from that which they told us at the time we were fighting for.

It would in fact suggest that behind the facade of Western-Soviet 'enmity' there has all along been Western-Soviet collaboration.

A look at the whole pattern of world affairs since 1945 lends much support to such a view. America and Russia have continued, growling at each other on the international stage, and as part of this have sustained armaments programmes at enormous expense — ostensibly in defence against each other; but where actually have the two come into **real** conflict?

Contrary to the supposition of conflict, there have been a number of areas of policy in which the US and Russia have been in close accord.

Both endorsed and assisted the dismantlement of the great European empires, and in accordance with the sentiments of President Roosevelt quoted earlier.

Both are today promoting the breakdown of the barriers separating white and non-white races, and in particular the destruction of White South Africa. Both in the 1960s and 1970s were in accord over the need to destroy White Rhodesia, and both worked tirelessly to that very end.

In the economic field, their collaboration has been constant.

Time and time again, when the Soviets have had a harvest failure the Americans have helped them out with food supplies on generous terms. EEC butter and other surpluses have time and time again been sold at knock-down prices to Russia, with no American disapproval.

And there has been a constant flow of western, particularly American, technology and money into Soviet industry, not least that part of Soviet industry occupied with arms manufacture. This has all been admirably documented by Professor Anthony Sutton in his book *National Suicide*. Sutton, probably the leading authority in the Western World on western technological and industrial aid to the Soviet Union, shows in his book how most of the ships in the Soviet merchant marine were either built outside Russia or equipped with engines of foreign, in all cases western, manufacture. In his own words:-

"About 100 Soviet ships are used on the Haiphong run (in Vietnam) to carry Soviet weapons and supplies for Hanoi's annual aggression. I was able to identify 84 of these ships. None of the main engines in these ships was designed and manufactured inside the USSR.

"All the larger and faster ships on the Haiphong run were built outside the USSR.

"All shipbuilding technology in the USSR comes directly or indirectly from the US or its NATO allies."

Sutton went on to describe the Gorki motor vehicle plant, until 1968 the largest in Russia. It produced, according to him, "many of the trucks American pilots see on the Ho Chi Minh trail" –- and military jeeps and rocket-launchers besides. And the Gorki plant was built by the Ford Motor Company.

Sutton also mentioned the well known FIAT deal, to build a plant on the Volga three times bigger than the Gorki one. But the Italian name and connections tended to hide the fact that "over half the equipment came from the United States."

"The Soviets," continued Sutton (the book was written in the early 1970s), "are receiving now — today — equipment and technology for the largest heavy truck plant in the world, known as the Kama plant. It will produce 100,000 ten-ton trucks per year — that's more than **all** US manufacturers put together." Said Sutton: "We have built ourselves an enemy, We keep that self-declared enemy in business. This information has been blacked out by successive administrations."

And, it might be added, blacked out here in Britain, in the press, by TV and radio and in the statements of our leading politicians on the alleged 'cold war'. The question must be asked: why — why if not to conceal the reality that, behind the appearance of conflict between the Soviet and Western worlds, there is taking place all the time an undercover collusion?

Compared with these major areas of collusion and common policy, those areas in which the western and communist powers have been in conflict have been small, and perhaps serve more to sustain the **image** of enmity than to give effect to any reality of it.

Then let us take a look at the theory that Russia has the ambition of conquering and occupying Western Europe and is only prevented from doing so by the American 'shield' (it must be remembered that it is a constant form of blackmail against Britons and other Europeans that if we do not continue in our subservience to US policy the Americans may pull out of Western Europe and leave us to the mercies of the Soviets).

Just a few minutes' clear-headed thought should be enough to convince us that the supposition of a Soviet intention to invade and occupy Western Europe is utterly preposterous. Just what purpose would this serve from the Russian point of view? At the present time, Russia has her work cut out keeping her East European satellites in subjugation — in addition to which she has also more recently had the headache of Afghanistan. As these words are prepared for the printer, the Soviets are getting ready for a withdrawal from the latter country, realising late in the day that policing it with 100,000 troops is an excessive price to pay for the questionable advantages of sovereignty there. And at Russia's far eastern end she is confronted with the potentially very real menace of Red China, requiring a continually large presence of forces in the Sino-Soviet frontier area. The very idea that the Russians, in this situation, would wish to add to their already considerable burdens by committing themselves to an invasion — at the risk of nuclear retaliation — of West Germany, France, Britain, Italy, Spain, Scandinavia and the rest, and then the permanent occupation of all those areas, belongs to pure fantasy. The simple question only needs to be asked: whatever for?

Certainly not for the purpose of showering on all the countries of Western Europe the blessings (as the Soviets would conceive) of communism. We must remember that the idea that nations go to war and risk their own destruction merely for the purpose of defending or promoting ideologies is one confined to the stunted brains of 'liberals', and certainly not taken seriously in the Kremlin.

The men who preside in that establishment, while certainly no friends of ours, are at least realists who would not dream of any overseas adventures except for the purpose of increasing their power, and they certainly are not interested in dissipating the resources of their country for philanthropic aims. They promote communism abroad, not for the purpose of benefiting the countries in which this is done, but only in order to subvert and weaken them. They are doing extremely well — thank you very much — by this method; why should they want to ruin it all by staging an invasion and waking us up when they are being so successful in putting us to sleep?

And just supposing that the inconceivable did happen, and the Soviet leaders one morning took leave of their senses and attacked westwards, are we seriously to believe that the Western European nations, with their combined populations of over 300 million and their vastly superior industries and technology, could not deal with such an attack with their own resources and without American protection?

Let us remember that in World War II **one** European nation, with the aid of some one million or so foreign auxiliaries, nearly defeated Russia, **on Russian soil** and **in the Russian climate**, and most certainly would have succeeded, as I have said, had she not had to deploy a part of her forces defending her western and southern flanks, and had Russia not been sent massive war supplies by her western allies.

And yet current propaganda delivers what must surely be the supreme insult to our intelligence by telling us that all the Western European nations **together**, on their own ground, without war on other fronts and, presumably, without their opponents being kept supplied with thousands of American trucks and jeeps, could not stop a Soviet invasion unless they had America present to hold their hands and direct the battle!

If this were true, it would indeed be a sad commentary on the degeneration of the Western European peoples in less than half a century, and would call into question whether there was anything they had left which indeed was even **worth** defending!

Of course, none of this is true, and the suspicion must exist that at least the more capable minds among those who peddle the idea **know** it is not true, but continue to maintain it as a myth for reasons and designs of their own. It is not the place here to go into the question of these reasons and designs, but only to say that a policy based on such a reading of the international situation must be a wrong policy, and should be scrapped.

As I have indicated, there can be no question of Soviet Russia being Britain's friend; that she is our enemy is evident from the vast machinery of subversion that she maintains against our country and against our interests all around the world. But as to whether she is an enemy that would use armed force to conquer and subjugate us as she has done the countries of Eastern Europe — that is another matter. The overwhelming evidence is that she is not, and could not be. Our foreign policy, when one day we actually again have one, must take cognisance of that fact.

It must do so because upon this question depends so much of the remainder of our foreign relations. If there is not a Soviet **military** threat to us, but only a **political** threat, we certainly are not required to enter into a complex system of defensive alliances based on the assumption of such a Soviet military threat, and in the process consent to debilitating limits on our national sovereignty and freedom of action, such as have been accepted by British governments of every colour, and to an ever increasing extent, since 1945.

Most of all, we are not required to regard our security and survival as dependent on the shield of America — as they most assuredly are not. Certainly we should seek, as far as is possible, to have good and friendly relations with the United States, but the time is long overdue for us to assert our independence from that country, just as two centuries ago its people asserted their independence from us.

Britain's future strength and security rests most of all, as I have made clear in the previous chapter, on her ability to build a close partnership with the white remnants of the old British Empire under a new dispensation, as described in that chapter. This is not a question of 'foreign policy', for the countries mentioned must not be classified as foreign. This relationship apart, it is most important, as I have also said, to come to a realistic decision as to what must be done with Africa. If, as is probable, we reject the proposition that we should leave Black Africa to stew in its own juice, this means that Europeans, in concert with one another, should again take control of Black Africa north of the Limpopo. An essential part of this policy would be to reinstitute good relations with the South African Republic, which for the foreseeable future will comprise the strongest combination of Europeans on the African Continent.

In the previous chapter I have acknowledged that Britain's old Dominion partners may by no means immediately be won over to the idea of a new partnership, and that sustained diplomacy over many years may be necessary to achieve that result. In such an event, good relations with South Africa would become all the more imperative. Here is a nation which, though it may not share a common heritage with us as do those where people of British stock are the dominant group, does share with us at the present time a common enemy — to wit, all those forces the world over bent on the destruction of the White Man. In a world situation in which Britain found herself to a great extent economically isolated, to have the co-operation of South Africa, with her enormous mineral wealth, would be a crucial asset.

The one major primary product that South Africa cannot supply is oil. On the other hand, in the Middle East there is oil in super-abundance. Common sense has always dictated that it is Britain's interest to maintain good relations with the Arab states, for this reason among many others. Yet, as in so many areas of policy, common sense has deserted us in the 20th century. We have alienated the Arab World, and contributed to permanent instability in the Middle Eastern Region, by our support for the State of Israel.

There never was a better opportunity to put a policy of close Anglo-Arab accord into operation than at the time following World War I, when, by co-operation between ourselves and Arab peoples, Turkish rule over large Arab areas of the Middle East had been removed. It will be recalled, in this connection, that T.E. Lawrence was able to enlist the help of considerable Arab guerilla forces in the recent war against the Turks by carrying to them the promise of the British government of Arab freedom and sovereignty over the whole Arab area in the aftermath of victory.

As history has recorded, this promise was cynically betrayed. At the very time that Lawrence was making it — with perfect sincerity in his own case — his government was behind the scenes making a wholly contradictory promise to allocate Palestine to the Jews, which promise later became enshrined in the infamous Balfour Declaration. The most pressing purpose of this double-cross, though there certainly were others, was to induce World Jewry to use its influence to bring the United States into the war. The very thinking behind this manoeuvre revealed the recognition, even at that early stage of our century, of the enormous power of Jewry in America. This promise to the Jews was of course kept, and the other one to the Arabs abandoned. The Middle East has been a troubled area ever since, and Britain's standing there has suffered grievously as a result of the loss of her reputation for keeping her word.

Of course, the claim of the Jews to Palestine was always an extremely slim one, resting on a presence in that area 2,000 years previously. If every nation in the world elected to make similar claims on territories based on occupation in the dim, distant mists of olden times, just where would we stand? Spain would presumably have to be given the Netherlands and Morocco a large part of Spain itself. Britain would be handed a substantial section of France and the modern descendants of the Huns great slices of Eastern Europe. The whole idea is of course ridiculous — and not even necessary; if the Jews really wanted their own homeland, there were at the time several other areas of the world that could have been given to them — Madagascar being one that was discussed then and afterwards. In the event, only a very small portion of Jewry has in fact settled in Palestine, and many of those settlers have, after a time, become disenchanted with the place and left.

Everybody who is knowledgeable in middle eastern affairs is well aware that the existence of Israel is not in the slightest way based on any genuinely valid historical 'right' of the Jews to that area, but rests solely on the fact of Zionist **power**, exercised over the governments of all the nations of the West but particularly over the government of the United States.

In the short term, solutions to the problem can only be adopted unilaterally. At the present time all Britain could do is withdraw her support from the Israeli State and refuse any co-operation to America in respect of actions in the Middle East undertaken in support of that state. In the longer term, we must envisage the possibility that America may choose to undergo a fundamental change in its attitude to this question and that a situation may arise in that country in which large-scale Jewish settlement there is not favoured. In that event, there would be grounds for co-operation between Britain and the United States, and possibly other nations, in the setting up of an alternative home for the Jews, quite possibly in an area somewhere in the immensity of Africa, where their presence would not be a threat to the peace and where their security could be achieved by international agreement — to which it would most certainly be in Britain's interests to contribute.

Indeed, so great has become the stranglehold of Zionism over US policy that it is difficult to imagine Americans tolerating indefinitely such a state of affairs. Should America throw off the Zionist shackles, an event of world-shaking importance would have taken place, and one which would fundamentally alter the circumstances affecting America's relations with the whole of the rest of the world.

I have earlier made some comment on the lunacy of Britain's current attitude to South Africa. It is difficult to know just how sincerely and seriously our politicians really believe the endless drivel that drips daily from their mouths concerning that country, and how much of it is just a cynical act put on to curry favour with another element that has been allowed, entirely without justification, to assume a persuasive voice in world affairs. I here refer to that amorphous entity we are accustomed to calling the 'Third World'.

This Third World has, by some curious chemistry, become a deity to which the leaders of all civilised nations are expected to pay regular homage. Its feelings must be taken solemnly into account in every decision of policy. We must beg its permission for many of our transactions of foreign trade. It has become the arbiter of our programme of international sports fixtures. It demands — and gets — its own special allocation of television time. Our whole educational system has to be disrupted, at enormous expense, to accommodate it. It stakes its claim to the budgets of our local authorities and to space for its places of worship in our towns and cities. It has every old-party election candidate chasing after its favours with an obsequiousness that stinks in the nostrils of every self-respecting Briton. It soaks up a large portion of our prayers and 'compassion' and occupies an equally large part of the working schedules of our priests and clergymen. And it occupies the energies of many of our crusading young people which would be much better spent relieving distress among their own kind. It makes the biggest and most aggressive noises at the conferences of the Commonwealth and the Assembly of the United Nations. And every British family is obliged to pay for it to the current tune of over £100 a year.

And in return for all this, what does the Third World actually do? What is its positive contribution to the peace, prosperity and progress of this planet? What is it that entitles it to thump the table and lay down the law to the leaders of the advanced nations? What are the achievements that earn the Third World the deference that we are all expected to show to it?

In fact, the Third World, as things are at present, is just a gigantic carbuncle on the advanced nations' backs — showing to the latter hardly a wisp of gratitude for all the charity it receives.

I believe that British people are sick of the sight and sound of pompous and self-important officials of Third World countries appearing on their television screens and lecturing them on every topic under the sun, from the selection of their cricket teams to the oranges they eat at their breakfast tables. And if there is any phenomenon that induces an even greater itch for the vomiting bowl it is the cringing response of the officialdom of our own country, which treats every demand, every stricture and every threat from these puffed up nonentities as if it came from the throne of the Almighty!

It is high time that Britain ceased treating the Third World as if it were some kind of 'power', warranting respect and attention, and instead went her own way in olympian disregard of the ravings of its upstart leaders. One of the myths with which we must certainly dispense is the idea that we rely on Third World goodwill for the maintenance of our export trade. In fact the portion of our exports to Third World countries that are actually paid for by those countries is a pretty small part of our overall economic output.

At the time of writing, we are currently dispensing aid to the Third World to the tune of about £1,300 million a year — and this is apart from the running cost of the Ministry for Overseas Aid and Development and other agencies that are needed to administer the huge scheme of hand-outs. When we come to our senses we will either stop this great national largesse altogether or link it to specific deals and arrangements with the receiving countries out of which Britain will obtain some reciprocal advantage. In another chapter I have spoken of the need for a vast programme of repatriation and resettlement of Britain's racial minority groups, and I have advocated that overseas aid projects should be linked to this programme and confined to those countries prepared to co-operate with us in absorbing the people involved. Another form of reciprocal advantage would of course be our assumption of sovereignty over certain parts of Africa by which, in return for aid, we would assume control of those territories and benefit from the exploitation, for our own purpose, of their resources.

As a general principle governing our relations with countries of the Third World, we should proceed from the recognition that, in terms of moral obligation, we owe them **nothing**. Once that is understood and established, we can then approach the question of our relationship with each such country on a businesslike basis: something for something in return. That is surely better for their self-respect as well as for our pockets.

And whatever our relationship, if any, may be with Third World countries, let us stop, once and for all, treating them as if they have some special right to be listened to in the councils of the world, let alone have their feelings taken into account in the formulation of British policy, whether domestic or foreign.

The final word about foreign relations must concern our near neighbours in Europe. It may seem an odd paradox to state that our party, with its firm policy of opposition to the Common Market, is in fact, of all the parties, the most **pro-European**. We desire to see the preservation of the ancient European **nations**, great and small, in their sovereignty and freedom and in the maintenance of their true national, racial and cultural identities. This is not to say that we would risk our own country's future by going to war to preserve the freedom of a particular European state — earlier in this chapter I have condemned the insanity of that type of thinking — but it does mean that, after the interests of Britain and her White Commonwealth, there is no better cause deserving our support than the preservation of Europe and its nations — above all its races.

From this standpoint, we can only see the EEC as fundamentally **anti-European** — a destruction of all that is finest in the European heritage and tradition, in the attempt to impose upon Europe a uniformity that is utterly alien to her character, and which in the end divides Europe much more than it unites it. And how in heaven's name can an institution set itself up as the guardian of the interests of the European peoples when it imposes no barriers to the settlement of our continent by millions of non-Europeans, when it makes no defence of the purity of European culture and when it declares political and economic war against fellow Europeans in South Africa?

There is one way, and one way only, to achieve a true and lasting unity of Europe, and that is the removal of the historic causes of conflict between Europeans and the creation of a Europe of **sovereign states**, each with the institutions and resources to meet its own individual needs — and, where necessary, with overseas spheres of influence in which it can develop its own special relations with its kindred peoples. In the previous chapter I have suggested the collaboration among Europeans in the recolonisation and development of Africa. This idea is not my invention; it was proposed in the post-war writings of Sir Oswald Mosley, although in a form which saw Euro-Africa as one single political and economic unit, whereas I advocate that it should consist of nationally demarcated areas working in co-operation but with each individually sovereign. My proposal is that where territorial disputes remain in Europe, such as over Alsace-Lorraine or South Tyrol, they may be resolved by the conceding party being given extra African possessions as compensation.

When all is said and done, peace and harmony in Europe rests most of all on a *modus vivendi* between Britain, Germany and France. If these nations can remove the historical bones of contention between them and live as good neighbours, there can be no major conflict in Europe — apart from that occasioned by the presence of Russia in our continent, something which at the moment we are not able to alter.

Britain has no interests in Europe other than to see it peaceful and stable. We have no territorial ambitions on the European mainland, nor are we the target of any such ambitions on the part of our neighbours. The European balance-of-power principle, of which I have spoken earlier, is, as stated, obsolete.

Germany, inevitably, has the desire for national reunification. We must understand that for Germans this means unification within the frontiers of 1914, or at the very least 1939. If this seems unreasonable to Britons, let us return to the hypothesis raised earlier and ask what would be our view if Kent or Norfolk had been detached from our country and handed to a Continental neighbour? We would believe it right, quite naturally, that they should return to Britain — and this belief would not be modified by suggestions that the loss of those areas was our just punishment for defeat in some distant war with which our generation had no connection.

Moreover, if it came to the day when the peoples of Germany and Austria decided that they should dispense with their border and unite into a single state, we certainly would have no right to stop them, nor would it be in our interests to try. If we believe, as we should, that peoples of common race belong to a common national community, then we cannot possibly deny that principle to Germans any more than we would deny it to ourselves.

Of course, giving effect to such principles in the case of Germany is another matter. The Soviet occupation of East Germany is a fact which will not go away, and there is no prospect in the foreseeable future of this changing except by means of the collapse of the Soviet system. Such events are beyond our power to regulate, and we can only say at this time that, should that collapse occur, and should Germany then take the opportunity offered to achieve the reunification to which it aspires, it would be the height of folly for Britain to oppose her. We should, by such a time, have achieved sufficient strength and security within our own sphere of interests that we would see no threat to ourselves in a Germany united, resurgent and powerful.

With France we have few differences that cannot be resolved by the dissolution of the EEC, or at least Britain's withdrawal from it. In the European reorganisation of Africa, it would be natural for France to resume control of her traditional spheres of influence in that continent, or at least a part of them. In the enormous African area, beside which our two metropolitan countries are no more than tiny specks on the map, there is ample room for French and British enterprise, without the likely occurrence of 'Fashodas' of the future.

Outside our partnership with the old Dominions, the peoples of Western Europe are our closest natural allies of the future, beside whom we can stand strong enough to meet any threat from anywhere — always providing we understand that a European alliance must be an alliance of **free nations**, and not an integrated mish-mash under a centralised authority.

America is a potential friend, but only when she has thrown off the shackles of what informed Americans call ZOG (Zionist Occupation Government). It is my view that this event, and not any staged 'agreement' with the Soviet Bloc, will provide the best opportunity for the withdrawal of US forces from Western Europe — a move that will, in my opinion, vastly improve US-European, as well as US-British, relations.

The Arab World is our friend, as stated before, if we decide to remove the cancer of Israel from the middle eastern region.

This impressive list of allies or friends, actual or potential, will naturally lead to the question: who then is our enemy? The immediate answer is that World Communism is our enemy — but a dangerous enemy only for as long as it is sustained by the forces of international finance and one-worldism that created it and to this day protect it. In the defeat of these forces lies the best prospect, indeed the **only** prospect of the defeat of World Communism. Russia, as a nation state, need not be an enemy, for only through communism do her ambitions become international. There are signs even now that marxist and national forces in Russia are vying for control over Soviet policy. If the latter prevail, they will find that their best course is that of withdrawal from world politics and the pursuit of single-minded internal development. In the words of Alexander Solzhenitsyn in his *Letter to Soviet Leaders*:-

> "And therein lies Russia's hope for winning time and winning salvation: in our vast north-eastern spaces, which over four centuries our sluggishness has prevented us from mutilating by our mistakes, we can build **anew**; not the senseless, voracious civilisation of 'progress' — no; we can set up a **stable** economy without pain or delay and settle people there for the first time according to the needs and principles of that economy. These spaces allow us to hope that we shall not destroy Russia in the general crisis of Western Civilisation."

The yellow races could be our enemy, in as far as they are the only ones outside the West so far to have shown signs of the West's aptitude for technology and economic and political organisation. They would certainly be a formidable enemy if the white nations dissipate their strength in further wars like the two world wars of this century. In that event the yellow races could well exploit such a moment to take possession of Australasia. It is in our vital interest to build up Australasia against such a threat and to ensure that never again, as in 1942, does that continent become exposed to invasion from the north while Britain is elsewhere fighting other nations' wars.

There is another respect in which the yellow races could represent a threat to us: entirely absent from their psychology are the series of hang-ups which go to make the outlook of **liberalism**. Neither the Japanese nor the Chinese is in danger of ever allowing himself to look at the world from the point of view of his enemies and to put their cause above that of his own people; nor does either race allow itself to be atomised and fragmented by the kinds of philosophies of private greed and selfishness that weaken the societies of the White Man, and especially that of the Anglo-Saxon. The yellow peoples are members of their nations before they are individuals, and they have a herd instinct to hang together and work together for a common corporate end rather than allow themselves to be divided easily, as we do, by internal conflicts. Despite the superficiality of 'democratic' institutions in Japan today, this remains a reality in the nation's life. Whether the yellow peoples are in rivalry with us militarily, as at times in the past, or just economically, as today, they will be a formidable thorn in our sides if we are unable to develop a social organism which achieves their teamwork and cohesion.

Over and above all this, let us never suppose that we and the yellow peoples will ever be bound together in common cause. We can certainly respect them — and they have without doubt in modern times earned our respect. But they will always see their interests as different from ours, and they will not deviate from the pursuit of those interests, whatever our own pleas to them to behave as 'world citizens'.

But far above and beyond Russia, Japan or China, the enemy we have to face in the modern age is one that cannot be identified in the form of a country or nation; that enemy is **internationalism**, and the forces which operate at global level to promote it. I have hinted at the shape of these forces in an earlier chapter when I spoke of the factor of conspiracy in national and world affairs. I believe it is certainly true today to say that there is a power in the world which, in our times, is more formidable than any single national power, and must be identified in the form that I have outlined: a network of people, consisting of the citizens of many states but who feel ties of allegiance to no state. In the councils of the United Nations, in the European Commission and Parliament, in the boardrooms of the multi-national corporations and in the citadels of international finance, they work to subvert and destroy the nations of the world as sovereign entities. It is the constant claim of this species that national borders and sovereignties must be removed in order for there to be world peace; but it is my view that it is this network dedicated to the cause of one-world internationalism that has caused more mischief and more conflict in this century than any nation. Total and everlasting world peace is a chimera; we will never achieve it. We can, with prudence, reduce international conflict to the barest practical minimum, and I am convinced that the way to do so lies through what might be termed 'co-nationalism', a policy of each nation minding its own business and coexisting with others on a basis of mutual respect. Precisely because of the passion we, in our movement, feel for Britain and the British Race, we are able to understand and appreciate the similar passions that others feel for their lands and races. Had this understanding existed in the minds of British and American leaders during this century, civilisation's death toll would have been much smaller.

A foreign policy is not, as liberals would have it, a blueprint for a perfect world of peace and harmony governed by abstract principles, whether they be 'democracy', 'socialism' or the 'brotherhood of man'. Foreign policy is the external arm of national policy, conceived for the purpose of national growth and development; it adheres to no ideologies but serves only national interests; it is concerned with what is happening in foreign countries only to the extent that it affects those national interests.

A foreign policy is not a charter to lecture other countries on the morality of their internal politics; least of all is it something to be determined by like or dislike of other countries' internal politics.

Most importantly, emotion — whether positive or negative — is no substitute for a foreign policy and no basis on which to formulate one. Foreign policy must at all times be carried out in accordance with the coolest and most practical considerations, and never to any purpose that is contrary to national advantage.

Foreign affairs are, as hinted earlier, like a game of chess. Moves are made in a calculated sequence aimed constantly at strengthening the position of one's own side and weakening that of one's adversary. The purpose of the game, of course, is to win — a truth so elementary that in ordinary times it would seem almost to be talking down to the reader to state it; but in these times, when political children are in charge of the ship of state and 'public opinion' is conditioned to believe in fairy tales, it is one that must be hammered home with repetition until it is grasped by all.

As I made clear at the beginning of this chapter, it is my belief that foreign affairs during the past century have been one big disaster area for Britain. In the analysis following, I have laid much stress on the naivety and illusions of 'liberalism' that have contributed to the succession of errors in this field. But references will also be noted which suggest that, in a number of places, other factors have been at work. In an earlier chapter I examined the theme of 'conspiracy' and asked whether there was some hidden and sinister force that had taken over the direction of British politics in modern times and was guiding us to national self-destruction. That question must be considered with particular seriousness when it comes to the field of foreign policy. I have cited here some examples of the possible workings of such a force, particularly in respect of the influences goading us on in the conflict with Germany which led to World War II. It is the popular pastime of those who scoff at the suggestion that there is conspiracy behind political events to label those who put forward this suggestion as people with unbalanced minds. The reader is invited to examine the facts and arguments set out here and then ask himself: is it the working of an unbalanced mind to question whether these turns of British foreign 'policy' fit into any logical pattern of national interest, or whether they do indeed suggest that, somewhere, there is a spanner in the works of state that is causing the whole machinery to malfunction?

The fact that current American policy in the Middle East is effectively run by the Israeli lobby in Washington, and in complete disregard for the real national interests of the United States, is today a matter of common acceptance even in 'orthodox' circles of politics and journalism. All that I am asking the reader to do here is extend the range of possibilities offered by this fact, and consider that in many other areas of policy, not just in the United States but also in Britain as well, decisions may have been made in modern times which defy all logic when looked at from the national point of view and which therefore must be attributed to the influence of pressure groups operating outside, and often against, the considerations of national interest.

Whatever the arguments, however, ultimately the test of a foreign policy (or lack of it) over an extended span of time — say, for the sake of simplicity, 100 years — is the results arrived at at the end of that time. These words are written in 1986. If we go back exactly one century and examine Britain's world position in 1886, we must acknowledge that it was a position of almost unrivalled strength. We were, if not the number-one world power, certainly one of the top two or three, while the territories and resources contained within the realm of the British Crown gave ample promise that this pre-eminent position would endure for a long time. In an earlier chapter I pointed out that there were then weaknesses lying beneath the surface of the imperial pomp and splendour, but these weaknesses were essentially internal, and capable of remedy by ourselves; they were in no way inherent in any disadvantageous global position.

Yet 100 years later we oscillate uneasily between the second and third rank of powers, while Japan, with none of the natural advantages of empire enjoyed by ourselves, has jumped far ahead of us in world rankings — and this despite a catastrophic war defeat which we never experienced in the same period.

At the end of the day, we are forced to concede that our present position has to be the result of a continuous misdirection of policy. The misdirection, as I have pointed out throughout this book, has been largely in the field of domestic affairs; but the field of foreign affairs cannot be excluded from the indictment; the two fields of failure, at root, form an integral whole, being simply common symptoms of bad leadership and a general national confusion as to what should be the aims and priorities of state. A disastrous domestic policy and a disastrous foreign policy are merely products of the same basic national rot. Cowardice, stupidity, lack of will, and almost total absence of true patriotic motive, will all become reflected in one sphere just as in the other, forming an integrated whole.

Again, to touch upon a theme raised earlier, however much we may attribute wrong turns of policy to the pressure of lobbies and interest groups with their own axes to grind, and to the conspiratorial methods by which these groups impose their will on events, we must lay the overall failure at the door of our own national 'leaders' — for if they were real leaders they would put such interest groups and lobbies in their place, allowing them no say in the making of great national decisions. Likewise, we must acknowledge that at the top of national affairs, and indeed running right through the classes dominating our society, there has prevailed an entirely wrong outlook on affairs, both domestic and foreign. Our values, to condense it into a few words, have been false values — entirely out of harmony with the real forces that regulate the rhythm of the universe and determine the rise and fall, the success and failure, of nations and peoples.

Seen against this background, the wrong turns in the British conduct of foreign affairs during this last century have been inevitable — given the nature of the kind of country we have become during that same century. We were bound to side with our enemies and against our friends; we were bound to act everywhere in violation of our own best interests; we were bound to do these things because that is the fundamental instinct of liberalism, as I have made clear in the chapter in which this tuberculosis of the mind and spirit was examined.

The restoration of sanity to our conduct of foreign relations will not come through some sudden revelation of truth to those responsible for that task — as long as the inner society of which they are a product remains unchanged. Sanity must come to reign within Britain itself, permeating every nook and cranny of our public life and producing a new type of public servant, as remote from the present type as from creatures of another planet. Then, and only then, will Britain's role in the big wide world outside have a direction and a purpose of the kind needed by a nation which wants to survive and prosper.

Chapter 20
Scenario of war

It is appropriate that an examination of the needs of British defence should follow a survey of foreign affairs, as the first consideration of any defence policy is that we should know what it is we are defending and what we are defending it against. British thinking on defence has for at least the past 40 years been dominated by a certain stereotyped view of the forces prevalent in the world, with friends and enemies neatly defined and scarcely ever questioned. This has led to what I would call a 'Maginot Line' defence mentality, which conceives a military threat coming, in serious terms, from only one quarter and only in one way, and which constantly commits the error of concentrating the bulk of defence resources towards meeting that one contingency, with the result that we are in peril of being unprepared for others.

Recruiting campaigns for our armed forces today make great play of what they call the defence of 'freedom'. This is of course just a shorthand term for the group of countries comprising the non-communist world which maintain institutions of parliamentary government. Whether there is any reality in this 'freedom' is a question that has been discussed elsewhere in this book and need not concern us here. What concerns us in this examination of defence policy is that the scenario of future war seems to be very simply and neatly decided: it will be a war between the 'democracies', led by the United States, and the communist world, led by Soviet Russia, and will most likely begin, if it begins, with an attack by Soviet forces across the so-called 'Iron Curtain' upon Western Europe.

Defence planning is directed towards meeting such an attack. The armed forces of most of the western nations are, for the main part, organised into a single integrated international body called the North Atlantic Treaty Organisation (NATO), which is always under the command of an American, irrespective of whether he is the most qualified man for the job. The forces are, so we are informed, deployed in such a way as to provide the best possibility available to deal with a Soviet attack along the lines described.

Because this scenario of the future war is taken so much for granted, there is increasing pressure for the forces in question to become even more integrated than they already are, with such developments as the standardisation of weapons, that is one single type of tank, one fighter-bomber aircraft, one type of each calibre of gun, and so on. The armaments industry of the United States, because of its size of budget and its economies of scale, is of course at the greatest advantage to corner the market where such weapons are concerned. In order, so we are told, to prevent the US obtaining a monopoly of weapon production and supply, arms manufacturers in Europe have in a number of cases pooled resources and developed 'all-European' products, the Tornado fighter-bomber being a case in point.

The result of all this is that, increasingly, national armed forces simply are not national in the sense they used to be. Not only is their deployment subject to a supra-national command but a large part of their weapons are likely to be made in foreign factories and therefore are reliant for their supply on the consent of foreign governments. If a particular government decides to back out of a multi-national scheme to produce a vital weapon, it may be that that weapon will be scrapped, and the forces relying on it thereby left stranded until an alternative weapon can be supplied from elsewhere — **if** it can be.

In the case of nuclear weapons, only three western countries have any producing capacity in this field: the United States, Britain and France, the latter not being a member of NATO. Instituted under President De Gaulle, the French policy has been to maintain forces strictly under national control and, for the most part, national sources of supply — though available to be used in collaboration with other western forces in the event of an attack on Western Europe. As part of this, France has insisted on the maintenance of her own independent nuclear capability.

Britain has retained her capacity to produce nuclear weapons but increasingly has come to rely for her effective nuclear defence on weapons supplied, and largely controlled, by the United States. We have committed most of our resources for the purchase of nuclear weapons to the Trident missile system, supplied by America at enormous expense.

All this means that for nuclear weapons immediately available for use Britain is heavily dependent on the United States, but does have the capacity to produce her own nuclear weapons should she have to. There is, however, a powerful political lobby in Britain in favour of abandoning even this very limited nuclear capacity and handing over to America our entire nuclear defence.

In the meantime, most of the training and conditioning of our armed forces is NATO-orientated, with regular joint manoeuvres with other NATO forces. Servicemen are encouraged to see their primary role as the defence of that abstraction referred to as the 'free world', rather than the defence of their own nation and its interests. Even where they are engaged in purely British operations, such as in Northern Ireland, they are not seen to be defending British territory but 'keeping the peace' between two warring communities.

I believe that this whole defence strategy is based on a dangerous misconception.

In the previous chapter I have, I hope, fairly thoroughly demolished the idea that a Soviet invasion of the West is remotely conceivable, other than in the unlikely event of the Kremlin being engulfed in a wave of insanity. And I have suggested that, should that ever happen, it is preposterous to maintain that the European nations could not quell such an attack by their own efforts and without American help.

If these conclusions are accepted, it follows that our conception of the needs of national defence in the late 20th and early 21st centuries is wrong from top to bottom.

I say **national** defence because that is in fact what it is. In the real world, armed forces are not brought into being and maintained, at great expense, for the purpose of defending political ideologies and systems; their function is to defend **peoples, territories** and **interests**. Where two or more nations happen to enter into an era when they have certain interests in common and face a common external threat, certainly it is a frequent practice for them to enter into military alliances. Even in this event, however, it is highly dangerous for any one party to place itself in such a position that it cannot take independent military action on its own behalf, for want of supply of vital weapons or other amenities for which it relies on a foreign source. Alliances, where they are useful, are supplements to national military strength, not substitutes for it.

Of course it will be argued that certain types of arms manufacture today are so costly as to impose a very heavy burden on those nations undertaking them alone, so that it makes economic sense for nations in alliance with one another to agree to a division of labour whereby production of one weapon is concentrated in one country and another weapon in another country, or else there is the kind of joint product to which I have referred earlier, where separate functions in the development and production of a single weapon are shared out among partners in an alliance.

This argument for economy is a seductive one and there are instances where it might be valid. It is an argument, however, which should have strict limits to its application. The further that a nation tailors its policy of arms procurement to such market-place considerations, the less it possesses a real national defence capacity. For certain small nations this may indeed be an unavoidable situation, but it is not recommended to any nation that truly values its freedom.

When a nation of the stature of Britain decides to submit defence policy to the judgement of accountants rather than adapt it to the needs of national freedom and security, that nation might as well abdicate from any self-respecting place in the world and place itself under the protection, and therefore effectively the suzerainty, of another. This is not, I presume, the purpose for which we British have fought the many wars of our history.

The first priority of any nation such as ours must be to have the capacity to defend itself and its interests with its own resources. Only after that do economic considerations come into the reckoning.

It is a frequently heard view that our forces must have the best weapons that money can buy, regardless of whether or not they are of British manufacture. Here again is an argument that sounds plausible — until one delves a little more deeply into the question.

Of course it is important that we should seek to put into the hands of our servicemen the very best possible weapons and equipment. But ultimately our ability to do this — and have an effective national defence capacity — rests on the maintenance of a strong national armaments industry. That is not going to be possible if our service chiefs, anxious for every little bit of momentary advantage, are allowed to rush off and purchase a foreign product in preference to a British one. The result of this is that British arms manufacturers will go out of business, and our ability to supply our own weapons of war will be reduced to a point of dangerous weakness.

If the British version of a vital piece of weaponry or equipment is clearly inferior to some foreign product, then the practical thing to do is obtain a sample of the latter and model a new British product upon it. This may involve greater expense, but that would be money wisely invested in national security and survival.

Sovereignty is not a thing that can be subjected to profit-and-loss considerations.

Recent history has demonstrated the folly of the rigid mentality which has placed most of our defensive eggs in the basket of NATO, on the assumption that a Soviet attack on Western Europe is the most likely contingency of war. Against all the predictions of the self-appointed 'experts' and professional theorists, the war that Britain had to face in the 1980s was not a NATO war but a national one, arising from the fact that British territory alone was attacked and British forces alone were available to expel the attackers. The Falklands episode completely vindicated the nationalist view of defence needs and completely discredited the internationalist one. Our expedition to liberate the Falklands from Argentina was by no means universally popular with our NATO 'allies', and from the start it was clear that we would have to undertake it and succeed in it by our own efforts. That we might in fact be faced with a war of this kind, while not wholly predictable, was much more so than any war in Europe along the lines for which our defence chiefs have planned. Yet when the Falklands War broke out our preparedness for it was almost non-existent. Victory was eventually achieved, but the affair was, as the Duke of Wellington would have called it, "a damned close-run thing."

British defence in the future — and with the Falklands episode before us as an example — must be based on much more flexible planning and a much broader appreciation of the contingencies of war in which we might find ourselves. The Falklands, of course, could again be attacked. As a safeguard against this, demonstration of the **will** to preserve British sovereignty over the islands is more important than the size of the permanent garrison there. The first Napoleon is on record as saying that, in warfare, the psychological prevails in importance over the material in a ratio of about ten to one; here, certainly, is a case where that rule applies. But we must indeed be prepared for a repetition of the events in the South Atlantic in 1982, and be ready to send a task force again to that area at a moment's notice.

Aside from this, our main areas of concern should be: the defence of the United Kingdom, including of course Northern Ireland; the security of Australasia; and the protection of any interests that we may re-establish in Africa. Canada could not seriously be threatened with military attack except, theoretically, by the United States — a contingency extremely unlikely but one which, for all practical purposes, it would be impossible to reverse if it occurred. The weapons used to win and retain Canada as a partner for Britain in whatever form of organisation replaces the old Empire and present Commonwealth would necessarily have to be entirely economic and political.

The important change of strategy, in pursuit of these commitments, must be to bring home our forces currently stationed in West Germany, which stand at the time of writing at the level of 58,000 men, and station them, as circumstances dictate, in readiness to act in the areas mentioned. By releasing ourselves from the burden of this pointless presence in Germany, we could make considerable economies which would go to balance greater commitments elsewhere.

It is not opportune here to enter into a detailed consideration of preferred types of weapon systems for the armed forces, as these are constantly changing with the rapid technological advances that are being made from year to year, and what might be written on the subject one year could become out of date the next. One further word must be said, however, on the question of nuclear weapons touched upon earlier. It is absolutely vital that Britain should retain her nuclear deterrent and the nuclear power industry that is a necessary adjunct to her nuclear capacity. To do this effectively, she does not have to enter into the nuclear arms 'race'. While it may be beyond our capacity to maintain a stock of nuclear weapons comparable to those of the US or USSR, it is perfectly within our means to maintain sufficient nuclear striking force to deter any would-be nuclear aggressor by a demonstration of the ability to inflict such damage upon him as to make no nuclear war against us — even if he could in the end win it — remotely worthwhile. Again we come back to Napoleon's statement about the psychological and the material, for this certainly applies to the deployment of nuclear weapons: **fear** of their possible use is a much greater factor in the international power stakes than their actual employment.

Far more important than the size of stockpiles of nuclear weapons is the knowledge that a nation has these weapons and, moreover, is ruled by leaders who would not hesitate to use them if the need should arise. In this respect, a world leader of strong nerve and will in control of a modest nuclear strike force is in a far more advantageous position than one with a much larger force but who is known to be weak-willed and vacillating — or controlled by others who are.

An essential weapon in a war of nerves involving a possible

nuclear holocaust is an adequate system of civil defence, for in a game of bluff — which such a confrontation would largely be — the side that is known to have civil defences that could protect most of its population in the event of a nuclear attack would enjoy an enormous advantage over the side that is known not to have this facility. For this reason, it is vital that Britain, whose civil defences today are wholly inadequate, should make a massive effort to make good this deficiency in the years ahead.

In the matter of nuclear weapons themselves, Britain should adopt what has in the last three decades been the French policy of *force de dissuasion*, that is the maintenance of a nuclear arsenal smaller than those of the US and USSR but sufficient simply to **deter** — and of course supplied from national sources and under complete national control. With such a force in our possession, we should dispense with all American bases in Britain, both nuclear and conventional, as these simply serve to make our country a target in a possible war of interests not her own.

What is then needed is a wholesale revolution in our institutions of national defence, proceeding first of all from a complete change in national attitudes towards all matters of a military nature.

Far more dangerous to the security of Britain than any momentary armed services manpower or weapons shortage is the climate of pacifism that runs right through our society like a deadly virus. It is not an exaggeration to say that our present-day 'intelligentsia' consists of people who, in the main, completely repudiate any concept of the value of soldierly qualities, ethics or traditions — and indeed any idea of the reality that war is an inevitable occurrence in international relations. Blind to all the lessons of history, these people have the conceit actually to believe that they are the prophets of a 'new history' that will proceed in the future according to an entirely different set of rules — rules under which armies will not be needed and patriotic fighting spirit will become redundant. They and their predecessors have been in the ascendant ever since World War I, and are today busy fashioning society in the image of their own cloud-cuckoo philosophy. They are the dominant force in our academic world. They write the scripts for most of the plays that are seen on television. And they are the architects of most of the ideas that go out to our youth through the rest of the popular entertainments industry. They have already had spectacular success. A large part of our so-called 'educated' classes are today so morally rotted that their preparedness to fight for their country in any future national crisis must be called seriously into question.

All commanders in war know that a spirit of defeatism, desertion and mutiny is infectious, and has to be stamped out the moment that it manifests itself in the smallest way, lest it spread throughout the army as a whole. By tradition, the time-honoured way to deal with this kind of disaffection in the ranks has been to single out the ringleaders and promptly have them shot. Only by such procedures have armies in battle ever been able to survive.

Yet an army in wartime — certainly in any major war — is merely a product of the civilian society that stands behind it. In such a large-scale conflict it is indeed that civilian society put into uniform — in the course of general mobilisation. Upon the will of that whole society to resist its enemy depends the question of national survival.

With this in mind, one has to ask: what is the point of having a military code instituting the severest measures against those who sabotage the war effort in the front line, while we tolerate thousands of similar saboteurs in the rear — saboteurs by reason of the way in which they preach defeatism and surrender within the nation as a whole?

A nation in which the dominant cultural and intellectual climate is hostile to the whole idea of national self-defence and derides the military hero as a comical anachronism (when he is not actually cast in the role of a dangerous evil) may as well dispense with what armed forces it has and offer up the national estate to the first bidder.

Our satisfaction in winning the Falklands conflict should not be allowed to obscure the fact that it was an extremely small-scale action involving never more than 10,000 men actually occupied in the fighting. These men were professionals, and were superbly fit, highly trained and well motivated to fight. Not entirely surprisingly, they performed with admirable courage and proficiency.

But in any major international conflict, of the scale of World Wars I and II, Britain would be required to send into the field armed forces of several million men, obtained by a mobilisation of most of the active manpower of the nation. When we consider the prevalent influences that I have described, the prospect this offers is truly frightening.

Clearly, no policy aimed at giving the nation strong defences has a hope of succeeding unless there is first a thorough transformation of British society and opinion, whereby the spirit of pacifism and national defeatism is rooted out wherever it appears. If this cowardly spirit is eliminated and the nation recovers its will to defend itself and conduct the battle for its interests with arms when the need arises, the business of providing ourselves with these necessary arms will be two-thirds completed. Our factories are capable of supplying the weapons. The British serviceman, throughout history, has been capable of taking on the best. Only weakness in government, and in the type of national mores and values prevailing on the home front, inhibits military capability.

It is for this reason that I believe that so much of present discussion on the subject of defence amounts to a putting of the cart before the horse. The discussion is of how to achieve an effective defence capability in complete isolation from the civilian society that is the font of our military strength. It is assumed that that society cannot, indeed should not, be changed. Questions of defence therefore revolve around how to get the best out of this fundamentally unfavourable national situation, working around, and in spite of, the widely prevalent pacifist spirit and conscience that rule so much of our national life — trying, as it were, to extract the silk purse of effective armed forces from out of the sow's ear of a society given up largely to the acceptance of decadence.

I believe that we in Britain will not achieve the defence capability that we must achieve for survival in this and the next century — unless we begin getting our priorities in the right order: we have to build a society **fit** to survive, and then from out of that recruit the manpower and formulate the organisation necessary to meet the contingencies of war.

When this necessary transformation has been brought about, the first task that must proceed from it is the re-establishment of universal national service. Earlier in this book I have spoken of the value of this institution properly organised and directed, and of the fact that Britain suffered from its abolition. It must return, suitably changed in places so as to ensure that the time spent by those involved in it is put to the maximum use in the way of training them, not only for national defence, but for citizenship as well.

I am well aware that one of the strongest arguments against national service comes from some of the chiefs of the armed forces themselves — thereby giving those arguments what some people might think is a special stamp of authority. The main objection in this regard is that conscript forces would place in the hands of the chiefs of the armed services large numbers of young men who were unwilling servicemen, poorly motivated, not of the highest physical standards, hard to discipline and generally not suited to the meeting of the nation's military, naval and air defence commitments as they stand at the present time.

To this argument I must reply that defence planning and organisation must take into account, not only currently existing needs of defence, but those needs likely to arise in the event of a major war. In that event, as I have stated, nearly the entire active manhood of the nation would have to be mobilised. It would also have to be mobilised, and made fit for battle, probably in the shortest possible time. If every man liable for call-up in that contingency has already had two years' experience of service life, is accustomed to basic disciplines, knows how to handle weapons and has had experience of some service trade or other, and if a due proportion of such men have held some rank and are used to a degree of command and responsibility, the process of such a national mobilisation in time of war would be much quicker and smoother.

As World Wars I and II both demonstrated, a perilous situation can exist between the time that a national mobilisation is decided upon and the time when the men being mobilised are ready to fight. All too often, the problem has been papered over by men being rushed to their active service units before they have been adequately trained; and this shortage of training has been all too often revealed in the incompetence of a number of our battle units.

A background of peacetime national service would do a great deal towards solving this problem. Of course, those whose period of peacetime service was not recent would need to be brought up to date with modern weaponry and changes in techniques and skills which had occurred since they were last in uniform, and that is a matter to which I will come in a moment. The point is that with some such background no man would be starting entirely from scratch. As a young soldier I was, as mentioned earlier, an artilleryman. Had a war occurred 20 years after my time of national service and I been drafted into the artillery again, I would have had to have become familiarised with new guns and new techniques accompanying their use (my original training being based on the old wartime 25-pounder field gun). There would undoubtedly have been something new to learn, but with a grounding in the basics already there the subject would not have been wholly strange to me, and the adaptation to new weapons and techniques would not have taken so long. In addition to this, the settling down into the even more basic routine of army discipline — marching, drilling and 'bull', etc. — would have been more rapid than with a recruit who was entirely new to these things.

Of course, to senior officers of the services there is something far more satisfying in the job of commanding limited numbers of men of high quality and enthusiasm who have sought to make the armed forces their careers than in that of having to contend with large numbers of unwilling recruits, and it is therefore not difficult to understand the preference that many of them have for the small but highly professional forces that are currently maintained. As a political leader, I am many times struck by the same feelings; the experience of working with a dedicated *elite* is far more agreeable than the problems often attendant upon having to organise and depend on large masses of followers, many of them of very weak motivation and quality.

But just as political power in the real world is inconceivable without the eventual achievement of mass support, so is victory in a major war inconceivable without mass armies. Britain took the longest time of all the European nations to face up to this truth, but eventually she was compelled by harsh necessity to do so. The 'top brass' of our service establishments who do not grasp it are simply fleeing from history.

I must make one concession to these service chiefs, however: extreme difficulty would indeed be experienced in building massed armed forces for war from out of some of the human material that would have to be recruited from our present society. National service under existing political and social conditions in Britain, and bearing in mind the contemporary culture and climate of education, would most certainly not work as national service needs to work to be effective.

The objections to national service of the kind one reads in the columns of today's newspapers are therefore to an extent understandable — presupposing as they do no fundamental change in the kind of nation we are in the 1980s.

Under present conditions, the fear of commanders of the armed forces that, with national service, they would be receiving large numbers of recruits totally unsuitable for service contains a good deal of truth. Possibly, these commanders' range of thinking does not extend to a comprehension of a nation and society radically different from those existing; hence their inability to conceive any circumstances in which national service could be effective.

In a previous chapter I have advocated rudimentary military

training for all boys of school age, combined with physical training and sports of an order that would promote in all of them much higher standards of physical fitness. In addition, I have proposed that schoolroom education should do much more than at present to inculcate patriotism and an appreciation of the military virtues. Young males should leave school in a frame of mind to welcome the experience of life in the armed forces as a continuation of this character-building development and as an apprenticeship for citizenship and, above all, **manhood**.

Along with this, the influences to which young folk should be subjected by means of the mass media should be of a complementary nature. Films, historical documentary programmes on TV and radio, newspaper and magazine articles, and even popular music, should have a large portion of content aimed at generating enthusiasm for armed service institutions and traditions and elevating the place of the armed forces in the esteem of the whole community. Young soldiers, sailors and airmen who have performed valiant feats in the service of their country in war should be foremost among the heroes of contemporary teenagers, not the drug-ridden half-men of the 'pop' industry who are lionised by the media today. Young males, by experience, upbringing and example, would then be thoroughly ready for their two-year 'stint' in the forces, and would be far easier then to form into efficient fighting units.

As I have stressed earlier when referring to my own experience in the 1950s, national service should be organised in a way that wastes not a single day's time in the lives of those who undergo it. A hard regime of physical fitness should prevail for the entire two years and not just for the initial basic training period. Everyone should be trained to a competent level in the use of small arms, regardless of whether they play an infantry role or not. And in every unit a greater degree of versatility should be promoted, with a view to an interchangeability of functions between members of a unit in case of incapacitation in battle.

The British soldier in World War II was often found to be lacking initiative when situations arose which had not been planned for in his training — and these were many. Contrary to popular propaganda, his German adversary was much less of a blind automaton, reliant on orders from above. In training, men, even of the lowest rank, must be confronted with situations in which their superiors have been put out of action and they have to think for themselves. This constant emphasis on the thinking soldier must permeate all training schedules. This is of course not neglected in the regular forces of today, but it would have to be given equal priority in the training of conscripts — which was most certainly not the case in my day.

A vital key to better forces is of course the recruitment of better men at officer level, and in particular at the level of regimental commanders. I have related earlier how the class system of officer selection was still far too prevalent in the 1950s. Some progress away from this has been made since, but probably not enough. In our guards regiments still today, a young recruit, even if he has real natural qualities of leadership, has almost no chance of obtaining a commission unless he comes from an upper middle class or aristocratic background and possesses private financial means — an asset apparently necessary because his schedule of 'social' duties involves an expense well beyond the limits of his army pay. This is a ridiculous anachronism in the 1980s and should be scrapped without further ado — if the pay cannot be expanded, then the 'social' duties should be reduced!

I have spoken earlier of the necessity for education in the fundamentals of patriotism and nationalism. This should not be neglected in forces life, as it quite clearly is today. The recruiting literature to which I have referred places scarcely any emphasis at all on the idea that men are in uniform to defend their country and people, but instead speaks in an insipid way of the 'alliances' of which we are part, and whose purpose is to defend, apparently, nothing more than a political system which an increasing portion of our young people might well question is even worth defending — for all that it has done for them!

Essential to the maintenance of discipline and morale in any armed forces is an absolutely firm belief on the part of all members that they are serving something really worth fighting for, and for which they would give their lives if necessary. My experience of national service is that there was no effort made in talks to the men to inculcate belief in anything. There is not any sign that very much has changed. I do not believe that it is in the nature of young men to rush bravely into battle prepared to die for parliamentary government, the universal franchise or 'liberalism' — least of all in the discredited circumstances of these institutions in modern times. **Land** and **people** are things that millions will face death for — because they are concepts that can be felt and understood. Even Russia today, with all its theoretical allegiance to 'socialism', understands this and injects such sentiments into its young soldiers by all means available. Stalin discovered in World War II that his subjects would not fight for a political system but would fight for their fatherland.

For national service to become effective as a preparation for national defence in time of war, it would have to be combined with some form of territorial service in which ex-national servicemen received regular courses to keep them acquainted with changes in the weaponry and equipment of their branches of the armed forces — thus minimising the problem of adjustment in war that I mentioned earlier.

Aside from the requirement of training men to serve their country in wartime, national service is vitally necessary as a school for citizenship and for life. In this respect it would be a continuation of the process begun in school and in youth organis- ation mentioned in an earlier chapter. The object must be to counteract all the potentially feminising influences in society that might infect young men at the most impressionable and vulnerable age of their lives. The values of manly pride, physical fitness, discipline and patriotism thoroughly absorbed at this crucial phase of entry from boyhood into manhood will create a population in every way better fitted for the tasks of the future, peacetime as well as wartime.

Recurring throughout this book has been the theme of building a stronger nation by means of a stronger people. I make no apology for the repetition, for the principle is crucial. One of the most troubling of modern phenomena is the very large number of young men we are today producing whose faces, voices, carriage, physique and attitudes betray a depressing 'wimpishness' and softness. I firmly believe that the effete political and spiritual doctrines that have come to hold sway in contemporary Britain are not unconnected with this national decline in manhood. The decline has to be stopped, and a new type of man made our ideal. Service in the fighting forces is a part — not the only part but a vitally important one — of the process of building this new man. This, above all things, is why it must become recognised as an absolute national necessity.

Chapter 21
The British National Party

Looking back on the development of the political ideas put forward in this book, I can say with truth that their foundations were laid early in my life, probably by the time I was 22 or 23 years old.

Much less clear cut has been the search for ways and means to promote the basic doctrine. I was convinced from the start that what was needed was an entirely new political movement, separate from, and different to, the established parties of the old system. But the exact form that this movement should take, what should be its strategy, tactics and type of organisation, have been questions over which my thoughts took much longer to develop — these being formed gradually in the hard school of experience, trial and error.

Throughout the 1970s and when Chairman of the National Front, I had worked within a framework of collective leadership not basically different from that operating in the political parties of the old system. I did so, as I have said, despite growing inner misgivings as to that procedure, avoiding allowing these misgivings to fester to the point of full-blooded conflict with my colleagues because I wished to preserve the unity of the party I led, and because I hoped always to find a way of improving the party's internal structure by common consent and peaceful change, rather than through a fight.

But it was not to be. At the end of the 1970s, as I have related earlier, the NF disintegrated into a number of warring factions. For two years after that I still hoped that it might be reunited under a new constitution and rules of leadership after this factional war had burnt itself out; but this was not to be either. I had to face the fact, albeit with the greatest sorrow, that the Front was now finished as an effective political force, although it may continue for a number of years more as a truncated relic of the party it had been. A new movement was needed with an entirely different leadership structure, controlled by a single individual who would be vested with complete executive and policy-making powers. I knew realistically that among those available I was the only person who could undertake this task.

No end of nonsense has been spoken and written on this subject. I have been accused by my adversaries within the movement of egotism, conceit, megalomania, intolerance of criticism and much else. And of course, as might be expected, the word 'dictator' has been borrowed from our political adversaries and used in just the same silly and mindless way as they are accustomed to using it themselves.

I have indicated before my belief that this word is one of the least understood, and therefore most abused, words in the English language. Like so many terms with a frequent political application, it is lacking in exactness and generally comes to mean what its user wants it to mean. But if 'dictatorship' means the institution of a strong executive power, and the concentration of all the resources of state (or party) on the task of assisting that power, rather than hindering it, then I am willing to aver that a great many people would approve such a system — in preference to the present party warfare.

I have described in an earlier chapter how the party with which I became involved in the 1970s was governed by a leadership committee, and with no one individual being granted the power to lead personally, and how this led to a reproduction in miniature of exactly the same conditions of politics as have given rise to an appalling standard of government in Britain. I determined that the new movement that we built from out of the ruins of that party would be run differently. It would not be allowed to become a battleground of warring factions; but, on the contrary, the moment that the first whiff of factionalism (as distinct from healthy debate) manifested itself it would be ruthlessly stamped out.

This itself involved power in the hands of a single individual, for a committee cannot stamp out factionalism when, as is probable, a section of that committee has a vested interest in maintaining it.

Furthermore, as I have stated earlier, a system of individual decision-making must prevail in preference to decision-making by the counting of heads. First, the larger the number of heads brought to bear on such a decision, the lower is likely to be the average of intelligence, wisdom and experience on the part of those concerned. Secondly, with individual decision-making power goes individual responsibility for decisions. The individual may decide wrongly — no-one is infallible — but if he does he can be called to account and can blame no-one else.

The conviction that I myself had to take this responsibility had nothing to do with egotism but was based purely on a knowledge of the other would-be runners in the field. It was simply a matter of answering the call of duty. I suspect that those who make a habit of seeing egotistical motives behind every such feeling are merely projecting onto others the very vices that lie within themselves. They are prone, in effect, to judge what prompts others in accordance with their own criteria. In actual fact, I have a pretty long, and I may say pretty good, record of submitting myself to the leadership of other people in the course of my life as a political activist; and this is especially borne out by the manner in which I contributed to the unification of factions out of which the National Front was set up in 1967.

I have always had the view that before one is fit to give orders one should learn how to take them. With every leader under whom I served in the past I faithfully carried out the instructions I was given, even when I strongly disagreed with them. Leadership involves onerous duties; with those duties should go certain rights. And one such right is the right to be obeyed on all occasions, including those occasions on which one is wrong. My attitude on these questions of leadership was, in spirit, a military one rather than a political one. You put a man in command, not because you expect him to be right all the time, but because his record shows that he is likely to be right more often than anyone else. When you think he isn't right, you tell him; but if your efforts at persuasion fail, you abide by his decision.

The pioneer socialist James Keir Hardie was reputed once to have said: "I believe in a committee of one." I can understand his thoughts. We should not confuse 'committees', which are usually elected and have the power of a majority vote, with groups of people assembled together for consultative purposes and chosen by appointment from above. While the latter are essential, the former, in the sense that I have here described them, are nothing but trouble.

Of course I realise that there are thousands of bodies up and down the country that have always been run by committees and probably always will be: societies, clubs, charitable and welfare organisations, and so on. Indeed the committee system will always probably operate in many more types of organisation than not.

But the important point to remember is that in the great majority of these cases the bodies in question are not dealing with real life-and-death issues. Such decisions as that of whether the cricket club annual dinner is going to be on the 20th September or the 27th of September, whether the village horticultural society's annual holiday should be in Switzerland or the South of France, these are decisions that may left to committees to make by majority vote because they are not decisions likely to make history, to determine the survival or collapse of nations. But when we come to those areas of decision where the stakes being played for are so much higher — and when, furthermore, the task in which we are engaged is one carried out in conditions tantamount, in effect, to war — such cosy formulae just will not suffice. They do not suffice in armed forces where men's lives, as well as a nation's freedom, may be at stake. Neither will they suffice, I will submit, in a struggle of the urgency of that in which our movement is involved — for on the outcome of that struggle will most certainly depend the question of whether Britain will live or die.

The people with whom I set up the British National Party in 1982 were people I had come to know, for the most part, during the previous decade. They were men with whom I was able to feel a meeting of minds on the questions of internal organisation that we had to face. They included some strong characters with ideas of their own who would by no means always agree with me on every point. They were people, however, who detested the faction-fighting and jockeying for power that had been a constant feature of our previous experience. They shared my basic view of how leadership should operate. There would often be lively discussion of the decisions to be made and plenty of frank speaking, but in the end one man had to decide and the rest had to back him up.

A constitution was drawn up for the new party which placed overwhelming powers in the hands of the party's head. During any year he could be replaced by the party members if he lost their confidence, but unless and until that happened he was in charge.

Enshrined in the party constitution were five basic principles concerning the party's commitment to the creed of British Nation-alism. These principles could not be altered by anyone, nor could any political course be adopted which ran contrary to them. Within that framework, the party's policy objectives could be adapted to suit the requirements of changing times and augmented to meet any new situation not previously existing. The prerogative for making these adaptations lay entirely with the party leader personally, although it would be normal for consultation to take place before that prerogative was exercised.

The rules governing internal organisation and discipline could be amended by the party leader at his discretion — save the one rule that I have mentioned making provision for his replacement. In other words, the party leader could not, by manipulation of the rules, instal himself for life.

All executive decisions concerning the running of the party were the responsibility of the party leader or of those deriving their authority from him. This included all appointments to offices within the party. Every such appointment is by the personal decision of a single official above rather than by election from below.

Geographically, the party was divided into regions, corresponding to counties or groups of counties. The heads of these are normally appointed by the leader of the party. Within each region, branches and groups are organised where the party has a concentration of active members making this possible. The eventual aim is a branch in every parliamentary constituency, but in the process of working towards that aim branches are set up to correspond to city, town, borough, rural district or whatever is the most convenient designation.

Where any number of members — even only one — is prepared to work actively in the promotion of the party in an area, a group is established. When this unit grows to a certain stage of strength and proficiency, and when the party is satisfied that it has capable leadership, it is given the status of a recognised branch.

Leaders of branches and groups are normally appointed by their regional leaders. They in turn appoint all other local officials.

There are no committees at local level anymore than at national level. The leader of the branch or group has full authority over his unit and is responsible to the regional leader above him. The latter has full authority over his region, being answerable to the party leader above him.

Party departments dealing with specific functions, i.e. administration, publicity, finance, etc., are organised on the same lines. A head is appointed by the party leader. That head may in turn appoint whatever subordinate officials may be required.

Any head of any region, branch or department within the party may organise whatever consultative body he may see fit to help him in his decisions, but it is always understood that the decisions themselves are the individual's prerogative and responsibility alone. A show of hands may be asked for to test opinion on any matter but that show of hands is never binding; it is for the leader in question to decide whether to act in accordance with it or not.

Along with this task of giving the party a clearly established chain of command, I took steps to set up a firm procedure for internal discipline. In the National Front, a specified list of disciplinary offences was given in the party's written constitution. If a member could be proved to have committed one of these, he or she could be made subject to disciplinary action; if not, no such action could be taken. It all looked fine on paper. In practice, it became subject to some appalling abuses. We soon came to see that there were a multitude of actions that members could commit which were thoroughly harmful to the party but which could not be placed within any of the specific categories of breaches of discipline stated. As we know in ordinary life, some of the worst villains against society are those who manage to operate within the law! But if the catalogue of offences against the law is extended to embrace their particular practices there is the danger that this may then render illegal numerous quite harmless, even socially beneficial, acts engaged in by others for entirely different and more praiseworthy reasons. In the end, the law has to avoid getting too technical but must leave the courts to recognise a natural evildoer when they see one and to act with discrimination and discretion.

This is doubly so in a political movement operating under what are, as I have said, conditions of war. The cohesion and functional effectiveness of the unit transcends in importance any abstract concept of 'justice'. If any individual is of a type that undermines this cohesion, he must be quickly thrown out — regardless of whether, technically, he has committed any breach of the rules. If this is not done, trouble is in store.

In the Front we had found that the existence of a code of rules and a procedure for trying, by tribunal and in accordance with standard court procedure, those accused of breaking the rules did not prevent the flagrant exploitation of the disciplinary process. Whatever faction controlled a committee, be it a national or local one, could ensure the selection of its own allies to sit on a tribunal. Thereupon the latter could drum out of the party practically any individual it didn't like — by finding him or her guilty of the offence charged, on whatever flimsy evidence. Ultimately, a corrupt ruling power will corrupt the law, no matter how fine the latter may be on paper. I have seen this in public life, as well as in political organisations.

Our new disciplinary procedure was much simpler. It gave to the senior officer locally, or to the party leader if the matter became a national one, the power to expel summarily any member it was seen fit to expel. The official concerned may, at his own discretion, set up an enquiry if he was in any doubt as to the guilt or unsuitability for membership of the person in question; but he was under no obligation to do so. The confidence on the part of the national leadership in any local leader had to include the confidence that the latter would act prudently and disinterestedly in such matters — otherwise he would not be in such a position in the first place. Obviously, a senior leader could overrule his subordinate in such cases, but in practice we have found that this is rarely necessary.

Such a system of course gives to local leaders very considerable powers, and in theory such powers could be abused; but this is no more the case than with tribunals selected by committees. The important thing is to pick the right man for the job, and then trust his judgement. If you do so, and he informs you that he has thrown one of his members out, you usually know that he has had good reasons.

The ultimate test of such a system is whether it works; and ours has worked. In the few years of our party's history we have had almost zero in the way of disciplinary troubles. At the same time we have been almost totally free of internal strife. In the first year of our existence two people in the London area tried to create a faction. One was thrown out so quickly his feet hardly touched the ground. The other, knowing the same was about to happen to him, pre-empted it by his rapid resignation.

Right from the start, we aimed at high standards of discipline among our members, and we have been successful in achieving them. It is my view that good discipline owes much more to the personality of the officer in charge than to a paper rulebook. The right man will tend from the beginning to attract around him the right nucleus. Then when numbers become expanded beyond this first nucleus by the winning of new supporters these latter, as they come in, will tend to adapt their behaviour to the company around them. Those who are of the type incapable of doing this usually soon find that they are square pegs in round holes and either drop out or get thrown out.

Right from the start, our policy has been to avoid recruiting any of the various brands of freak or yobbo that tend, if allowed, to hitch themselves to radical political organisations. We are conscious of the orientation of the mass media — a subject to which I have devoted a whole chapter in this book and about which my opinions will have been made clear. It is the purpose of the media to depict people in our type of politics as comprising hooligans, and just one single hooligan amongst us — even if he is in a tiny minority — will get media attention focused on him the moment that he manifests himself. For instance, if we stage a march with some hundreds of marchers on the column, including just one or two Neanderthals, we can be quite sure that the TV or press cameras will 'zoom in' on these Neanderthals and give them prominence while ignoring the remainder present. It is for this reason that we discourage as much as we can the recruitment of any elements that might appear or behave in such a way as to discredit us. It is my observation that those who have set themselves up as rivals to us in the business of promoting British Nationalism have failed appallingly in maintaining the same standards.

Around the country we have now built a cadre of excellent local leaders, who act completely as a team. This would not have been possible except by the method of appointment from above. My experience of leaders chosen by the electoral process is that the person who gets the position is often the biggest talker, the most expert in self-publicisation and who will, on the right occasion, buy everyone the most drinks. These credentials do not always go hand in hand with ability. By exercising the prerogative of appointment — usually done in consultation with the men I most trust in each area — I have succeeded in acquiring colleagues of the highest quality and aptitude.

The majority of our recruits have been young. There is in the young population of Britain today a very large number just looking for a strong cause and creed in which they can believe and with which they can identify. They constitute an immense reservoir of potentially good adherents, but when they are recruited it must be on our terms and not theirs. If they have picked up certain silly fashions and behavioural patterns, they will soon discard them if they are set a good example and shown something better. But if, in an eagerness to recruit them in vast numbers overnight, we identify **ourselves** with the very decadent cults that they have been taught to follow by the trendsetters of this modern age, our party will have been won over to them rather than they to us. From then on they, and not we, would dictate party styles and tactics. This is something that I am not prepared to let happen.

At the centre of our movement there has been formed an 'inner circle' of active zealots whose whole lives are dominated by their cause and revolve around that cause — who live, eat, sleep and breathe that cause every moment of every day and night. It would not be stretching the language to call these people 'fanatics' in their approach to British Nationalism. We should not recoil from the word 'fanatical' and assume that it always means something bad. We may disparage the fanatics of the left, but we can never ignore them and we should never underestimate them. It is precisely because the left has been able to attract people who give so much of themselves to their cause that it has become powerful all over the world. Minorities of hard-line left-wingers take over trade unions and other bodies precisely because they are fanatical, precisely because they do so consecrate their lives to their political work that they become simply invincible — which of course they are to those who do not have the same fires burning inside them to fuel their activity. It has long been my contention that this single-minded dedication on the part of the crusaders of the hard left can only be effectively combated by opposition consisting of people of equally total commitment. Conservatism and the 'respectable' right can never meet this need. Everything about their approach to politics is tepid. Only ideals of mighty force can inspire the strongest commitment of the strongest people, and no such ideals exist in the spectrum of the parties which represent 'moderation' in politics. It has always seemed to me a symptom of decadence that our society in Britain looks down upon as 'odd' anyone who makes politics a thing of passion. The enemies of our nation of course find this thoroughly suitable because it leaves the field clear to them to establish a monopoly of that commodity. The passage from Yeats that I quoted earlier sums it up.

At the centre of our movement is a band of *elite* activists whose commitment to their cause has about it the fervour of the apostles of a religious order. They are people who have very largely, in some cases almost totally, subordinated everything in their private lives to their political work. Their choice of residence and job is adapted to the demands of politics rather than the other way round. They eschew career promotion and financial advancement if these get in the way of their party duties. They travel all around the country several weekends in each year, often sleeping rough, and entirely at their own expense, to promote the party on a nationwide basis. They face opposition violence on the streets when selling party newspapers or handing out leaflets. They are prepared to go to jail for their beliefs — something that I could not ask them to do if I had not undergone such an experience myself.

Indeed, I would never be in a position to ask for such commitment from my leading colleagues were they not aware of how total has been my own dedication, over many years, to the cause for which we fight. Having organised my own private life, such as it is, around this cause, I am well placed to summon others to do the same; and in the case of my senior associates that is exactly what they do. Not unreasonably, I listen to their opinions on matters with an attentiveness that I would not accord to the half-hearted activist. I make it my business to give an ear to every viewpoint within the party, but it is only right that I should give special consideration to the views of those whose commitment is the greatest. In an organisation structured according to the rules of 'democracy', this would not of course be possible; everything would be decided by votes and everyone's vote would be worth the same. Only in the type of organisation we have developed can I adhere to the rule of giving the greatest weight to the opinions of those who make the greatest contribution — and of course to those whose experience and track record entitles them to speak with the greatest authority.

I have no time at all for those who whine about the power enjoyed by dedicated left-wing activists in the trade union movement, when that power is simply such people's natural reward for the level of their dedication and commitment. While I totally oppose most of the policies they stand for, I admire and respect their devotion and zeal, and I regard the fact that they possess much more influence than the ordinary run-of-the-mill payer of union dues as perfectly just. The way to beat them is to oppose them with people with a dedication and commitment — if you like, a 'fanaticism' — equal to their own, not to talk of taking power out of their hands in order to give it to the legions of the lazy, the apathetic and the half-hearted.

I have referred to the violence that our activists often have to face, and there is no doubt that this has intensified in recent times. The political left in Britain has spelled out abundantly clearly what its policy is towards the nationalist movement: we must be prevented from exercising our rights of free speech at all costs, and whenever we manifest our presence in an area we must be physically smashed. We regard this, of course, as a compliment: it is an acknowledgement that the left looks on us as 'dangerous' — and also that it has no answer to us in the way of rational argument. If these people did not react to us in this way, but took the view that we could be left to promote our political views in the ordinary way, we would begin to worry that we were failing somewhere.

It is our general rule that the correct response to left-wing violence is to leave the job of keeping order to the police. In practice, however, this is not always possible; the police cannot be everywhere at once, and in the numbers necessary to deal with all such disorders. This means that we must be prepared to act in our own defence on occasions; and indeed our members frequently have to do just that. The announcement that we are about to hold a public meeting (on the limited occasions when we can obtain the facilities for doing so) is something that the left regards as a 'provocation' and a challenge to their authority over who may or may not speak in public. We therefore can take it as read on such occasions that the meeting will be subject to attempted attack. Similarly, where the left finds that our paper-sellers are manifesting their presence in town centres and enjoying good sales, it feels bound to remove those sellers from their pitches, in the first instance by violent threats, and, when these fail (as they always do) by actual physical assault. If we were not prepared to stand up to the thugs of the left and give them a dose of their own medicine, we would effectively be abdicating our right to make our voice heard or read anywhere.

I have laid down to our activists a few basic rules to be followed in respect of this situation. The first is that no offensive action should be taken to prevent our political opponents exercising their right to promote their opinions. This would be entirely counter-productive. In a previous chapter I have called for national leadership vested with much stronger authority than presently exists. At the same time, I have insisted that the right of people opposed to us to voice their opinions should be respected, and that those opinions should be answered by superior argument rather than silenced by law or by force. We should act today as we intend to carry on, and any attempt to use force to curb our opponents' rights of free speech would be taken as a sign that we were frightened of what they had to say and had no answer to it.

Therefore, whatever the provocation involved in left-wingers attacking us, we should not stoop to the same level by attacking them.

Self-defence in the event of an attack on our people by their opponents, however, is an entirely different matter. As I have said, where such an attack is made and the police are present to deal with it the latter should be left to do their job. On the other hand, where and when the police are not present our members are perfectly entitled to take what measures of self-defence are required by the situation. Here the rule is to hit back — and hit back **hard.** There is a reason for this rule, as I shall explain:-

Almost everywhere around the country where our members are under physical threat from the mobs of the left, the latter are able to mobilise greater numbers for such confrontations than we can. In such situations, it will sometimes happen that, if a battle does ensue, the left is bound to win in the end by sheer numerical weight. Our only safeguard against this happening is to drive home to the thugs of the left the message that, even if in the end they are able to swamp our people by means of overwhelming odds, before that happens a number of them are going to get badly hurt in the process. This, we have found, has acted as a very effective deterrent. Not all that many of these 'comrades' are endowed with great physical courage; few of them want to go home after an affray nursing purple eyes or ruing several missing teeth, let alone even worse infirmities. By our tactics, the word has gradually got through to these people that it is not in the interests of their own good health that they should 'take on' BNP activists in a fight, even where they are at a numerical advantage. This has not stopped the incidents of assault on our people, but has considerably reduced them.

On the ethics of this matter, we have no agonies of conscience. A good number of these left-wing rowdies are absolute animals. I have seen them engage in vicious attacks on groups of nationalists, in the 1970s and more recently, where they have picked deliberately on elderly women. I have a vivid memory of an encounter in Bradford, for instance, in the mid-seventies, when I saw a lady supporter of ours of 65 or so with her face streaming with blood after having been hit over the head with a half-brick by a member of a jeering red mob. Such incidents are not untypical, and any reader of this book, whether he or she is a political activist or not, will probably know of some incident in which left-wing thuggery has manifested itself with the result of injury to innocent people. Our rule when we get attacked by these creatures is not to treat them with kid gloves but to administer a thrashing to them which they will not forget or want to experience again. I deplore the fact that the political climate in Britain has reached the level at which these attitudes are necessary, but merely deploring it will not change it; we have to act according to the *de facto* conditions of our time — until we are able to change them.

Liverpool is just one area where we have experienced some of the nastiest left-wing thuggery. As many will know, this city is a stronghold of left-wing militants — until recently they controlled the council there. Frequently on weekends our activists have gone to sell the party paper in the city centre. After a while, the local left decided that this would no longer be permitted. They first tried verbal intimidation, informing our people that if they continued showing themselves and peddling their 'racist filth' in the city they would be set upon and 'smashed'. To this, the leftists got a very brief two-worded reply that it would be improper to reprint here.

The left-wingers then set about carrying out their threat. Gangs would appear of about four times the numerical strength of our men, and the latter, though putting up a stout resistance, were eventually overwhelmed. Not liking the injuries that some of them sustained in this unequal encounter, the left would then come back with even heavier numerical odds. Paper sales were seriously disrupted for a number of weeks.

Eventually, our people did the only thing that could be done. One day they called in some reinforcements from adjacent areas. The usual number of sellers set up in business in the customary place while the reserve team waited *incognito* around a nearby corner.

Duly the red mob arrived and, seeing our men in what appeared to be modest strength, they made their attack. The 'extras' thereupon came from around the corner and tore into action. In the ensuing scuffles our men went in very hard and a number of red warriors ended up in a considerably poorer state of heath than they had enjoyed when they woke up that morning. The result of this? For a considerable time after that occasion BNP paper sales were able to proceed in Liverpool centre in complete peace.

The tactics of the left at nationalist meetings have been described in an earlier chapter; they scarcely ever vary. The left gets a large mob of its own supporters into the hall, and as soon as the meeting starts the mob sets up a barrage of massed chanting which makes it quite impossible for the speaker to be heard. We then have a situation in which it is obviously out of the question for the meeting to proceed unless the mob is ejected. Of course, this is the left's way of provoking a fight while being able to say that our side struck the first blow.

Usually there is a police presence at the meeting, and when the police tell us that they wish to attend to the ejection of these troublemakers we comply. The problem about this is that the police, for reasons that are perfectly sound when looked at from their point of view, prefer to carry out their job of ejection piece-meal — one or two disrupters at a time. In this way the likelihood of a large-scale riot is diminished. The adverse side of it is that the process is very slow. A few words are spoken by the speaker, then the chanting drowns him. The meeting stops. The police come in. They remove one or two rowdies. The meeting starts again, and so does the chanting. The procedure is repeated.

The result of all this is that a great deal of time is lost. A lot of people who may have come in with a genuine interest in what we had to say may get impatient and leave. Often half of the time for which we have hired the hall is taken up with the slow and laborious job of removing people who have come to stop the meeting.

I do not criticise the police in this matter. Their chief aim is to avoid a disturbance. In that respect their priority is different from ours, which is to hold the meeting. We want to avoid a disturbance if possible, but holding the meeting and getting through the agenda come first.

For this reason, we always prefer, when an attempt is made to stop a meeting, to deal with it quickly — even if this involves a larger disturbance. It is better to get all the troublemakers out of the hall with the minimum delay, so that the meeting can then proceed in peace and according to schedule.

We therefore would always rather sort out this kind of trouble ourselves, and by our own methods, than have the police do it.

At one meeting in London's Bethnal Green area in 1986, at which I was present, we were already far behind in our timetable when the meeting started, as the usual mob had turned up and surrounded the gates of the premises with a view to stopping us getting in. We were ready to force our way through this mob and I requested the senior police officer present to let us do just that. Not entirely surprisingly, he refused my request. This involved a very long delay as the police devised a method for getting us into the premises by another entrance. In the end, the meeting started an hour and a half late, and with little more than an hour left before our booking of the hall was due to expire.

A part of the mob, about equal in number to our own people present, got into the hall, and as soon as the chairman of the meeting rose to speak the usual din started. After two requests to stop, it continued. Quite obviously, the intention was, as usual, to stop the meeting taking place.

In view of the time, had the police taken charge of the job of clearing the hall of troublemakers and done it in their customary way, the meeting would never have finished. I therefore decided that we had to act quickly. I gave a signal, and our men pitched into the mob and threw them out in little more than a minute. In some cases, more than the minimum force was used, and, as at Liverpool, some members of the opposition sustained injuries that will probably have made them think twice about causing trouble at BNP events again. A number of these people, however, did not need very much persuasion to go; seeing our men coming for them and being mindful of these men's reputation as highlighted in their own propaganda, they bolted for the exit before even a hand could be laid on them — this of course all making our job much easier.

The hall was clear and the meeting was finished on time. In any other circumstances it would not have been.

I saw no reason to reprimand any of our men afterwards for the way they acted; on the contrary, I commended them. With these red gangsters there is absolutely no other way. It has to be driven home to them that it simply is not healthy for them to try to break up our meetings by force. This is the only language they understand. On this occasion I was myself engaged in a scuffle with one red disrupter, who tried to pin an assault charge on me for not allowing him to smash up our meeting! Nothing came of it, since the police knew very well that our opponents had started the trouble and only got what they deserved.

As I have said previously in this book, we do not glorify violence; on the contrary, we would far rather that political argument took place in an atmosphere of rational debate. But confronted with the type of intimidation which is standard practice from left-wing elements in Britain today there is only one policy that can be adopted: you have got to teach them a lesson so that many of them will not want to come back for more. This is the time-honoured rule for dealing with bullies across the ages.

At these meetings, we do not object to opposition as such. A good argument is healthy, and heckling is particularly welcome. We sometimes have a question time and people are then allowed to make points from the floor; these points are always listened to and answered politely, however hostile they may be. What will not be tolerated is any attempt to break the meeting up. At the London meeting that I have mentioned, one female member of the opposition who had been particularly vociferous was allowed to stay during the subsequent question time and was given a hearing without any attempt to silence, let alone intimidate, her — something that most certainly would not have been allowed with one of our supporters, female or not, at a meeting of the left.

Notwithstanding all the actual circumstances of this meeting as I have described them, the affair was written up in the left-wing press the following week in such a distorted way that we had to laugh aloud at the nerve of our opponents. According to them, they had just gone along to heckle 'peacefully' and were set upon, without any provocation, by 'Tyndall's thugs'. One group of them had the cheek to send a letter along these lines to *The Guardian* newspaper. The paper's editor allowed the letter to be printed without the slightest attempt to contact us to hear our side of the story. I was prompted thereupon to send in a reply. *The Guardian* printed this in an abridged form, allowing it much less space and prominence than the letter of our opponents. Sometimes even this right of reply is not observed, and the press prints write-ups of incidents of this kind as they are informed about them by red propagandists. In this way, the image is built up in the public mind of 'fascist violence'. It was the same with Mosley's movement in the 1930s. Fleet Street does not change its spots.

My letter to *The Guardian* made the facts clear. The left had come along with the deliberate intention of starting a fight, and its supporters were now squealing because they had got the worst of it. This, I have found, is standard left-wing practice — the eternal bully again: when he meets his match, he runs blubbing to teacher!

It has been my observation that our men are, on average, of much better physique, and are fitter and more courageous, than are their opponents; and whenever numbers are anything like equal, or even when there is a slight superiority on the opposition side, our men will always win. It is a good thing that the opposition gets to know this, for that will minimise the probability of trouble.

No matter how provocative the circumstances, our men are

always instructed to deal with trouble in a disciplined way. One of the popular tactics of the reds is to use women as their front-line troublemakers. Some of the women they manage to produce are the most ghastly representatives of the female species imaginable, and their language is often as offensive as their appearance. Nevertheless, our men are under strict instructions when dealing with them not to lose their temper. Here the rule about 'minimum force' does indeed apply. Female members of the opposition, however provocative, are never roughly handled. The same rule is not observed by our opponents towards our own women, as I have related. Our practice, however, is always to try to shunt our female members to a safe corner before a fight begins; we never, if we can help it, place them in the battle zone, as does the opposition.

In the face of this pattern of left-wing violence, we are at a considerable disadvantage due to restrictions imposed upon us by the state. As I have explained previously, the inappropriately named 'Public Order Act' prevents any political group properly organising its own self-defence in a really methodical way. We are not permitted to adopt any kind of paramilitary structure, equipment or training to prepare our men for these contingencies — although of course the same legislation is never used against those who organise violence on our opponents' side. We have to bend over backwards to comply strictly with the law in this regard, otherwise we would immediately be prosecuted. Our opponents are organised in advance to smash up meetings; we are not permitted to organise to defend them — as the 1962 prosecutions clearly established. When trouble starts, we have to act spontaneously, and without the systematised form of self-defence that would allow us to do the job so much more effectively, and thus cut the violence down.

By the time the BNP was founded in 1982, I had available a small but solid network of men around the country on whom I knew I could rely. I have said that they were, as I was, sick of faction-fighting and wanted only to devote themselves to promoting nationalism. They were men of good character who had acquitted themselves with honour in the struggles of the past. In contrast to some who, in the internecine warfare with which the patriotic movement has been plagued, had chosen sides according to the promptings of opportunism and self-interest, these men had shown that they were prepared to take the side they knew to be right, and regardless of personal advantage. I have said that they shared with me the same basic views on the type of organisation we now needed.

It is my natural instinct to acknowledge each of these men by mentioning his name. With the odd exception in this book, I do not do so because in giving such a list there is always the risk that someone may be excluded whose contribution, unbeknown to me, has been equal to those mentioned, and who therefore would be done an injustice by being left out. I will therefore content myself here with a very general comment on the men who have worked beside me in the British National Party, and this is that my debt to them is beyond anything to which words can do justice.

With these men, and here and there women also, we have built the BNP on really solid foundations. It is still, at the time that I write these words, a very small organisation. As it is expanded in the future, it will develop from the very firm base that we have laid down; and in the constitutional arrangements that we made right at the start it will be ensured that this base will remain, however large the structure subsequently erected on top of it.

So far, the 1980s have been a time for gradual and patient consolidation rather than rapid growth in support. The tide of recruitment to nationalism that we witnessed in the previous decade has for the time being levelled off a little. There has been for the past few years a certain degree of public euphoria over 'Thatcherism', to which many have looked to solve the crippling national problems that have hung over the country. In an earlier chapter I have described how the Tories won the general election of 1979 with a set of entirely bogus promises and postures on law and order, immigration control and economic revival in which many believed. It will take time for these promises and postures to be revealed for the mere vote-catching stunts that they were. In addition to this, the nationalist movement has been divided, its resources depleted and, in places, the morale of its adherents has been at a low ebb. With all these factors in mind, no dramatic breakthrough to mass support was to be expected for a time after we set up our organisation, and I counselled everybody that the way ahead for a while would be slow and laboured. In this situation the important task would be to build an organisation of **quality** without expecting too much progress in quantity. We also knew that the schism in nationalism would only be healed ultimately by means of events proving the correctness of our own position. Gradually, this has happened, but it has taken time.

I have learned that in politics one sometimes has to be prepared to be cast for a while into the wilderness, listened to only by a few, while the tide of affairs flows on far from one's control. It is at such times that the true political crusader — the one to which his cause is a life's vocation — is separated from the dilettante and the hobbyist, who are essentially fair-weather politicians looking for short cuts to success and drop out when the gates to these are closed. The really dedicated ones will not slacken in their resolve in times when things appear to be standing still, or at the best moving forward very slowly, but will put these times to good use preparing for later times when the opportunity to break through will again occur. Mass inertia and stupor will often render many people immune to persuasion of the need to make great changes, and then only the evidence before their eyes of the collapse of those things in which they had previously believed will convince them of the need to set out on new paths. Before the time is ripe for this to happen, the most persuasive oratory in the world will be of no avail. But when it happens the men who warned of it in the past, mostly to deaf ears, are vindicated; and the time then belongs to them. It is their moment of opportunity.

What is important is that when that moment comes such men are still there, having not been demoralised by their isolation but stood their ground in readiness for such a change in events.

The trials and tribulations of the 1970s enabled me to sort out the fair-weather patriots from those who recognised the fact that our struggle involves a lifetime's work, with its stagnant periods as well as its fruitful ones. The latter were of the type around whom we formed the BNP.

One of the great mistakes made by some people in the stagnant situation that I have described is to vent their frustration at the slowness of progress by blaming the common multitude, saying of that multitude that because it is not prepared, so far, to listen to the message of its salvation it is in fact "not worth saving." The assumption here is that all we have been doing is merely for the benefit of that multitude — seen as an aggregate of individuals. This is a fundamental error. The great majority of people, of any nation and in any era, are not especially good or bad, not especially heroic or unheroic. That they may not be moved by the vision of a great ideal is something we must attribute essentially to the fact that there are not mobilised, in the presentation of that ideal, the great resources of propaganda that are necessary to promote it. When we say that what we are doing is 'for' the British people, what we mean is that we are working for the British people

as a national entity, as a strictly impersonal concept — and one which is **timeless**; that is to say we are working for the British people of the past and of the future as much as of the present: we are working for an historical and racial entity rather than just for so many millions of individuals who happen to be living at the present moment.

But, more than this, we are working for an **ideal** and a **vision** which far transcend 'people', taken at the level of the average individual. That ideal and vision, because of their greatness, are always worthy of our highest dedication and sacrifice, quite regardless of how 'people', at any one juncture of time or place, may measure up to them. Such ideals and visions are in this world only ever truly understood by a few. It is for those few to get their hands on the **machinery** whereby that ideal and vision can be communicated down to the ordinary masses in language by which they can understand their value in terms of those things that affect their own ordinary lives. Before this task is accomplished, it is futile to expect the masses to respond to any great message sent out on behalf of such things.

As long as we begin our mission by taking the ordinary man in the street exactly for what he is, not expecting from him any more than he is able to give, and recognising that he will only ever be moved by the mighty currents of affairs set in motion by active minorities, we will not be despondent when he fails to heed our call, and we will not take this as a signal to give up the struggle.

Our first task after forming the new movement in 1982 was to establish its name. Up till then, the name of the National Front had been the one synonymous with our politics nationwide, and for a long time my own name had been indelibly linked with that of the Front. There were some who believed that because of these factors the surviving remnant of the NF would be bound to emerge again as the dominant force in British Nationalism. These people mistook shadow for substance: they imagined that it was the Front's well-known name that had created its former strength and that therefore that name would forever remain a source of such strength. In fact they had got things entirely base-about-apex. The fame attached to the name of the National Front in the 1970s was wholly the result of the public impact made at the time by its growth and success, and that growth and success were above all the work of certain **people**, that is to say a team of capable and energetic individuals who had put the party on the map. The name had been made by the party's progress, not the other way round.

Now that the people who had, for the most part, been the architects of the Front's success in the 1970s had severed their connections with it, the idea that its impetus could be revived and then sustained just by its name was pathetic. Only the brand label remained; the winning product had gone.

Gradually, we started to succeed in winning recognition for the name of the British National Party by forcing our way into the public eye by a series of bold activities. Our biggest chance to do this came with the general election of 1983.

When this election was called, the BNP was barely more than a year old, and considerably smaller in membership and resources than the National Front had been when it took on the (up till then) unprecedented challenge of fighting 50-plus seats in the election of February 1974. I decided nevertheless that this somehow had to be done. Our reward would be to qualify for broadcasting time, and this, more than anything else, would help to make the name of our new party known to the British public. But could it be done with our slender resources and with so little time to mobilise them?

It was done — by a miracle of determination, effort and sacrifice. I am proud to have shared in that achievement and led it, but it was really the work of a team. The men and women in whom I had come to place sure faith rose to the occasion magnificently and performed prodigious work to get us ready in time.

I stated as a rule a little earlier that I would not mention names — but for the occasional exception. Here I must mention such an exception. Among the unsung heroes whose efforts enabled us to meet the great challenge in 1983 was John Smith, of our Hertfordshire branch. Somehow this man will forever remain for me symbolic of the spirit of our movement.

John Smith had perhaps the most ordinary name in the English-speaking world, but he was an extraordinary man. In 1944, when in the British Army, he took part in the D-Day landings in Normandy, being no politician then but a simple patriot doing his bit, as he saw it, for his country — like millions of others.

This D-Day soldier gradually became disillusioned with the post-war world that his generation had helped, without knowing it, to create. Believing in his youth that Britain had won a victory, he came, as he grew older, to see that in effect his country, and the whole of European civilisation, were in the throes of defeat. He began to take an interest in politics in an effort to understand what forces were at work.

John Smith was in his fifties when he joined the National Front in the 1970s. He became one of its finest active workers, but never sought the limelight nor any position for himself. For this reason he came only slowly to my notice. He was one of those who followed me out of the NF in 1980, and partook in the formation of the BNP two years later.

John Smith was a postman. When the 1983 election came, he was in his sixties and not far from retirement. He got together with his colleagues at a London sorting office and raised with them nearly £1,000 towards election deposits. Without that money, we would not have fought the 50-plus seats that we needed. In addition, he worked like a Trojan in his local Hertfordshire area in the promotion of a number of campaigns, in one of which he was a candidate.

John Smith was one of the many inconspicuous people who, shunning personal glory, worked almost around the clock to make our achievement possible. Somehow, however, he symbolised all of them.

A year afterwards, he crossed over to the Normandy beaches to join his old regiment in a D-Day reunion. As he and his comrades visited a graveyard of the fallen, he told his friends: ''They died for nothing.''

Within a short time afterwards, John himself was dead. It was in the last years of his life that he fought the real battle for his country, as he himself well knew. Nations sometimes erect monuments to what they call 'The Unknown Soldier'. When our movement is triumphant, as one day it will be, our 'Unknown Soldier' will, I hope, bear the features of this man, whom it was a privilege to know.

In the end we contested 54 seats, winning the right to one five-minute TV broadcast and one radio broadcast of the same length. This was a far more noteworthy achievement than that of the National Front in fighting the same number of seats in February 1974. Apart from the tremendous efforts of certain individuals, we owed this achievement, beyond any doubt, to the strong spirit of authority and discipline that permeated our party from top to bottom. Had the procedure of committee rule and *laissez-faire* democracy prevailed, the thing would never have been done. When majority decisions carry the day, and when those who comprise that majority are themselves elected by the votes of majorities at a lower tier of organisation, inertia, over-caution and cowardice usually prevail, and the word 'impossible' is all too often accepted as a welcome refuge from the responsibility of seizing destiny with both hands at those rare moments that it offers itself. Every rational calculation told us that we could not bring the thing off, that the available time and resources simply would not permit us to find over 50 candidates and the deposits to finance them. And a committee would most certainly have taken this rational view. But we defied such reasoning and did the 'impossible'.

I remember spending many hours on the telephone talking to people around the country — there just was not the time to go and see them — during which, on occasions, I had to be teacher, father, coach and psychologist all rolled into one. Some of these people had to be infused with will power and a faith in their own potentialities. Some of them had to be promised financial assistance which at the time I hadn't the slightest idea how we were going to acquire. There had to be cajoling, pleading, provoking and sometimes downright bawling out — depending on the make-up of the person to whom I was talking.

One branch, which shall be unnamed, still had not accustomed itself to the new spirit and procedures that had been adopted for the running of the party. It convened a meeting of its members and took a vote on whether it could fight a seat or not. The majority, in its great wisdom, decided not. On hearing this, I immediately dispatched a colleague to this branch (a man who shared my view of how things had to be done) and he curtly told the branch that they would fight a seat, and that was that. They did!

As expected, our votes in the election were not high. By the time that we had found 54 candidates and deposits, we had very little left to back them up in the way of campaign literature. In only five areas was the latter possible, and there our votes were twice as high as elsewhere. In addition to our own meagre campaigning resources, a further disadvantage was that the public just was not in a frame of mind for a big change in voting allegiances. Four years of thoroughly bad Conservative government were to a great extent glossed over by what became known at the time as the 'Falklands Factor'. A war caused by political ineptness and won by military valour was turned, quite falsely and wrongly, to the credit of Mrs. Thatcher; and the Tory sheep remained in the fold.

Nevertheless, our TV broadcast had been seen by over 13 million people and the party name had been put on the map. While it would be an exaggeration to say that the publicity had made that name a household one, at least it had been lifted from almost total obscurity. In the following weeks, we received a flood of enquiries, which we duly answered with literature giving information about the BNP, and then dispatched, where possible, to local leaders for following up with personal visits to the enquirers. From this publicity we won some notable new members, whose contributions have helped enormously in the strengthening of our organisation. And from then on the name of the British National Party was no longer unknown.

After 1983, the party underwent something of a change of strategy. The main purpose of contesting the election of that year had been, as I have said, to obtain broadcasting time and make the name of the party known nationwide; it was not anticipated that many votes would be won. In the aftermath, and looking back over previous elections in which the nationalist movement had taken part, we were bound to acknowledge that the right conditions for nationalism to make an impact at the polls just did not yet exist in Britain. It was not a question of the electorate being hostile to our policies; over a wide area of these policies millions thought and felt in the same way as we did. The problem lay in the nature of the British electoral system, which tended to condemn to irrelevance small parties lacking in the resources to get their message over in a way that made them appear to 'count'. A large number of British electors today vote 'tactically'. That is to say they vote to keep out the party or candidate they dislike most rather than to show their support for those with whom they are in greatest sympathy. The 'first-past-the-post' electoral procedure followed in Britain places at an enormous disadvantage any party which cannot demonstrate that it has a chance of winning a majority in a particular electoral area — this being different from the system prevailing over most of the European Continent, where a reasonable number of votes for a party over a whole country can obtain seats for it in the country's parliament, even if it is not able to come first in any one area.

To overcome this handicap, the nationalist movement needs to get over to the electors that by voting for its candidates they **can** employ their votes decisively — in as much as, even if the candidates do not win, a demonstration of increasing support for them can create a snowballing effect, encouraging yet more people to vote for them in the future — and to the point at which they can actually begin to be among the front-runners, with a chance of getting elected. At the same time, it must be equally demonstrated to these electors that their decision to vote for this or that of the established parties will make very little difference to the ultimate course being pursued by the country.

I am convinced that it **is** possible to drive this message home eventually, but it is not possible with the campaigning resources at present at our disposal. We need to have access to means of communication far in excess of those presently available. The printed election addresses that we are able to get delivered through every letter box at election times are utterly inadequate when compared with the heavy artillery of our opponents' propaganda, with their massed canvassing teams, their daily newspapers and their regular access to television and radio.

From 1983 onwards, I therefore resolved that our party would concentrate its entire resources, such as they were, on a programme of **long-term** organisational development, with a view eventually to acquiring the resources necessary to make its voice heard properly by the nation, rather than continually butt its head against the brick wall of the electoral system in circumstances in which, as at present, it had no hope of making any significant dent.

This would not mean that electoral activity would be abandoned in its entirety; occasions could arise in which the investment of money and effort in election campaigns would pay off in terms of those campaigns providing us with a platform by which to make our name known and get our message across; but the choice of when and where to do this would have to be made very selectively, and with a view to such forays absorbing only a small portion of our overall resources and energies.

This strategy has become particularly necessary in view of the increase in parliamentary election deposits to £500.

For this reason and for others, it was decided that the party would not take part in the general election of 1987, although by that time the party was stronger, and its resources greater, than in 1983. The decision, though it caused some controversy at the time, was vindicated: in the aftermath of the election, the party remained in a healthy condition financially, and was thus able to go ahead with the next stage of its organisational development. Had it taken part in the 1987 election, the effort would have left it financially exhausted, and almost certainly with few votes to its name in a political climate that had not changed fundamentally since four years earlier.

I am in no doubt that, ultimately, the ballot box is the only possible path open to British Nationalism to win political power. Those who talk of other means being employed are just emitting so much hot air which betrays a woeful incomprehension of political conditions existing in Britain. 'Armed uprisings' and other similar fantasies do not stand the slightest hope of success, and even the tiniest steps in such a direction would set us all back to square one by landing our entire leadership and active cadres in prison for decades to come. I have, furthermore, analysed in a previous chapter the possibilities of achieving political success for our movement by working within one of the established political parties. I regard those possibilities as amounting to a big zero, as I have made clear.

An open nationalist challenge at the polls therefore remains the one possible avenue by which we may succeed; but, while accepting this, we must be realistic in recognising that it must be a challenge mounted under conditions far more favourable to us than those we have encountered in the past. Two vital needs must be met in this regard: we must have at our disposal the organis- ational machinery — in particular, the facilities of mass media — to make our challenge effective; secondly, conditions in the country must have evolved yet further in the direction of disintegration and collapse than has hitherto been the case.

I am not in the slightest doubt that this is going to happen. I take no pleasure in the prospect of it happening, any more than one takes pleasure in seeing one's dearest friend or relative suffer intense physical pain. Yet there are times when the pain is necessary as part of the process whereby the patient must be convinced of the need for the surgery that has to be undertaken for his recovery. It is the same with nations that have reached the condition now afflicting Britain.

Our party is small today — that I have acknowledged. But I do not consider its size at the present time to be of prime importance.

What is of prime importance is that it develops to the right size — at the right time and with the emergence of the right opportunity. All our efforts at the present moment are dedicated to preparation for that event. The event will come, and when it does come we shall be ready to fulfil our role and our mission. My life is dedicated to this purpose, and with me are many more who are of the same dedication. With every week our numbers grow. No power on earth will now stop the force that we have created.

Our immediate task in the time ahead of us is to create a new climate of public opinion. A part of that task is already accomplished, in so far as there is already a strong consensus of support for our policies on such issues as Immigration, Law and Order, the Common Market and many more besides. What still remains to be done is to convince millions that only through the vehicle of British Nationalism can their aspirations on these issues be properly realised, and that only by placing massed support behind an entirely new political movement can they make possible the victory of British Nationalism.

As will have been made clear in what has already been said in this book, I regard the **mass media** as a greater enemy of everything we fight for, and everything that is good for Britain, than any of the opposing political parties. It therefore follows that, in the coming phase of our struggle, the task of creating an effective challenge to the power of that mass media, of beating the media in the battle of ideas, is more important than anything we do in the arena of pure party politics. We must build an alternative machinery of mass communication, and through it perform an educating role that will entirely change the climate in which political issues in Britain are judged. Only after that task has been largely accomplished should we attempt again to make a strong impact in parliamentary or local elections.

We will engage in specific projects in the latter field, where and when an opportunity exists for us to obtain some concrete benefit from so doing. But this activity will for the moment have a lesser priority than the opinion-forming campaign which must for the present occupy most of our attention.

At the same time, we have to continue the work of building a firm and indestructible nationwide organisation. This means finding, by patient pruning and sometimes by trial and error, the right personnel, with the right attitude and necessary commitment, to staff and lead our movement in every area of the country and in every department of affairs. Here, as I will have made clear, I am looking, not for 'politicians', but for dedicated crusaders for a great ideal, who are prepared to work and fight for that ideal through fair weather and foul, through good times and bad. Of course such people, or at least a portion of them, must be capable of working effectively in the political field — as a means to an end; but in their attitudes and motivation they must be as remote from today's conventional parliamentarians as if they belonged to a different species.

And these party operatives, in addition to their individual attributes, must be capable of working together as a **team**. As I have indicated before, at the smallest sign of factionalism those responsible will find themselves on the outside in the twinkling of an eye. This is of course without prejudice to their right to engage in constructive argument and criticism at the right place and time.

Though the aims of our movement must be pursued primarily through political methods, those aims embrace a field of human activity that ranges far beyond the merely political. It is our purpose, as we develop and as available personnel and resources permit, to become an embryo of the kind of society we want to see created in Britain. We must identify ourselves with every force and every tendency for national regeneration, in social, cultural, spiritual and recreational, as well as political, fields. My desire is to see instituted, long before our political victory becomes possible, many of the organisations, movements and policies advocated in this book, such as rural renewal, artistic, musical and literary counter-revolution, and the formation of associations for the promotion of physical culture and fitness — particularly among the young.

In this way, the target of political power for nationalism becomes merely one — albeit the most important one — of our goals. It means that target no longer represents a point of progress before which everything is impotence and after which everything is victory, success and power; victories, successes and a degree of power can be won far in advance of the achievement of this target — by the mere creation and expansion of these healthy trends which we wish to see implanted in Britain.

In effect, our purpose is to be a force for everything that is healthy, wholesome and regenerative in British life. Already we are able to record small victories in this regard, and quite soon we will be able to record bigger ones. Far better that we fix our eyes on these immediately or shortly feasible objectives and work to realise them rather than be obsessed with more distant objectives that at present are far beyond our means.

This then is the role of the British National Party. It is a role in which idealism is harnessed to realism, the distantly desirable reconciled with the immediately possible. The former **will** be attained, but I cannot and will not set a timetable for its attainment. The latter we are attaining already, with progress visible with every day that goes by.

Chapter 22
The way ahead

We live under a state that is terminally sick, in the manner of a political, economic, social and spiritual AIDS. Lacking the built-in natural immunity that is to be found in all healthy body organisms, it is vulnerable to every germ and shock that the world climate may blow its way. For this state, every week is a crisis, as it wriggles vainly to cope with some fresh problem arising from out of its own insoluble internal tensions and contradictions. Its death is certain; the only remaining uncertainty is that of the precise moment when it expires.

It is a state whose entire structure is built on foundations of untruth. Firstly, there is the regular diet of untruth ladled out to the people concerning the meaning of the daily events reported in the newspapers — on those occasions, by no means without exception, when such events are allowed to be reported at all.

Secondly, there is the untruth concerning the nature of the society and political system under which we live: an untruth which proclaims, as part of daily catechism, that we are all 'free' people, whereas we are in reality slaves, spiritually incarcerated within prison walls of conformity which most of us cannot see. Only those of us know those walls are there who have made the effort to cross over them.

Day in, day out, when trains do not run, when factories are on strike, when inner city mobs are rioting and when national assets are being sold off to the highest foreign bidder, the soothing lullaby is purred in our ears that we must consider ourselves lucky because we enjoy a heritage of 'freedom'; but in the end, when the sleep is washed from our eyes we find that this 'freedom' consists of no more than the facility to mark a cross, every so often, beside the name of one or other of the ventriloquist's dolls of parliament or town council seated on the knee of the grinning Moloch of money power who pays all the party pipers and calls all the tunes.

Finally, there is the supreme untruth concerning the nature of our world and history, which has become standard teaching everywhere. Conservatives who rail against left-wing propaganda in the classroom seem to have only the tiniest conception of the phenomenon of which they speak, for were it otherwise they would know that this propaganda is only the apex of a pyramid of falsehood underpinning almost the whole of the education of the last three or four generations. Historical untruth got its foot in the school door a long time ago, and today's perverted textbooks are merely the logical end product of an educational process that started swapping fiction for fact before most of us were born. Few people understand that in this gigantic intellectual swindle the left is no greater offender than the conventional 'right'.

And in the mass media, as much as in education, the world we live in, and the history giving rise to it, are mere distorted images, designed to give backing to the policies of state no less than in the Soviet system to which we are thought to be opposed. In these images the great men are villains and the villains great men, the good works evil and the evil works good. Triumphs are disasters and disasters are triumphs. Friends are enemies and enemies are friends.

Total honesty is impossible in politics, just as it is in war, where subterfuge naturally has to be employed to deceive one's enemy. But there is a difference between the small fib employed as a necessary manoeuvre in the game of power — and power itself built on top of a Mount Everest of deceit, with the entire ideology of state maintained by means of a fraudulent prospectus. Yet the latter is not an inappropriate description of the racket by which life in Britain is presently governed.

Politically, we are currently in the midst of a period of Conservative hegemony, which shows no sign of abating for some while. But this is a hegemony which owes nothing whatever to any merit of achievement in national government, only to the almost complete absence of any strong and credible opposition — this and the maintenance of a propaganda offensive, backed up by most of the press, which puts across daily the fable that Britain is embarked on a programme of 'recovery', whereas the truth is that she is sliding ever more deeply into ruin.

In every aspect of contemporary British politics the habit is to try to 'square the circle', to make work that which will not work. The present form of parliamentary 'democracy' as a method for the translation of the popular will into political action has become a stale joke. Yet the greater the evidence of this the greater the intransigence with which the system is defended and the shriller the cry of 'wolf!' against those who would question it. An economic doctrine that has emaciated industry and delivered over

3 millions to idleness is persisted in as if no other were conceivable. The response to inner city deterioration is yet more promises of open cheques, bearing the signature of the taxpayer, while almost everyone with a wit to rub against the other knows that money has almost nothing to do with the problem. Pious speeches against mounting crime are a weekly ritual, while those making them know in their bones that, within the limits of what is 'acceptable' policy, nothing will be done, or can be done, to reverse the trend.

Meanwhile, the lunacy of 'race equality' has become the national religion in a manner reminiscent of pre-reformation frenzy, with every unbeliever a candidate for the stake.

And in the global field the phantoms of internationalism and 'one world' paralyse all searchings for a policy that will ensure British survival.

In the great institutions of state an abiding putrescence is everywhere. The councils of every imaginable public body are packed with squalid, mediocre little time-servers, drawing inflated salaries and expenses while they reduce to shambles almost every enterprise they undertake. About our political leaders there is a depressing sameness which transcends superficial party differences, as they lisp the familiar slogans of the parliamentary custard-pie fight that everyone has heard a thousand times before. They are of course, without exception, merely sales assistants, messenger boys and clerks, working in the service of much more powerful people who, behind the scenes, determine real policy. The little tricks that they try to pull over each other in order to score points in the party game are nauseating to the nostrils of anyone with the instinct to perceive the reality of national decay surrounding them.

The political rot, however, is only a part of a much more general rot. Our entire national life is in the grip of degenerative forces, which barely leave one small area of affairs unaffected, as they run amok like maggots invading a diseased carcass, filtering through everywhere as resistance wanes. As I have indicated in an earlier chapter, from Cornwall to Caithness, from Londonderry to Kent, as the daily toil ends and the working members of the family return home, the press of a little knob condemns the nation to another evening of poison, spewed out into every drawing room by highly specialised professional liars, misinformers, mindbenders and traders in dirt and drivel. By this technique, and in a manner perceptible only to an informed few, a once vigorous and healthy race is being alienated from its roots, robbed of its heritage and held spiritual captive while being deluded that it enjoys 'liberty'.

And if those same people who sit and swallow the pigswill served up to them by means of the silver screen should on a Sunday morning venture out to their local place of worship they will in all probability receive a message from the pulpit which counsels them in the virtues of marxism, pacifism, race suicide, national defencelessness and prayers for the mugger and the rapist — while saying almost nothing in support of the morals that lead to the rule of law, good health and the stability of home and family.

Almost every influence, every example and every suggestion to which our people are today subjected by their 'leaders' in thought and behaviour is in fact conducive to the further disintegration of our national life and culture, and the rendering of Britain a permanent invalid among the nations.

Having stated these facts, I would be wrong to say that they are not widely recognised; indeed they are a regular topic of conversation almost everywhere where normal people meet and talk. I claim no novelty in such a diagnosis of the national situation. Even in our controlled daily press, admission of the state of things, albeit very incomplete, is by no means unknown.

But what is not yet fully grasped is the depth of the root of the sickness and the radical nature of the means needed to overcome it. Too many people still see and talk about only the **symptoms** of what is wrong. Only a few are prepared to give their minds to the **causes** — and fewer still to the **causes of the causes**. It is my conviction that if we really are to understand the ills of Britain in the 1980s we must see them as the logical and inevitable result of a process of faulty national development extending well back into the previous century. Institutions do not lend themselves to infiltration, take-over and internal corruption on the present scale unless they possess in the first place some fundamental weakness. Likewise the fashionable doctrines of national degeneracy that hold such wide sway today could not ever have infected a climate of ideas that was basically healthy.

What many people regard as the 'lunatic left', for instance, is a growth that first needed fertile soil for its germination. That soil existed in the atmosphere of **liberalism** that preceded the growth, and in the system of values which in that atmosphere had gained widespread acceptance in our society. It was liberalism which, over many decades, eroded the once sturdy national and racial spirit of our educated classes, thus paving the way for a marxist creed which requires the elimination of that spirit as an essential precondition for its advance. It was liberalism which, over many decades, undermined belief in a strong state authority, thus removing society's armour against all the forces of subversion within the national borders. It was liberalism which hastened moral deterioration and atrophy of clear and robust thought, helping to create legions of sick morons who have now become the commissars of our town councils and world of 'education'.

It is liberalism that lowers society's defences against the marxist infection by paralysing that society's faculty for recognising its enemies, to say nothing of its will to fight and defeat them.

If we are seriously to grapple with the chaos of the present day and formulate a creed and movement for national rebirth, our thinking must begin with an utter rejection of liberalism and a dedication to the resurgence of authority.

As such, it must entail the embrace of a political outlook which is, in relation to the present, **revolutionary**.

Nothing less will suffice. If our established institutions of state were basically sound but just in a momentary condition of misuse, a conservative position would be, as I have said before, still tenable, and I would be among those who would support that position. As it is, I believe that these institutions are rotten at their very foundations, and are destined inexorably to succumb. As I have also said previously, the only question is when they will do so — to which should be added the question of by what they will be replaced.

I am certain that they will inevitably be replaced by institutions rooted in marxism and communism — unless we are prepared to opt for a radical and dynamic alternative, and do so soon. The revolutionary left, whatever the falsehood of its doctrine, has a certain crude vitality and dynamism that make it irresistible when confronted only by the rearguard of the old 'liberal democracy'. Alone among the political movements in present fashion, it can summon great enthusiasm and dedication in its followers. Alone, it has a vision of the future for which people will fight. Alone, it has that certainty of faith that is essential to the will to win.

The future belongs to marxism and communism unless they are opposed by a doctrine and movement equal in the fervour with which they are believed in, equal in their certainty of faith and equal in the dedication of their followers.

At a recent Conservative conference, Mrs. Thatcher called for her party to enter into a crusade.

That is certainly what is needed; but equally certainly Conservatism is incapable of undertaking it. Just a look around at the faces in the conference hall revealed that they were not those of people who are crusading material by the wildest stretch of imagination. And a look at the most recent Conservative election manifesto will show that it has about as much crusading flavour as a limp kipper.

The policies set out in this manifesto appeal only to material ambition, selfishness and greed. They are unheroic. They are static.

And it is precisely a creed of heroism that is needed now to turn the tide of British history at this eleventh hour, a creed that will call forth all the finest attributes of manhood that sent our forebears across the oceans in their small boats in the drive to empire, a creed that will unite the British Nation into a true **community**, capable of undertaking the gigantic works of national reconstruction to which we must apply ourselves if we are to have a future, a creed by which we may achieve a new renaissance of the British genius in all the creative arts and sciences and hurl back the forces of decadence that now threaten to engulf us.

I have attempted in this book to present the outlines of such a creed. The book is not an election manifesto — although victory at elections must be the ultimate means by which we attain the power to act. It makes no attempt to pander to the idiocies and prejudices that are the political currency of the moment. It is addressed to a select circle of people in Britain and elsewhere with minds unrestricted by conventional boundaries of debate, people who are seriously concerned for posterity and are prepared to work for it.

It will be recognised from what has been written that the doctrine being put forward is much more than just political. It embraces every aspect of the life of the nation and its members, for nothing less than a total reformation of personal, as well as national, values can bring about the renewal that we need.

Indeed, it is within the individual that this renewal must begin. No revolutionary change in society can occur except through every person aspiring to that change first undergoing a revolution within himself. This means an adjustment, where necessary, to new habits of living as well as to new values. It means a wholesale rejection of our contemporary civilisation, with its worship of the deformed, the diseased and the decayed, and the quest for a new order of truth and beauty, built by a higher breed of people.

Ironically, those who wish to save Britain and open up a splendid future for her must be prepared to reject many ideas popularly but quite falsely held to be 'British', even 'patriotic'. We must not confuse those real national virtues that led to our mighty success and expansion as a race with the traits with which today our enemies flatter us — precisely because they are the traits that make us a 'soft touch'. True patriotism, as I have hinted before, lies in the nurturing of all that is strong, healthy and vital in our nation, and the casting out of everything that weakens, however deeply instituted.

In every way possible we must draw from the best of our own national traditions the inspiration for the movement of British revival of which we are part. Every great nation must stage its own awakening in its own way, and with methods appropriate to its own particular national character and genius. In an earlier chapter I related my brief involvement in, and later my decisive rejection of, politics resting on imported terminology, paraphernalia and symbolism, and with its pantheon of heroes who, whatever their merits or demerits, have no part of **our** history. Today, down to the minutest detail I strive to ensure that our movement draws its building materials from home sources, even to the point of a preference for melodies originating in the British Isles as the music for party songs.

Nevertheless, it is inevitable that parallels are going to be drawn between at least some of the policies we advocate for national reconstruction in Britain and policies carried out in similar fields by other nations at other times, and with the lumping of all together under some blanket description, the most popular of which is 'fascism'. Our opponents will see to it that this is done, whatever we may do or say to the contrary.

So what is 'fascism'? It is a word of Italian origin used to describe the programme carried out in Italy by Mussolini between 1922 and 1943. It is no part of our language and we do not need it. Be that as it may though, 'fascism' has entered the dictionary as a term employed to cover almost every conceivable kind of patriotic and national doctrine of the 20th century, and in so doing has lost all its original precision. Today it means just about anything that people want it to mean, according to their viewpoint.

There are two extremes of reaction to this state of affairs, and both are equally foolish.

One is to copy to the letter the name, programme, symbols and ritual used by some foreign movement of the past, be it that of Mussolini or Hitler, and attempt to resurrect it — right down to the last belt buckle.

The other is to jump like a scalded cat and bolt in panic in the opposite direction, trying so hard to prove to the world that one is not a 'fascist' or a 'nazi' that one abandons one firm political position after another, to the point at which there is none left. Nothing creates such a pathetic spectacle as those people who live in daily dread of being branded as 'fascists' or 'nazis' and are thus deterred from adopting any robust principles of politics at all.

We should reject both these foolish courses and be prepared to look at every political idea on its merits, regardless of the names people give to it and regardless of who may have adopted it, wholly or partially, in the past.

We must see today's professional 'anti-fascists' and 'anti-nazis' for what they are: people whose purpose is to impose a psychological terror which puts an end to all rational thought and discussion about anything — in a way similar to the 'anti-racism' of which I spoke in an earlier chapter. We must not allow the process of public debate to be controlled according to these people's rules.

If I happen to believe that a particular policy is good and right for Britain in our time, I am not going to be frightened of advocating it by the fact that a similar policy may have been carried out by fascists or national socialists in another country at another time.

And if British people generally are going to take effective action to win back control of their country and rebuild its prosperity and strength, they must first decide to immunise themselves psychologically against the shock impact of the 'fascist' label. There is absolutely no chance of doing anything meaningful to help the patriotic cause while escaping this label, and so everyone may as well learn to live with it and not worry about it.

Indeed, one of the barriers that has to be overcome is that of convincing people that there simply is no easy and comfortable way of winning this battle. A great many people would like to see the victory of a patriotic movement in Britain but delude themselves that there is some route to this objective in which we can avoid the confrontational politics of the kind in which people like me have been involved for years. Such people simply fail to comprehend the forces arrayed against our side and the fact that these forces will compel confrontation with us, whether we wish it or not. When such confrontation occurs, we have the option of standing our ground and defending ourselves or packing up and going home. We have chosen to stand our ground. Inevitably, when this happens disorders occur. They are not of our making and not our wish. Almost invariably, however, they are reported in the media in such a way as to suggest that they are at least as much our fault as that of our opponents. People see or hear these reports and form the view that we go about deliberately looking for trouble. "If only you did not do that," they often say to us, "you would get so much more support." The truth is of course that we do not look for trouble at all, but it pursues us and will continue to do so as long as the forces of left-wing mob power are allowed the licence they presently enjoy in Britain.

As the old system slides ever further into anarchy and chaos, the moment for the emergence of a dynamic new force in British politics draws nearer. Can we establish such a force and win political power in the time left to us? In affirming that we can, I am in no doubt as to the formidable obstacles that first have to be overcome.

The first and most obvious of these is the entrenched power of the establishment and interests against which we fight. While these enemies have shown complete ineptitude in governing and managing Britain, they are highly organised and capable when it comes to defending their own positions and institutions against any movement of real change. Something of the workings of this system of power and corruption I have attempted to reveal in this book.

The second major obstacle is a strong indisposition on the part of many British people, not only towards political action, but towards political radicalism of any kind. This observation is today true of white, western peoples generally but it is particularly true of our own people.

A consequence of this national temperament is that great political changes, when they occur in our country, do not occur quickly. The first Labour government in Britain, for instance, was formed in 1924. The idea of British Socialism, however, had been present in these islands for much longer, its development extending back into the distant mists of the 19th century.

It will be clear from what I have said earlier that British Nationalism as an idea is by no means new. It is only new as an instrument of action, in which role it has yet to be applied. Earlier in this book I have given accounts of its early infancy in the pre-1914 period, its coming to maturity between the wars and its revival after the Second World War. British Nationalism, like British Socialism, has been no overnight growth.

It would be wholly wrong to draw from this, as some pessimists do, that because nationalism has not in all these years achieved political power, or even won widespread mass support, it cannot do so in the future. Such a conclusion would be as mistaken now as it was about socialism earlier this century.

The pioneers of socialism had to wait with patience for their moment of destiny, allowing natural historical forces to make possible the advent of socialism as a power factor in Britain. The important thing is that, when that moment arrived, socialists had ready the political machine needed to exploit it, and thus turn into a potent political force what had previously only been an idea and a vision in the minds of a comparative few.

Exactly the same rule governs the coming of the moment of destiny for our own movement.

I have emphasised earlier that all great historical changes in societies are brought about, not by masses, but by highly organised minorities.

If a particular political ideology has no mass support, it is not necessarily because there is no disposition within the mass to support it; rather is it much more likely because there simply is not a sufficiently strong and organised minority to provide the apparatus by which such mass support can be mobilised.

A very high proportion of the population may hold opinions on current issues which are in accord with the policies of a particular reforming movement; but that does not mean that that movement is certain to enjoy practical support in the same proportion. If it does not possess the necessary organisational apparatus — and popular confidence — for it to be considered a **power factor** in the politics of the nation, its support will be mostly silent and passive; it will not be translated into either mass membership or large numbers of votes.

There is another factor of enormous importance. There is a deep-rooted timidity, even cowardice, in the masses which inhibits them from supporting any cause which, while on the one hand seeming to be highly controversial and attracting strident opposition, does not on the other hand seem to have powerful forces working for it to defend it in this controversy and combat such opposition.

This is a strange and interesting phenomenon. In times of war, large numbers of people from out of the mass of a population can be capable of displaying a high order of courage, with many men, young and not so young, willing to risk their lives in battle, and many of all ages and both sexes on the home front showing great fortitude in the face of bombing and the several privations that attend their lives in such a situation.

Yet these same people, even including men who have been fighter pilots or tank or submarine commanders, can become petrified rabbits in the face of pressures to conform to the current political orthodoxies and to avoid identification with any brand of politics deemed to be current heresy. This paradox is particularly common among Anglo-Saxons.

I am certain that it is this factor that lies behind the customary protestation by many British people that they are against any form of political 'extremism'.

In an earlier chapter I looked a little into the question of 'extremism' and identified the term as an entirely relative one, the meaning of which is determined by those in a position to fix the central location on the map of politics and thereby decide what is to be the ruling 'orthodoxy'. If tomorrow these masters changed, and a new 'orthodoxy' became the vogue, the masses in Britain, and probably any other Anglo-Saxon country, would find no difficulty whatever in embracing it. That which had been yesterday's 'extremism' would today become a quite respectable viewpoint!

In fact, what we have today is the maintenance of an entirely artificial climate of opinion by means of the creation of an atmosphere of **fear**. In this respect Britain has become similar to the very 'totalitarian' countries to which she is always proclaiming herself morally superior.

Lurking in the minds of many millions are feelings of discontent about present policies, deepening into disgust with the whole established order. But these feelings are largely suppressed due to the psychological intimidation of the state machine and its various agencies, of which the mass media are by far the most important.

In the case of many people, these natural inner feelings are suppressed by the individual even before they can crystallise into actual thought. A kind of 'policeman' of the mind tells him: "No, attractive though that idea may be, you are not allowed to hold it!" With others, the process may go a stage further: the policeman is disobeyed, and feelings and thought become one. 'Heretical' opinions are actually held, with no inhibitions of the 'liberal' conscience suppressing them when they stir. But they continue to be held secretly. Thought of social ostracism, even harm to one's business or career, is a deterrent to open profession of faith. In some there is even the preparedness to go further than this and actually give voice to such opinions, but even here there is a widespread reluctance to think through and acknowledge their full political consequences in terms of the national changes needed to give effect to such wishes. The end is desired, but there is a shirking of the means.

And finally there is the factor that has been mentioned earlier. The politically discontented individual still has the tendency to clutch at straws. Even when he has reached the point of recognising the desirability of an entirely new political force in the country, the fact that he cannot at the moment see one on the horizon that is likely to win power within the short time-scale of his own thinking drives him back into the arms of whomever he sees as the least evil among the political options currently on offer. He votes, as I have indicated, to influence the outcome of today's election rather than create possibilities for tomorrow's.

These are in the forefront of the difficulties we face, but none of them is insurmountable; they can be overcome by an intelligent grasp of the factors of mass psychology making for them, and then a determined application of the lessons thus learned.

The first and most vital point we must understand is that millions who do not support us while we are weak will in fact support us when we are strong.

The very evidence of the growth in the strength of a movement and idea confers a corresponding growth in the respectability of it. Just as in business money makes money, so in politics strength generates strength.

The left knows this rule very well. By applying it, it has made a great number of habits, cults and ideas which in the past were not accepted now widely accepted — by the simple method of persuading people that so many now adhere to them they have become quite normal — and cannot anyway be stopped!

We, on our part, must understand that only a little way beneath the surface is a vast wave of support for what we stand for, which today is withheld due to the thought that we are small and weak, but which will burst forth as we demonstrate that we are becoming larger and stronger.

Every great reforming movement in history has begun by being built around the nucleus of a tiny minority. It has begun by being shunned by most people, not because of the repellence of what it stands for, but because of its **weakness**. In that situation, only a few intrepid spirits join it.

Provided that those spirits stay together and retain their inner cohesion, while determinedly fighting to promote their ideas, a few more will, bit by bit, enlist in their ranks. Initial progress may well be tortuously slow. Some of those who joined will be discouraged by this and will drop out. This should not be a matter for dismay, for it only indicates a sound process of natural selection at work, weeding out the weaker elements.

At times, whatever the energy with which the cause is promoted, progress may stand still — because existing conditions do not permit growth. But always, if the cause is right, those conditions will change: some new event will occur which will alter the situation and give a new impetus to growth.

Gradually, the tiny nucleus will expand into a somewhat more substantial force. The movement will still be very much outside the 'mainstream', and therefore will retain the aspect of 'non-respectability' — but not quite so much so as previously. Its growth potential will correspondingly widen.

And so on until eventually it breaks through by the sheer force of its own crusading will, combined with the pressure of the events happening around it, which will vindicate its stand. At every stage, it will be the magnetic pull of **growing strength** that will provide a large part of the impetus for development. Without that strength, neither the dedication of its adherents nor the evidence of its intrinsic rightness, would ever provide the necessary attraction to the masses to support it.

I have always therefore seen our movement as having the task of breaking through a certain credibility barrier, which we have to do by demonstrating, not the soundness of our ideas, but the evidence of our growing strength. In terms of membership size, the first 10,000 is the hardest to recruit, the job of turning that 10,000 into 20,000 less hard, and so on. In terms of votes at elections, it will be the first 5 per-cent of the poll that is the hardest to win. After that, people are likely to become persuaded that we may eventually have a chance to get candidates elected, and thus will our vote be increased.

I always urge upon our various active units that getting our message across to the public is useless if it is done in such a way as to display weakness. If public demonstrations are mounted in any area, extra members must be drafted in from other areas so as to give an impression of numbers. This is not only necessary from the standpoint of the physical safety of our demonstrators in the face of likely attacks by our opponents; it is also important as a psychological weapon.

In our circles, the questions are often asked: "When will the British people wake up and rise against their misgovernors? When will the big backlash come that ought to come against the appalling policies that have been imposed upon the nation for so many years?"

The very phrasing of such questions shows a misunderstanding of how great political changes really occur. 'The people' as a whole never 'wake up' or 'rise' against anything. In the mass, they are totally inert. There never is any 'backlash' in the sense implicit in the question quoted.

Any awakening must always be on the part of a public-spirited and politically active minority. Any backlash is the backlash that that minority sets in motion. For even when a political movement has attained sufficient strength to become a real national force, contending for political power, its members still comprise, along with the members of all the other political parties put together, a relatively small part of the population.

It is this reality that renders so inane the slogans currently adopted by the other parties about 'people's power' and those parties' claims that people (the mass of the people, that is to say) should "take a greater part in the decision-making process." Such ideas are wholly contrary to the true nature of people in the mass, who want neither 'power', nor the right to make decisions (other than at a purely personal and domestic level). People in the mass **do** want a strong and purposeful national authority that will exercise power and make decisions for them — albeit that those decisions should be in accordance with their own deepest instincts of right and wrong; but that is something else entirely.

The British people in large numbers will translate their inner feelings about national affairs into support for nationalism at the polls when, and only when, a national and patriotic political force has been established which is big enough, strong enough and with a voice loud enough to make its presence felt throughout the land on a scale that puts it among the front runners in politics and gives it the image of irresistible **power**. Until then, that public will shirk the decisive step needed, and cling instead to its old political habits.

Such power as I have described must of course include the

capability to expose, by information and enlightenment, any attempts by political parties of 'establishment' pedigree to head off the nationalist challenge by the fraudulent adoption of what appear to be similar policies — tactics which, as I have demonstrated earlier, were widely employed by the Conservatives in the general election of 1979.

Supporters of our party express a great deal of outrage when the party or its representatives are in some way viciously and unjustly treated, whether this be by the imprisonment of its leaders, the denial to it of its rights of assembly or some distorted reporting on it in the media. Of course such outrage should be felt and expressed, and whatever protest is within our means should be mounted. But I always counsel our people to recognise that this is going to be our fate just for as long as we are small and without power. If 50 to 100 people hold a protest demonstration against a particular injustice, no notice is likely to be taken of it. If 10,000 to 20,000 do so, it is a very different matter. The injustice may be equal in both cases: the merits of the protest may be the same. But in the latter instance the protest is much more likely to hit home. We British like to indulge in a little national narcissism concerning our supposed sense of 'fair play'. My own observation, based on much experience, is that there is little real 'fair play' in this country, or anywhere else, for the opponent of the system who does not have the muscle to defend himself and hit back. In this world, weak political movements, like weak nations, are liable to be kicked, and assuredly will be kicked. Only the strong can ultimately assert their right to justice.

The supreme challenge to our movement is the test of our capability to stand firm and persevere through the process of maturing from a small nucleus into a viable and nationally recognisable political force in Britain, after which the momentum of our own gathering strength will be the fuel driving us forward. In this maturing process the most vital need of all is that our movement becomes and remains **united**, and that we guard against the suicidal tendency to splintering that has wrecked past opportunities. This is the reason for my policy of ruthlessly throwing out any elements that show signs of exercising a divisive role.

Running constantly throughout this book has been the theme of an 'enemy within', contriving the destruction of British nationhood; and the manner in which that enemy has been portrayed may well convey the impression of formidable power intruding into every corner of British life. That power should certainly not be underestimated. We would be in grave error, however, if we fell into the trap of regarding it as omnipotent. Evident everywhere in 'the system' is the proof of its weakness: the meagre calibre of public men that it brings to the fore, its puerile level of public debate, its terror of allowing into that debate people and ideas to which it has no answer, its manifest failure in every branch of national affairs to which its resources have been applied.

I began this chapter by saying that this system is headed for inevitable collapse, and that is indeed my conviction. Every development in public affairs points to it.

Concomitant to this, we should not underestimate the potentially titanic strength of the forces opposed to what is being done within the system and which belong, in fact, on our side. These include many tens of thousands of ordinary members of, not only the Conservative Party, but the Labour and other parties too, not to forget the many active and public-spirited people in the ranks of Ulster Unionism, in its various factions. Finally, we should not exclude those thousands who were active in the nationalist movement in the 1970s but who subsequently dropped out, not because they had changed their opinions or sentiments, but because of their frustration at our failure to break through into the 'big time' of politics as quickly as they had hoped.

All these elements amount to what is potentially a gigantic army of national resistance and resurgence. It only needs to be mobilised into a single and co-ordinated force for political action. Somewhere a catalyst must, and will, emerge that will bring about this mobilisation. When it comes, the force it will represent will be irresistible.

But before this can happen a number of prerequisites are needed. One of them I have touched upon already earlier in this chapter, and that is that a great many people must overcome this hypnosis exercised by the words 'extremist' and 'extremism'. Apart from the considerations I have mentioned, it must be understood that Britain today is in a situation of **extreme crisis**, in which forces of **extreme evil** threaten her on all sides. 'Extremism' in the way of opposition to these forces is in no way wrong. The way to fight the extreme of evil is by means of the extreme of good. People must cast away their fear of this 'extremist' label, and concentrate their minds on what is wrong and what is right; they must look at the issues and judge those issues on the merits of the arguments raging over them, not be led astray by mere catchwords.

Another vital need is that people, in the tens of thousands, break out of the straightjacket of the old parties, and rid themselves of the idea that only within those parties can they accomplish anything politically useful. The fact is that the precise opposite is true. The old parties, and the not so old Democrats and SDP, simply tie down great numbers of people in a political dead end who could otherwise be organised to bring about great national change — for these parties are so constituted, controlled and led that they will do precisely **nothing** to halt the slide to disaster upon which Britain is presently set.

There is a further need which needs strong emphasis. In various places throughout this book I have pinpointed the role of **money** in making for political power. It is indeed the crucial role, for behind every degenerative and nationally ruinous tendency that we can see in British life money will be found providing the fuel and giving the direction.

If a great movement with policies for national recovery is to be created, vast resources of money will be needed to make that movement possible. Money is required for the construction of an effective political machine, with full-time professional operatives in every area. Money is needed to create a counter-media to oppose the mass media of the present, with the inestimable billions that it has behind it. Money must purchase the amenities for the patriotic message to be properly heard.

In this regard, patriots of the British race must learn something from the example of those of other races, notably the Jews, whose money power has set up the juggernaut of World Zionism. Zionism is today powerful — some would say all-powerful — precisely because within the Jewish community everywhere there is ample number of people prepared to put huge funds at the disposal of those who operate the international Zionist power machine. As long as this remains a fact, and as long as those who are the victims of this power machine are unprepared to put their own money where their sentiments are and finance a machine to counter it, it could be said that there is some justice — however disagreeable it is to ourselves — in the hegemony that the Zionists enjoy.

Just half a dozen patriotic British millionaires prepared to make available a mere 10 per-cent of their wealth to finance the nationalist movement in this country would make possible a huge stride forward in that movement's development. Of course it would only be a start, and many millions — indeed billions — more would be needed to continue the process. But such a start would give us a momentum which would in time generate much further growth, and in accordance with the laws that I have stated.

Such sacrifices would be small in relation to the means of such people — far, far smaller than the sacrifices made by humble people of my acquaintance over many years. As I write these words, I am reminded of an elderly couple in the western part of the Greater London Area who regularly send us cheques of £100 or £50. I know their means are very modest, and that they cannot really afford this generosity, any more than we can afford to refuse it! These people put to shame others of much more substantial means whose contributions do not even match theirs in absolute terms, let alone proportionately.

If the people of wealth in the ranks of the British Race are not prepared, at this time of crisis, to finance properly those who are working to save their race, then the race assuredly will not deserve to survive and most certainly will go under.

But if such financial backing is forthcoming, and if the vast legions of those with patriotic instincts find the will to coalesce together in a proper movement for political change, the forces of darkness, degeneracy, subversion and treason now rampant in our land can be swept away and the dawning of a new era of national greatness be heralded.

In this book I have emphasised the national and British interest, and called for the building in Britain of a movement of nationalism. This is necessary because Britain is our country and it must come first in our priorities — along with those other countries sharing with us the British heritage.

But none of this should obscure the fact that, at a certain level, our struggle is global — just as we are confronted by a global enemy. I have acknowledged our spiritual and intellectual debt to nationalist thinkers of the era preceding 1914, and it is a considerable one. But in our thinking today and in the future nationalism must take on something of a different dimension to the one dominant at that stage of history. Over and above the rivalries of nations, there is the transcendent interest of Western Civilisation, Western Culture and — as the creator of these things — the White European Race. Here we must see 'The West', not in the form currently fashionable: as a coalition of nations organised in mutual defence of the dubious blessings of 'liberal democracy' and 'capitalism', but as a **cultural** and above all **racial** entity. In this regard, the peoples of Eastern Europe currently under communist rule are in truth part of the same entity.

In the policy of the future, notwithstanding the vigour with which we must pursue national interests, we must grasp the reality that such pursuit will in the end be counter-productive if it is at the expense of the wider interest of the white western peoples as a whole.

It is not necessary for me to spell out how these peoples have been, during this century, driven to mutual destruction in bogus 'national' causes by forces that were the common enemies of all. Nationalism in the future must be directed within, and not against, the greater cause of white western survival.

It is important for us to understand this particularly with respect to our relations with the United States of America. Present circumstances of politics compel us to take a stance of opposition to those currently controlling US policy. But this should not blind us to the fact that the vast mass of ordinary Americans in the hinterland behind these controllers are for the most part fellow Europeans and to no small degree Europeans of the same stock as our own. They, just as much as we, are the slaves and victims of the evil forces controlling both of our nations, and if those forces can be defeated both sides of the Atlantic nothing need stand in the way of a happy relationship between our peoples — though it may not be 'special' in the sense believed in by British Tories of the present day.

For all these reasons, our creed and cause, though they must begin with nationalism, must ultimately rise beyond nationalism to serve the paramount interest of **race**. This does not mean a repudiation of the national idea and the search for panaceas of 'world order' of the kind that are the present mode and which have been firmly rejected in this book; what it does mean is that our national concept must attain a maturity not present in some of those older ones, which set one white, western nationalism against another, sometimes in dispute over stretches of territory minute in proportion to the overall racial blood sacrifice in which such conflicts resulted.

For it is the West — the **true** West — and not just Britain and the lands of her overseas kindred, that is in deadly danger. The danger was seen by Oswald Spengler earlier this century and set out in his monumental work, *The Decline of the West*. Spengler was a German and a nationalist, but his vision and concern extended far beyond Germany and embraced the whole racial family and culture of which his own nation, like ours, is a part.

His thesis was that Western Civilisation, like other civilisations before it, had its natural life span, and that the West was coming to the end of its life span, having been drained of all the vital life forces that had given it its former strength and dominance. Spengler saw as symptoms of this impending death: political liberalism, internationalism and the dominance of money over politics. And he saw in the modern city, particularly, the quintessence of all the degenerative tendencies making for this creeping demise; he further saw in the modern intellectual the quintessential occupant of that city. Speaking of this relationship, he said:-

> "No wretchedness, no compulsion, not even a clear vision of the madness of this development, avails to neutralise the attractive force of these daemonic creations...Once the full sinful beauty of this last marvel of all history has captured a victim, it never lets him go. Primitive folk can loose themselves from the soil and wander, but the intellectual nomad never. Home sickness for the great city is keener than any other nostalgia. Home is for him any one of these giant cities, but even the nearest village is alien territory. He would sooner die upon the pavement than go 'back' to the land. Even disgust at this pretentiousness, weariness of the thousand-hued glitter, the *taedium vitae* that in the end overcomes many, does not set them free. They take the city with them into the mountains or on the sea. They have lost the country within themselves, and will never regain it outside."

Expanding on the same theme, Spengler then perfectly summed up the crisis of civilisation created through the reign of urban intellectualism throughout most of the Western World, saying:-

> "And then, when being is sufficiently uprooted and waking-being sufficiently strained, there suddenly emerges into the bright light of history a phenomenon that has long been preparing itself underground and now steps forward to make an end of the drama — **the sterility of civilised man**. This is not something that can be grasped as a plain matter of causality (as modern science naturally enough has tried to grasp it); it is to be understood as an essentially **metaphysical** turn towards death. The last man of the world-city no longer **wants** to live — he may cling to life as an individual, but as a type, as an aggregate, no; for it is a characteristic of this collective existence that it eliminates the terror of death. That which strikes the true peasant with an inexplicable fear, the notion that the family and the name may be extinguished, has now lost its meaning. The continuance of the blood-relation in the visible world is no longer a duty of the blood, and the destiny of being the last of the line is no longer felt as a doom. Children do not happen, not because children have become impossible, but principally because intelligence at the peak of intensity can no longer find any reason for their existence. Let the reader try to merge himself in the soul of

the peasant. He has sat on his **glebe** from primeval times, or has fastened his clutch in it, to adhere to it with his blood. He is rooted in it as the descendant of his forebears and as the forebear of future descendants. **His** house, **his** property, means, here, not the temporary connection of person and thing for a brief span of years, but an enduring and inward union of **eternal** land and **eternal** blood. It is only from this mystical conviction of settlement that the great epochs of the cycle — procreation, birth and death — derive that metaphysical element of wonder which condenses in the symbolism of custom and religion that all landbound people possess. For the 'last men' all this is past and gone. Intelligence and sterility are allied in old families, old peoples and old cultures, not merely because in each microcosm the overstrained and fettered animal-element is eating up the plant-element, but also because in the waking consciousness that being is normally regulated by causality. That which the man of intelligence, most significantly and characteristically, labels as 'natural impulse' or 'life-force', he not only knows, but values causally, giving it the place among his other needs that his judgement assigns to it. When the ordinary thought of a cultivated people begins to regard 'having children' as a question of *pros* and *cons*, the great turning point has come. For nature knows nothing of *pro* and *con*. Everywhere, wherever life is actual, reigns an inward organic logic, an 'it', a drive, that is utterly independent of waking-being, with its causal linkages, and indeed not even observed by it. The abundant proliferation of primitive peoples is a **natural phenomenon**, which is not even thought about, still less judged as to its utility or the reverse. When reasons have to be put forward at all in a question of life, life itself has become questionable. At that point begins prudent limitation of the numbers of births. In the classical world the custom was deplored by Polybius as the ruin of Greece, and yet even at his date it had long been established in the great cities; in subsequent Roman times it became appallingly general. At first explained by the economic misery of the times, very soon it ceased to explain itself at all. And at that point too, in Buddhist India as in Babylon, in Rome as in our own cities, a man's choice of the woman who is to be, not mother of his children, as among peasants and primitives, but his own 'companion for life', becomes a problem of mentalities. The Ibsen marriage appears, the 'higher spiritual affinity' in which both parties are 'free' — free, that is, as intelligences, free from the plantlike urge of the blood to continue itself; and it becomes possible for a Shaw to say 'that unless woman repudiates her womanliness, her duty to her husband, to her children, to society, to the law, and to everyone but herself, she cannot emancipate herself.' (Shaw, *The Quintessence of Ibsen*)."

In the last lines here we find an echo of 'modern' woman's objection to the restoration of the anti-abortion laws, in her claim that she has the 'right' to decide what to do with her own body. Of course! — just as everyone has the 'right' to destroy his or her own health by dissolute living — so long as, in the ethics of liberalism, it does not 'harm one's neighbour'. Gone is the duty to posterity, to the blood, to the task of continuance of family and race which Spengler pinpointed in the quoted passage. In the individual there may still exist the will to life; but in the stock there is only the will to extinction.

Parallel with the 'free' woman in this twilight of great cultures is the womanish man, who has been spotlighted in this book and who is the principal high priest and personification of liberalism in all its forms. Both are complementary components of racial decay, having both rejected the primary impulse of all healthy social organisms: the impulse to perpetuate the life of the species, in particular the life of the **strongest** and **best** of the species. Today the impulse of self-perpetuation survives only among the darker peoples of the world — a condition that, if not changed, and changed soon, will render the European White Man an obsolete breed.

The one central weakness in Spengler's analysis is that he did not anticipate the revolutionary challenges against these death forces that were to occur later in our century and which, though they have been momentarily defeated at the political level, live on as ideas and signposts from which we can draw the inspiration and the understanding that there exists a lifeline for the renewal of our civilisation that is there for the grasping if we can summon the determination to fight our way to the attainment of it. We can, in other words, prove Spengler wrong in his assertion that the West is finished; for the remedy to its potentially terminal sickness is indeed available, contrary to his own supposition when he wrote its epitaph. The formula for rebirth and renewal is on offer. Whether we have the wisdom and the will to take it is the great question that yet remains unanswered. Recent events in France, however, suggest that there is in that country a not insubstantial part of the population of a modern western state that is prepared to take the necessary step across the intimidating chasm between national death and national life — and this despite the fact that that people has been subjected over past years to all the same degenerative influences as those afflicting the people of our own land. This French example shows that the will to resurgence has not by any means been extinguished but burns strongly in the hearts of millions.

Here in Britain the instrument for the awakening of a similar will is still only in the infancy of its creation; and for the moment at least the political scene is doomed to be dominated by party combinations which, whatever their surface differences, are representative of the same underlying forces of national and western self-destruction. But behind the stage on which the old-world politicians enact their mock battles new forces and new ideas are stirring, though they are yet to be formed into a single powerful coalition that can make its strength felt in a contest for mass support, as has happened across the Channel.

I have attempted in this book to make some contributioɴ towards the ideas that will form the basis of, our own British movement of rebirth and reawakening that must take its place, alongside others, in the desperately needed renaissance of the West. Many of these ideas will seem strange, even outlandish, to those whose minds are still shackled within the perimeters of contemporary debate. In the foreword to the book I have stated my task as being to point forward to new horizons of political thought and action. I hope that those to whom the book is addressed will see in these horizons a vision of **grandeur** — for is it not grandeur that has become a despised, almost laughed-at, commodity in the politics of today, preoccupied as these are by the small and the mean, by the petty perspectives of the petty people who rule over them? We are told to deride as 'dangerous' the dreams of grandeur and greatness; yet is it not such dreams that have inspired all the mighty movements of men and ideas that have propelled the world forwards since the dawn of recorded history? Let us never dismiss those grand visions from our souls, for without them we become merely the lotus-eating remnants of exhausted nations and cultures. Let us acknowledge the fact that we fight for the coming of a new age of grandeur, beside which the present will appear as a mere anthill at the side of the road of British destiny. Let us march to the music of grandeur as we proceed along that road — and let the ideals of grandeur be our guiding stars as we call from within us those needed reserves of human resolve and spirit to sustain us in the epic struggle against the powers of decay that confront us at every bend!

This book has been given its title because of my belief that our country and people are approaching a time of supreme decision and supreme reckoning, at which, if the wrong path is taken, we will be committed to a course of self-destruction from which there will be no possibility of turning back.

Will Britain take that course and lapse into a dark age in which all vital forces of the national genius are extinguished and in which she abdicates from the world scene, immersing herself in ever more frivolous pleasures and childish amusements while history is made elsewhere? Will the degeneration of national life that has been evident for most of the present century, and at accelerating speed since World War II, continue unabated, while small-time political careerists, poseurs and shysters carry on their squalid and pathetic party fight like heirs of a fallen dukedom battling for the few pots and pans remaining of the family estate?

Should this be our choice, I see, as I have indicated, no prospect ahead but a gradual slide towards a type of society increasingly akin to communism, the tendencies of which can be seen today like a creeping green slime, filtering through into every branch of our political, intellectual, cultural and religious affairs.

Or will we take the alternative road, the road of resurgence and renewal, hurling back the degenerative forces in a mighty effort of the national will, and asserting again the qualities of manhood that in past ages gave us world leadership?

This vital question will be answered and resolved by our generation, and we should count it a privilege that we live at a time of great decision, a time that does not permit escape from the hard realities of historical choice but throws us down at the crossroads of destiny and confronts us with the options: life or death, future or extinction, the manly fight for national rebirth or the resigned acceptance of the descent into senility, ending with the expiry of every real asset of nationhood and every inheritance of race.

This book is addressed to those who have already made the former choice, and to those many more whose instinct is to make it if given the opportunity. Nowhere have I concealed the fact that the road ahead for us is long and hard and the pitfalls dangerous. We face the concentrated enmity and fury of the whole of the old world of politics. We face the lies and distortions of a corrupt press. We face the violence of the hate-crazed red mob. And we face the apathy born of false illusions of security and affluence. All these obstacles make our mission a hazardous one which will demand from us the highest exertions of staying power and valour of which man is capable.

Our creed is one of heroism, and the coming epoch calls for the return of the heroic virtues. Not for us the cosy tranquillity of the political soft option; for us only the long march through the cold night — which must precede the glorious dawn. These conditions demand a special quality of steel in those who rally to our banner, and if the forthrightness of the message put forward in this book frightens and puts off the delicate of fibre and of spirit, that is good; for their place is not with us and we would not wish to encumber ourselves with their presence.

Today, from out of the chaos and the ruins wrought by the old politics, new men are rising. These new men of the new age are now working night and day across the land to forge the sinews of the movement to which their lives and mine are dedicated. Above them as they work are the spirits of legions of mighty ancestors whose bones lie at the bottom of the oceans and beneath the soil of five continents where the men and women of our blood have borne the British flag and stamped the mark of British genius. Today we feel the voices of these past generations calling down to us in sacred union, urging us to be worthy of their example and their sacrifice. To them we owe it to fight on, and to dare all, so that a great land and a great race may live again in splendour.

INDEX

Abortion: 62, 264, 278-9, 313, 605
Abyssinia: 512
Aden: 473
Afghanistan: 528
Africa: 94-5, 123, 138, 305, 352, 459, 471, 473, 475, 479, 495-8, 503, 530, 534-6, 547
Afrikaners: 471-3
Agincourt, Battle of: 432
Agriculture: 119, 268, 278, 376-80
Alexander, A.: 421
Alliance (Lib/SDP), the: 155
Alsace-Lorraine: 536
American Colonies: 464-5, 471, 502-3
American Indians: 305, 467, 487
American War of Independence: 464, 471, 503, 523
Anglo-Irish, the: 440
Anglo-Irish Agreement: 163, 446-7, 450, 453
Anglo-Japanese Alliance: 524-5
Anglo-Saxon-Celtic peoples: 72, 77, 302, 312-3, 424, 478, 487, 495, 521-3, 538, 595
Anti-Defamation League: 110
Anti-Nazi League: 232-4
Anti-Racism: 138-9, 142-3, 161, 233, 326, 412-3, 435, 592
Anti-Semitism: 52-3, 56, 107-113
Apartheid: 138, 267, 427, 429, 473, 496
'Appeasement' party: 512
Arabs/Arab World: 418, 531, 537
Argentina: 128-30, 547
Aristocracy: 34-5, 59, 157, 169-70, 267, 279-80, 308-10, 410
Arts, the: 16, 62, 298, 403-7, 410
Arts Council: 405
Asia: 416-8, 423
Athens, State of: 267, 522

Attenborough, Sir R.: 333
Australasia: 538, 547
Australia: 356, 389, 403, 421, 426, 430, 462-3, 467, 471, 474-5, 477, 483-7, 489-91, 520
Australian Aboriginals: 467, 487
Austria: 504, 512, 517, 536
Austrian Succession, War of: 502
Austro-Hungarian Empire: 513

Babylon: 605
Balance of power principle: 502, 516, 536
Baldwin, S: 271
Balfour Declaration: 106, 522, 531
Baltic States: 416, 475
Bank of England: 352
Bantus: 479
Barnett, C.: 15, 70-2, 374, 521, 523
Bavaria: 80, 105
BBC: 159, 176, 226, 231, 242, 262, 323-8, 329, 342-3, 344
Bean, J.: 64, 181-2, 185, 203, 416
Beckman, R.: 384-5
Beethoven, L. van: 333
Belgium: 121, 379
Belloc, H.: 108
Bengalis: 479
Benson, I: 111, 420-1
Bentham, J. 117
Best, Capt.: 517
Bismarck, Otto von: 60, 467, 504-5
Birth-control: 312-3, 460-1, 497-8, 604-6
Blunt, A.: 315
Boer War: 472
Bonaparte, Napoleon: 34, 73, 312, 432, 502-3, 507, 547, 548
Brahms, J.: 333

Bretton Woods Agreement: 355
Bristol Univ.: 155,165
British Army: 26-35, 121, 505, 507, 514, 577
British Brothers' League: 77
British Commonwealth: 356, 389, 459, 484, 486-90, 492-5, 498-9, 533, 535, 548
British Empire: 10, 38-40, 45, 49, 55, 62, 69, 73-5, 78, 93-4, 120-1, 156, 158, 164, 233, 333, 348-51, 353-6, 389, 431, 457-60, 463, 465, 469-75, 477-81, 483, 489-90, 499, 502-5, 509-10, 512, 514, 518-22, 530, 541, 548
British Exped. Force, 1914: 507
British Exped. Force, 1939: 514
British Fascism: 80-1, 83, 87-8
British Foreign Policy: 61-2, 93-4, 100-2, 121, 500-543
British industry: 58, 61, 72-3, 79-80, 85, 95, 104, 118-9, 151-4, 158-60, 172-3, 282, 321, 327, 348-51, 353-4, 356, 360-77, 379, 389-90, 392-3, 431, 486, 493, 508, 510, 512, 521, 546
British Movement: 204
British National Party (1960s): 182-3, 185-6, 203-5
British National Party (1980s): 254, 557-84
British Nationalism: 40, 55, 61, 65, 67-91, 135, 175, 182, 202, 206, 208, 217, 228, 231-2, 241, 243, 245, 248, 255, 337, 339, 411, 455, 564-5, 582-4, 593-4, 598, 600, 602
British political system: 17-19, 61, 71-2, 77-8, 82, 84-6, 176-7, 258-91, 350, 355, 357, 384, 396, 398, 580, 600
British Steel: 367-8
British Union of Fascists: 48, 83, 188, 208
Britons Publishing Co.: 96
Brooks, A.: 49
Brown, S.E.D.: 131-2, 136
Buddhism: 605

Burma: 473
Burnham, J.: 43, 134-5

Caesar, Julius: 115
Campaign for Nuclear Disarmament: 224
Canada: 389, 421, 426, 465, 471, 475, 483-4, 486-7, 489-91, 503, 523, 547-8
Candour newsletter: 50, 64, 97, 212
Candour League: 212
Canterbury, Archbishop of: 197
Cape Province: 472, 496
Capitalism: 22, 58, 118, 151-2, 294, 306-7, 350, 352, 355-9, 391-2, 395, 448, 480, 602
Capital Punishment: 264, 267, 278-9, 454
Catholic Church/Catholics: 445, 447, 454, 514
Censorship in Britain: 96, 98-100, 104-5, 108-10, 231, 272, 287, 299, 336, 339, 342, 345-6, 420
Central America: 473
Chamberlain, J: 73-6, 86, 354, 478
Chamberlain, N: 73, 512-3
Chesterton, A.K.: 50, 53, 64, 97, 111-3, 181-2, 186, 199, 203-6, 208-12, 214, 221-2, 416
Chesterton, G.K.: 108
Chiang Kai-Shek: 520
China: 112, 418, 457, 520, 528, 538-9
Christianity: 435
Church, the: 16, 43, 90, 233, 314, 417, 440, 588
Churchill, Sir W.S.: 338, 519-20
Cinema, the: 16, 406-7
City of London: 120, 157, 327, 353-4, 372
Civil Defence: 549
Class war: 35, 307-8
Clausewitz, Gen. K. von: 114, 501
Cleon Skousen, W.: 112
Clive, Baron R.: 479

Clydesiders: 82
Collective leadership: 212-5, 557-60, 578
Colonialism: 45-6, 94, 458, 470-1, 495, 497-8, 534-5
Coloured races: 12, 24-5, 45-6, 68, 77, 123-4, 126-7, 138, 143-4, 161, 164-6, 184, 193, 231, 243, 298-9, 312, 328, 330, 332, 339, 412-3, 416-26, 428, 437, 440, 463, 480, 526
Common Agricultural Policy: 376
Commonwealth Office: 482
Communism/Communist World: 53, 80, 85, 95, 97, 105, 112, 123, 136, 145, 150, 152, 169, 214, 232, 327, 332-3, 336, 338, 362, 518, 523, 525, 528-9, 537, 543, 589, 608
Community Relations: 167
Community Service: 402
Conservatism/Conservative Party: 20-22, 39-40, 48, 50, 56-60, 62-3, 65, 94, 95, 140, 145, 152-3, 155-77, 181-2, 194-5, 229-30, 237, 242-3, 258-9, 263, 270, 274, 308, 311, 326-9, 337, 365, 368, 371, 382, 390, 394, 421, 433, 440, 444, 459-60, 481-2, 521, 565, 574, 579, 585-6, 589-90, 599-600, 603
Conservation: 399-400
Conspiracy Theory: 50-51, 92-116, 139, 290, 336, 420, 422, 539-40, 542
Cook, Capt. J.: 42, 479
Crime: 62, 127, 133, 150, 160, 167, 224, 293-4, 296, 310, 400-401, 418, 424, 587-8
Cromwell, Oliver: 68

Darwinism: 70
Day, Sir R.: 327
Decimalisation: 278-9
Defence: 30-31, 40, 61, 95, 103, 133, 144, 271, 282, 292, 296, 300, 305, 315, 317, 321, 469-71, 477, 492-3, 04, 507, 509-

10, 512, 521, 529, 543-556, 588
De Gaulle, Pres. C.: 544
Degeneration of British Society: 16, 42-3, 62, 114, 116, 126, 158, 233, 315, 319, 342, 405, 408-9, 587-8, 603
Democracy: 17-19, 45, 71, 84, 104, 114, 229-30, 239, 241, 246, 248-9, 250, 260-93, 299, 305, 316, 319-20, 329, 336, 337-8, 410-1, 479, 525, 538-39, 543, 566, 587, 586, 589, 602
Denmark: 379, 421
Dictatorship: 83-5, 99, 134, 284-5, 288, 299, 558
Discipline: 28-30, 40, 301, 320-1, 357, 402, 432, 510, 553, 556, 562-4, 573, 578
Disruption of patriotic organisations: 179-80, 185-6, 208-15, 221, 236-41, 244-5, 247-8
Dominions, the: 39, 74, 86, 302, 353-6, 430, 458, 471, 474, 477, 481-2, 485-6, 493, 503, 530, 537
Domvile, Adml. Sir B.: 516, 524-5
Drake, Sir F.: 42, 507
Drugs: 62, 150, 167, 173, 233, 278-9, 311, 315, 317, 334-5, 409, 434, 554
Dunkirk: 121
Durham Miners' Gala: 224
Dvorak, A.: 33
Dyer, Gen. R.E.H.: 333

East, industrialisation of the: 353, 409
Ecology/Ecology Party: 231, 398
Economic Nationalism: 70, 353, 370, 395
Education: 15, 29, 47, 62, 70-1, 81, 153, 160, 278, 284, 286, 295, 298, 301-8, 311, 314, 326-7, 344, 398-9, 430, 440, 443, 448, 454, 470, 533, 585, 589

Edward I: 68, 109, 416
Edwardian era: 78
Egalitarianism: 46, 259, 351-2
Einstein, A.: 284
Emigration: 313, 461-2, 494
England: 301, 309, 375, 402, 439, 446, 502
English Revolution: 169
Enlightenment, the: 264
Entente Cordiale: 504-6
Environment, the: 397-9, 410-1
Epstein, J. 346
Eskimos: 487
Estonia: 475
Ethiopia: 138, 403
Eton College: 479
European Commission: 539
European Common Market: 49, 95, 103, 158, 263-4, 298, 355-6, 377-80, 450, 482, 488, 492, 498, 527, 535-6, 583
European Free Trade Area: 482
European Parliament: 539
European Union: 48-9, 94, 103, 164, 380, 482, 488
'Extremism': 162-4, 247, 595, 600

Falkland Islands: 426, 473, 498
Falklands War: 128-131, 547, 550, 579
Fascism: 80-1, 83, 86-88, 128-30, 133-4, 191, 233, 285, 512, 591-2
Feminism: 62, 303
FIAT Motors: 527
Finance, power of: 84-5, 97, 150-3, 178, 262, 265, 277, 283, 288, 294, 336, 351-4, 384, 485, 492, 511, 519-20, 585, 601-2, 604
Financial System, the: 381-9, 391
Foch, Marshal F.: 506
Ford Motors: 527
Foreign & Commonwealth Office: 482
Foreign Office: 482, 519
Forster, E.M.: 315
Fountaine, A.: 185, 203-4

Fractional Reserve System, the: 352
France: 72, 76, 109, 121, 169, 309, 312, 349, 378-9, 435, 442, 448, 502-3, 505-7, 513-4, 519-20, 528, 532, 536-7, 544, 549, 606-7
Franco, Gen. F.: 512
Franco-Prussian War: 505
Freedom, erosion of: 122, 165-6, 229-30, 232, 285-7, 299, 315
Free enterprise: 22, 58, 90
Free Market Economy/Free Trade: 58, 70, 72, 74, 78-9, 86, 118-20, 173, 174, 275, 320, 352, 360-3, 367-70, 375-6, 406, 508
French Empire: 121
French Revolution: 136, 169, 435
Frost, R.: 30

General Election (Feb. 1974): 217-20, 242, 577-8
General Election (Oct. 1974): 220, 242
General Election (May 1979): 224, 240-4, 574, 599
General Election (Jun. 1983): 577-81
General Election (June 1987): 581
Gaitskell, H.: 81
Galtieri, Gen. L.: 128
Gandhi, Mahatma: 39, 135, 333
Genetics: 399-401, 411, 438
Germany: 25, 30, 35-7, 42, 60, 72, 76, 80-81, 88, 93, 100-2, 106, 108-9, 120-1, 186-7, 312, 327, 332-3, 349, 374, 378-9, 407, 421, 434-5, 440, 478, 503-7, 511, 513-9, 528-9, 536-7, 540, 548, 554, 603
Gibbon, E.: 42
Giles, F.: 129-30
Gladstone, W.E.: 123
Goebbels, Dr. P.J.: 327
Goethe, J.W. von: 512
Gold Standard: 517
Gorki Motor Plant: 527

Greater Britain Movement: 199-201, 203-4, 206
Greater London Council: 144
Greece: 379, 475-6, 605

Haiti: 428
Handel, G.F.: 334
National Health: 59-60, 278, 300, 302-3, 311-2, 318, 320
Heath, E. 421
Herbert, A.: 505
Hillingdon B.C.: 230
Hitler, A.: 25, 30, 36, 82, 88, 100-102, 106-8, 152, 186-7, 434, 508-9, 511, 513, 516-8, 520, 526, 592
Ho Chi Minh Trail: 527
Hohenzollern, House of: 506
Holland: 379, 421
Hollywood: 332
Holmes, Sherlock: 95
'Holocaust', the: 338, 434-5
Home Office: 166
Homosexuality: 42, 62, 143, 231, 233, 246-7, 264, 298, 314-5, 334, 340
Hong Kong: 159, 360, 473, 475
Honeyford, R. 142, 156
Howe, Sir. G.: 124-7
Humanism: 401
Hungarian Uprising: 338
Hungary: 80, 105, 338, 416
Hunger: 496-7
Huns, the: 532

IBA: 325
Ibsen, H: 605
ILEA: 143
Immigration: 12, 24, 164, 415-7, 419-22, 426-7, 458, 477, 489-91, 535, 583
Imperial Federation: 74-6, 474-8, 504
Imperialism: 457, 462, 466-77, 478-9, 481-2, 490, 495
Imperial Preference: 74, 86, 478, 486
India: 192, 333, 420, 473-5, 522, 605
Industrial Relations: 158, 293, 363-5, 390-3
Industrial Revolution: 348, 352, 356, 377
Infiltration of patriotic organisations: 180, 208-9, 213-4, 221, 244, 248-9, 253
Inflation: 152, 381-2, 385-8, 390-1
INLA: 143
Internationalism: 11, 66, 80, 82, 89-90, 97, 103-7, 135-6, 153, 164, 175, 275, 286, 326-7, 336, 339, 351, 354-5, 369, 372, 411, 443-4, 467, 478, 485-6, 489, 493, 501, 537-8, 544-6, 587, 604
IRA: 135, 144, 156, 444-6, 451-2
Ireland: 7-8, 10-11, 35, 73, 163, 247, 301, 375, 439, 453, 455-6
Irish Nationalism: 135, 163, 444-6, 450-1, 453-4, 456
Irish Republic, the: 440-1, 446-7, 450, 453, 456
Irving, D. 338, 519-20
Israel: 55, 94, 98, 101, 106-7, 111, 475-6, 495, 531-2, 537, 541
Italy: 80, 81, 88, 378-9, 407, 475, 519, 528
ITV: 232-3, 325

Jabotinsky, V.: 515
Jacobinism: 169
Japan: 93, 120, 349, 360-1, 365, 369-71, 418, 457, 524-5, 538-9, 541
Jehovah's Witnesses: 284
Jews/Jewish Question, the: 52-6, 67-8, 77, 98-113, 184, 188, 192, 332, 337-8, 412, 415-6, 421, 434, 453, 472, 475-6, 511, 515-6, 522-3, 531-2, 601
Jingoism. 472
Jordan, J.C.C.: 182, 184-6, 188, 192-3, 195, 197-9, 203, 416

Kama Motor Plant: 527
Kashmir: 418

Keir Hardie, J: 559
Kenya: 498
Kerr-Ritchie, I.R.: 192-3
KGB: 334, 340
Kibbutzim: 495
Kipling, J.R.: 248, 412
Kleist, Gen. E von: 514
Kremlin, the: 528, 545

Labour Govt. (1924): 593
Labour Govt. (1929-31): 82-3
Labour Govt. (1964-70): 82
Labour Party: 222-3,· 50, 82-3,
    141-5, 151, 153, 155-8, 162,
    182, 224, 229, 232-3, 274,
    326-7, 337, 351, 390-1, 394,
    440, 511, 593, 600
Lansbury, G.: 351
Lassalle, F.: 105
Latvia: 475
Lawrence, T.E.: 531
Leadership: 80, 82, 85, 209-10,
    212-4, 235, 237-41, 244-5,
    249-51, 256, 259, 265-6, 268-
    70, 272-3, 281-2, 287, 289,
    290, 298-300, 304, 306, 321,
    349, 354, 358-60, 365, 374,
    410-11, 438, 557-63, 578,
    583
League of Empire Loyalists: 49-
    52, 178, 181, 186, 203-5, 212
League of Nations: 73, 507
Lecky, W.E.H.: 309
Leese, A.: 112
Left, the: 48, 52, 56, 61-3, 84,
    90, 94, 122, 135-6, 141-56,
    161, 165-66, 168-69, 171-2,
    177-8, 182, 191-2, 195, 197,
    225-6, 228-30, 232-3, 243,
    259, 286, 308, 326-8, 336,
    352, 358, 405, 480, 565, 573,
    585, 588-9, 593, 596
Leicestershire, Chief Constable
    of: 226
Lend-Lease: 519
Lenin, V.I./Leninism: 122
Lewisham, Battle of: 226-7
Liberal · Establishment: 264-5,
    273-4, 280, 324, 326-7, 336,
    338-9, 444, 473

Liberalism: 43-4, 46, 51, 62, 70-
    2, 75, 86-7, 90, 117-42, 154,
    158, 175, 197, 214, 232, 264,
    267, 270, 279, 286, 292-300,
    303, 305, 309, 315-20, 326,
    336, 339, 354-5, 365, 368-9,
    398, 401, 409-11, 424, 435,
    443-4, 449-50, 452, 466, 470,
    475-6, 483, 486, 495-7, 501,
    506, 513, 528, 538-40, 542,
    555, 588-9, 596, 602, 604,
    606
Liberal Party: 48, 50, 62, 65, 73-
    4, 127, 223, 270, 274-5, 327
Liberal Unionists: 73
Liddell-Hart, Capt. B.: 514
Lie, use of the: 148-9, 158, 234,
    240, 272, 286, 347, 585-6
Lilienthal, A.: 111
Lithuania: 475
Little Englanders: 463
Lloyd, G.: 345
Local Government: 142-5, 153
    293, 314, 398-9, 589
Lords, House of: 279-81
Ludovici, A.: 136-7, 309-10
Luther, Martin: 108
Lutyens, Sir E.L.: 405

Macedon, State of: 522
Madagascar: 532
Maginot Line: 543
Malaysia: 473
Malta: 473
Mandela, N. 135, 144-5
Maoris: 467, 487
Marches: 223-8
Marshall Aid: 519
Marx, K./Marxism: 63, 94, 105,
    119, 121-2, 136, 145-6, 154,
    286, 346, 537, 588-9
Mass Media, the: 54-5, 90, 95,
    97-111, 116, 125, 127, 134,
    137, 148-9, 151, 153-4, 158-
    9, 173, 187-8, 220, 225-6,
    228, 230-2, 234-6, 242-3,
    252-3, 260-5, 267-8, 271-2,
    277, 283, 285-6, 288. 296-9.
    306, 314, 323-47, 407-9, 417,
    441, 443-4, 485, 487-8, 494,

496, 500, 511, 516, 527, 533, 554, 564, 581-3, 586-8, 599, 601, 608
Methodists: 284
Middle East: 94, 106, 531-2, 537
Mid-West, American: 378
Milner, A. Lord: 76-7
Miners' Strike, 1984: 366, 393
Monday Club: 175
Montgomery, Field Marshal. B.L. Lord: 469
Moore, Sir H.: 346
Morality: 16, 42-3, 62, 158, 173-4, 313-5, 317, 319-20, 340, 345, 409, 432
Morocco: 532
Morse, J.: 412
Mosley, Sir O.E.: 25, 48, 81-8, 184, 188-9, 199, 208, 277, 287, 350-1, 355, 416, 510-11, 524, 535
Mugabe, R.: 124
Muggeridge, M.: 117, 452
Munich Conference (1938): 512-3
Murdoch, R.: 485
Music: 16, 36, 194, 298, 318, 330, 332-5, 403-4, 409
Mussolini, B.: 81, 512, 591-2

Napoleonic Wars: 312, 502-3
Natal: 472
National Debt: 387
National division: 259-60, 273, 290, 307
National fitness, need for: 60, 300, 302-3, 311-2, 407
National Front: 204, 206-57, 337, 557-9, 562, 576-7, 578
National Front (Constitutional Movement): 245-6
National Government (1931-45): 355
National Independence Party: 211 5
Nationalism: 11, 40, 55, 61, 67-91, 106-7, 135, 151, 175, 182, 206, 217, 228, 231-2, 242-3, 245, 248, 255, 301-2, 333, 336-7, 339, 477-8, 485, 539,

547, 555, 598, 600, 602-3
National Labour Party (1958-60): 181-3, 186
National Service: 30, 40, 69-70, 78-9, 304-5, 402, 504, 551-6
National Socialism: 25, 36-7, 80, 88, 107-8, 121, 186-7, 191, 232-3, 327, 332, 401, 416, 434-5, 508-9, 516, 518, 592
National Socialist Movement: 186-7, 196-8
National sovereignty: 44-5, 61, 103-4, 131, 158-9, 163-4, 469, 476-7, 489-90, 530, 546
National Union of Journalists: 232, 235, 242, 262
National Union of Mineworkers: 364
National unity: 259, 284, 299, 357, 430
NATO: 527, 543-5, 547
Netherlands: 6
New England: 378
'New Harmony' Community of Equality: 146
New National Front: 251-4
New Party: 83
New Zealand: 377, 389, 426, 462-3, 467, 471, 474, 483-4, 486-7, 489, 494, 520
Nietzsche, F.: 132, 410
Nigeria: 420
Normandy Landings (1944): 577-8
Northern European races: 72, 76-7
Northern Ireland: 145, 156, 163-4, 265-6, 325, 439-56, 521, 545, 547
Norway: 356, 421
Nuclear disarmament: 144
Nuclear power: 548
Nuclear weapons: 544-5, 548-9

O'Brien, J.: 214
Occupational franchise: 277-8
Oliver, Prof. R.P.: 114, 139
Old Bailey: 192
Orange Free State: 472
Orwell, G.: 47

Ottawa Conference (1933): 355
Overseas Aid: 46, 124, 429, 458, 496-7, 534
Overseas Aid & Development, Ministry of: 534
Owen, Dr. D.: 141
Owen, R.: 146

Pacifism: 549-51, 588
Pakistan: 420
Palestine: 522, 531-2
Paramilitary organisations: 451-2, 454
Parker, J.C.: 256
Parker, V. (Mrs.): 257
Parker, W.H.: 8
Parliament: 83-5, 144, 154, 156, 158, 175, 264-8, 270, 273, 327, 417, 450, 555, 585
Party warfare: 85, 268-70, 273, 276, 284-5, 288, 290, 297, 321
Patriotism: 9-11, 21-2, 44, 79-80, 94, 122, 133, 158-60, 170, 175, 177, 232, 235, 241-3, 255, 300-1, 304, 306-7, 321, 326, 340, 344-5, 353, 360, 390-1, 439, 445, 450, 453, 455, 472, 480, 488, 495, 554-6, 591-2, 598
Pavlov, Prof. I.P.: 233, 434
Peel, Dr. P.H.: 505, 522-3
Pirie, D.A.: 192-3
Plymouth Brethren: 284
Poland: 93, 416, 453, 475-6, 513-4, 517
Police: 7-8, 62, 127, 149, 166-8, 183-4, 188, 226, 229, 424-5, 567-8, 570-1
Pope, H.H. The: 454
Population growth: 61, 72, 75, 89, 312-3, 409
Populism: 236
Powell, J.E.: 76, 416-7
Poverty: 57, 82, 152, 308, 480, 508
Premiership, new system of: 282-4, 287-8
Presbyterians: 284
Privatisation: 371

Profit-sharing: 359
Protection of industry: 74, 86, 104, 535, 362-3, 366-9, 377
Protestantism: 445
Prussia: 440, 504
Public Order Act: 184-5, 188-92, 573

Queen Elizabeth II, H.M. the: 160
Quigley, Prof. C.: 112

Race: 12, 24-5, 43-6, 55, 61-2, 65, 67-8, 72, 76-7, 86, 94, 97, 104-7, 123-8, 133, 138-9, 141-4, 151, 155, 158-9, 161-2, 164-7, 176, 182, 184, 227, 229, 231-3, 243, 263-4, 275, 298-9, 302, 312-3, 316, 326, 329-30, 332, 336-7, 339-40, 352, 400, 403, 412-38, 439-40, 450, 463, 475, 480, 496, 504, 526, 587-8, 592, 603
Race riots: 127, 159, 166-8, 231, 310, 329, 417, 424, 430, 585
Racial Preservation Society: 221-2
Rachman, P.: 54
RAF: 507
Ramsay, Capt. A.H.M.: 514
Red Army: 518
Reed, D.: 111
Read, J.K.: 221-2
Repatriation/Resettlement: 427, 429-30
Representation of the People Act: 230
Rhineland, Hitler's occupation of: 512
Rhodes, C.J.: 77
Rice, J.B. 309
Right, the: 155-177, 352, 400, 565, 586
Roman Empire: 42, 115, 432, 467, 522, 605
Roosevelt, F.D.: 106, 519-20, 526
Rothermere Press: 101, 516
Round Table, the: 76-77
Royal Irish Constabulary: 7

Royal Navy: 507
Royalty: 159-60, 282, 410
Royal Ulster Constabulary: 445, 451-2
Rural regeneration: 377, 401-3
Russia (Imperial): 109, 170, 503
Russia (Soviet): 76, 80, 85, 93-5, 98, 102-3, 105, 109, 123, 145, 152, 169, 162, 264, 307, 324, 327, 334, 358, 421, 435, 457, 478, 509, 515, 517-8, 520, 525-30, 536-9, 543, 545, 547-9, 555-6
Rundstedt, Field Marshal G. von: 514

Scandinavia: 439, 528
Scarman Report: 166-7
Schellenberg, W.: 517
Scottish Nationalism: 135
Scotland: 301, 375-6, 402, 415, 439, 446, 494
Searchlight magazine: 222
Seely, Prof. J.R.: 75-6
Sellers, P.: 157
Selwyn-Gummer, J.: 433-4
'Sexism': 63, 143, 298-9
Shakespeare, W.: 108-9, 115
Shaw, G.B.: 605
Siberia: 170
Simonstown Naval Base: 473
'Simple, Peter': 142, 325-6
Singapore: 473
Sinn Fein: 144
'62 Group: 192, 196-7
Skidelsky, R.: 81
Small business: 294, 296
Smith, J.: 577-8
Smith, T. Dan: 399
Snowden, P.: 351
Social Credit: 387
Social Democratic Party: 62, 65, 141, 270, 275, 327, 601
Socialism: 22-3, 38, 40, 48, 52, 56-62, 82, 87, 152-3, 171, 174, 177, 182, 270, 306-7, 326, 350-1, 356-8, 395, 435, 448, 539, 555, 594
Socialist Workers' Party: 231, 233

Social and Liberal Democratic Party: 141, 263, 440, 601
Solzhenitsyn, A.: 538
South Africa: 94, 123-6, 128, 131, 138, 210, 267, 328-31, 426-7, 429, 435, 443-4, 449, 471-3, 495-7, 526, 530-1, 533, 535
South America: 520
South Tyrol: 536
Spain: 82, 109, 379, 435, 473, 502, 512, 528, 532
Spanish Armada: 432
Spanish Inquisition: 109, 435
Spanish Succession, War of: 502
Sparta, Kingdom of: 305
Spearhead magazine: 178, 200-2, 217, 251, 414
Spengler, O: 288, 306, 319, 331, 338, 603-6
Splintering: 179, 185-7, 197, 214-5, 245-8, 253, 256, 557, 560, 563, 573, 599
Sport, value of: 13-14, 60, 303, 407
SS, the: 517
Stael, Madame de: 364
Stalin, J.V.: 293, 435, 520, 523, 556
Sterilisation: 401
Stevens, Maj.: 517
Stock Market Crash (1929): 348, 385
Struggle, law of: 89, 114, 120, 132, 320
Sudan, the: 403
Suez Crisis: 522
Suttee: 470
Sutton, Prof. A.: 527
Sweden: 356, 374, 421
Switzerland: 356, 374, 421

Tariff Reform: 74, 86, 354-5, 478
Teheran Conference (1943): 520
Terraine, J: 507-8
Territorial forces: 556
Terrorism: 135, 144-5, 445-6, 452, 454
Teutonic Knights: 513

Texas: 378
Thatcher, Mrs. M.: 156, 176, 242-3, 364, 366-7, 390, 406, 495, 574, 579, 590
Third World: 138, 429, 483-4, 533-5
Thomas, J.R.: 351
Thompson, C.: 196
Tolpuddle Martyrs: 393
Tornado fighter-bomber: 544
Trade & Industry, Ministry of: 371
Trade Unions: 232, 235, 242, 262, 265, 293-4, 327, 390, 565-6
Transvaal, the: 472, 496
Trevelyan, Mrs. V.: 201-2
Trident Missile System: 544
Trotsky, L.D.: 145
Tudor England: 70
Turkey: 531
Tyndale, W.: 6, 17
Tyndall, Rt. Rev. C.J.: 8, 10
Tyndall, G.F.: 8-9, 11-12, 48
Tyndall, Prof. J.: 7
Tyndall, J.F.: 7, 41, 453
Tyndall, John H.: Family origins: 6-7, 439; Birth & childhood: 9; Adolescence: 11-25; Sporting interests: 12-14, 24, 30-31, 33, 38, 41; First political stirrings: 16-25, 32, 38; Army service: 26-40; Years of political study: 19, 22-3, 38, 41, 47, 87, 95-7, 99, 100, 182; Further political development: 41, 47-8, 50-2, 92, 148; Joined LEL: 51; Joined NLP: 182; Joined BNP (1960-62): 182; Joined NSM: 186; Set up GBM: 198-9; Joined NF: 206; Set up NNF: 251; Political writings: 64, 178; Political speaking: 64, 183, 188; Journey to Russia: 51-6; Adoption of firm position in politics: 65; Years of political apprenticeship: 178-207; Launched *Spearhead*: 200; Brushes with law: 183-4, 188, 192; Imprisonment: 193-5, 412, 566; Became Deputy leader NF: 214; Became leader NF: 215; Deposed as NF leader: 221; Reinstated as NF leader: 223; Married: 256; Became father: 257; Set up BNP: 557-60
Tyndall, Miss Marina H.V.: 257
Tyndall, Mrs. N.: 8-9, 25
Tyndall, Mrs. Valerie D.: 5, 256-7

Uganda: 498
Ukraine, the: 475-6
Ulster Loyalists: 145, 163, 440, 444-53, 455-6, 600
Unemployment: 57, 82, 104, 152, 159, 171-4, 294, 300, 308, 351, 355, 361-2, 365, 369, 372, 380-1, 386, 392, 394, 420, 480, 587
Union Movement: 48
United Nations: 134, 467, 533, 539
United States of America: 76, 95, 105-6, 109, 111, 114, 118, 139, 159, 170-1, 282, 293, 333, 338, 378-9, 389-90, 395, 406, 421, 427, 440, 441, 457, 465, 475-6, 478, 485, 490-3, 507, 509, 515-6, 518-33, 537, 539, 541, 543-9, 603
United States Constitution: 171
Untermeyer, S: 515
Urban Renewal: 398, 403, 405-6, 408, 430, 587
Usury: 372

Value-Added Tax: 299
Vaughan-Williams, R.: 333
Venice: 309-10
Venlo Incident: 517
Versailles, Treaty of: 506, 508
Victoria, H.M. Queen: 72, 499
Victorian Era: 72-3, 77-8, 357, 473, 499
Vietnam: 527
Viking invasions: 439
Vincent, J.: 155-6

Violence: 65, 83-4, 144-5, 148, 155, 165-8, 183-4, 188-93, 196-7, 224-30, 232, 235, 336-7, 566-73, 592-3, 598, 608
Voltaire, J.F.M.A. de: 336

Wagner, R.: 108
Wales: 301, 375-6, 402, 439, 446
Wallace, H.: 520
Washington Conference (1922): 507, 524
Webster, Mrs. N.: 146
Welfare State: 57, 60, 149, 172-4, 294, 300, 312, 394-5
Wellington, Duke of: 547
Welsh Nationalism: 135
West, the: 139, 214, 288, 305, 319, 335, 409, 421, 443, 464, 483, 497, 504, 526-8, 532, 538, 543, 545, 602-4, 606-7
West Indies: 420, 473, 475
White Defence League: 182, 204
White Races: 24-5, 45-6, 68, 123-6, 128, 131, 139-40, 143-5, 158, 161, 299, 303, 312, 328, 330, 333, 337, 414, 417-9, 423-4, 428, 435-7, 440, 449, 453, 463, 480, 497, 526, 530, 538, 602-3, 606
Wilhelm II, H.M. Kaiser: 503

William the Conquerer: 67, 416, 442
Wilson, H. Lord: 82:
Wilson, Woodrow: 106, 506, 520
Wolfe, Gen. J.: 479
Workers' Co-operatives: 359
'Workfare': 394-5, 403
World Government: 489
World War I: 77-80, 106, 120, 212, 259, 321, 320-1, 374, 380, 479, 481, 505-8, 517-8, 522, 530-1, 538, 549-50, 552
World War II: 9-11, 81, 100, 102, 106, 120-1, 138, 152, 259, 320-1, 332-3, 338, 352, 355, 380, 420, 435, 479, 488, 510, 516, 518-20, 522, 524-6, 538, 540, 550, 552, 554, 556, 594, 608
Wren, Sir C.: 405

Yalta Conference (1945): 522-3
Yeats, W.B.: 150, 565
Yellow Races: 538-9

Zambia: 124-5
ZANU: 124
Zimbabwe: 124-6
Zionism: 55, 98, 337-8, 532, 601
Zollverein, the: 504